Travel and Exploration

The history of travel writing dates back to the Bible, Caesar, the Vikings and the Crusaders, and its many themes include war, trade, science and recreation. Explorers from Columbus to Cook charted lands not previously visited by Western travellers, and were followed by merchants, missionaries, and colonists, who wrote accounts of their experiences. The development of steam power in the nineteenth century provided opportunities for increasing numbers of 'ordinary' people to travel further, more economically, and more safely, and resulted in great enthusiasm for travel writing among the reading public. Works included in this series range from first-hand descriptions of previously unrecorded places, to literary accounts of the strange habits of foreigners, to examples of the burgeoning numbers of guidebooks produced to satisfy the needs of a new kind of traveller - the tourist.

A Hand-Book for Travellers in Spain, and Readers at Home

Targeted at both intrepid travellers and 'readers at home', this two-volume account of Spanish history, topography and culture by Richard Ford (1796–1858) combines the rigour of a gazetteer with the humour and pace of a private travel diary. First published in 1845, as part of John Murray's series of guidebooks, the work made an immediate impact upon the reading public, and it was celebrated in the press as the 'most comprehensive and accurate account of that country' hitherto produced. Starting in the Kingdom of Leon, and again using a series of hand-picked routes, Volume 2 leads readers to the pilgrim shrine of Santiago de Compostela and through Galicia and the Basque provinces, introducing them to castles, universities, art collections and the 'inhospitality of Madrid'. The result is an engaging account that will be of interest to modern tourists and historians alike.

A Hand-Book for Travellers in Spain, and Readers at Home

VOLUME 2

RICHARD FORD

CAMBRIDGE
UNIVERSITY PRESS

CAMBRIDGE UNIVERSITY PRESS

Cambridge, New York, Melbourne, Madrid, Cape Town,
Singapore, São Paolo, Delhi, Mexico City

Published in the United States of America by Cambridge University Press, New York

www.cambridge.org
Information on this title: www.cambridge.org/9781108037549

© in this compilation Cambridge University Press 2012

This edition first published 1845
This digitally printed version 2012

ISBN 978-1-108-03754-9 Paperback

HAND-BOOK

FOR

TRAVELLERS IN SPAIN.

A

HAND-BOOK

FOR

TRAVELLERS IN SPAIN,

AND

READERS AT HOME.

DESCRIBING THE

COUNTRY AND CITIES, THE NATIVES AND THEIR MANNERS;

THE ANTIQUITIES, RELIGION, LEGENDS, FINE ARTS, LITERATURE,
SPORTS, AND GASTRONOMY, PAST AND PRESENT:

WITH NOTICES

ON SPANISH HISTORY.

———

PART II.

CONTAINING

LEON, GALLICIA, THE ASTURIAS, THE CASTILES (OLD AND
NEW), THE BASQUE PROVINCES, ARRAGON,
THE PYRENEES, AND NAVARRE.

With Travelling Maps and a Copious Index.

———

LONDON:
JOHN MURRAY, ALBEMARLE STREET.
———
1845.

THIS BOOK IS PUBLISHED
AT GIBRALTAR, BY GEORGE ROWSWELL; AT MALTA, BY MRS. MUIR.

LONDON: WILLIAM CLOWES AND SONS, STAMFORD STREET.

CONTENTS OF PART II.

SECTION VIII.

LEON.

SECTION IX.

THE KINGDOM OF GALLICIA.

SECTION X.

THE ASTURIAS.

SECTION XI.

THE CASTILES, OLD AND NEW.

SECTION XII.

THE BASQUE PROVINCES.

SECTION XIII.

KINGDOM OF ARRAGON.

SECTION XIV.

KINGDOM OF NAVARRE.

SECTION VIII.

THE KINGDOM OF LEON.

CONTENTS.

The Province; its History; Character of the Country and Natives; the Charros and Charras.

The very important kingdom of Leon, because lying out of the hacknied track of travellers, is not visited as it deserves. It abounds with sites of unrivalled military interest; the painted sculpture is of the first class; the scenery in the Vierzo and Sierras is magnificent, and the fishing excellent. The chief cities, Salamanca, Valladolid, and Leon, are full of architectural and artistical interest, while to the historian the archives of Spain lie buried at Simancas. The Summer months are the best for the hills, the Springs and Autumns for the plains.

THE KINGDOM OF LEON.

El Reino de Leon runs up from the plains of the Castiles into the spurs of the Gallician and Asturian Sierras. It is one of the most ancient of the once separate and independent kingdoms of the Peninsula, for the natives, being situated near the mountain-den from whence the Lion of the Goth soon turned upon the Moor, were among the earliest to expel the infidel invader, whose hold was slight and resistance feeble when compared to his deep-fanged retention and defence of Andalucia. Nor, when we behold the dreary steppes and rugged hills of Leon, and pass over the mountain barrier into the cold damp Asturias, can we be surprised that the Arab, the lover of the sun and plain, should turn readily to the more congenial south. The Christian dominion was extended by Alonzo el Catolico, who, between A.D. 739-57, overran and reconquered the plains down to the Duero and Tormes. The Moors nevertheless continued to make annual *Algarus* or forays into these parts, more for purposes of plunder than reconquest. Thus this frontier arena was alternately in the power of Christian and Infidel, until about the year 910 Garcia removed the court from Oviedo to Leon, and gave its name to his new kingdom, to distinguish it from those of Castile and Navarre, and other counties and lordships. Indeed, the ranges of hills which from Catalonia to Gallicia separate district from district, divided the country politically as well as geographically, and the dislocated land seemed to indicate distinct petty principalities, to prevent national unity, and foster local partition, and that *isolated independence* which is the inveterate tendency of this unamalgamating land; the early Christian counts, lords, dukes, or kings (sheikhs in reality), were rivals to each other, and when not at war with the Moor, quarrelled among themselves after the true Iberian fashion, " Bellum quam otium malunt; si extraneus deest, domi hostem quærunt" (Just. xliv. 2). The male line of the Leon kings failed in 1037 with Bermudo III., whose daughter carried the crown to her husband Ferdinand of Castile; he redivided his domains by his will, which, however, his son Sancho reunited, and Leon and Castile were finally joined in the person of St. Ferdinand, and have never since been separated.

The kingdom contains about 20,000 square miles, with a million inhabitants. These hardy, ill-educated agriculturists neither change their homes nor habits; creatures of routine and foes to innovation, they cling to the ways of their forefathers; yet although purely tillers of the earth, their practice is barbarously backward, and they plough in the primitive style of Triptolemus and the Georgics; most farmers are slow to improve, and these are no more to be hurried than their mules. Their minds, like their cumbrous creaking wheels (see Index, *Chillo*), are blocked up with the dirt and prejudices which have been accumulating since the deluge.

The minor traits of Leonese character are influenced by local differences, and the peasant is modified by the nature by which he is surrounded. Thus near the Sil, the Leonese resemble the Gallician mountaineers, as in the Sierra, near the Asturias, they partake of the Asturian, while in the southern portions they differ very little from the old Castilians (see Sect. xi.). These plains produce much corn and *garbanzos*, and a strong red wine is made near Toro. The hills to the N. are well timbered, and their valleys are filled with pastures and refreshed by beautiful trout streams. In these rarely visited localities the stranger will find a simple but cheerfully offered hospitality. The marly fresh water basin, or *tierra de Campos*, between Zamora, Leon, and Valladolid, is the land of Ceres; but although bread is a drug, and there are no corn-laws, nowhere are the people more scanty or miserable; they dwell in mud hovels made of unbaked bricks, or *adobes,* the precise Arabic *toob-ny,* and vie even with La Mancha in discomfort. The country is as uninteresting as the ventas are uncomfortable; woe betide him who rides across these interminable plains in winter or summer, the apologies for roads are then either axle or ancle deep in mud, or clouded in a salitrose dust, which seems to be on fire under the African sun.

Near Salamanca, however, matters improve, and many of the yeomen are wealthy, and live on isolated farms, *Montaracias,* growing much corn, which is exported into Andalucia. They are also breeders of cattle on a large scale, which they manage with the primitive sling, or *honda,* as near San Roque. The *conocidores,* or herdsmen, ride down the animals, *les agorachan a caballo,* just as their descendants do in South America. At their cattle brandings and family feasts, *herraduras y fiestas de familia,* as at their marriages, they keep open house with much eating, drinking, singing, and dancing the *habas verdes;* such feasts are truly described in Don Quixote at the wedding of Camacho. They are the unchanged convivia *festa* Carduarum of Martial (iv. 55, 17); and such were the Oriental sheep-shearings of Nabal (1 Sam. xxv. 36), who " held a feast in his house, like the feast of a king."

The houses of the humble Leonese, like their hearts, are always open to an Englishman ; they have not forgotten the honesty, justice, and good conduct of our triumphant soldiers, which contrast with the rapine, sacrilege, and bloodshed of the defeated foe. They remember Salamanca, and him whom they call the " great lord," *El gran Lor,* the Cid of England; and many years after his victories over the French, imagined that he was coming back, possibly to become king of Castile. Their houses are substantially furnished and clean, for here, as elsewhere in the unvisited portions of the Peninsula, dirt and discomfort lodge at the public inn, whose accommodations are fit for the beasts and muleteers who use them. One peculiarity in their houses is the loftiness of the beds; the mattresses and pillows, *colchones y almohadas,* are often embroidered with lions and castles, and the coarse, but clean home-spun sheets are fringed with *flejos y randas.*

The peasant's dress near Ciudad Rodrigo and Salamanca is peculiar and expensive; his Sunday costume is worth more than that of all the peers who attend early service at Whitehall chapel, *El gran Lor`s* included. The Leonese *Charro y Charra* are here what the *Majo y Maja* are in Andalucia, at least as far as goes gay and costly apparel, the joy of half-civilized nations ; but these sons of the Goth have none of the *Zandunga* of the Oriental Southron, and the two costumes differ altogether. The *Charro* wears a low, broad-brimmed hat ; his shirt, or *camison,* is richly worked in front, with a gold knob-brooch, or *boton ;* his *chaleco,* or waistcoat of figured velvet, is cut square and low down to the pit of the stomach, to display this shirt ; it is garnished with square silver buttons and cross ribbons ; his jacket is open at the elbow, and edged with black velvet; his sash is a broad belt, a *cinto* of leather not of silk ; his long dark cloth gaiters are embroidered below the knee ; he wears large silver buckles in his shoes; a stick in his right hand and a cloak over his left shoulder, complete the rustic dandy. The gay *charra* is worthy of such a beau. She wears a *caramba* in her hair, and a mantilla of cloth cut square, *el cenerero,* which is fastened by a brooch or silver clasp, *el colchete,* and this hood is richly embroidered ; her red velvet boddice, *jubon,* is adorned with bugles, or *canutillo,* worked into fanciful patterns; her wrist-cuffs are wrought with gold ; her sash is tied behind ; her petticoat, *manteo,* is usually scarlet *de grana,* which, with purple *morado,* is the favourite colour, and like her apron, or *mandile,* is embroidered with birds, flowers, and stars. She has also a handkerchief, *rebocillo,* which is worked in gold ; she wears many *joyas,* jewels and chains bedecked with coloured stones, which descend as heirlooms from mothers to daughters. But these fine clothes have not corrupted the wearers, whose honest simplicity of character, "*La honradez y sencillez de los Charros,*" is proverbial; thus one of them being at a theatre, where in the play a traitor was deceiving the king, cried out, thinking the transaction a reality, "*Señor, Señor, no crea V. M. á ese*"—"Sire, Sire! do not believe him." The Leonese rustic disputes with the *Sanchos* of La Mancha the palm of being the *Juan Español,* or Goody Gaffer of the Peninsula.

CIUDAD RODRIGO rises on a slight eminence above the Agueda, which flows under the walls to the W., being here intersected by small islands. A bridge communicates with a suburb, and leads over the plains to Portugal, which is distant a few miles. This fortified place, although " weak in itself, is," says the Duke, " the best chosen *position* of any frontier town that I have seen." Hence the important part it played in the retreats and sieges during the Peninsular war : and in these consist its present interest, for otherwise it is dull and poverty-stricken, and, as usual, miserably provided with every requisite for defence.

Ciudad Rodrigo was so called after the Conde Rodrigo Gonzalez Giron, who founded it in 1150. Three Roman columns brought from ancient Malabriga are preserved in the *Plaza,* and are borne by the city for its arms. It is the see of a bishop, suffragan to Santiago. Pop^{n.} about 5000. There is only a poor posada. As this is a *Plaza de Armas,* much jealousy is exhibited towards curious strangers, who are suspected of making plans with a design to take the citadel. All who wish to examine the positions, and make sketches, had better apply for permission of the governor, which probably will be refused.

There is little worth notice in the town. The cathedral was begun in 1190 by Ferd. II. of Leon: the architect, Benito Sanchez, lies buried in the cloister. The edifice was enlarged in 1538 by Card. Tavera, Archbishop of Toledo, and previously bishop here. An inner door of the old cathedral exists near the entrance, with curious statue work and alto-relievos of the

Passion. The quaint Gothic *Silla.* *del Coro* is by Rodrigo Aleman. The classical *Colegiata,* or *Capilla* de Cerralvo, was built in 1588 by Fr^{o.} Pacheco, Archbishop of Burgos, and *was* very fine. Being converted into a powder magazine, it was blown up in 1818 by what here is called an accident, but which, as in the East, is the common result of a careless want of ordinary precautions. The shattered fragments were left for many years exactly as they fell, pictures flapping in the *Retablo,* &c. The cardinal's coffin had been torn from its sarcophagus by the French to make bullets of the lead, —unplumbing the dead to destroy the living. The uncovered corpse was cast into a niche, and then moved to a loft, where we saw it lying in the tattered episcopal robes. The chaplain, on this indecency being pointed out, merely shrugged his shoulders : yet he was a descendant of this prelate, and enjoyed the revenues of his endowment; although he duly dined himself, he never buried his dead, neglectful of the conditions of the national proverb, *Los vivos a la mesa, los muertos a la huesa.* The cathedral being placed at the N.W. angle of the town, and exposed to the *Teson,* has suffered much during the sieges. The walls were built by Ferdinand II., and the large square tower by Henry II. in 1372.

The Duke, when here, lodged at *La Casa de Castro;* observe its portal with spiral pillars. The costumes of the *Charro* and *Charra* are to be seen in Ciudad Rodrigo in great perfection on holidays.

Ciudad Rodrigo, uninteresting in itself, has been rendered illustrious by the great events which have taken place in it and its immediate neighbourhood. The chief of these are the siege by the French, the failure of Massena's invasion of Portugal, the siege and capture by the English, and the Duke's retreat from Burgos ; while in the vicinity are *El Bodon, Sabugal, la Guarda, Fuentes de Oñoro*, and other sites where the moral and physical superiority of our chief and his troops over the enemy was signally manifested, in spite of their great gallantry and our inferiority of numbers. Near, also, are *Celorico, Fuente Guinaldo, Freneda*, and other villages, long the head-quarters of the Duke, while hovering on the borders of Spain and planning her deliverance. From these once obscure places some of his most remarkable dispatches were written : then and there, while all at home and abroad despaired, his prophetic eye saw in the darkest gloom the coming rays of his glory.

The first siege was undertaken in the spring of 1810 by Massena and Ney, almost in the presence of the English army, which was stationed on the Coa, within the Portuguese frontier. This siege was a gross mistake, which the French found out when it was too late ; they here wasted precious time, during which the Duke prepared his lines at Torres Vedras, and thus out-generaled and defeated the enemy. Ciudad Rodrigo, when invested by the French, was miserably supplied with means of defence, owing to the usual want of foresight and means of the government, but the commander Herrasti was a brave and skilful officer. The Duke, although anxious to relieve him, refused to risk an action against an enemy " double," as he said, "his number in infantry, and three times so in cavalry." He disregarded the sneers of Spaniard and Frenchman alike " at his coward selfish caution," for he knew that the fate of Spain did not depend upon Ciudad Rodrigo's fall or relief, but on the preservation of the little English army, the salt of the whole, and which eventually drove the invaders countless legions headlong over the Pyrenees.

After a most desperate resistance, the accidental explosion of a powder magazine forced the gallant Herrasti to surrender July 10, when every article of the capitulation was forthwith violated by Ney (Toreno xii.).

After the fall the Duke remained patient, through fair and foul report, until his *time to act* at Ciudad Rodrigo was come. He foresaw that Buonaparte would make a third attempt on Portugal, to "drown the leopard," and efface the disgraces of Junot and Soult : and accordingly he was prepared. In July, 1810, Massena crossed the frontier with overwhelming numbers. Busaco checked his fool-hardy advance, where, Sept. 26, Ney was repulsed by Beresford and the Portuguese. Massena, however, pushed on to Sobral, and there, Oct. 10, found out for the first time the deep pit which his greater rival had in his prescience dug for him. Massena's whole campaign was a complete failure : begun in fanfaronnade, carried out in rapine and butchery, it ended in total defeat, in the loss of 30,000 men, and of every pretension to generalship. His only strategics were rash, rapid advance, and reliance on great numerical superiority. "His retreat in March, 1811," says the quiet Duke, "was marked by a barbarity seldom equalled, and never surpassed." Women were regularly foraged for and sold in the market, while the abominable horrors and filthy slime of their foul quarters were "revolting and degrading to human nature" (Pen. Camp. iii. 54).

While Ney and Massena differed on the field of battle, Soult at a distance was influenced by those rivalries which sapped the French cause (see Barrosa. p. 221). Instead of hastening day and night, as he ought, to his comrade's relief, he never moved from Seville until December, when it was too late, and then loitered at Olivenza and Badajoz, where, but for the misconduct of Mendizabal at Gebora, of Imaz at Badajoz, and of Lapeña at Barrosa, Soult and Victor would have both been beaten at

2 B 3

the same time as Ney and Massena. The Duke was thus robbed by others of his full reward; he could deserve success, but 'tis not in mortals to command it.

Massena soon made a desperate effort to restore his faded laurels, and crossed the Agueda, May 2, 1811, with 45,000 infantry and 5000 cavalry, to relieve Almeida, which the Duke was blockading with less than 36,000 infantry and 2000 horsemen, and those out of condition; accordingly he fell back on the hills, which are seen from Ciudad Rodrigo, rising S.W. on the Portuguese frontier. His object was, in spite of inferior numbers, to protect both his approaches to Almeida, and his line of retreat into Portugal by Sabugal; hence he was obliged to over-extend his line; his centre was the village on the ragged hill of *Fuentes de Oñoro*, now truly *Fountains of Honour* to England; this point rises above the stream *de dos casas*, and was made, May 5, the grand object of Massena's attack, whose repulse was complete. Nothing ever surpassed the charge of the 71st and 79th Highlanders, who, their colonel being killed, raised the war-cry of the Camerons. The 88th cleared the streets, and bayoneted down the " finest body of French grenadiers ever seen." Our cavalry, feeble in number, caught the generous inspiration, and crushed the splendid French horsemen under Montbrun, whose hesitation lost what Picton called their " golden moment," for they might have destroyed the whole light division. But Massena withdrew, just at the critical moment when a real general would have pressed on; he retreated, having lost 5000 men and his entire military reputation. Our loss was 2000 men. This day settled the "spoilt *child* of victory," who under the Duke's tuition had grown up to be a finished *man* of defeat. He surrendered on the 11th his command to Marmont, and retired to Bordeaux, having carried off 800,000 dollars, " extorqués par le sang et le pillage, une malédiction générale le

suivit " (Schep. iii. 252). Plunder, indeed, says the Duke, was the original motive of Massena's Santarem expedition, " against every military principle, and at an immense sacrifice of men " (Disp. Dec. 29, 1810).

He lived to prove false to both Buonaparte and the Bourbons. "Signalez-le," say the French (B. U. xxvii. 407), " à l'horreur de la postérité, ses rapines lui ont acquis une honteuse célébrité." He died, April 4, 1817, the disgusting death of a low debauchee, an end worthy of his origin. The son of a Jew pothousekeeper at Nice, hooted out of the ranks for theft, he rose from being a fencing master to be a favourite of Buonaparte, and obtained a great name by easy victories over feeble enemies; tested against the Duke he was always found wanting.

The next year the Duke pounced upon Ciudad Rodrigo, and took it in 11 days, being in less than half the time which he himself had expected. His secresy and boldness of plan, rapidity of attack, and admirable strategics baffled Soult and Marmont alike. Now, as afterwards at Badajoz, the French scarcely began to move before the deed was done. This fortress, which when weak had defied Ney and Massena for three months, had in the meantime been rendered much stronger by General Barrie, an able officer who worthily commanded a gallant garrison; he had thrown up new works, and fortified the two convents, Sᵃ· Cruz to the N.W. and San Francisco to the N.E. into redoubts. The Duke, in spite of the winter season, appeared before the place Jan. 8, 1812, and at dusk that very evening took the strong fortified *teson* to the N.; Graham, with the light division, having converted a proposed reconnaissance into a real attack. This determined the rapid fall of the fortress, as precious time was gained, and breaching batteries securely established. On the 19th two practicable breaches to the N.E. were nobly carried by Picton and Crawfurd, the latter receiving his death-wound. After Ciudad Rodrigo was taken the Duke rode back to Gallegos, sorrowful at the loss of brave Crawfurd ; he outstripped his suite, and arrived alone and in the dark. Marmont was so taken aback by the rapidity and brilliancy of this capture, that in his official report he observed, "There is something so *incomprehensible* in all this, that until I know more I refrain from any remarks." What can be greater praise to those who thus puzzled him? Yet Foy (i. 259, 302) refuses to the Duke and our engineers even a knowledge of the "alphabet of their art," and sneers at their profound ignorance and bungling in every siege ; and this when Cadiz, Tarifa, Gibraltar, and Alicante were attacked by the French, and *not* taken, because defended by the English, while Ciudad Rodrigo, Badajoz, Salamanca, Almaraz, Sⁿ· Sebastian, &c., defended by the French, *were* taken, because stormed by the English. So also did a handful of our soldiers capture at a hand-gallop both Cambray and La Pucelle Péronne, to say nothing of Paris. In truth, whether in Spain or France, the British army never took up a position which it did not hold, and never attacked a position of the enemy which it did not carry, and it accomplished both, although the French in numbers were generally as two, often three to one, and fought like truly brave and first-rate soldiers. In both the sieges and captures of Ciudad Rodrigo of Badajoz, the scholar will be struck with the parallel of Scipio's feat at Carthagena (Polyb. x. 8): he too jumped upon his prey, while two enemy armies were just too far apart to be able to get up in time to relieve it ; he too concealed his scheme so profoundly that the vulgar attributed the results of deep design to the "gods and luck," to which none ever owed less than the Duke.

The Duke, for this splendid feat of design and execution, was made an English earl ; the Cortes bestowed on him the rank of *grande*, making him duke of his recovered fortress ; and by this title,

Duque de Ciudad Rodrigo, Spaniards are fond of calling him, as it Espanolises to their ears our victorious general, while Wellington, a *foreign* name, grates harshly because inferring services rendered by a superior.

The Duke gave over captured Ciudad Rodrigo to Castaños and the Spaniards. This act for a time conciliated our allies, who had before suspected that England would keep this frontier key for themselves. Our confidence was miserably disappointed, for Don Carlos de España,* who was placed in command, forthwith broke all promises ·of pay to his men, and a mutiny ensued, the repairs were neglected, and even the stores furnished by England not moved in ; but the *Boukra, bab boukra* of the Oriental is the *Mañana, pasado mañana,* of the Spaniard, whose *to-day* is ever sacrificed for to-morrow ! By this unpardonable procrastination the capture of Badajoz was neutralized and Soult again saved, as by Lapeña at Barrosa, from ruin. " If (says the Duke) Ciudad Rodrigo had been provisioned as I had a right to expect, there was nothing to prevent me marching to Seville at the head of 40,000 men " (Disp. April 11, 1812).

The traveller will visit the English position, walking out to the suburb by the Alameda to Sⁿ· Francisco, then to the smaller *teson*, now called de Crawfurd, and then to the larger *teson*, now *elfuerte de Wellington ;* he may return by Sᵃ· Cruz and the Agueda ; it was on its banks, Oct. 11, 1811, that Julien Sanchez the *guerrillero* surprised the French governor Reynaud while out riding, and carried him off. He treated his prisoner with hospitality, and yet he himself had taken up arms because his house had been burnt and

---

* This man was created a grandee by Ferd. VII., and became the celebrated Conde de España, long the terror of Catalonia. Ennobled, he claimed descent from the Foix of Bearn. He was originally a French adventurer, and when the war began, was in prison at this very Ciudad Rodrigo for smuggling. For his tragical death see Urgel (p. 502).

his parents and sister had been murdered by the French, and he himself at that very moment was proscribed as a *brigand* by Gen.Marchand (Toreno, x.).

Ciudad Rodrigo became in the hands of the Duke an important base for future operations, and its capture may be termed the first blow by which he struck down the invader. It was to this point that he retreated Nov. 17, 1812, after raising the siege of Burgos; this sad conclusion of a campaign in which he had taken two fortresses, won Salamanca, delivered Madrid and Andalucia, and traversed Spain a conqueror, in spite of the great gallantry and numerical superiority of the enemy, was no failure of his. The neglect of our ministers at home, and the misconduct of our allies abroad, robbed him as usual of his full reward. He had much less to fear even from the French, his valorous enemies, than from his worst opponents, his so called friends.

EXCURSIONS FROM CIUDAD RODRIGO.

A morning's ride may be made to *El Bodon*, and to *Fuente Guinaldo*, which lie to the S.W. up the basin of the Agueda. " Here," says the Duke, " the British troops surpassed every thing they had ever done before." In Sept. 1811, while the Duke was blockading Ciudad Rodrigo, Marmont and Dorsenne advanced with 60,000 men to its relief. The Duke, whose forces barely reached 40,000, fell back towards *El Bodon*. Fifteen squadrons of superb French cavalry under Montbrun charged the 5th and 77th in squares, attacking them on three sides at once : they were repulsed at every point, and the two magnificent regiments retreated some miles in the plain with all the tranquillity and regularity of a parade. Marmont on that day proved that he was no great general ; he failed to take advantage of the most favourable moment of the war to crush the English army (Nap. xxiv. 6).

On the 26th the Duke took up a position at Fuente Guinaldo, and Mar-

mont, as if to amuse his opponent, went again through certain beautiful manœuvres in the plain below like a ballet-master. A little behind flows the Coa, and here, near the heights of Soito, the Duke offered Marmont battle, which, notwithstanding all his numbers, he declined. Remembering Massena's defeats, he was shy of advancing into Portugal.

Those who have leisure may prolong their excursion by making a circuit into Portugal, and coming back by Almeida, thus visiting many spots the scenes of the Duke's victories, and long his head-quarters. The author, who had planned this trip, was unfortunately prevented, but this was the route furnished by a friend in Ciudad Rodrigo. Take, however, a local guide, and attend to the provend. The distances are given approximatively.

ROUTE LXII.—EXCURSION FROM CIUDAD RODRIGO.

El Bodon	2
Fuente Guinaldo	1¼
Alfayates	2¾
Guarda	3
Celorico	4¼
Almeida	7
Freneda	2¾
Fuentes de Onoro	1¼
Gallegos	2½
Ciudad Rodrigo	3

Leaving Ciudad Rodrigo, bear S.W., keeping on the ridge with the valley and river to the l., passing *El Bodon ;* the plain to the r. of the road is the spot where Montbrun's charges were made in vain. From *F*ᵗᵉ *Guinaldo*, strike W. to *Alfayates ;* and entering Portugal, wind over the spurs of the Sierra de Meras, and by *Torre* to the Coa at *Sabugal ;* thence proceed N.W. to *Pega*, where, says Walter Scott, March 30, 1811, the French rearguard was overtaken by our cavalry ; thinking themselves safe from the strong position, they played " God save the King" in derision ; their minstrelsy was deranged by the *obligato* accompaniment of our artillery, and the rout complete ; they were pursued and cut up for four long miles.

Continuing from Pega we reach *Guarda*, an ancient Portuguese episcopal town, on the Sierra de Estrella, pop^{n.} about 2300. Observe the old walls and Cathedral. The town took its name from the castle, which *guarded* the frontier against the Moors. It is about 6 L. from the Spanish *raya*. Water here is most abundant, and the descents to the rivers Mondego and Nocyme, together with the mountain ravines, are very picturesque. These almost impregnable heights were abandoned, March 29, 1811, by Massena, who, with 20,000 men, retired without firing a shot, from Picton, who had only three English and two Portuguese regiments. Thence on by *Prades* and *Salgaraes*, over a hilly peninsula formed by a bend of the Mondego, to *Celorico*, pop^{n.} about 1500. The country is full of streams with decent bridges. Cross the river and strike N.E. by Baracal, Alverca, Carvajal, to Valverde, and then cross the Coa to *Almeida*, distant about ¼ L. This frontier fortress of Portugal rises on a gentle eminence, almost surrounded by a desert *plain*, or table as the word signifies in Arabic; it is distant about 1 L. from the Spanish *raya*, and about 7 from Ciudad Rodrigo; in times of disturbance the only route usually permissible is by the Val de la Mula, and the Aldea del Obispo, where the Spanish advanced posts are placed.

Almeida contains about 1200 inhabitants, and has a good church and tower; the citadel, which as in Spain has never been properly repaired since the Peninsular war, is still one of the finest in Portugal, although on the south side the rise -of the land is in nowise favourable to military operations. It has six bastions of hard thick granite, with other six ravelins, together with a noble platform, which commands a full view of the surrounding country. It is flanked by wide trenches, covered way, and esplanades; and in the centre stands a castle celebrated for its style of architecture and strength, as also from its magazines being bombproof. It

has wells and two fountains. On the 25th August, 1762, it was taken by capitulation, after a heroic resistance, by Count O'Reilly, with forty thousand Spaniards and French, for Portugal had then no force sufficient to oppose a siege. By the peace of 1763, it was restored by the Spaniards. The first result of the Duke's victory at *Fuentes de Oñoro* was the capture of Almeida, to relieve ·which Massena risked the battle. Such was his fright and flight after which, that he left the garrison to shift for itself without even communicating his retreat to Gen. Brennier, the governor, who blew up the bastions, and managed by his skill and bravery, aided by another blunder of Sir Wm. Erskine (see Miravete, p. 539), to save his troops. This, said the Duke, "is the most disgraceful military event that has occurred to us; I have never been so much distressed as by the escape of even a man of them " (Disp. May 15, 1811); but, as he then remarked, he could not be everywhere at once.

The rivers Coa and Turones divide Spain and Portugal, at these the smuggler laughs; from Almeida ride S. by the ridge to Freneda, under Monte Cabrillas, and distant about 5 L. from Ciudad Rodrigo; thence to Villa Formosa and so on to Fuentes de Oñoro; visit the village, cross the Dos Casas, and make for Alameda, or Gallegos, a poor hamlet of 600 souls, and distant about ¼ L. from the Agueda. The events which have occurred at these sites have been described a few pages previously.

ROUTE LXIII.—CIUDAD RODRIGO TO
SALAMANCA.

Santi Spiritus . . .	3	
Martin del Rio . . .	2	.. 5
Boveda de Castro . .	4	.. 9
Calzada	3	.. 12
Calzadilla	2	.. 14
Salamanca	2	.. 16

There is a sort of coach conveyance; the road is bad and uninteresting. Those who are riding and do not seek hospitality (and it is seldom or never denied *here* to any Englishman) in some *Montaracia*, will find an isolated *posada* near the church at Boveda. The memorable field of the battle of Salamanca may be visited the next morning by turning out of the high road to the r., through Tura and Miranda de Azan; coming out of which and the trees which fringe the Zurguen, is the point where Pakenham headed and checked the extreme French left; instead of following the road straight on to Torres, keep now to the r.; in front of Azan was the scene of the grand cavalry charge of Le Marchant, which shivered the superb French lines, and decided their defeat. Thence descend to the poor village of Arapiles. About 1½ mile E. rise the two knolls, the Arapiles, by which the French call this important battle. Salamanca with its domes rises about 4½ miles N. of the village.

This glorious victory took place July 22, 1812. The battle was the result of a false move made by Marmont. He and the Duke had long been manœuvring in face of each other, like two chess-players, or as Turenne and Montecuculi did in 1673; Marmont's disposable forces amounting to more than 100,000, the Duke's being under 60,000 (Nap. xviii. 4), of which scarcely half were British. This gave Marmont the power of every initiative, and reduced the Duke to act on the defensive. Marmont was goaded on by the reproaches of Buonaparte to risk a battle, and having lost it, was accused of rashness by his inconsistent master. The Duke's own account to Graham is short and sweet. "I took up the ground which you were to have taken during the siege of Salamanca. We had a race for the large Arapiles, which is the more distant of the two detached heights; this race the French won, and they were too strong to be dislodged without a general action. I knew that the French were to be joined by the cavalry of the army of the North on the 22d or 23d, and that the army of the centre was likely to be in motion. Marmont ought to have given me a *pont*

d'or, and he would have made a handsome operation of it; but instead of that, after manœuvring all the morning in the usual French style, nobody knew with what object, he at last pressed upon my right in such a manner, at the same time without engaging, that he would have carried our Arapiles, or he would have confined us entirely to our position; this was not to be endured, and we fell upon him, turning his left flank, and I never saw an army receive such a beating. I had desired the Spaniards to continue to occupy the castle of Alba de Tormes; Don Carlos de España had evacuated it, I believe before he knew my wishes, and he was afraid to let me know that he had done so, and I did not know it till I found no enemy at the fords of the Tormes; when I lost sight of them in the dark, I marched upon Huerta and Encinas; if I had known that there had been no garrison in Alba, I should have marched there, and should probably have had them all " (Disp. July 25, 1812).

The Duke's position was in the village of Arapiles. The battle began about three in the afternoon, for Marmont then extended his line towards Miranda de Azan. The Duke was writing when this false move was reported. He jumped up, and with eagle-eyed intuition exclaimed, "Egad! I have them:" and so he had. He " fixed the fault with the stroke of a thunderbolt." A few orders issued from his lips like the incantations of a wizard, and the English masses advanced; Pakenham to the l. about five o'clock breaking the head of Thomières's splendid column into fragments with the force of a giant. Then the 4th and 5th divisions attacked the French centre, gaining manfully the crest of *La Cabaña*, on which hill some desperate fighting took place; then and there the English cavalry, under Le Marchant, trod to the dust 1200 Frenchmen, " big men on big horses," says Napier, " trampling down the enemy with terrible clamour and disturbance, smiting mass after mass with downright courage and force," then 800 sabres overwhelmed Buonaparte's superb "columns of granite." The 3rd, or "Old Picton's fighting division," all but destroyed the 7th French division, which was posted on the brow of the hill and commanded by Foy.

The Duke broke through the French line here as Buonaparte did through the Russian at Austerlitz.

Marmont was wounded, and the command fell on Clausel, who with great talent and bravery endeavoured to repair the battle by changing his front; but the Duke turned round and smote him, then he fled behind the Arapiles, having abandoned everything that can constitute an army, and writing in the first agony of truth that not 20,000 men of the French army could even be reorganised. He retreated on Burgos, sending Col. Fabvrier to convey the news to Buonaparte, whom he reached on the Borodino, Sept. 7.

The late hour at which the battle began saved the enemy. " If we had had an hour more daylight the whole army would have been in our hands" (Disp. July 28, 1812). So again wrote he at Nivelle when there crushing Soult, and such were the very words used by Marlborough at Oudenarde, and by Stanhope at Almenara.

Salamanca was indeed a victory: the Duke in 45 minutes beat 45,000 Frenchmen. The shortness and completeness of the affair arose from the combatants being nearly equal in numbers; the English and Portuguese amounting to 46,000, the French to 45,000, but in fact very superior, in being of one nation, and in artillery and position, insomuch that Marmont was only afraid that the Duke would *escape* to Ciudad Rodrigo. He made so sure of victory, and was so desirous of monopolising all the glory, like Victor at Talavera, that he would not wait for Joseph, who was coming up with 15,000 more men. The French lost 2 eagles, 11 cannon, and 14,000 men; our loss amounted to 5200. Although the full

bowl of joy was dashed from the Duke's lips by the left-handed Carlos de España, yet the victory was most important; Madrid and Andalucia were delivered, the Opposition was silenced in England, and the traitor members of the Cortes of Cadiz were prevented from making terms with Joseph; while the recoil shook Buonaparte even in Russia, and raised the courage of the rejoicing world. The Duke now felt his growing power : " I saw him," says Col. Napier, a soldier portraying a soldier, " late in the evening of that great day, when the advancing flashes of cannon and musketry, stretching as far as the eye could command, showed in the darkness how well the field was won. He was alone,—the flush of victory was on his brow, and his eyes were eager and watchful; but his voice was calm, and even gentle. More than the rival of Marlborough, since he had defeated greater warriors than Marlborough ever encountered, with a prescient pride he seemed only to accept this glory as an earnest of greater things."

The peasant who attended the Duke as guide was named Fr°· Sanchez; he lost a leg in the fight, and was therefore always called afterwards *El Coco.* He had a pension of six reals a day, which the *Liberals,* so he told us, took from him in 1820.

These plains, bleak, commonplace, and such indeed as elsewhere would be hurried over without notice, are henceforward invested with an undying halo; and little is that man to be envied who when standing on such sites, does not feel his patriotism grow warmer. Now every vestige of the death-strife of giant nations has passed away. Nature, ever serene, has repaired, like a bountiful parent, the ravages of these quarrelsome insects of a day. The corn waves thickly over soil fertilised by the blood of brave Britons who died for ungrateful Iberia; and the plain for twenty years afterwards was strewed with their bleaching bones, left to the national undertaker the vulture; nay for want of cover in these denuded steppes, the sculls were strangely tenanted, *quœque ipse miserrima vidi:*

> "Beneath the broad and ample bone
> That buckled heart to fear unknown,
> A feeble and a timorous guest,
> The fieldfare built her lowly nest."

And, for another trait of character, the peasant *El Coco* assured us that although 6000 Spaniards, under even Sarsfield, in whose veins flowed Irish blood, had been quartered two months in Salamanca in 1832, not one man or officer had ever been to visit this battlefield; and truly there, as at Barrosa, no single blow was struck by Spanish sabre: nor has delivered Spain reared any chronicle of stone, or filled any niche at Salamanca with aught to record an English ally; nor does Mellado, in his Guia of 1843, even allude to the victory at all; yet he can devote pages to the paltry bushfightings of Carlists and Christinists.

But there still stand those grey Arapiles, those pillars of the Hercules Britannicus, and engraved with his sword. They will exist for ever, silent but eloquent witnesses of a glorious truth, which none can ever rail from off the bond.

The results of the victory of Salamanca were neutralised by the misconduct of our ministry at home, and of Ballesteros and the Spaniards in the Peninsula. The siege of Burgos was raised, and in November, 3 months after Marmont's disaster, the Duke stood again on these plains: then, as he had predicted, the relief of Andalucia threw on him the additional army of Soult, who, joining Jourdan on the Tormes, now commanded 100,000 infantry, 12,000 horse, with 120 cannon. The Duke and Hill were resting their weary forces, which did not exceed 52,000 men; but he knew his old ground, and wished to fight and to conquer again and again: deprived by some absurd proceedings of the Cortes of his usual sources of information, he lingered at Salamanca, challenging the French to battle one day

too long. Jourdan, who had forgotten Talavera, wished to engage at once; but Soult, who remembered Oporto, hesitated, and his discretion was backed by Clausel, who disliked les souvenirs des Arapiles, and thus lost the precious chance. Both, although brave and skilful, were cowed by the mere presence of the Duke; they hoped, relying on vast superiority of numbers, to cut him off from Ciudad Rodrigo, *par des savantes manœuvres.* Then it was that the Duke made that magnificent move, defiling as at Burgos in the face of the enemy, who did not even molest him: thus he gained on them the advance, and bringing his army to the river Valmuza, marched hence by the upper road through Vitigudino to Ciudad Rodrigo; a retreat unparalleled in daring and complete success, and more glorious than many aggressive campaigns. Never was exhibited a more perfect conception of difficulties —never were they met and mastered with greater presence of mind; every step evinced far-sighted prescience and sagacity, and the happy divination of genius.

The French account is characteristic (V. et C. xxvi. 204): Soult rejète les Anglais en Portugal, en leur faisant éprouver une grande perte, quoiqu'ils *precipitassent* leurs mouvements pour *éviter* une affaire générale. The truth being that the Duke's only error was the not sufficiently hastening his retreat, and that because he *courted* a general action to which Soult prudently demurred.

After leaving these plains, and riding over a bleak, treeless, unenclosed country, cold in spring and winter, and scorching in summer, we reach Salamanca rising nobly with dome and tower on its hill-crest over the Tormes, which is crossed by a long Roman bridge of 27 arches, and which better becomes a learned university than the Folly bridge of our Oxford.

SALAMANCA is without even a tolerable *Posada.* The Ledesma diligence starts from *La de los Toros: La de Navarra,* near the Pl^{n.} Mayor, is but a mere *parador;* but gastronomy never was an Iberian science, and if Salamanca has produced 100,000 doctors, it never has reared one good cook. The food for body and mind, however copious in quantity, is equally unsatisfactory in quality, the *panes pintados* not excepted: it has not even the " brawn and puddings" of Oxford, which heads of houses digest. However bad the inns, there are many *posadas secretas,* or " private lodgings," and *tiendas de Uveceria,* and *Botillerías,* where the undergraduates lodge, and drink bad aniseed brandy, with or without Castalian streams, as copiously as German Burchen do beer. Salamanca is the capital of its modern department; the see of a Bp. suffragan to Santiago; pop. under 14,000. The town is dull, cheerless, and cold; the air bites shrewdly, and as fuel is very scarce, the sun is the fireplace of the poor : hence "the South" takes precedence in the three " Marvels" of Salamanca : *" Medio dia, medio puente y medio claustro de S^{n.} Vicente."* The city has an antique old-fashioned look. The beautiful creamy stone comes from the quarries of Villafranca, distant about a league, and is infinitely superior in colour and duration to the perishable material used at Oxford. This university however is altogether deficient in those academic groves and delightful gardens of her English rival. The traveller must inquire whether the contemplated *Museo* is formed; meanwhile the principal pictures and objects of art will be described in their pristine localities, and if they are moved there will be no difficulty in identifying them. Salamanca is built on three hills, in a horseshoe shape; the Tormes forms the base, and the walls which overlook it are very ancient, especially near the *Puerta del Rio.* The Tormes rises in the Sierra de Gredos, near Tormelles, and after a course of 45 L. flows into the Duero near Fermosella; it contains fine trout, some have been caught weighing 18lb.; the

best fishing is nearer the source : at Salamanca the dingy waters rather resemble the Cam than the Isis, and they are supposed to produce similar effects. *" Ha bebido de las aguas del Tormes,"* is either a compliment or a satire, and alludes either to the waters of Castalia, or to those of oblivion, as the case may be, and generally to the latter; for Salamanca is presumed to be learned, because all bring to it something, and few take away anything : thus Fabricio advises Gil Blas not to go there, because having some natural cleverness he risked its loss.

Salamanca (Salmantica) was a large and ancient city of the *Vettones.* Plutarch (De Virt. Mul.) calls it μεγαλη πολις ; he relates how, 532 u.c., Hannibal raised its siege, the Spaniards having " promised to pay" 300 talents of silver and give 300 hostages. No sooner was he gone than they did neither, whereupon he came back and destined the place up to plunder, having ordered the male population to come out in jackets, and without arms or cloaks. The women, however, hid swords under their *sayas* (as the Manolas still do knives); and when the Massæsylian guard placed over the prisoners left their charge to join in the pillage, these Amazons armed the men, who killed many of the plunderers; Hannibal re-appeared, and the Spaniards ran to the hills, but he was so pleased with the *brave* women, and so anxious to do what would the most gratify them, that he allowed them to re-people Salamanca (see Tortosa, p. 467). The ladies only spoke Iberian, and Hannibal only Punic, but he had an interpreter named Bacon.

Under the Romans Salamanca became the IXth. military station, on the *Via Lata,* the broad road from Merida to Zaragoza. Trajan (Pontifex maximus) built the bridge, of which the original piers exist. The prophetic Goths patronised Salamanca; here they coined money in gold, which they seldom did elsewhere (see Florez, ' M.' iii. 272). It was ravaged by the Moors, and finally reconquered in 1095. It abounds with early specimens of architecture, thus, the old cathedral is of 1102; S⁰. *Tome de los Caballeros* of 1136 ; Sⁿ. *Cristobal* of 1150; Sⁿ. *Adrien* of 1156 ; Sⁿ. *Martin* of 1173; S⁰. *Tomas a Becket* of 1179, having been built only four years after his murder at Canterbury, thus offering a singular proof of the rapid extension among churchmen of the fame of this champion of ecclesiastical pretensions over the civil power.

Salamanca, called by Spaniards *Roma la chica*, from its number of stately buildings, is truly a university to any *architect* who wishes to study style from the earliest periods; it contains most superb specimens of the simple and florid Gothic, as of the richest cinque-cento and plateresque, down to the most outrageous *Rococo ;* for Josef Churriguera, the heresiarch of bad taste, and whose name is synonymous with absurdity in brick and mortar, was born here about 1660. This man and his style were only another ulcer, an exponent of the then universal corruption of Spain, religious, political, and artistical.

The French spared his works, which were the models of their gewgaw style of Louis XIV. ; they selected the noblest monuments of religion, art, and learning on which to set the mark of their *empire*, as if its greatness was to be tested by extent of injury. " Operæ pretium est cum domos atque villas cognoveris in urbium modum exædificatas, visere templa quæ nostri majores religiosissimi mortales fecere. Verum illi delubra Deorum pietate, domos suas gloriâ, decorabant; neque victis qnidquam præter injuriæ licentiam eripiebant: at hi contra ignavissimi homines per summum scelus omnia ea sociis adimere quæ fortissimi viri victores hostibus reliquerant ; proinde quasi injuriam facere, id demum esset imperio uti." So thought the Roman philosopher (Sall. B. c. 12); and thus wrote the indignant English conqueror, June 18th, 1812:

" The enemy evacuated on the 16th, leaving a garrison in the fortifications which they have erected on the ruins of the colleges and convents which they have demolished." " It is impossible to describe the joy of the people of the town upon our entrance; they have now been suffering more than three years, during which time the French, among other acts of violence and oppression, have destroyed 13 out of 25 convents, and 20 of 25 colleges which existed in this celebrated seat of learning." Again, Feb. 10, 1813, " I have lately received intelligence that the enemy have destroyed the remaining colleges and other large buildings which were at Salamanca, in order to use the timber for firewood." There are some people (says Bacon) who will set fire to a man's house to roast their eggs. The western portion is now quite a heap of ruins; thus conceive Oxford, if Monsieur Joinville should " enter" and " *écraser*" Christchurch, Corpus, Merton, Oriel, All Souls', the Ratcliffe, Bodleian, Brazennose, and St. Mary's.

Salamanca, for a town of 14,000 souls, was previously very tolerably supplied with spiritual establishments; besides the cathedral, and its splendid chapter staff, there were 25 parish churches, 25 colleges, 25 convents, and 11 nunneries; but to understand what it was before Messrs. Ney and Marmont went into residence, consult ' *Historia de Salamanca*,' Gil Gonzalez de Avila, 4to., Salᵃ· 1606 ; and ' *Compendio Historico*,' Bernardo Dorado, 4to., Salᵃ 1776 ; Ponz, xii.; Florez, ' E. S.' xii. Spaniards, like Orientals, seldom repair anything, nor in their recent poverty have they the means of re-erecting monuments, the work of centuries of wealth, piety, and learning, which the armed foe has reduced almost to nothing, and for which there is no demand now, for the scholastic age is here past, although that of railways is hardly begun : nor have they imitated our Hookers and Lauds, who, when the Reformation had despoiled the church of funds, being unable to rebuild old edifices with stones, reared new monuments with their pen, to the honour and glory of their sacred order.

Salamanca is the Oxford of Spain. The first university in Castile was that founded at Palencia by Alonzo VIII., which induced Alonzo IX. of Leon to establish this for Leon. When the two kingdoms were united under his son St. Ferdinand, Palencia was incorporated with Salamanca, and he gave the united universities new statutes in 1243. Alonzo el Sabio, his son, being learned, *not* wise, favoured this seat of learning, and endowed professorships in 1254; here were calculated his celebrated astronomical tables; but, like Thales, who, when star-gazing, stumbled on the earth, this poor pedant's political career was one entire failure: *Mucho sabia del cielo, y poco del suelo.* The university was first governed by its own rector, and code drawn up in 1300: this officer of great authority was chosen for a year every 11th of September, and entered into his functions on the 25th. The discipline of the university was placed under his tribunal. The details of office, the *Becas,* or distinctive hoods, the *Maceros,* silver bedels, &c. will be found in Davila and Dorado, and in that quaint old 'Handbook' for Spain, ' *Grandezas de España,*' Pedro de Medina, 1566, p. 97.

On the important head of tufts, we may just mention, that a *white* tassel in a cap signified divinity; *green,* common law; *crimson,* civil law; *blue,* arts and philosophy; *yellow,* medicine, the proper tint of bile and jaundice— but these colours were only hoisted on gaudy days and grand occasions.

The colleges were divided into *Mayores* and *Menores:* at the *larger* were taught divinity, law, medicine, and the classics; at the smaller, grammar and rhetoric. The *Escuelas,* or schools, were three: first the *Mayores,* or greater, teaching theology, canonical law, medicine, mathematics, philosophy natural and moral, languages, and rhetoric; next the *Menores,* or smaller, teaching grammar and music; and last, the *Minimos,* or smallest, teaching the mere accidence, reading, and writing. The *larger* colleges were aristocratical foundations, for the rigid proofs of birth and purity of blood, *Hidalguia y limpieza de sangre,* monopolized them in the great families, insomuch that simply to be a member of one of them ensured immediate subsequent promotion in law and church. Of these *Colegios Mayores* there were only six in all Spain; one at Seville, one at Valladolid, and four at Salamanca, which were Sⁿ· Bartolomé, Cuenca, del Arzobispo, and del Rey. The others are, or rather were, 21 in number, and by name, Monte Olivete, Sᵒ· Tomas, Oviedo, Sⁿ· Millan, Sᵃ· Maria, Sᵃ· Cruz, La Magdalena, Alcantara y Calatrava, de los Angeles, Sᵃ· Susana, Guadalupe, Sⁿ· Pelayo, Sⁿ· Bernardo, Los Irlandeses, Sᵃ· Catalina, Las Viejas, Sⁿ· Juan, Jesus, Sⁿ· Miguel, Sⁿ· Pedro y Sⁿ· Pablo, and Burgos.

These colleges are not of very early date, for the wealthy pious of primitive times founded convents, until their abuses turned the charity of the thoughtful into a better direction, to the erection and endowment of schools, colleges, and universities, to all of which a religious character was given. The dawn of classical literature in the 15th century tended to add to these foundations; while some of the long-sighted, who must have foreseen the eventual downfall of the monkish system, wished to invest their bounty in securer objects.

The *Colegios Mayores* were first curtailed of their privileges by the minister de Roda, who, having when young been rejected at one from his low birth, persuaded Charles III., about 1770, to *reform* them; thus, they were deprived of their patronage and remodeled. These changes, ostensibly made for the public good, were really the effects of private revenge: Blanco White (Lett. 104) gives the secret history of this job.

Salamanca, which in the 14th century could reckon 14,000 students, had already, in the 16th, declined to 7000, and it continued to languish until the French invasion : now it is a comparative desert. The establishment of local universities in large cities has broken up the monopoly of granting degrees; and now, in the stagnation of payment of pedagogic salaries, sad abuses occur ; degrees are granted without residence, forged certificates are obtained from tutors and lecturers, who must live. The advantages also of an academical education to the better classes are much diminished since the rich sinecures in cathedral chapters and courts of justice have been diminished ; the poorer students, who aspire only to be humble curates, have always been the subject of witticisms and satires. *Un Estudiante* has long been synonymous with an *impertinente.* The inferior orders of them were simply beggars " licensed by act of Parliament," just as our "poor scholars " were by 7 Richard II.; they were permitted by law (Recop. lib. i. tit. 12, ley 14) to vagabondize and finish their education by soliciting charity. Thus they took their degrees gratis; and many rose to be Spanish ministers, and masters of arts in begging loans. Their costume is remarkable, especially their tattered cloaks or gowns; but *debajo de una capa rota hay buen bebidor,* there is many a good drinker under a bundle of rags, and l'habit ne fait pas le moine. These students are among the boldest and most impertinent of the human race, full of tags and rags, fun, frolic, *licence,* and guitars. Their peculiar compliment is the throwing their cloaks of shreds and patches on the ground for well-dressed handsome women to walk over. Sir Walter Raleigh's similar delicate attention to Queen Elizabeth helped him to a better suit. This "spreading garments in the way " is truly oriental and classical (Matt. xxi. 8). Thus the troops of Cato testified their respect to him (Plut. in vit.), as before had been done to Jehu (2 Kings ix. 13); and Roa

(Singularia i. 144) mentions the usage as continued among the Moors of Granada. They wear also a quaint oilskin cocked hat, in which a wooden spoon was placed, such a one as those with which paupers relieved at convent doors used to eat their gratuitous soup: hence these *Estudiantes* were also called *Sopones Soperos Sopistas,* soupers not sophists; and few in sad truth were born with a silver spoon in their mouths, or a superfluity of anything, except impudence. But modesty is of no use to a beggar or monk, as *Fray modesto nunca fue guardian,* and still less if he be hungry, which these students proverbially are, and worse than hounds, *Hombre estudiantina peor que la canina :* they are gregarious, generally hunting in packs, but one, the *gracioso,* or wag of the party, begs in verse, accompanying his improvisation with a guitar. These students figure in all low life picaresque novels of Spain, *El bachiller de Salamanca* and such like, and the character was frequently assumed by young nobles as a mask for indulging in tricks upon travellers and adventure ; the real pauper students went their rounds with real beggars, and according to Quevedo, those of the eating-houses as regularly as pilgrims.

" *Romero el Estudiante, con sotanilla corta,*
   Y con el quidam pauper, los bodegones ronda."

Many of such students were as ill-conditioned as their vagrant habits : they almost appropriated to themselves the epithet *tuñante,* rogue, a word derived from the Persian *tuni,* a vagabond beggar. They always loved low company, especially that of *muleteers,* who represent in Spain the blackguardism of our fraternity of the whip ; hence the proverb *Estudiante sin recuero, bolsa sin dinero ;* and their purses, whether from absence or impatience of coin, were, like Valentian stockings, open at the end. By them the " *Freshman* " was always victimised, and among other summary initiations, crowned with a foolscap mitre; hence, as among our irreverent dealers in horseflesh, he was said to be *Obispado*, "Bishoped," a term equivalent in Spanish slang to being *done*. No tradesman in Salamanca was allowed to trust any student for anything without the previous authority of his tutor or parent. This law of Charles V., 1542, might well be extended to Oxford.

The academical career of the better classes is dull indeed compared to the boatings and Bullingtons of Oxford; it rather resembles the Calvinistic routine of Geneva, without even the musical snuff-boxes. Oxford takes precedence of Salamanca: this nice question was decided at the Council of Constance in 1414, when Henry de Abendon, warden of Merton, advocated his university. Compared to the learning, scholarship, order, and wealth of Oxford, Salamanca is what the Spanish "Lines" are to Gibraltar.

The "Dons," as far as *Puchero* commons go, are hospitable, nor is vino de *Toro* wanting, which, like port elsewhere, is said to promote prejudice. These siestose men of protruding and pendulous abdomens, " Dediti ventri atque somno (Sallust says, ' B. C.' 2, indocti incultique" reside, " duller than the fat weed which rots itself at ease on Lethe's wharf." They indeed studied the oriental philosophy of indolence, preferring unctuous *ollas*, and fat bacon to the feast of reason and the sage of Verulam : and those who have much to digest ought to think proportionately little. 'Tis folly in well beneficed rectors to cultivate the cerebral secretions at the expense of the gastric juices, for dispepsia, says the learned Portuguese Amati, follows study as a shadow does the body, or a *Dueña*, all eyes and toothless, does a pretty damsel ; accordingly all systems elsewhere exploded here took deepest root, especially the *Averoista*, or corrupted Aristotelian. Even up to 1747 it was considered a heresy to assert that the sun did not revolve round the earth ; so that the capon revolved round the spit, what cared the senior fellows and drony Doctors, contented when

not sleeping to suck in the milk of *Alma Mater,* indifferent as to the history and origin of their separate foundations. Nor were they in good humour when cross-questioned by the *impertinente curioso* or foreign " chiel '' taking notes, for " faith he'll prent it."

Let not the book collector fancy that he will pick up any choice thing in this seat of supposed learning. The commonest editions of the classics are hardly to be had (see on this matter p. 138).

Inquiry should be made whether any new library has been formed out of the recent sequestrations. The *Salamantinos* were quicker with their *coliseo,* for *Pan y toros* is a more popular cry than "Arma virumque cano." However, during the Peninsular war, the gownsmen, all and every one, from the rector down to the scout, hated the invader, by whom their funds were stolen, their " commons " eaten, and their colleges destroyed. They furnished the Duke with secret information, and the names of Curtis and Guillen are immortalized in his dispatches as good men and true.

Salamanca, in times of yore, when not disturbed, was renowned for useless and unentertaining knowledge, for polemics, casuistry, dogmatic theology, and papal orthodoxy—for the defence of this, or, as they termed it, " *La Fe*," *the* religion, and the " immaculate conception of the Virgin," colleges were founded. The University has produced very few really eminent men, or over honest, for it always has been ready, when mitres and preferment were held out, to give opinions in favour of the king, whether Don Pedro in 1355 wished for a divorce, or Philip II. *not to pay* the dividend of his loans. This University, which burnt as *magical,* the library of Villena, the Mæcenas of Spain, and which condemned as visionary the scheme of Columbus, was declared by the infallible Clement VII. to be "Turris David inexpugnabilis cum propugnaculis, ex quâ mille clypei doctorum virorum pendent, omnisque armatura fortium, quæ Ecclesiam Dei Sanctam, contra virulentos Hereticorum impulsus extreme tuentur." *"Nous avons changé tout cela,"* said the French, who, having pulled the Pope out of his throne at Rome, found no difficulty in ejecting his Salamantine professors from their chairs, and in converting these metaphorical, theological bulwarks into real bastions and barracks.

To those who are not artists, architects, or antiquarians, a day or two will suffice to see the marvels of ruined Salamanca. The superb Plaza *Mayor* is indeed the *largest* square in Spain: it was built by Andres Garcia de Quinones, in 1700-33. A colonnaded arcade is carried on each side, underneath which are shops, the post-office, and *Casa del Ayuntamiento*, or mansion-house, which is churriguerresque and corporate. In this Plaza, bull-fights are given, and 16,000 to 20,000 spectators have been accommodated. The façades are adorned with busts of kings and worthies of Spain, and blank spaces have been left for future great men. These vacua, hateful to nature, have gaped for a century, hiatus maxime deflendus (see p. 214). Even the struggle for independence, which calls spirits from the deep, did not give birth to one Spaniard, civil or military, who attained even mediocrity. No bust of Wellington decorates any yawning niche in these walls, which overlook those plains where he won back this city and Madrid (and compare Pamplona); yet Arguelles, in his ' *Historia* ' (i. 20), cites as a proof of Spanish gratitude the *paper* decree of the Cortes, Aug. 17, 1813, to erect a memorial to the deliverer of Salamanca. This ended in being a vox et præterea nihil, since the performance is deferred until the Greek calends and the payment of what was *promised* to Hannibal. Below this new square is the old Covent Garden, *La Plaza de Verdura :* observe the peasants in this picturesque market. Over the portal of Sⁿ· Martin is a rude sculpture of the

Saint dividing his capa, a charity which the Castilians of all people best estimate, and least imitate. In the interior the *Retablo,* concealed by a trumpery tabernacle, has the same " partition." Observe the Santiago and the Crucifixion and Glory above. In this church some of the pointed arches and capitals are very remarkable.

The cathedral is splendid florid Gothic of the age of Leo X.; it was begun (see the inscription at the grand entrance) in 1513; a consultation was previously held of all the chief architects in Spain; see the curious documents printed by Cean Bermudez (Arch. i. 293). Nor is this at all a singular instance (see Gerona), but the mediæval age in Spain, which now-a-days is called the dark one, was that of ecclesiastical magnificence, munificence, and knowledge; then were reared those cathedrals, colleges, and schools, whose founders may well rise from their graves, and rebuke their critics, the soi-disant leaders of modern civilization. Centuries then passed during the erection of the house, the "*palace* of God " (1 Chron. xxix.): the completion was a solemn duty, handed down from one generation to another. The church, built like a rock and on one, rose as if also to endure for ever, for no expense of thought or gold was ever spared in this labour of love. The homes and houses of those who raised it were indeed poor, but they, like the old Romans (Sall. B.C. 9), stinted nothing for the dwelling of him who had given them everything. Now private luxury and decoration contrasts with religious poverty in art and meanness in feeling, nay the Gothic devotional sentiment has almost become too mysterious to be comprehended in modern contracts, whereby it is provided in eighteen months to finish off so many pews and so many " free sittings," distinctions and postures unknown in more Christian ages, and the very bane and destruction of ecclesiastical architecture.

After much deliberation at Salamanca, the plan of Juan Gil de Ontañon was selected. The edifice was built under Bp. Fr⁰· de Bobadilla, son of Beatrice the dear friend of Isabella, who had the good sense not to pull down the old cathedral, to which this is now joined, and from whence service was removed March 25, 1560, *Lady day* being chosen by the mariolatrous chapter. The entrance is exquisite. Observe the infinite ornaments and statues of the rich portal, and the beautiful cream-coloured stone in which they are wrought. The towers are inferior and are of later date; over *La Puerta de las Palmas*, is the Entry into Jerusalem; outside is a walk, a Gradus, or " Grees," as at Seville. There are three aisles, of which the central is the highest. At the sides of the two lateral ones are enclosed chapels as at Seville, and the whole is in admirable condition and well kept. The roof is supported by graceful shafts, with small capitals painted in blue and gold : the Gothic roof is studded with gilded rosettes. The gallery is most delicate, with a double frieze of birds, animals, and scroll-work. Observe above, the busts projecting from gold circular frames. The octangular *cimborio* is very light and elegant. The *coro*, as usual, blocks up the centre, while the *silleria* is heavy and bad, and the exterior churrigueresque. Observe, however, the statues of St. John and a cross Sᵃ· Ana teaching the Virgin to read : both are ascribed to Juan de Juni. Visit the *Dorada* chapel, built by Fr⁰· Sanchez; observe the profusion of small saints, on gilt pedestals, picked out in blue, white, and gold. The tomb of the founder is dated 1524 ; he is sculptured as asleep in his robes ; above is his portrait in black. Observe the *azulejos*, and the sepulchres of 2 prelates railed off like lions' dens. In the *Capilla del Sepulcro* is a copy of Titian's " Deposition." In the *Cᵃ· del Presidente* are some paintings by Morales, two heads of the Saviour and a doubtful Virgin with the Infant and St.

John. Visit next *La Pieza,* the vestry of the canons; observe the delicate foliage and ornament, and the Louis XIV. mirrors fit for a fine lady's toilet. In the adjoining *Oratorio* the relics are kept, but the French carried off the silver mountings. Here is *El Crucifijo de las Batallas,* a small bronze, which the Cid always carried before him in fight, as the Pagans did their *Victorias*. It is very curious and authentic. The crown is black, the apron gilt, and girdled with a white belt, studded with gilt checquer work. This semimiraculous crucifix has actually had its historian. (See ' *El Christo de las Batallas,*' Gil Davila, 4to., Salam. 1615.) It was brought here by Geronimo, the Cid's own bishop, and remained over the prelate's tomb from 1120 to 1607, when it was removed to the Relicario.

In the *Cᵃ· de Sⁿ· Antonio* are some fine pictures, possibly by Zurbaran, of the Beheading St. John, and, in the next chapel, a Crucifixion, with two Bishops. Below were buried the family of the founder, Antonio Corrionero. The small box, dated 1633, is said to hold, not bones, but parchment title-deeds. In an adjoining chapel is a St. Jerome beating his breast, by Gaspar Becerra. Observe the 3 Gothic sedilia in the *Cᵃ· de Abajo* behind the choir, and a circular concave *Retablo* with more than 50 paintings set in white and gold frames. The sepulchres are of the date 1466. Observe the ancient arches and capitals.

The old cathedral which lies below is simple and massy, and half a fortress; hence the epithet " *Fortis* Salmantina," to distinguish it from " *Sancta Ovetensis,*" Oviedo rich in relics ; " *Dives Toletana,*" Toledo rich in tithes ; " *Pulchra Leonina,*" Leon beautiful in art. This *Fortis Ecclesia* was built in troubled times of frontier danger, by a prelate of the Church militant, by Geronimo, the confessor of the Cid. He was a Frenchman, born at Perigord, and was brought to Spain by his countryman Bernardo, primate of Toledo ;

he was made Bishop of Valencia, in 1098, by the Cid. They were in every battle, like true Bishops of a Church militant, and worthy sons of their martial country. Geronimo, after his master's death, was translated to Zamora. He next induced Count Ramon, the husband of Queen Urraca, to build this cathedral at Salamanca, in 1102, which Calixtus II., own brother to Ramon, elevated to episcopal dignity, both sees being held by him, and in both his cathedrals he introduced the Norman-French style of architecture; the exterior of his *Iglesia vieja* is best seen from *La puerta del patio chico;* the simple solidity contrasts with the elaborate portal of the later edifice. Observe the Norman square billet as at Tarragona, the salient balls as at Toledo, and the peculiar scaly tiling of a pyramidical tower top. The old cathedral is low, damp, and neglected. Geronimo lies buried in the 2nd chapel to the l. Some have read the word *Visquio* as his name, others as old Spanish for *Vixit.* His tomb was opened in 1606, when a delicious smell issued forth, worthy of one born in the town of odoriferous pies, but this odour is one of the sure proofs of monastic sanctity after death. Although a goaty, shirtless, illote, unshod Capuchin when alive never reminded the olfactory nerves of "the sweet south breathing over a bed of violets," being exactly one of the soapless Pagan prophets, the Σιλλοι ανιπτοποδες of Homer (Il. π, 235); yet the orthodox belief in Spain, the result of repeated experiments, is that the grave and corruption, which rob beauty of her fragrance, do but perfume a deceased friar. It is clear from all Spanish ' *Flores* Sanctorum,' that these holy carcases have always been miraculously re-discovered, like truffles, from their peculiar subterraneous bouquet, but this notion of *L'esprit de mille nonnes,* was, however, borrowed from Ovid:

" Mansit odor, posses scire fuisse Deam."

On those snowdrops of odour of sanc-

tity, the *live* nuns of Spain, a few praises have been sung at p. 72. They, too, are precise imitations of the Pagan *Flaminicas* (Ovid, ' Fast.' vi. 229).

" Non mihi detonsos crines depectere buxo,
  Non ungues ferro subsecuisse licet."

Among other, although not inodorous tombs, observe that of Mafalla, daughter of Alonzo VIII., 1204; of the Dean Fernando Alonzo, 1285; of Juan Fernandez, Rico Ome, 1303. Some of the *Retablos* are extremely old. In the *Capilla del Colegio Viejo,* which is painted blue, and studded with stars of gold, is the tomb of Diego de Anaya, 1374, Archb. of Seville and founder of Sⁿ. Bartolomé. The ceiling of this chapel, now a lumber room, is quite Moorish, and doubtless the prelate brought hither some of the Granada workmen who had adorned the Seville Alcazar for Don Pedro; near it is a beautiful sepulchre of an armed knight and his sister, and a " Beheading of St. John " by Fernandus Galecus (Gallegos), by whom also, in the *Cᵃ· Sⁿ· Clemente,* is a " Virgin with the Saviour who takes a rose from St. John." These are among the earliest of Spanish paintings, yet they have been scandalously neglected. Gallegos was born at Salamanca in the middle of the 15th century, and is the Van Eyk of Spain. The old cloister, built in 1178, has been partly modernized; here formerly the schools were held. In the Cᵃ· de Talavera, founded by Rodrigo Maldonado, the Musarabic ritual was continued (see Toledo); in the *Cᵃ· de Sᵃ· Barbara* degrees were confirmed; and in *Sᵃ· Catalina* synods were held, and " wranglings " for honours and professorships open to competition or *de oposicion,* were contended for, until the regular schools were built, which are close adjoining, for the university, strictly speaking, is a jumble of buildings. *Las Escuelas,* " the schools," were commenced in 1415 by Alonzo Rodrigo *Carpentero*—no bad name for a builder, and one probably derived from his vocation—and were removed here from the cloister in 1433. This was the age of Juan II., the patron of literature and the troubadour: see the inscription over the gate *de las Cadenas.* The chapel was dedicated to St. Jerome, the *Doctor Maximus* of the church, who was flogged by angels for reading the classics instead of theology, a warning not forgotten by Salmantine students. Medina gives the details of this once most curious chapel, which was modernized and ruined under the Bourbons, when good taste, at all events, was not taught. The *Retablo,* rich in material and poor in design, contains some bad pictures, by Fr°· Cachaniga, of doctors swearing to defend the "immaculate conception:" over the door of each of the *aulas,* "halls," or lecture rooms, are tablets denoting the science which is or ought to be taught in them; inside each is a pulpit for the lecturer, or *catedratico,* with rows of benches for the students, and a sort of ledge for them to write their notes on. The *Patio* is modern, and the royal portraits, in *chiaro oscuro,* are very bad. Ascending the staircase, observe the morris dancers and foliage by way of bannisters; in the anteroom are other royal portraits, from Philip II. downwards, and all equally devoid of merit; the roofs of the ceilings are in rich *artesonado,* and stalactitical. The handsome library is fitted with Louis XIV. bookcases and gallery; in a smaller room are confined the books prohibited by the *liber expurgatorius;* thus, as in the appendix of some improved classics, all the objectionable matter is creamed together for the initiated, who obtained a papal dispensation for such reading. The library was rich in theology, editions of Aristotle, and works of Tostado (see Avila). Near the anteroom was the chamber in which the student about to "dispute" or "wrangle" was placed, with a sentinel at the door, for 25 hours, to consider his subject quietly; it was filled with huge folios, fit for the leisure of cloistered pedants, but

now seldom read save by yellow parchment-faced bibliomaniacs, whose skins took the colour of their food, as the bones of rabbits fed on madder become pink, or the stockings of learned ladies blue: now all is quiet, and the worms either die of old age or eating nonsense. The smell is truly musty, and must be conducive to learning if knowledge could be acquired by the nose. Many of the polemical books were formerly chained to the reading-desks, like mastiffs, more to prevent collision than removal.

Passing through some quaint tapestry-clad rooms, as the *Sala del Claustro,* a modernish saloon, the Golgotha in which the doctors and heads of houses assemble in conclave. The size of these now-deserted halls bears witness of past crowds; how much has been here disputed, how little decided! how much wasted research, what a much-ado-about-nothing, how much taught of what it would have been equally profitable to have remained ignorant; the modern system of education in Spain is now modelled on that of France; the schools are divided into different classes, according to the age of the instructed and nature of instruction. The teachers are clergymen, and their salaries are defrayed by the state, or ought to be, for they are seldom paid now; hence every sort of neglect and abuse. Education is in some degree compulsory, being defrayed out of the public purse; but a child may lead a Spanish *burro* to the fountain of Castalia, while an army of tutors cannot make him drink. There are no public schools as in England, but the students are day pupils, and return home to board with their parents; accordingly the domestic ties are longer kept up, and filial and parental relations better maintained than with us, at the expense, however, of the sciences of boating, foot ball, and cricket, in which young Spain is lamentably in arrear; and the rising generations lack an early initiation into the miniature world, such as Eton and Winchester where conceit is taken out, and all fin their level; where *fair play and h*

2 c

principle and true manliness are taught; where " *English gentlemen* " are formed, that πρωτη ὑλη, that first and best material for everything else.

Coming out of the schools the grand façade of the library is alone worth an architect's visit to Salamanca: it is the triumph of the decorative and heraldic style; here the creamy stone has been as wax in the hands of the artist, and no Moor ever embroidered lacework, Cachemire *Lienzo,* more delicately. It is of the richest period of Ferd. and Isab., whose medallions and badges are interworked with scrolls: the inscription is in Greek, " The fear of God is the beginning of wisdom." In the *Plazuela* opposite is the hospital of poor students, and some of the smaller *Escuelas;* they are very ancient, especially Sⁿ· Millan, and *Pan y Carbon,* bread and coal, food for the body rather than the mind, which recalls our *Brasinghouse,* now Brazennose, nomenclature.

Hence to San Bartolomé, the oldest of the *Colegios Mayores,* and therefore called *El Colegio Viejo,* but New College would be more appropriate, for it has been completely modernised. The rawness of the new tasteless work ill accords with the venerable date of the older buildings, which, like aged men, look better in their contemporary russet coats than in " the last " spick and span fashions. This college was founded, in 1410, by Diego de Anaya, Archb. of Seville, who, returning from the Council of Constance, had seen Bologna. The object was to " defend *the* faith ;" hence it was so thronged in 1480 that the proverb ran " *Todo el mundo está lleno de Bartolomicos;*" here was devised the fatal *Limpieza de sangre,* which neutralized all conversion from Jew and Moor, by distinguishing between new and old Christians, the *nuevos o rancios,* thus cursing Spain, already sufficiently unamalgamating, with a new caste, and another fatal germ of disunion. These religious distinctions were borrowed from the Moors, by whom those of the old Goths

who renounced Christianity were called *Môsalimah,* or *new* converts to Islam. They were despised just as the renegade Moors were among the Christians. Arabicè *Muraddin,* their equivalent for the Spanish *Cristiano nuevo.* The term *Mulatto,* half-caste, is Moorish, *Mnwallad,* " any thing or person not of pure Arabic origin," and which being pronounced then, as it is now, in Barbary, *Mulad,* became in Spanish *Mulato* and *Mula* (Moh. D. ii. 458); the primitive root was doubtless the Latin *Mula,* mule.

The college of San Bartolomé was " *beautified* " about 1767 by one Josef *Hermosilla.* The Salmantines admire it prodigiously, but the Ionic portico is heavy, the cornice clumsy, and the square windows of the entresol mere portholes; the *Patio* is simple and better, but the staircase is somewhat narrow, and the pictures in the chapel by Sebastian Concha are indifferent; this college produced *El Tostado,* very renowned in Spain, and elsewhere very much unknown; see Avila.

Cuenca, the next *Colegio Mayor,* was founded in 1506 by Diego Ramirez, Bishop of Cuenca, by whom Charles V. was baptized. This most exquisite cinque-cento edifice, fair daughter of Cuenca's elegant cathedral, was, before M. Ney " entered," the marvel of Salamanca; men wondered where artists could be found to design it, workmen to execute, and wealth to defray the cost. Of this gem of Berruguete art, only a fragment of the front, with the founder's motto γνωθι σεαυτον, remains, and by their fruits shall ye know those who demolished the rest. A few medallions of prelates, knights, and elegant ornaments about the windows show what was the original character of this splendid pile. In a ruined quadrangle portions of sculpture mutilated by the invaders still encumber the weeds.

Passing hence to *San Blas,* the full extent of this French devastation is evident. In order to fortify this commanding quarter, they demolished Sⁿ·

Benito, Sⁿ· Vicente, La Merced, and Los Cayetanos, and levelled all the houses up to Sⁿ· Bernardo, to make a glacis as at the Alhambra and Valencia. From these ruins the eye ranges over the river, the cathedral, and the enormous Jesuitas. These forts were stormed by the Duke in person, June 27, 1812, and although defended by 800 picked men and 20 cannon, they surrendered at once, like the *Teson* at Ciudad Rodrigo. Thus were captured in a few hours bastions which it had occupied the enemy three long years to construct, and this in the face of Marmont's superior army, which did not venture to interfere. Now Monˢʳ·Guetin (Guide en Espagne, p. 478) tenderly deplores how much "Salamanque eut à souffrir en 1812, du feu des batteries Anglaises, qui tiraient à boulet rouge sur cette malheureuse cité."

Adjoining is *El Colegio Mayor de Santiago*, or, as it is usually called, *del Arzobispo*, from the founder, Alonzo de Fonseca, Archbishop of Toledo, who was buried in the Ursolas. It was begun in 1521 by Pedro de Ibarra, at the best period of the cinque-cento style. Observe the most airy elegant *Patio*, the fluted pillars, and Pierino del Vago medallions, which glitter in the sun, like a rich chasing by Cellini. The boys and heads, some in caps, some in helmets, are full of grace and variety of design. Ibarra was aided by Alonzo de Covarrubias and Berruguete; thus the three great artistic architects of their age, tria juncta in uno, were simultaneously employed, each vying in honourable rivalry to outdo the other. Some of the work is in the transition period, from the Gothic to the Renaissance. Berruguete in 1529 undertook to "build, carve, and paint" the *Retablo* of the chapel : Ponz (xii. 234) gives an extract from the original agreement. The noble work was finished in 1531, but whitewash has done its worst, and a portion only of the original colouring has escaped near the altar. The precious *Retᵒ·* when

seen from a distance, looks like a silversmith's work of gold and enamel. The eight paintings are rather coldly coloured, and the drawing resembles that of Juan de Bologna ; the upper four are the best, but the figure of the student in the centre niche is not by Berruguete.

The last of the *Colegios Mayores* is that *del Rey*, "King's College." It was commenced in 1625 by Gomez Mora, and was founded by the military order of Santiago. The quadrangle is Doric, serious and simple. The chapel was unfortunately modernised and bedaubed with gilding and *churrigueresque*, by a S. American bishop of more wealth than taste.

Close by is *Sⁿ· Esteban*, a Dominican convent so called, because, when one near the Tormes was destroyed by a flood in Nov. 1256, this parish church was assigned to that order. It was one of the finest enriched Gothic buildings in the world. The benefactors were Juan Alvarez de Toledo, uncle to the great Alva, and Diego de Deza, tutor to Prince Juan (who died at Salamanca, Oct. 7, 1497) and afterwards Archbishop of Seville. This true Dominican and ferocious Inquisidor was nevertheless, like Philip II., a patron of art, and protector of Columbus, and he was sincere even in his bigotry. He also founded the College of Sᵒ· Tomas at Seville. Observe the elaborate façade and portal ; it almost rivals that of the library. The eye is bewildered with the details, which are thrown like an embroidery or filigree work, over the whole ; the creamy stone is worked into saints, apostles, candelabra, and richest caprice. The martyrdom of the tutelar is by Juan Antonio Ceroni of Milan. The noble church is a Latin cross. The entrance is under a *dark* elliptical arch which supports the *coro* as at the Escorial, but beyond all is brilliant, nay the altar is overdone with gilding. The dome is painted in fresco by the feeble Antonio Palomino ; the subject, the "Triumph of Religion," is a failure of art. The roof is richly studded; the *Retablo* has a good Martyrdom of St. Stephen by Claudio Coello. Observe to the r. a precious door worked with riding children and scroll-work. In the light cloister remark the pillars and capitals in the angles, and the basso-relievos sculptured by Alonzo Sardina. Observe also the *sala capitular* built in 1627 by Juan Moreno, the grand staircase, the beautiful *sacristia*, and library. This exquisite pile was vandalised by the French, who made a magazine of the church and stables of the cloisters.

Columbus in 1484-6 was lodged here; and the monks and Deza, to their honour, espoused his scheme, which the " *Golgotha* " of the university had pronounced to be " vain, impracticable, and resting on grounds too weak to merit the support of the government." The sable conclave was held at Valcuervo, " the Valley of *Crows*," Jackdaws, 2 L. off, to secure quiet for deliberation. Here the arguments of the great Genoese were rebutted by texts from St. Augustine; here he was thought to be an atheist, a reckless adventurer, a fool, by real fools, who despised what they could not understand, and this occurred in the palmy days of Salamanca; such then were her pedants, Dons of " fat paunches and lean pates;" who, ignorant of the world, nursed in routine, and steeped in prejudice, from long custom of teaching others, were incapable of being taught themselves: but Salmantine pedagogues, from the habit of measuring their intellects with their pupil inferiors, frequently form a false standard of their own powers and acquisitions, and when they come into the world, and are grappled with by men, they are either thought bores and quizes, or are hooted at like owls, whose proper place is the darkling cloister, not the bright daylight.

These convocated heads of houses, who could decide against a vision *foreigner*, who was in the *right*, always gave an opinion in favour of Spaniards

of place and power, albeit in the *wrong;* their decisions, as in the case of Don Pedro's divorce, are a sore subject in Salamanca, and over which Gil de Avila says " He must draw a veil, as the dutiful son did over the nakedness of Noah."

Opposite to the palace of the Alvas, with its two turrets, all gutted by the French, is *Las Agostinas Recoletas*, a once magnificent convent, founded in 1626 by Manuel de Zuñiga, Conde de Monterey, and favourite of Philip IV. This "good slow man," according to Clarendon, had married a sister of the all powerful Conde Duque, and was by him appointed viceroy at Naples. He became so rich, that a poor pregnant woman who had a longing, *un antojo*, to see Philip IV., when thanking him for granting an audience, prayed that " God might make him viceroy of Naples." The Palace of Monterey should also be looked at, on account of its elegant turrets, and upper line of arcaded windows, which remain, the rest having been terribly ruined by the French. The convent built by Juan Fontana is a noble pile with red marble fluted Corinthian pillars, and a simple cupola: it has an Italian character. The church, a pure Latin cross, is one of the finest in Salamanca. Observe the Florentine pulpit of *Pietre dure*, in which S^{n.} Vicente de Ferrer is said to have preached, and the *Retablo* to match, with Corinthian red marble pillars, and the gilt bronze tabernacle, with spiral columns and *lapis lazuli;* the tombs of the founder and his wife are by Algardi; observe the armour and costume: many pompous titles are inscribed below the kneeling figures, which but enhance the triumph of death, who has cropt them all to form a garland for his victor brow; now his turn is come, and all is nothing and neglect. Monterey, if he did make his fortune in office, at least was a splendid patron of art; many pictures which he gave to Philip IV. are still at Madrid; he reserved for this convent ' S^{n.} Januario kneeling on the clouds," by P. Veronese, doubtful; an "Annunciation," by Lanfranco; a "Nativity," Ribera: the child is much repainted; some very fine Stanzionis (Caballero Maximo). Observe also a S^t. John-like Guido, S^t. Joseph, a fine dark S^n. Agustin, and the meeting of the Virgin and Elizabeth, and a Nativity, fine; also a San Nicolas, Lanfranco; a *Virgen del Rosario*, Ribera, and the grand altar-piece, the *concepcion*, signed Jusepe de Ribera, Español, Valentiano, F. 1635. In this the Virgin's feet are shown, a liberty allowed to artists in Italy, but prohibited in Spain by the Inquisition: as Monterey was viceroy at Naples at the precise moment when Ribera, Stanzioni, Lanfranco, and others had really created a school of art in that city of Sybarites and macaroni, this convent was once a museum of Neapolitan paintings; now they flap rotting in their frames, but yet are pure in surface, having never yet been defiled by harpy cleaners or restorers. It is, or was, proposed to send them to the local *Museo*. There are more paintings inside, which cannot be seen by the male sex, as the nunnery is *en clausura*. Of the famous cartoons by M. Angelo, "the Swimmers," mentioned by Carducho (Dial. 151), we could obtain no information, and yet probably they exist mislaid and unappreciated; for Don Alejo Guillen, who had often been inside, assured me that during the French occupation he managed to secrete there many precious things, which thus escaped the spoiler.

Another nunnery, *S. Espiritu*, destined like Las Huelgas at Burgos for noble ladies, is a fine pile of granite. Observe the superb roof over the *coro*, and the portal by Berruguete. The church of *Carmelitas Calzadas*, is a pure simple Doric of Juan de Herrera. The quadrangle of the *Colegio de Guadalupe* is incredibly rich in minute decorations, a lace-work of form and figure, animal and vegetable. The tower of *S^o. Tome de los Caballeros* is of the 12th century. Observe the an-

cient sepulchres with pointed arches near the altar. The elegant and pathetic Luis de Leon was buried in 1591 in the *Agustinos Calzados*. Observe the portal of *Las Dueñas*, founded in 1419, as inside Santa Teresa received her Divine revelations (see Avila).

The *Jesuitas*, built in 1614 by Juan Gomez de Mora, is enormous. The chapel and transept are grand, but the *Cimborio* has been cracked, and the *Retablo* is vile churrigueresque. The portals, towers, and cupolas, are more striking from size than good art. Here the Irish students were lodged, after the suppression of this order; their original college was founded in 1592 by Philip II., and dedicated to St. Patrick, in order that "some priests of the true faith might yet be educated for unhappy England in the hopes of finally extinguishing pestilential heresies;" and merry old England did profit thereby, for the honest rector, Dr. Curtis, did his countryman the Duke good service during the war, and was recommended warmly by him (Disp. Feb. 22, 1813).

Philip II. was married Nov. 13, 1543, at Salamanca to Maria of Portugal, when the city outdid itself in bull-fights, to wipe away all memory of the part it had taken against his father in the outbreak in 1521. The leader of the Patriots, or *Comuneros*, was one Valloria, a *Botero*, or maker of wine pigskins. This agitator plundered the colleges, their plate-chests, butteries, and cellars so effectually, that the mob were so pleased that they made every one swear this oath of allegiance:— " *Juras a Dios no haber mas Rey, ni Papa, que Valloria*." This Spanish Jack Cade, or rather "Best, son of the tanner of Wingham," was very properly hanged April 23, 1521.

Near the churrigueresque *Merced*, is the *Colegio de la Vera Cruz*, so called from the apparition of white crosses on the dresses of the Jews during a sermon of S^n. Vicente Ferrer. The *Refectory* of the convent was once the synagogue. This St. Paul and tutelar of Valencia visited Salamanca in 1411, where he converted 8000 Moors, 35,000 Jews, and 100,000 other sinners. This seems a good many in so small a town; but it was one of his common *miracles* (see Valencia, p. 448); indeed, such things were so much of every day occurrence, that the operator, when he was asked by one of the doubting doctors for a sign, replied, " What more do you require than that up to this day 3000 miracles have been wrought by means of this sinner" (see, for details, Gil de Avila, p. 354, and Dorado, 286). Sⁿ. Vicente was second only to Father Matias, 30 years first cook to the Dominicans at Salamanca, who used to remain in an ecstatic state while his dinner dressed itself, the dishes running after the spoons, and a pretty *puchero* it must have been (see Dorado, p. 22 ; and compare this miracle with Sⁿ. Isidro's ploughings,— Madrid). These are saints after the Castilian's own heart, who loves to doze with folded arms, while Hercules does the work, stands the fire, and then is not even allowed to share in the *olla.*

Among the houses best worthy observing in Salamanca, is *La Casa del Sal,* or *Salinas,* with its arched front, granite pillars, ornamented windows, and singular *Patio.* Observe the projecting roof and gallery upheld by quaintly carved and grotesque figure supports. The Maldonado family have a fine old house opposite La Trinidad. Near the Jesuitas is the *Casa de los Conchas,* ornamented on the exterior like the Mendoza Palace at Guadalajara ; the interior is much degraded : observe the fine Patio, and minute Gothic ornaments. In the *Plaza Sⁿ. Agustin,* observe the ruined front of the convent destroyed by the French, and a singular old house with the arms of Ferd. and Isab., and most delicately shaped windows.

The *Calle de las Muertes* is so called from the house built by Archbishop Fonseca, whose bust, with those of his two nephews, are sculptured in front. Under the windows are placed sculls, which give the name to the street ; here lived our kind and hospitable friend Don Alejo Guillen, prior of the cathedral, and one mentioned so often with honour in the Duke's Dispatches, and thus embalmed and immortal ; see particularly Aug. 18, 1812. His Grace himself, when at Salamanca, lodged in the house of the Mˢ· de Almarza, in the *Plaza de Sⁿ. Boal.* Every Englishman will of course visit it, and observe the rosette-studded arch at the entrance, and the medallions in the *Patio,* especially a young lady with a ruff, and the heads of the founder and his beautiful wife, whose drapery is free and flowing.

In the *Plaza Sº. Tomé* is an ancient mansion with red brick Moorish arches and *Azulejo,* and another with a Berruguete front and portal, with the medallions of the founder and his wife— a very common Spanish *cinque-cento* decoration.

The *Torre de Clavel* is a good specimen of the mediæval Castilian keep, with those little turrets at the corner which occur at Coria, Coca, Segovia, and elsewhere. In the *Cuesta del Seminario* was the *Aula,* the hall where Villena endeavoured to restore learning. Here he taught natural philosophy, which the monks thought heretical and magical. The University at his death appointed Lope de Barrientos, Bp. of Avila and Inquisidor-general, to inspect his library ; two cart-loads were sent him, which he forthwith proceeded not to read, but to burn. Ponz (iii. 105) prints a curious letter written at the time by Fernan Gomez, physician to Juan II., to the poet Juan de Mena, lamenting this Omar vandalism. According to him, Lope de Barrientos " could not understand the books more than the Dean of Ciudad Rodrigo would have been able." Juan de Mena grieves (Coplas, i. 126) over such " exequies" of the patron of literature and " honour of Spain ;" but profane learning, and especially Moorish, had long been condemned by the cowl, who, like Swift's

— " Clowns on scholars as on wizards look,
And take a folio for a conjuror's book."

Thus Gerbert—Sylvester II.—from having gone in 985, to study Arabic in Spain, was held afterwards to be a sorcerer. Some few of Villena's volumes escaped, and among them that singular treatise on carving, *arte cisoria*, which was printed at Madrid in 1766 from the MS. then existing in the Escorial, but in no country have libraries fared worse than in Spain. Ximenez burnt at Granada 80,000 Moorish volumes, under pretence that they were Korans, just as his friend Torquemada burnt Hebrew books at Seville. Monks of convents, like the librarian at Alcalá de Henares, sold treasures to rocket and glue makers, while the French made parchments into cartridges, and systematically bombarded libraries. Thus, in unhappy Spain, the bonfires of fanaticism and revolutionary ignorance have blazed far and wide : " in libros sævitum,"—the impotent malice which provoked the magnificent indignation of the Pagan philosopher,—" Scilicet *illo* igne vocem populi Romani, et libertatem senatûs, et conscientiam humani generis, aboleri arbitrabantur." —Tac. Agr. 2.

Descend now to the Tormes, and observe in the way the *Puerta de Sn. Pablo,* with the infinite statues of saints, the Pope or St. Peter in the centre. Examine the foundations of the old walls, and the Roman bridge. The *Medio Puente* is one of those pavilions or shrines so common to Spanish bridges, in which some tutelar river god or local saint is worshipped. On this bridge was placed one of those strange animals, which, whether wild boar or rhinoceros, are classed with the *Toros de Guisando* (see Index); and the Oxford of Tauromachian Spain has taken for its arms " a bull on a bridge crossing a river "—a Bull-ford. Having passed the Tormes, turn to the r. and cross the rivulet Zurguen to view the

noble city rising proudly in front. This *Zurguen* was to the poet Melendez what the " *Bonny Ayr* " was to Burns. If the traveller will ascend the cathedral tower, and walk some afternoon out of the gate S° Tomas, and make the circuit of the walls, passing the gates of Toro, Zamora, and Villamayor, and entering again at San Vicente, he will have seen something of Salamanca.

There are three routes from Salamanca to Madrid, and a sort of public coach ; No. 1, the shortest and mos$_t$ uninteresting, is through Peñaranda.

ROUTE LXIV.—SALAMANCA TO MADRID.

Aldea luenga	.	.	2	
Ventosa	.	.	.	3	.. 5
Peñaranda	.	.	.	2	.. 7
Fontiveros	.	.	.	3½	.. 10½
San Pascual	.	.	.	3	.. 13½
Blanco Sancho	.	.	2½	.. 16
Venta de Almarza	.	.	1	.. 17
Madrid	.	.	.	15	.. 32

Huerta is a poor village in a plain near the Tormes, which occasionally inundates the road; and thither it was that the Duke marched after the victory of Salamanca, imagining that the bridge lower down to the r. at Alba de Tormes was secured by the Spaniards as he had ordered, which it was not. Hence crossing the Ventosa to *Peñaranda de Bracamonte,* a decent town of 4000 souls, well supplied with water from a fine aqueduct. The parish church is simple and well built. The road is next carried over the rivers Trabancos, Zapardiel, and Adajas, which flow down from the Avila chains rising to the r. After travelling over an uninteresting slovenly-cultivated country, this route joins the high Madrid and La Coruña road at the *Venta de Almarza.*

The second route makes a circuit by Valladolid.

ROUTE LXV.—SALAMANCA TO MADRID.

Pedrosillo	.	.	.	2½	
Cañizal	.	.	.	3½	.. 6
Alaejos	.	.	.	3	.. 9
Siete Iglesias	.	.	1	.. 10
Tordesillas	.	.	.	4	.. 14

Simancas	3	..	17
Valladolid	2	..	19
Segovia	19	..	38
San Ildefonso	2	..	40
Escorial	8	..	48
Madrid	8½	..	56½

This route cannot be recommended except to those who are pressed for time and do not propose returning from Madrid to France by Burgos and the western provinces. However, they will thus see Valladolid, Simancas, Segovia, and the Escorial, and be able to go on to Valencia by Toledo, Aranjuez, and Cuenca.

The country to Tordesillas is dreary, from thence excursions may be made to Toro and Medina del Campo: for all these and other towns in this route, consult R. lxxv.

The 3rd line is through Avila, and, if continued through Guisando and the Escorial, is full of interest to the artist, antiquarian, and angler (see R. cxvii.).

ROUTE LXVI.—SALAMANCA TO MADRID.

Alba de Tormes	4		
La Maya	2½	..	6½
Piedrahita	3	..	9½
Villatoro	3	..	12½
Sa. Maria	3	..	15½
Avila	4	..	19½
Escorial	7½	..	27
Madrid	8½	..	35½

Alba de Tormes, whence the family of Toledo take their ducal title, is in the centre of their vast possessions. It has a noble bridge over the Tormes, which Don Carlos de *España*, true man of *Spain*, by neglecting to secure as ordered, rendered a *Pont d'or* to the French after Salamanca. The palace-fortress overlooks the town, with its round towers and machicolations, but it was ruined and gutted by the enemy, and the superb armoury stolen. Observe the spiral pillars of the chief patio and the plateresque façade. The interior was painted in arabesque, and frescos relating to the battles of the great Alva. The grand gallery to the S. was upheld by marble pillars, and filled with busts. In the *Carmelitas descalzas* are the fine sepulchres of the founders, Fro. Velazquez and Teresa his wife; observe their effigies, the Doric pilasters, and also the sepulchral statue of Simon Galarza, and Juan de Ovalla and Doña Juana de Ahumada with a child at their feet. Near the town is the fine Jeronomite convent, with two quadrangles, and the superb tomb of Gutierez Alvarez de Toledo, Archbishop of Toledo: proceed hence through a broken country, studded with oak-woods, to *Piedrahita*, built on a slope, with the palace of the Alvas, erected in the last century at a cost of more than 400,000*l*. Jacques Marquet, a Frenchman brought to Madrid in order to pave the streets, gave the design. The gardens, with temples and terraces, rendered this the Stowe of Spain, but all was ruined, like Abadia, by the invaders.

Alba de Tormes, besides being the scene of *España's* negligence after the battle of Salamanca, witnessed the disgrace of the Duque del Parque. He (Oct. 19, 1809) had defeated Gen. Marchand at Tamanes, distant 2 L., and the success turned the Seville Junta's heads, who, thinking that they now could reconquer Madrid without the aid of the English, planned the campaign of Ocaña, in defiance of all the Duke's warnings and advice. The defeat of Areizaga recoiled on del Parque, who forthwith commenced his retreat; and here at Alba de Tormes, within 2 L. of his former victory, he was surprised, Nov. 28, 1809, by Kellermann: alarmed, says the Duke, at the appearance of 30 French dragoons in his rear, the army dispersed, abandoning guns and everything; fortunately there was no enemy at hand to take advantage of this panic.

The road soon enters New Castile, and is carried through the *Puerto de Villatoro*, and thence by gentle descents through a wooded sporting country to Avila (see R. cxvii.).

When once at Salamanca, we strongly advise the traveller to make the pilgrimage to Compostella, visiting the trout streams and monasteries of the

Vierzo, and then turning into the Asturias to Oviedo, and coming down to Madrid through Leon, Valladolid, and Segovia. This ride in summer is delicious, as the country is alpine, and to the angler, unequalled. Many of the cities are full of interest to the antiquarian, as it was to this mountain-corner of Spain that the remnants of the Goths fled in 712, and where they first reconstructed the monarchies of Leon and Castile.

ROUTE LXVII.—SALAMANCA TO LUGO.

Calzada	3	
Cubo	3	6
Corrales	3	9
Zamora	3	12
Piedrahita	3	15
Riego	2	17
Sta. Eufemia	2	19
Benavente	3	22
Pozuelo	3	25
A la Bañeza	3	28
Toral	2	30
Astorga	2¼	32¼
Manzanal	3¼	36
Bembimbre	3	39
Cubillos	2½	41½
Villafranca	3½	45
Ambas Mestas	2½	47½
Castro	3	50½
Doncos	3	53½
Santa Isabel	2½	56
Sobrado	2½	58½
Lugo	3	61½

First we may mention that Toro lies 12 L. from Salamanca by an uninteresting carriageable road, through Fuente - Sauco, 6 L., and along the river Guarena (for Toro, see R. lxxv.).

The celebrated warm baths of *Ledesma* lie about 6 L. from Salamanca to the W., and there is a diligence to them in the season. The district is of great antiquity, and is still divided into *Rodas*, districts, Arabicè *Rauda*, garden. *Ledesma*, Bletissa, the chief town, is very ancient and picturesque; its singular walls are thought to be earlier than the Romans. It stands on the Tormes, the fine bridge over which was built on Roman foundations. Many inscriptions are found here, and outside the *Puerta de los Toros* are two of those strange antique Bulls of Guisando (see Index). The baths lie

about S.E. 2 L. off. The waters are warm, ranging from 29 to 30 Réaumur, and are used both internally and externally, being very beneficial in cutaneous and rheumatic complaints. The season is from June 1 to Sept. 30. From Ledesma to Zamora there is a cross-road through Sⁿ. Marcial.

The road to Santiago passes between those to Toro and Ledesma. To Calzada it runs over a desolate waste of *Xaras y encinas;* a living creature is rare: here we were struck with flocks of wild hawks of a large size, with greyish white bodies and tails and wings tipped with black. About Cubo the country improves; and here, in a sheltered valley, is *Val Paraiso,*—the vast convent in which St. Ferdinand, one of the best and greatest of kings, was born; it is now a ruin, as the French converted this *paradise* into a wilderness. The peasants about here become as churlish as their country, no longer saluting the stranger like the *Estremeño* or *Charro.* They either wear *Monteras*, or "shocking bad" and Irish-looking hats. The red-stockinged women veil their heads with handkerchiefs, and all seem poverty-stricken and starving amid corn and wine: the latter, fine and good, sells for about 3 reals the *arroba*, or 6d. for 16 bottles. Although here are no corn-laws, and wheat is a drug, yet what avails all this cheapness and plenty, when wages are at the lowest ebb, and none have even a mite wherewith to make purchases; nor are there any outlets for the over-production; roads, canals, and customers are all wanting, yet this *Vino de Toro* is far superior to what is commonly sold in England as port.

From Salamanca to Corrales under its windmill-studded hill is a 6 hours' ride; we slept at the decent *Posada;* continuing the route from the hermitage *El Cristo de Morales*, Zamora is seen rising grandly, with its ancient walls, over the waters of the Duero, *Fluminaque antiquos subterlabentia muros.* The long embattled line is terminated to the l. by the castle and ca-

2 c 3

thedral. The old bridge, to the r., has three of those towers on it which are so common in Spain ; the arches are very pointed ; the river above and below is dammed up with water-mills. The piers of another ruined bridge are seen below the cathedral. The Duero, as it approaches Portugal, has few bridges, and being now deep, and with dangerous ferries, becomes a most important military line in time of war. The river rises in the bleak Sierra de Urbion near Soria, receiving the affluents of the hills above Logroño and the Montcayo. It flows west through a dreary country, which improves near Zamora, below which it forms the boundary between Spain and Portugal. The whole course is about 500 miles. The name Ur, ὕδωρ, the Celtic Dwr, simply means *water*, as *Gave* does in the Pyrenees. This water *par excellence*, is indeed an αριστον μεν ὕδωρ, since according to the proverb it is equal to chicken-broth in nutriment: *Agua de Duero caldo de pollos*, an axiom which our readers may well distrust, and put a real *poule* in their *pot ;* the river moreover has the honour to give the title of Marquis to the Duke, as on its banks he foiled the enemy, especially Soult at Oporto. Below Zamora are some wild passes and ferries, used by smugglers ; the most remarkable are *El Paso de las Estacas*, that of the Stakes, and *El Salto de la Burraca*, the leap of the great she-ass, not the heaven-ascending mule of Mahomet.

Zamora is a decayed place. Pop^{n.} under 10,000. There is a tolerable *Posada* on the *Plaza Sa. Lucia*. The cathedral is the see of a bishop, suffragan to Santiago. The city bears for arms its bridge, with two towers and a flag. The name is said to be derived from the Moorish *Samuráh*, a city of " turquoises," of which it possesses none. Conde, however, suggests " Diamond," and considers it a mere metaphor for its hardness as a rock-built citadel. In the early Spanish annals, being placed on the barrier river, the Duero, it was an important frontier

town against Moorish invasions. It was recovered from the infidel in 748 by Alonzo El Catolico. It was besieged in July, 939, by Abdu-r-rahman, when a desperate battle was fought for its relief by Ramiro II., and the Moslems were defeated. Zamora was then enclosed by 7 lines of walls, and the spaces between were defended by moats ; 40,000 Moors are said to have been killed in these trenches. Ramiro, from being in want of everything, was unable to follow up his victory. Zamora was retaken and destroyed in 985 by the great Al Mansúr, but was rebuilt by Ferdinand I., who gave it in 1065 to his daughter Urraca, who must not be confounded with her niece Urraca, the wife of Ramon of Burgundy, and *Reina propietaria* of Spain; this once common name, which still exists in these parts, is pure Arabic, and means " brilliant in colours;" hence Mahomet's mule, on which he ascended to heaven, was called *El Burac*. The term is also given to a delicious pear in Gallicia, and to a chattering pie, *habla mas que una Urraca*.

Ferdinand, like Louis le Débonnaire, by his impolitic devise, dismembered a monarchy which his whole life had been spent in consolidating, and like his 7th namesake, bequeathed a civil war to his heir Sancho, who, resenting the unjust partition, besieged Zamora in 1072. Then it was the well-walled city, *Zamora la bien cercada*, and proverbially almost impregnable: *a Zamora, no se ganó en una hora*. Sancho being enticed near the walls by Vellido Dolphos, was assassinated on the 7th Oct. in an unseemly position, according to the old ballad, the Cid from want of spurs being unable to catch the traitor; but every one will read his *Romancero* on these sites.

The Spaniards, after the king's death, wanting a fit leader, their emphatic *want* in all times past and present, disbanded, like true Orientals, each man to his own home. It was at this siege that 5 Moorish kings (sheikhs) brought tribute, and saluted Ruy Diaz de Vibar with the title of Cid Campeador—the champion prince, just as our Wellington is now called here *El Lor, El gran Lor,* " *The* Lord," exactly as we say " *The* Duke."

Pass out by the *Puerta de la Feria* into the pleasant Alameda with its fountains and stone benches, and hence to the palace of Urraca, which occupies the extreme point of the city. The walls follow the irregularities of their rocky bases; the palace is a ruin. A mutilated bust of Urraca still remains over a gate, and an inscription said to be the " *Afuera! Afuera! Rodrigo el soberbio Castellano*" of the old ballad, and allusive to the Cid's being shut out when the traitor-assassin Dolphos was let in. Near the cathedral is the bishop's palace, with its corridors and open gallery.

This cathedral is very ancient. The see, which had fallen into abeyance during the time of the Moors, was restored by Alonzo VI., son of Ferdinand I., whose heiress, Urraca, had married Ramon, brother to Pope Calixtus II. ; and thus through family interest at Rome many difficulties with contending prelates were got over. The Archbishop of Toledo was a Frenchman named Bernard, who filled the sees of Spain with his countrymen, and they introduced the Norman style of architecture, exactly as occurred at Tarragona. Geronimo, the confessor of the Cid, when deprived of the see of Valencia at its reconquest by the Moors, was appointed to Zamora with *quasi*-episcopal functions. The S. and dilapidated entrance deserves particular notice. Observe the four round or Saxon arches, and the singular pattern-like rolls of linen. The capitals of the pillars are the bastard Norman-Gothic Corinthian. The rose windows are fine, and the massy square tower and *cimborio* are quite cognate with the *Iglesia Vieja* of Salamanca. The two lateral aisles in the interior are low. The dome is picked out with a wavy pattern of gold on white. The

altar mayor is composed of reddish marble pillars, with gilt bronze capitals, and the Transfiguration sculptured in marble is modern, and of inferior art. The old retablo was moved to the convent of San Geronimo. The *coro* is carved in a tedesque manner like Rodrigo Aleman, and dated 1490. Observe the open Gothic spire of the bishop's seat, and the saints and figures above the dark-coloured stalls of the canons. Remark the carved door with figures and Gothic work to the l. of the high altar. Among the tombs observe those of Bernardus, the first bishop, 1149, and near the door that of Bishop Pedro, 1254, confessor of St. Ferdinand, opposite to that of Bishop Suerus Perez, 1286. Other old tombs are in the *Capilla del Cardenal*, viz. Alvaro Romero, cloaked, observe his sword ; and in the *Ca. de Sⁿ. Miguel* that of Canon F. M. de Baltas, 1308. The very ancient *Retablo* is parted into 6 divisions, with paintings like Fernando Gallegos. The original cloisters were burnt in 1591, and the present, in simple Doric, were rebuilt in 1621. The N. entrance to the cathedral has unfortunately been modernised in the Corinthian style, which ill accords with the primitive Gothic.

La Magdalena was a church of the Templars, which was, at their suppression, given to the Order of St. Juan of Jerusalem ; it is a simple solid edifice of the twelfth century. Observe the masonry of the exterior, the deeply-recessed entrance, with remarkable circular arches above, highly enriched, partly with Norman, partly with Moorish patterns. The absis is circular. In front is the high altar, with a beautiful round arch and mouldings: observe also the rose window above, formed with small columns, precisely like that in the Temple church at London. Before entering the inner portion, on each side of the lofty pointed arch are two ancient tombs of members of Sⁿ. Juan. Observe the cross and the spiral pillars which support the canopies, also the enriched portal. Zamora contains much quaint mediæval architecture, now sadly decayed, as if to enhance its merit for the painter; visit, for instance, *La Plaza de los Momos*, and observe the singular façade of a *casa solar*, with *ajimez* windows, and the peculiar Valentian doorway, with large fan-like stones in the arch-work; but what foreign vandals have spared is allowed to go to ruin by national neglect.

Zamora, the once proverbial strong city, which resisted even the Cid, lost caste with the monarchy's decrepitude. Yet the natural position remained most important; and in vain did Moore urge the Junta of Salamanca to repair the defences, and receive there his stores, for his retreat had *commenced* before they had done deliberating. (Schepeler, ii. 119.) Had Zamora been put into a state of defence, he would have fallen back on it instead of on La Coruña, and thus Portugal would have been spared the ravages of Soult. The sins of the Junta were visited on Zamora, as it was soon after taken by the French. Darricaut and Maupetit gallantly scaled the walls of this once *bien cercada*, and although no resistance was made, the town was sacked, neither age nor sex were spared, and the principal persons executed. Zamora was afterwards occupied and plundered by M. Foy, and it has never recovered these visitations. The victory of Salamanca delivered Zamora; its evacuation by Foy was a blundering operation, for had he held it, the Duke's plans would have been deranged (Disp. Aug. 18, 23, 1812).

On quitting Zamora, the wretchedness of the peasantry increases; their cabins are of mud, their furniture and agricultural implements are rude in form and material. Their carts, and they prevail all over the N.W. provinces, are the unchanged *plaustra*, with solid wheels, the Roman *tympana*, a mere circle of wood, without spokes or axles, much like mill grinding-stones or Parmesan cheeses, and such as the old Egyptians used, as seen in hieroglyphics (Wilk. i. 369), and no doubt

exactly resembling those sent by Joseph for his father (Gen. xlv. 19). The type is Oriental, and still is used among the Affghans and Spaniards, who are unadvanced coachmakers. The whole wheel turns round together with a piteous creaking, which whines all over the N.-western portion of Spain. The drivers, whose leathern ears are as blunt as their edgeless teeth, delight in this excruciating *El Chillar*, *El Chirrio*, Arabicè *charrar*, to make a *noise*, which they call music. They, moreover, think it frightens wolves, bears, and the devil himself, which it well may, for the wheel of Ixion, although damned in hell, never cried more piteously. The shrill sounds, however, serve as warnings to other drivers, who, in narrow paths and gorges of rocks, where two carriages cannot pass, have this notice given them, and draw aside until the coast is clear.

From Zamora the naturalist might make many excursions: the botanist should visit *La dehesa de San Andres*, 1 L., and the geologist go to *Muelas*, 4 L., in the angle of the confluence of the Esla and Duero: here, curiously formed and marked, calcareous stones and crystals are found, and the peculiar clay is considered the finest in the Peninsula for making kitchen ware. The sportsman and angler will also find a fine wild country, covered with aromatic underwood, and intersected with splendid trout streams all the way from *Zamora* to *Villafranca del Vierzo*. Those who can rough it might first visit *Carbajales*, 4 L., a town belonging to the Duque de Frias, popⁿ· 1200. The neighbouring *La Peña colorada* and *monte Valdoradas* abound in *Caza mayor y menor;* of course the stranger will take local guides. The trout-fishing is first-rate, as a network of rivers come down the fan-like offshoots of the serpentining *Sierra de Culebra*, and empty themselves into the *Aliste*. From Carbajales the sportsman might either strike off W. to *Alcañices*, which is a small town with 600 souls, on the confines of Portugal, where there is excellent cover, or he might cut across to *Puebla de Sanabria*, and thence over the *Vierzo* to Villafranca, through some of the best fishing districts in Spain. (See R. lxvii., lxviii., lxix.)

Leaving Zamora, the road continues to be uninteresting until after passing *S^a· Eufemia*, when an opening discloses *Benavente* in the distance, with its fine castle rising on a knoll to the l. out of a girdle of trees. Before arriving at the town, the Esla, one of the large tributaries of the Duero, is crossed in a clumsy ferry-boat, and, as generally is the case, the boatmen are either on the other side or absent. Here one of the first encounters took place between the British and French cavalry ; early in Moore's retreat (Dec. 29, 1808), Lefebvre Desnouettes, commanding 600 of the imperial guards, attacked the English rear. He was met by Col. Otway with only 200 men, and checked ; Lord Paget then came up with some of the 10th, and in "an instant" (says Napier) "the scene was changed, and the enemy were seen flying in full speed towards the river, the British close at their heels." Lefebvre Desnouettes was taken prisoner, when his indignation was increased by the derisive laughter which his sullen looks and torn coat excited among the English soldiers—du sublime au ridicule il n'y a qu'un pas. Buonaparte, an eye-witness of this event, wrote the following account for Paris in his 21st bulletin :—" Le général, emporté par cette ardeur qu'on a si souvent reproché au soldat Français, passa la rivière à la nage pour se porter sur Benavente, où il trouva *toute la cavalerie* de l'arrière garde Anglaise : alors il s'engagea un *long* combat de 400 hommes contre 2000 ; il fallut enfin céder au nombre. Cette échauffourée a dû convaincre les Anglais de ce qu'ils auraient à *redouter* des pareilles gens dans une affaire générale."

Lefebvre's subsequent breach of parole is well known, but Buonaparte, instead of sending him back "a pri-

soner," as the Duke would have done, had any English officer been capable of such dishonour (Disp. Oct. 20, 1809), approved of his conduct, and reinstated him in the command of his chasseurs. Can it be wondered, under such " circumstances, that the Duke could place no confidence in the parole of any French officer " (Disp. June 30, 1811), not even on Soult's, their chief (Disp. Sept. 11, 1813). Yet now, M. Foy having ascribed the bravery of English soldiers to beef and rum, thinks "that honour is a motive too delicate for their dense organization, and that even our officers lack the exclusive idolatry to it of the French " (i. 235, 241). Alas for ancient France, on whose Good John's lips truth set up her throne,—Oh land of Henri IV. and Bayard, *sans peur et sans reproche,* how wert thou then revolutionised! *Ruse doublée de force,* in the words of De Pradt, was thy tyrant's policy; with him, as in the dark ages, a breach of word was but a familiar jest, and a breach of parole and a perjury only a *façon de parler :* "Francis familiare erat *ridendo* fidem frangere " (F. Vopiscus Proculus). " Gens Francorum infidelis est, si pejeret Francus qui novi faceret, qui perjurium ipsum *sermonis genus* putat esse, non criminis " (Salvien. *de G. D.* iv.).

Crossing the Esla, *Benavente,* with its long, mud, *cob* walls and ruined castle, rises on a gentle eminence ; pop^n· about 2500. There is a decent *Posada* outside the town on the road to Astorga ; the town dull and poverty-stricken. The castle, the Alcazar of the Pimentels, now merged in the Osuna dukedom, was once the great lion. Southey, who in his Letters (i. 139) tells us that he arrived here too late to see the inside of this edifice, indulges in his *History* in the following *poetical* romance : " We have nothing in England which approaches to its grandeur : Berkeley, Raby, even Warwick and Windsor, are poor fabrics in comparison" (ch. xv.). All which is pure Poet Laureate fiction, as this

Château en Espagne is far inferior in size and details to many of our Welsh castles, while the material is a reddish coarse ignoble stone, with a considerable portion of mere *cob.* The ruin is entered by a gentle ascent; passing under an arch between two towers, a defaced Santiago on horseback is over the portal. The *Torre Pastel* bears the date Maio 20, 1462. Here are the arms of the Pimentels, once the powerful Counts of Benavente, the Sheikhs or Lords of all around. The inside is all a ruin, having been gutted by Soult, when retreating from Oporto. The Patio is still strewed with fragments of sculpture, which were then wantonly destroyed. In the upper story was the state gallery, where yet are some remains of Moorish *Tarkish* and *azulejo* in the windows: a portion of the grand staircase exists. The view over the bald plains of Leon and mountains towards *la Puebla de Sanabria* is extensive; the river front is the strongest; the masonry is coarse and ornamented with a huge stone chain and the projecting balls so common at Toledo: below are what were the gardens of the Duchess, but destroyed by the enemy. A pretty walk, *el Caracol,* leads under the trees and by a trout stream. The *Sa. Maria* church in Benavente has a remarkable tower, circular chapels, and round Saxon arches.

There is a carriageable communication from Benavente to Leon, 11½ L., over a most uninteresting country, through *Torral de los Guzmanes* 4½, *Ardon* 3½, and Leon 3½. That to the l. to Orense, 33½, is full of alpine and river beauty (see R. lxviii.).

At Benavente (Dec. 28, 1809) Moore's retreat may be said to have commenced : here the laurel was wreathed with the cypress, and the sins of official epigrammatists washed out by brave men's blood. In October he had been sent to the Peninsula with some 25,000 men, without any specific instructions, beyond a direction to act in concert with *Spanish* generals; the

bleak Castiles were chosen because in winter they are almost impracticable from cold and rain. Moore reached Salamanca Nov. 13, and there he heard that three Spanish armies had melted like a snow-wreath almost before attacked. He crossed the frontier Oct. 11; Blake, on that same day, was beaten at Espinosa, Belvidere having on the 10th been routed at Burgos; and when Moore reached Salamanca in November, he heard how Castaños had been crushed at Tudela; soon after Somosierra gave Madrid to Buonaparte, and thus the unassisted English were left to bear the whole real burden of the war; thus 25,000 British troops were now opposed to 250,000 French veterans, flushed with victory : yet the Duke of York had counselled our ministers not to send less than 60,000 English to the Peninsula, which he was prepared to furnish; he felt that no little war ought to be carried on; but pedling, paltry politics prevailed,—this (says Napier) mere handful was embarked, and then without money, plans, or scarcely ammunition.

Moore, who had now become the principal instead of the auxiliary, for " Il n'y a que les Anglais à craindre," said the shrewd emperor, was next lured into the Castiles by the juntas, and by our ambassador, Mr. Frere, who, Hispanis Hispanior ! believed the ministers of Spain to be honest, the generals skilful, and the raw undisciplined levies fit to cope with the magnificent legions of Buonaparte, and he did his best to deceive and destroy Moore, by enticing him on to Sahagun. At that moment the emperor rushed (Dec. 12) like lightning from Madrid, and in ten days, defying the elements, reached Astorga with 80,000 men. Moore, ignorant of his peril, remained the 22nd and 23rd of Nov. at Sahagun, urged even then by Frere and Morla to advance on Madrid, when one step would have caused certain ruin. But the truth flashed across his mind, and he retreated with unexampled decision, baffling even Buona-parte, who arrived twelve hours too late at Benavente, and found that his victim had escaped, and all the glory of a thunderbolt coup de main was lost; then the *échauffourée* of the Esla gave him some forebodings of what might happen in a general engagement, and remembering Acre, and prescient of Waterloo, he would not risk his reputation in the fastnesses of Gallicia; he delegated that to Soult, and only advanced to Astorga, where (Jan. 1, 1810) he reviewed 80,000 Frenchmen in pursuit of 19,053 English infantry, 2278 cavalry, and 63 guns, magnified by him into 30,000 or 40,000, and then departed, falsely pretending that he had received important intelligence from Germany which required his return; but he in reality was so little in a hurry that he daudled ten days at Valladolid, routing the English in his bulletins—the paper pellets of his brain. Moore, although never any-where beaten during the campaign, ima-gined that the whole French army was in pursuit, hence his movements too often resembled a flight rather than a steady retreat.

Moore was by nature the very anti-thesis of the sanguine Frere; of a de-sponding temperament, he saw at once the difficulties of his position; he de-spaired from the first, and amid his vague undetermined plans, always turned his secret thoughts to the sea; he sank under responsibility, the in-cubus of all but master-minds. This true soldier, who would have acted brilliantly as second in command, overrated the enemy and underrated himself; he began by a mistake, think-ing that "when the French had Spain, Portugal could *not* be defended." How thought the Duke? " If I hold Portugal, France cannot and will not hold Spain," and *shall not*, he might have said, and *"no* mistake," as he drove her worsted legions over the Py-renees. Moore, although always me-ditating a retreat, never made any preparations for one, either by sending

to reconnoitre routes, or to prepare ma-gazines and halting-places. He met with little aid from the Castilians, still less from the Gallicians. "They" (and these are some of his last words), " although armed, made no attempt to stop the passage of the French through the mountains; they abandoned their dwellings at *our* approach; they drove away their carts, oxen, and everything that could be of the smallest aid to the army," *socorros de España.*

Napier (iii. 3) has rescued the fair fame of Moore, and has exposed those by whom he was sacrificed. " In Sir John Moore's campaign" (said the honest Duke), " I can see but one error; when he advanced upon Saha-gun he should have considered it as a movement of retreat, and sent officers in the rear to mark and prepare halt-ing places for every brigade: but this opinion I have formed after long expe-rience of war, and especially the pecu-liarities of Spanish war, which must have been seen to be understood; finally, it is an opinion formed after the event." The Duke was soon after-wards sent to Portugal, where the re-treat to Corunna was more than wiped off by that from Oporto, from whence Soult, after a defeat, which Moore never received at all, fled under cir-cumstances of horror and precipitancy which far exceeded that of our ill-fated hero.

The ten long leagues from Benavente to Astorga are dull; the country is studded with vineyards and small vil-lages: at *Sⁿ. Roman de la Valle* the mud hills are excavated into *bodegas* or wine cellars, whose contents were more fatal to Moore's troops than any foe, but Bacchus has ever been more formidable to our brave men than Mars; they succumb at once to the temptation of drink (Disp. Nov. 2, 1810), and then all is over : the enemy in the mouth discharges honour, duty, valour, for vini potio est veneni potius. " Oh thou invisible spirit of wine, let us call thee devil." The rude pea-santry wear *madreñas* or wooden *sabots* like the French, turned up at the toe, and supported by clogs; they hobble along in torture, even youth looking care-worn and old; the churches are mere barns, with a wall in front built up to a point whereon is placed a niche for a bell, to which a staircase conducts. Passing *La Bañeza* with its fine alameda of poplars, the snowy cloud-capt mountains close in as an amphitheatre, and seem to bar further approach. Soon Astorga appears looking both warlike and picturesque; its broadside is defended with walls and countless semi-circular towers. There is a tolerable *posada* just before entering the town.

Astorga—Asturica Augusta—was, in the days of Pliny (N. H. iii. 3), a "magnificent city," now it is miserable and decayed. The bishopric, founded in 747 by Don Alonzo El Catolico, is suffragan to Santiago; the town bears for arms a branch of oak, indicative of strength. The local histories are 'Fundacion,' &c., Pedro de Espeleta, 4to. Mad. 1634; and 'Fundacion,' &c., Pedro de Junco, 4to., Pamplona, 1639. Humboldt considers *Astorga* to be a vernacular Iberian name, and derived from *Asta*, "a rock, a rock-built place," e. g. *Astures, Astaba, Astigi.* The Spaniards finding in Sil. Italicus (iii. 334) that *Astyr,* son of Memnon, fled to Spain, consider him the founder of *Asturica.* Certainly it is most ancient; the walls are singularly curious, and there are two Roman tombs and inscriptions near the *Puerta de Hierro.* Seen from the outside it has a venerable imposing appearance, with its infinite semi-circular towers, which do not rise higher than the level of the wall; like Coria and Lugo, it gives a perfect idea of a Roman fortified city, of which so few specimens remain, since most of them were dismantled by Witiza.

Astorga ranks as a grandee, for Spanish cities and corporations have *personal* rank. It gives the marquisate to the Osorio family, a ruin of whose palace yet remains: the fine library now belongs to the advocates at Edinburgh.

The Gothic cathedral was raised in 1471, on the site of one more ancient; it has since been much modernised and disfigured; one tower is built of grey stone, the other of red, which is capped with a slated top, that of the grey tower having been destroyed by an earthquake in 1765. The exterior and entrance is churrigueresque, and the two lateral aisles are lower than the central one; observe the *Reja* and elaborate *Silla del Coro,* in the tedesque style of Rodrigo Aleman. The ridiculous drummers, naked women, and monsters, which *ornament* the organ, contrast strangely with the venerable saints and bishops. The *trascoro* is very bad; the pulpit, with its medallions, is more clerical; the cloisters are modern. The enormous *Retablo* is by Gaspar Becerra, who was born at Baeza in 1520, and studied under Michael Angelo, in Italy, and was patronised by Philip II.; his finest works are in the Castiles and centre of Spain. This *Retº.*, executed in 1569, was perhaps his master-piece; and is one of the most remarkable of its kind in the Peninsula, but unfortunately it has been much repainted; it is divided into three parts; the frame-work of the under story is supported by Berruguete pillars; the second tier has fluted columns and enriched bases, the third pilasters, in black and gold. The carvings represent subjects from the life of the Saviour and Virgin; observe, especially the Pieta, the ascension and coronation of the *Santissima,* and the fine recumbent females and Michael Angelesque "Charity." These nudities gave offence and were about to be covered, when the *Consejo* of Madrid interfered; these grand carvings are very Florentine and muscular (compare this *Retº.* with that at Medina del Rio Seco). In the *Capilla de Sn. Cosmo* is the tomb of King Alonzo, obt. 880, with ancient marble sculpture in low relief, from subjects of the New Testament: the former glory of the cathedral was the *Relicario*, the gem of which was a grinder, and part of the jaw of S¹· Christopher, *cosa monstruosa*, says the admiring Morales; it weighed 12 pounds, and never had an equal, save and except that ass's jawbone with which Sampson killed a thousand men (see also p. 440).

Astorga, when, as usual, utterly unprovided, was assailed in February, 1810, by the French under the cruel Loison, who was nobly repulsed by the gallant José Maria de Santocildes, with a few raw soldiers. Junot came next, March 21, and threatened to put the whole town to the sword; and then, in spite of the advice of his engineers, rashly tried to storm the town by the *Puerta de Hierro*, but was beaten back. Santocildes, deserted by the coward Mahy, who ought to have relieved him, and having expended his scanty ammunition, capitulated April 22, after a defence as glorious as those of Gerona and Ciudad Rodrigo. The French then dismantled the works and destroyed the fine palace of the Astorga family, of which only two turrets and some armorial shields remain, and are best seen from the garden of the Moreno family, in whose house Moore was lodged.

In 1812, Castaños, with 15,000 Gallicians, was here detained three months by the gallant Gen. Remond and only 1500 brave Frenchmen; few things in the whole war were more disgraceful to Spanish arms. This was the manner in which the "Hero of Bailen" co-operated with the Duke, at the moment when Marmont was in his front; the Duke was so inconvenienced that he thought of coming himself, for, as he said, " It is ridiculous to talk of Astorga as a fortified place; it is a walled town, which could not have stood *one day* against a regular attack" (Disp. Feb. 23, 1811).

Astorga is the capital of *La Maragateria*, or the country of the *Maragatos*, which is about 4 L. square. It contains 36 villages, San Roman being one of the best. The name *Maragato*

has been derived by some from Mauregatus, the king who was forced to pay, as an annual tribute to the Moors, 100 Spanish virgins. The Maragatos, however, are not proud of having descended from such a stock, and probably the whole tale is fabulous. Others trace the name to *los Moros Godos*, i. e. those Spanish Goths who continued among the Moors, like the Musárabes; and now, live the Jew and gipsy, the Maragatos like exclusively among their own people, preserving their primeval costume and customs, and never marrying out of their own tribe. They are as perfectly nomad and wandering as the Merinos *trashumantes* or the Bedouins, the mule only being substituted for the camel. They are almost all *arrieros, ordinarios*, or carriers, and their honesty and industry are proverbial. They are a sedate, grave, dry, matter-of-fact, business-like people. Their charges are high, but the security counterbalances, as they may be trusted with untold gold. They are the channels of all traffic between Gallicia and the Castiles, being seldom seen in the S. or E. provinces. They are dressed in leather jerkins, *jabonetas*, which fit tightly like a cuirass, leaving the arms free; their linen is coarse but white, especially the shirt collar *Gorguera* (gorget), or *Lechuguilla*; a broad leather belt, in which there is a pouch (the purse of the Roman Zona), is fastened round the waist. Their breeches, " breeks," *bragas*, are called *Zaragüelles*, like the Valencians, a pure Arabic word for kilts or wide drawers, and no burgomaster of Rembrandt is more broad-bottomed. They wear long brown cloth gaiters, or *polainas*, with red garters; their hair generally is cut close, sometimes, however, strange tufts are left; a huge, slouching, flapping hat completes the most inconvenient of travelling dresses, and it is too Dutch to be even picturesque; but these fashions are as unchangeable as the laws of the Medes and Persians were; nor will any Maragato dream of altering his costume until those dressed models of painted wood, which strike the hours on the clock on the *pláza* of *Astorga*, do theirs; *Pedro Mato*, also, another figure *costumé*, who holds a weather-cock at the cathedral, is the observed of all observers; and, in truth, this particular *traje*, or costume, is, like that of Quakers, a sort of guarantee of their tribe and respectability; thus even Cordero, the rich Maragato deputy, appeared in Cortes in this local costume.

The dress of the Maragata is equally peculiar; she wears, if married, a sort of head-gear, *El Caramiello*, in the shape of a crescent, the round part coming over the forehead, which is very Moorish, and resembles those of the females in the basso-relievos, in the *Capilla real*, at Granada. Their hair flows loosely on their shoulders, while their apron or petticoat hangs down open before and behind, and is curiously tied at the back with a sash, and their boddice is cut square over the bosom. At their festivals they are covered with ornaments, *La Joyada*, or jewelry, of long chains of coral and metal, with crosses, relics, and medals in silver. Their earrings are very heavy, and supported by silken threads, as among the Jewesses in Barbary. A marriage is the grand feast, then large parties assemble, and a president or *Padrino* is chosen, who puts into a waiter whatever sum of money he likes, and all invited must then give as much. The bride is enveloped in a *Manto*, which she wears the whole day, and never again except on that of her husband's death. She does not dance at the wedding-ball. Early next morning two roast chickens are brought to the bedside of the happy pair. The next evening ball is opened by the bride and her husband, to the tune of the *gaita*, or Moorish bagpipe. Their dances are grave and serious, but such indeed is their whole character. The *Maragatos*, with their honest, weather-beaten countenances, are seen with files of mules all along the high road to La Coruña. They generally walk, and,

like other Spanish *arrieros*, although they sing and curse rather less, are employed in one ceaseless shower of stones and blows at their *Machos*.

The whole tribe assembles twice a year at Astorga, at the feasts of Corpus and the Ascension, when they dance *El Canizo*, beginning at 2 o'clock in the afternoon, and ending precisely at 3. If any one not a *Maragato* joins, they all leave off immediately. The women never wander from their homes, which their undomestic husbands always do. They lead the hardworked life of the Iberian females of old, and now, as then, are to be seen everywhere in these W. provinces toiling in the fields, early before the sun has risen, and late after it has set; and it is most painful to behold them drudging at these unfeminine vocations.

The origin of the *Maragatos* has never been ascertained. Some consider them to be a remnant of the Celtiberian; most, however, prefer a Bedouin, or caravan descent. To this Capt. Widdrington (ii. 61) is decidedly opposed: he suspects them to be of a Visigothic origin. It is in vain to question these ignorant carriers as to their history or origin, for like the gipsies they have no traditions, and know nothing. *Arrieros*, at all events, they are, and that word, in common with so many others relating to the barb and carrier-caravan craft, is Arabic, and proves whence the system and science were derived by Spaniards. Thus purely Arabic are the names of animals, *Recua, Jaca, Acemil, Alfana, Alhamel, Almifor;* their colours and qualities, *Alazan, Lozano, Zaino, Haron, Haragan, Rodado;* their helpers, instruments, burdens, and language, *Zagal, Albeitar, Alforjas, Telliz, Fardo, Forrage* (forage), *Zalea, Atahorre, Grupa, Acial, Albarda, Almohaza, Jamuga, Atahona, Guiar, Arre, Anda,* etc.

The *Maragatos* are celebrated for their fine beasts of burden; indeed, the mules of Leon are renowned, and the asses splendid and numerous, especially the nearer one approaches the learned university of Salamanca. The *Maragatos* take precedence on the road: they are the lords of the highway, being *the* channels of commerce in a land where mules and asses represent luggage rail trains. They know and feel their importance, and that they are the rule, and the traveller for mere pleasure is the exception. Few Spanish muleteers are much more polished than their beasts. However picturesque the scene (see p. 46), it is no joke meeting a *recua* of laden *acemilas* in a narrow road, especially with a precipice on one side, *cosa de España.* The *Maragatos* seldom give way, and their mules keep doggedly on, and as the *tercios* or baggage projects on each side, like the paddles of a steamer they sweep the whole path. But all wayfaring details in the genuine Spanish interior are calculated for the *pack;* and there is no thought bestowed on the foreigner, who is not wanted, nay is disliked. The inns, roads, and right sides, suit the natives and their brutes; nor will either put themselves out of their way to please the fancies of a stranger. The racy Peninsula is too little travelled over for its natives to adopt the mercenary conveniences of the Swiss, that nation of innkeepers and coach-jobbers.

The difficulties and over-haste of Moore's retreat began after Astorga, for up to then he had hoped to bring the enemy to a general action. The high road to Lugo is magnificent, and a superb monument of mountain engineering. The leagues are very long, being *de marco*, or of 8000 yards each ; they are marked by mile-stones. The climate is cold and rainy, and the accommodations fit only for swine; both (*experto crede*) are bad even in summer and in time of peace : how fearful must they have been during the snows and starvation of a December retreat.

Leaving Astorga we ascend over a heath-clad "highland" country to Manzanal, and enter *El Vierzo*, the Switzerland of Leon. This is a district of alpine passes, trout-streams, pleasant meadows, and groves of ches-

nuts and walnuts. *Bembimbre*, where so many of our soldiers were lost through drunkenness, lies on the rivers Noceda and Baeza, a splendid trout stream, in a sweet valley amid gardens and the vineyard, whose wines were more fatal to Moore's soldiers than the French sabres. The ruined castle looks Moorish. *Ponferrada*, Pons ferrata, lies to the l., on the confluence of the Sil and Baeza. You do not enter it : the bridge was built in the eleventh century, for the passage of pilgrims to Compostella, who took the direct route along the Sil by Val de Orras and O-rense. The town afterwards belonged to the Templars, and was protected by the miraculous image of the Virgin, which was found in an oak, and hence called Nª· Señora de la *Encina ;* it is still the patroness of the *Vierzo.* Ponferrada is a good point of starting to see the ancient convents of this Thebais (see post, p. 598). For the communication with Orense, see R. lxix. Ponferrada is an excellent quarter for the angler, amidst virgin trout-streams, which have never been whipt by fly-fisher. The fish rise with all the eagerness of Gallician hunger, and their ignorance of mechanical art. *Cacavelos* is a wretched hamlet. Between this and Prieros 400 of the 95th and a picket of cavalry were attacked (Jan. 3, 1809) by Gen. Colbert and 8 squadrons. The French were beaten back everywhere, and their leader killed. Buonaparte's version of this *defeat* ran thus in his 25th bulletin : —" L'arrière garde Anglaise était composée de 5000 hommes d'infanterie, et 600 chevaux ; cette position était fort belle et difficile à aborder. Le Général Merle fit ses dispositions : l'infanterie approcha ; on battit la charge, et les Anglais furent mis dans une entière déroute."

Villafranca del Vierzo is truly Swiss-like, and placed in a funnel of mountains, with painter-like bridges, convents, cottages, projecting balconies, and vines, and the glorious trout-streams the Burbia and Valcarce, yet it is the abode of dirt, misery, and poverty. At the entrance is a large square fortress mansion, with round towers at the corner, which belongs to the Alva family. Here Romana, in 1809, took 1000 of the French garrison prisoners. Villafranca contains about 2500 souls, and is good head-quarters for the trout angler. We dined off a splendid fellow of 4 lb. Fleshly comforts are rare in the Vierzo, although fish and fruit abound. Rye-bread, or *Pan de centeno*, affords scanty staff of life to a squalid population. This town was formerly the halting-place of the French pilgrims bound to Santiago, and hence was called Villa Francorum. It was given to a brotherhood of monks from Cluny, and the name of the present ancient *Colegiata* is *Na· Sᵃ· de Cruñego*, or *Cluniego*. 1 L. E. on the road to Corullon, is another most ancient church, *La Sᵃ· Marina*. The enormous Franciscan convent which overlooks the town on the r. was founded to expiate his proportionate crimes by Don Pedro de Toledo, the Viceroy of Naples, who, aided by Paul III., tried to introduce into it the Inquisition. The populace, in profane joy at this persecutor's death, exclaimed, " He has descended into hell for our salvation." He bequeathed to the monks his fine library of Greek manuscripts, which is now lost for ever, for the village was sacked both by the French and English in 1810. The latter vented on the wretched peasantry their indignation against the non-co-operation of Spanish juntas and generals.

Here in 1808 Filangieri, governor of La Coruña, was murdered by his troops because slow in proclaiming the cause of independence. He was an Italian by birth, and had the common military sense to see that Fabian and defensive strategies were those which history, and the character of this country and people, demonstrated as the best suited; this offended those who were eager to rush into general actions and defeats, and his prudence was imputed to treachery ; he was, moreover, a *foreigner*, whereat *Españolismo* took huff,

and his conduct was called a *Judiada—the deed of a Jew* (Schep. i. 404) ; an accusation always enough in Spain to ensure death : thereupon his troops fixed their bayonets in the ground, with the points uppermost, and then tossed their general on them, leaving him to die in torture. Thus the Carthaginians spiked Regulus. But to murder their generals is an inveterate Iberian trick. The Junta took no steps to prevent this crime ; and Blake, who succeeded to Filangieri, only sent a battalion after the deed was done ; *socorros de España tarde o nunca :* for this pedant, feeling confident that he could lose battles even as well as Cuesta, was ambitious to get Filangieri's command (see Schepeler, i. 412).

Continuing our route over a noble road, now the mountain barrier of Gallicia is to be scaled by the Alpine pass *el Puerto de Piedrahita*, near Doncos. The Burbia to the l. is the perfection of a trout-stream ; this pleasant, brawling companion to the dusty highway is tracked upwards and upwards, until it becomes a rivulet heard but not seen, amid its fringed banks. The rivers are most piscatorial and picturesque in these N.-western districts; the joy alike of the angler and artist, they boil along over their rough beds, their fair course hindered ; now they impatiently rage, *iræ amantium*, then, on reaching the pleasant meadow, all is peace and reconciliation, and the appeased stream—

" Giveth a gentle kiss to every sedge
He overtaketh in his wanton course."

The road after the *Puerto* descends to wretched *Nogales*. In the Posada, kept by the daughter of Don Benito, Moore was lodged. Here his despondency increased, and he needlessly precipitated his retreat, abandoning baggage, tools, and treasure. The country is pastoral, but without the charms of Switzerland or the plenty of England. It is very damp, with all the discomforts and none of the luxuries of the Alps; no cream, butter, or strawberries. The squalid natives, tattered and half-clad, almost starve in ill-constructed hovels, fitter for beasts than men, and formed to admit, not exclude, the evils of the climate; the very swine have lost their Estremenian rotundity. The ascent continues to Sᵃ· Isabel, where the slate-roofs are kept down by heavy stones as a protection against the winds. The women turn their brown *sayas* edged with white over their heads, which forms the genuine national *mantilla.* The grand road now winds up the heights, with a tremendous precipice to the r., and rapid river deep below; all around the grey rocks peep out of the cistus and heath. The fine bridge of Corcul spans with three arches a terrific ravine, and its creamy-coloured masonry is worthy of the Romans; here, from Moore's previous hasty destruction of heavy fourgons, the engineers failed from want of even tools in mining the bridge, which would have arrested the French pursuit at once; and although Moore was a whole day in advance, here 25,000*l.* in dollars were thrown down the precipices; then, according to Buonaparte (bulletin 27), the French took "2 millions of francs, the English carrying off from 8 to 10 millions more;" thus magnifying into 660,000*l.* a sum proved by parliamentary papers to have only been between 60,000*l.* and 70,000*l.*

After Sobrado the country improves, and looks more English. As we emerge from the mountains, the noble Miño winds through pleasant meadows, but *Lugo* is not seen until nearly approached. There is a decent posada in the Barrio de Sⁿ· Roque before entering the town. For Lugo see Gallicia, and for the continuation of routes to Santiago and the N.W., see R. lxxxiv.

The kingdom of Leon stretches both to the r. and l. of Benavente; the portion to the l. is called *El Vierzo* or *El Bierzo*, a name corrupted from the Roman *Bergidum*, the *Interamnium Flavium* of Ptolemy. The site of this river-girt town was near Carucedo at *Castro de la Ventosa*, a wind-blown eminence, a Windsor which commands the district, and traces of walls yet remain; the Vierzo is one of the most interesting nooks in the whole Peninsula, and is all but unknown to the English antiquary, artist, angler, and sportsman. The singular ecclesiastical details have only just been nibbled at by Southey (Letters, i. 105); here, indeed, is a fresh ground open to all who aspire in these threadbare days to book something new; here is scenery enough to fill a portfolio, and subject enough for a quarto; how many flowers pine unbotanised, how many rocks harden ungeologised; what views are dying to be sketched, what trout to be caught and eaten, what valleys expand their bosoms longing to embrace the visitor, what virgin beauties hitherto unseen await the happy member of the travellers' club, who in ten days can exchange the bore of eternal Pall Mall, for these untrodden sites; and then what an accession of dignity, in thus discovering a terra incognita, and rivalling Mungo Park.

Nor are old printed books altogether wanting; for the ecclesiological branch the best is honest Ambrosio Morales, who was sent here in 1572 by Philip II. to inspect the archives and relics. His report was published by Florez, ' *Viaje de Morales*,' fol. Mad. 1765, who has also dedicated the 14th, 15th, and 16th volumes of his *España Sagrada*, to these parts and the vicinity; his maps of the bishopric of Astorga by *Manuel Sutil*, 1761, and of that of Orense by *Joseph Cornide*, 1763, will be found very useful in threading this intricate and alpine country. The traveller should visit *El Vierzo* in the summer time, bringing plenty of tackle, and of course taking a local guide, and especially attending to the "provend."

The Vierzo is a district which extends about 10 L. E. and W. by 8 N. and S. It is shaped like an amphitheatre, and is shut out from the world by lofty snow-capped mountains raised as it were by the hand of some genii to enclose this simple valley of Rasselas. The great Asturian chain slopes from *Leitariegos* to the S.W., parting into two offshoots; that of *El Puerto de Rabanal* and *Fuencebadon* (Fons Sabatonis) forms the E. barrier, and the other, running by the *Puertos de Cebrero* and *Aguiar*, forms the frontier; while to the S. the chains of the *Sierras de Segundera*, *Sanabria*, and *Cabrera* complete the base of the triangle : thus hemmed in by a natural circumvallation, the concavity must be descended into from whatever side it be approached; the crater, no doubt, was once a large lake, the waters of which have burst a way out, passing through the narrow gorge of the Sil, by Val de Orras, just as the Elbe forms the only spout or outlet to hill-walled-in Bohemia, the *kettle-land* of Germany.

The vicinity of mountains and the natural elevation render the winters cold, but the summers are delicious. The central portion, which is bounded to the E. and S. by the Sil, and to the W. by the Cua and then the Burbia, is in some portions a Swiss paradise, where Ceres and Bacchus, Flora and Pomona, might dwell together. The snow-clad *sierras* are the alembics of crystal streams which descend into lochs, and feed rivers which teem with trout, while the woods and aromatic wastes abound in game of all kinds, both *caza mayor y menor*. Here grow hay, turnips, and potatoes, rare productions in the *tierras calientes ;* which, with the thyme-clad verdurous meadows and green hills, afford pasture for flocks of sheep, to tend which is one great occupation of the simple primitive natives, who, far away from cities, are without either the advantages or drawbacks of civilization, for they are rude and poor among plenty, having neither industry, commerce, nor education. These secluded districts, shut out from the world, attracted the notice of the recluse in the 7th century. The spirit of that age was monastic, and the good work consisted in flying from the living into solitude; for the essence of

the monk was to be alone and in the desert, μονος εν τῷ ερημῷ : and never was nature more enthroned in loneliness than here ; nor are water and herbs, hermit's fare, wanting. Accordingly the *Vierzo* soon became a Thebais, and rivalled the holiest districts of Palestine in the number of its sanctuaries and saints, which, says Florez (E. S. xvi. 26), God alone, who can count the stars of heaven, could enumerate. The first founder was San Fructuoso, the son of the count or petty sovereign of *El Vierzo*,—a sheikh shepherd, for his wealth consisted in his herds and sheep; to which his heir, about the year 606, as Florez says, preferred flocks of holy monks. With this view, having surrendered his worldly goods, he settled near the *Puerto de Rabanal*, and founded the convent of *Compludo.* His princely example, the fame of his sanctity, and the number of his miracles, attracted numerous disciples, insomuch that these districts soon became as densely peopled as they previously had been uninhabited. Thereupon Fructuoso, in order to escape the pressure from without, retired from one cave to another, and on one occasion was nearly killed, having been mistaken for a wild beast by a hunter. After this he lived to a good old age, as is recorded in his biography, which was written by Valerio, one of his disciples.

At the Moorish invasion these Christian valleys were utterly ravaged, the monks dispersed, and their edifices destroyed ; but the *religio loci* was indestructible, and when the Gothic kingdom grew in strength, a second founder arose about 890 in the person of San Genadio. Those curious to see the infinite number of early monasteries are referred to the 'E. S.' xvi. Many of them have crumbled away from sheer age, others have been converted into parish churches for their respective hamlets, and many were burnt by the French. We shall briefly point out those which are best worth investigation, and suggest a few routes which include the finest scenery and the choicest trout-fishing. To the military man, these localities are interesting as being the line by which Soult retreated in 1809 after he was surprised and beaten at Oporto by the Duke. These happy valleys, in which amid a simple peasantry hermits and philosophers had long dwelt in peace, were visited by the enemy, who, infuriated by defeat and disgrace, vented his rage on the poor villagers: he spared, says Monsr. Durosoir (Espagne, 146), neither sex nor age. Loison led the way; in the Val de Orras he is better known by the nickname *Maneta*, the bloody *one-handed.* He was the Alaric of Evora, the forager of women. "His misdeeds (says Southey, 35) were never equalled or paralleled in the dark ages, uncivilised countries, or barbarous hordes." "Le congé des Français (says Schepeler, ii. 374) en Galicie fut signalé le 27, par les flammes de 31 villages incendiés dans le Vierzo." Their progress is thus described by Foy (i. 62), quæque ipse miserrima vidit, et quorum pars magna fuit: "Ainsi que la neige précipitée des sommets des Alpes dans les vallons, nos armées innombrables détruisaient en quelques heures, par leur seul passage, les ressources de toute une contrée; elles bivouaquaient habituellement, et à chaque gîte nos soldats demolissaient les maisons bâties depuis un demi-siècle, pour construire avec les décombres ces longs villages alignés qui souvent ne devaient durer qu'un jour: au défaut du bois des forêts les arbres fruitiers, les végétaux précieux, comme le mûrier, l'olivier, l'oranger, servaient à les réchauffer; les conscrits irrités à la fois par le besoin et par le danger contractaient *une ivresse morale* dont nous ne cherchions pas à les guérir."

Who can fail to compare this habitual practice of Buonaparte's legions with the terrible description in Hosea (chap. ii.), of the "great people and strong" who execute the dread judgments of Heaven: "A fire devoureth before them, and behind them a flame burneth; the land is the garden of Eden before them, and behind them a desolate wilderness, yea, and nothing shall escape them."

ROUTE LXVIII.—BENAVENTE TO ORENSE.

Sistrama de Tera . .	2	
Vega de Tera . . .	2½	.. 4½
Mombuey	3	.. 7½
Remesal	3	.. 10½
Puebla de Sanabria .	1½	.. 12
Requejo	1½	.. 13½
Lubian	2	.. 15½
Cañizo	2	.. 17½
Navallo	2½	.. 20
Ferreiras	1½	.. 21½
Monterey	1½	.. 23
Villar del Rey . . .	2½	.. 25½
Abavides	1	.. 26½
Ginzo de Limia . .	1	.. 27½
Allariz	2	.. 29½
Taboadella	1	.. 30½
Orense	2	.. 32½

Before plunging into the mountains, this, the main communication between Vigo and Madrid, must be described. The road is far from good, especially after Requejo to Monterey. A new *Carretera* has long been in contemplation, but every sort of obstacle has been raised by the intrigues and jealousies of other towns, who fear to lose their petty traffic. Were it once completed, a really good communication would be opened from the Atlantic to the capital.

After leaving Benavente and recrossing the Esla, at Sistrama, the beautiful Tera flows to the l., and is tracked upwards by its lovely *Vega.* At the village on the *Rio Negro*, a tributary stream which comes down from *Carbajales*, is a remarkable image, called *Na. Sa. de Farrapos*, Our Lady of Rags and Tatters, because the beggars who are cured of diseases by her miraculous intervention dedicate their votive wardrobes as a fee to the priests. *Mombuey*, with some 600 souls, has a fine oak-clad hill. *La Puebla* is the chief place of the small mountainous *partido* or district of *Sanabria:* pop^n. under 1000. The town is built on a slaty slope, with the noble *Sierra de Segundera* rising to the N.W. As this is a sort of frontier *plaza*, it has some old walls and a castle on the eminence. It is a good point from whence to make excursions into the Vierzo, and especially to the lake and convent of *Sⁿ. Martin de Castañeda* (see next page). The romantic road now turns towards *Requejo*, winding under an offshoot of the Segundera, and is often almost impracticable in winter. It continues to be very indifferent by Padornelo to *Lubian*, where the Sierra rises to the r., and the frontier of Portugal, distant about 2 L., expands to the l. This is a district of smugglers; indeed, the whole intricate indented *raya* from Ciudad Rodrigo to Orense and Tuy is peopled by bold *Contrabandistas*, who constitute one-fifth of the male population, and alone carry on any traffic, in localities where regular trade is in a state of congestion: they have a perfect understanding with the *Carabineros* and other preventive guards, who, being duly bribed, take care that none shall molest them (see pp. 323, 463). *Canda* is placed in the *portilla* which divides Leon from Gallicia. At *Cañizo* another road to Orense branches off to the r., by which 7 L. are saved; but it is an *atajo*, and very rough riding over hills and valleys. The line, however, is as follows :

Erosa	.	.	.	1
Porto de Camba	.	.	2	. . 3
Laza	.	.	1	. . 4
Alverguería	.	.	1¼	. . 5¼
Pedreda	.	.	1¼	. . 7
Orense	.	.	1	. . 8

Laza, popⁿ. 900, is charmingly situated, with the *Sierra de Mamed* rising to the N. The valley is delicious, and watered by two streams which flow into the *Tamega*, a superb trout river, which meanders down to *Monterey*. Near *Pedreda* a rivulet is crossed which flows into the *Laguna* of the Limia.

It is better to continue the under line, and proceed W.S.W. to *Verin*, popⁿ. 800. This hamlet is placed on the l. bank of the Tamega, with the

hill and castle of Monterey rising on the opposite side. There is a good stone bridge, but the river often in high floods inundates the village. The valleys above and below are charming, the district is fertile and abounding in fruit and vines, and the trout-fishing is capital. S. of Verin, at *Villar de Ciervos*, near the Portuguese frontier, are some neglected tin mines. Ascend to the castle of the Condes at *Monterey* to enjoy the fine view. The road now winds more N. up to *Villar del Rey* and *Abavides*, by the ridge which divides the basins of the Tamega and Limia. The latter is crossed at *Ginzo*, a hamlet placed below the *Laguna* in which the waters flowing from the *Sierra de Mamed* are collected, as it were, into a *Pantano* or reservoir. This *Limia* is the real river of Oblivion, which has been confounded with the *Guadalete*, near Xerez (see p. 235): it is a splendid water for trout and *salmon*. The Roman soldiers, when on its banks, were apprehensive of forgetting their wives, but they were no fishermen, for the real fear will be the not recollecting to bring enough tackle. Another ridge is next crossed, which divides this basin from that of the *Arnoya*, also a first-rate trout river, and tributary of the Miño. *Allariz*, a pleasant town on its banks, will be a good quarter: popⁿ. 1500. It is a walled place, and has a castle and two good bridges. The Franciscan convent, *Sª. Clara*, was founded in 1292, by Violanta, wife of Alonzo el Sabio : in it she is buried; and there are very ancient tombs in the *Coro* of sundry *Infantes* and of the Biedma family. The grand saint is one *Brandeso.* Those who fish up the stream will find another pleasant village called *Junquera de Ambia :* popⁿ. 1400. Here is an old priory, founded in 876 by Gundisalvo and Ilduara, who are buried here. W. of Allariz is the celebrated convent of *Celanova.* For it and Orense, see R. lxxxvi.

EXCURSIONS IN THE VIERZO.

Good starting points are from Puebla

de Sanabria, Benavente, Astorga, Ponferrada, Villafranca, and Puente de Domingo Florez, within which circle this preserve of monks and trout fishers is enclosed. The chief monasteries worth notice, out of some score, are *San Martin de Castañeda, Santiago de Peñalva,* and *Carracedo el Real.* The best trout streams are the Tera, Eria, Tuerto, and Orbigo, which go to swell the Esla, and the Cabrera, Burbia, Cua, which are tributaries of the Sil, itself a prince of rivers. Starting from *Puebla de Sanabria,* taking a local guide, ascend the Tera to the *Lago,* distant about 2½ L. : this is the reservoir of that sweet river, which rises in the mountains behind, near the Portillo, and after flowing about 2 L. into its charming *cueva,* falls into the lake, which is hemmed in by a horseshoe of hills, the spurs of the Segundera. This crystal loch, like the filled crater of a volcano, is about four miles round; its depth is unknown. The monks indeed are gone, caught in one fell swoop by the casting-net of Mendizabal, but the trout, *lo que hace al caso,* defy reformers and poachers; they are noble in size, inexhaustible in number, and when in season pink as chars. A boat and an attendant may be hired at the prettily placed village : pop^n. 300. In the lake is an island on which is built a castle by way of fishing-box of the old Counts of Benavente, which retains a something of its former decoration. The Bernardine monastery was founded in 952, but the ancient building was accidentally burnt: it is well placed with a warm S.E. aspect on the mountain slopes.

From the Puebla de Sanabria to Astorga is 13 L., mountain leagues: the scenery is wild and grand, and the rivers beautiful. Return to Remesal, and thence by *Carbajales de la Encomienda* 2 L. to Muelas, in a plain, near which are some iron mines and excellent shooting; then cross a ridge to *Castro contrigo* 3 L.; pop^n. 800: it is placed under the snowy Telado and Peña Negra. The river Eria is all that an angler can desire.

From the Puebla de Sanabria the lover of sweet-aired highlands may cross the *Sierra* to *Puente de Domingo Florez,* taking the following route:— Start by Vigo and ascend the Vega de Tera to the *Portillo de las Puertas,* keep then to the l. to the *Fuente de los Gallegos,* and thence to *Campo-Romo,* descending by *San Pedro de Trones* to the bridge over the *Cabrera.* This small village, a good fishing-quarter, lies under the *Campo de Braña,* near the confluence of the Cabrera and Sil ; the former of these noble trout streams comes down from the ridge of the Cabrera, a district divided into *alta y baja,* and from which waters part, flowing E. and W. Thus the Eria descends in a contrary direction to the Cabrera. The whole of the Cabrera may be fished up, turning at its bend near Robledo up to the reservoir lake at La Baña.

There are several routes E. from the Puente: first, either follow the r. bank of the Cabrera to *Lavilla,* and then ascend the *Cuesta de Llamas* to Odollo, and so on to Castrillo and Corporales, descending by *Truchas* (the name tells its produce) to Quintanilla and El Villar, and then crossing the Eria ascend to Torneros, whence either proceed N. to Astorga or W. to La Bañeza. From El Villar the angler might fish down the beautiful Eria, keeping on the l. bank to see the monastery of San Esteban de Nogales, or on leaving *El Puente de Domingo Florez* the Cabrera may be crossed and the ascent gained to *Robledo sobre Castro,* and thence up to Piedrafita, descending to Lomba and reascending to the beautiful Portillo *de la Baña,* and thence to La Baña and over the Cabrera ridge to Truchas and Castro Contrigo. Excursions might be made from *El Puente,* and first to the W.; cross the bridge over the Cabrera and then pass the arrowy Sil at *Puente Nuevo ;* go on to the *Barco de Valdeorras* 2 L., where Gallicia begins; hence 2 L. more to La Rua, a village of some 1200 souls. The bridge over the Sil is of Roman

2 D

foundation, and is called *Cigarrosa*, a corruption of *Sigurra*, the ancient town which once stood here. Quitting now the road to Orense make for San Miguel de *Monte Furado*, the "pierced hill" which lies about 2½ L. on the r. bank of the Sil : pop^n. 600. The mountain rock by which the course of the river was impeded was called by the Romans *Mons Lavicus*, and was dedicated to Jupiter, as an inscription on it recorded. It is tunneled through for the space of some 300 yards, a work the object of which is uncertain; some imagine that it was for the purpose of draining the upper country, and others that it was a shaft cut by miners in search of gold (consult ' E. S.' xv. 63; Morales, ' Anti.' 16; Molina, 14).

The Roman road to Orense crossed the Sil at *Cigarrosa* and continued to *Laroco* : the windings and elbow turns are called *los Codos* de Ladoco, a corruption, says Molina, of Lavico, whence Larouco. The *Puente de Domingo Florez* is distant 5½ L., but we will give the whole route from Ponferrada to Orense.

ROUTE LXIX.—PONFERRADA TO ORENSE.

Borrenes.	2	
Puente Domingo Florez.	2 ..	4
Barco de Valdeorras . .	2 ..	6
Larouco	3½ ..	9½
Puebla de Trives . . .	2 ..	11½
Burgo	2 ..	13½
Villarino Frio	2 ..	15½
Niño Daguia	2 ..	17½
Orense	3 ..	20½

This is a Swiss-like ride by fell and flood, hill and vale. *Borrenes*, pop^n. 400, stands in a plain girt with hills : there are iron mines near it, and to the r. near the Sil is the lake of *Carucedo*, about 3 miles round, which abounds with fine eels. *Las Medulas*, 1 L. on, was the ancient Argentiolum, and is placed under the *Campo de Braña*, but the mines so much worked by the Romans are now abandoned. Molina (p. 24) describes some curious caves and strange tower-like mounds, called *Torres de Barro*, which have been formed out of the marl and soil by the action of the waters : hence by a line just described to *Larouco*, a large village of 1000 souls. Crossing the Bibey is *Puebla de Tribes*, near which the Navea rises, after which we emerge from the hills, keeping the *Sierra de San Mamed* to the l. This district, called *La Tierra de Caldelas*, is celebrated for its hams. A détour to the r. may be made after passing *Villarino Frio*, and the Arnoya may be ascended to *Junquera de Espadañedo*, where there is a Cistercian monastery founded in 1225; and thence the traveller may proceed through *Rocas* to *Rivas de Sil*, in order to see the Benedictine convent of S^n. Esteban, which was founded on a most secluded hilly and romantic bend of the river by Ordoño in 961. The curious old tombs of nine bishops in the cloisters have been broken up and used for building materials, *Cosas de España*. This convent is 3 L. from Orense, through Faramontaos. Keeping on the l. bank of the Sil the fisherman will cross over the ferry and look at the rivers Cabe and Miño, which flow into the Sil : the Miño, although smaller, now robs its beautiful absorbent of both waters and name. Picturesque *Monforte de Lemos* lies distant 3 L. The route to Orense runs through Pombeiro, Peroja, and Rivela, after crossing the Bubal. For Orense see R. lxxxvi.

CONVENTS IN THE VIERZO.

The pilgrim must visit the sites to which the Saints Fructuoso and Genadio retired. Ponferrada will be the most convenient starting point; and first for *Santiago de Peñalva*, which lies by direct road about 3 L. from it; but we suggest the following longer circuit, which will include other interesting sites :—Make first for *Campo*, on the banks of the Boeza, amid its turnips and potatoes, thence to *Espinoso*, 2 L., on the Rio de Molina, from which *Compludo* in its plain is distant 2 L. more. Here was the first convent founded by S^n. Fructuoso, who dedicated it to S^n. Justo y

Pastor, the tutelars of *Complutum* (*Alcalá de Henares*). The monks have long disappeared. Now pass through *Bouzas* and ascend the ridge, the *Monte Irago*, which forms part of the E. barrier of the *Vierzo;* the way is rough and rugged, and the distance may be some 3½ mountain leagues to *Santiago de Peñalva*, now a miserable village. The Benedictine convent is placed about half-way up the W. side of the ridge, and takes its name from the *white* snow-capped peak. San Fructuoso chose this spot on account of the natural caves, which still remain, defying the destroyer, looking E. and hanging over the *Rio de Silencio*, which flows into the Oza, and thence by the Valduesa into the Sil. These caves, five in number, are still called *las Cuevas de Silencio*, and in them the ascetic monks used to pass their Lent, fit retreats for taciturn anchorites: a wild goat path leads up to this retreat for a San Bruno, and subject for a Salvator Rosa. The Benedictine convent was begun by Sⁿ· Genadio in 920, and completed after his death in 937; afterwards a sort of cloister cemetery was built around the original chapel, in which are several much dilapidated tombs of great antiquity. However, to visit them is still a religious duty, and the 25th of May is a grand day of pilgrimage, on which the peasants of the Vierzo flock here in great numbers: then is the time for the artist. The chapel, now the parish church, is of an oval form, with a circular termination at the E. and W. ends. It is entered from the S. from the cloister or cemetery; near the opposite door is buried the abbot Esteban, ob. 1132. The high altar is placed in the E. absis, and the sepulchre of San Genadio and Urbano in that to the W. The whole is a treat to the antiquarian.

Sⁿ· Fructuoso's next retreat from the Caves of Silence was to *San Pedro de Montes*, which lies about 1½ L. W. under the desolate hills of *Aguilanas*, the "Eagle's haunt," a name now corrupted into *Sierra Aguiana:* here

he made himself a cell which was so narrow that he could not turn round in it. The building was destroyed by the Moors, but restored in 895 by San Genadio; the chapel was finished in 919 by an architect named Vivianus (see the curious inscriptions, 'E.S.' xvi. 132; Cean Ber. 'A.' i. 9). It was raised, as is there stated, "non oppressione vulgi, sed largitate pretii et sudore fratrum." Here San Genadio died, and bequeathed to the convent his curious library; Morales saw some of the books (Viaje 173), but the careless Benedictines had allowed them to be much torn and injured. On the summit of the Sierra, above Sⁿ· Pedro, is a *high place* sacred to the Queen of Heaven and Earth, to which pilgrimages are made in summer. One league from San Pedro, in a cold, elevated, and bleak situation, is *Ferradillo*, whose woods supply fuel for the neighbouring iron forges: descend hence half a league to *Sᵗᵃ· Lucia*, once a convent, and distant 2½ L., to Ponferrada, passing through *Rimòr*, 1 L., and *Toral de Merayò*, where the meadows are pleasant, and an excellent bridge.

From Ponferrada another excursion may be made on the r. bank of the Sil to the royal Cistercian monastery of Caracedo, which stands on the l. bank of the Cua. It was founded in 990 by Bermudo II. for the place of his sepulture. It was restored in 1138 by Sancha, daughter of Queen Urraca. The library was numerous, before the monks, as Morales tells us (Viaje 170), had given them away for old parchment. Compare *Alcalá de Henares*.

Having thus described the portion of Leon which extends to the l. of Benavente, we must next proceed to the districts which stretch to the r., and include the capital and Valladolid. For Benavente to Leon, see R. lxxii.

ROUTE LXX.—ASTORGA TO LEON.

Hospital de Orbigo	.	2
Villadangos	3	.. 5
Leon	2	.. 7

This flat country is uninteresting

2 D 2

and lonely, albeit in ancient times it was very much frequented by pilgrims to Santiago; it therefore was chosen, July 11, 1434, as the site of the celebrated *paso honroso*, where Suero de Quiñones, 15 days before the feast of that Apostle, defied for 30 days all passengers at the bridge of the river Orbigo, which here divides the village; 727 *carreras*, or courses à l'outrance, were run; consult the quaint old account by Pedro Rodriguez de Lena.

These single combats for pure honour's sake, and the display of personal prowess and bravery, are perfectly in accordance with the deep feeling of every Spaniard, who thinks Spain the finest country in the world, his native province the best of its provinces, his native village the best of its villages, and himself the best man in it. *Pundonor* and self-respect are the key-stones of character in the *individually* brave Spaniard; he is ever ready, when personal consideration is at the stake, to find a quarrel in a straw, and think it but an easy leap to "pluck bright honour from the pale-faced moon;" he resents to the death the slightest personal affront, or *desaire*, and any *desden* or *menosprecio* rankles never to be atoned except by blood: *Sana cuchilladas pero no malas palabras*. It is not easy for an Englishman to estimate the touchy sensitiveness of a punctilious Spanish *Hidalgo*, so *peletero y quisquilloso*, or to reconcile his disposition to take offence, and to suspect imaginary, unintentional slights, with his real high caste and good breeding; none except those who have lived long and intimately with them can conceive what a drawback to social intercourse is this Quixotic porcupine fretfulness. Based in inordinate self-appreciation, it is increased by their present fallen fortunes; but the feeling has always formed a marked feature in the national character, and exhibited itself in duels and challenges at a time when the nice point of modern honour was quite unknown to the Greeks or Romans; thus Livy (xxviii. 21) gives an account of an Iberian trial at arms by volunteers of high rank, who contended before P. Scipio at Carthagena. It was usual also among the Spaniards for a champion to step forward and defy the enemy to single combat. This monomachia is evidently Oriental: thus the type of the *Campeador* of Intercatia, who was killed by Scipio when quite a youth (App. 'B. H.' 480) is a precise parallel to the case of Goliah and David (1 Sam. xvii.).

Nowhere did the spirit of knight-errantry take a deeper root than in Spain, whether in church or camp. Hercules became in both the model, as a redresser of wrongs and an abater of nuisances, and a Santiago or Roland *à la Grecque*. The challenges of Sciron and Antæus shadowed out *los Pasos honrosos*, just as the troubadour of Catalonia and the old ballads represented Pindar and the songs of the Olympic Games; but at every step in Spain we stumble on the classical and pagan, *warmed up*, as it were, and suited to modern taste and habits. The valour and address of the Spaniard as *an individual* are unquestionable. The champions of the Great Captain at Trani had no difficulty in defeating their French antagonists; nor were the troops of Buonaparte ever a match for an equal number of *guerrilleros* man to man, and in a broken country, where military science and manœuvre could not tell: left to *himself* the Spaniard knows well how to defend his honour and his life; it is only in the *collective* that disgrace attends him, and this arises from his mistrust in others, and his want of confidence in unworthy chiefs.

To the *individual* Castilian one may cheerfully confide one's purse of untold gold, one's life and honour, which none but a maniac would do to *Nosotros collectively*. When two or three Spaniards are gathered together *juntados*, then envy, hatred, and all uncharitableness rules as regards each other, combined with perfidy, desertion, and non-co-operation in respect to all others : see also some remarks at Ocaña and *Cortes,* Madrid.

LEON has a tolerable posada on the *Rasgo,* which is the best point for quarters ; the other inns are *La del Sol ; Meson del Gallo ;* and *de Cayetanon.* Capt. Widdrington recommends M. Dantin, a respectable Frenchman of the old school, who lives in a remnant of S°· Domingo, and occasionally receives travellers.

LEON, the time-honoured capital of its ancient kingdom, stands on the verdant banks of the trout-streams Vernesga and Torio,which unite below the town at *Aguas Mestas,* "waters meet," and then flow into the Esla ; their sides are well planted with poplars trimmed up like hop-poles. Leon is the residence of the provincial authorities, has a superb cathedral, a bishop, and had a mitred abbot of San Marcos ; pop^n· 5000. In common with other ancient and now deserted capitals, it is dull and decaying. The best time to visit it, as we did, is June 24, during the horse-fair, which, like those of Ronda and Mairena, attracts all the fancy and picturesque rogues, *chalanes,* gipsies, and honest *maragatos* of Spain.

The name Leon is a corruption of Legio, as the 7th Legio gemina was quartered here by Augustus, to defend the plains from the forays of the Asturian Highlanders. This frontier town was built extremely strong, in the form of a square, according to the cardinal points. The walls were 25 feet thick, and defended with towers ; four marble gates opened into four chief streets, which crossing each other at r. angles, intersected the city. It long survived the empire, and continued as a Roman independent city, which the Goths could never subdue, down to 586, when it was taken by Leovigildo, who changed the name to Leon. The Goths highly valued their prize, and the city was one of the few exempted from the fatal decree of Witiza, by which almost all others in Spain were dismantled, and thus left without defences against the Moors. Gothic Leon yielded at

once to the Moorish invader, but was soon reconquered ; then Ordoño I., in 850, reversed its pristine intention, and made it the defence of the mountains against the infidel invaders from the plains. Leon (Liyon) was stormed by Al-Mansúr in 996. This ravager of Veled Arrum, or the land of the Romans, as they called the Christian territory, entered it after a year's siege ; the Roman gates and walls were then perfect, for the Moorish annalists describe them as " 17 cubits thick ;" but every thing was destroyed, neither age nor sex were spared : for the inhuman atrocities see the account of an eye-witness (E. S. xxxiv. 307) ; nor do the Moors deny them (Moh. D. ii. 114). They gloried in a "sublimity of destruction " as the best test of power.

Leon was soon recovered after Al-Mansúr's defeat at Calatanazor, "the castle of eagles," of which Mariana (viii. 9) details such miraculous apparitions in favour of the Spaniards, and the crushing result is still remembered in the distich—*En Calatanazor Almanzor, perdió el tambor ;* the victors, says Risco (E. S. xxx. 2), writing in 1786, killed exactly 60,000 foot and 40,000 horse of the infidel ; how were they fed, when alive ? Sounds, moreover, of the battle were heard at Seville, 90 L. off ; but the date and results of the battle are in reality uncertain. Mariana places it in 998, and claims the victory for Spaniards ; Conde gives A.D. 1001 ; Gayangos (Moh. D. ii. 197), 1002, and states that Al-Mansúr was not only not beaten at Kal -at-An-nosor, but that he overcame the Conde Sancho Garcez with great loss. One thing is quite clear, that the formidable Al-Mansúr sickened soon afterwards, and died at Medinaceli (see R. cxii.).

Leon was re-peopled by Alonzo V., who rebuilt the walls in *Tapia,* which were taken down in 1324 by Alonzo XI., who enlarged the city to the S., and altered part of the defences ; the walls are best preserved on the N. side of the town, and there resemble those of

Lugo and Astorga in the number of semi-circular towers. Their mode of construction is slovenly; the huge stones worked into the bases no doubt belonged to the Roman work : the rubble walls to the S. are still more inferior; the city is divided by a wall which runs from the *Plaza S^n· Marcelo* to the *P^a· del Peso.* All the walls are much built up against. The city thus defended continued long to be the capital of the kings of Leon, until Don Pedro removed the court to Seville at Alonzo XI.'s death, since which it has lost all its former importance. It bears for arms, argent a lion rampant gules. Consult '*Historia de las Grandezas*,' Atanasio de Lobera, 4to. Valladolid, 1596; '*España Sagrada*,' vols. 34, 35, 36; and the excellent '*Historia*,' Manuel Risco, 4to. 2 vol. Mad. 1792.

This ancient bishopric is *extenta*, or subject to no primate. Urban II. wished to annex it to Toledo, but its independence was confirmed, in 1105, by Pasqual II. Ordoño II., when he fixed his court here, was its great patron, and gave up, for the new cathedral, a portion of the royal palace, which was formed out of the Roman Thermæ, and built on the eastern walls. St. Froylan, who was bishop from 900 to 905, and an eminent architect, filled the city with churches and convents, and was consequently made a saint; all these edifices were, however, totally destroyed by the Moors.

The present cathedral, which is dedicated to *S^a· Maria de Regla*, is an early specimen of the pointed style, and was commenced on the site of the former by B^p· Manrique de Lara, about 1199, proverbially one of the most graceful and elegant in the world, *Pulchra* Leonina—*Leon en Sutileza ;* in delicate elegant sveltura, as well as in lightness, proportion, and masonry, it is unrivalled, and the inscription near *N^a· S^a· La Blanca* does but express the truth, as regards its beauty of holiness.

" Sint tamen Hispanis ditissima pulchraque templa,
Hoc tamen egregiis artibus, ante prius."

First examine the exterior; the *gradus* or platform around it is enclosed by chains; the grand W. entrance is seen to much advantage from the open *plaza*, with its fountain, old brick houses, and arcade; the three doorways of pointed arches are enriched with much elaborate sculpture, in which saints contrast with the sufferings of the wicked. On each side is placed a tower : that to the r. is terminated with a filigree pyramid of open Gothic work ; the other is of more modern plateresque. A smaller pinnacle rises above a noble rose window, with detached lanterns on each side. The S. front also has a *plaza*, but narrower. Opposite the Cathedral is the Colegio de S^n· Froylan and the bishop's palace : here also the entrance is by three arched doors, enriched with Gothic sculpture. The N. façade has been modernised with balustrades and candelabra; the E. is circular and Gothic, with flying buttresses and pinnacles. The masonry throughout is admirable, and the stone of a warm, creamy, and beautiful colour.

The lightness and simplicity of the somewhat narrow interior is charming ; the *Coro* alone cuts up its fair proportions, otherwise no lateral chapels with paltry wooden altars disfigure and darken the sides. The walls rise up from the pavement to the roof; formerly they were pierced by two tiers of windows, divided by an *ambito*, or gallery. The upper, or clerestory, is enriched with gorgeous red and green painted glass, the effect of which is brilliant as an illuminated missal, or rich enamelled jewel work. Remember to visit this church about sunset, for then, as the interior darkens, the windows brighten like transparent rubies and emeralds. The under tier has been bricked up, and painted with figures and scrolls, in a poor academical chiaro oscuro, probably copies of the original painted windows. The edifice, in its pristine state, must have sprung into the air like a majestic conservatory far surpassing the abbey church at Bath, the "lantern of England."

The interior has been barbarously whitewashed, and the capitals of the piers coloured with that Wyat-like nankeen dye with which our Salisbury cathedral is daubed. The *Sill*ª· *del Coro* is of different periods; the upper and oldest is carved in dark wood, with saints and apostles, in the tedesque style of Rodrigo Aleman. The king and the Marques de Astorga are hereditary canons of Leon, and have their appropriate stalls. Philip III. and the Marques both sat in quire Feb. 1, 1602, and received their fee for attendance; this marquisate enjoys a canonry ever since, because an ancestor of the Osorios fought at Clavijo in 846, side by side with Santiago. The *trascoro* is sculptured in white alabaster and gold, with figures painted like waxwork. The subjects are the Annunciation, which is the best, the Nativity, the Adoration, and Offering of the three Kings, and their Berruguete richness baffles description; but the effect is injured by a wooden door put in by the barbarian canons for their convenience, which cuts up the composition. In 1738 the chapter removed the ancient *Retablo*, and erected the present fricassee of marble *El trasparente*, which in absurdity and expense rivals its model at Toledo; in both cases marble is tortured into every possible form into which it ought not to be. This *mamarrachada* was made by Narcisso and Simon Gavilan Tomé, followers of the Heresiarch Churriguerra. In few cathedrals has the bad taste of modern Spanish deans and chapters been more perniciously indulged.

On each side of the altar are buried San Froylan, and San Alvito, Bᴾ· in 1057-63; the possession of the precious body of the former created vast disputes, which, on one occasion, were determined, as usual in Spain (see p.501), by placing them on a mule, and letting the beast take them where he liked

(E. S. xxxiv. 194). The body of the latter was placed here in 1565, and his tomb was one of the most glorious silver works in Spain. The precious *frontal* was carried off by the French, but the *Urna* remains a specimen of exquisite art; and the host is deposited on Good Friday in its central division. Observe the silver temple or tabernacle, with the statue of St. Froylan, the Corinthian pillars, the sides adorned with alto-relievos and saints, and the rich pilasters: on the doors are sculptured St. Paul and Sⁿ· Melchisadeck. The church plate was kept in a room near the Sacristia, where now the empty cases of the chief articles alone remain. The contents were removed to Gijon to escape the Gallic Scylla, and fell, as usual, into the Spanish Charybdis. A viril in silver and gold, and another square and gilt, which have escaped, are beautiful specimens; but the cross and custodia are gone, alas! for they were masterpieces of Enrique d'Arphe, in 1506, the great silversmith of Spain. The latter was one of the finest pieces of plate in the world; Morales (Viaje 55) describes it, and the curious mechanism invented by a Fleming, by which it was moved in processions through the streets; such exactly was the contrivance of the *Paso* of Bacchus (Athen. v. 7). See Valladolid for church plate.

To the r. of the high altar is the *sacristia;* observe the triple Gothic sedilia, in the *ante-sacristia.* The *sacristia* itself is of the best period of Ferd. and Isab., but the pictures are all bad copies of Raphael and Italian masters. Coming out, observe a fine Gothic sepulchre, and adjoining it that of Bp. Pelagius, Mense Aprilis, Era 916. The *trasaltar* is most curious; here is the tomb of Ordoño II., obt. 923, and coeval, it is said, with the edifice: he lies at full length in his robes, a herald stands at his head, and a monk, his architect, holds at his feet a scroll inscribed, "Aspice," as much as to say, like Wren, "Si monumentum quæris, circumspice." The angels, holy subjects, and lions and castles have been painted, and these armorial badges infer a later period, as they were not generally used before the end of the 12th century. Observe a singular old painting on a gilt ground, into which a miserably drawn and coloured Christ has been introduced.

The chapel of Santiago, of the time of Ferd. and Isab., is one of the most airy, elegant Gothic piles in Spain, although a churrigueresque gilt *retablo* mars the *religio loci;* the lofty windows are painted with apostles, saints, virgins, kings, and bishops; the reds and greens are splendid; indeed, these are among the finest specimens of this art in Spain, and as usual they are by Flemish artists. The admirable masonry in this chapel seems only to have been finished yesterday; the circular chapel near is of great antiquity. In the *Capilla de N^a. S^a. del Dado,* our Lady of the Die, is a miraculous image, so called because a gambler, who had been unlucky, threw his dice at it, and hit the infant's face, which immediately bled; here is buried the founder of the cathedral, "Præsul Mauricus jacet hic, rationis amicus." Opposite to the tomb of Ordoño is that of the Condeza Saucha, a great benefactress to churches, for which she was murdered by her nephew and heir, who was torn to death by horses for it, as represented in the sculpture. In the *C^a. de San Pedro* lies B^p. Arnaldo, ob. 1234, the friend of St. Ferdinand, and a bitter persecutor of the Albigenses protestants. Behind the confessional of the *Penitenciario,* is a curious tomb with a sculptured procession of priests. Passing through a passage in which the canons keep their dresses, and looking at the old tombs on the walls, we enter the cloisters; the most curious ancient stucco paintings of events of the Saviour's life are fast going to ruin from damp and neglect, once they must have resembled those of Toledo. These fine cloisters were partly modernised in the 16th century; when the Gothic and Plateresque were brought into a singu-

lar juxtaposition : observe the roof with rich Berruguete shells and stalactites painted in white and gold, and the interior of the niches of the old sepulchres, especially that of S^a. Veronica, and the Gothic temple in the corner ; here is the *Madonna del Foro,* to which the corporation, on the 15th of August, made an offering of 260 reals, called *La offerta de la Regla ;* here also are some Roman inscriptions, one with the name "Legio VII Gem." The once wealthy canons nestled close to the mother church in the spacious street out of the Plaza, *calle de la Canongia.*

Leaving the cathedral, visit San Isidoro el real on the N. side of its *plaza,* which opens by the *Postigo* through the W. wall of the city. It is entitled Royal, from its founders, Ferdinand and Sancha ; in 1063 this great king, the terror of the Moors, applied to Ben Abeth, King of Seville, for the bodies of S^as. Rufina and Justa. As he sent an *armed* embassy, headed by Bp. Alvitus, the wily Moor, glad to pay only such a tribute, consented at once: the only difficulty was where to find the virginal corpses, when San Isidoro, the great Gothic Archbp. of Seville, appeared three times in a vision to Alvitus, and said, "I am the Doctor of the Spains, and *mine is* the body to be removed." In furtherance of this rather ungallant proposal, the doctor next made known his burial place, and his body, revealed by the usual divine odours, was taken up and removed to Leon in triumph, working miracles all the way, " curing the lame and blind, and casting out devils!" Wherever the corpse rested at night, it was found so heavy the next morning that it could not be moved until the inhabitants promised to found and *endow* a church on the spot; that done, it miraculously became again transportable. The whole particulars are detailed in the 'E. S.' ix. 234, 406, and were reprinted in 1827 as *credible facts,* by Matute (*Bosquejo de Italica,* 144); but however true, they are not new, for thus

Cimon the Athenian by a *divine* revelation discovered the remains or λείψανα of Theseus at Syros, which were moved in similar pomp to Athens, after an absence of 400 years, and the oracles directed that they were to be worshipped (Plut. in Cim.). When San Isidoro's body reached Leon, Alonzo, Ferdinand's son, destroyed for this *new* tutelar a temple erected in 960 by Sancho I. to St. John the Baptist, " Vana superstitio *veterumque* ignara deorum." He began in 1063 the present pile, employing for architect Pedrus de Deo Tamber, or Vitambena, who, besides understanding his trade, was a saint, and worked miracles (Risco, ii. 144); his tomb still remains, a large dark stone coffin, near the square *Pila* or font.

San Isidoro, declared by the 8th council of Toledo to be the " *Egregious Doctor of Spain*," although a man of letters while alive (see p. 31), became a man of arms when dead ; he was the Hercules, the Santiago of Leon, and in that capacity fought at the battle of Baeza armed with a sword and cross ; again, when Don Diego and a mob attacked this convent, the egregious doctor struck him blind, nor was his sight restored until he restored the stolen plate. Thus Hercules, when Theron wished to plunder his temple, appeared and fired his fleet (Macrob. ' Sat.' i. 21). San Isidoro was polite enough to leave the winning the victory of *Navas de Tolosa* to Sᵃ· Isidro, the patron ploughboy of Madrid, for these nearly namesake saints must not be confounded with each other: nevertheless during that battle the egregious doctor could not rest in his sepulchre, out of which sounds of arms were heard to issue, showing the interest which he took in the event : Risco (ii. 69) gives all the authorities. Thus the " Ancilia" were heard to clatter of their own accord, just before the Cimbrian war was concluded (Livy, Ep. lxviii.) ; and a voice louder than mortal gave warning in the temple of Vesta of the invading

Gaul (Livy, v. 32). The doctor was silent in the case of Soult, yet Santiago had clashed his arms in his tomb after the *Dos de Maio*, at least so Foy says (iii. 199), who eloquently enough adds, " Si la superstition peut trouver grace devant le philosophe, c'est lorsqu'elle s'associe á la défense de la patrie." Those who wish to know more about San Isidoro, should consult his life written by José Manzano Salamanca, 1732, and for his countless miracles, *Los Milagros* de San Isidoro, composed in Latin by the Bishop of Tuy, and translated by Juan Roblez, Salᵃ·, 1525. This is the sort of knowledge which that eminent university particularly disseminated.

The egregious doctor became the Cid of Leon, and is styled *El Señor* San Isidoro, the *Lord*, the title given to the Almighty, and his shrine became, with those of *El bujo de San Vicente* at Avila, and *El cerrojo del Cid* at Burgos, one of the three *Iglesias Juraderas* of Spain ; and persons swore by his altar as the pagans did at Cæsar's, " Jurandasque tuum per nomen ponimus aras :" all who swore falsely were struck with illness : compare the similar penalties at the *Dellos* or *Crateras* of the pagans (Macrob. 'Sat.' v. 19).

His convent, the *Real casa*, is built on the walls, and by going out of the *Postigo del Rastro*, portions of the original edifice may yet be seen ; of these, observe also the two entrances, the circular chapel, and the ancient square tower, with round Saxon arches built into the walls. Over the S. entrance is the egregious doctor, arrayed *in pontificalibus*, and mounted as he rode down the Moors at Baeza ; his white and gold painted dress, and a royal blazon of arms, contrasts with the time-stained portal ; remark the rude bastard Corinthian pillars and the capitals, which are made of strange animals and scrollwork. The Doric cornice is of later date ; observe beneath some most ancient bassi-relievi, and the two rams' heads, the statue of San Isidoro, and the sacrifice of Abraham, a work of the

2 D 3

12th century. This front has been recently fortified with loop-holes and defences, at which time the beautiful *Puerta del Perdon* was concealed by a new wall : get, however, a ladder, and look over it, for the old work was not injured.

The Gothic church has three naves; the pier-shafts are square, with half-columns projecting from each front; the strange Gotho-Corinthian capitals are formed of groups of children and animals. This royal church was entirely bemired and desecrated by the invaders; when they departed it was cleansed of their slime, whitewashed, and the pillars and capitals picked out in white and buff. Thus between French defilement and Spanish restoration, the pile, now bedaubed and be-painted in the most barbarous taste, is only an incongruous shadow of the past.

The high altar shares with Lugo the rare privilege of having the Host always visible, or *manifestado:* the effect at night, when all is lighted up, with figures of angels kneeling at the side, is brilliantly melodramatic. This *Capilla Mayor* is of later date, and was erected in 1513 by Juan de Badajoz; while it was building the body of the doctor was moved to the chapel of *San Martin*, not the cloak-dividing rival of Santiago, but a pilgrim canon and idiot (an exact Moorish *santon* or *Wellee*), to whom, in 1190, San Isidoro appeared in a dream, and gave him one of his books to eat; whereupon the sleeper awakened a wise man, and preached in Latin, which the people did not understand. However, he continued to work miracles alive and dead; for authentic particulars consult Morales, ' *Viaje*,' 49; and 44 pages printed in 1786, of the ' *Esp. Sagr.*,' xxxv. 365.

The precious silver *reja* and plate of the egregious doctor's tomb was mostly removed by the French, against whom, both here as elsewhere in Spain, all previously protecting miracles seem to have strangely failed; they also burnt the extraordinary library and archives, of which Morales has preserved a record (p. 51), and fortunately Risco has printed many of the earliest deeds, now so many brands rescued from this modern Al Mansúr's fire. The tomb of the tutelar was originally of pure gold ; this Alonzo* of Arragon, second husband of Queen Urraca, carried off, substituting one of silver ; the fragments and the sepulchre deserve the notice of antiquarians. The *Camarin* was gutted by the modern invaders, a few bits of plate only escaping; then was melted the reliquary, made in 1095, containing the jaw of St. John the Baptist, and the enamelled crucifix which worked miracles, the gift of the Infanta Sancha, daughter of Ramon and Urraca; she also offered her virginity to the egregious doctor, and however ungallantly he had behaved to the low potter's daughters at Seville, the prelate felt what was due to royalty, which commands obedience :

" For when a *lady's* in the case,
All other things of course give place."

He accepted her proposal, and she, according to Risco (ii. 139) became his mystical spouse ; the egregious doctor came often to her down from heaven, and not he alone, for San Vicente (and probably under the usual form of Spanish monks) visited her, and said, " *Sancha, esposa muy amada del Doctor San Isidoro, el Señor ha oido tus ruegos por amor de tu esposo.*" Nevertheless she died a virgin, and was buried near her mother, who, according to popular

* He was the celebrated soldier-king *El batallador*, a hero, like some modern marshals, of a hundred razzias, and a noted pillager of churches and convents : after the death ;of Count Ramon, Urraca became *Reina Proprietaria*, or Queen of Spain in her own right ; as Alonzo disputed some claims, a compromise was effected by their marriage, which ended in a separation. Urraca, however, like many other queens of Spain ill-used by Hymen, continued devoted to Venus, and died in child-birth of a bastard in 1126; as there are so many Alonzos and Urracas these facts may be useful. The best book on the queens and royal concubines of Spain is ' *Las Memorias* de las Reynas Catholicas,' by Florez, 2 v. Mad. 1761.

outcry, was "*Meretrix publica y engañadora.*"

This convent became the Escorial or burial-place of the early kings of Leon and Castile; the *panteon* is in the adjoining cloisters, which have been partly modernized in the Ionic style, when the Gothic roof was hideously picked out in leaden greys and white; the side nearest the church has escaped with its round brick arches, and some very ancient painted work remains ; these Capt. Widdrington (ii. 51) thinks "so decidedly Byzantine that the artists must have come from Constantinople," but they appeared to us very early Gothic.

The *Panteon* is a small low chapel, dedicated to Sª· Catalina, whose three-quarter bust, in red and blue tinsel, disfigures the altar. This home of so many kings, queens, and royal personages, was torn to pieces by the French soldiery, who violated the tombs and cast the royal ashes to the dust, as they had done those of Henri IV. at Sᵗ· Denis. The chapter of Leon, in 1825, endeavoured to repair these outrages, *en lo posible,* i. e. as far as they could, and a tablet records simply the event, and leaves the reader to make his own comment. " *Este precioso monumento de la antigüedad, deposito de las cenizas de tantos poderosos Reyes, fue destruido por los Franceses año de* 1809." The restorations, like those of Murillo at Madrid, are scarcely less deplorable than the outrages; the low pillars are rudely painted, to imitate *Verde antique,* which they do not; the tombs consist of plain boxes, piled one upon another, without *order* or *decency* to the dead ; the smallest ones contain the bones of *Infantes,* and are packed on the larger; some few have inscriptions, which are scarcely legible, and they are curt enough, *e. g.* " hic jacet in fossa Geloiræ Reginæ pulvis et ossa." Remark in some the title *Domna* (Domina), not Doña, which is given to the ladies. The epitaphs are all printed by Risco (ii. 148). Now the miserable remains are made a show of, and a sort

of mummy is called the body of Doña Urraca. The roof, being out of the reach of pollution, remains in the original state; observe the stars and herring-bone patterns on the arches, and the singular paintings of architecture, the Saviour, Apostles, and holy subjects, inside the vaults : they are of the 12th century; explanatory labels are appended.

To the W. of the entrance is the once splendid library, a noble lofty room, much out of repair; the books were once among the most curious in Spain, and there were many MSS. of the seventh and eighth centuries, but they were destroyed by Soult, who having routed Romana, was the first enemy who entered Leon, which was dreadfully sacked Dec. 21, 1808: nor was this all, for the unfortunate town and vicinity were frequently ravaged afterwards by his countrymen, and especially by Kellermann and Bessières.

Outside of Leon, near the bridge over the Bernesga, is the enormous convent of *San Marcos de Leon,* once so richly endowed (see p. 289), and whose abbot was mitred ; this convent was founded in 1168, for the knights of Santiago, and here Suero Rodriguez professed ; it was rebuilt in 1514-49, by Juan de Badajoz ; observe, on entering the chapel, a circular arch, and a door fringed with rich Gothic nichework ; the upper part is unfinished ; the royal arms placed between two heralds are of the time of Charles V. The edifice, left incomplete, and now never likely to be finished, stretches to the l., and is a noble Berruguete pile, of most beautiful stone ; the magnificent façade has few equals in the world : observe the medallions and plateresque work ; over the door is Santiago on horseback, and above a clumsy modern construction by Martin de Suinaya, 1715-19, whose Fame blowing a trumpet adds very little to his fame. The arched entrance to the chapel, now a storehouse, is enriched with niches and most elaborate Gothic detail. The *Silla. del Coro* was originally a fine work, by Guillermo Doncel, carved in 1537-42, but it was repaired and ruined in 1721, an epoch fatal to the fine arts of Leon.

To the N. of the rose-perfumed Alameda, also, outside the town, is the huge *Casa de Espositos*, where the sinless children of sinful parents, who escape starvation, manufacture a coarse linen. Opposite is *San Clodio* (Claudio), rebuilt in 1530, with a lofty elegant cloister of light pointed arches with a rich roof; the *Sacristia*, 1568, is beautiful with its white and gold ceiling, which escaped the invaders, who made it a magazine. Passing out of the gate of *So. Domingo*, is the convent of that name, plundered and burnt in 1810 by the French, who then mutilated the noble Ionic sepulchre of Juan Guzman, Bishop of Calahorra, ob. 1575, and that with Corinthian ornaments, of another Guzman, 1576, whose armed effigy is kneeling: this convent has recently been all but demolished, and some of these sepulchres cast out near the entrance of the town. The materials were destined by the *Junta* of Leon to build forts against the Carlists, and which were not *begun* until after Gomez had taken Leon.

Alonzo Perez Guzman, *El bueno* (see Tarifa), was born at Leon, Jan. 24th, 1256; his *casa solar* on the *Pa. San Marcelo* was a palace worthy of the "good soldier;" but this his cradle was entirely gutted by the invaders, and now is the abode of paupers and degraded, still the *patio* shows how noble it once was. Observe, on this *plaza*, part of the old wall, the fountain, the Doric and Ionic *Casa de Ayuntamiento*, built in 1585, by Juan Ribera; and close to it, remark the parish church and the *Santo Hospital.*

Nearly opposite *La Casa de los Guzmanes*, and close to the old southern wall, is the *Casa de los Condes;* this palace of the Lunas was also sacked by the French, and is now almost a ruin; observe the tower, and at the entrance a circular arch and a singular window, with four antique columns; the fine *patio* was never finished, and never will be; the natives say that Queen Urraca lived in this palace. The *Plaza mayor* is a handsome regular square, with the *consistorio* on the W. side; the market-place is spacious, and should be visited for costume and natural history. Leon has several gates, of which the northern, *La del Castillo*, rebuilt in 1759, serves as a state prison, a Newgate.

The communications with Leon are very indifferent, and few travellers come this way. There is a diligence to Valladolid, which occasionally on its return passes on to Oviedo and Gijon; it is in contemplation, however, to place a permanent line, when the new road now constructing is completed, and there is a prospect of a rail-road to Oviedo and Aviles, and to Madrid through Valladolid; meanwhile the Maragatos (see p. 593) are the usual and a most trustworthy channel of intercommunication from one town to another. For the routes to Oviedo, see R. xcv., xcvi.

ROUTE LXXI.—LEON TO BENAVENTE.

Onzonilla	1½	
Ardon	2	3½
Toral de los Guzmanes	3½	7
Villaquejida	1½	8½
Sn. Cristobal	2	10½
Benavente	1	11½

This is carriageable: the dull plains are altogether uninteresting.

ROUTE LXXII.—LEON TO PALENCIA.

Mansilla	3	
Burgo	2½	5½
Sn. Pedro de las Dueñas	3	8½
Villada	2	10½
Paredes de Nava	3	13½
Palencia	3½	17

Dreary and wearisome are these routes, whether in the dust of summer or the mud of winter; the villages in these wide corn plains are as wretched as the population; they resemble La Mancha and the Castiles, and offer no interest or entertainment to man or beast. On leaving the poplar plantations of Leon, the boggy grounds continue almost to the fine and long bridge of Villarente, over the Porma, with its seventeen arches; it is not well built, and was much broken by the inundations in 1843; soon the corn steppes begin, which are fertile, but hideous, from want of water, trees, houses, and signs of human life. The villages are built of *cob*, i. e. mud and straw, for there is little fuel wherewith to burn bricks; most of them have no windows, and the few that have are seldom glazed; a large door answers all purposes, and lets in air, light, men, and pigs: the outsides are daubed over, and rude flowers are scrawled on them in red and white. The Esla is crossed at Mansilla, a town of ruined walls, pop. 700, and a decent posada; the cultivation is everywhere slovenly. The people are simple, wearing almost black jackets, breeches, and very white stockings. The marshy and stagnant waters of the Esla, which overflow these flats, breed agues and *Tercianas*. Here, Dec. 30, 1808, the gallant Franceschi routed the Ms. Romana, who fled without even destroying the bridge; thus leaving an easy access to Soult to take Leon, and then attack Moore's flank.

At *Paredes de Nava*, a townlet situated on a pestilential lake extending towards Palencia, Alonzo Berruguete was born, about 1480; he was the introducer of the classical or rather *cinque-cento* style, to which he has, in Spain, given his great name; he studied in Italy, and is mentioned by Vasari as copying Michael Angelo, at Florence, in 1503; he went with that great master to Rome the next year, and, like him, became an architect, sculptor, and painter; he returned to Spain about 1520, and was soon patronised by Charles V., and afterwards employed all over the Peninsula, which he adorned with magnificent works, in which, although too many have been destroyed by vandals foreign and domestic, no country can even now compete with Spain. He died at Toledo, in 1561.

At *Husillos*, a poor place 2 L. from Palencia, to the N. of the lake, exists or existed a fragment of antiquity which called into action the dormant genius of Berruguete, just as Vasari tells us, that Nicolas Pisano was led to revive the art of sculpture by the study of an ancient sarcophagus; but so long as the physical and moral qualities of man are the same, similar combinations of facts must produce similar results. This sarcophagus was about 8 ft. long by 3½ high, and contained the history of the Horatii and Curatii sculptured in some 50 figures. Berruguete, after his return from Italy, used to say that he had seen nothing finer there; and Card. Poggio pronounced it to be worthy to be placed at Rome among the choicest antiques (see Morales, '*Viaje*,' 26). It will be worth inquiring after this precious relic. For Palencia see R. lxxvi.

ROUTE LXXIII.—LEON TO SAHAGUN AND BURGOS.

Mansilla	3	
Al Burgo	2½	5½
Sahagun	2½	8
A las Tiendas	3	11
Carrion	3	14
Revenga	2	16
Fronista	2	18
Guadilla	1½	19½
Castroxeriz	2½	22
Ontanáz	1½	23½
Rabé	3½	27
Burgos	2	29

This route is carriageable; dull in itself, it interests from the recollections of the ballads of the Cid and Moore's self-sacrificing advance (see p. 590), whereby alone Spain and Portugal were saved from the clutches of Buonaparte, whose plans it deranged, by withdrawing forces which then must have subjugated the whole defenceless country. This diversion gave time to England to send out her armies, which eventually defeated and drove out the invaders: Napier xxiv. 6. Sahagun contains about 2500 souls, with vestiges of its walls and castle. The Cea flows by it, and refreshes a few plantations on its banks. The celebrated Benedictine abbey of San Facundo was founded in 905, by Alonzo III. el Magno; it was *nullius* diocesis, being subject directly to the Pope. Alonzo VI. was almost its second founder, and his Gothic church was begun in 1121 and finished in 1183. The *Retablo*, ascribed by some to Gregorio Hernandez, represents the martyrdom of the tutelar, who was beheaded near the Cea Nov. 27, 304. Alonzo made this abbey the burial-place of himself and his 5 wives. The marble sepulchre is superb, with a statue of the king; the *Urna* is supported by lions. Among other tombs are those of Alonzo Peranzurez, and Bernardo the first archb. of Toledo after its reconquest: who had before been abbot here. The glories of this abbey passed away in 1810, when it was plundered by the French: for its former silver, altars, treasures, relics, and library, consult Morales, ' *Viaje*,' 34; and for its history, that written by Joseph Perez, and published and augmented by Romualdo Escalona, a learned Benedictine of the convent. The monastery was partly repaired in 1814 by the Abbot Albibo Villar. To this holy asylum many early kings of Spain retired like Charles V., and died monks; e. g. Bermudo I. in 791, Alphonso IV. in 931, Ramiro II. in 950, Sancho of Leon in 1067.

The name Sahagun is a corruption of an ancient and once venerated Saint Facundo—San Fagunt, who, however, is now superseded by *San Juan de Sahagun*, a santon of more modern creation. The curious in hagiography may consult a poem on his life and miracles, by Julian de Almendraiz, Roma, 1611; and a prose biography by Ag. Antolinez, the saint's personal friend, 8vo., Salamanca, 1605.

About 1 L. from Carrion to the l. is the Augustin convent of Benevivere, "*good-living*," and no doubt the holy cœnobites did their duty both in chapel and kitchen; it was founded in 1161, by Diego de Martinez, who, having served the kings Alonzo VII., Sancho,

and Alonzo VIII., retired, like so many noble Spaniards, to end his days as a monk; he died era 1214 (A.D. 1176), and was buried in the chapel Sⁿ. Miguel. Observe the singular portico and round arched niches. The church was built in 1382 by Diego Gomez Sarmiento; now this ancient and interesting monument is in a melancholy state of neglect.

Carrion is called *De los Condes*, because it belonged to the *Counts* Diego and Fernan Gonzalez, so well known to ballad-readers as the false sons-in-law of the Cid. The Campeador appealed to Alonzo VI., and a trial of arms took place, when the counts and their uncle Siero were beaten by the Cid's champions, Pedro Bermudez, Martin Antolinez, and Nuño Bustos. The city was then taken from the counts, who were disgraced and declared traitors.

Carrion, in 1366, gave the title of Count to Hugo de Carloway, or Calverley, an English knight, who was serving in the Spanish army until recalled by the Black Prince, whereupon Henrique III. deprived him of his rank after the death of Don Pedro.

Carrion stands on its river of the same name, which has a good bridge : pop. under 3000. It is a city of " the plains," or *Tierras de Campos*. Much corn is grown in these districts, which is preserved in *silos*, or underground *Mazmorras*, granaries. The Benedictine convent in the suburb, Sⁿ. Zoil, was one of the finest things in Spain, until the French plundered and desecrated it. The cloisters remain, and are in the richest plateresque Berruguete style. The infinity of ornaments, saints, medallions, arms, &c., cannot be described. It is an ensemble worthy of Cellini. The under tier was begun in 1537 by Juan de Badajoz, who finished the E. side : the others were completed by Juan de Celanova, and the upper gallery added in 1604. The principal sculptors in the under portions were Miguel de Espinosa and Antonio Morante, by whom is the Christ over the entrance, and the Ecce Homo in the *Capilla de los Condes.* The church is in a sort of pseudo-Doric. The rich plate and pictures were swept away by the invaders. In Carrion is an old temple, *Na. Sa. de la Victoria,* raised to commemorate the attack made by certain bulls on the Moors (compare *Ejea de los Caballeros*), who came here to receive the 100 virgins, the annual tribute agreed to be paid them by Mauregato. A sermon was preached every year, called *El Sermon de Doncellas y Toros;* the legend of lady rent is altogether apocryphal, and a Doric frieze, with the Capita Bovis in the façade, was probably the origin of all this taurumachian nonsense (see Ponz, xi. 201).

Near Carrion, in 1037, was decided the battle between Bermudo III. of Leon and Ferd. I. of Castile, in which the former was killed; the 2 kingdoms were then united by the conqueror's marriage with Sancha the heiress.

Villalcasar de Sirga, vulgo Villasirga, lies about 4 m. from Carrion on the Burgos road. The parish church, which once belonged to the Templars, contains the very remarkable tombs of the Infanta Felipe, son of Sⁿ· Ferd., obt. 1274, with that of his wife Inez de Castro. The figures, larger than life, repose on enriched *urnas,* and the sculpture, although coarse, is full of expression, and the costume very interesting.

Crossing a ridge which separates the basins of the Carrion and the Pisuerga, below extend the endless plains, through which the *Canal de Castilla* was to unite Reinosa with Segovia, and serve both as a means of transit and irrigation. This admirable work, which would have infused life into these dead districts, was begun in 1753; the work in those parts where it is complete is worthy in execution of the conception (see p. 640).

Fromista, an ancient decayed town, stands close to the canal: a few miles S.E. is *Santoyo,* whose church contains

a superb *Retablo* wrought in 1570 by Juan de Juni for Sebastian de Navares, secretary to Philip II.

Near *Itero de la Vega,* the Pisuerga is crossed; it forms the boundary between Leon and Old Castile; thence passing through *Castroxeriz,* a town of 4000 inhab., with a *colegiata* and a sort of palace, and placed between the rivers Odra and Garbanzuelo, we reach Burgos (see R. cxiii.).

ROUTE LXXIV.—LEON TO VALLADOLID.

Mansilla	3	
Matallaua	3	.. 6
Mayorga	3	.. 9
Ceinos	3	.. 12
Berruecos	1	.. 13
Medina del Rio Seco .	3	.. 16
A la Mudarra . . .	3	.. 19
Villanubla	2	.. 21
Valladolid	2	.. 23

There is a slow and bad diligence between these two towns. Crossing the Esla at Mansilla (see p. 613) a loose broken road, dusty in summer and muddy in winter, leads to *Mayorga,* a mud-built village on the Cea, with, however, a decent *posada.* Here Moore made the (Dec. 20, 1808) effected his junction with Baird, and here took place the first encounter of English and French cavalry; thus Mayorga was to the British *sabre,* what Maida was to the British *bayonet.* Then Lord Paget, with 400 of the 15th, charged 600 of their splendid French dragoons, riding them down horse and man. In vain (as at Fuentes de Oñuro) was brandy served out to the foe, the better man prevailed, as must be if the foe can be but grappled with at close quarters, either with sword, bayonet, or boarding-pike. Then, in a bulldog struggle for life or death, blood, bone, and bottom must tell : a purely *physical* superiority generates from consciousness of its power a *moral* confidence. Mons. Foy, however, attributes the accidental success of the English horsemen first to their invariably vast superiority of number and next to rum, as he does the courage of our infantry to beef. "Le rhum vient à propos ranimer ses esprits dans le moment du danger " (i.

231). Again, "Nous avons vu plus d'une fois de faibles détachements charger nos battaillons à fond, mais en désordre. Le cavalier ivre de Rhum lancait son cheval, et le cheval emportait le cavalier au délà du but" (i. 290). Be that as it may, such was the moral superiority felt by our cavalry, that the Duke was obliged to issue a general order to prevent mere companies from charging whole French regiments. Such was, to use his words, "the trick our officers of cavalry have acquired of *galloping at everything*," by which, of course, occasionally they got into scrapes, by falling unexpectedly on strong reserves of infantry, commanded by brave and skilful officers.

On these very plains, ten short days afterwards, did Blake with his whole leader-lacking army run away, scared by one daring charge of Franceschi's dragoons, which two companies of British infantry would have riddled to shreds.

At mud-built *Ceinos* is a curious brick and limestone tower to the ruined church, now used as a *camposanto*, and formerly belonging to the Templars. A wearisome steppe leads to *Medina del Rio Seco*, "the city of the dry river," the Roman Forum Equrrorum. It stands in what was once, like the Alcarria from which it is separated by the Guadarrama chain, a vast lake, before the basin of fresh-water limestone was drained by the Duero and its tributaries. This mud-built capital of a clayey marly district was a noted emporium in the fourteenth century. The fairs of cloth and linen then ranked among the chief of the Castiles, but now life is extinct, and the carcase is returning to the earth of which it was made, dust to dust: the city will become a " heap"—pulvis et umbra nihil : a shadow of the fairs is held April 19 and Sept. 18 ; what is wanting are goods and customers.

Our readers are cautioned against believing even half the natives' exaggerations of their great former commercial prosperity. The essence of the Gotho

Spaniard was a contempt for commerce, as among the Romans those who sprung from trade were disqualified for the senate ; such persons were also despised among the Teutonic nations, the ancestors of the Goths, with whom war and the chase were considered the only occupation of the gentleman. In-door sedentary habits, and delicate manufactures, which require the finger rather than the arm, have in their nature a contrariety to military disposition ; since even Hercules, with the distaff of Omphale, *manufactured* fewer threads in a year than one little white slave of a Manchester cottonocrat turns out in a day. In the best period of Castilian power, the mechanical arts were only imperfectly practised, while the higher speculative and less operative branches of commerce were almost unknown. When the sciences of banking, exchange, and insurances crept slowly into Spain from Italy and the Low Countries, these exotics withered in an uncongenial soil. Then, as now, and in the East, there were no bankers except in the great towns : the vocation of money-scrivening being left in the hands of the despised Jew, the Genoese, Flemings, Alemanes, and other foreigners, who have consequently borne the odium of extracting the wealth of Spain, by entering, as Moncada says, "through the breach of national idleness made by the devil ;" and to this *indolence* he might have added ignorance and insecurity. When, indeed, could commerce flourish in Spain ? (Catalonia excepted) : during the Moorish struggle and constant *algaras y talas*, property was insecure, and scanty capital was wasted in war. Spain, like ancient Rome, rose without trade to pride and power, and when the Moor was conquered, other objects engrossed her ambition. Accordingly, commerce has here always been passive, and at best is a mere exportation of *raw* materials, furnished by a kind soil and climate, which were received back again in a manufactured state from the scientific industrious foreigners, for the consumption of the rich only, since the rude wants of the country at large were and are scantily supplied by a coarse home-made article (see Segovia), each family generally providing for itself, and procuring a few additional articles at periodical fairs, while every luxury was imported by foreigners, and in foreign ships. To this day the shops of the local interior cities, as in the East, demonstrate a most backward stagnant commerce; and they probably are better since the loss of the S. Americas than in former times. That *loss* has indeed been rather an advantage, since necessity has given a spur to Peninsular *enterprise,* if to use such a word be permissible.

The bragging of past commerce, like "the boasting of present strength," is pure rodomontade, but a reference to some bygone period of old and better times is the fond and allowable dream of all who suffer under the evil of the day; and where, however, are the positive proofs of commercial prosperity? The grandee and the church have indeed left memorials of their indubitable power and magnificence, but where are the remains or even records of roads, canals, docks, quays, warehouses, and other appliances? They are not; while everything that tends to the contrary is evidenced in all Spanish feelings and institutions, their exclusive nobility, their disqualifications, their marble-cold spirit of caste, and still existing contempt; all these obstacles of opinion are more difficult to be overcome than those of natural causes. The bulk of the nation despises trade, and as the Moors think all Franks were merchants, so, adopting the sneer of Boney, that grandest of phrase-makers, it considers England to be a country of shopkeepers, who with their operatives would starve without the custom of rich and noble Spain.

Again, at all past periods, the constant lamentations of all writers and every Cortes, the "paper" remedies and plans for amelioration, are negative evidences that the merchants of Spain never were princes, and never attained the wealth, intelligence, honour, and *power* in the commonwealth, which broke down the feudal entails in England, and trampled on the barriers of aristocracy in Venice and Bruges. And as at home, so abroad, few Spaniards, when forced to leave their country, have ever raised themselves in trade, for whether in Spain or out of Spain, the operatives are, in mere handicraft, much below those of most European nations.

The church of Sᵃ· Maria is Gothic; the *Retablo* is one of the finest in the Peninsula. It is divided by fluted Corinthian pillars, with bases and pediments supported by naked children. It was carved in 1590 by Esteban Jordan, and painted by Pedro de Oña, his son-in-law; reds and blues predominate. Observe in it the grand ascension of the Virgin. The whole *Retablo* recalls the noble work of Becerra at Astorga. *La Capilla de los Benaventes* to the l. was once a gem of art, but now all is decay and neglect. The plateresque *Reja* was made by Frᵒ· Martinez 1553: observe above an arch the medallions of the founder's family and their arms. The *Retablo* was carved by the bold and fiery Juan de Juni; observe the Sⁿ· Joaquin and Sᵃ· Ana, and above the *Buena Venturanza,* or the mystical beatitude of the Saviour in the Apocalypse, with a sea filled with the bodies of those rising to judgment. The gilding is much perished by damp and neglect, which have also ruined the Creation of Adam and Eve, and the paintings of Juni on the semicircular arch. Observe over the door the portrait of the founder, Alvaro Benavente, æt. 50, and the 3 fine tombs, separated by caryatides. The paintings at the back of the niches have been ascribed to Juni. Observe the Sᵃ· Ana in bed, and two kneeling figures. The stucco ceilings and ornaments are in the finest Berruguete taste. Cean Berm. '*Ar.*' ii. 69, 221, has printed the curious original contract and specification of these works by Juni.

There are 4 fine pictures in this church either by Murillo or Tovar, for it is not easy to decide, owing to their dirty condition and position; the subjects are a large oblong Nativity, a charming St. Catherine, a kneeling Magdalen, and full-length Madonna and child, which is the finest. These paintings flap in their frames covered with dust, which might be expected from the men of Rio Seco, whose plains and brains have been dried in the sun.

The church of *S^a. Cruz* has a classical façade, which, although much admired here, is somewhat heavy. The sculptured sibyls, the finding the Cross, and the two tiers of Corinthian pilasters, give it a serious character, notwithstanding which, it was pillaged by Bessières, who made it a brothel for the army, selecting nuns for the victims. It was founded by the great Don Fadrique Enriquez, Admiral of Castile, of whose palace in the town a gate is all that has escaped ruin. The tombs and kneeling figures of himself and his wife, Ana de Cabrera, were in S^{n.} Francisco, where were some good *terra-cotta* statues of St. Jerome and St. Sebastian, and much Berruguete work, and a very fine ivory crucifix. This convent was built with the materials of the old castle which withstood so many sieges in the time of Don Pedro and Charles V., but which the Franciscan monks levelled; now, in the cycle of destruction, their turn is come.

The last blow to decaying Rio Seco was given July 14, 1808, after its battle, which placed Joseph on the throne of Madrid, and was compared by Buonaparte to the crowning victory of Villa Viciosa. Previously the incompetence of Savary had compromised the French position in the Castiles, as Filanghieri hovered on their flanks in Gallicia, wisely abstaining from battle; suspected, therefore, by the Juntas of treachery, he was murdered and succeeded by Blake, who effected a junction with Cuesta, only, however, to end in quarrel. Such

seems ever to be the curse of this unamalgamating climate, for Scipio's great hopes of subduing Spain were based on the mutual dissensions of the Iberian generals (Polyb. x. 6, 7). It infected the French cause; the rivalries of Buonaparte's marshals (see p. 221) contributed to the Duke's successes.

Now, either Blake or Cuesta alone, would have been enough to secure a reverse, which two such great masters of defeat being together rendered certain, and in order to ensure it they led 50,000 men, worthy of better chiefs, into the plains of Monclin, near Palacios. Bessières had only 12,000 French, but beholding the absurd arrangements of his enemy, which rendered even defence impossible, ordered La Salle to charge with some cavalry, whereupon the Spaniards, mistrusting their leaders, ran away instantly. The French soldiers, thirsty in the pursuit and burning sun, finding the river dry, exclaimed, "even Spanish water runs away." The Spaniards lost 6000 killed and wounded, the French not even 500.

Bessières, who was no real general, did not know how to follow up his victory, and he was afraid to advance into Gallicia, alarmed at the report of the English having landed. Rio Seco, unarmed and unresisting, was however sacked; neither age nor sex was spared, and yet the inhabitants had illuminated their houses in token of friendly feeling to the French (Toreno, iv.). Schepeler (i. 434, 37) details the horrors of fire, lust, and rapine, accompanied with cold-blooded murder of prisoners, with which we cannot stain these pages. Bessières, who began life like Suchet, a barber, was sent to his last account at Lutzen. This just man, according to Buonaparte's bulletin, was "recommandable par ses qualités civiles," and as he wrote to the widow, "a laissé une réputation sans tache." The widows and nuns of Rio Seco never penned that epitaph.

Rio Seco is a good central point from whence to make excursions to several ancient cities.

ROUTE LXXV.—RIO SECO TO
VALLADOLID.

Villafrechós	2¼	
Villalpando	2¼ ..	5
Sⁿ Esteban	2 ..	7
Benavente	2 ..	9
Zamora	10 ..	19
Fresno	3 ..	22
Toro	2 ..	24
Pedrosa del Rey . .	3 ..	27
Villalar	2 ..	29
Tordesillas	1 ..	30
Rueda	2 ..	32
Medina del Campo. .	2 ..	34
Valdestillas	4 ..	38
Puente Duero . . .	2 ..	40
Simancas	1¼ ..	41¼
Valladolid	2 ..	43¼

As far as country villages and people are concerned, nothing can be more bald or wretched than this circuit, which, however, includes towns of former fame, and sites of important events. *Villalpando* in its vast plain was once a city of 50,000 souls, but it decayed when Rio Seco rose at its expense; now the popⁿ is under 3000. The original city, being built of mud, has mostly disappeared, while the French gutted the more solidly constructed Franciscan and Domenican convents; the misery is now complete inside, and outside a vast tract of land, a *valdio* or "common" of the townsfolk, is left almost uncultivated. Benavente and the route to Zamora have been described (see R. lxvii.). Those who do not wish to go there, may cross the plains directly from Rio Seco to Zamora, 13 L. through Bustillo, which is about half way: for Zamora, see p. 586.

Ascending the Duero from Zamora, is the ancient and decayed city of *Toro*, with its fine bridge and the pleasant walk on it, from which we look at those *Almenas de Toro* chaunted by Lope de Vega. This city, like Salamanca, takes its bridge and a "canting" *Toro*, one of its Guisando breed, for its arms. It lords over the plains, those *campos* which were the granary of the Goths. Toro is dull and backward; it contains about 9000 souls. The iron *rejas* to the windows give it a

prison-like look, and the streets are dirty and ill-repaired; the civic fund, *La Meaja*, has long, as usual, been eaten up by the commissioners of improvement. The traveller may visit the ruined Alcazar of Garcia, in which the French kept a garrison. Gen. Duvernay captured the unprepared city, Jan. 6, 1809, with a handful of cavalry; for Moore had in vain urged the *junta* of Toro to fortify their town, which, like Zamora, might have formed an important place for him to fall back on, and as the French at that time had no artillery for sieges, they must have been arrested, and the retreat on *la Coruña* avoided, but, as usual, nothing was done by the procrastinating imbeciles.

It was at Toro that the Conde Duque, the disgraced minister of Philip IV., died in 1643, haunted, as he imagined, by a spectre—the ghost of his country's departed greatness, which he had so mainly contributed to destroy.

Toro, of course, has a *Plaza de Toros*. The architect may also observe *La Torre del Reloj*, the house of *Los Fonsecas*, and the *Casa del Ayuntamiento*, built by Ventura Rodriguez, and the granite *Colegiata*, of which the façade of the clock-tower, with its solid buttresses, deep recessed entrance, and circular arched work, deserve notice.

Toro was a city of great former importance. Don Pedro entered it in 1356 by the gate Sᵃ. Catalina, and thus put down the rebels. Near it was fought in 1476 the battle between Alonzo V. of Portugal and Ferdinand, which gave the crown of Castile to Isabella, and defeated the faction of La Beltraneja. Here again was held in January, 1506, the celebrated Cortes by which, after her death, Ferdinand's authority was recognised.

Leaving Toro, and continuing on the r. bank of the Duero, near the river Hormija is the most ancient abbey Sⁿ. Roman, founded by the Gothic Recevinto for the burial-place of his wife: thence to *Villalar*, where (April

23, 1521) the Conde de Haro defeated the *Comuneros* under Juan de Padilla, and crushed this popular insurrection against the foreign favourites of Charles V. Padilla was beheaded the next day at Tordesillas. Southey, when young, wrote verses on this martyr to mob patriotism. The conduct of the *junta* was precisely such as we have seen in our times; for they exhibited, says Robertson, " the strongest marks of irresolution, mutual distrust, and mediocrity of genius," incapable alike of carrying on war, or of making peace. Padilla fell a victim to their combined baseness and ignorance : he was the husband of Maria Pacheco, to whom before his execution he wrote that most touching and manly letter preserved by Sandoval, and translated by Robertson.

Tordesillas stands in its weary *Paramos de Leon*, those bald steppes, those seas of corn, which are bounded only by the horizon; it has an old bridge over the Duero, and therefore always is an important strategic position. Visit the church *Sⁿ. Antolin*, as the *Retablo* contains a fine Crucifixion, which is attributed to Juan de Juni. The superb marble sepulchre of the Comendador Pedro Gonzalez de Alderete, was wrought in 1527 by Gaspar de Tordesillas; it is equal to Berruguete, and is designed in the style of the royal tombs at Granada, with caryatides at angles, figures and cinque-cento ornaments : the founder lies armed, with his helmet at his feet. The other tomb in a niche is inferior. The nunnery Sᵃ. Clara is of good Gothic, so is the chapel of Esteban Lopez de Saldaña, 1435 : observe particularly the *Retᵒ.*, and the four sepulchres in niches with armed figures; the architect Guillem de Roam is buried near it; ob. Dec. 7, 1431. This convent has received eminent personages; here Juana la Loca, " crazy Jane," the mother of Charles V., died, April 11, 1535, aged 76, having watched for 47 years, with jealous insanity, the coffin of her handsome but worthless husband, in which she buried with tears all her earthly joys, and which was so placed in the chapel that she could see it from her apartment; a sad remembrance fondly kept. Memory may indeed be sometimes the renewer of great sorrow, but often is the sole friend and consoler of the mourner. In her case it amounted to monomania, for the object of her regret was undeserving, and there was no justice in her affliction, no duty in her lamentation. It was a pure indulgence of the selfish luxury of grief, the joy of a melancholy half-cracked temperament,—who can administer to a mind diseased ? and the morbid taint broke out again in her descendants; it induced her son Charles V. to die a monk at San Yuste; it tinged the gloomy bigotry of Philip II., and ended with the Austrian race and dynasty in the confirmed imbecility of Charles II., a sovereign who kept pace with the decline of his kingdom and dynasty.

In this convent Buonaparte was lodged, Dec. 25, 1808, and he thus wrote in his bulletin, " Sa majesté avait son quartier général dans les batimens extérieurs du Couvent Royal de Sᵗᵉ. Claire — c'est dans ce batiment que s'était retirée, et qu'est morte la mère de Charles V. Le couvent à été construit sur un ancient palais de Maures, dont il reste un bain et deux salles, d une belle conservation ; l'abbesse a été présenté à l'Empereur."

Much red wine, strong and heady as port, is grown in these districts; a détour should be made of 2 L. to the r. to *Nava del Rey*, as the Corinthian *Retablo* in the *parroquia* is a noble architectural and sculptural monument by the great Gregorio Hernandez : observe particularly the two St. Johns.

Rueda, popⁿ. 2500, has also a fine parish church, and a handsome long street. It is one of the best of the towns in this district, as the quantity of good wine grown here is a source of profit to the inhabitants. The vineyards lie on a stony broken soil ; the wine is kept in deep cellars in large oaken barrels, and is considered to be a specific *against* the gout. To this town the *Maragatos* and wine-merchants of the north come to make their purchases, bringing iron and colonial produce in exchange. At Rueda, as at El Bodon, the Tormes, Zubiri, and so many other places, the name and presence *alone* of the Duke saved his army in the retreat from Burgos: here Caffarelli, Oct. 21, 1812, with 40,000 splendid French infantry and 5000 cavalry, came up with "not 20,000 British and Portuguese;" in spite of all this numerical superiority, the enemy declined giving battle; thus protected by the halo of his glory, he passed on unmolested, and this is his record: "I was shocked when I saw how the Spaniards fought, and when I saw the whole of the enemy's army, it was *very clear to me* that they ought to eat me up. I have got clear off in a handsome manner out of the worst scrape I ever was in " (Disp. Oct. 31, 1812). That scrape was occasioned by our ministers at home, and by Ballesteros in Spain, while the " getting off" was the fair reward of superior tactics, by which the enemy were cowed, outgeneraled, and baffled. Nothing ever exceeded the Duke's self-possession, presence of mind, and nerve; he was calm in the greatest dangers, and sustained by a confidence that he was equal in himself to every emergency: the character of Turenne as sketched by Michaud (Bio. Uni. xlvii. 59), is far more applicable to our English hero: " Conservant dans ses revers comme dans les succès ce calme stoïque, ce sang-froid imperturbable, qui sert si bien à réparer les uns et à compléter les autres, il ressemble plus qu'aucun de nos grands hommes aux *Héros de l'antiquité*, marchant toujours à son but, du même pas, ne s'emportant jamais, et repoussant par son calme et sa froide raison les sottes prétensions et mêmes les injures!"

Medina del Campo, the city of the plain (Methimna Campestris), is another important strategic point, as it is equidistant from Zamora, Salamanca, Palencia, Avila, and Segovia, being

about 14 L. from each. The town is placed on the swampy Zapardiel, whose neglected waters breed pestilence. The Moors had corrected this, and cut a canal, which also served for irrigation; some remains only of their work may be traced at *La Cava*, for all as usual was let go to ruin by their successors.

Medina was the capital of the *Campo*, or level district, which is one of the finest wheat countries in the world; corn is here worth about 25s. the quarter, but from want of roads and transport 18s. must be added before it is on board at Santander, from whence to England a freight of 6s. must be calculated on.

Medina was once a royal court and much-frequented emporium: the pop[n], said to have been 50,000, has now dwindled down to 3000. It was, however, thus described by the Bishop of Mondoñedo, even in 1532: "This towne, to my judgement, hath neither grounde nor heaven; for the heavens are always covered with cloudes, and the grounde with dyrte, in such wise that if the neighbourhood call it Medina of the field, wee courtiers doe terme it Medina of the dyrte. It hath a river that is so deepe and dangerous, that geese in summer go over it dry-footed "—'Guevara's Letters,' p. 101, translated by Fellowes, London, 1584.

The city was plundered in Aug. 1520 by the *Comuneros*, when Antonio de Fonseca and the patriots burnt 900 houses. It never entirely recovered, and during the recent war was impoverished by frequent French pillage and exaction. The church S[a.] Antolin was founded in 750, and made collegiate in 1480, of which date are the tower, and the figures that strike the hour. The *Ret[o.]* is very grand, and consists of five tiers, with the life of our Saviour and Berruguete ornaments. The crucifix is by Gaspar Becerra; the Doric *Sill[a.] del Coro* came from Guadalupe. The hospital was built by Juan de Tolosa in 1591, for Simon Ruiz Embito, the Heriot of this town. As usual, it is unfinished, because most of the funds were eaten up by the junta, and the rest was invested in *juros*, or government stock, all of which was lost in the usual national bankruptcy. The quadrangle is grand. The *Ret*º· in the chapel is adorned with a miracle of the charity-dispensing San Diego. Observe the iron *reja*, and the tomb of the founder kneeling with his two wives, and his portrait painted by Pantoja de la Cruz. Part of the hospital was recently made a cavalry barrack.

The city shambles, *Las Carnecerias*, are much admired, as the *patio*, with granite pillars, was built in 1562 by Gaspar de Vega. Look at the plateresque *Casa de los Dueñas*, and walk in the Chiopal. Visit the *Castillo de Mota*, erected in 1440 by Fernando de Carreño, for Juan II., on the site of the Roman Methimna. Isabella employed Alonzo Nieto to increase it in 1479. It crowns the hillock, and its slim *Torre del Homenaje* has the turrets at the angles, which are so common in these districts. Here the notorious Cæsar de Borgia was confined for two years, until he escaped by the aid of the Conde de Benavente. And here, a little before noon on Wednesday, Nov. 26, 1504, died Isabella, in the 54th year of her age and 30th of her reign. Peter Martyr, writing the same day from the spot to the Conde de Tendilla, and to Talavera the good Archbishop of Granada, thus truly sums up the just eulogium of his mistress, a pattern of her sex, and the purest sovereign by whom female sceptre was ever wielded : " Cadit mihi præ dolore dextra; orbata est terreæ facies mirabili ornamento, inaudito hactenus : in sexu namque fœmineo et potenti licenciâ nullam memini me legisse, quam huic natura Deusque formaverit, comparari dignam " (Epis. 279). Her body was moved to Granada in December, after a journey replete with horrors, over roadless tracks, amid storms and torrents, of which Peter Martyr, who accompanied his mistress to her last home, gives a faithful picture. For her character, see Granada, p. 388.

From hence to Valladolid is 8 L., either returning to Tordesillas, or taking the direct road to Puente del Duero, and thence diverging to *Simancas*, where the archives of Spain, a yet unexplored mine of historical information, are interred. The town and castle rise boldly on the opposite side of the Pisuerga, here crossed by a stone bridge of 17 arches, which the French injured Sept. 8, 1812, when they retreated before the Duke. The river is deep and rapid ; and the proverbs say, " *El Duero lleva la fama, y Pisuerga lleva la agua;*" " *Duero y Duraton, Arlanza y Arlanzon, en la puente de Simancas juntos son.*" Like the Guadiana and Guadalquivir, the stream is turbid and discoloured by the clayey soils through which it eats its way. Some geographers make this river the boundary between Leon and Old Castile.

Simancas was a town and castle originally belonging to the Henriquez, the Grand Admirals of Castile, until it was taken from them by Ferd. and Isab., and destined for the national archives. The strong edifice, which rises over the river, was a safe and well-selected site when the court resided in the neighbourhood, but now its distance from Madrid is very inconvenient, and the Escorial would do better. The interior was altered for Philip II. by Herrera, Berruguete, and others (see Cean Ber. '*Ar.*' ii. 325). The papers were very complete from 1475. Most of the earlier were destroyed by the *Comuneros* in 1520.

Those relating to S. America were sent to Seville in 1783. The French, on arriving, in 1809, at Simancas, took all the papers relating to their diplomacy with Spain, and the captivity of François I. In vain did Ferd. VII., at the restoration, reclaim them of his Bourbon kinsmen; few ever were returned. A worse fate remained for many documents which had no French interest, as Kellermann used them as waste paper; his troops lighted their fires with the archives, and cut open the bundles for the sake of the string by which they were tied. In vain did Joseph remonstrate to Buonaparte; the precious documents were destroyed by waggonloads, as Manuel Gonzalez saw done, and related to us on the spot. The French troops were quartered in the rooms: and not contented with daily destruction during their stay, when they evacuated the castle they set the whole on fire, as a parting legacy; then the N. wing was burnt down, which has since been rebuilt. The remnant of Kellermann's spoliation and fire at Simancas was entirely re-arranged by Don Tomás Gonzalez, canon of Placencia, who with his brother classified the most curious papers, and placed them in the *Patronato viejo,* and in *el cubo.*

Visit first the old chapel of the *Henriquez* family, with a blue and gold roof, and a saloon richly decorated by Berruguete. Each traveller will of course inquire for the class of papers which most interest himself. Among those of general curiosity, observe *El Becerro,* the book of nobility of Alonzo XI.; the original deed of capitulation at the taking of Granada, signed by the queen; the title-deeds of the *Soto de Roma,* now the D. of Wellington's domain; the *cuentas del Gran Capitan,* and many of his original dispatches, written in a loose large handwriting; the *Recamera,* or inventories of Isabella's jewels, her library, and treasures at Segovia, and the swords: among them are noted La Tisona del Cid, *La Giosa del bel cortar of Roldan,* the one with which he divided the Pyrenees; notice particularly her last will, a parchment signed by her, Oct. 12, 1504, Medina del Campo; the codicil of Charles V., Sⁿ· Yuste, Sept. 9, 1558, written in a trembling hand, yet enjoining the extirpation of heretics. There are many letters of Charles V., Philip II., and his fit wife, our bloody Mary: many and most curious papers regarding the "*Invincible* Armada," the outfit and expenses. The documents relating to our Elizabeth, from

1558 to 1576, have been made the groundwork of Gonzalez's admirable paper (Memˢ· de la Acad. Hist. vol. vii. 249): he also prepared from the original documents *La Retirada,* or retreat of Charles V. at Sⁿ· Yuste. The original drafts of Philip II.'s dispatches to his ministers and ambassadors are most numerous: they are corrected and interlined with his own royal loose and straggling handwriting.

In the plain below the castle was fought (July 19, 939), one of the most bloody battles between Moors and Christians. The bridge of Simancas is worth notice, so after crossing it is the view back, with the towering castle. The celebrated Irish rebel, Hugh Roe O'Donnell, died at Simancas September 10, 1602: he had fled after the defeat of Kinsale, with many of his adherents, to Philip III., because the most decided enemy of England. He had pined for some time at la Coruña, sickening under the hope deferred of broken promises, and coming to urge the king died here, cursing punic Spain, and remembering his sweet Argos. From this date commenced the influx of Irish priests, outlaws, and Pat-riotics, who settled in Spain, and from whom were descended the Blakes, O'Donojus, &c., who were the bitterest opponents of their great fellow-countryman the Duke, in his efforts to deliver their newly-adopted *Patria.*

Soon we enter Valladolid by its noble *Campo Grande.* The best inn is *El Parador de las Diligencias,* kept by *La Bilbaina.*

VALLADOLID, the Roman Pincia, was called by the Moors *Belad-Walid,* the city or "Land of Walid" (*El Weléed I.*) under whose kalifate Spain was conquered. Some Spaniards, who dislike Moorish recollections, derive the name from *Valle de Lid,* the scene of strife; others from *Vallis Oliveti,* there being few olives in this cold elevated district. *Belad-Walid* was recovered in 920 by Ordoño II., who raised a sculptured lion, a memorial of his victory, on the site of *El Leon de la Catedral.* The domain was granted by Alonzo VI. to his son-in-law, the great Count Rodrigo Gonzalez Giron, who gave the city his coat of arms, " gules 3 banners or." Some heralds, however, hold these "*girones* " to be "flames of fire;" others " waves of the river;" an orle of eight castles was afterwards added.

When the male race of this Giron failed, the domain was regranted in 1090 to the Conde Pedro Ansurez, who is the real founder of modern Valladolid ; by him were rebuilt the bridge, Sⁿ· Nicolas, La Antigua, and the Hospital of the Esqueva. He died leaving only a daughter, and the grant again soon relapsed to the crown. The city rose gradually in population and wealth ; especially in the beginning of the 15th century, when it was made the residence of Juan II. Then, according to the proverb, it was without its equal in Castile : " *Villa por Villa, Valladolid en Castilla.*" Under Charles V., it was adorned with splendid edifices, and his son Philip II., born here, favoured his native town ; he gave it the title of city in 1596, having induced Clement VIII. to elevate it to a bishopric the year before.

Madrid rose on the decay of Valladolid, as when the court removed, the sources of its prosperity were cut off. Philip III. feeling how much better the situation of the ancient capital was than the upstart new one, determined to re-establish it, and quitted Madrid in 1601 ; but, after a five years' absence, the attempt was found to be impossible. Thus a position on a fine river, in a rich fertile country abounding in fuel and corn, and under a better climate, was abandoned for a mangy desert, exposed to the death-pregnant blast of the Guadarrama. Navagiero (35) details what Valladolid was in all its glory, when filled with rich nobles, and foreign merchants established here, on account of its vicinity to the great cities and fairs: nor social pleasures were wanting, or, as he observes, " se vive con *gualque poco meno* de se-

verita, che non si fa nel resto de Castiglia." It then contained more than 50,000 inhab., now it scarcely numbers 24,000.

Valladolid pined slowly away, keeping pace with the decay of Spain, until the invasion of the French, when ruin came on with frightful celerity : Buonaparte gave the signal himself ; here he lodged and loitered from Jan. 6th to 17th, 1809, while defeating Moore in his bulletins. Here he wrote paragraphs in praise of the Benedictines, to be *read* in Paris, while he directed executions of monks to be *seen* in Valladolid. Here at his presence, as at Burgos, Hope withering fled and Mercy sighed farewell ; his first feu de joie was the burning the *Trinitarios Descalzos,* which was utterly destroyed, with the glorious *Retablo* by Berruguete, on the third night after his arrival. He next dismantled the Dominican college, the grandest building in the city, then his imitators proceeded to gut the *Carmen de los Calzados,* where they tore down the *Reto·* of Hernandez, broke his finest works, for he lived and died in this convent, violated his grave, and turned the chapel into a hospital. They then pillaged the *Sⁿ· Juan de Letran,* and stole the Rincon paintings. Next they emptied the magnificent *Agostinos Calzados,* and made it a straw magazine ; now it is a barrack. They subsequently entirely ruined *San Pablo,* and desecrated *Santiago,* destroying the master-pieces of Juni and Tordesillas.

The city had been previously sacked, Dec. 26, 1808, the day on which the invaders first entered ; it afterwards became the head-quarters of Kellermann, who, fit successor to Bessières, spared neither church nor cottage, age nor sex, man nor beast. Some partial restorations have since taken place ; but the impoverished citizens were no longer able to emulate their more magnificent ancestors ; barely able to live, they had no *surplus,* by which alone great works are done, *obra de lo que sobra,* and to little purpose was done, the little that was effected; civil wars and sequestrations have carried out what the foreign foe commenced; and there are few cities in Spain where the lover of antiquarian and religious pursuits will be more pained than in Valladolid. Nowhere has recent destruction been more busy; witness San Benito, San Diego, San Francisco, San Gabriel, &c. almost swept away, their precious altars broken, their splendid sepulchres dashed to pieces; hence the sad change from the treasures of art and religion which are recorded by previous travellers.

VALLADOLID lies on the l. bank of the Pisuerga, which is here joined by the Esqueva; the latter divides the town, acting as a sewer. These rivers sometimes overflow, and occasion infinite damage. The inundation of Feb. 4, 1636, destroyed entire streets. The abundance of water, however, favours cultivation. The *Alamedas* on the river banks are pleasant: to the N.E. is *El Prado de la Magdalena*, on the Esqueva, which is crossed by the central bridge *de las Chirimias*. On the Pisuerga are *El Espolon nuevo*, and *El Plantio de Moreras*, pleasant and shady walks which lead up to the fine bridge, or rather bridges; for the ancient one being narrow, another was built alongside of it by the Conde de Ansurez. The grand suburban Alameda is on the *Campo Grande.*

Valladolid is placed in a concave valley; the sloping hills on the r. bank of the Pisuerga look barren and clayey, with reddish streaks or strata. The *Canal de Castilla*, which begins at Alar del Rey, terminates at Valladolid, and if ever completed, will do much to restore a portion of former prosperity. The university is attended by nearly 2000 students, and just now is perhaps the first in the Peninsula.

Valladolid is the capital of its province, and the residence of the captain-general of Old Castile; the see is suffragan to Toledo. It has 16 parishes, an academy of fine arts, a university, a liceo, a new museo, public library,

hospitals, *Casa de Esposítos,* and usual public establishments, and high court of Chancery. The town has few social attractions: the climate is damp in winter, and cold from its elevation, while the summer suns scorch fiercely; but it is not, however, unhealthy like Madrid. The inhabitants are genuine old Castilians, grave, formal, and honourable. Here Columbus died, May 20, 1506; here Philip II. was born, May 21, 1527. For local histories, consult '*Las Excelencias de Valladolíd,*' Ant°· Daca, duo. Val^d· 1627; and especially for the hagiography of its tutelar saint, Pedro Regalado: '*Viaje Artistico,*' oct°·, Isidoro Bosarte, Mad. 1804, p. 99; Ponz, '*Viaje:*' these explain the artistical treasures before the invasion. The '*Compendio Historico Descriptivo,*' published by Julian Pastor in 1843, is useful, and contains a catalogue of the contents of the new Museo. There is a map of the city by Diego Perez Martinez.

The *Esqueva* is the aorta and imperfect sewer of the town. We will commence our sight-seeing above the bridge *de las Chirimias,* keeping on the r. bank: in the first street is the site of the Inquisition, the *chancelleria,* and the *prison,* the latter being the natural consequence of these tribunals, too often the engines of superstition and injustice. The great Chancery, or court of appeal for the N. of Spain, was fixed here by Juan II. in 1442, and was moved to the present building by Ferd. and Isab., who appropriated the mansion of the ill-fated Alonzo Perez de Vivero. Over the court of this Chancery is the motto "Jura fidem ac pœnam reddit sua munera cunctis," which to all who know what Spanish *Justicia* is, let alone chancery in general, seems a bitter mockery, an addition of insult to injury.

This Chancery was in the N. what that of Granada was to the S., a monopoly; as the distances from other provinces were great and inconvenient it was divided in 1835, and an audiencia

2 E

established at Burgos, in order to render the court of appeal nearer to suitors
from Arragon and Catalonia. Previously, however it might ruin suitors,
it benefited the practitioners and Valladolid, as it encouraged the residence
of lawyers, and occasioned an influx
of clients, witnesses, and students:
hence jurisprudence has always been,
and still is, one of the chief studies of
this city's university. The jurisdiction
of the *Audiencia* of Valladolid extends
over 965,300 souls: the number of
tried in 1844 was 3256, which is about
one in every 296 persons.

Passing next into the *Plaza de S^n.
Benito el viejo*, and then into the larger
one *del Palacio*, is the royal palace of
Philip III. Although the exterior is
commonplace, it has a noble Berruguete staircase and two *patios ;* the
smaller is called *El Zaguan*, and the
larger has a fine gallery, *la Saboya*,
which was restored by Pedro Gonzalez
for Ferdinand VII.: observe also the
busts of Spanish monarchs. In this
house Buonaparte was lodged, and
looking out of his window every morning on two of the noblest specimens of
religious Gothic art in the world, destined both to desecration and ruin.
The first was the Dominican convent
San Pablo, which was rebuilt in 1463
by Card. Juan Torquemada, originally
a monk of the older convent, and the
ferocious inquisidor of Seville. The
rich façade attributed to Juan and
Simon de Colonia, consists of two
divisions : observe the beautiful portal,
and elaborate oval, with niche-work
and figures ; the upper portion is
crowned with the arms of the Cardinal
Dnke of Lerma, its subsequent patron,
who was buried here ; his splendid
tomb is in the Museo. The church is
lofty and noble, but disfigured by a
paltry modern high altar, which has
been erected in place of the former
magnificent one which the French
broke to pieces. The picture of St.
Paul struck blind is by Bartolomé
Cardenas : observe the beautiful portals at each side of the altar, and the

roof, which, being out of reach, is not
defiled. The exquisite statues by Hernandez, a glorious sepulchre, the pictures, plate, library, &c. were all swept
away by one sentence of Buonaparte :
" Sa majesté," says he himself, " a or-
donné la suppression du Couvent des
Dominicains, dans lequel un Francais
a été tué :" but even this pretext was
untrue, for an eye-witness on the spot
assured us that this soldier died a victim to his own brutal excesses. San
Pablo was next made by the invaders a
storehouse for forage, and now is a prison
for galley slaves, and a den of thieves !

Adjoining to *San Pablo* is the
Dominican *Colegio de S^n. Gregorio*,
founded in 1488 by Bp. Alonzo de
Burgos. The architect was one Macias
Carpintero of Medina del Campo, who
killed himself in 1490, a rare instance
in Oriental Spain, where suicide is
almost unknown, being opposed to
their fatalist principles and singular
resignation ; his plans, however, were
worked out. The Gothic façade, if
possible, is more elaborate than that of
San Pablo ; observe the basket-work of
interwoven trees, the armorial shields,
the wild men and boys. The Berruguete cornice, with heads, festoons,
and angels, is of later date and by
other artists. For this once splendid
temple Juan de Juni carved a grand
Ret^o., in which the founder was represented kneeling ; he was buried before
it, and his effigy clad in his episcopal
robes lay on a marble sarcophagus,
resembling the royal tombs of Granada,
a work ascribed by some to Berruguete ;
and the device, " Operibus credite,"
referred both to the *good works* of the
artist and the prelate. He was a magnificent patron of art and learning,
and the friend and confessor of Isabella : his library was superb, and a
part of the room yet remains with its
splendid *artesonado* roof, for Buonaparte
ordered the pile to be destroyed, and
it was done ; the fragments in the
courts, doorways, &c., now only await
a final demolition, for Spain at least
is energetic in destruction.

At the back of the Palacio is the Calle de Leon, so called from the lion carved over the house No. 2; thence pass through the *Plaza de los Leones* and Sⁿ· Miguel up a narrow street to that of *El Almirante*, opposite to whose ancient mansion with quaint windows is *El Penitencial de las Angustias*, or *Sᵃ· Maria de las Angustias.* The façade is seen to advantage from the open space in front; according to an inscription over the *coro*, it was built by Martin Sanchez de Aranzamendi in 1604, after designs, it is said, of Herrera; the under portion of the Corinthian facade contains good statues of St. Peter and St. Paul, and a Pietá. The interior was once a museum of painted sculpture, but most of the finest things by Hernandez have been removed to the Museo. The dead Christ in the arms of the Virgin, by Hernandez, was a truly Michael Angelesque composition of maternal grief. The *Retablo* of Corinthian order, with black and gold ornaments, contained the Annunciation; and several "*Pasos*" are still stowed away here-: visit this chapel to see the celebrated *Dolorosa*, by Juan de Juni, placed in a churrigueresque chapel under a tinsel red and gold temple. It is also called *La Señora de los Cuchillos*, from the seven swords which pierce her breast (compare the three-barbed arrow by which Juno was wounded, Iliad E 393); the blades are modern, and mar the image, which, a master-piece of Juni, is graven out of Sorian pine; it is larger than life, clad like a widow, and seated on a rock. Nothing can be deeper than the expression of grief; but the natives never have felt this work of art, as a Conde de Rivadavia wished to cover over the noble draperies with modern finery; and when the figure was taken out as a *Paso* in the holy week, for which it was never intended, the carvers of regular portable figures laughed at it, calling it *La Zapatuda*, the clumsy-shod. Thus are art and religion equally degraded.

Leaving the Angustias, we approach

the *Esqueva*, whose bridges, arches, and narrow overhanging streets are very Prout-like. Crossing the *Puente de Magaña*, is the Plaza of the University, founded in 1346 by Alonzo XI., and at present one of the most frequented in Spain, especially by students in jurisprudence. It has always been the nursery of *Justicia*, the harpy of Spain, which has done more to impoverish the land than plague, pestilence, drought, or the *guitar*, that cause and effect, that instrument and excuse for *idling*. The two colleges, one for the Scotch, and the other for the English, are now merged into one, and for the Irish. The *universidad* has been modernised; but one old Gothic gate yet remains, which leads into the *Calle de la libreria.* The facade is overdone with churrigueresque, Corinthian and nondescript ornaments, and an abortion of heavy statues, which profess to represent those sciences which are here set at nought. The interior is not so bad; the chapel altar is surrounded by an iron railing, and when honorary degrees are granted is filled with doctors. In *La Sala del Claustro* are some second-rate portraits of Spanish kings.

Near it is what was *El Colegio Mayor de Sᵃ. Cruz*, one of the six larger colleges in Spain (see Salamanca, p. 571). Founded in 1494 by Cardinal Pedro Gonzalez de Mendoza, it was built by Henrique de Egas. The excellent Gothic is well seen from its plaza. The frontal is elaborate, and the cornice and parapet striking. The founder kneels before the Virgin over the studded door. Unfortunately, in 1719, some modern attempts to "beautify and repair" have marred the general effect. The *colegio* is well kept; observe in the *Patio*, the ball ornaments, the arms of the founder, and the balustrades.

This edifice has recently been destined for the *museo*, in which are got together the pictures, carvings, and images of the suppressed convents. The *indifferent* paintings are arranged

2 E 2

in three galleries in the *Patio*, while those which are somewhat better are placed in separate saloons in the interior. In the second *galeria* is the fine college library, consisting of some 14,000 volumes, and very rich in civil law and topography; there are also some maps and coins. The garden front is plain and decorous.

We shall refer to the numbers of Pastor's *Compendio* for the contents of the *Museo*, otherwise it is as meagre in regard to historical and artistical information as an auctioneer's catalogue. There is no attempt to distinguish the older masters, no clue to tell posterity from what particular convent ney came. Many of the early pictures are curious, but a large proportion of the collection is rubbish. Pictorial art was never so much studied as sculptural in this province of Leon, and the best painters were foreigners, Vicente Carducho, Rubens, Arsenio Mascagni, a Florentine; Bartolomé Cardenas, a Portuguese, 1547-1606, and patronised by Lerma and Philip III. The pictures of Rubens, of Diego Valentin Diaz and of Diego Frutos (both native artists), deserve most notice. The other objects best worth attention are the bronzes of P. Leoni, and the wooden-painted sculpture; of these the finest are by Berruguete, Juan de Juni, and Hernandez. Here are gods and goddesses of every age and colour. These images, now removed from the altars, are as it were dethroned from Olympus, and the prestige is gone; they have become objects of admiration to artists, of pity, nay derision, to Protestants, instead of veneration and fear (see our remarks on these *Pasos*, p. 110). This is indeed a Pantheon, and the lust of the eye is over-satiated. The severe colourless naked simplicity of the Greek has been metamorphosed into gaudy tinsel-clad colossal dolls. However mistaken the piety which could adore them, and the bad taste which compelled the artist to degrade his talents, it is impossible to deny the startling merit of some of these works. This *Museo* is

the creation of *accident* and *individual* energy. Don Pedro Gonzalez, director of the Academy, by his own activity and love for art, rescued these brands from the burning in a moment of general vandalism. He alone did it, and to him be the glory, for the *Diputacion provincial*, a true Spanish junta, cared for none of these things; their sole assistance was the lending *six galley-slaves*, to move the objects: *cosas de España.*

One word, before entering, on two great sculptors whose names have scarcely escaped from isolated Spain; first and foremost is *Juan de Juni*, the Herrera el Viejo of Castilian sculpture. He felt the grandiose and daring style of M. Angelo, and emancipated sculpture from the timid fetters of conventional attitudes, as Dedalus did among the ancients. Nothing is known of his country or birth, and Cean Bermudez suspects that he was an Italian. It is certain that he studied in Italy, and was brought to Spain by Pedro Alvarez de Acosta, Bp. of Oporto, and afterwards of Leon and Osma (see Aranda de Duero). Juni was a much more profound anatomist than most Spaniards. The Inquisition, by prohibiting dissection, kept surgery in the hands of barbers; while again, by prohibiting nudity, a knowledge of draperies, not of anatomy, sufficed for the artist. Juni, fierce and fiery in design, bold and learned in execution, was occasionally extravagant in his attitudes: his was what the Germans call a " stürm und drang" style, one of sound and fury; but it signified something, expressed the sentiment of *Action*, such as suits the impassioned temperament of the South. From his aiming at scientific display, his forms often bordered on contortion, and his colour was over-Florentine and hard leaden, such, indeed, as that of his friend Berruguete, a co-pupil of Michael Angelo, and all three architects, sculptors, and painters; but flexibility and transparency of skin is always lost in painted sculpture. Juni, like his great master, joyed in daring strokes of the chisel, as if in conscious pride of his mastery over a difficult material, by which inferior minds are every moment hampered; they triumphed like creators, when breathing the divine spirit of life into senseless blocks.

His successor, Gregorio Hernandez, was born in Gallicia in 1566, but lived always in Valladolid, where he died Jan. 22, 1636. Many of his finest works were burnt and broken by the French, who destroyed his tomb, and scattered his ashes to the dust, as they did those of Velazquez and Morillo, and Hernandez was the Murillo of Castilian sculpture; he loved the gentler passions, and idolized nature in preference to the ideal. He avoided the violence of Juan de Juni, and the attitudinarian anatomical style. His soul was in his work, and a deep true religious sentiment elevated his vocation to the high character of the artist combined in the priest. He felt the awful responsibility of the maker not merely of " stocks and stones," or objects of beauty and art to be admired, but of representations of the Deity, to be bowed down to and worshipped. He, like Angelico da Fiesole and Juanes, never proceeded to his task without purifying his soul by prayer, and endeavouring to elevate his mind to his holy task ; thus his refined art rendered intelligible those touching and pathetic passages from holy writ which otherwise in the negation of the translated Bible to the people, must have remained buried in an unknown tongue: he spoke to the many through the universally-understood language of the eye, and thus made sculpture a means of religious education, for rarely in his hand was it prostituted to monkish hagiology and deception. Truly devout, his works of relaxation were those of charity ; he attended the sick, and buried the friendless dead. Visit, therefore, the humble dwelling where he lived 23 long years, and produced such immortal works (see p. 636).

There is much commonplace in this museum. As at Granada, the French and Spaniards have picked out most of the plums. The sculpture and pictures by Rubens are down stairs ; the paintings are above. Commencing at *La Entrada del Museo* (p. 85 catalogue), is the portrait of the founder, the great Cardinal Pedro Gonzalez Mendoza, long the " Tertius Rex" of Castile. Who and what this mighty churchman was is detailed in his interesting ' *Chronica de el gran Cardenal de España,*' Pedro de Salazar, fol. Toledo, 1625. In the *Galeria primera* are some bad paintings from Franciscan convents. The carved walnut choir seats ranged round the room, and some statues, are better. Passing on to the *Salon grande*, No. 4, is a Virgin and Child by F⁰· Meneses, the favourite pupil of Murillo. The *Escalera principal* is hung with portraits of monks and now venerable forgotten friars. In the *Galeria segunda* observe Nos. 1 and 2, Chapters held at Valladolid and Rome, painted by Diego Frutos. Nos. 3 to 24 represent divers passages in the Life of Fray Pedro Regalado, the tutelar saint of Valladolid, to understand which refer to Daça's Life (see p. 625), who devotes 204 pages to such imposture and nonsense, which, if it were not actually printed, none would believe possible to have been palmed on intellectual beings. In the *Escalera segunda*, No. 15, St. Francis feeding 6000 Friars in the Desert, in imitation of Christ; Diego Frutos. In No. 4, the same saint raises 30 dead to life at once; in the *Galeria tercera* are 30 other pictures of Regalado's astounding miracles, etc., and a series of bad portraits of Benedictine monks.

Quitting these subjects of mortification (see p. 115), and sad proofs of the subjection of art to base purposes, enter the *Gran Salon*, which is 127 feet long, 25 wide, and 50 high (see p. 45 catalogue). Here are the celebrated pictures by Rubens, which long formed the boast of the nunnery at *Fuen Saldaña ;* sent to the Louvre by the French, and disgorged after Waterloo, they were then much neglected by the nuns, who wanted the means of even framing them. The subjects are, No. 1, an Assumption of the Virgin.—No. 12, San Antonio of Padua.—No. 14, St. Francis receiving the Stigmata. The Spaniards, who, however they dislike foreigners, admire foreign things, rave about these rather sprawling tawdry compositions, which will no more stand comparison with Velazquez or Murillo than a Flemish cart-horse with an Andalucian barb. The Assumption is the largest and finest, but the saints are sensual commonplace Dutchmen, while the cherubs, with their wigs of hair, are most unangelic. The landscape in the St. Francis is very fine, painted in those grey sober tones which Rubens must have caught from Velazquez.—No. 4, San Diego, by Vicente Carducho, 1585-1638.—No. 5, an Annunciation, by Jose Martinez, who lived in Valladolid in the 16th century, and imitated the Florentine school. This picture was saved from Sⁿ· Agustin, when the French destroyed the others, with the glorious azulejos, finished in 1598, after designs of Martinez.—No. 6, a Bodegon ascribed to Velazquez.—No. 13, The Last Supper, Antº· Pereda, born in Valladolid, 1599, ob. 1678.—No. 24, a Conception.—No. 16, San Elias, Diego Diaz. In the centre of the saloon are the gilt bronzes of the Duke and Duchess of Lerma, by Pompeio Leoni of Milan, rescued from San Pablo, when it was all but destroyed by Buonaparte's order.—Nos. 3 and 4, the two Angels near the Assumption of Rubens, are sculptured by Hernandez.—Nos. 5 and 6, Sⁿ· Miguel and Sⁿ· Juan, are by Berruguete, by whom also are the carved walnut choir seats round the saloon, which came from Sⁿ· Benito: he was assisted in these very fine works by his worthy pupil Gaspar de Tordesillas. The saint over each stall and coat of arms indicate the particular seat of the heads of each Benedictine convent in Spain, when they

assembled in grand chapter at Valladolid.

In the Sala primera : Nos. 5 and 9, Sⁿ· Francisco, are by V. Carducho, and fine.—No. 8, the Jubilee of La Porciuncula (see Index), by Diego Valentin Diaz.— No. 15, Sº· Domingo bestowing alms ; Bartᵉ· Cardenas.— No. 33, a Descent from the Cross ; Bassano (Leandro). In the Sala segunda : No. 2, St. Peter ; Ribera.— Nos. 4 and 10, Adoration of Kings and Shepherds ; B. Cardenas. In the Sala tercera, observe No. 29, Virgin and Child ; and No. 33, Sª· Ana and Infant, and several others equally curious from their antiquity. In the Sala cuarta : No. 1, Holy Family, from Sⁿ· Benito, a truly Florentine picture, and the master-piece of the author ; it is signed Didacus Dizas pictor, 1621 (not 71, as stated in the catalogue, p. 58), for he died in 1660.—Nos. 4, 5, and 6 are attributed to Rubens (?). On a scagliola table is a model of the Convento del Prado, by Col Leon Gil de Palacios, by whom there are such admirable works of the same kind at Madrid.

The Sala quinta contains some poor performances of the feeble Bayeu and Palomino.—Nos. 20 and 22, Passages in the Life of Sº· Domingo ; B. Cardenas. Observe a fine bronze crucifix by Pompeio Leoni. In the Sala sesta, No. 3, is a Sⁿ· Joaquin and Child, attributed to Murillo, and, if so, it is in his earliest manner.—No. 8, St. Peter ; Ribera. In the Sala setima, No. 24, a carved Retablo, with early pictures of St. John, the Virgin, and St. Benedict. In the Sala novena, No. 16, a San Bruno, by Zurbaran.—No. 18, an Annunciation ; Alessandro Bronzino. In the Sala decima, No. 13, the Legend of the Vine Stock, curious for subject (see p. 636).—No. 24, Christ, the Virgin, and Magdalen ; Ribalta (?).

But the sculpture is far more interesting, nor can the great Castilian school be any where better studied than here. Begin therefore at p. 75 of catalogue, Sala primera : No. 1, three little statues; Berruguete.—No. 2, Sᵃ. Teresa de Jesus, from La Carmen, a masterpiece of Hernandez.—No. 3, by do., St. Francis.—No. 7, do., Christ bearing the Cross; a superb *Paso.*—No. 11, Sepulture of Christ; Juan de Juni, very fine.—No. 14, another Sᵃ. Teresa, by Hernandez.—No. 16, San Antonio, by Juni.—No. 18, Juni, a most Murillo-like Virgin giving the Scapulary to Simon Stock.—No. 20, San Bruno; Juni, very grand.—No. 22, a beautiful Virgin by Hernandez, from La Carmen.—No. 24, Sᵃ. Antonio, the first Hermit; Juni. Observe also all the small statues by Berruguete. *Sala segunda :* No. 5, a curious Gothic bas-relief.—No. 28, S. Dimas, the Good Thief; Hernandez.—No. 29, Death of the Saviour, do., fine. Observe also the small statues by Berruguete. *Sala tercera,* are some *Pasos* by Hernandez; and No. 23, the *Pietá,* do., very grand; also Nos. 26, 27, from the Angustias; the Good and Bad Thief, by Leon Leoni.—No. 36, Baptism of Christ; Hernandez, fine.—No. 37, do., Burial of Christ.—Nos. 39 and 40, 2 Letterns. In the *Sala de Juntas :* No. 16, Portrait of Card. Mendoza. Observe the small statues and crucifixes; and Nos. 34, 35, the *Escritorios* and tables, and various articles of altar furniture.

Quitting the *Museo,* and returning by the *Universidad,* next visit the cathedral. The older *Colegiata* was taken down by Philip II., who directed Herrera in 1585 to prepare plans for a new edifice; these and a wooden model exist in the archives, which are very complete, and should be looked at. Philip granted as a building fund the monopoly of the sale of children's horn-books; the works proceeded during his life, and then, as usual in the East and Spain, were discontinued. *If* they had been completed, the edifice, as Herrera said, would have been "*un todo sin igual.*" Fatal, however, are those little words *if* and *but* to most Spanish conceptions. The design was a pure Græco-Romano elevation; but unfortunately his design was tampered

with by Alberto Churriguera in 1729, and the abominable Sun, Moon, Ave Maria, &c., were added.

The façade is Doric, the favourite order of this severe master. The noble arch above the principal entrance is 50 feet high by 24. Only one of the four intended towers was finished : it was simple and well proportioned, rising to the height of 260 feet, and terminated with a cupola, but it fell down in May 31, 1841, and has not been rebuilt. The interior bespeaks the classical proportions of Herrera in its simple, unadorned, untinseled condition, and, like the chapel of the Escorial, it breathes the true grandeur of architecture. It is disfigured by an oversized *reja* and a huge wall which the barbarous canons have reared up, and which in these days of pulling down ought instantly to be removed. The form of the interior is an oblong quadrangle 411 feet long by 404 broad. A *trascoro* of later date cuts up as usual the size, and the *Silleria del coro,* which belonged to the old Gothic *colegiata,* is misplaced in this classical pile of Corinthian pilasters; that from *San Pablo* is more appropriate, and was designed by Herrera for the Duke of Lerma, and cost the then enormous sum of 30,000 ducats. In the *altar mayor* is an Assumption by Zacarias Velazquez.

The fine Florentine picture, possibly by one of the Allori, of the Crucifixion, was rescued from the Agostinos at Medina del Rio Seco, during the ravages under the Constitution of 1820, by our kind friend the Prior Jose Verdonces. It, as well as the Transfiguration opposite, by Luca Giordano, has, however, been repainted by Pedro Gonzalez. Observe the chapel of Conde Pedro Ansurez, the lord and benefactor of Valladolid in the 12th century; his sepulchre is emblazoned with arms, sable chequered or, and with two metrical epitaphs, and the head of the recumbent figure is fine. The Doric cloister is unfinished; the archives are perfect from 1517. Here are kept the plans and the fine drawings by Herrera for the cathedral, and a collection of bad portraits of bishops of this cathedral.

The noblest memorial of past days of religious splendour is the magnificent silver *custodia*, which none should forget to see. This masterpiece of Juan d'Arphe, 1590, which escaped by a miracle from the French melting-pot, stands six feet high. The chief subject is Adam and Eve in Paradise; this indeed is a specimen of what once was wrought in this city of silversmiths. A few chalices and a golden *viril* studded with jewels are the scanty remains of many other chests which were plundered by the invader.

Leaving the cathedral, pass into the heart of the city to the *Fuente Dorada*, and thence to *El Ochavo*, whence, like at our *Seven Dials Street*, a multitude of smaller streets lead like veins to the *Plaza Mayor*. The bridge *de la Plateria* runs from the Ochavo, and, as at Florence, is peopled by silversmiths. They indeed exercise the same craft of the D'Arphes, but are fallen in proportion as Spain has since the days of Charles V., when Navagiero (p. 35), writing in 1525, stated that there were more workers of plate here than in any other two countries.

The church plate and goldsmith's work of Spain is highly deserving of notice in an antiquarian and artistical point of view, as the workmanship and design has far surpassed the comparatively paltry material, which has too often tempted the aurivorous sacrilege of vandal robbers, foreign and domestic, who have consigned to the melting-pot what ought to have been deposited in museums; and how much exquisite art would have escaped, had iron and copper been employed instead of gold and silver!

Spain herself was the bullion mine of antiquity (see for details, p. 415), while in modern times, by being mistress of the ores of South America, she has again supplied the world with the precious metals; her rulers in church and state have always reserved large portions for religious and royal magnificence. Spain has always deserved the eulogium of Claudian (de Lau. Ser. 54), who coupled her metallic charms with her fecundity in producing *pious* princes—Speciosa metallis, principibus fœcunda piis. The national disposition to adorn and enrich the house of God was encouraged by the clergy, who never were more powerful than when Spain was possessed of her widest dominion and greatest affluence. The sacred edifices became, as in olden times, the treasure-houses of the offerings of wealthy piety, and of the splendid outlay of a clergy always distinguished for the pomp and dignity with which they clothed their stately and imposing system. The vessels of silver and gold, the consecrated plate, were handed down from one generation to another; they were protected by the inalienability of church property, by the dread of sacrilege, the moral defence which the unarmed clergy have ever thrown over their physically unprotected treasures, and by being concealed in moments of national convulsion and foreign aggression.

Nothing could exceed the beauty and richness of the chased plate in the Donarium, i. e. the *Relicario y Tesoreria*, of the temple of Hercules at Gades. It was the Oviedo, Guadalupe, and Monserrat of Iberia (see Philostratus, v.). Every victor contributed a portion of spoil (Livy, xxi. 21; Sil. Ital. iii. 15), which every enemy respected as sacred.

The use of gold and silver plate is of Oriental origin, and was carried to the pitch of luxury by the Phœnicians and Carthaginians; the latter sneered at the poverty or frugality of the Romans from finding at every grand dinner the same service of plate, which was borrowed by all who entertained, there being only that one in Rome (Pliny, 'N. H.' xxxiii. 2); but the iron of these simple soldiers soon won the gold and silver of their deriders, whom they next imitated and then surpassed in metallic magnificence: *e. g.* one Rotundus, on being made *dispensator*, or true fortune-making treasurer in Spain, had a silver dish which weighed 500 lbs. After the downfall of the empire, the Goths had very correct notions as regarded plate, in which San Isidoro (Or. xx. 4) required only three points—workmanship, weight, and brilliancy; in those dark ages, as they are now complacently called, a polish was required which was unknown to the Romans, who, like the modern Spaniards, only washed and never cleaned their plate (Juvenal, xiv. 62). The splendid magnificence of the Gothic silver-work astonished even the Moors, accustomed as they were to the gorgeous jewellery of Damascus; the quantity is proved by the Arabic details of the spoils, especially at the capital Toledo (Moh. Dyn. i. 282). The art of working it was improved by the conquerors, who introduced their rich chasings and filigree style from Damascus to Cordova, insomuch that in the tenth century the tiara of the pope was made in Spain, and called *Spanoclista;* and the peculiar church plate *Spanisca* was so beautiful that, as at Oviedo, the clergy palmed it off as the work of angels.

But all these vessels of gold and silver were confined to the temple, as the medieval Spaniards, like the earlier Romans, were simple in their homes, reserving their magnificence for the home of the deity; their boast was rather to conquer those who ate off plate than to possess such luxuries. Haro relates that Juan I., coming to dine with Alvarez Perez Osorio, first Count of Trastamara, found nothing but wooden trenchers—plates, doubtless, on a par with the cookery—his soldier host telling him that he never had time to eat except standing, and out of his hand; so the king sent him some silver dishes; but soon after, dining again with the veteran, found nothing but the old trenchers as before, and on inquiring what had become of his gift, Alvarez took him to the window, and showed him a hundred men armed in shining cuirasses, ex-

claiming, "That, Sire, is the only plate which a soldier ought to have"* (*Nobiliario*, i. 275).

As the conquest of Spain and Asia introduced the luxury of silver among the Romans (Justin, xxxvi. 4), so the conquest of Granada and discovery of the new world corrupted the Spaniard; silver was now accounted as nothing; and as wrought plate was exempted from the agio on coined silver and the duty on bar bullion, it became the form in which governors, *i.e.* robbers on a grand scale, sent home their accumulations. Spain being a land without bankers' security or confidence, these hoards of plate became, as in the East, the available property of rich individuals. The quantity was enormous: the duke of Alburquerque was employed, says Mad*e·* d'Aunoy (ii. 173, ed. Haye, 1715), for six weeks in weighing his; he had 1400 dozen silver dinner plates, 1200 dishes, and 40 silver ladders to ascend to the buffet. All these golden and silver ages are passed, and Spaniards as a nation have returned to the primitive and Oriental fork the finger, varied with a wooden or horn spoon and sharp *cuchillo.* Few even of grandees are now born with a silver spoon in their mouths, for the French invaders, like their ancestors the Gauls in Italy, carried off plate by waggon-loads, stripping alike church and palace, altar and sideboard; and much of what escaped has either been sold by the impoverished owners, or swept away during the civil wars and governmental appropriations. Very few indeed out of Madrid have

* Under the Roman republic a silver cup and salt-cellar was all that the law allowed even to a commander-in-chief (Pliny, 'N. H.' xxxiii. 11); who also mentions that *Catus* Ælius returned the plate which the Œtolians sent him on finding him dining off earthenware, *Loza.* Plutarch relates that Cato, when commanding in Spain, dined off radishes, which he pared himself, and thought the sweetest eating, ἥδιστον ὄψον; nor was the medieval fare better, as, according to the proverb, these delectable roots were dinner for knights a la Alvarez—*Rabanos, son comida de caballeros.*

2 E 3

now a complete service, and silver is so scarcely seen at the tables of the provincial nobility that an Englishman who gave balls at Seville was cautioned by the natives to place none on the supper-tables. As to carry away sweetmeats is allowable, the transition to the fork and spoon is very easy; but so it long has been: compare the theft committed at Lord Digby's table in 1622 (Somers, 'Tracts,' ii. 504), with the *Señor Diputado*, who pocketed these matters only the other day at Madrid.

Fortunately for Spain, at the very moment of her greatest influx of bullion, and in the age of Leo X., there arose a family of goldsmiths, who carried the art of plate-making to its highest perfection. The founder was Enrique de Arphe, or Arfe, a German, who settled at Leon about 1470, and worked in the then prevailing rich florid Gothic style. His son Antonio, following the changes of fashion, adopted the Græco-Romano taste, while in the age of Leo X., there grandson, Juan de Arphe y Villafañe, born at Leon in 1535, excelled in the human figure, and was the greatest artist of his family. Antonio and Juan settled at Valladolid, which was then the court of the great emperor Charles V. These d'Arphes were almost entirely employed by the rich cathedrals, churches, and convents of Spain, for whom have been worked those magnificent articles, after which every traveller should inquire, when visiting ecclesiastical treasure-rooms, asking particularly whether they possess any specimens of these elegant masters. This family not only wrought these beautiful objects, but created and fixed the style of religious plate in Spain, which we term *cinque cento* from the period, but which is called in Spain *el gusto plateresco*—the silversmith or Berruguete *gusto* (see p. 123). Juan de Arfe y Villafañe, who was appointed by Philip II. Master of the Mint at Segovia, published a treatise on his art, with exact designs for every piece of church-plate, and his elegant models have fortunately been generally adopted

and continued. This work, which every collector should purchase, is entitled ' *De Varia Commensuracion ;*' it has gone through many editions. Those now before us are, first, that of Seville, 1585, by Andrea Pescioni; and Villafañe was fortunate in securing for his printer this Italian, who had a kindred soul, and whose works are among the few in Spain which can be really called artistical. Another edition is that of Madrid, Francisco Sanz, 1675; and a later, Mad., 1773, Miguel Escribano, in which the original woodcuts have been copied. The work embraces the science with plans, details, geometry, dials, the anatomy of man and animals, architecture, and church-plate; for each particular of which, drawings and exact measurements of proportions are given. Juan also published a ' *Quilatador de Plata*,' duo. Vall[d.] 1572, and Mad. 1578. He was the Bezaleel of the Peninsula (Exod. xxxvii. 22), the Cellini of Spaniards; and his family in the W. rivalled that of the Becerriles of Cuenca; for the names, etc. of the chief pieces of sacred plate, see p. 125.

Valladolid retains its silversmiths, but the magnitude of their works has passed away; their articles want also the fine finish of skilful workmanship; the forms are better than the operative execution, for they are classical and antique, nor are former models much departed from; the working, as in the East, is carried on with the rudest implements. The chief wares are ornaments for the peasantry, and the usual talisman's crosses, saints, and penates; these are made in thin silver, but even baser materials are now resorted to, since the wares are suited to financial capabilities, as in the days of Isaiah (xl. 18): "To whom, then, will ye liken God? a graven image which the goldsmith spreadeth over with gold, or of a tree that will not rot for him that is *impoverished.*"

Next observe the elegant and classical façade of *La Cruz*, which finishes the view, and has been attributed to

designs by Herrera. The interior contains some very fine *Pasos*, indeed it is
a museum of Hernandez: observe particularly the Ecce Homo: "The
Christ in the garden;" the Christ at
the pillar, coloured like Morales; the
magnificent Descent from the Cross,
especially the draperies of St. John;
La Dolorosa, or *La Virgen de Candelas*,
is an imagen *à vestir*, and which, when
dressed up, is as fine as tinsel can make
her; *Sᵃ· Cruz* is exactly a Pagan
Favissa, or magazine where old damaged idols were stored away, and
where the "properties" of the processions were kept when the melodrame
was over. Valladolid used to rival
even Seville in the pageants, and bearing forth of images, during the holy
week (see for details, p. 112).

The *Plaza Mayor* is very imposing
in size and style. This central spot
owes its present space and regularity
to a fire in 1561, which lasted three
days, and burnt down many streets.
Philip II. ordered the rebuilding to be
carried out on a fixed plan, and it
became the model of that of Madrid;
the granite pillars brought from the
quarries of Villacastin, which support
the arcades, give an air of solidity and
perhaps of gloom; yet this is the most
frequented spot of the town, and where
the circulation, such as it is, flows the
liveliest, as here are the best shops.
The S. side, *La Acera de San Francisco*,
is the lounge of idlers and gossips, and
is a minor *Puerto del Sol*. In this
Plaza all grand spectacles, executions,
and bull-fights take place; here was
beheaded in June, 1453, that spoilt
child of fortune, Alvaro de Luna, the
favourite of Juan II., *El valido* (Arabicè Walid, Welee); he was deserted,
after long services, by his false, feeble
master, a shallow, skipping king, influenced by poets and courtiers, and
alternately their dupe and tyrant. The
Chronicle of Luna was edited by
Florez, Mad. 1784; Chʳ· 127 contains
the truly Froissart account of this
memorable execution by an eye-witness. Here the cold-blooded bigot,

Philip II., celebrated, Oct. 7, 1559, a
memorable *auto-de-fe*, gloating on the
details, as Calvin did at Geneva when
Servetus was burnt. Even Nero, says
Tacitus (Ag. 45), " substraxit oculos,
jussitque scelera et non spectavit; præ-
cipua sub Domitiano miseriarum pars
erat spectare et aspici."

Now cross a small bridge to what
was *San Benito*, and formerly one of
the finest convents of that order, and a
museum of piety, art, and literature;
but now all is hastening to ruin. Once
a royal palace, it was given in 1390 by
Juan I. to the monks, and it was increased in 1499 by Juan de Arandia; the
old palace gate stood near the tower;
the modern Doric and Ionic portal was
built by Rivero, imitating Herrera;
the cloisters were fine, and in the same
style. The church, once of good Gothic,
was bedeviled during the Churriguera
mania, and plundered by the invaders,
and during the recent civil wars converted into a fort. The fine old convents
built in troubled times, and of substantial masonry, became admirable
shells for modern defences; and as
the French engineers had taught the
Spaniards how to convert chapels into
casemates, then the revolutionary *Exal-
tados* purposely selected the noblest
monastic buildings, because their desecration evinced a philosophical en-
lightenment and contempt for their
original religious purposes, of which
Don Carlos was assumed to be the
supporter.

The *Retablo*, soon destined to be
among the things which were, both as
to its architecture, sculpture, and painting, was a chef-d'œuvre of Berruguete,
1526-32. The figures were somewhat
too small, the Virgin and tutelar saint
alone being as large as life. The colouring was rather leaden; the best
compositions were a Nativity, with a
fine Virgin and angels kneeling behind;
a Flight into Egypt; two grand subjects
in *chiaro oscuro* on a gilded ground,
a Sibyl, and a female approaching
a seated man, are quite Michael-
Angelesque. This *Retᵒ·* resembled that

at Salamanca (p. 579). Bosarte (p. 359) has printed the original contracts and specifications, and subsequent disputes.

The splendid carved seats of the choir have been moved to the new *Museo :* inquire, however, for the light *Reja*, a masterpiece of Juan Tomas Celma, 1571, and the beautiful Facistol; here also were the pictures by F. Gallegos, and the glorious *Retablo* of San Antonio Abad, by Gaspar de Tordesillas, 1597 ; the *Cristo de la Luz*, by Hernandez, and Holy Family, by Diego Valentin Diaz. The library, first ravaged by the invaders, has now disappeared. Those curious in Benedictine antiquities are referred to the ' *Historia General de la orden Sⁿ· Benito*,' by Antº· de Yepes, 7 vols. folio, 1609-21.

This chapel of San Benito was frequented from far and near by pious worshippers of its celebrated miraculous relic, for which inquiry should be made, or at least for the shrine in which it was guarded ; it was called *El Cristo de la Cepa*, " the Christ of the vine stock," and being made from one of these roots, it has the appearance of a misshapen idol of the Bonzes : the magnificent silver *Urna* was enriched with appropriate vines. The legend is this : A Christian and a Jewish labourer (for names, date, and place are not preserved in this authentic fact) in a vineyard were disputing on their respective creeds ; the Hebrew said, " I will believe your views when your Messiah comes out of this vine." The image instantly appeared — *credat Judæus* — and was given to the convent in 1415, by Sancho de Roxas, primate of Toledo : consult Palomino, *Museo Pittorico*, i. 208, where in 1795 all this was printed for Spaniards as gospel truths ; but even Morales (*Viage*, p. 7), in the relicomaniac age of Philip II., had ventured to allude to the Mandragora, those anthropomorphic mandrakes, the Dodaim, for which Rachel gave somewhat a large price for a jealous wife (Gen. xxx. 14). The Valladolid *Cepa* lacks

originality, for the Argonauts made a goddess Rhea out of a stump of an old vine στιβαρου στυπος αμπελου (Ap. Rh. i. 1117). The Populunians also cut a Jupiter out of a similar root (Plin. ' N. H.' xiv. i.). But the *Fetish* deformity called in the principle of *fear*, which the Pagan priests knew well how to make use of. Lucan describes (Phar. iii. 411) the *horror* inspired by trees, by the sad *simulacra*, which

    " Arte carent, cæsisque extant informia truncis,
    Numina sic metuunt, tantum terroribus addit."

The barber-bred Bessières, accustomed as a boy to blocks, was too great a " philosophe " to be frightened at these carved monsters ; while he took the silver custodia which weighed 22,000 ounces, he left the vine-root ; and the worthy canon who accompanied us was anxious to pass this relic unnoticed, and could not refrain from a smile ; so the Pagan Parmeniscus was cured of an inability to laugh by seeing an absurd image of Latona (Athen. xiv. 1), and Cato, a sufficiently grave man, used to wonder how any soothsayer ever could meet another without laughing at the tricks they palmed off on their flocks (Cic. de Div. ii. 24) ; but, qui decipi vult, decipiatur.

Now pass on to the celebrated *Campo grande*, through which the road from Madrid enters Valladolid, by the fine *Puerta del Carmen*, on which the baboon-headed Charles III. figures ; first, however, visit the house of Juni and Hernandez, which is at the r. corner of the *Cᵉ· de San Luis*; small and low is the cradle from whence such vast and lofty works came forth, when whole forests of Sorian pines were carved into gods or goddesses, as the sculptor's genius or caprice willed, as in the days of Horace, when, instead of making a trunk, maluit esse deum. The studio was in the room looking into the street, but the window was blocked up in 1828 ; few in Valladolid ever visit this former abode of genius now, and as bats make homes in deserted palaces, the inmates are unworthy of the master spirits who once dwelt there. The house was built by Juan de Juni in 1545, who died in it early in the 17th century: it was then purchased by Hernandez of the daughter and heiress of his predecessor, June 15, 1616. Thus they succeeded each other in art and local habitation, nor is the latter course either unusual or unreasonable, as the peculiar fittings-up and the good-will and the public knowledge of a particular trade being carried on there, would naturally make the residence more desirable to one of a similar profession than to any other.

Close by is the noble Alameda, the *Campo grande,* which in the palmy days of Valladolid, was the site of the burnings of the *auto-de-fe,* of jousts, tournaments, and royal festivities. This *great field,* or appropriate court of approach to the capital of Charles V., is surrounded with noble convents, hospitals, and palaces, many of which were gutted by the invaders, while others have been recently demolished, and all impoverished; however, the fine Corinthian portal which formerly belonged to Sⁿ. Gabriel has been carefully taken down, and is intended to be re-erected to adorn Campo grande. On this open space the Castilians proclaimed St. Ferdinand their king, when his prudent mother Berenguela surrendered the sceptre. Here Buonaparte reviewed 35,000 men. The open space is laid out in public walks and avenues, with flower gardens and seats: the traveller will of course visit it at the proper time to study the rank, fashion, beauty, and costume of Valladolid. Among the buildings which fringe it, the San Juan de Letran is a specimen of abominable churrigueresque. Visit, however, the *Casa de la Misericordia,* or *Colegio de Niñas huerfanas,* founded for female orphans by the painter Diego Valentin Diaz. He was a familiar of the Inquisition, and dying here in 1660, was buried in the chapel with his wife; their por-

traits, painted in the style of Pantoja, deserve notice; he was a grey-haired, sharp-eyed old man with mustachios, she a dark-haired dame. The *Retablo* of the chapel is painted by him; observe the linear perspective: the colours are somewhat leaden, and the manner very Florentine: observe also a " Charity with children," and a Virgin working in the temple, excellent pictures: the *Cimborio* is painted in stucco, with a Virtue in each angle. The smaller *Retablos* contain paintings of Sⁿ. Nicolas, our " Old Nick," the portioner of fortuneless maidens, and of San Luis, the ransomer of poor captives, subjects selected because having reference to good works and *charity.*

The *Hospital de la Resurreccion,* or *El General,* contained a marble representation of that subject, 1579, and inside, *La Virgen del Escapulario,* by Hernandez, with a painting of the Resurrection by Pantoja, 1609. Adjoining is the small but once magnificent *Portaceli,* founded by Rodrigo Calderon, son of a common soldier of Valladolid, and the ill-fated favourite of the D. of Lerma, with whom readers of Gil Blas are so familiar, and himself the ill-fated favourite of Philip III. Rodrigo having made a vast fortune by peculation was put to death by Philip IV., who wished to squeeze out the sponge, and appropriate the treasure for himself—a truly Oriental and Spanish proceeding. The *Retablo* and high altar in the chapel are splendid, and composed of marbles and gilt bronze. The fine paintings of St. Francis and Sᵒ. Domingo are attributed to Caballero Maximo (Stanzioni). The body of the founder lies interred in a noble *Urna.* Adjoining the Portaceli is the abode of the Augustine mission, an edifice reared in 1768 by the academical Ventura Rodriguez.

The convent of *Carmen Calzados* was once the ornament of the *Campo* which Hernandez laboured to adorn, and the invaders laboured to defile; they made it a military hospital, now it is a barrack. Here Hernandez was buried, with Maria Perez, his wife, but neither was doomed to rest, for the enemy disturbed their ashes, next also broke up for firewood the splendid *Retablo*, which Hernandez had filled with his choicest sculpture, and carried off his fine portrait.

The ecclesiologist, among the surviving relics of church and convent, may visit the Gothic *Parroquia de la Magdalena;* the arms of the founder, Pedro de Gasca, Bp. of Palencia, decorate the façade, and the church was built in 1570 by Rodrigo Gil. The grand Corinthian *Retablo* is a masterpiece of Esteban Jordan: observe especially the apostles St. Peter and St. Paul, and the Magdalen, and among other sacred subjects, the Ascension of the Virgin, and an Adoration; the figures are somewhat stumpy, but the feeling is grand. The bishop founder is buried here; his white marble figure in episcopal robes reposes on a fine sarcophagus, the work also of Jordan. He was the prelate sent by Charles V. in 1556 to S. America to restrain the violences of Pizarro.

In *San Lorenzo* were some paintings by Matias Blasco, 1621, viz. a martyrdom of the tutelar, and others relating to miracles effected by an image in this church: observe a pretty "Holy Family," and a repetition of the *Virgen de las Candelas,* by Hernandez. In the *Sacristia* is a singular representation of a procession when the Virgin was brought to Maria, queen of Philip III.

The *Antigua* is a Gothic parish church of the 11th century, and is so called because the citizens, not content with rearing one temple to a female divinity, were building this and the *Colegiata* at the same time, and both in honour of the Virgin: this having been the one first finished accordingly obtained the epithet of the ancient or earliest. The *Retablo*, by Juan de Juni, is one of the remarkable sculptures in Valladolid: observe the crucifix at the top of the Sᵃ. Barbara and Sᵃ. Ana in a niche; in some other of

the figures the peculiar violence and twists of this sculptor are overdone; while the blue and tinsel is also injurious to artistical effect.

The *San Miguel,* once belonging to the Jesuits, and now a parish church, has a fine nave, with well-wrought Corinthian pillars and pilasters. The classical *Retablo,* with carvings of the Nativity and Circumcision, has been attributed by some to Becerra, but it more probably is the work of Jordan. The *San Miguel* is by Pompeio Leoni. In a chapel to the r. observe the kneeling figure of Pedro de Vivero, ob. 1610, and of his wife, ob. 1625. The Sacristia is a fine room.

Las Huelgas Reales is a Corinthian edifice in the style of Herrera; here is the fine alabaster tomb of the foundress, Maria de Molina, wife of Sancho el Bravo. The *Retablo* is a superb work of Hernandez: observe the Ascension of the Virgin, San Bernardo kneeling, and two St. Johns dated 1616; paintings have been attributed to the Zuccaros.

The *Retablo* of the *Delscalzas Reales* contains many paintings by Vicente Carducho, in a Caravaggio manner; the Marriage of Sᵃ. Ana and Sⁿ. Joaquin is fine in tone, with great breadth of draperies, while the two boys to the r. are truly Spanish. The Assumption and Coronation in the centre are by Matias Blasco; the Virgin with joined hands is quite Michael-Angelesque. In addition to these fine pictures, observe in *Las Colaterales* a Sᵃ. Clara, with a graceful Virgin and child, and architecture; and a Sⁿ. Francisca in ecstasy, in a rich wooded scene: they are grand compositions, and painted in a coarsish but bold manner by Arsenio Mascagni in 1610, a pupil of Ligozzi.

The *Sᵃ. Ana* is the most modern church in Valladolid, built on plans by Sabatini. This bald academical thing is much admired by the natives, who energetically destroy their fine old Gothic because out of fashion. The paintings inside by Goya and Bayeu seem placed there to show that a sister art shares in the decline; and this in the city of Diaz and Hernandez.

The brick-tower belfry of *San Salvador,* and the *Retablo*-like portal, are better. The sculpture represents the Incarnation, Transfiguration, &c.; inside are some sepulchres of the Alba Real family.

The once splendid *Agostinos Calzados* was made into a straw magazine by the French. The *Cimborio* was superb. The chapel in which Fabio Nelli is buried was adorned with Italian arabesques by Julio de Aquilez, who decorated the Alhambra. The enemy desecrated and destroyed the building and paintings: a portion of an Adam and Eve only escaped.

The antiquarian artist and lover of ancient mansions may look at some of the palaces of the nobles, those once sumptuous edifices of former grandeur and opulence, but now the crumbling abodes of humble paupers, whose present misery mocks past magnificence— *Cosas de España;* for such melancholy changes of fickle fortune occur in most of the former time-honoured capitals of Spain, which have been deserted for the upstart Madrid, and abandoned to the *administrador,* whose type is the " *unjust steward* " of the East. In the first house to the r., going out of the *Plazuela Vieja,* into the *Cᵉ. de Sⁿ. Martin,* Alonzo Cano is said to have killed his wife. Berruguete, who began life as an *Escribano del crimen* to the Chancelleria, lived near *Sⁿ. Benito el Real,* or crown side attorney to the *Chancelleria;* from the desk of chicanery he passed into the noble studio of Michael Angelo, and thus putting off corruption became immortal. The inesthetic authorities of Valladolid, so far from raising a monument to his glory, converted his house into a barrack, as the palace of the princely Benavente was turned into a foundling hospital.

Fabio Nelli, the Mæcenas of Valladolid, lived in the *plaza* which still bears his name; observe his fine old house with Corinthian *Patio* and me-

dallions. In the *Casa de las Argollas,* so called from the "iron links," Alvaro de Luna was confined before his execution; the *artesonado* ceiling of his dungeon of state is or (perhaps now) *was* magnificent : look also at the *Casa de Villa-Santes,* in the Cᵉ. del Rosario; and the *Patio* of the *Casa Revilla,* corner of the Cᵉ. de la Ceniza, with its arabesques, and rich roofing of the staircase. The *Diputacion Provincial* is lodged in the former palace of the Admirals of Castile; a fulsome motto was placed there allusive to the pardon obtained by Don Fadrique of the *Comuneros* from Charles V. The *Casa del Sol,* opposite to San Gregorio, has a fine portal; this, now a quarter for recruits, was the house of Diego Sarmiento de Acuña, the celebrated Conde de Gondomar, ambassador of Philip IV. to James II., and by whom James was led by the nose, the wily diplomat speaking faulty Latin on purpose, in order to give the royal pedant the triumph of setting him right; his library was one of the finest in Spain, but what the worms spared, the fire of modern destroyers has consumed, and no trace of it remains. What must Valladolid have once been—cum tales sunt reliquiæ!

Those who have not visited the archives of Simancas, will, of course, ride out there (see p. 622). The village of *Fuen Saldaña,* now that the Rubens pictures are in the Museo, scarcely deserves a visit. It lies about 4 L. N. of Valladolid, and belongs to the Alcañiçes family; the castle of excellent masonry is a specimen of the medieval Castilian fortress, with the usual small turrets at the corner of the donjon-keep and machicolations. It was built by Alonzo Perez de Vivero, treasurer to Juan II., who was cast down from a tower by Alvaro de Luna, jealous of his influence over the king; the whole event (see chʳ· 113-4 of the Chronicle) was a most Oriental tragedy watered by Punic tears; the scene of the letters, "Read this and this," is quite Shaksperian. The armorial shield of Vivero is still over the portal. The castle is now degraded into a granary. In the chapel of the small convent near it were long kept the Rubens pictures, which have been mentioned at p. 629.

Communications from Valladolid : these are numerous. There are regular diligences to Palencia and Santander, to Leon, to Burgos, and to Madrid, and occasionally to Oviedo and La Coruña. There are *galeras* and *ordinarios* to Zamora and Avila, and a passage boat on the canal to Palencia. There is much *talk* of improving the roads to Olmedo, to Salamanca by Tordesillas, and to Leon by Mayorga, and of railway communications with Santander, Leon, Aviles, and Madrid.

ROUTE LXXVI.—VALLADOLID TO SANTANDER.

Cabezon	2	
Venta de Trigueros .	2 ..	4
Dueñas	2 ..	6
Palencia	2 ..	8
Fromista.	2 ..	10
Herrera de Pisuerga .	8 ..	13
Aguilar del Campo .	3 ..	16
Quintanilla	1 ..	17
Quintela	1 ..	18
Reinosa	4 ..	22
Barcena	3 ..	25
Las Caldas	4 ..	29
Torre la Vega . . .	2 ..	31
Santander	2 ..	33

This is performed in a day by the *Castellana* diligence.

Cabezon in May, 1808, witnessed one of the first actions in the Peninsular war between the French and the Spaniards, and was a fair type of most of the subsequent. The brave but undisciplined troops, instead of acting on the defensive, courted a combat and defeat. The Junta had told the people that they were invincible, and the mob compelled Cuesta to engage; had he hesitated they would have murdered him for a traitor (Schep. i. 420). Cuesta, as usual, made every disposition to ensure failure, and even neglected to secure the bridge, leaving it open as a *pont d'or* to an advancing not retreating foe. The disheartened Spanish artillery abandoned their guns before even 50

bold French dragoons could get near them ; and yet, as Foy (iii. 278) observes, " La position de Cabezon défendue par des bonnes troupes, eut été impregnable."

The road to *Cabezon* has the Pisuerga and the canal on the l. hand ; the river is soon crossed, and then the canal at *Dueñas*. Here the *Burgos* road continues to *Baños*, and then branches off to *Palencia* to the l. The engineer should examine the canal at Dueñas ; the works were completed in 1832 by Epifanio Esteban, and in magnificence of execution and scientific arrangements would do credit even to England. This canal was planned in 1753 by the minister Ensenada, whose object was to unite Segovia with Reinosa and Santander, taking up at Palencia the canal of Arragon, which was to come from the Mediterranean, while another branch was to communicate with the Duero at Zamora; thus the Mediterranean and Atlantic were to be connected, and an outlet afforded to the Castiles for wines and cereal productions to be exchanged with the iron and timber of the Asturias and colonial produce imported through Santander. For these splendid lines of circulation nature had supplied easy levels, a light soil for excavation, and fine rivers as feeders : thus irrigation would have ensured fertility, while a means of transport would have favoured commerce, and a vitality moral and physical would have been infused into the *corpus mortuum* of these districts. The plan, as usual in Spain and in the East, was begun with ardour, and the works progressed during the life of the originating minister, and then decayed. The affair lingered, was now taken up and then let down, until the French invasion blighted it altogether, in common with most other ameliorations of Spain. Ferd. VII. in 1830 granted a lease to a company, who recommenced the works ; but when they will be finished, *Lo sabe Dios !* Spain, which under the Moors presented a most scientific system of artificial irrigation ;

which in 1528, under Charles V., devised the canal of Arragon, and contemplated under Philip II. in 1581 the navigation of the Tagus; which thus long preceded England in these works, so essential to commerce, is now as in other things far far behind; she has stood still, while others have sailed on, and yet water under her sun is the very blood of life, the principle of fertility and wealth.

The morris-dances of the peasantry at Dueñas are the combined Pyrrhica Saltatio of the Romans and the *Tripudium* of the Iberians (see p. 189); we witnessed here one Sunday a quadrille performed by eight men, with castanets in their hands, and to the tune of a fife and drum, while a master of the ceremonies in party-coloured raiment like a pantaloon directed the rustic ballet; around were grouped *payesas y aldeanas,* dressed in tight boddices with *pañuelos* on their heads, their hair hanging down behind in *trensas,* and their necks covered with blue and coral beads; the men bound up their long locks with red handkerchiefs, and danced in their shirts, the sleeves of which were puckered up with bows of different-coloured ribands, crossed also over the back and breast, and mixed with scapularies and small prints of saints; their drawers were white, and full as the *bragas* of the Valencians, like whom they wore *alpargatas,* or hemp sandals laced with blue strings; the figure of the dance was very intricate, consisting of much circling, turning, and jumping, and accompanied with loud cries of *viva* at each change of evolution.

Before leaving *Dueñas* ascend to the square castle on its conical hill : the view sweeps over the treeless *Parameras,* or *Tierras de Campos;* below the Pisuerga has deserted its old bed and bridge, which stands high and dry (see Coria). In the distance rises *El Monte de Torozos,* now almost bare, but once covered with forests. Those who thus denude their hills ensure to their children a want both of timber

and water, wants which are the twin curses of central Spain. This tract, which forms the boundary of Old Castile, commences at *Villa Nubla,* and extends to *Villa Garcia,* being in width some 3 L. In this *Monte* is the Bernardine *Convento de la Espina.* The portal is Ionic ; the cloister classical. Before the ancient *Retablo* kneel the statues of Queen Leonora and Doña Sancha.

Thence to *Palencia,* Pallantia. The best inn is that of Gabriel Papin. This is an ancient city and university, founded in the 10th century, and afterwards moved to Salamanca in 1239 ; pop^n. about 10,000. It stands on the Carrion, having a good stone bridge, and another called *Los Puentecillos.* The Alamedas round the ancient walls were laid out in 1778 by the Intendente Carrasco. Those on the little island by the bridge, built by the Archdeacon Aguarin, occupy the site where a grand tournament was given to Charles V. The air of Palencia is keen and cold, as it stands with its trees an oasis in the wide shelterless plains. One long street, *El mayor,* intersects the town, running from the gates Monzon and del Mercado. Near the latter is imbedded a Roman sepulchral stone of the sons of Pompey. The town is well placed for commerce on its river and canal, and has some manufactories of rude blankets and counterpanes. The Gothic cathedral is light and elegant, and was built after the type of that of Leon in 1321-1504, on the site of one more ancient, and raised by Sancho el Mayor over the cave of San Antolin, to whom this church, in common with many others in these districts, is dedicated. This saint was a Frenchman, and lived in a den in the woods with and like the wild boars : it so fell out that the king, when hunting them, was about to shoot his arrow at one which had fled into the anchorite's cave, whereupon his extended arm was instantly withered up ; but it was restored again by the intercession of the recluse, thereupon the king immediately granted the district to the church. The den was made a chapel, and to this day the bones of the saint and the boar are worshipped by the peasants, and are indeed the lions of the cathedral. In the *Capilla Mayor* are the tombs of the Ms. del Pozo and his wife, 1557. The *Silla. del coro* is fine, and of the cinque-cento period. Observe the *reja* and the pulpits with bassi-relievi of boys and festoons. The *Respaldo del coro* contains plateresque Berruguete sculpture. The Custodia was made in 1582 by Juan Benavente. The coffin of Queen Urraca, 1149, is still preserved. The tower, cloister, and chapter-house are Gothic, and the door of communication between the latter is worth the architect's notice. In the Dominican convent were the superb sepulchres of the Rojas family: one on the l. of the altar of Juan de Rojas and his wife, 1557, was in the richest Berruguete taste; the other opposite, after designs of Herrera, was Doric, and composed of black and coloured marble, with fine kneeling figures of Fro. de Rojas and his wife Fra. Cabrera, who raised it in 1604.

The hospital of San Lazaro was once the palace of the Cid, and the reader of ballads will remember that this saint appeared to the Campeador in the guise of a pilgrim. Here the Cid was married to Ximena, whose father he had slain; the ladies of Palencia were most valiant also, as they are said to have beaten off the Black Prince. These Pucelles de Palencia were allowed by Juan I. to wear a gold band on their head-gear (compare them with the ancient Amazons of Tortosa). The modern men of Palencia, like those of that town, behaved very differently, for Gen. Milhaud took the city without difficulty, Nov. 13, 1808. It was afterwards frequently occupied and plundered, and particularly by Foy in October, 1812; consult the Local '*Historia*,' by Pedro Fernandez del Pulgar, and the '*Descripcion*' by Domingo Largo.

The road passing the ridge at Fromista follows the line of the canal into the basin of the Pisuerga. These bald plains produce vast quantities of corn, the flour of which is exported to Cuba from Santander. At Aquilar del Campo the river turns to the l., and the road to the r., and enters Old Castile (for the *Montañas* and Reinosa see R. cxiv).

ROUTE LXXVII.—VALLADOLID TO BURGOS.

Cabezon	4	
Dueñas	3	7
Torquemada	3	10
Villadrigo	4	14
Celada	4	18
Burgos	4	22

This is the diligence road, and it is very dull. Buonaparte, according to M. Savary, rode this distance in 1809 in less than six hours (for Dueñas, see preceding route). At Torquemada in June, 1808, the Spanish army, mis-led by Cuesta, fled even before the battle began, frightened at one gallant cavalry charge of La Salle. The village was then sacked and burnt by Bessières, by whom neither age nor sex was spared.

The Arlanzon coming down from Burgos joins the Pisuerga, crossing which we enter Old Castile. Leaving the Pisuerga, the road now continues along the basin of the Arlanzon, passing Celada and its corn-plains, to the walls of ancient Burgos (see R. cxiii.)

ROUTE LXXVIII.—VALLADOLID TO MADRID.

Puente del Duero	2	
Valdestillas	2	4
Olmillos	2	6
Olmedo	2	8
San Cristobal	3½	11½
Martin Muñoz	2	13½
Sn. Chidrian	2	15½
Labajos	2	17½
Villacastin	2	19½
Fonda San Rafael	3	22½
Guadarrama	2	24½
Torrelodones	2½	27
Las Rosas	2	29
Madrid	2½	31½

The sandy road to Olmedo has recently been repaired, but its dulness never can be removed. *Olmedo*, a decayed town, is celebrated for the bloody battles in 1445 and 1467, during the civil wars in the reigns of Juan II. and Enrique IV. It contains 2000 souls, and is situated in a plain, irrigated by the Adaja, which comes down from Avila, and by the Eresma, which descends from Segovia, and which were destined to feed the canal up to that city. The dreary sandy plains extend almost to Labajos, but produce, however, much and tolerable wine. Soon we enter the province of Old Castile; and at S⁰. Chidrian the road joins the *camino real.*

From Oviedo to Madrid, after Labajos, the granitic ranges of the Carpetanian mountains commence. The stone of Villacastin is excellent. The Guadarrama range separates the basins of the Tagus and the Duero. The name is by some derived from Ash-Sherrat, alxarrat, the dividing sierra. Conde (Xedris, 167) reads *Wadarrambla,* " the river of the sand;" it being a chain of granite. The road made in 1749 by Ferdinand VI. ascends to the *Puerto,* where a marble lion on the extreme height, said to be 5094 feet above the sea, marks the boundary between Old and New Castile, the former lying spread below like a map. The line of road is well chosen, and the engineering excellent, but in winter it is occasionally impassable from the snow. The bleak winds of both the Castiles produce an intensity of cold which the French never experienced in the winter campaigns of Friedland. It was on Christmas eve, 1808, that Buonaparte started from Madrid, having heard of Moore's advance, which deranged all his certainty of conquering Portugal and Andalucia at one blow. His new plans were conceived with his usual decision, and carried out with corresponding rapidity. He led his army over these prison caves of the storm and nurseries of death, like lightning amid glaciers; his own impatience was so great, that he leaped off his horse and walked through the snows himself in order to encourage his troops. " Shall a mole-hill in Spain (cried he) check the conquerors of St. Bernard ?" He leant on the arm of Savary, and arrived greatly exhausted at Espinar, where he slept, resting the next day at Villacastin. The losses suffered by his army were very great, yet the brave men pushed on; but in vain their courage and rapidity, for Buonaparte, in spite of unexampled exertion, reached Benavente just 12 hours too late (see p. 590). Passing the *Puerto,* and leaving the Escorial to the r., we descend into the dreary mangy wastes which encircle Madrid. The immediate approach, however, by the Florida with the noble palace is striking. A better route will be to proceed from Valladolid to Olmedo in the diligence, and then ride to Segovia.

ROUTE LXXIX.—VALLADOLID TO MADRID BY SEGOVIA.

Olmedo	8	
Villequillo	2	.. 10
Coca	1	.. 11
Sª. Maria de Nieve. .	3	.. 14
Garcillan	2¼	.. 16¼
Segovia	2¼	.. 19

At *Villequillo* Old Castile is entered. *Coca,* a small town between the Eresma and Voltoya rivers, possesses a grand specimen of a genuine Castilian castle of the Gothic medieval period. Observe the projecting *Balistaria,* bartizans, the angular turrets of the great donjon-keep *La torre mocha.* The superb towers rise like the Alcazar of Segovia, and the barbican frame-work is remarkable. This strong castle was quite perfect and used as a state-prison until the French reduced it to its present ruin. In the parish church are some fine marble pillars. Nothing of interest now occurs until we reach Segovia.

ROUTE LXXIX. A.—VALLADOLID TO MADRID BY CUELLAR AND SEGOVIA.

Tudela del Duero	. .	3
Monte mayor	3	.. 6
Cuellar	3	.. 9
Sancho Nuño . . .	2	.. 11

<table>
<tr><td>Navalmanzano</td><td>.</td><td>.</td><td>.</td><td>2</td><td>..</td><td>13</td></tr>
<tr><td>Escarabajosa</td><td>.</td><td>.</td><td>.</td><td>2</td><td>..</td><td>15</td></tr>
<tr><td>Segovia</td><td>.</td><td>.</td><td>.</td><td>3</td><td>..</td><td>18</td></tr>
</table>

The country on this route is cereal, and interspersed with vineyards and pine trees. *Tudela*, pop. 1400, stands on its river, and has a stone bridge which was damaged during the war; the magnificent façade of the noble *parroquia* is in the Ionic and Græco-Romano style, and consists of three tiers ornamented with sculpture, representing subjects from the life of the Saviour, with the Apostles, and the Ascension of the Virgin in the central place of honour; all this is the work of one Martin, who finished it in 1614, and who deserves to be better known: inside is a fine *Retablo* which has been attributed to Hernandez from its grandiose character: by him also is a Virgin *con el Niño*, and another *del Rosario*. This church was begun in 1515, and finished in 1555, but the tower was only completed 60 years later.

Continuing amid pines between *Montemayor* and *Cuellar*, is the celebrated and much-frequented sanctuary of the Virgin *del Henar*, "the river." *Cuellar*, Colenda, lies on a slope of a hill which is crowned by a fine castle. Pop. 3000; the streets are steepish and badly paved; the environs are very fertile, and the game and turkeys renowned: Cuellar had ten parish churches and three convents, a tolera-bly sufficient spiritual supply for 3000 souls. The façade of the convent *San Francisco* is in good Ionic; here were interred in splendid sepulchres the great family of Alburquerque, to whom the castle belonged: ascend to it, as the views over the interminable plains with the distant Sierra are fine. This palatial alcazar was granted in 1454 by Henry IV., the Impotent, to his favourite, Beltran de la Cueva, who was to him what Godoy was to the wittol Charles IV. The edifice was rebuilt in 1550, and before the fatal French invasion was one of the best preserved in Spain, and furnished with its ancient ornaments, armoury, and gallery of pictures; these, however, were much neglected, as is usual in the provincial mansions of absentees (see the account in Ponz, x. 5). The *patio* is very noble, with upper and lower corridors, and solid granite colonnades. It was at *Cuellar*, Feb. 20, 1843, that Serjeant Garcia, the Granja revolutionist, died in poverty and just neglect, for in Spain *la traicion aplace pero no el que la hace*; from Cuellar to Segovia there is little to notice.

Cuellar communicates with *Peñafiel*, which lies N. distant 4 L. through *Moraleja*, which is half way; *Peñafiel* itself being half-way between *Valladolid* distant 8 L. and *Aranda del Duero* distant 7½. For ancient and picturesque Segovia, see R. xcix.

SECTION IX.

THE KINGDOM OF GALLICIA.

CONTENTS.

The Kingdom; the Character of the Country and Natives; Books to Consult.

The proper period for visiting Gallicia is during the warm months. The objects best worth notice are Santiago, and the mountain scenery and fishing, especially in R. lxxxviii., xc., xci., and xcii. The angler might spend three months with much pleasure and profit in taking the following *unwhipped* line :—Vigo, Orense, Puente San Domingo Florez, Cabrera alta y baja, Lago de Castanedo, La Bañeza, Ponferrada, Villafranca, and then crossing the mountains by R. cxi. to Cangas de Tineo, Grado, and Oviedo. (See for details, Index.)

EL *Reino de Galicia*, or the kingdom of Gallicia (Spaniards spell its name with one L, although they use two in that of the inhabitants *Los Gallegos*), forms the N.W. angle of the Peninsula, and is bounded by Portugal, the Bay of Biscay, the Asturias, and Leon. It contains 15,000 square L., and a popⁿ· of one million and a half. The grand river is the *Miño*, called by the ancients Minius, from the vermilion found near it. It rises not far from Mondoñedo, and flows S. to Orense and Tuy, forming the boundary on the side of Portugal. The fishing in it and its tributaries is admirable, especially for salmon, the *Savalo*, trout, and lampreys: the latter were sent to the epicures of old Rome. In 1791 a project was formed to render the *Miño* navigable, but nothing was done beyond a *Memoria* by Eustaquio Giannini.

The climate of Gallicia is temperate and rainy, as the surface is very mountainous. This European barrier to the Atlantic extends from Cape Finisterre to the Pyrenean spurs in the Basque provinces. The hills are well clothed with timber for building and shipping, while the chesnuts and acorns afford food to men and swine ; the hams and bacon rival those of Estremadura. The meadows are verdurous, for this N.W. coast of Spain resembles Switzerland in its pastures: any quantity of cattle might be reared ; and no doubt the operation of our new tariff will give a great impetus to breeding stock, which will be exported from Vigo and La Coruña. The woody hills are full of boars and wolves, that descend into the plains, which are irrigated by rivers, whose pleasant banks have an English aspect:

" Nunc frondent silvæ, nunc formosissimus amnis."

The natural productions in the higher localities are chiefly maize, rye, and flax, with such fruits as flourish in Devonshire, apples, pears, nuts, and those of the *berry* kind, which are rare in the hotter portions of Spain ; the potatoes also are excellent, although not yet used as an article of general subsistence, but rather as a culinary addition to the tables of the richer classes. As the eastern mountain boundary is covered almost all the year with snow, especially the *Pico de Ancares* and the *Peña Trevinca*, while the sea-coasts and riverain valleys bask in a latitude of 42°, having scarcely any winter, the range of botany is very wide and interesting, and never has been properly investigated. The warmer and lower valleys of the Miño, and the country about Tuy, Redondela, and Orense, are perfect gardens of plenty and delight ; Nature there retains all her " wealth," and is still " *smiling amid flowers*" as in happier days of old (Sil. Ital. iii. 345 ; Claudian, ' Lau. Ser.' 71). The contrast between the backward ignorance and poverty of the peasants is painfully striking ; art, science, and literature languish, where the olive and orange flourish, and rich wines are produced ; of these the best are those of Valdeorras, Amandi, Rivero, and the Tostado of Orense, and they would rival the vintages of Portugal, were the commonest pains taken in the making ; but here, as on the eastern coast (see Benicarló), everything is managed in the rudest and most wasteful manner. Gallicia is to the N.W. of Spain what Murcia is to the S.E., its Bœotia, and to the bulk of Spaniards it is almost unknown, as few ever go there. They form their idea of Gallicians from those who come from it, emigrating, like the Swiss, from the mountains to the plains ; thus the district of La Coruña supplies the Castiles, as Pontevedra and Orense do Portugal. The emigrants generally are absent from four to five years, after which they pay their homes a visit, and start forth again : others only go down for the harvest time, returning, like the Irish, with their hard-earned gains. Those who settle at Madrid become *Riposteros*, and managers in families, where, however boorish their exterior, they are sufficiently cunning to find out in the *kitchens* the secrets of every menage ; just as the Nubian slaves do in the establishments of the wealthier Arabs at Cairo, and, like them, they herd and pull together. Many, for they are as thrifty as their neighbours the Asturians, scrape up much money, with which in after-life they come back to their loved and never-forgotten hills. The humbler emigrants, and they are well qualified by their muscular frames, do the *porters*' work of Spain and Portugal ; hence the term *Gallego* is synonymous with a boor, *ganapan*, or a " hewer of wood and drawer of water," the biblical expression for the over-worked. Lisbon is filled with them, as Portugal is nearer to their homes, and there is a greater affinity of language than in the Castiles. The Portuguese, who do not love a neighbour, modestly contend that God first made *men*, i. e. Portuguese, *viros* " gentlemen," and then Gallicians, i. e. *homines* or slaves to wait on them. These white niggers frequently wear wooden shoes *Madreñas*, which, according to Goldsmith's porter when reasoning

on Frenchmen's *Sabots*, is another proof of their being only fit to be beasts of
burden. Good land is scarce in Gallicia, as much of the country is hilly and
broken, and unfit for agriculture, while other wide tracts or *Dehesas* (called
here *Gándaras*, from their barrenness) are abandoned to heaths and aromatic
herbs : there is, consequently, a struggle for land in the valleys and favoured
localities ; and hence, as in Ireland, the over-rented peasant toils day and night,
and eats a scanty bread of the lowest quality, either of maize or millet, *pan de
Centeno, de Borona,* for corn is scarce. The cottages are full of dirt, smoke,
and damp, true *Arcas de Noe,* says Gongora, from the close packing of various
beasts within, where the same room does for nursery, stable, kitchen, pigstye,
" parlour and all ;" but no flood natural or artificial ever gets into these Noah's
arks : the *Ventas* in the hills and out-of-the-way localities, are no better; *attend to the provend,* for in these dens, ravenous wolves, who are not particular in
their cuisine, would be badly off, much less honest Christians ; the fire-places
often have no chimneys, and the damp wood, which won't burn, will smoke ;
this is as distressing to the visual organs as the prospect of no roast is to the
digestive ones, however satisfactory all this classical lacrymoso non sine fumo
may be to readers of Horace. In the plains and more favoured valleys the
accommodation for travellers is not quite so bad, but Gallicia is seldom visited
except by muleteers, according to whose wants and demands these discomforts
are regulated. It need not be said where people sup without chimneys and
sleep without beds, that vermin which were deemed a plague in Egypt, are here
held to be free denizens by long prescription.

When the Gallician men migrate the females do all the drudgery at home
in house and field, and a painful sight it is to see them labouring at the plough,
which is no duty of woman ; in the field or out their hands are never idle, and
the *Rueca* or distaff is part and parcel of a Gallega, as is a fan of an Andaluca.
A fare as hard as their work, coupled with exposure to an uncongenial climate,
nips their beauty in the bud ; few, indeed, are born good-looking, or even then
retain their charms long ; they are aged before thirty, and then look as if they
never could have been young, or had anything of the feminine gender ; they resemble mummies or cats which have been found starved behind a wainscot, things of
skin, bone, and fur ; the men are boorish and rude, seldom giving a direct answer ; seen in their wretched huts, they are scarcely better than their ancestors,
who were little better than beasts, since, according to Justin (xliv. 2), Feris
propriora quam hominibus ingenia gerunt, while Strabo (iii. 234) pronounced
them even worse and Θηριωδεστεροι. Nevertheless, these beasts thought themselves lions, and now as then, like true highlanders, are proud of their birth and
their illustrious pedigrees : compare the Τα γνωριμα εθνη of Strabo (iii. 228)
with the *nobiliarios* of Gándara, and others. They claimed Teucer of old as
their founder, who, they said, came from the east to select this damp remote
province, just as the moderns predicate of Santiago, and in both cases without
the slightest foundation in truth.

These ancient gentlemen also left to their ladies all tasks, except war, robbery,
and the chase (Justin xliv. 3) ; they delighted, as now, in wild dances and rude
songs, or " howls" according to Sil. Ital. (iii. 346), which still are no less
grating to fine ears, than is the *chirrio, el chillar,* or creaking of their solid cart-
wheels (see p. 588). The women dug and delved in the fields as now (Sil.
Ital. iii. 350), and their *travail* was not simply agricultural, for, according to
Strabo (iii. 250), they merely stept aside out of the furrows to be brought to
bed, if such a term may be used, returning back to their other labour just as if
they had only laid an egg. The men were worthy of such Amazons, and
their physical forms are cast in nature's best mould ; they are not effeminated

by residence in large cities, nor dwarfed by manufactures, which reduce men to " hands," and the breed and general ways of life remain very little changed. The males are fine animals; they are a good recruiting raw material, and if properly fed and led would make capital soldiers; yet such was the incubus of their inefficient chiefs, that Moore found them the very worst-off soldiers among Spaniards. " In your life (wrote the Duke, Disp. Dec. 10, 1812), you never saw anything *so bad* as the Gallicians; and yet they are the finest body of men, and the best movers I have seen." " They are but a miserable mob, on which we have no reliance," said old fighting Picton.

The language of Gallicia is a patois, harsh and uncouth to the ear; it is quite unintelligible to Spaniards; yet from it and the *Bable* of the Asturias the modern Castilian has sprung. Had Spain been the land of philologists, this curious key to the origin of their language would have been investigated as it deserves, and some remnants preserved of ancient ballads and usages; to all strangers the dialect is as impracticable as Gallician ventas and cross-roads— Cependant, as Laborde would say, les Galliciens s'entendent entre eux.

Their wrong-headed litigious character has long been a butt to other Spaniards, who think it almost hopeless to attempt to improve them: " *No se les puede negar á los Gallegos mas legos. que vale por mil Gallegos, el que llega á despuntar,*" says Fro. de Salas. Want of roads and communication with other provinces has confined the Gallician in this *cul de sac* corner of routine and ignorance. The presence of the apostle at his star-paved city, *Compostella*, has done nothing in enlightening his chosen province, which his priests, barring fire-works, seem to have sedulously preserved in impenetrable *obscurantismo*.

There is only one great road which runs from Madrid to La Coruña; on this, in 1842, Carsi and Ferrer established a diligence, which occasionally runs through Villacastin, Valladolid, Tordesillas, Benavente, and Lugo. It has long been in confemplation to cut a shorter direct road between Vigo and the capital, by Orense and El Vierzo; thus nearly 100 miles might be saved, instead of making, as at present, a wide détour. This scheme, which would benefit vast districts, has been, is, and will be thwarted by local jealousies, the old curse of Spain; each selfish town wishing to monopolize the traffic to itself, and to injure its abhorred neighbour; accordingly most of the cross-roads resemble those in the *Serrania de Ronda*, but the country is not infested with robbers, for there are few travellers, and the Gallicians pilfer rather in kitchens than on the highway.

The rider who comes from Andalucia will probably find (as we did) that his faithful barb will fall sick in these parts from change of fodder; for now, instead of the Oriental "barley and straw," he will only meet with hay and oats, and a reedy rubbishy *broa* for litter. It is prudent in the large towns to buy a little barley to mix with the oats, as the oat contains much less nourishment and more husk. Remember also that a stallion horse is constantly kept on a fidget here from the pony-mares which the peasants ride (see p. 54); and as the horse-flies are very troublesome, a net will be of much service. Again, the roads being very stony, the horseshoes soon wear out, and it is not easy to replace them, except in the towns, since the country farriers seldom keep a ready-made full-sized horseshoe, for which there is no demand, ponies being here the ordinary cattle. Take therefore some nails and a spare set of shoes ready made for your own horse—*Hombre prevenido nunca fu vencido;* " for want," says poor Richard, "of a nail the shoe was lost, and for want of the shoe the horse was lost."

The ecclesiastical antiquities of Gallicia occupy no less than nine volumes of the '*España Sagrada,*' and are most curious: consult also *Viage de Morales;* the works of Felipe de Gándara, his *'Nobiliario,'* and *'Armas y triunfos,'* 4to., Mad. 1662; the metrical *'Descripcion,'* by El licenciado Molina, 4to., Mondoñedo, 1551; *'Descripcion Economica,'* Jose Lucas Labrado, El Ferrol, 1804; *'Ensayo sobre la Historia de Galicia,'* Jose Verea y Aquiar; *'Anales de el Reyno de Galicia,'* F.X.M. de la Huerta y Vega, 2 vol., Santiago; *'Descripcion Geognostica de Galicia,'* thin 8vo., Guillermo Schulz, Mad. 1835. This slight geological treatise has also a useful lithographic map of the kingdom. The author is a German, for the Gallician, like the Oriental, leaves to the foreigner the investigation of her natural history. The *'Viage a Galicia, por dos Amigos,'* Mad. 1842, is a paltry performance.

LUGO has a decent *posada* outside the town, on the road to Astorga, in the *Barrio de San Roque.* This, the most central town of Gallicia, is described in the xl. and xli. vol. of the *'España Sagrada.'* It has also its own *'Historia,'* by Pallares y Gayoso, 4to., Mad. 1700. *Lugo,* Lucus Augusti, was celebrated under the Romans for its warm sulphur baths; the waters still exist because the work of nature; but the *Thermæ,* the work of men, have disappeared: some remains of a dyke against inundations testify their former magnificence. The present incommodious baths are placed on the l. bank of the Miño; the season is from June 15 to Sept. 30, when they are beneficial in cutaneous and rheumatic disorders. The poor pay *dos cuartos* for the liberty of immersion, and there they lie like porpoises, or immundæ sues, in the steaming waters among the loose stones. Hard by is a mineral spring, which contains nitre and antimony. In the town, in the *Calle de Batitales,* was discovered (Sept. 1842) a Roman mosaic pavement, with designs of animals, fish, &c. It probably is now either reburied or destroyed.

Lugo contains about 7000 souls. It is nearly a square, with the corners rounded off; the walls resemble those of Astorga, and are defended by countless semicircular projecting buttress towers, which do not rise much above the line of circumvallation; on them is a broad and agreeable walk round the town; here the ivy, a creeper rare in the torrid parts of Spain, mantles the ruins. The oldest portion,

with solid Roman granite work, is best seen near the tower of Santiago. The *Plaza* has an arcaded colonnade, which is necessary in this rainy climate; the fountain, which is supplied from a rude extramural aqueduct, is so ill-contrived, that women come with long tin tubes to coax the water into their vessels. This water, coupled with a rye-bread diet, produces frequent gout, to which even females are subject. The old castle is not remarkable beyond a singular turreted chimney. Lugo, once the metropolitan, is now suffragan to Santiago. The see is one of the most ancient in restored Spain, having been founded in 734 by Alonzo el Catolico. The granite cathedral was built in 1129 by Don Ramon, husband of Queen Urraca, and as in that of Astorga, the two lateral aisles are lower than the central. The exterior was injudiciously modernized in 1769 by Julian Sanchez Bort; the whole granite facade and statues are heavy: observe in the pediment, Faith holding the Hostia. The unfinished towers have hideous slated pigeon house-tops, and a chiming apparatus of iron, which, so common in the Netherlands, is very rare in Spain. The cloisters also have been modernized, but two lateral doors retain some of their pristine character; observe the hinges of the N.W. one, and the Saviour seated in the mystical *Vesica Piscis.*

The interior has low arches on each side, with a gallery above, and below rows of sentry-box confessionals, with the names of especial tutelars over each. The *Silla del Coro* of good

2 F

carving is by F^{ro}· de Moure of Orense, 1624. The bishop's seat bears the arms of Alonzo Lopez de Gallo, who defrayed the cost. This cathedral is privileged to have the consecrated Host, *i. e.*, the actually then and there present and incarnate Deity, always exposed, or *manifestado.* This immemorial right is shared only with San Isidoro of Leon. In reference to this high distinction Gallicia bears the *Host* on its shield, and Lugo " two towers supported on lions, and the wafer in a monstrance." This is said to indicate that Lugo, Lukoh, was never taken by the Moors (which, by the way, it was by Al-Mansúr); for in captive Christian cities the wafer was always concealed, or rather shrouded, in sign of grief. According to Molina (p. 22), a wafer near Lugo actually became flesh, in the hands of a sceptical clergyman, and was preserved in the monastery of Zebrero (see Daroca). The *Hostia* in other Spanish churches is put away in a tabernacle, except in those great cities which have the privilege of the *cuarenta Horas,* or exhibition of it by routine in different churches for 40 hours, when the same spiritual benefits may be obtained by the faithful who kneel before it, as by an actual pilgrimage to St. Peter's. This spectacle was first introduced at superstitious Valencia in 1697, having been established at Rome in 1592 by Clement VIII. Thus is reversed the custom of the pure primitive church, which almost concealed the sacramental emblems from all except the initiated. At Lugo the incarnate *Hostia* is always manifested in a glass *viril;* one made by Juan d'Arphe was given in 1636 by Bp. Castejon. The Host is always here surrounded with burning tapers, candles for Him to see by, who made light itself. The glass-enclosed high altar is modern, tawdry, and theatrical, especially the painted oval, with angels of white marble with gilt wings. The *Baldaquino* is supported by coloured marble pillars and gilt capitals; behind, in a modern circular chapel overcharged with ornament, is an image of the Virgin, which, surrounded by tinsel and gilding, is the *real* object of popular adoration. This highly privileged cathedral rejoices also in a Maria *de los ojos grandes,* the Juno Bow$_{\pi s}$ of the Pagans, and the phrase *ojos de buey* is a common Spanish compliment to mortal women. Those who happen to have a headache at Lugo will be cured by visiting the tomb of Froyla, mother of S^n· Froylan, in this cathedral. See ' E. S.,' xxxiv. 175. This saint's brother is buried on the Gospel side of the high altar.

It was at Lugo that Moore halted for a few days, Jan. 6, 1809; he had retreated with most unnecessary haste from Villafranca in 48 hours, during which the misery produced by cold and starvation was intense, but no description, says Lord Londonderry, can come up to the reality. All discipline was at an end, except when the enemy appeared in sight; then, as the famished eagle bursts into strength on beholding its quarry, so did our footsore hungry troops recover at once order, power, and the bayonet; wherever and whenever the French ventured to advance, they were signally beaten back; and now Foy, who was an eyewitness, has the face to state (forgetting the old parallels of Agincourt and Cressy), " On ne dira pas des Anglais qu'ils étaient braves à telle rencontre, ils le sont toutes les fois qu'ils ont dormi, bu, et mangé : leur courage, plus physique que moral, a besoin d'être soutenu par un traitement substantiel. La gloire ne leur ferait pas oublier qu'ils ont faim, ou que leurs souliers sont usés " (i. 230).

Soult came up with Moore at Lugo, and ordered a partial attack under Lallemand, who was beaten back at every point with a loss of 400 men; and although the English offered him battle on the 7th and 8th, he declined, and thus, as on the Tormes and at Zubiri, missed the nice tide of the affair, for had he pressed his attack, such was the exhaustion of our troops and want of ammunition, that numbers might have prevailed. But he thought that Moore was much stronger than he really was, and thus, as often elsewhere, the French exaggeration of our numbers recoiled, by a poetical justice, on themselves, being deceived by their own inventions. Buonaparte saw, but salved over his lieutenant's error: his 28th bulletin stated (Œuv. v. 378) that at Lugo Soult took 300 of our wounded, 18 cannon, and 700 prisoners; adding, that the English had now lost 2500 horses, being exactly 320 more than Moore had at starting. The simple truth was, that Soult, with 24,000 troops, did not even molest the retreating English rear-guard on the 9th, when they fell back on La Coruña. Four short months afterwards this same Lugo beheld, May 29, 1809, this very Soult flying from the Duke at Oporto, his troops having thrown away their arms, and arriving like famished wolves, in almost a state of nature.

Then he and Ney rivalled each other in sacking the wretched place, which they had made a Plaza de *armas*, destroying for that object nearly one-third of the town, as was done at Salamanca, and the Alhambra, and Valencia. Many of the houses have since been rebuilt, which gives to *old* Lugo a *new* character rarer even than ivy in Spain, where much is destroyed, and little is repaired.

Lugo is in the centre of many branch and bad communications; for those S. by Astorga, see R. lxvii.: first, therefore, to La Coruña.

ROUTE LXXX.—LUGO TO LA CORUÑA.

Otero del Rey . . .	1½	
San Julian de la Roca .	2 . .	3½
Gueteriz	2 . .	5½
Vª. de la Castellana .	2 . .	7½
Vª. de Monte Salgueyro	2 . .	9½
Betanzos	3 . .	12½
El Burgo	1¼ . .	14
A la Coruña. . . .	1¼ . .	15¼

This country abounds with first-rate streams for the angler. Quitting *Otero del Rey*, is the Miño, with its tributaries the Tamboga, Lama, and Azu-mara; next comes the superb trout river, the Ladra, running to the l., and crossed before reaching *Gueteriz*, and afterwards before coming to the *Vª. de la Castellana;* the Mandeo is also a charming stream, and flows along the road to *Betanzos*, which is placed between it and the Cascas.

Betanzos (Brigantium Flavium) is an ancient city of some 5000 souls, and a good fishing quarter, since many rivers disembogue into the *ria*, and there is, moreover, an excellent *Posada*. Betanzos is placed on a sort of peninsula, and some of its narrow streets, or rather lanes, are still defended by ancient granite gateways. The road to La Coruña is delightful, as the rich country is well cultivated, and the views, which sweep over mountain and water, superb. After crossing the Cascas, we soon reach *El Burgo*, on its river and ria. This was the route taken by Moore, whose troops here lost their way, and suffered much in the dark wintry night.

La Coruña, since the Audiencia and captain-general have been removed to it from Santiago, has made much progress in every kind of improvement; popⁿ· 25,000, and increasing. The best inns are *El Comercio*, Calle Real; the charge is about 16 reals, 3s. 4d., per day,—and the *Cafe del Correo*. Sometimes a local steamer in the summer time coasts up and down from Cadiz to San Sebastian. *La Coruña*, which we call Corunna, is the chief seaport of Gallicia, and stands on a headland of the three bays, or rias, of Coruña, Betanzos, and El Ferrol. The sea-board, *Las Marinas*, is picturesquely indented, and the iron-bound coast rises bluffly out of the waters, proclaiming to the Atlantic, thus far shalt thou go and no farther. La Coruña, formerly called by the English the *Groyne*, is about half-way between the Capes Ortegal and Finisterre.

Founded by the Phœnicians, it was captured by the Romans, u. c. 693, when Gallicia was overrun by Junius

2 F 2

Brutus, who called it Ardobicum *Corunium;* nevertheless, the present name has been derived by some from *Columna,* the tower, the Phœnician Pharos, and this is still called *La Torre de Hercules.* It was repaired for Trajan by an architect named Caius Servius Lupus, as is conjectured from a damaged inscription in a rock hard by. The present edifice is square, and rises above 100 ft. high, with walls more than four feet thick. The Spaniards let it go to ruin; but the repeated entreaties of the English and Dutch consuls to restore it into a lighthouse were at last attended to by Charles III., only, however, when El Ferrol rose into importance. The Coruñese contend that Hercules built this Pharos over the bones of the Geryons, whereat the Gaditanians and Geronese are justly wroth. The Gallicians now, as of old, are great claimers of persons' bones who have never even visited their province either dead or alive, for Geryon is but the type of Santiago; nevertheless, *La Coruña* blazons boldly on its shield "a tower on rocks, a lamp, two crossed bones, and a scull above crowned with an orle of eight scallops in honour of Santiago :" consult ' *Averigüaciones,*' José Cornide, 4to., Mad. 1792, with plates.

In the 12th century, *La Coruña* was called *La Villa de Cruña;* Cor Car is a common Iberian prefix connected with height—*coro*na, crown. In 1563 La Coruña was raised to the seat of the *Audiencia,* which in 1802 was removed to El Ferrol, and under the *Sistema,* or Constitution of 1820, to *Santiago,* to the infinite subsequent bickerings and hatreds of the cities, to say nothing of La Coruña's mercantile horror and jealousy of Vigo and Santander, two rival ports to the S. and N. The jurisdiction of the *Audiencia* extends over 1,472,000 persons : the number tried in 1844 amounted to 3903, being about one in every 377.

La Coruña, like Trujillo, has an *alta* or upper quarter, and a *baja* or lower one; the former contains the principal official and ecclesiastical buildings, La Coruña has two ancient churches. That of *Santiago* was commenced in the 11th century : observe the tower and arched crown-like work at the top, the bull's head at the S. door, the absis in the interior and the pulpit, with carved groups of females at the pedestal. The old font is in a circular lateral building, which has been recently repainted in a most ridiculous manner. The other church is *La Sa. Maria* or *La Colegiata,* with a W. porch in the Norman style; the tower has been finished off with a pyramidical structure as at Leon; the interior is dark. The great altar is in an absis.

The new town, which was once *La Pescaderia,* or a mere refuge of fishermen, has now eclipsed its former rival. It is well built, and principally with granite; the *Calle Real* is a broad, well-paved, busy, and handsome street; so is that *de Espoz y Mina.* The lines of balconies with glazed windows are the favourite boudoirs of the women, who sit in them at work— spectant et spectantur. In the evening they saunter out *tomar el fresco* on *La Marina,* which is a charming walk. The town is well supplied with everything, the produce alike of sea and land, and is very cheap. Here butter, strawberries, and potatoes abound, luxuries rare in central Spain; the asparagus is excellent, and the hams and sweetmeats celebrated ; coal is brought from Gijon. The sea-bathing is very good, and winter is almost unknown. The natives are cheerful and fair-complexioned ; the better female classes wear the *mantilla ;* the lower tie handkerchiefs on their heads, with the hair in long plaits or *trensas ;* their walk and *meneo* are remarkable : the men are clad in *Paño pardo,* and have singular *monteras,* with a red plume and a peacock's feather. Such were the Mitræ of the Iberians (see p. 308). In the lower town is the large theatre, the custom-house, the seat of commerce, and a good reading-room or club. The convent *Sn. Agustin* has been suppressed, but the handsome modern classical church serves for the parish, while the rest of the edifice is converted into municipal offices. There is no fine art here; some poor *Pasos* of San Nicolas, the Virgin, and San Ignacio are paraded on *fiestas* for the amusement, edification, and adoration of the populace.

La Coruña, except to the military man, has little worth seeing. The entrance, or *Boca del Puerto*, is defended by the castle San Anton, and the land approach by the *cortadura*. A line of fortification towards the old town is about to be turned into a glacis. Meanwhile everything necessary for real defence is wanting, and a boat's crew of Billingsgate fish-fags might surprise and take the place. La Coruña in war-time used to be a nest of privateers, who molested the chaps of the British channel, which armed steamers will in future prevent. Herrings and pilchards abound on this coast, and afford occupation to the many fishermen. Although the entrance is not very good, the port is safe and deep.

La Coruña is now easily accessible from England, viâ steamer to Vigo, and there is a talk of the steamer touching here also. The vicinity is almost virgin ground to the angler. The circuit, including Betanzos, Varmonde, Villalba, Mondoñedo, the Valles de Oro and Vivero, to Puentes de Garcia Rodriguez, includes superb trout streams; among the best are the Allones, Eume, Ladra, Miño, Lamia, Azumara, Parga, Turia, Eo, Masma, and Jubia. The map by Tomas Lopez, in the ' Esp. Sag.' (vol. xviii.), is of great use for the localities between Lugo, La Coruña, and Mondoñedo.

Ascending the heights and looking down on the quiet bay, what glorious and sad recollections crowd on the English sailor and soldier's memory. Here, in May 1588, was refitted during four weeks the Spanish *Invincible Armada*, which sailed in June out of this port after the first false start from Lisbon, to easy and immediate defeat.

The squadron consisted of 130 ships, whose tonnage amounted to 57,868, and cannons to 2630. It was manned by 19,275 sailors, and carried 8450 soldiers. They made as sure of conquering and making slaves of the English, as if they had been wild S. American savages. This Armada, which had taken 4 years to prepare, was settled in 9 days, a true 9 days' wonder. "Off Callice," writes a Spaniard, "all our castles of comfort were builded in the aire, or upon the waves of the sea." Drake, with 50 little ships, had attacked 150 of the floating monsters, and beat them just as Nelson did at St. Vincent. "In all these fights," wrote our Spaniard, "Christ showed himself alone a Lutheran." The admiral, the Duke of Medina Sidonia, during the combat "lodged himself in the bottom of the ship." He had been chosen, after the death of the M⁵·de S⁴· Cruz, simply from his high rank: *Cosas de España.* And to complete this characteristic expedition, the Duke of Parma, who was to have co-operated at Dunkirk with 35,000 men, was *hors de combat* in the nick of time: *Socorros de España.*

Thus beaten and betrayed, the Spaniard, scared by fire-ships, determined on flight—venit vidit fugit; and not venturing to repass the channel, made a circuit of Scotland; but when off the Orkneys and the Irish coast, the disabled runaways were caught in storms, when 32 more ships and 10,185 men perished. The Armada, as usual in Spanish expeditions, was so ill provided, that from 4 to 5 men died per day of hunger on board even the admiral's ship: but to such cruel shifts and such incompetent leaders have the brave people of Spain, worthy of a better fate, been always exposed; nor has the valour with which the Spanish sailors fought on this occasion ever been questioned. Medina Sidonia arrived at Santander about the end of September, "with noe more than 60 sayle oute of his whole fleete, and those very much shattered." The defeat of this Armada sunk deep in the mind of the nation, which ever sees clearer than its mis-governors; " then arose in the fleet the common brute (saying, *bruit*), that if ever they got back again, they never would meddle with the English any more." This was embodied in a pro-verb, Con todo el mundo guerra, y Paz con Inglaterra ; and it was acted upon as a state maxim, until the Bourbon and French succession; then family compacts and alliances with Buona-parte brought Spain into hostile contact with her natural and best ally, and cost her her navy and colonies. The reader may consult two curious tracts from which we have briefly quoted; viz., ' A true Discourse of the Armie which the King of Spaine,' etc., trans-lated from the French by Daniel Archdeacon : London, John Wolfe, 1588. Also ' The Copie of a Letter,' etc., of Bernardin Mendoza : bk. lr. London, J. Vantroller for Rich. Field; Septemb. 1588. All the idle tale of the *elements* having destroyed this Armada was got up to salve over the humbled pride of Philip II. ; and such too was Buonaparte's ex-planation of Trafalgar (see p. 222), for the deed was done by the English Jacks—a race not yet extinct. They heed not when the stormy winds do blow, but fight all the better, emulat-ing the elemental war; while your fair-weather foreigner is kneeling to San Telmo or Notre Dame de la Garde, and deprecating the untoward combination of the battle *and* the breeze.

Next let our soldier reader turn his eyes inland, sweeping over *Corunna*, whose name alone suggests *the* battle, the triumph, and the victor's death. This hard action was fought Jan. 16, 1809, on the heights of Elvina, behind the town. Moore arrived here on the 11th, and found no fleet, for, by the advice of others, it had been ordered to Vigo, and now could not round Cape Finisterre; it only arrived on the 14th, when the heavy artillery was em-barked, and thus a vast advantage was given to the French.

Narrow, indeed, now was Soult's escape, for had Moore not over-des-ponded, this fleet of transports might easily have brought fresh troops from Portugal, nay, it ought to have done so, for the intelligence of the real ill-condition and limited numbers of the French had long before been conveyed to Oporto, by channels to which un-fortunately no credence was given by the presumption of official ignorance. Then was lost by Sir John Craddock the nick of time, and the chance of being a Wellington : had he arrived with his brigades Soult must have been annihilated. This was one of the pos-sibilities which his sagacious master foresaw when he pretended to be ob-liged to return from Astorga.

Moore's position was bad, but from no fault of his, for with only 13,244 men he could not defend the stronger but more extended line of the outer heights against the superior numbers of the French, and he lacked his embarked artillery; he was thus obliged to oc-cupy the range nearer the town. About two in the afternoon the French, ex-ceeding in number 20,000, attacked brilliantly and with great superiority of cavalry and artillery, and were every-where most signally repulsed ; the 4th, 42nd, and 50th, under Baird, putting to flight at Elvina a whole French co-lumn commanded by Gen. Foy, whose defence was most "*feeble*" (Nap. iv. 5). Meantime, as at Vitoria, different bat-tles were going on in different parts of the ground, and at every one the foe was simultaneously beaten. La Hous-saye, the plunderer of the Escorial, Cuenca, and Toledo, next turned and fled with his dragoons, Paget riding down the enemy, and threatening their whole left; and then had Frazer ad-vanced, Soult must have had recourse to flight. The English loss amounted to 700, and that of the French exceed-ed 3000 ; as their column was riddled by our steady lines at Elvina, and for-tunately before the battle our men were supplied with fresh muskets and am-munition. Moore, like Wolfe, Abercrombie, and Nelson, lived long enough to know that the foe was defeated, and therefore, like them, died happily, having "done his duty." His last words, and the tongues of dying men enforce attention like deep harmony, were in anticipation of his posthumous calumniators; "I hope the people of England will be satisfied; I hope my country will do me justice." The despatch of Gen. Hope is one of the most simple, manly, pathetic, and beautiful compositions ever written by a soldier's pen, and the very antithesis in taste and truth to Buonaparte's bulletin. "Les Anglais," says he (Œuv. v. 383), "furent abordés franchement par la première brigade, qui *les culbuta*, et les délogea du village d'Elvina. L'ennemi culbuté de ses positions, se *retira* dans les jardins qui sont autour de la Corogne. La nuit devenant très-obscure on fut obligé de suspendre l'attaque : l'ennemi en a profité pour s'embarquer en toute hâte; nous n'avons eu d'engagés pendant le combat qu'environ 6000. Notre perte s'élève à cent hommes [*i.e.* 3000]: l'opinion des habitans du pays, et des déserteurs, est que le nombre des blessés [English] excède 2500—des 38,000 hommes que les Anglais avaient débarqués, on peut assurer qu'à peine 24,000 retourneront en Angleterre. Les régimens Anglais portant les numeros 42, 50, 52, ont été entièrement détruits. L'armée Anglaise avait débarqué plus dès 80 pièces de canon, elle n'en a pas rembarqué 12; le reste a été pris, ou perdu; et de compte fait, nous nous trouvons en possession de 60 pièces de canon Anglais." "Lord! Lord! how this world is given to lying," says the comparatively veracious Falstaff.

The *truth* was, that the embarkation took place with perfect order, and was unmolested by the worsted foe; and had the English army only then been turned against Soult, he himself must have retired, and he knew it.

The Corunnese distinguished themselves both before and after the battle. Their first step was to detain Baird and his 6000 English on board their transports from Oct. 13th to 31st, although coming to aid them against the invaders, refusing even to let them disembark without an order from Madrid; and then they never gave them, or even offered, any assistance ; so the Moorish Berbers treated their foreign allies. When Moore arrived here, the Spanish officer in charge of the powder magazines, which had been filled by the English for the use of the patriots, reported them to be *empty ;* and the truth was only accidentally discovered, when 5000 barrels found in them were exploded, and thus rescued from the enemy. See Ker Porter's letters, p. 290.

While the English remained at La Coruña, the town was safe, but no sooner were they embarked than the commander, Don Antonio Acedo, hastened on the 19th to surrender to Soult, who otherwise, from having no battering train, never could have taken the place and citadel. Soult, thus provided with Spanish cannon, turned them against *El Ferrol* on the 22nd. This important arsenal was garrisoned by 8000 men, but the governor, Fr°· Melgarejo, and his colleague Pedro Obregon surrendered also on the 26th, by which Soult obtained the stores provided by England for these patriots, and also 8 Spanish ships of the line. He was thus enabled to conquer Gallicia and invade Portugal. To complete their infamy, Acedo and Obregon became *Afrancesados*, and the latter was made French commandant of *El Ferrol*.

Turn we to better men ; and ascending to the extremity of the upper town visit the *Campo de San Carlos* and the grave of Moore, whose mourners were two hosts, his friends and foes. His requiem has been sung by Charles Wolfe, and rivals the elegy of Gray ; and where can it be read to such advantage as on this site, the "churchyard" of the Man himself ?

" Not a drum was heard, not a funeral note,
    As his corse to the rampart we hurried;
Not a soldier discharged his farewell shot
    O'er the grave where our Hero we buried.

" We buried him darkly at dead of night,
   The sods with our bayonets turning,
By the struggling moonbeam's misty light,
   And the lantern dimly burning.

" No useless coffin enclosed his breast,
   Not in a sheet or shroud we wound him,
But he lay like a warrior taking his rest,
   With his martial cloak around him.

" Few and short were the prayers we said,
   And we spoke not a word of sorrow; [dead,
But we stedfastly gazed on the face that was
   And we bitterly thought of the morrow.

" We thought, as we hollowed his narrow bed,
   And smoothed down his lonely pillow,
That the foe and the stranger would tread
   o'er his head,
And we far away on the billow.

" Lightly they'll talk of the spirit that's gone,
   And o'er his cold ashes upbraid him :—
But little he'll reck, if they let him sleep on
In the grave where a Briton has laid him.

" But half of our heavy task was done, [ing,
   When the clock struck the hour for retir-
And we heard the distant and random gun
   That the foe was sullenly firing.

" Slowly and sadly we laid him down,
   From the field of his fame fresh and gory;
But we carv'd not a line, and we rais'd not a
   stone,
But we left him alone in his glory."

Moore was interred by a party of the 9th on the ramparts, but the body was afterwards removed by the Marquis Romana to its present resting-place, and a monument was raised, the expense being defrayed by the British Government; this was soon neglected by the Corunnese, and became a temple to Cloacina Gallega. In 1824 it was restored and enclosed by our consul Mr. Bartlett, also at our government's order and expense, as a stone within the barrier records: the place was again soon bemired by the Corunnese, and so continued until 1839, when Gen. Mazaredo, who had lived much in England, raised a subscription among the English, cleansed and repaired the tomb, and planted the ground for a public *Alameda*, having had the greatest difficulty to induce the *Xefe-politico* to give his consent; now a sentry is placed here, and the walk is a fashionable lounge: read Mazaredo's inscription in the summer-house.

Napier (iv. 5), in his ultra-advocacy of Soult, says, that " He, with a noble feeling of respect for Moore's valour, raised a monument to his memory ;" now what say even the French themselves :—"The marshal being informed of the spot where Gen. Moore had been killed, caused an inscription to be cut on the adjoining rock to record that event, and the victory *gained* by the French army " (Le Noble, 45). In justice to his Grace of Dalmatia, Soult, who knew how handsomely he himself had been *beaten*, said nothing about this *victory*, as his inscription simply ran, " Hic cecidit Joannes Moore, dux exercitus, in pugna, Jan. xvi. 1809 ; contra Gallos a duce Dalmatiæ ductos" (Mald. ii. 101).

How long even this monument to Moore will remain is now uncertain. Already the " *Dos Amigos,*" two afrancesado bagsmen from Madrid, in their recent Viage, p. 44, have wished to efface the inscription, because it *ofende algun tanto la delicadeza Española ;* that delicacy which made a dunghill of a sepulchre raised and paid for by others, to a brave ally who died fighting for the independence of Spain.

El Ferrol should by all means be visited from La Coruña. The land route is about 9½ L.; after Betanzos it coasts the *Ensenada de Sada* by a rough road, with fine views over sea and land. Then the Eume is crossed, and afterwards the Jubia at Neda. *El Ferrol* lies opposite to the r. higher up to the l. At Jubia is a considerable copperwork establishment, founded by Eugenio Isquierdo. The better plan, however, is to cross over from La Coruña, from whence it lies distant about 4 L. N. E., in the steamer (when there is one) in about two hours. Formerly this was very troublesome to sailing boats, from the swell on this ironbound coast, especially near the rock *La Peña de la Marola ;* hence the proverb, " Quien *pasa la Marola, pasa la Mar toda.*" On entering the landlocked channel between *Monte Faro* to the r., and *Cabo Prioriño* to the l., the glorious situation of this harbour scooped out by nature is very striking, while art has defended the narrow entrance by the two castles of San Felipe and Palma. The *Posada de San Felipe* is tolerable. The name of *El Ferrol* is derived from an ancient *farol* or light; originally it was a mere fishing town, and was not wanted for marine purposes or as an arsenal, since the Spaniards, while possessed of Italy and the Low Countries, procured their artillery from Milan, and their fleets, ready built and rigged, from Holland. Hemp they bought of Russia, having in Granada the finest in the world; copper from the Swedes and Germans, having themselves Rio tinto; lead from England, having themselves Berja; and sail-cloth from France (Bourgoin, ii. 24).

The Spanish Bourbons, when deprived of these foreign resources, endeavoured to replace them by native industry. Charles III., who never forgave the English for having sailed into Naples, and who added to that feeling all his family's fear and hatred, selected this spot, for which nature had done so much, and created what then was the finest naval arsenal in the world; it was destined exclusively for the royal navy; see the careful details in Miñano, iv. supp. 276, with the good map by Col. Angel, del Arenal. The landside was fortified in 1769-74 with a wall on which 200 cannon might be mounted, and which now are not. The new town was next built between the old one and the planted *Esteiro;* the one is all irregular, the other a parallelogram of 7 streets in width by 9 in length, intersecting each other at r. angles; it has 2 square plazas, by name *La de Dolores* and *La del Carmen.* In this, Gen. Abadia erected in 1812 a fountain in honour of one Cosme Churruca, killed at Trafalgar. The pleasant public Alameda lies between the new town and the *Astillero* or gigantic dock-yard. Here is the *Parroquia San Julian,* rebuilt in 1772. We enter the dock-yard or *Darsena* at the *Puerta del*

Parque; to the r. is the Doric *Sala de las Armas.* The dock-yard is divided into a smaller outward, and a larger inward portion, the whole space exceeding 115,000 square yards. Behind the inner dock or *dique,* are the dwellings of the operatives, and in the N. angle are the founderies, ropewalks, and magazines, now full of nothingness; but throughout, the grandeur of conception, style of execution, and finish of masonry is truly Roman. Passing out of the *Puerta del dique,* to the r. is the *Esteiro,* the hospital, the arsenals *Carranza* and *Carragon* for timber, the *Presidio* or prison for the convicts, and the *Gradasde Construccion,* or building slips. Everything is on a colossal scale, but the clay-footed giant now wants vitality. Don Angel triumphantly alludes to the comparative smallness of Portsmouth and Plymouth; yet from those poor little docks went forth those poor little ships with which Nelson made short work à la Drake with his "old acquaintances," the gigantic three-deckers of imposing *El Ferrol.*

The authorities are jealous in admitting strangers to see their beggarly empty boxes. Because Mr. Pitt was here in 1776, they think that every gaping Englishman is his *double,* and coming to take plans to capture this arsenal, the terror of our navy. *El Ferrol,* however dilapidated, still retains what nature has done for it, a land-locked bay ; while Gijon can supply coal, the forests of Asturias timber, and Cargadelos iron for cannon and shot. The water, especially that of *La Grana,* is delicious, while that in the *Darsena* is free from the *teredo navalis,* the Carcoma; but what can cure the misgovernment of Spain, dry-rotten to the core? El Ferrol, like *La Carruca* and *Cartagena* (see pp. 217, 414), is a sad emblem of Spain herself; the population has dwindled down to some 13,000, and is poverty-stricken and unemployed; just now there is much talk of restoring the navy of Spain to its former splendour; mean-

2 F 3

while the immense bay is almost without a sail, the basins and magazines empty, a rotten hull or two float like carcases, whose sailors, stores, and life are wanting. It is the silence and decay of the church-yard, not the bustle and vigour of the dock-yard, in which, in 1760, 50,000 men toiled, and where, in 1752, 55 men-of-war floated. France, which induced Spain to *force* a navy at the cost of millions, has since urged her dupe into ruin at Cape St. Vincent, while at Trafalgar (as at Vigo) she deserted her in the hour of need.

The navy of Spain, in 1793, consisted of 204 vessels, 76 of which were line of battle ships, 56 being in commission; of these three only now remain, two of which, *El Heroe* and *El Guerrero*, are at this place, and little better than wrecks. But Spain (Catalonia excepted, which is not Spain) never was really a naval power, for the confinement of a ship, like that in a garrison fortress, is hateful, as the Duke says (Disp. May 3, 1812), to their nomade wandering habits.

The Ferrol was menaced August 25, 1802, by Adm. Walker and Gen. Pulteney. This peddling paltry expedition, sent out with no precise object, failed, like that of Antwerp, from the combined indecision of the leaders. Had they sailed boldly up to the Ferrol, the Gallicians were only waiting to surrender, being, as usual, absolutely without means of defence either by sea or land. But the "*surf was high*," as at the failure at Tarragona, and the barometer gave signs of untoward events; so with the mercury fell the resolution of the chiefs, and the fleet departed *re infectâ*. Now the Ferrolese are all heroes, and the failures of others are imputed to them as merits; the "*Bizarria* of a *puñado* of Spaniards baffled 12,000 to 15,000 English," says Paez (i. 302). El Ferrol could and would no more have resisted English sailors than it did French soldiers. When Ney (July 22, 1809) evacuated it, after Soult's defeat at Oporto, he destroyed the stores, and disabled the defences.

Capt. Hotham landed on the 26th with a handful of seamen, and compelled the Spanish garrison, allies of the French, to surrender.

Those who are going from La Coruña to Aviles and Oviedo have the choice of two routes; one, which is the shortest, passes from El Ferrol to Mondoñedo.

ROUTE LXXXI.—EL FERROL TO MONDOÑEDO.

Jubia	1	
Espinaredo	4	5
Lousada	3	8
Mondoñedo	5	13

After *Jubia*, where there is a copperwork establishment, the river of the same name is crossed, and then, after *Espinaredo*, the Eume at the *Puente de Garcia Rodriguez :* a dreary wild *dehesa* or *gándara* leads to the crystal Ladra, which is crossed before reaching *Lousada ;* after which the country becomes more hilly (for Mondoñedo, see R. lxxxix.). This is the shortest line; but the route is intricate, and the accommodation bad; however, to the angler nothing can be more favourable.

The other route makes a circuit by *Betanzos* (see p. 651), whence after crossing the Mandeo, which is kept to the l., we reach *Labrada* 4 L.; and thence over a dreary track, part moor, part swamp, passing tributaries of the Ladra to that sweet trout stream itself, after traversing which is *Villalba*, about 3 L., where sleep, and as there is a decent *Posada*, it might be made the head-quarters of a fisherman. The antiquarian will observe a curious old tower in the walls. Next day cross a *cuesta* which divides the basins of the Ladra from those of the Tamboga and Lama, tributaries of the Miño, and all made for Izaak Walton. N.B. Take a local guide.

LA CORUÑA TO SANTIAGO.

The corner of Gallicia between La Coruña, Vigo, and Orense is interesting to the reader of Froissart, as being the scene of the expedition in 1386, when John of Gaunt, "time-honoured

Lancaster," landed, claiming the crown of Castile in right of his wife, daughter of Don Pedro. He was three days marching the 9½ L. to Santiago, for the hardships of Spain remain unchanged, and such as Moore found this district in our times did he do then. Oh *dura* tellus Iberiæ! exclaimed the ancients, where the harsh, hard, and arid prevail in climate, soil, and man, where so little is tender, delicate, or gentle. Well did Froissart then describe thee as "pas douce terre, ni aimable à chevaucher ni à travailler." The city of Santiago surrendered at once to the English, as it did in our times to the French. John of Gaunt resided in it during the *guerrilla* carried on by his men-at-arms, he himself ingloriously idling away his time with his court and ladies like a Sardanapalus. He lost out of 5000 men more than half, without striking one blow, who perished from sickness and want in hungry Spain, where the commissariat is ever *the* difficulty, even in time of peace. He, however, accomplished part of his object by marrying one daughter, *Philipa*, to the King of Portugal, and the other, *Constanza*, to the son and heir of John of Castile. Such, however, were the fears and suspicions of the Spaniards that they refused after this to allow even English pilgrims to visit Compostella (Mariana, xviii. 12). Don Pedro had ceded part of these N.W. provinces to the Black Prince, and when the French enabled Enrique II. to murder his brother, they stipulated that no Englishman whatever should enter Spain without permission from the King of France. So long has the Peninsula been the bone of contention and battle-field between the two great rivals of Europe.

ROUTE LXXXII.—LA CORUÑA TO SANTIAGO.

Palabea	. . . . .	1	
Carral	. . . . .	2	.. 3
Leira	. . . . .	2	.. 5
Siqueiro	. . . . .	3	.. 8
Santiago	. . . . .	1½	.. 9½

The diligence, bad and dear as it is (that of Jose Pou is the least bad), is the best mode of performing this uninteresting route, which is done in from six to seven hours. After 1 L. of tolerably cultivated land, a long hill is ascended, and then the dreary moor-like country continues to Santiago, which, like Madrid, has neither gardens nor inclosures to mark the vicinity of a capital, and holy city of pilgrimage.

Those proceeding from Lugo to the Asturias, may either reach Santiago by La Coruña, or ride across the country direct. There are two routes, and both equally bad; however, there is excellent fishing in the Ulla below Mellid.

ROUTE LXXXIII.—LUGO TO SANTIAGO.

San Miguel de Bocorrin.	2		
Puente ferreira	. . .	2	.. 4
Mellid	. . . . .	3	.. 7
Arzua	. . . . .	2	.. 9
San Miguel de Salceda .	2	.. 11
Omenal	. . . . .	2	.. 13
Santiago	. . . . .	2	.. 15

The other, which is equally bad, is even a better line for the angler. The distance is about the same; the leagues, although we have twice ridden every one of them, are guess-work, and very long.

ROUTE LXXXIV.—LUGO TO SANTIAGO.

Santa Eulalia	. . .	2½	
Carvajal	. . . . .	2½	.. 5
Sobrado	. . . . .	2	.. 7
Buy muerto	. . . .	2	.. 9
San Gregorio	. . .	2	.. 11
San Marcos	. . .	3½	.. 14½
Santiago	. . . . .	½	.. 15

After crossing the Miño by a noble bridge, ascend the chesnut-clad heights, and look back on the grand view of Lugo, with its cathedral and long lines of turreted walls. Hence over swamps, moors, rivers, and detestable roads, to *Sobrado*, situated on the fine trout-stream the Tambre. The village clusters round a Bernardine convent, once lord of all around. The noble domain is enclosed with tower-guarded walls; everything is in contrast with the lowly village, but the fat and portly monks are gone. The, edifice was pillaged and injured by the French, but was repaired in 1832. The principal facade is Doric. The grand *patio* is unfinished. The over-charged ornate front of the chapel, with fluted pillars and lozenge-enriched pilasters, is in imitation of that of the Lugo cathedral, and in the bad taste of 1676. Under the dark *coro* are some fine tombs of recumbent warriors in twisted mail, of the Ulloa family, 1465. The court-yard and stabling are spacious. This convent was founded in 950, and originally for both sexes: an arrangement " fit as the nun's lip to the friar's mouth." Hence a 9 hours' ride over a desolate country to Santiago; the road is however better, having been smoothed for the convenience of the holy brotherhood. Midway some wild moors lead to *Sⁿ. Gregorio*, a hermitage which, with its clump of storm-stunted firs, is seen from afar. The shooting here is excellent. Next we reach *San Marcos*, thus correctly described by the old pilgrim in Purchas, " Upon a hill hit stondez on hee, where Sent Jamez ferst schalt thou see," and from hence still the dark granite towers of Santiago first catch the wayworn traveller's eye, and the deep-mouthed tolling bells salute his ear. It is indeed a grand and impressive sight. To the r. rises the barren rocky *Monte Dalmatico*, while the green slope to the l. is crowned with the convent Belvis, and beyond stretch undulating hills and distant mountains; here the pilgrim of yore uncovered and proceeded, the very penitent, on his knees, singing hymns up to the holy city's gates. There droves of mendicants snuff the stranger's arrival, and congratulate him on his escape from the pains and perils of Gallician travel, and beg charity for the sake of his deliverer, the great apostle, concluding, supposing they get anything, with prayers for the donor's safe return to his home and wife; " may Santiago give you health and defend you from all enemies" (see post, p. 667).

SANTIAGO : the best inns are those of *La Viscaina*, a respectable Basque widow in La Rua Nueva, it is clean and orderly; and *La Posada de Martin Morena* en las Cases Reales. The Maragatos put up in the *Rua de San Pedro*. They go to Valladolid in about 12, and to Madrid in 15 days; and those who, having landed at Vigo, propose a riding tour, may safely trust them with the conveyance of any heavy baggage (see p. 593).

Rey Romero (King Pilgrim), 16, Cᵉ· de la Azabacheria, is a good bookseller for those about to start on Spanish travel.

The town of Santiago is so named after St. James the Elder; it is also called *Compostella*, Campus Stellæ, because a star pointed out where his body was concealed. Those who wish at once to hurry to sight-seeing may pass on to p. 668, but it is impossible to understand many important portions of Spanish fine art and religious character, without an acquaintance with the history of this St. George of the Peninsula, which has never been fully detailed to English readers.

The Spanish legend of St. James the Elder, or of "Santiago, as," says Southey, " he may more properly be called in his *mythological* history," when not purely Pagan, is Mahomedan. The Gotho-Spanish clergy adapted these matters from the ancients and the Moslem, just as Mahomet formed his creed from the Old and New Testament, making such alterations as best suited the peculiar character and climate of their people and country; hence the success, and their still existing hold over their followers.

The custom of choosing a tutelar over kingdoms and cities prevailed all over the ancient world, and when by the advice of Gregory the Great the Pagan stock in trade was taken by its successor into the Roman Ca-

tholic firm, the names being merely
changed, the system of patron-saints
was too inveterate to be abandoned.
The Spaniards contend, without a
shadow of real evidence, that St. Peter,
St. Paul, and St. James, came all
three to the Peninsula immediately
after the crucifixion. Rome, however, having monopolized the two
former for her tutelars, Spain was
obliged to take the latter. The making
his burial-place a place of pilgrimage
was next borrowed from the East, and
was one of the results of Sᵗ. Helena's
invention (and a rare one it was) of the
cross at Jerusalem in 298. The principle of visiting a sacred spot was too
inspiring to be overlooked by Mahomet, when he adapted Christianity
to Arabian habits, and pilgrimage became one of the four precepts of his
new creed, Mecca being selected in
order to favour his native town by
this rich influx. The ill-usage of the
Christian pilgrims led to the crusades,
in which Spaniards took little part;
nay, they were forbidden to do so by
the Pope, because they had the infidel
actually on their own soil. Yet Spaniard and Moor felt the spirit-stirring
effect of a particular holy spot, and
determined on having a counterpart
Jerusalem and Mecca in the Peninsula
itself. The Spanish Moors were accordingly absolved by their clergy
from the necessity of going to Mecca,
which being in possession of the Kalif
of the East, was inaccessible to the
subjects of his rival in the West; and
Cordova being the capital of his new
state was chosen by Abdu-r-rahman,
who, like Mahomet, wished to enrich
his new city; and a visit to the *Ceca*,
where some of the bones of Mahomet
were pretended to be preserved, was
declared to be in every respect equivalent to a pilgrimage to Mecca.(see
p. 299).

Thereupon the imitating Spaniards,
who could not go to Jerusalem, set up
their local substitute; they chose their
mountain capital, where they, too, said
their prophet was buried: thus the

sepulchre at Compostella represented
alike those of Jerusalem and Mecca.
The Arragonese, whose kingdom was
then independent, chose for their *Ceca*
their capital Zaragoza, where they said
the Virgin descended from heaven on
a visit to Santiago; and the religious
duty and saving merits of pilgrimage
became as much a parcel of the orthodox Spaniard's creed as it was of
the infidels, whom they always fought
against with a weapon borrowed from
their own armoury (see also p. 120).
As the Moors had established soldier-
monks or *Rábitos* to guard their fron-
tiers and protect their pilgrims, so the
next imitation of the Spaniards was
the institution of similar military religious orders, of which that of Santiago
became the chief. Founded in 1158
by Fernando II. of Leon, it soon, like
that of the Templars, from being poor
and humble, became rich, proud, and
powerful, insomuch that *El Maestre
de Santiago*, in the early Spanish annals,
figures almost as a rival to the monarch. When Granada was conquered their assistance was no longer
needed, and Isabella, by bestowing
the grand-mastership on Ferdinand,
absorbed the dreaded wealth and power
of the order into the crown, without
having recourse to the perfidy and
murders by which Philippe le Bel
suppressed the Templars in France.

This was now accomplished without
difficulty, for these *corporate* bodies
lacked the security of *private* properties, which every one is interested
in upholding. They were hated by
the *clergy*, because rivals and independent brotherhoods, half priest, half
soldier, without being either one or the
other, although assuming the most
offensive privileges of both. The
people also stood aloof, for they saw in
the members only proud knights, who
scorned to interchange with them the
kindly offices of the poor monks; while
the *statesman*, from knowing that the
substance was no longer wanted, held
the order to be both obsolete and dangerous. All parties, therefore, aided

Ferdinand, who was greedy of gold, and Isabella, who was determined to be really a queen, and the order virtually ceased to exist, save as conferring a badge on nobles and courtiers.

But in the mediæval period it was a reality, as then a genuine lively faith existed in both Moor and Spaniard; each grasped the legend of their champion prophet as firmly as they did the sword by which it was to be defended and propagated. Proud towards men, these warriors bowed to the priest, in whom they saw the ministers of their tutelar, and their faith sanctified and ennobled such obedience: both equally fanatical, fought believing that they were backed by their tutelars: this confidence went far; to realise victory, possunt quia posse videntur, and especially with the Spaniard, who has always been disposed to depend on others; in the critical moment of need, he folds his arms and clamours for supernatural assistance; thus the Iberians invoked their Netos, and afterwards prayed to the Phœnician Hercules. All this is classical and Oriental: Castor and Pollux fought visibly for the Romans at Regillum (Cic. 'N.D.' ii. 2); Mahomet appeared on the Orontes to overthrow Count Roger, as Santiago, mounted on his war-horse, interfered at Clavijo in 846 to crush the Moslem. There was no mention of Santiago, or his visit to Spain, or his patronage, in the time of the Goths (Sⁿ· Isidoro, 'Or.,' vii. 9), and simply because there being no Moors then to be expelled, he was not wanted.

For this Hagiography consult ' El Teatro de Santiago,' Gil. Gonzalez. Florez (E. S. iii.) has collected all the authentic facts which different infallible Popes from Leo III. have ratified. The best book is ' Historia del Apostol de Jesus Christo, Sanctiago Zebedeo, Patron y Capitan General de las Españas ;' Mauro Castellá Ferrer, fol. Mad. 1610, for this is the correct title of the apostle in Spain. The conferring military rank spoke the spirit of

the age and people when bishops rode in armour and knights in cowls, and a nation of caballeros never would have respected a footman tutelar. Accordingly Santiago, San Martin, and San Isidoro are always mounted, and represent the Fortuna Equestris of the Romans.

Froissart felt the full rank of this chief of a religious chivalry, and of a church-militant, and, therefore, like Dante, he calls St. James a Baron— Varon, Vir, a gentleman, a man emphatically, in contradiction to Homo, Hombre, or a mere mortal clod of earth. So Don Quixote speaks of him as " Don Diego," the Moor-killer, and one of the most valiant of saints. The Cids and Alonzos of Spain's dark ages at least had the common sense to choose a male tutelar to lead their armies to victory ; it was left to the enlightened Cortes of Cadiz in 1810 to nominate Sᵃ· Teresa, the crazy nun of Avila, to be the fit commandress of-the Cuestas, Blakes, and suchlike spoilt children of defeat.

According to church-authorised legends, St. James was beheaded at Jerusalem in 42, but his body was taken to Joppa, where a boat appeared " nutu dei," into which the corpse embarked itself, and sailed to Padron, which lies 4 L. below Santiago; it performed the voyage in seven days, which proves the miracle, since the modern Alexandria Steam Company can do nothing like it. It first made for Barcelona, then coasted Spain, and avoiding the delicious S. (probably because polluted by the infidel), selected this damp diocese, where the wise prelate Theodomirus, who planned the self-evident trick, resided. The body rested on a stone at Padron, which hollowed itself out, wax to receive, and marble to retain, although some contend that this stone was the vessel in which it sailed. The corpse was then removed to a cave sacred to Bacchus, and the whole affair was forgotten for nearly 800 years, when, says Florez, " Spain breathed again by the discovery of the body, which occurred after this wise :—Pelagius, a hermit, informed Theodomirus, bishop of Iria Flavia, *Padron,* that he saw heavenly lights always hovering over a certain site. It was examined, and a tomb found which contained a body, but how it was ascertained to be that of the apostle is not stated: that unimportant fact was assumed. Thereupon Alonzo el Casto built a church on the spot, and granted all the rich land round for three miles to the good bishop. In 829 the body was removed for greater security to the stronger town of Santiago, wild bulls coming by " divine inspiration," *Toros guiados divinamente,* to draw the carriage, as a delicate compliment to the tutelar of the land of Tauromachia. Riches now poured in, especially the corn-rent, said to be granted in 846 by Ramiro, to repay Santiago's services at Clavijo, where he killed single-handed 60,000 Moors to a fraction. This grant was a bushel of corn from every acre in Spain, and was called *el Voto* and *el Morion,* the votive offering of the quantity which the Capt.-General's capacious *helmet* contained. The deed, dated Calahorra 834, convicts itself of forgery (see however Mariana, vii. 13). This roguery in grain recalls that in oil of Hinckmar, who, 360 years after the right date, forged the story of the Sainte Ampoule being brought down by a dove from Heaven for St. Remy in 496 to baptize Clovis at Rheims.

This corn-rent, estimated at 200,000*l.* a-year, used to be collected by agents, although not much eventually reached Gallicia, for grains of gold and wheat stick like oil to Spanish fingers, and *Quien aceite mesura le unta las manos.* The jokes in Spain on these and other corn-collectors were many : *Quien pide por Dios, pide por dos; anda con alforjas de fraile, predicando por el saco.* This tax was abolished in 1835. When corn-rents were given to discoverers of bones, revelations never were wanting if the land was good ; hence every dis-

trict had its high place and palladium, which however tended indirectly to advance civilization, for the [convents became asylums in a rude age, since in them the lamp of learning, of the arts and religion, flickered. The duty of visiting Compostella, which, like that of a pilgrimage to Mecca, was absolutely necessary in many cases to take up an inheritance, led to the construction of roads, bridges, and hospitals,—to armed associations, which put down robbers and maintained order: thus the violence of brute force was tempered.

The scholar will see in the whole legend a poverty of invention worthy of this Bœotia of the North. " Lucida Sidera," strange constellations, eclipses, and comets, are the common signs of Pagan mythology, palmed on an age ignorant of astronomy. These star-indicated spots were always consecrated. Compare this *Compostella* with the Roman Campus Stellatus (Suet. ' Cæs.' 20). The Gallicians, however, of old, were noted for seeing supernatural illuminations, and what was more, for interpreting their import (Sil. Ital. iii. 344). Thus when the gods struck with lightning the sacred hill, gold (not bones) was sought for (Justin, xliv. 3). But ancient avarice was straightforward and unblushing : the results nevertheless were the same, and the invention of the modern priests gave them the philosopher's stone, the magnet wherewith to attract bullion.

As to marvellous transportations by sea in miraculously sent ships, Lucian, *de D. Syriis* (and Santiago too came from Syria), tells us, that the head of Osiris was carried to Byblus by water θειη ναυτιλιη, and also in seven days ; again Herodotus (iv. 152) records that Curobius was transported θειη πομπη by sea, and *also* to Spain and also through the Straits. Pausanias (vii. 5. 5), particularly names Tyre as the port whence an image (which Faber, ' Cabiri,' i. 109, says was one of Hercules) was carried by a ship conscious of its sacred cargo to Priene, and there became the object of pilgrimage; so, according to the Greeks, Cecrops sailed from Egypt in a boat of papyrus. But it would be mere pedantry to multiply instances extracted from Pagan mythology, and for every one a parallel might be found in papal practice in Spain. See, e. g. *El Cristo de Beyrut* at Valencia, and *El Cristo de Burgos.* That rocks soften on these occasions, all geologists know well. Thus the stone at Delphi, on which the Sibyl Herophile sat down, received the full impression, second only in basso-relievo to that grand stone on which Silenus reposed, and which Pausanias (i. 22. 5) was shown at Trœzene: so among the Moslem, when Mahomet ascended to Heaven, his camel's hoofs were imprinted on the rock (just as those of Castor were at Regillum, Cic. 'N. D.' iii. 5); and his own footmark is shown near Cairo, at Attar é Nebbee, and in the Sahara or sanctum of the *Haram* at Jerusalem. Such a saxeous metamorphosis was an old story even in skeptical Ovid's times (Met. i. 400).

"Saxa, *quis hoc credat?* nisi sit pro teste
    vetustas,
Ponere duritiem cœpere, suumque rigorem
Mollirique morâ."

Some antiquarians, with sad want of faith, have pronounced this stone to be only a Roman sarcophagus; if, however, people can once believe that Santiago ever came to Spain at all, all the rest is plain sailing; yet this legend, the emphatic one of Spain, is not yet disbelieved, for see Mellado's Guide, 1843, p. 275, on Santiago and his Cockle Shells; but the Phœnix of the ancients is no bad symbol of the vitality of superstitious frauds, which, however exploded for a time, rise up again from their ashes. As the inventive powers of man are limited, an old story comes round and round like the same tune in a barrel organ. There is nothing new under the sun, said the wisest of kings, il n'y a rien de nouveau, que ce que l'on ait oublié, says the cleverest of lady letter-writers. The

Pontifex maximus of old and modern Rome have alike fathomed the depths of human credulity, which loves to be deceived, and will have it so, "and the priests bear rule by their means :" Jer. v. 31.

The first cathedral built over the body was finished in 874, and consecrated May 17, 899; the city rose around it, and waxing strong, the Cordovese felt the recoil of the antagonist shrine and tutelar, even at their Ceca; whereupon Al-mansúr, dreading the crusading influence, determined on its total destruction, and in July, 997, he left Cordova on his 48th *al jihad,* or holy crusade, having also sent a fleet round to co-operate on the Duero and Miño. He advanced by Coria, and was met at Zamora by many Spanish counts, or local petty sheikhs, who with true Iberian selfishness and disunion sided with the invader, in order to secure their own safety and share in the spoil (see 'E. S.' xxxiv. 303). Al-mansúr entered Santiago Wed. Aug. 10, 997; he found it deserted, the inhabitants having fled from the merciless infidel, whose warfare was extermination; then he razed the city, sparing only the tomb of the Spaniards' *Prophet,* before which he trembled : so close was the analogy of these cognate superstitions.

Mariana (viii. 9), however, asserts that he was "dazzled by a divine splendour," and that his retiring army was visited by sickness inflicted by *La divina venganza.* Had this taken place *before* Al-mansúr sacked the town, it would have been more creditable to the miraculous powers of Spain's great tutelar. The learned Jesuit, however, dismisses this humiliating conquest in a few lines, and these contain every possible mistake in names, dates, and localities. Thus he fixes the period A.D. 993, and kills Al-mansúr, whom he calls Mohamad Alhagib, at Begalcorax in 998, whereas he died in 1002 at Medinaceli (see Index).

Shant Yakoh, the "Holy City of Jalikijah" (Gallicia), is thus described by the more accurate contemporaneous Moorish annalists (see ' Moh. D.' i. 74; ii. 193); and it affords a curious proof of the early and wide-spread effect and influence of the antagonistic tutelar and tomb on the Moors. The shrine was frequented even by those Christians who lived among the Moors, and the pilgrims brought back minute reports. "Their *Kabáh* is a colossal *idol*, which they have in the centre of the church; they swear by it, and repair to it in pilgrimage from the most distant parts, from Rome as well as from other countries, pretending that the tomb which is to be seen within the church is that of Yákob (James), one of the 12 apostles, and the most beloved of Isa (Jesus): may the blessing of God and salutation be on him and on our prophet!" "They say that the Moslems found no living soul at Santiago except an old monk who was sitting on the tomb of St. James, who being interrogated by Al-mansúr as to himself, and what he was doing in that spot, he answered, I am a familiar of St. James, upon which Al-mansúr ordered that no harm should be done unto him." The Moslem respected the *Faquir* monk, in whom he saw a devotee borrowed from his own Caaba of Mecca. His great object was to destroy the idols of the polytheist Spaniards, as the uncompromising Deism of the Hebrew, and his abhorrence for graven images, formed the essence of Islamism. Al-mansúr purified the temples according to the Jewish law (Duet. vii. 5), and exactly as the early Christians in the 4th century had treated the symbols of Paganism. Thus, by a strange fate, the followers of the false prophet trod in the steps of both Testaments, while Christianity, corrupted by Rome, was remodelling and renewing those very Pagan abominations which the old and new law equally forbade.

Al-mansúr returned to Cordova laden with spoil. The bells of the cathedral of Santiago were conveyed to Cordova on the shoulders of Christian captives, and hung up reversed as lamps in the

Great Mezquita, where they remained until 1236, when St. Ferd. restored them, sending them back on the shoulders of Moorish prisoners. Al-mansúr is said to have fed his horse out of the still existing porphyry font in the cathedral, but the barb, reply the Spaniards, burst and died. Possibly, coming from Cordova, the change of diet had affected his condition, and certainly we ourselves nearly lost our superb *haca Cordovesa* from the "hay and oats" of Gallicia.

Al-mansúr could not find the body of Santiago, at which some will not be surprised; however the soundest local divines contend that the Captain-General surrounded himself when in danger with an obfuscation of his own making, like the cuttle-fish, or the Lord Admiral of the Invincible Armada (see p. 653); and to this day no one knows exactly where the bones are deposited: de non apparentibus et non existentibus eadem est lex. *It is said* that Gelmirez built them into the foundations of his new cathedral, in order that they never might be pried into by the *impertinente curioso*, or removed by the enemy. Thus it was forbidden among the Romans to reveal even the name of Rome's tutelar, lest the foe, by greater bribes, or by violence, might induce the patron to prove false. The remains of Hercules were also *said* to be buried in his temple at Gades, but no one knew where. However, Santiago *lies* somewhere, for he was heard clashing his arms when Buonaparte invaded Spain (see p. 609); so, before the battle of Leuctra, Herculis fano arma sonuerunt (Cic. *de Div.* i. 34), so the war-horse neighs at the trumpet's sound. The Captain-General, valiant at Clavijo, had already given up active service in 997, and it could not be expected that such an invalided veteran should put on, like old Priam, arma diu senior desueta, and turn out of his comfortable resting-place to oppose Soult 812 years afterwards. After all it is just possible that the veritable Santiago is not buried at

Compostella, for as the Coruñese claimed a duplicate body of Geryon, to the indignation of the Gaditanians, so the priests of S⁺· Sernin at Toulouse, among 7 bodies of the 12 apostles, said that Santiago's was one ; and when we remember the triumph of Soult at Santiago and his trouncing at Toulouse, it is difficult not to think that the real Simon Pure is buried at S⁺· Sernin, and helped our Duke.

Be this as it may, for non nobis talem est componere litem, all Spanish divines lose temper whenever this legend is questioned ; volumes of controversy have been written, and the evidence thus summed up :—*Primo*, The *veneras* or scallop shells found at Clavijo, prove that they were dropt there by Santiago, in killing 60,000 Moors. *Secundo*, If the Virgin descended from Heaven at Zaragoza to visit Santiago, of which there can be no doubt, it follows that Santiago must have been at Zaragoza. However the honest Jesuit Mariana (vii. 10) thinks no proof at all necessary, because so great an event never could have been believed at first without sufficient evidence ; while Morales concludes that "none but a heretic could doubt a fact which no man can dare to deny ;" be that as it may, the Pope soon became jealous of this assumed elevation, which the sons of Zebedee excited even while alive (Mark x. 41); and Baronius resented pretensions which rivalled those of St. Peter, and were pretty much as unfounded. Accordingly Clement VIII. altered the Calendar of Pius V., and threw a doubt on the whole visit, whereat the whole Peninsula took alarm (see M'Crie's excellent 'Reformation in Spain,' p. 5). The Pontiff was assailed with such irresistible arguments, that his virtue, like Danäe's, gave way, and the affair was thus compromised in the Papal record : "Divus Jacobus mox Hispaniam adisse, et aliquos discipulos ad fidem convertisse apud Hispanos receptum esse affirmatur." This would not do ;

and Urban VIII. in 1625, being "refreshed" with golden opinions, restored Santiago to all his Spanish honours.

The see, now an archbishopric, was formerly suffragan to the metropolitan Merida, at that time in partibus infidelium. It was elevated in 1120 by the management of Diego Gelmirez, a partisan of Queen Urraca, who prevailed on her husband Ramon to intercede with his brother Pope Calixtus II. Diego, the first primate, presided 39 years, and was the true founder of the cathedral ; and although the people rose against him and Urraca, he was the real king during that troubled period when Urraca was false to him and to every one else. There is a curious Latin contemporary history, called 'La Compostellana,' which was written by two of his canons, Munio Hugo and Giraldo ; it is given at length in 'E. S.' xx., and none can understand this period without reading it. The city and chapter of Toledo opposed the elevation of a rival Santiago, for as in the systems of Mahomet and the imitating Spaniard, religion went hand in hand with commerce and profit, as it had since the days of the Phœnicians. A relic or shrine attracted rich strangers, while its sanctity awed robbers, and shed security over wealthy merchants ; hence an eternal bickering between places of established holiness and commerce, and any upstart competitors: as Medina hated Mecca, so Toledo hated Santiago.

But Gelmirez was a cunning prelate, and well knew how to carry his point ; he put Santiago's images and plate into the crucible, and sent the ingots to the Pope. Such was the advice given by the Sibyl to the Phocæans, to "plough with a silver plough ;" and they too, in obedience, converted their holy vessels of precious metal into unconsecrated cash, and conquered. He remitted the cash to Rome (where no heresy ever was more abominable than the non-payment of Peter's pence, for, no penny no paternoster), by means of pilgrims, who received from his Holiness a number of indulgences proportioned to the sums which they smuggled through Arragon and Catalonia, then independent and hostile kingdoms, and the "dens," say these historians, " not of thieves, but of devils," for Spain in those unhappy times resembled the Oriental insecurity of Deborah's age, " when the highways were unoccupied, and travellers walked through the byways."

Following the example of the Pagan priests of the temple of Hercules at Gades, Gelmirez now extolled the virtues of making a visit and an offering to the new tutelar at Santiago. The patron saint became *el* santo, *the* saint par excellence, as Antonio at Padua is *il* santo. He never turned a deaf ear to those pilgrims who came with money in their sacks : " exaudit quos non audit et ipse Deus !" and great was the stream of wealthy guilt which poured in ; kings gave gold, and even paupers their mites. Thus all the capital expended by Gelmirez at Rome in establishing the machinery was reimbursed, and a clear income obtained; the roads of Christendom were so thronged, that Dante exclaims (Par. xxv. 17)—

" Mira mira ecco il *Barone*
Per cui laggiu si visita Galizia!"

At the marriage of our Edward I., in 1254, with Leonora, sister of Alonzo el Sabio, a protection to English pilgrims was stipulated for; but they came in such numbers as to alarm the French, insomuch that when Enrique II. was enabled by them to dethrone Don Pedro, he was compelled by his allies to prevent any English whatever entering Spain without the French king's permission. The capture of Santiago by John of Gaunt increased the difficulties, by rousing the suspicions of Spain also. The numbers in the 15th century were also great. Rymer (x. xi.) mentions 916 licences granted to English in 1428, and 2460 in 1434.

But the pilgrimage to Compostella began to fall off after the Reforma-

tion ; then, according to Molina, " the damned doctrines of the accursed Luther diminished the numbers of Germans and *wealthy* English." The injurious effect of the pilgrimage on public morals in Gallicia was exactly such as Burckhardt found at Mecca; it fostered a vagrant, idle, mendicant life; nothing could be more disorderly than the scenes at the tomb itself; the habit of pilgrims, once the garb of piety, became that of rogues (see Ricote's account in Don Quixote). It was at last prohibited in Spain, except under regulations. But smaller pilgrimages in Spain, as among the Moslems, are still universally prevalent; every district has its miracle-shrine and high place. These combine, in an uncommercial and unsocial country, a little amusement with devotion and business (see p. 121). The pilgrims, like beggars in an Irish cabin, were once welcome to a " bite and sup," as they were itinerant gossips, who brought news in an age when there were no post-offices and broad sheets; now they are unpopular even at Santiago, since they bring no grist to the mill, but take everything, and contribute nothing ; they are particularly hated in *Ventas,* those unchristian places, from whence even the rich are sent away empty; hence the proverb, *Los peregrinos, muchas posadas y pocos amigos.*

A residence in holy places has a tendency to materialize the spiritual, and to render the ceremonial professional and mechanical. Thus at Santiago, as at Mecca, the citizens are less solicitous about their "lord of the apostles," than those are who come from afar; as at Rome, those who live on the spot have been let behind the scenes, and familiarity breeds contempt. They are, as at all places of periodical visit ancient or modern, chiefly thinking how they can make the best of the "*season,*" how they can profit most from the *fresh* enthusiasm of the stranger; and as he never will come back again, they covet his cash more than his favourable recollections.

Accordingly the callous indigines turn a deaf ear to the beggar who requests a copper for Santiago's sake, he gets nothing from the natives but a dry— *perdone Vmd. por Dios, Hermano!* Therefore the shrewd mendicant tribe avoid them, and smell a strange pilgrim, for whom even the blind are on a look-out, ere he descends the hill of Sⁿ· Marcos; he enters the holy city, attended by a suite hoarse with damp and importunity—*quære peregrinum, vicinia rauca* reclamat. For Spanish beggars, see p. 171.

SANTIAGO, although much shorn of its former religious and civil dignities, is still the see of an archbishop, with a cathedral, 2 collegiate, and 15 parish churches. Its numerous convents were plundered and desecrated by the invaders in 1809, and since have been suppressed: built for monks, and fit for nothing else, they now remain like untenanted, rifled sepulchres going to ruin, and adding to the melancholy appearance of this melancholy town, on which the Levitical character is still deeply impressed, notwithstanding the Reformation, by withdrawing the rich English and German pilgrims, and the French Revolution, by sapping not only the buildings of religion, but the very principle, have dried up the pactolian streams of offerings and legacies.

The removal of the captain-general and the *audiencia* to La Coruña, a blow dealt by the liberals against a *priest-ridden* city, has completed the impoverishment, by taking away the military, the legal profession, and clients. No wonder that the two cities hate each other with more than the usual Spanish detestation of a neighbour. This measure was alike uncalled-for and injudicious, since La Coruña possesses no single advantage over Santiago, which, besides the *religio loci*, abounds in noble and suitable edifices. The university alone remains, which has a good library, and is much frequented by Gallician students.

Santiago is built on an uneven, irregular site, thus the convent of San

Francisco lies almost in a hole: the cathedral occupies the heart of the city, and indeed it was the origin of its life; from this centre many veins of streets diverge, and the tutelar's tomb may be compared to a spider in the middle of its web, catching strange and foolish flies. Santiago itself is damp, cold, and gloomy-looking. It is full of arcades, fountains, and scallop shells, and has a sombre look, from the effect of humidity on its granite materials. From the constant rain this holy city is irreverently called *El orinal de España*, therefore every body carries an umbrella : the peasants add also a stick, for their courage is not dampt, and they love broils as if their patron had been St. Patrick. The rivulets Sar and Sarela, better known as the toad streams, *Los rios de los Sapos*, flow to the N.W. The best streets run parallel to each other, such as *La rua nueva* and *La rua del villar*. The wet weather, however disagreeable to those coming from the adust Castiles, is favourable to vegetable productions, and the clouds drop fatness; in consequence the town is cheap and well supplied with fruit, among which the Urraca pear is delicious; the sea and river fish, especially trout, is excellent, and here we find fresh butter, a luxury rare in the central and warmer provinces.

The situation of Santiago is very picturesque: for general views ascend the cathedral tower, taking up the good map of the town by Juan Freyre; walk up to the *Monte de la Almaziza* to the E. near the quarries, and looking over *Sᵃ· Clara*, it commands a noble view ; saunter also to the *Alameda de Sᵃ· Susana*, going out at the *Puerta Fajera*, on to the *Campo de Feria*, and thence to the *Crucero del Gayo*, and if you have time up to the *Monte Pedroso*, from whence the panorama is as extensive as beautiful.

Of course the cathedral is the grand object of every pilgrim to Compostella : first let him examine the exterior (for the interior go to p. 673); each of its four fronts looks on to an open plaza; the largest of these lies to the W., or the grand entrance; it is called *El Mayor,* or *El Real,* and is really royal.

The first cathedral was commenced in the 9th century by Sisnandus, when Alonzo III. and Ximena gave the site, and the materials of destroyed mosques. This cathedral was razed to the ground by Al-Mansûr; but in the 11th century Bermudo II. and the Bp. Cresonio restored it, and erected strong towers against the Moors and Normans. Gelmirez in 1082 rebuilt the pile, which was completed in 1128. The primitive character has been injured by subsequent alterations; one singularity is, that most of these have been built up against the original walls ; thus the old edifice is as it were encased, and accordingly is well preserved from the effects of weather in this damp climate.

The grand façade is quite modern, and is placed between two overcharged towers, which terminate in pepper-box cupolas, but which are not unsightly : the churrigueresque entrance is adorned with the statue of the tutelar, before which kings are kneeling; although the work looks older from the action of moisture, all this was only raised in 1738, by Fernando Casas y Noboa, whose original designs are to be seen in the cathedral ; here damp and mosses, which are so much wanted in the dry South, have tinted the already sober granite. To the r. rise the square towers of the cloister, with pyramidical tops, and a long upper row of arcaded windows. These grand cloisters, simple and serious in the inside, were built in 1533 by Fonseca, afterwards Archbp. of Toledo ; his library was placed in a noble suite of rooms above them : here also are the *oficinas,* or offices of the cathedral ; to the l. of the portal is the gloomy simple palace of the prelate. On the N. side of this Plaza is the *Hospicio de los Reyes,* the hospital for pilgrims, built for Ferd. and Isab. by Henrique de Egas in 1504. This *was* one of the finest establishments of the

age, and Molina mentions in 1551, that there were seldom less than 200 patients ; hardships on journey, contagious disease, and religious madness peopled these dwellings, which, unknown to the ancients, were first founded in 1050 by Godfrey of Bouillon, for the use of pilgrims to Jerusalem. Many infirm persons went purposely to Santiago, in order to die there with comfort, just as the Hindoos do to Benares, believing that the patron would take them to heaven with him at the resurrection. This notion was borrowed alike from Mecca, and from Jugannât-ha, " the *captain-general of the universe,*" whose region, consecrated to death, is strewed with pilgrims' bones; but superstitions of purely human invention must necessarily reproduce themselves.

The hospital is a grand building, but badly conducted, as since the appropriation of church revenues, it was much impoverished by losing a revenue of tithes. It is square in form, and divided into four quadrangles, with a chapel in the centre, and so contrived that the patients in the different stories can all see the service performed. The elaborate portal is enriched with saints, pilgrims, chainwork under the cornice, and the badges of Ferd. and Isab. Two of the patios have arches and delicate Gothic work : observe a fountain gushing into a tazza from four masks. The chapel is plain, but the portion within the railing is unequalled in Santiago for delicacy and richness of work ; the roof springs from four arches with Gothic niches and statues. The other two patios are of later date, and in the Doric style; in the entrance hall are bad portraits of Ferd. and Isab.

The *Seminario* fronts this façade of the cathedral ; it was built by the Archbp. Rasoy in 1777, for the education of young priests; in the celibate system of Rome those destined for the altar are instructed apart from the sons of laymen, in order, as at ladies' schools, that they may be brought up in certain sexual ignorances, which is not always the case in either.   In this fine palace the captain-general used to reside and the audiencia sat; it is now partly assigned to the *Ayuntamiento;* the now suppressed *S*ⁿ· *Jeronimo* lies to the S., and from the poverty of its accommodations it was commonly called *Pan y Sardina.*   The front is ancient, but the interior has little worth notice.   Some idea of this assemblage of architectural piles may be formed from the charming view which our good friend Roberts made from a drawing by the author of these humble pages (Landscape Annual, 1838, p. 108), but the letter-press account of Santiago is neither by him or us.

On the noble plaza the bull-fights take place, and fire-works are let off on San Juan, June 24, and Santiago, July 25.   This city, in spite of the rain, was and is the Vauxhall of Spain, and every saint's day was kept with consecrated crackers, and at every convent, when a member obtained a dignity, rockets were let off, starring again this Campus Stellæ, with a St. Peter's *Girandola,* on a small scale; then the spectators crowd together in pious and picturesque groups, and the Protestant pilgrim finds it difficult to say which are the best or most numerous, the Roman candles or Catholics; but explosions are very naturally thought to please the son of thunder, and blue lights to conciliate the *Luz* y Patron de las Españas.   So among the Hindoos (the inventors of all superstitions) pyrotechnics are a favourite act of devotion, especially to their female goddess Kali.   Reform and church appropriation have put out many of these meritorious squibs, but still, among the *Cofradias* and rich and pious laity, money seldom is wanting for them.   Santiago being a Levitical town which depended on the church for amusement, indulgences, and expenditure, now must decay like Toledo.   Hence it is not over-pleased with the *progreso,* or march of intellect; so when the Cortes abolished the In-

quisition, and wished to appropriate the church revenues, "it depended," said the Duke, "on the Archbp. of Santiago whether the N.W. of Spain should rise or not against us, who were supposed to uphold the constitutional changes."

Leaving the Plaza by the S.W., observe the now suppressed *Colegio de Fonseca,* founded by the Primate of Toledo, and then turn into the *Plateria,* situated at the S. entrance of the cathedral.   This is the most ancient front; observe the *Torre del Reloj,* one of the original towers, into which Gelmirez and Urraca fled from the populace.   The mob tried to burn them out—a very Oriental and Spanish custom.   Thus Abimelech destroyed those who fled to the tower of their "captain-general" Berith (Judges ix. 52).   Formerly the tower was called *Torre de Francia,* as the long street is still *del Franco.*   The French then supported and enriched the shrine, and Louis le Jeune came here in person as a pilgrim; but *La Jeune* or revolutionary France has since laboured to undo what her forefathers contributed to adorn, for Ney was sent by Soult on one of the usual plunder expeditions; he arrived here Jan. 17, 1809, and remained until May 23, when Soult's defeat at Oporto forced him to fly, carrying off, says Toreno, 10 cwt. of sacred vessels of the temple, the time-honoured gifts of former kings:

"——— Grandia templi
Pocula adorandæ robiginis, aut populorum
Dona, vel antiquo positas a rege coronas!"

and now Bory, an accomplice, turns king's evidence (see his Guide, 259; and Laborde, iv. 460), and laments with unspeakable naïveté the poorness of the "swag;" alas, says he, the solid silver candelabra were "*plus mince que du billon, et de peu de poids;*" "ce fameux St. Jacques d'or massif avec des yeux en diamant, était de *Vermeil;* et n'avait que des prunelles en pierres fausses."   Hannibal, more clever in pillage, never needlessly incurred the odium of sacrilege, for he, sharper than M. Bory, *bored* church plate first, and *if solid,* then, and only *then,* stole it (Cic. *de Div.* i. 24). The chapter thus took in both the intelligent French and the pious pilgrims, by imitating their pagan predecessors (see Baruch vi. 10), and converting the solid offerings into dollars *for themselves,* and cheating the vulgar eye with tinsel substitutes, just as they foisted empty forms and ceremonies, instead of the spirit and practice of religion. According to Bory, " On n'a pas tiré en lingots la somme de cent mille écus, quand *la nécessité* des temps força d'employer, pour la solde des troupes Françaises de la division du Gén¹· Marchand *le don* qu'en fit le chapitre au corps d'armée du M¹· Ney." This necessity (the old plea by which a certain person excuses his deeds) was the necessary consequence of the Buonaparte maxim, " La guerre doit nourrir la guerre;" the precise Bellum se alet of Portius Cato, who razed the cities and razziad the plains of Spain, filling every place "fugâ et terrore" (Livy xxxiv. 9). Possibly the plundering of Santiago s altars may have been forced on the French officers, since Foy (i. 67) states that "ils eussent cru s'avilir en prenant part au pillage, tant ils avaient la cœur *haut* placé:" a eulogy, however, which Toreno and Maldonado think pitched a trifle too high: at all events a portion of the cathedral treasure was spared, because the spoilers feared the hostility of the *Plateros,* the silversmiths who live close to the cathedral, and by whom many workmen were employed in making little graven images, teraphims and lares, as well as medallions of Santiago, which pilgrims purchase. Thus Alexander the coppersmith of Ephesus, and Demetrius the silversmith, called together their operatives, " Sirs, ye know that by this *craft* we get our wealth;" and they became the bitter opponents of St. Paul, who preached against image and female worship. Thus the Agrigentines rose

against Verres (to whom Toreno compares Soult), when he attempted to steal their golden tutelar Hercules.

The *Plateros,* like those at Zaragoza, are loud in the praises of their images, phylacteries, and preservative talismans, and swear that they keep these shops solely for the benefit of their customers' souls; they assert that a silver *Santiago* on horseback is an infallible security against ague and robbers; and certainly as such a *Santito* only costs a few shillings, the insurance is not an unsafe speculation, as it is like a waterman's protection badge. We appended such a medallion to our *Zamarra,* and travelled hundreds of leagues over every part of Spain, without sickness, sorrow, or ever being robbed except by innkeepers; all which was attributed by an excellent canon of Seville to the special intervention of the " Captain-General of the Spains;" and certain it is that very few Gallician soldiers ever omit to stow away in their *Petos,* or linen gorget waddings, a *Santiagito* and rosary which ought to turn aside bullets and bayonets.

In the *Plaza de los Plateros,* observe a gushing fountain supported on Triton horses. To the left is the *Quintana de los Muertes,* the former cemetery of the canons. The very ancient portal of the cathedral on this side is only opened in the Jubilee year; over it is Santiago in pilgrim attire, and below in square-niched compartments are 12 saints, 6 on each side. This is the door by which pilgrims enter. On the E. side of the *Quintana* is the church dedicated to *S*ⁿ· Payo, Pelayo (for who he was see Oviedo, p. 702). The altar is said to be the identical one on which Santiago offered, but Morales (Viage, 132) discovered, to his horror, that it was only a Roman tomb converted to this new office. He obtained the effacing of the Latin and Pagan inscription, to the indignation of the Gallicians, who contended that D.M.S. *i. e.* Diis manibus sacrum, meant Deo maximo sacrum : " Who shall decide when doctors disagree?"

The ground on which the cathedral is built is far from being level on this side, hence the steps; and here yet remains a circular portion of the first building. The fourth and last side opens to the N. on the *Azabacheria* or *Plaza de S^{n.} Martin*. The former term is derived from *Azabache*, jet, of which vast quantities of rosaries used to be made and sold on this spot to the pilgrims as they entered, just as is done at Jerusalem, and in the Great Court of Mecca. The whole thing is borrowed from the Oriental : thus *Azzabach*, the Persian *Schabah*, signifies "small black beads." The making these chaplets constitutes a lucrative trade in all pilgrim cities, whether in the East or in the Peninsula. The mendicant monks manufacture their *cuentas*, counters, from a brown sort of mais berry, which were the precise Moslem *Sibhá*, counters, and made of berries, *Hab ;* the divisions were marked by cuttings of vines, *sarmientos*. They presented these holy beads as a great favour to those who put money into their purses, and the counting them affords an occupation to the indolence of devout Spaniards,—so the pious Moors are always telling their *Twer*. The modern Egyptian Mahomedan's chaplet, the *Seb'hhah, Soob'hhah*, consists of 99 small beads, with marks of divisions between them (Lane i. 92). At each of these beads the Moslem repeats an epithet in praise of God, whose name is reserved as a climax for the last and largest. In the jealous worship of one God, the Mahomedan contrasts with the Marian Spaniard, who, having borrowed the *Rosario* from him, has adapted it to his female worship. Few Spanish females ever go to church without this Oriental appendage; and their devotion is

"To number Ave-Marias on their beads."

The Dominicans were the managers and great preachers of its virtues and miraculous properties, the Virgin having given her own chaplet of beads to St.

Dominic, which was called a rosary from the sweet perfume which it emitted. It is carried in the hand, or tied round the neck, while the excellent rope of St. Francis is only worn round the waist. The hands of many Spanish monks have been observed after death to be perfumed with attar, from their constantly holding the *rosary*, and never washing off its fragrance, just as the cigar has the same effect on profaner fingers. The illiterate, both Moors, Chinese, and Spaniards, find these beads to be a convenient help in the difficult arithmetical operations of counting the "long prayers" and frequent repetitions which Christianity especially condemns, and the Pope and Mahomet especially require, since such mere repetitions have in both creeds an actual saving virtue of themselves, where *forms* have been substituted for spiritual essentials. The *Rosario* ought to contain 150 beads, in which only one *Paternoster*, one Lord's prayer, is allowed for every ten *Ave-Marias ;* "but one halfpennyworth of bread to this intolerable deal of sack!" The prayers are divided by certain breaks in the string. Santiago, and Seville (see p. 265), were the great cities of the Rosario. The peculiar chaunt re-appears here, but the hymn sounds harshly, sung by sore-throated Gallicians, who *howl* in their catchcold climate as *barbarously* as in the days of their ancestors : "Barbara nunc patriis ululantem carmina linguis" (Sil. Ital. iii. 346). Nor are these jet chaplets less gloomy when compared to those made in the bright south. Few, however, of the *Rosarios* of the golden age of Spain have escaped the sacrilegious melting-pot. Those of Cordovese and Mexican manufacture are exquisitely wrought in pure gold filigree, and studded with precious stones, but the virtues of the rosary would form a handbook of themselves.

The second name of this N. *Plaza, de S^{n.} Martin*, is in reference to the enormous convent of that saint, which was founded here July 26, 912, by King Ordoño II. San Martin is honoured at Santiago next to Santiago; and in fact, as among mortal captains-general in Spain, he is *el Segundo Cabo de la Provincia*, the deputy lord lieutenant: so among the pagans Castor and Pollux, and always on horseback, presided in couples, and such was the aboriginal Iberian belief before Rome introduced her particular polytheism. Now Santiago is their *Bandua*, the god of war, and San Martin is his associate, like their *Vexillor.* It is the precise arrangement of the early inscription, mutato nomine, " Deo Vexillor Martis socio *Banduœ*" (Masdeu, ' H. C. ' v. inscrip. 86). The Romans, who cared very little about the abstract religion of their new subjects, provided they paid taxes and obeyed the Prætor, at once admitted concurrent local gods into their capacious pantheon, and gave them *ad eundem* rank and ceremonials, thereby setting an example to Gregory the Great.

San Martin, if the whole of Christendom were polled, would be found to be more universally worshipped than Santiago, whose influence is a thing of local isolated Spain,—for where, indeed, is there a city in Europe without its Saint Martin? He was the great raiser of convents in the fourth century, whose monks naturally elevated shrines to their champion and benefactor, thus the first Christian church built in England was dedicated to him. As he was the great iconoclast, and destroyer of graven images and idols of the Pagan, how he would now be pained, could he revisit Santiago and the Peninsula, where more statues are now erected to his own worship when dead, than ever he brake down while alive. Tours is his real Compostella, where the mere exhibition of his relics scared away the Normans. The modern term chapel has been derived by Ducange from the small chamber in which his cope or cloak was adored (Capa, Capilla); for when alive he had divided it in order to cover a naked beggar, and this

is the especial action in which he is usually painted and carved by Spaniards, and with reason, since no nation can better appreciate this act of charity than the *gens togata* of modern times, although none is less likely to follow the example, even were a lady in the case—*Da mihi et beatæ Murtinæ.* This ancient convent has been almost entirely modernised. It is on an enormous scale; a portion hangs over a ravine; it has a fine garden, and commands noble views from its magnificent long corridor upstairs. Formerly it was one of the most wealthy of the Benedictine establishments, now it is a barrack.

The heavy modern Doric entrance is the work of Casas y Noboa, in 1738. The grand patio was rebuilt in 1636, and finished in 1743, as the dates over the arches indicate. This was the vile period of bad taste, when models were afforded to our half-convent, half-bastile, half-barrack, new poor-law Unions, by which the sweet country of England is disfigured; but cheapness and accomodation of numbers was the principle. Observe, however, the handsome fountain with three falls and satyrs' heads. The interior is commensurate with the exterior, as one corridor is 205 paces long. The library *was* superb. The Benedictines were a learned order, and promoters of schools and antiquarian research. The chapel, now a parish church, is in bad taste, with a heavy tesselated trunk-headed roof. The *Retablo* is of vilest churrigueresque, but in it Santiago and San Martin ride quietly together, like the fratres Helenæ, lucida sidera, in a fricassee of gilt ginger-bread. The pulpits are composed of rich marbles: the circular *sacristia* is fine. From the Azabacheria to the opposite great *Plaza* there is an arched communication under the archbishop's palace.

Now enter the cathedral from the *Azabacheria*, first looking at the modern encasement, which, with its Doric and Corinthian tiers, its heavy pediment, supported by caryatides of

2 G

Moorish slaves, with Santiago above dressed as a pilgrim, etc., was erected in 1765 by one Domingo Ant°· Lois Monteagudo, a Gallician, *i. e.* a Bœotian builder. The original façade had been previously tampered with by one *Sarela*, a worthy who ought to have been cast into his namesake's river (see p. 668). The interior has escaped much better, and is very striking. It has purposely been kept somewhat dark in order to increase the effect of the illuminations at the high altar, thus rendering the image of the tutelar the emphatic feature. The cathedral forms a beautiful cross, of which the lateral chapels do not injure the general effect. The three grand naves are narrow in proportion to their height and length, the central being the highest. The piers are light and elegant, and contrast with the enormous thickness of the outer walls. Low galleries are carried round the Coro, and above, with an open arcade of double-rounded arches. The two transept ends of the ancient cathedral remain as they were, and the new fronts built outside them add to the strange effect. The dark side aisles, which almost look like *corridors*, are filled with confessional boxes, dedicated to different saints, while on those destined for foreign pilgrims are inscribed the languages which the priest in them is supposed to understand. This once was necessary when strangers came from all countries, but now the *Gallego* confessors can only speak strange tongues " comme des vaches Espagnoles." *Polyglot* confessionals are in like manner provided at St. Peter's by his Holiness, *El vivo Oraculo*, as was done at the pilgrim shrine at Delos, where hymns were composed in all languages—παντων δ' ανθρωπων φωνας (Hom. ' Hym. Apol.' 162).

Near the *Capilla de los Reyes* is the grand confessional, in which the *Penetenciario* alone may sit; and in order that he may do so, this great dignitary is excused attendance in *coro:* his box is inscribed "Tabula post Naufragium."

To him alone the monks, clergy, and men of rank and rankest crimes confessed, and he had proportionate powers of absolution, since his capacious ears were the *cloaca maxima* of offences not to be named to minor auriculars. He pardoned, through the merits and intercession of Santiago, *les forfaits, que le courroux des dieux ne pardonne jamais.* Nor were those who had come so far ever used harshly ; the natural interest of the chapter to attract rich sinners rendered them very indulgent, and the previous grades of ordinary repentance—to wit *Contricion,* the sorrow for having sinned, because it is offensive to God, and *Atricion,* the sorrow for having sinned, because of fear of punishment—are assumed by the *ipsum factum* of pilgrimage. The confessors, it must be confessed, for we looked at them all, will disappoint most readers of Mrs. Radcliffe ; they have little of the unearthly Schidoni scowl which rends the soul ; they are mostly fat and well-fed, with a dormouse look of bore, especially when subjected to the communications of a garrulous aged woman, and the pleasing prospect of coveys of similar hags, squatting around waiting their turn, like patients at a doctor's door who gives advice gratis ; the confessors, like hospital nurses, soon become callous from long habit, and like Spanish Sangrados, they doubt in the efficacy of their own remedies. A desire to confess, and a belief in the magical effect produced by a tap of a white wand, through which the penitent is spiritually whitewashed, is daily diminishing among male Spaniards, who would gladly see their wives and womankind rescued from this abominable private cross-examination, by which the priest pries into the innermost arcana of every family; thus he can apply a moral screw to the weaker sex, who under the most favourable circumstances seldom keep any secret except that of their age. The confessional is a most awful police and inquisition, from whose polluting scrutiny no Spanish man or woman is safe. "The strictest delicacy," says Blanco White (Letter 3), "is inadequate fully to oppose its demoralizing tendency; without the slightest responsibility, and not unfrequently in the conscientious discharge of what he believes to be his duty, the confessor conveys to the female mind the first foul breath which dims its virgin purity." That author, who knew the whole truth, did not dare to continue the subject; the sort of questioning may be seen in *Sanchez de Matrimonio*, or in any of the *Promtuarios*, sold for the use of young confessors, to which Dr. Dens and his filth is untrodden snow.

In former times, *to confess* was absolutely necessary to obtain the benefits of the Apostle, and to convey information on that point was the object of the mediæval *Mrs. Starkes*; thus, in the earliest English *Handbook for Spain*,[*] full details—fuller, indeed, than ours—are given of the power of "Confessourez," confessors, to absolve and name penance, and to "assoyle thee of all thinge." This taking off the soil of moral dirt was particularly to be had on the north side, where " there is pardon and much faire grace."

The sacred effigy of the martial intercessor is placed, as it was when Al-mansûr arrived here, on the chief, and here an isolated altar: this was usual in all ancient Asturian Gotho-Spanish churches. This *Simulacro* is the identical Iberian idol " Neton, *Martis Simulacrum*, quod maximâ religione colebant" (Macrob. ' Sat.' i. 19). The base is composed of richly polished marbles, enclosed by gilt pillars, adorned with foliage and grapes, possibly in remembrance of the cave of Bacchus (see p. 662). But every sentiment of antiquity and veneration is marred by the abominable, immense, and lofty canopy, or Baldaquino, which is reared above and behind the image, instead of the usual *Retablo;* this *Hojarasca*,

carved and gilt in the worst *churriguerismo*, is a mixture of the Pagan, classical, and Salominic styles, and anything indeed but Christian, while the heavy supporting angels savour nothing of heaven. The image was graven by Mateo for Gelmirez, out " of a stone good for nothing, by an ancient hand" (Wis. Sol. xiii. 10). In his left hand he holds the *Bordon*, or pilgrim's staff, with a gilt gourd, *Calabaza*, fastened to it: cum baculo perâque (Mart. iv. 53); for the derided cynic of the Pagans is the type of the Catholic pilgrim's god. In his right hand is a label inscribed, " Hic est corpus Divi Jacobi Apostoli et Hispaniarum Patroni." The face is painted,—the expression is chubby and commonplace, with a bottle-nose and small twinkling eyes, more like a pursy minor canon than a captain-general, a destroyer of 60,000 Moors at one time, and one of the sons of Thunder, Boanerges: but the idols of rude people preceded fine art, and in time obtained a conventional sanctity independent of form; nay, when beauty and grace were substituted, the stern deep religious sentiment was lost. Reverence was then merged in artistical admiration, and the altars, as at Rome, were visited as picture-galleries, and the siren beauty seduced the pilgrim and anchorite. Thus, when Leo X. succumbed to the fair sin (for the cinque-cento, or *resurrection* of the antique, was almost the *renaissance* both of Pagan creed and art), the severe majesty of insulted religion avenged herself in the iconoclastic Reformation.

Great importance is attached to the hood worn by the image, the *Esclavina*, which resembles those worn by policemen in London, and Cardinals at Rome. It indeed is also called *Denque*, from a sort of mantilla worn by women, or a modern " *Cardinal*." It was once made of gold, which M. Ney secured, thinking, like the tyrant Dionisius, when he stole the golden mantle of Jupiter, that a woollen hood would be more comfortable in this damp

* See Purchas' ' Pilgrimes,' ii. 1230. The metrical guide is entitled ' The Way from the Lond of Engelond unto Sent Jamez in Galiz ;' it was written in the 14th century.

Gallicia. The present *Esclavina* is studded with such ornaments as become a saint and a captain-general, to wit, with canons and *shells*, both scallop, *veneras*, and projectiles, *bombas*; possibly artillery might have been miraculously used at Clavijo in the year 846, as Spanish was spoken by San Cecilio (Granada, p. 390). Mass can only be said before this image by bishops, or by canons of a dignity called *Cardenales*, of which there were seven on grand occasions. Then the altar is decorated with the exquisite silver Custodia by Antonio d'Arphe, 1544, and with the small gilt figure of Santiago, whose glory, *Aureola*, is composed of rubies and emeralds bright as a peacock's tail. Most of the silver lamps disappeared in 1809; but under the Cimborio still hangs the large Incensario, which is swung backwards and forwards by an iron chain, filling the *Crucero* with perfumed wreaths. The tabernacle is also cased with silver.

Through the influence of a friend in the chapter, we, Protestantism notwithstanding, were conducted through the ceremonial of the pilgrimage. The newly-arrived ascends some steps behind the image, places his hands on the shoulders, and kisses the hood. This is called *el fin del Romaje*, the end, the object of the pilgrimage. This osculation (see p. 124) is the *essential* homage; thus the people of Agrigentum *kissed* their idol of Hercules (Cic. in Ver. iv. 43), as the multitude at Rome now do the old Jupiter, with a new St. Peter's head. All kiss; some the toe, some the shoulders, for the part kissed is a matter of local convention: thus, at Mecca, the Moslem Hadji kissed the black stone of the Kaaba (and see Toledo).

After this osculation the pilgrim proceeds to one of the "Confessourez," makes a clean breast of it, and is "assoyled," or scoured from all moral dirt, like a dyspeptic after a course at Kissingen. He next communicates, and receives his certificate, or, as it is called, his "*Compostella*." This is a

printed Latin document, signed by the canon, "Fabricæ administrador," which certifies that he has complied with all the devotional ceremonies necessary to constitute a *Romero* or Hadji, a pilgrim, and returns quite whitewashed from having taken the benefit of the act. This *Compostella* was often deposited with the family title-deeds as a voucher of the visit, as otherwise lands under certain entails could not be inherited.

The *Silla del Coro* was carved with holy subjects in 1606 by Gregorio Español; the two bronze *Ambones*, or pulpits, on each side of the *Reja* of the high altar, are masterpieces of cinquecento art, by Juan Bauª· Celma, 1563. Observe the 6 exquisite gilt alto-relievos, carved with battles and sacred subjects, for here the strong restoration of Paganism struggles with Catholicity, and mermaids and battles mingle with holy subjects. There is not much other fine art in this cathedral, for Gallicia is a Bœotia. The pictures of St. Peter and St. Andrew are by Juan Antonio Bonzas, a Gallician imitator of Luca Giordano, his master.

Behind the apostle is a small room which contains what has escaped of the church plate. Observe two very ancient gilt *pixes*, a Saviour seated under a Gothic niche with two angels, and some ewers and basins in the shape of scallops. Next visit the *Relicario*, in which are many exquisitely wrought shrines and goldsmith work, containing the usual assortment of bones, rags, &c., which we do not detail because printed catalogues of the items are given gratis in Latin, Spanish, and French, to which "eighty days' indulgence" for one Paternoster and Ave-Maria repeated *delante de esta Imagen*, are also added and also gratis by the grace of the Archbishop. The relics are pointed out by a clergyman with a long stick, who goes through the marvels with the rote and apathy of a wearied showman. Formerly there were *Lenguageros*, linguists, who explained what he said in all the tongues of the earth. Observe some milk of the Virgin, quite fresh and white; a thorn of the crown which turns red every Good Friday; sundry parcels of the 11,000 Virgins, and a mighty molar of San Cristobal. We were much struck with a smaller tooth of Santiago himself, the gift of Gaufridus Coquatriz. This *Relicario* is also called *La Capilla de los Reyes*, in which the royal tablets have been barbarously modernised. Some of the sepulchral statues are of remote antiquity, e. g. Don Ramon, era 1126; Fernandus II., era 1226; Berenguela, era 1187; Alonzo IX. of Leon, 1268; Juana de Castro, 1412. The enamelled tombs of San Cucufato and Fructuoso are curious, so are the chased *relicarios*. The rich chased crucifix, which contains a portion of the real cross (Morales, alas! found it to be *palo de Peral*, or made of peartree) is one of the oldest authentic pieces of Christian plate existing. It is a gilt filigree work, studded with uncut jewels, and is inscribed, " Hoc opus perfectum est in era ixoo et duodecima. Hoc signo vincitur inimicus, hoc signo tuetur pius; hoc offerunt famuli Dei Adefonzus princeps et conjux." It was therefore made about 874, and resembles the cross of Oviedo, the work of angels; the figure of the Christ on it is more modern. Here are two chandeliers of gilt arabesque, studded with jewels and bassi-relievi of the Rey Chico, and said to have been taken in 1492 in the Alhambra, but they are modern, and of the date 1673. The *Tesoro*, upstairs, has a fine *artesonado* roof. Here is the *Urna*, the silver sarcophagus, with the star above, in which the host is deposited on Good Friday, when it is placed in a beautiful *viril*, made in 1702 by Figueroa, of Salamanca.

One of the ancient entrances to the transept remains, having been encased by a modern facing, and deserves close inspection; it consists of three arches: in the centre is *La Gloria*, or Paradise, with the Saviour surrounded by angels and saints, with prophets on the pillars.

The small arch to the r. is called *El Infierno*, the Hell, from the appropriate subjects. Observe the musicians, and their costume and instruments. All this was designed and mostly erected by Maestro Mateo, who is named in an inscription, bearing date era 1226, A.D. 1188. Of the chapels one of the most interesting is that behind the high altar, which is dedicated to La Virgen del *Pilar*, in memorial of her descent from heaven on a *pilar*, when visiting Santiago at Zaragoza. Observe the jaspers and precious marbles, and the elaborate *Retablo*. The founder, Antonio Monroy, 1725, a rich Mexican prelate, is buried here: the head of the fine old kneeling man is admirable. The *Capilla del Rey de Francia* retains a delicate white and gold Berruguete *Retablo;* otherwise the ancient tombs and screens in the cathedral have been sadly modernised and concealed, and many ancient sepulchres swept away: take the *Cª. del Espiritu Santo* as a specimen; observe the recumbent effigy of Didacus de Castilla, and then the traveller may look at the *Virgen de las Angustias*, in the *trascoro*, and on leaving the cathedral visit *La Cortesela*, or parish church, which, as usual, is a separate building. It is a fine specimen of early style, with three naves, roundheaded arches, and absises. It has recently been abominably repainted in a style, says Capt. Widdrington, fit for the green-room of a provincial theatre.

The university of Santiago is much frequented, as the minor colleges have been suppressed and incorporated into it. The building is heavy, with an Ionic portal, but the simple Doric patio is better. The library is a fine room, and well provided with books, not indeed of much value, being the sweepings of convents: here, however, are several French works, and (rara avis!) Cobbett's parliamentary debates, in truly Britannic half-russia, contrasting with the vellums of Spain, as our rubicund soldiers at Gibraltar do with the sallow-faced Spaniards at the Lines. The once splendid convents of Santiago are in the usual desecrated, half-ruined, and untenanted condition: visit, however, that of San Francisco, as the chapel, which has been converted into a parish church, is fine, and has a good roof: behind the altar is a portrait of a *Monroy*, a former benefactor. The cloisters of the half-destroyed *S^{n.} Agustin* deserve notice, and the square belfry of *S^{to.} Domingo*. Among the parish churches, that of *S^{n.} Felix de Solorio* is the work of Martin Paris, 1316, but it has been much modernised. In *Las Animas* is some good painted sculpture, principally representing our Saviour's Passion, by one Prado.

The public walk called *Susana* is charming. It was destroyed in 1823 by the Royalists, because planted by the Constitutionalists, who, for the reciprocal reason, and, at the same time, *beheaded* a statue in the Plaza del Toral ; but see p. 229 for Spanish revenge on works even of benefit.

The artist and naturalist will of course go to the market on the *Plaza del Pan*, to study natural history and costume. The women are clad in white or striped linen, which they throw over their heads for mantillas, exhibiting their dark *sayas*. The men wear a singular helmet-shaped *Montera* (the *mitra cristata* of their forefathers), which is worked in many-coloured cloths by their *Queridas*. Sunday, as is usual in Gallicia, is the great market-day ; then, after mass, the peasants enjoy their dances and bagpipes, the *Gaita Gallega*, put on their best costume, and play at singlestick.

The roads to and from Santiago are detestable. There has been for many years much talk, and many plans prepared on paper, for their improvement, especially in opening a good carriage communication between this capital and Lugo and Orense. In other provinces of Spain, the star-paved milky way in heaven is called *El Camino de Santiago*, but the Gallicians, who know what their roads really are, namely, the worst on earth, call the milky-way

El Camino de Jerusalem. The Pagans poetically attributed this phenomenon to some spilt milk of Juno. Thus the monks, our early gardeners, changed Juno into the Virgin, and called the milk-thistle Carduus Marianus.

Meanwhile the roads in Gallicia are under the patronage of Santiago, who has replaced the Roman Hermes, or Macadam; and they, like his milky-way in heaven, are but little indebted to mortal repairs. The Dean of Santiago is waywarden *virtute dignitatis*, and especially " protector." The chapter, however, now chiefly profess to make smooth the road to a better world. They have altogether degenerated from their forefathers, whose grand object was to construct bridle-roads for the pilgrim ; but since the invention of carriages and the cessation of offering-making Hadjis, little or nothing has been down.

ROUTE LXXXV.—SANTIAGO TO CAPE FINISTERRE.

Puente Maceira. . .	3	
Buen Jesus	4	.. 7
Corcubion	3¼	.. 10¼
Finisterre	1	.. 11¼

Every lover of wind scenery by sea or land should make this picturesque excursion, which is also full of interest to the sailor. Take a local guide and some sort of introduction to Corcubion, for the people are as savage as their country. The readers of Borrow's ' Bible in Spain ' will remember his hair-breadth escape from being shot for Don Carlos, just as Lord Carnarvon was nearly put to death in the same districts for Don Miguel ; Capt. Widdrington also was arrested in these parts on suspicion of being an agent of Espartero. But no absurdity is too great for the petty local " Dogberries " in Spain, who rarely deviate into sense ; and when their fears or suspicions are roused, they are as deaf alike to the dictates of common sense or humanity as are any Berbers. All classes, in regard to strangers, generally take some absurd notions into their heads; and, instead of fairly and reasonably endeavouring to arrive at the truth, they pervert every innocent word, and twist every action, to suit their own preconceived nonsense, and trifles become to their jealous minds proofs as strong as holy writ. Mr. Borrow was luckily delivered by the alcalde of Corcubion, who, if alive, must be a phœnix worth pointing out in any handbook, as he was a reader of the "gran Baintham," *i. e.* our illustrious Jeremy Bentham, to whom the Spanish reformers sent for a paper *constitution,* not having a very clear meaning of the word. *Corcubion,* its sheltered bay and rich valley, are well described by Basil Hall, who was there before the Benthamite man in office. In April, 1809, the Endymion frigate was sent to assist the patriots. The swagger, cowardice, and imbecility of the Junta are truly recorded by him. They, however, were only a sample of every other such congregation in the Peninsula. As soon as Ney's troops appeared, the Junta took to their heels. Then the unresisting inhabitants were butchered, the houses burnt, and the women ravished as a matter of course.

Corcubion, pop. about 1200, is a poor fishing town placed on a slope on a charming *Ria;* the port is safe, and was once defended by two now dismantled forts. The *Pescada* and sardines caught here are excellent: the noble Cape *El Cabo,* which is seen in all its glory from *El Pindo,* rises grandly about 2 long L. distant. Now we have reached the western end of the old world—the Promontorium Nerium, *Finisterræ.* This Land's End was the district of the Arotebræ, Artabri, a word which fanciful Celtic etymologists interpret as *Ar-ot-aber,* a " hanging over the sea." The Atlantic is indeed glorious, even had it not been rendered doubly so by British victories.

Here (May 3, 1747) Anson encountered the combined E. and W. Indian French squadrons under La Jonquiere.

He gave them the Nelsonic touch, that is, took *all* the six line-of-battle ships and four armed Indiamen. Then the captain of the *" Invincible "* (a name foreigners like to give to their armadas), when delivering up his sword said to Anson, " Vous avez vaincu *' l'Invincible,'* et *' La Gloire '* (another of the prizes) vous suit." The English action and French compliment were equally pretty.

Here again, Nov. 4, 1805, Sir Richard Strachan caught Dumanoir, and captured the four runaways from Trafalgar, " *Le Formidable,*" Dumanoir's own ship, being the first to strike its flag.

On these same waters Sir Robert Calder had before met Villeneuve, July 22, 1805. The English fleet consisted only of 15 sail of the line and 2 frigates; the French of 21 sail of the line, 3 of them very large ships, and 5 frigates. Although 17 were thus opposed to 26, ·Calder attacked the enemy, and took two ships of the line; a thick fog came on, and the French escaped into El Ferrol, from whence they sailed to be settled at Trafalgar. The French claim this day as their victory, because, accustomed to lose all their ships in sea engagements, here they had only lost two; and the English, a " shopkeeper nation," but in the habit of doing wholesale business in this line, almost felt this success to be a reverse; they could not understand how 17 of their ships could have failed in taking at least half of the 26 French, and the gallant Calder was brought to a court-martial for the incompleteness of his victory. His defence, however, was unanswerable; and Nelson, just to a brave man, like the Duke to Moore, manfully asserted, " that he, with so *small* a force, might not have done so much."

Buonaparte received the news of his naval *victory* with infinite discontent, as it entirely deranged his invasion and conquest of England. The summing up of the ' V. et C.' (xvi. 143) is characteristic : " Ainsi, par une bizarrerie que nous ne chercherons pas à expliquer, l'amiral Français, après avoir été réellement vainqueur dans l'action du 22, lassait entre les mains de son adversaire le gage de la victoire, deux bâtimens qui allaient être considérés comme la preuve matérielle que 15 vaisseaux Anglais en avoient battu 20 Français et Espagnols ".—say rather 17 English having beaten 26 French.

Those going into the Asturias, and wishing to visit this corner of Gallicia, may make the following circuit. Ladies should go in a *litero*, or sedan-chair, slung between two mules.

ROUTE LXXXVI.—SANTIAGO TO LUGO.

Al Padron	4	
Caldas del Rey	3	.. 7
Pontevedra	2	.. 9
Puente San Payo	1	.. 10
Redondela	4	.. 14
Vigo	2	.. 16
Porriño	2	.. 18
Tuy	2	.. 20
Codesas	2	.. 22
Tranqueria	2	.. 24
Rivadavia	3	.. 27
Orense	4	.. 31
Readago	1¼	.. 32¼
Chamada	3¼	.. 36
Taboada	2	.. 38
Naron	2¼	.. 40¼
Lugo	4	.. 44¼

The descent from Santiago is long and monotonous. Towards the bottom of the valley is a church of the Virgin, which formerly was a sanctuary for every kind of criminals, who have testified their gratitude to their patroness by numerous votive offerings. These asylums of crime, once so common in Spain, are now shivered by the explosion of public opinion : of Oriental and Pagan origin, they, in times of violence, were a sort of rude equity, which even armed power respected. Higher up is the *Pico Sagro*, a conical hill of crystallized quartz; its *holy* epithet is simply a translation of the old Gallician *Mons Sacer* described by Justin (xliv. 3); the country is green and pleasant, abounding in maize and fruit, and the whole line up to *San Juan de Coba* is extremely picturesque.

El Padron—el patron, the Patron—is the ancient Iria Flavia, a name still retained in the *Colegiata de Sa. Maria*, which ranks as a cathedral. This town, population about 3500, is situated on the Sar, which soon flows into the Ulla; a stone bridge divides El Padron from Dodro and Lestrobe. Easter Monday is a grand day here, as it is a much frequented mule and cattle fair. Iria Flavia was a see of greater antiquity than even Compostella; the *Colegiata* outside the town contains tombs of the early prelates.

El Padron being the spot at which the body of Santiago landed itself (see p. 662), was formerly a pilgrim city ; the *Romeros* came here after having visited *Compostella ;* Morales, in his ' *Viage*,' p. 137, gives the details of their proceedings; first they visited the church of Santiago, ascended and kissed the image over the high altar, and then walked round and kissed the stone to which the miraculous boat moored itself, and which is evidently the pedestal of a former Roman statue. Then they went to see the stone on which the body reposed after its voyage, and lastly, which was most important, ascended the *Montaña ;* going up is a hermitage or church built on the spot where St. James preached when alive here, and from under the altar gushes a stream which the pilgrims drink and then perform their ablutions with; after which they ascended on their knees, to the broken and perforated rocks which St. James pierced with his staff, in order to escape from the pursuing Gentiles ; two of the holes or *agujeros* were particularly holy, and over these the devout stretched their bodies. All this is simple imitation of the Moslem, who drank at Mecca of the waters of Zemzem, who encompassed the black stone, and who ascended on his knees the hill of Merva. The Ulla, with its tributaries the Pambre, Furelos, Arnego, Deza, and Sar, abounds with fish ; it is crossed at the bridge, *El puente de Cesures*, Pons

Cæsaris, built on Roman foundations, in 1161, by Maestro Mateo, for
the passage of pilgrims from Portugal;
the tide flows up to it.

Thence to *Caldas del Rey*, Calidas,
the warm mineral baths, of which the
season is from July 1 to Sept. 20. The
temperature of the odourless and tasteless waters is about 32° Réaumur.
Their effect in softening the skin is
marvellous. The bath is of granite,
with a partition. Thus about five men
and five women can bathe and talk to
each other at the same time. About
1 L. up the river are the *Caldas de
Cuntis,* warm hydro-sulphuric baths,
which also benefit the cutis. The season is from July 1 to Sept. 30. The
accommodations, as usual in Spain,
are indecent, but much frequented.

The country continues to be rich
and fertile, but the peasantry are ill
clad and poverty-stricken, and have
a truly Irish-pauper look. Crossing a
ridge, *Pontevedra,* Pons vetus, with its
long bridge, rises on a slope overhanging its beautiful ria and the estuary
of the Lerez. It is a clean, well-built,
well-paved town. Pop^n. about 5000.
There is a decent *Posada* in the Calle
del Puente. In the upper part of the
town is a modern church, which is seen
from afar, like the Superga near Turin.
Farther on is a convent of Augustines,
ruined by the French, and now a picturesque ivy-clad ruin. Adjoining is
the *alameda,* with its charming views
of the environs, studded with villas,
farms, and woodlands. The old *Palacio de los Churruchaos* deserves a look.
The Pontevedrans are good haters, and
regard their neighbours of Vigo as the
men of Santiago do their brethren at
La Coruña. The Gallicians, during
the war, detested the Asturians worse
than the Jews did the Samaritans; their
respective juntas would not even meet
each other to devise plans of self-defence
against the common foe; not a man of
either province ever marched to assist
the other in the hour of danger. Neither
the cold nor damp of the climate
could repress the fierce fires of local

hatreds, nor could all the stars of
the *Campus stellæ* enlighten them on
the folly and weakness of divisions.
There is a little work on *Pontevedra*
published there by the bookseller
Garcia.

There is a direct rout from Pontevedra to Orense by which Tuy is
avoided; it is 14 L. passing through
S^n· Jorge de Sacos 3, Cerdedo 2, Bo-
boras 4, Maside 2, Orense 4. The
grand Cistertian convent of *Acebeiro* to
the l. after leaving Cerdedo, and before .crossing the ridge of hills, lies
in its valley near the source of the
Lerez under the heights of the *Candan
Sierra.* The founder was Alonzo VII.
A.D. 1135: the tombs of Pedro Martinez and the Abbot Gonzalo still
remain.

The ride to *Redondela* is one continued garden, with charming views of
the ria of *Vigo* to the r. Soon we pass
El puente de San Payo, famous for
oysters and the complete defeat which
Ney, commanding 7000 men, received
June 7, 1809, from some rude peasants
under Noroña, backed by the English
marines, and a battery under Colonel
M'Kinley, and a handful of Moore's
stragglers, who did the work, although,
as at La Bispal, Spaniards now claim
all the honour. This non-success is
now explained away by the French, as
resulting from the misunderstanding
between Ney and Soult; as if *Le
Brave des Braves* would have allowed
himself to be beaten to oblige a hated
rival. Ney being a first-rate soldier
probably saw the military mistake of
remaining in Gallicia, as this remote
corner was open to English attack from
the sea, and offered strong mountain
positions inland for Spaniards to hem
in an invader.

A good deal of the stolen church
plate, &c. was recovered in the captured baggage of the French, but so
disproportionate to the quantity known
to have been taken, that a notion
exists in these parts that much of it is
buried; hence the wild treasure-hunting
speculations. Borrow has graphically

2 G 3

detailed those of the Swiss adventurer, Benedict Mol; and only in Dec. 1843 another exhibition of avarice and credulity was publicly made by the authorities in the vain search of some of Ney's deposits, guided by a common French soldier, a former accomplice, like Bory. All this is very Oriental and classical. Thus the Punic Bassus took in the respectable Nero, by *promising* to find treasure hidden by Dido, which he did *not* (Tac. ' *An.*' xvi. 1). Bait the trap well, and universal Spain is caught, from the finance minister downwards, for all are dreaming of Aladdin discoveries. *Oh si urnam argenti fors quæ mihi monstret!* No doubt much coin is buried in the Peninsula, since the country has always been invaded and torn by civil wars, and there never has been much confidence between Spaniard and Spaniard; accordingly the only sure, although unproductive, investment for those who had money, was gold or silver, and the only resource to preserve that, was to hide it.

The exquisite scenery continues to *Redondela*, which is divided by its river, and connected by a bridge. It stands on the charming lake-like *ria* of Vigo, which now opens to the S.W., and is one of the finest bays in this indented coast. It is secured by a natural breakwater, the isolated *Cies*, the *Siccas* of Pliny, and which are also called *las Islas de Bayona. Bayona* lies 4 L. of bad road from Vigo, about half way to the mouth of the Miño. It is very ancient, was sacked by the Normans, and is alluded to by Milton in ' Lycidas :' " Namanco's and Bayona's hold." Bay-on-a is said to signify the " good bay." There are passages into the *ria* outside the Cies islands, and also one between them, which is called *la Porta*, the gate. These were the islands which the Duke, always prescient, wished to fortify, in order to have a strong point in Gallicia on which to fall back in case of reverse, but the suspicious Junta of Cadiz refused permission (Toreno,xiii.),

just as they had done in regard to their own port, which in their hour of incapacity of self-defence they begged the Duke to garrison and defend.

Vigo, Vico Spacorum, is a most ancient port. The establishment at El Ferrol did it a serious injury, and the towns abhor each other. Now it is reviving, and is the point where the Peninsular steamers touch when going up and down the coast. They generally arrive here, coming from England, in less than four days. Accordingly accommodation has improved, and the *Posada de los Viscainos* is decent. Vigo probably will become a point of export for Gallician cattle under our new tariff. The British vice-consul, Don Leopoldo Menendez, an enterprising and intelligent gentleman, has already taken steps for the improvement of the breed of oxen, by importing bulls of a high caste from England. The Spanish graziers are as jealous of their bulls as the Moors were of their mistresses. They are strictly conservative, and never, with Sir Robert Peel's liberality, offer their favourite *toro* to their neighbour's cow. The Gallician bullocks are much used as animals for draft and the plough : a fine one is worth here about 10*l.*

Vigo has a theatre, a lazareto, a pleasant alameda by the *Puerta del Placer*, and a good port. The heights behind are crowned with the castles San Sebastian and *del Castro*. The view from the latter is superb. The pop^{n.} is under 6000. The sea furnishes fish in abundance, and the environs the fruit of the earth : it is very cheap. Here foreign vice-consuls reside. The modern church at Vigo, although unfinished and unadorned, is a simple architectural temple, with a double row of noble columns supporting the arched nave. There is a ' *Descripcion de Vigo*,' by Dr. Nicolas Taboada, Santiago, 1840.

Vigo has often been attacked and almost destroyed by the English. Drake was here in 1585 and 1589, singeing the King of Spain's whiskers, until his name alone scared the whole coast; and setting an example to Adm. Rooke and Gen. Stanhope, who returning from their failures at Barcelona and Cadiz, here heard that the Plate galleons had arrived, Sept. 22, and that the bullion was still on board, not having been landed in consequence of remonstrances from the selfish Cadiz authorities, whose port alone had the privilege to import silver; the English, Oct. 22, instantly attacked the Spanish fleet and the French convoys under the Count Chateau Renaud, who fled in the middle of the action, and left his allies in the lurch like Dumanoir at Trafalgar. The English victory was complete, and the hostile fleets were destroyed. Now, according to our ingenious neighbours, this Chateau Renaud is a naval hero, and his modest epitaph ran thus :—

" C'y gît le plus sage des Héros : [eaux.'
Il vanquit sur la terre, il vanquit sur les

He died, at all events, immensely rich; and therefore it is conjectured, that all the Spanish treasures were not lost and sunk in Vigo bay. Rooke, who fluttered this invincible, died poor, and his will records the reason :—" I do not leave much, but what I do leave was honestly gotten : it never cost a sailor a tear, or the nation a farthing." Like the Roman of old, " gloriam *ingentem,* divitias *honestas* volebat" (Sall. ' B. C.' 7). The bulk of the treasure *was said* to have been cast into the sea; at all events much more money has since been thrown away after it in idle diving speculations; but Gallicia is the land for treasure-seeking, whether under earth or water. The losses at Vigo nearly ruined Philip V., as those at Cadiz had Philip II.

Vigo was again attacked and almost destroyed, Oct. 11, 1719, by Lord Cobham ; nor, in case of a future war, would it give our steamers much trouble, although apparently well fortified by the castles *Alaje, del Castro,* and *San Sebastian,* for the works, as usual, are much neglected, and amply fur-

nished with nothing necessary for real service. The little fort at *Cangas* is sometimes used as a place of refuge in periods of civil outbreaks and blockades.

The examples of La Coruña and El Ferrol (see p. 655) were not lost on the citizens of Vigo, who, in Feb. 1809, surrendered at once to a simple charge of bold French dragoons under Franceschi ; but the town was retaken, March 27, by a motley band of students and peasants under the *Abbad de Valladares,* for in Gallicia the *curas* are called abbots. Then the since notorious Morillo was created at once a colonel, because the French would not treat with peasants. This man, ignorant of the rudiments of war, accepted from Chalot a convention of Cintra, by which the enemy with all their spoil would have been transported to France : but Capt. M'Kinley, who was blockading Vigo with the " Lively " and " Venus " frigates, demurred, and 1300 Frenchmen surrendered, with some of the pillage taken from the Escorial by La Houssaye (Southey xix.).

All *this* aid and *that* misconduct is blinked by Toreno (viii.), Mellado, &c. who ascribe the whole glory to " Gallician patriotic impulse," and *el benemerito* Morillo. This well-deserving gentleman was sent out of France by the Duke for encouraging plunder, and next was employed by Ferd. VII. to " put down " the S. American insurgents; his more than Punic bad faith, his more than Iberian bloodshed and inhumanities at New Granada horrified even Spaniards; defeated in 1818 by Bolivar, and again by the English legion, he returned to Spain, and after proving false to every one except self, died at Paris in 1838 a disgraced exile.

The uninteresting mule-track from Vigo to Tuy joins the Santiago highroad at Porriño. Tuv, *Tude ad fines,* where there is only a bad *Posada,* was founded, *se dice,* by Ætolian Diomede, the son of Tydeus (Sil. Ital. iii. 367);

and Morales (Viage, 145) here discovered a Greek altar and a Greek sculpture of wrestlers. Witiza made Tuy his residence in 700. It was destroyed by the Moors in 716, but the site was recovered in 740 by Alonzo el Catolico, and the old town rebuilt in 915 by Ordoño I.; next the new city was removed from the original site to the present in 1170 by Ferd. II. Tuy, which once was an important frontier town on the Miño, is regularly built and walled round, but now it is decayed and decaying; yet the climate is delicious, and the fertility of the *vegas* unbounded. In this happy corner of Gallicia the valleys, especially *La Vega de Louro,* with its oranges, rival Andalucia, and speak for the soil and sky of a land which Providence has so much blessed, and man so disregarded. The wines are excellent; the salmon, *savalos,* and trout abundant. The best rivers are the Louro, Tea, and Avia. The strong and almost castle cathedral was begun in 1145; the see is suffragan to Santiago. The cloisters are fine. The great saint here is naval, not military as at Santiago, for Pedro Gonzalez, *San Telmo,* the hope and patron of Spanish mariners, represents the *San Antonio* of Italians, the *San Nicolas* of Greek pirates, or our "Old Nick," and the god of Spanish thieves; he was the companion of St. Ferd., and furnished the fair wind, like Circe, by which the bridge of boats at Seville was broken through. San Telmo was canonised by Innocent IV. in 1254, and Florez (E. S. xxiii. 131) has written his life and numerous miracles He always appears in storms at the mast-head in a lambent flame, after the fashion of the pagan "Fratres Helenæ, lucida sidera:" accordingly the Spanish sailors, when it begins to blow hard, fall to prayers to him instead of lowering topsails and reefing; their midshipmen are brought up in his college (see Seville, p. 280). The tomb of this "*Nautarum Patronus,*" with gilt *rejas* and arches, was raised

here in 1579 by Bishop Diego de Avellanada. His friend Don Lucas de Tuy, the historian, commonly called *El Tudense,* and the persecutor of the Albigenses, lies buried near him : for his life see Florez (E. S. xxii. 108). The episcopal palace was in the Alcazar, but this and other defences were much injured by the French. As there is no bridge here across to Valenza, the strongly fortified Portuguese frontier, Soult, Feb. 10, 1809, desired Thomières (who made the false move which lost the battle of Salamanca) to force a passage in boats, in attempting which he was beaten back by the Portuguese Ordenanzas; and by this failure Soult was obliged to go down to the bridge at Orense. On what small hinges do mighty destinies turn! This trifling delay prevented Soult from reaching Lisbon at once, and gave time to England to send forth her squadrons to Portugal, which, had Soult previously overrun it, in the depression of Moore's retreat and disgust at Spanish misconduct, would not have taken place. The Duke landed, and for the second time expelled the French, and thereby led the way to the deliverance of Spain and Europe. Consult, for local history, '*Antigüedad de Tuy,*' Prudencio de Sandoval, 4to., Braga, 1610; and for the ecclesiastical, Florez, 'E. S.' xxii. 3.

The pleasant road to *Orense* borders the Miño. *Rivadavia,* with some 2000 souls, is an irregular, dull place on the "bank of the Avia," which flows down from its rich basin. The province of Orense is the most fertile of this corner of Spain, especially near the banks of the Sil, Avia, and Miño. Linen is the chief manufacture. The hams made at Caldelas are excellent. Mem.: always have one in the commissariat, and a *bota* full of *Tostado* wine. The wines are renowned, although the process of making them is more rude and classical, if possible, than on the eastern coasts (see Benicarló). Orense, should the grand road between Vigo and Madrid be completed, which is to pass by it and Puebla de Sanabria, will become an important point, as an outlet will be afforded for these rich port-like wines. This *Carretera*, if ever finished, will also form the most expeditious line of communication between England and Madrid.

Orense, aquæ *urentes,* Warmsee, was celebrated in antiquity for its "*warm baths,*" and these, called *Las Burgas,* are still frequented from July to September. They gush forth at the W. of the town from a granite rock, almost boiling, and are turned to many useful purposes besides medical ones. Orense, a nice clean town, is the capital of its province, and the residence of local authorities, and of a bishop, suffragan to Santiago: pop[n]. under 6000. It is pleasantly situated, rising gently above the Miño, and girdled by hills. The bridge is very striking, being 1319 ft. long, and 18 wide: it is defended by a castle on the town side. The grand arch is 156 ft. wide, and 135 high from the bed of the river, on account of sudden inundations. It was built in 1230 by Bishop Lorenzo, and repaired in 1449 by Bishop Pedro de Silva.

Orense was patronised by the Goths, and here the Suevi-Gothi first renounced Paganism. A cathedral, dedicated to St. Martin, was built so early as 550, but the Moors, in 716, levelled Orense to the ground, and it remained a heap of ruins until 832, when it was rebuilt by Alonzo el Casto, and granted to the bishop in 1131. The present Gothic cathedral was raised by Bishop Lorenzo in 1220. S[a.] Euphemia is the local patroness, and has a chapel near the high altar. A shepherdess, on the confines of Portugal, first discovered her body, which put out its hand, from which the girl took off a ring, and was struck dumb, but recovered her speech by putting it on again. The body was then brought to Orense in 1157, working miracles all the way (Morales, '*Viage,*' 148). Observe also *El Paraiso,* so called from the infinity of saints and angels. The *Silla. del Coro* is

good, and the *Cimborio* and the transept deserve notice, as well as the quaint mediæval shrines of S[n.] Facundo and S[n.] Primitivo, local and primitive saints, which are much venerated. Visit the *Capilla del Cristo Crucificado,* founded in 1567 by Bishop F[ro.] Triccio; also that of S[a.] Juan B[a.], rebuilt in 1468 by the Conde de Benavente, in atonement for the ravages done to the cathedral during his family feuds with the rival house of Lemos. The antique cloisters were erected in 1804 by Bishop Ederonio: observe the inscription. The *Ca. de la Maria Madre* was restored in 1722, and connected by the cloisters to the cathedral: eight of the canons were called *Cardenales,* as at Santiago, and they alone did service before the high altar. This custom was recognised as "immemorial" by Innocent III., in 1209. For this diocese consult Florez (E. S. xvii.), and the useful map by Cornide and Lopez, Mad. 1763.

Orense is an excellent head-quarters for the angler. The best rivers in the vicinity are the Avia, Arenteiro, Miño (higher up), and crossing it, the Sil, Cave, Nabea, Arnoya, and Limia.

It was from Orense that Soult invaded Portugal, having Loison and Foy for his lieutenants. They met with no resistance up to Oporto, which they sacked without mercy, butchering in cold blood some 10,000 men, women, and children: but the avenger was at hand, and the Duke pounced upon Soult, who fled May 12, 1809, performing a retreat unequalled in horrors, both suffered and committed, even by that of Massena. Thus was Moore most nobly avenged. The cruel coward Loison proposed to open a Cintra convention, but the bold and skilful marshal preferred setting an example to Massena, rather than following that of Junot. He abandoned everything that constitutes an army, but impedes rapidity; thus he saved his men by sacrificing guns, baggage, and plunder. The French reached Orense almost naked, from whence 76 days before they had set forth with 26,000 men and 78 cannon, now reduced to 19.500 unarmed stragglers. They fell back on Benavente, venting their irritation under military repulse on the homes and persons of the defenceless peasantry (see R. lxix.)

The Portuguese frontier on the route to Chaves begins near *Feces de Abajo*, 12 L. from Orense. To the r. of *Allariz* (see p. 600), and about 3 L. on the other side of the Miño, and near a stream that runs into the Arnoya, is the once wealthy abbey of Benedictines at Celanova, founded in 973 by San Rudesinto. In the garden is one of the oldest chapels in Spain, supposed to be the work of Vivianus, and before 973. In the abbey-church are the ancient sepulchres of Ilduara and Adosinda, the mother and sister of the founder, who was buried in a curious sepulchre supported on four pillars and constructed after the fashion of that of San Torcato, one of the companions of Santiago. This inestimable miracle-working-corpse was deposited by the Christians at the Moorish invasion at Santa Comba, distant 4½ L.: being near the frontier, some Portuguese stole it, when a mist came on, and losing their way, they brought it to Celanova, whose convent bells began forthwith to ring of their own accord, which Spanish bells often used to do: see Velilla.

Many other ancient tombs lie here in sad neglect; among them was one inscribed with the well-known epitaph, A. D. 1324:—"Era 1362: *Aqui jaz Feijoo Escudeiro, bon fidalgo e verdadeiro, gran casador e monteiro.*" Hence passing by Allariz to the Laguna is the Limia, the real river of oblivion, which the soldiers of Junius Brutus hesitated to pass over (see p. 235).

Communications with Orense. For the line to Benavente, and hence on to Madrid, see R. lxviii. When once at Orense an excursion should by all means be made to the *Vierzo* (see p. 597), or at all events as far as *Monte Furado del Sil.*

ROUTE LXXXVII.—ORENSE TO SANTIAGO.

Bouzas	2	
Piñor	1½	3½
Castrodozon	1	4½
Gesta	1½	6
Fojo	2	8
Castrovite	2	10
Barca de Ulla	1	11
Susana	2	13
Santiago	1	14

This is a bad cross-road. After passing the ranges at Piñor and Castrodozon, we descend into the rich basin of the Ulla, which is crossed near *Castrovite*, leaving *El Padron* to the l., and the conical hill *El Pico Sacro* to the r.

The bridle-road from Orense to Lugo ascends the Miño, which divides the Chantada and Puerto Marin districts from Monforte.

ROUTE LXXXVIII.—ORENSE TO LUGO.

Readego	1½	
Chantada	3½	5
Taboada	2	7
Naron	2½	9½
Puntin	1	10½
Lugo	3	13½

This road is rough, and often flooded in winter, but the fishing is excellent, as about six miles from Orense the river branches off: the grand stream comes down by Chantada and Puerto Marin. *Puerto Marin* lies to the r. of Naron, and is a capital angling quarter, for the trout are very fine. It is a pretty place, divided by the river, with a good bridge. It belonged first to the Templars, and then to the knights of St. John. The *Colegiata*, dedicated to Sn. Nicolas, is a fine unfinished Gothic edifice of excellent masonry. Observe the delicate bassi-relievi over the doors. The palace of the *Bovedas*, the hospital for pilgrims, and the whole place was dreadfully sacked by the French under Maurice Mathieu.

The angler may go down the rich valley of Lemos to *Monforte*, on the Cabe, and thence to its confluence with the Sil and Miño, near *Sn. Esteban.* The country is rich and pastoral, the bacon delicious, and the *Biscochos de Monforte* renowned. Near the town is a curious tidal fountain. From Monforte the angler may proceed by *Montefurado* to the *Vierzo*, and either ascend to Ponferrada, or work down to *Puebla de Sanabria* (see p. 599). The summer is the best period. Take a local guide, and attend to the "Provend" and look to your tackle, for hereabouts are some of the finest salmon and trout fishing quarters in Spain; here are virgin unwhipped streams, which would make old Izaak Walton's mouth water. The whole mountain W. barrier of Spain from Gallicia through the Asturias to the Pyrenean spurs and the Bidasoa, abounds in alpine valleys, each with its own river, which form the tributaries of larger trunks, that disembogue themselves into the sea, and up which salmon and the *Savalo* run.

From central Lugo there are two communications with the Asturias: one coasts the sea-board, the other threads the inland valleys: and first by the coast.

ROUTE LXXXIX.—LUGO TO OVIEDO BY SEA-COAST.

Quintela	3½	
Bean	3	6½
Mondoñedo	3	9½
Villa Martin	2	
Rivadeo	3	12½
Franco	3	15½
Navia	2	17½
Luarca	3½	21
Las Ballotas	3½	24½
Muros	3½	28
Aviles	2½	30½
Villadoveyo	2½	33
Oviedo	2½	35½

Although we have ridden every inch of this route, we can only give the distances approximatively. The leagues are very long, and the road after Navia to Aviles is a constant up and down. The accommodations are tolerable: the fish everywhere, both sea and river, is excellent.

Leaving Lugo, an uninteresting swampy country intervenes to *Bean*, after which the road ascends and descends, overlooking pleasant nooks, with the distant sea filling up the gaps in the mountain horizon with a border of blue. *Mondoñedo*, Britona, stands in an oval and highly cultivated valley, under the hill Infiesta, and surrounded by the clear tributaries of the Masma. It is the see of a bishop, suffragan to Santiago, pop$^{n.}$ about 6000, and is quite uninteresting. The cathedral, with two pepper-box towers, was begun in 1221: in 1595-99, four chapels were added behind the *Capilla Mayor*. The *Sanctuario* is the only object worth notice, as the image is called *La Inglesa*, because brought from St. Paul's, London, at the Reformation, and also *La Grande*, from its full-grown size. Mondoñedo, and the districts of Vivero and Navia, were completely sacked by Maurice Mathieu. He surprised the old blockhead Worster and his Gallicians, who were swaggering and feasting under the delusion that the French were running away from them, which they forthwith did from the French. Well did the old Cid, in the ballad, understand these Gallicians, their carelessness, their national propensity "to boast of their own strength," and underrate that of their foes. He too came upon them like Mathieu, and put them to rout.

"*Ça ellos han por costumbre*
Quando ganan algun campo,
Alabarse de su esfuerzo
Y escarnecer al contrario;
Gastarian toda la noche,
En placer y gasejado,
Y dormiran la mañana
Como homes sin ciudado."

At *Sargadelos*, on the sea near Cape Burela, is an iron foundry, established in 1792 by Antonio Ibañez. Here the shot and shells for the arsenals of El Ferrol were cast. The ore is found at *San Miguel de Reinante*, near Barreiros, and is embarked at Foz on the Masma, to the l. of Rivadeo.

Leaving Mondoñedo, at 1 L. on the Masma is the fine Benedictine convent of San Salvador at *Lorenzana*; it was founded in 969 by the Conde Gutierre Osorio, who afterwards became a monk, went to Jerusalem, died, and was buried here in a superb marble and mosaic ornamented tomb: for his life and miracles see 'E. S.' xviii. 296: here also is buried his sister Urraca. The convent was pillaged by the French. The last league into Rivadeo is called *La legua de Rochella*, and is the longest in Gallicia. The country is full of farm-houses and village. Much flax and maize are produced : the latter is dried in buildings pierced with slits, like windows for arrows.

Rivadeo is a sweetly situated town on its beautiful *ria* or bay, abounding in fruit, vegetables, and excellent fish. There is a decent Posada: also a small house with good accommodation, kept by the Spanish widow of a Frenchman. The alameda is pretty. Here also is an Alcazar, with two towers and a Moorish-looking gate. The *Castillo* commands the lovely bay, which is spread out like an indented lake. The cannon were thrown into the sea during the war, and there they may be still seen, unrecovered by the apathetic Spaniard. The towns of Figueras and Castropol rise on eminences opposite. Froissart describes the siege of Rivadeo, which held out for a month against Sir Thomas Percy, in 1385, to his surprise, for they " were but peasants, and not one gentleman in the town." He prepared a battering ram, which scared the townsfolk, who wanted to surrender, when the English laughed, and said, " we don't understand your Gallician." They sacked the town, plundered the rich Jews, ate so much pork, and drank so much wine, that they were disabled for two days. Wine is and has ever been the only foe which surely triumphs over the English soldier. Rivadeo was once the seat of a see, and now has a *colegiata* dedicated to the Virgin.

The river Eo, famous for its oysters and fishing, flows into the bay, and divides the provinces of Gallicia and Asturias. The salmon-fishing at *Abires*, 2 L. up, is first-rate. Now the road continues to Aviles, 17 L. along the coast, with the sea close to the l. It is beautiful, but tedious; the spurs of the hills come down to the shore, and through their dips flow infinite streams. Thus it is one continual up hill and down hill, *cuesta arriba y cuesta abajo*, and one ferrying and fording. so that very little real progress is made after much labour to man and beast.

On leaving *Rivadeo*, a ferry-boat, after a passage of a quarter of an hour, lands the traveller at *Figueras*, the first town in the Asturias. If the weather is very bad, it will be necessary to go round the *ria*, crossing over to *Castropol*, a steep clambering fishy town, near which some workings of an old tin-mine have been discovered by Mr. Schultz. The country soon becomes wild and boggy, and we reach *Navia*, built on its splendid salmon river; here the *Meson* is decent, and the fish capital. *Luarca* is not seen until it is entered, as this pretty spot is nestled in a sheltered cove between the points *Las Mugeres* and *Focicon*. The trout-stream Rio Negro comes down into the bay. The houses are most picturesque, and a chapel, with a whitened tower, hangs above on a rock, a landmark to ships, and put into the picture to please painters. The little inn, with its pretty garden, is clean and comfortable, and here the angler might put up. The natives are simple and industrious, and the whole country is thickly peopled and cultivated with maize. The peasants have less of the misery of the interior of Gallicia. Their homes are more comfortable, and their windows oftener glazed. The costume and manner changes and improves as we advance into the *Asturias* : see Heading of Sect. x.

Hence to the river Caneiro, 1 L., and then into *Las Ballotas*, as a jumbled series of hills is called, which extend to *Muros*, 6 L. Romantic, indeed, are the glens and precipices, but fatiguing to the horseman; however, the broken and dislocated strata afford fine sections to the geologist, while the botany and trees on the slopes delight the artist and lover of natural history; unfortunately, their stems are too often trimmed up, and the lateral branches lopped off. The road is very intricate. At *Soto* the lemon and orange reappear. There is an excellent Meson, or Posada, at *Soto de Rudinia*, placed amid noble chesnuts, in a charming Swiss-like valley, which lies a little out of the road, and is strongly recommended by Capt. Widdrington as head-quarters for the naturalist.

The 7 L. to *Muros* took us nine hours' riding. It was at Muros that Jovellanos, one of the few *real* patriots of Spain, was wrecked and insulted by the petty authorities : he died Nov. 27, 1811, at Vega, near Navia, worn-out with age and fatigue, and heart-broken at the ingratitude of his country, which too often uses worst those who have served her the best (see B. White, ' Letters,' p. 480).

Crossing the deep blue and glorious fishing river the Pravia, is the *Castillo de la Barca*, the castle of the ferry-boat, where an ancient square tower defends the passage. The scenery here resembles that of Devonshire, with sloping wood-clothed banks, dipping into the water, damp and green as Mount Edgecombe. 2½ L. of infamous road, up and down over ruts and broken stones, lead to *Aviles;* before which, about 1 L. to the l., on the sea-coast, are the rich coal-mines of Arnao, which are now worked by an Hispano-Belge company. The engine for drawing up the mineral is moved by bullocks, while women do the drudgery of lading the craft below. The adit to the mine hangs about 30 ft. above the sea, the shaft runs about 1200 ft. deep, and runs below the water's level. The seam of coal is about 40 ft. thick. Nothing can be more primitive than the process of mining; and Capt. Widdrington (ii. 135) justly remarks that these, in common with the ballads of the peasantry, carry one back to the times of Pelayus — aye, and much earlier.

Aviles, with a very tolerable *Posada,* is situated about 1 L. from the sea, with an open *ria,* which is flooded at high-water, and well stocked with wild-fowl in winter. An embankment is now making, by which a portion of these valuable salt-marshes will be redeemed. The dull red roofs, and absence of any spire, announce this gloomy old town, which is entered by a causeway over a swamp, passing the large old church of San Nicolas.

Aviles, Argenteorolla, the capital of its *Consejo,* and one of the cradles of the monarchy, contains some 6500 souls : it is cheap, dull, and well provided with fruit and fish. The streets are irregular, damp, and arcaded; the *Plaza* sombre. The women are pretty, and walk with elegance, especially the maidens, who come out to draw water after an Oriental and classical fashion : light and sure is the chamois step of these graceful Rebeccas and Hebes; upright their figure, and picturesque their bearing. The well or fountain in Spain, as in the East, is the morning and evening Tertulia of the womankind, who here pause a moment from a life of toil, to criticise and abuse their friends, for scandal everywhere refresheth the sex. Their costume is quite à l'antique ; a handkerchief, tightly drawn, defines the form of the head, while the hair and knots are collected behind, and fall quite in a Greek model. The boddices are of velvet, or coloured cloth, with a tippet crossed over the bosom.

Aviles has little worth seeing : the architect may look at the houses of the Marquises of Santiago and Ferrera, which are better, and deserve notice. A portion of the rude old walls remains near the quay, which, with the *Puente de San Sebastian,* is respectable. The frontal of *San Nicolas,* built in the Norman style, is very ancient, composed of animals, flowers, zigzag and engrailed patterns. In the interior is a statue of *Nª· Sª· del Carmen,* by Antonio Borja, with lengthy fingers, and an old tomb of the La Sallas family, supported by eight Alhambra-like lions. The font is hollowed out of a Corinthian capital. The *Capilla de Solis* was built in 1499 by Rod°· de Borceros, for Pedro de Solis, who also founded the hospital in 1515. In the San Francisco were three old tombs, and a Santa Rosa by Borja; an Asturian sculpture of the time of Philip III. Juan Carreno de Miranda, the painter, was born here, March 25, 1614. At *Mansanara*, about 1 L. from Aviles, Capt. Widdrington (ii. 127) discovered, in 1843, a curious ancient church of the Norman style, which deserves a visit. It stands isolated in a field. The arch over the high altar is extremely beautiful, and the masonry admirably preserved: the corbels and roof deserve notice. This building is of the 11th century, and belonged once to the Templars.

Aviles may possibly be converted ere long into the most important place on this coast, by one touch of the magic wand of English gold, enterprise, and science. It has been selected by the *North of Spain Railroad Company* to be the terminus of this grand line to Madrid, which has been projected by Mr. Keily and Rembel, and which is intended to pass through Oviedo and Leon. To the former city there can be no difficulty, and in its immediate neighbourhood are some of the largest coal-fields in Europe. It is also contemplated to run steamers from Falmouth to Aviles, a passage which may be effected in two days: thus, in a few years Madrid, the so long isolated central capital of Spain, will be brought within four days' journey of London, the capital of the world, the stronghold of peace, order, and liberty, the fountain of moral civilization. These are gifts worthy of the ocean's queen, and which must inevitably influence, in an incalculable degree, the future progress of Spain to new wealth, honour, power, and prosperity : so be it.

Oviedo lies distant from Aviles 5 L., the first 3 very hilly; at the second, and to the l., a most extensive view opens, with *Gijon* projecting on a tongue of land. Entering the superb *Camino real* is Oviedo, with a glorious background of misty cloudcapt hills towering one above another, the fit mountain capital of the wild Asturias. For Oviedo, see p. 697.

For Oviedo, see p. 697.

ROUTE XC.—LUGO TO OVIEDO.

Gondar	2	
Fontaneira	3	5
Fon Sagrada	3	8
Acebo	2	10
Puente Salime	3	13
Berducedo	2	15
Pola de Allende	2	17
Cangas de Tineo	5	22
Tineo	4	26
Salas	3	29
Grado	3	32
Oviedo	4	36

This inland route is rough riding at all times, and in winter is scarcely practicable, from snow in the passes, and river floods in the valleys. In the summer it is truly Swiss-like and pastoral, and delicious to the artist and angler. It was by it that Ney advanced, in May 1809, on Oviedo; then the relentless invaders converted these happy valleys into scenes of misery, and turned the quiet villages into dens of thieves: they burnt, robbed, and destroyed everything within reach. However fiction be allowable to poets, neither Byron, when he sung of the progress of "Gaul's locust host," nor Walter Scott, ever came up to the reality of horrors which the French then and there perpetrated :—

" When downward on the land his legions
      press,
Before them it was rich with vine and flock,
And smiled like Eden in her summer dress,
Behind his wasteful march a reeking wilder-
      ness."

Take a local guide, and attend to the commissariat. After passing over a broken mountainous district below *Fon Sagrada*, runs the Navia, a glorious salmon and trout river. It rises near Nogales, and enters the sea at Navia, having wound down a Swiss-like valley, with the high range which divides it from the basin of the Eo, walling it up to the left.

The village *Berducedo*, in the heart of the *Consejo* de Allende, is good angling quarters, and the shooting in the broken hills is excellent. The Navia is crossed before reaching Berducedo at a stone bridge. The province of Gallicia is quitted soon after Acebo: another ridge separates the valley of the Navia, which now turns up to the l., from that of the Narcea, on which *Cangas de Tineo*, the head of its *Consejo*, is built. Visit *La Cueva de Sequeras,* which has singular stalactites. The angler will find this neighbourhood an excellent fishing quarter ; on all sides are *Cordales*, or hills, with defiles, and each with its stream. The best rivers will be found to be the Luina, Naviega, and the Pequeña, lower down.

Cangas de Tineo (*Concha,* a shell, a valley) is a central point for the artist and angler. The fishing near the Benedictine monastery of *Corias* is capital : this was founded in 1012, by the Conde Piñelo. In the *Iglesia de la Vega*, are some ancient sepulchres ; here Bermudo *el Diacono* was buried. There is another Benedictine convent at *Obona*, about 1 L. from Cangas, which was founded in 680 by Aldegaster, son of the king of Gijon, who is buried here. The situation on the slopes of the Guadia hill is wild, and the chesnut woods are infested with wolves. Visit also the curious tidal fountain, *La Cornellana.* Now you may either continue on to Oviedo, or sketch and fish down to Villafranca, in the Vierzo, or to Leon. In either case the wild route will ascend to *Naviego* and the *Brañas*, where the *Puerto de Leitariegos* commences. Those proceeding from Cangas to Oviedo, will descend with the Narcea, which empties itself into the Pravia, and both afterwards into the sea near Muros. The salmon are plentiful. *Grado* is another good quarter : the angler will fish up the valley to Oviedo by *Peñaflor,* where he may dine on a trout like Gil Blas. Near this is *Trubia,* famous for its foundry for cannon balls, and Langres, which

contains vast coal-beds, hitherto too much neglected and unappreciated. From Grado, up stream, is the Nalon, with its tributaries, the Lugones, Noreña, both full of trout, and the Nora, which with its feeder, the Aller, is considered one of the best fishing streams in the N.W. of Spain. *Mieres* is a good quarter, and at *Ujo,* about three miles, is the junction of the rivers. The smaller rivulets, Cot and Cannedo, join near *Pola de Somiedo :* Miranda and Silviella are also good quarters ; and the fishing in the Arce and Pequeña is excellent.

Those who are not going directly to Oviedo may branch off from Cangas de Tineo either to Villafranca and the Vierzo (see R. lxvii.), or to Leon (see R. xcii.).

ROUTE XCI.—CANGAS DE TINEO TO VILLAFRANCA.

Naviego	2	
Puerto de Leitariegos .	2 ..	4
Laceana	3 ..	7
Palaceos del Sil . .	3 ..	10
Toreno	3 ..	13
Cacabelos . . .	2 ..	15
Villafranca	1 ..	16

The *Puerto* is the pass through the mountains which divide Leon from Asturias, and being extremely elevated is buried during winter in snow. The *Brañas* are very interesting : the word means a "high place." They are small hamlets of chalets, *chozas*, mountain huts, like the *Bordas* of Navarra, to which the breeders of cattle, or *Vaquieros*, migrate from the plains in the summer. These nomad pastoral shepherds remove in caravans like gipseys, carrying all their household goods, children, and cattle. They thread the intricate passes of the elevated heights, where they pasture their flocks, and make provisions of hay for winter, herding entirely with their cattle, and holding no commerce with the villagers below, or even the other *Brañas* on high. Each little clan stands alone and aloof, in Oriental and Iberian isolation, hating, shunning, and despising its neighbour : they fence themselves in against mankind, as they do their flocks against the wolf. As in Genesis xxiv. 37, they never marry out of their own tribe; and as all are too closely connected for the canonical rules of wedlock, the fee for dispensations is considerable, and robs them of their scanty hard-earned gains. Although they pay no taxes, live without doctors, and die without lawyers, they cannot escape the priest, who works on their superstitions, which are commensurate with their ignorance. The truly Oriental and Spanish spirit of love of self and hatred of all others, extends even to the churches, where a bar divides the flock from their fellow-shepherds and villagers, whom they curse even while at prayers. These Bedouins of the mountain, not desert, have retained many Pagan observances, especially as regards their dead and funerals; in fact, they are unchanged Iberians, savage as the Berbers of the Ereefe mountains, yet not without a wild hospitality to the stranger. Civilization cannot reach these wandering children of Ishmael, who again leave no print of their feet on the earth, for their occupancy is no longer than the herbage of the season.

Laceana is the first town of the Vierzo. Now the route follows the beautiful Sil, thence to Toreno, with a good bridge to Ponferrada (see p. 595).

The route to Leon first ascends to the Puerto, and if the rider takes the line by *Carballo*, then thus :—

ROUTE XCII.—CANGAS DE TINEO TO LEON.

Puerto de Leitariegos .	6	
Villableno	2	.. 8
Puerto de la Magdalena	2	.. 10
Riello	3	.. 13
A la Magdalena . .	2	.. 15
Campo Sagrado . .	1½	.. 16½
Lorenzana	2	.. 18½
Leon	1½	.. 20

Nothing can be wilder than all this rarely-trodden Sierra. To the l. of the pass of Leitariegos are many others; first that of Zerezal, then of Somiedo, then of La Mesa, thus offering openings through the mountains all the way to Pajares (see R. xcvi.), through which the grand road is carried. All the Consejo of Somiedo is alpine. The country is broken, and almost impracticable, and quite so in winter. The woods abound with birds and beasts of prey, as well as game; but in the sheltered valleys an abundance of fruit is raised. The rivers, with their Swiss bridges, are made for the artist and trout fisher. The Orbigo is a beautiful stream, and rises near the *Puerto de la Magdalena ;* but the Luna, which joins it near *Llamas de Ribera,* is perhaps the best of all these trout streams. It flows before its junction through the Consejo de Villamor de Riello. The road then strikes more to the l., and enters the charming valley of the Bernesga, which flows down from the *Puerto de Pajares :* of course the traveller will take a local guide, and attend to the " Provend." For Leon, see p. 605.

SECTION X.

THE ASTURIAS.

CONTENTS.

The Principality; the Character of the Country and Natives ; *Los Montañeses;*
Early History.

The best periods of visit are the warm Spring and Summer months. The chief object is Oviedo, with the fishing and geology in its neighbourhood. The scenery and antiquities of R. xciv., and the scenery and fishing of R. xcv. and xcvi. are highly interesting.

EL *Principado de las Asturias,* the Principality, the Wales of the Peninsula, was the mountain refuge of the aborigines, unconquered alike by Roman or Moor, and afterwards became the cradle of the Gotho-Hispano monarchy. It is a narrow strip, separated by an inner barrier of hills from Leon, and bounded to the N. by another outward range, *La cordillera de la costa,* which fringes the Bay of Biscay, while both of these grand dorsal spines have lateral offshoots or *cordales,* which run into the valleys and dips. The entire area contains about 310 square leagues, and is divided into 69 *consejos,* councils or districts. In climate and natural characteristics it is closely analogous with the Basque provinces and Gallicia : refer, therefore, to the headings of Sect. ix. and xii. The Asturians hate their neighbours, and the Gallicians especially (see p. 681). The Principality is a land of hill and dale, meadow, river, and forest, and as the bosky dells are homes for the dryad, so the limpid streams are haunts for the naiad and the disciple of honest Izaak Walton. The climate is damp; cold in winter, and temperate in summer. It is our Wales on a larger scale, for some of the elevations rise to 10,000 feet above the sea level. The clouds with shadowy wings, always hover above these mountain ranges, which thus become a huge alembic to catch and condense the sea-mists from the Atlantic. Wheat is scarce in these humid regions, and the staple food is maize ; a bad bread is made of rye, or of *escanda,* a sort of spelt wheat which ripens in August. A considerable quantity of cattle is reared here, and, as in Gallicia, the bullocks draw carts and the plough, for they do the work of horses, as women do of asses and men. The pastures and hay feed the cows, who give much milk; and recently some attention has been paid to the dairy, and good fresh butter is made, long a luxury rare in central, southern, and eastern Spain.

The natural timber of oak, chesnut, silver and Scotch firs, and the Pinus Uncinata, is very fine, although the woods are generally either neglected or destroyed, but in remote districts, where safe from the axe, it is superb, as in the forest of Leibana. There is also an abundance of coal and turf for fuel, and of cider for drink; the fruits, flowers, and vegetables resemble those of Devonshire; the hills abound with game, and the rivers with salmon, shad, trout, and eels. The horses (see p. 52) are safe and active: Nero rejoiced in one (Suet. 46). Being small they never were fit for cavalry,—"Hic parvus sonipes nec marti notus" (Sil. Ital. iii. 335); but these mountaineers are better walkers than riders; and the stubborn cobs, hardy as the people, bear the same analogy to their biped masters as the fanfaron Cordovese barb does to the gas-conading *Andaluz*. The Asturian uses his arms quite as actively as his legs, and he is an excellent single-stick player and dancer. The national jigs are *La Muneira* and *La Danza prima*, and a cudgel capering of remote antiquity closely resembling *La danza dels bastons* of the Catalans (see, however, p. 189).

In the Asturias, a country which was so much less exposed to the Moorish and Spanish forays than Andalucia, a greater security of person and property has long existed. There are few robbers, for they would starve in these poor and untravelled hills. Accordingly the peasantry, instead of herding for protection in walled towns, live in small farms, and often own the land which they cultivate. Land in general is more subdivided here, as in the Basque provinces, than in the south, where large districts were granted to the *conquistadores* who assisted in ousting the Moorish occupants. As this distant nook has comparatively escaped the horrors of wars, foreign and domestic, the farms and cottages have less of the misery of the Castiles and Gallicia. The costume of the lower classes is Swiss-like; the females when drest in their best wear boddices of yellow or green, laced in front with gold *joyas*, and coral necklaces. Dark coloured serges are also in great vogue, which with black mantles or *dengues* are thrown over the head; sometimes pretty handkerchiefs are used, which are tied closely over the front, while the hair hangs down behind in long plaits or *trensas*. The Gallician *madreñas*, or French-like *sabots*, wooden shoes, are also replaced by leather ones, and a small sock, edged with red or yellow, is worn over the stockings. The men generally have white felt caps turned up with green, and delight in skittles. Both sexes are kind, civil, and well-mannered, especially the women, who are gentle and attentive to the stranger. Their homes may indeed be humble, and their costume homely; but, far away from cities, commerce, and manufactures, the best qualities of the heart have never been corrupted; a tribute which none who, like ourselves, have ridden over these rugged districts, and shared in their unbought courtesies and hospitalities, will ever deny them.

The Iberian word *ast* implies elevation, thus *ast thor* has been interpreted the "gate of lofty rocks." And these mountains are as unchanged as the original character of those who are born and bred among them, where their native air braces up mind and body. The remnant of the autochthones are active, robust, and industrious, simple, honest, and loyal. These hills, natural fastnesses if defended by brave men, are not to be conquered. It is therefore useless to invade them with a small army, while a large one would be starved. The *Astures* were scarcely known before the reign of Augustus, and were then, like the Cantabrians, serâ domiti catenâ, and subjected more in name than in reality. Nor were they mastered by the Goths, against whom they constantly

rebelled (S⁰· Isid. er. 641). The Saracenic deluge, which swept unresisted
from the East, was first checked and beaten back from these mountains, to
which the highlanders are fondly attached : and here, in spite of damp, hard
fare, and harder work, the average of life is long, and the population swarming,
for which there is neither room nor adequate employment. Hence the males
migrate, like the Nubians to Cairo, and do the work at Madrid of hewers of
wood and drawers of water. They also become valets and indoor servants, and
are the Swiss of Spain, faithful, but interested—point d'argent point d'Astu-
rien. They are among the best cooks in Spain, or rather the least bad in
this land of gastronomic Erebus, where people only eat to live, like the beasts
that perish.

Many of the Asturians, and especially *Los Montañeses* and those who come
from the hills (*Las Montañas*) near Santander, keep the chandlers' and small
grocery shops in other parts of Spain ; and, besides their avarice, they are noted
for tricks in trade, and particularly for the adulteration of their wares: *aguan
el agua*, they water even their water, says the proverb. Many migrate from their
damp homes to arid Andalucia, and seek employment at Xerez and the wine
districts, where they frequently become very rich, for, like their ancestors (Astur
avarus, Sil. Ital. i. 231), they are thrifty and careful of their hard-earned gains.
They return from torrid Andalucia to their sweet-aired hills, like many Scotch,
who have made fortunes in India, do to their heath-clad birth-places. If
debarred a hope of return, they pine from Nostalgia or Heimweh ; but this ma-
ladie du pays—home-ache, like the goitre or itch, is a disease of the highlander,
who cannot live in peace if not sure that his grave will be near his cradle.

Those who do not leave their home remain poor, and, like the Gallicians, are
hardly-worked and ill-fed, both male and female, young and old. They are
much subject to bronchocele or *goitre—Papera, Lamperon.* This, probably a
disease of race, is at all events called into action in most alpine localities, either
by the drinking snowy water, or by something peculiar which finds a matrix in
the predisposing principle in the constitution. *Pero hay remedio para todo*, and
these *Lamparons* are cured by the miraculous oil of the lamps of S⁸· Engracia
at Zaragoza, quite as certainly as the king's evil was by a royal touch. The
Asturians are also afflicted with the *Mal de Rosa*, a sort of erisypelatous scurvy,
which some attribute to an insufficiency of good linen and living.

The Asturias during the Peninsular war produced many notorious personages,
of whom the best was Jovellanos. From this his native province Toreno set sail,
to crave that aid from England which he lived to try to write down. Riego, the
leader of the constitutional rebellion in 1820, Arguelles el divino, Cayetano
Valdes, and sundry stars of the Cadiz Cortes, rose also in these misty hills.
Rivals to them in the field, here Blake and Ballesteros jumped into command
and defeat. Few men, in council or camp, could be named of larger plethora
of vanity, combined with greater infeasibility of practice ; but the modern
Asturians, whatever they may have been and have done before, under Pelayus,
have wofully degenerated. Their character was soon found out by Lord
Lynedoch, who thus wrote to Moore: "The deputies sent over knew nothing
but just concerning their own province, and, *pour se faire valoir*, they exaggerated everything : for example, those of the Asturias talked louder than
any body, and Asturias as yet has never produced a man to the army ;" and
never did since. Again, Carrol writes to Baird : "This province, the first to
declare war with France, has during seven months taken no steps that I can
discover to make arrangements against the event of the enemy's entering the
province. What has been done with the vast sums of money that came from
England? you will naturally ask. *Plundered and misapplied*, every person,

who had or has anything to do with money concerns, endeavouring to keep in hand all he can, to be ready, let affairs turn out as they may, to help *himself* (Nap^r. i. Ap. 57-62). In this money *selfishness* the Astur avarus merely exhibited *one* quality in which, however heterogeneous in other matters, all Spaniards have a common homogeneity, for, as the Duke says of the Spaniards, the first thing they require uniformly is *money* (Disp. May 7, 1811).

The travelling in the Asturias is on the primitive mule or horse, as the roads are like those star-paved highways in Gallicia which are superintended by Santiago, and fit for no carriages but King Charles's wain; one magnificent *Camino real* being the only exception, which traverses the principality from Gijon and Leon to Madrid, and which cost so much that Charles IV. inquired if it were paved with silver. Soon, *it is said,* an iron railway is to be constructed with the gold of England—that fond ally, who fights and pays for Spain. If this grand project—"there is much virtue in If," according to Touchstone—be ever realized in a land of mountains, and where mountain throes bring forth mouselike abortions, the benefit conferred on Madrid and Spain will be incalculable; the dear and ill-provided capital will be readily supplied with colonial produce, foreign ideas, timber, fuel, fresh fruits, fish, butter, and an outlet of export afforded for the corn and wines of the central provinces.

Meanwhile—for even railroads creep *con despacio* in Spain, the cross and interior communications are impracticable for carriages; alpine in character and accommodations, but delightful to the young, the artist, and the angler, whether he wanders inland or coasts the Bay of Biscay, nothing can be more charming than this "sweet interchange of hills and valleys, rivers, woods, and plains, now land, now sea." The antiquarian and lover of romantic annals will remember that this is the corner to which the soldier remnant of the Goth fled, and from whence Pelayus sallied forth to reconstruct the shattered monarchy and religion of Don Roderick. Here, therefore, will be found sites and churches of the eighth century, and whose nomenclature, which like form often outlives substance, is remarkable. The extreme antiquity of the creed is evidenced by the primitive names of the parishes, and the odd quaint saints who are their tutelars, although elsewhere either unknown, or obsolete in the changes of papal hagiology, but here the localism of the Asturian is riveted by his own old and peculiar gods. The Gothic church was very independent of the Pope, whose ritual and dominion were only established in Spain about 1086, and then by foreign and French influence. Here in these wild mountains will be found the cave-palaces and grotto-shrines at which her early champions lived and worshipped when Spain was free and uncorrupted. Many have been pillaged and desecrated by the French, or barbarously neglected by the Spaniard; yet enough exists from which the ingenious architect may reconstruct and understand the former system. The Asturias, poor and out-of-the-way, have been comparatively free from the rage for gilding and *churriguerismo* which came over the more wealthy localities, when the old gods, the Cabiri, the Dii majores gentium, the saints and tutelars of the mediæval centuries, were turned out to make room for men newly raised to heaven, those " ex hominibus Deos," as Cicero says (N. D. iii. 15), who were the exact Pagan types of the modern saints, the Semidei, Ανθρωποι Δαιμονες, of the great puppet-maker, the Κυροπλαστης and *Titiretero* of the Vatican, by whom these canonizations or elevations to demigodhood are managed.

The patois spoken by the peasantry differs from the Gallician, and is called Bable; it was one of the first approaches of the Gotho-Spaniard to the Romance and present Castilian idiom. It is much to be lamented that no one has collected its remains, whether in proverbs or ancient ballads, for in these, besides being the germs of language, many curious relics of early manners and history are doubtless preserved, soon, alas! to be among the things that were, for the Spaniard in the mass lives only for himself and for to-day, and, speaking no language but his own, scarcely knows what philology means: for some remarks on this *Bable*, see Duran, iv. 41.

The antiquarian may consult for this province ' *El Viage de Morales*,' published by Florez, in folio, Madrid, 1765 ; also the ' *Esp. Sag.*' vols. 37, 38, and 39; ' *Antigüedades—de las Asturias*,' Luis Alonzo de Carvallo, Madrid, 1695. The natural history is described by Casal; and the German Professor Schultz is employed in preparing a geological and mineralogical survey and map, a resumé of which has already been printed in the Oviedo ' *Boletin*,' in June and July, 1839; meanwhile what little is known must be searched for in the works of other foreigners, especially Mr. Walton and Capt. Widdrington.

The Asturias gives the title of prince to the heir apparent, which was done in professed imitation of our Prince of Wales, and at the desire of the Duke of Lancaster in 1388, when his daughter Constance married Enrique, eldest son of Juan I. Like that of the Welshman, the pedigree of an Asturian mounts up to the deluge at least, and his *Bable* from the tower of Babel; and he is equally proud of the purity of his religion and excellence of his cheese, although in truth double Gloucester and Puseyism are preferable.

OVIEDO, a name familiar to all readers of ' Gil Blas,' is the mountain capital of this mountain principality. It is a good head-quarter for the fisherman, who will here obtain a guide and replenish his commissariat. There are two posadas, *La Tinaña*, which is very tolerable, and *La Catalana*, where the traveller will be better used than Gil Blas was when he came to bury his father.

Oviedo is a nice clean town, with some 10,000 inhab. It is the residence of the provincial authorities, has an *audiencia territorial*, a theatre, and a reading society, to which foreigners are readily admitted. The university, a fine modern building outside the town, has a decent library. Oviedo has several regular streets : the four principal ones follow the line of the roads to Gijon, Leon, Grado, and Santander, and terminate in alamedas, of which *La Tenderia* and *Chambel* or *Chamberri*, are the most frequented. The streets meet in a handsome Plaza. The town is well supplied by an aqueduct called *Pilares*, which brings pure water from Gitoria: it was planned in 1553 by Juan de Cerecedo, and built in 1599 by Gonzalo de la Bercera. The name

Oviedo is derived from the rivers *Ove* and *Diva*, on which Pelayus defeated the Moors. Previously to 791 the Gothic princes resided at Cangas and Pravia, until Alonzo el Casto made this place his court and capital.

Oviedo in the war of independence was barbarously treated by the French. When Soult, after Moore's retreat, advanced into Portugal, he sent Ney from Lugo with 6000 men to pillage the Asturias. Ney, taking the inland line (see R. xc,), arrived at Oviedo before the careless Asturians even knew of his departure; and while Romana and the Junta were entirely occupied in their own local and base intrigues, the armed spoiler pounced down upon them, May 19, 1809. Thereupon Romana, Worster, and Ballesteros instantly fled, setting an example to their troops which they followed to a man. Although no defence or resistance was made, the city was mercilessly sacked for three days. The thinness of the silver plating of the holy relics, and the earnest prayers of the chapter, who *gave* M. Ney their solid bullion lamps and images (compare p. 671), saved these contents of the *Camora Santa*, which there was no time to con-

2 H

ceal. Thus the " work of angels" was rescued from the sacrilegious crucible of mortal men. The defeat of Soult at Oporto recoiled on Ney, who fled from the N. W. with somewhat tarnished laurels. But miserable Oviedo was again plundered by Bonnet, who re-entered after the misconduct of the Spaniards at Columbres, where Bonnet, in order to decoy his arrogant enemy, had pretended to retire: Barcena fell instantly into the trap, and advanced, like Cuesta at Talavera, on what he supposed were flying deer, but he found them tigers, for Bonnet turned round and scattered his pursuers like sheep. This man, who rose from the revolutionary ranks, was the Alaric of the Asturias, where his name is held in no less execration than Sebastiani's is at Granada or Murcia.

The see of Oviedo was founded in 810 by Alonzo el Casto. At first it was a metropolitan, and afterwards became an *Iglesia estenta*, an excepted church, and not suffragan to any archbishop. The cathedral is called *La Santa*, on account of the relics, and the city *civitas Episcoporum*, because here, in 808-14, a council was held of all the Spanish prelates whose sees were in the possession of the Moors, in partibus infidelium; it was the Glastonbury of the Peninsula. The cathedral, although not large, is very elegant and beautiful. It is not very old, having been begun in 1388 by Bishop Gutierez de Toledo, who in an evil hour took down most of the previous edifice, which was built in 802, and dedicated to San Salvador. With the exception of the *Camara Santa*, the other portions which were spared have subsequently been removed by the modernising chapter. The W. façade, although unfinished, is striking. A noble porch stands between two towers, only one of which is complete, and that, unfortunately, not according to the original design; the chapter, in 1575, having preferred adding an open filigree pyramidical spire, to finishing the opposite larger and incongruous tower,

which they only carried up to the height of the nave. Observe the singular arch of the northern tower. The interior of the cathedral rather disappoints: the central nave is higher than the aisles on each side, and the windows to the l. are not painted. A gallery runs under the clerestory. The *Retablo* of the high altar is of the date 1440, and is divided into five tiers. A modern gilt wooden custodia replaces the former one, which, with a silver *reja*, was stolen by the invader. The *Silla del Coro* is ornamented with inlaid marqueterie.

Many of the lateral chapels are disfigured with *churrigueresque* and modern abominations. The *trascoro* has also suffered, the elegant Gothic centre having been whitewashed, while on each side incongruous altars of dark marble have been erected in a bastard classical style. The chapels at the *trasaltar* are abominable. Here was that of the Virgin, the Escorial or burial-place of the early kings: it was a portion of the original building, which was pulled down in 1712 by Bishop Tomas Reluz, who built the present contemptible abortion, of the very worst period of art. The *Cimborio* is overcharged, and the low pillars, and Corinthian pilasters, and heavy disproportionate cornice, are gross failures. This is now called *La Capilla del Re Casto* (Alonzo II., obt. 843), as he here lies buried, with many of the earliest kings and princes, to wit, Fruela I., Alonzo el Catolico, Ramiro, Ordoño I., Alonzo el Magno, Garcia I., Doña Giloria, wife of Bermudo; Urraca, wife of Ramiro I., &c. Six niches in the walls contain stone coffins. All the original sepulchres, epitaphs, and inscriptions, so carefully described by Morales, have been ruthlessly swept away, and now a paltry modern tablet records their names. The cloisters are small, but solid; the windows are in a good pointed Gothic.

The glory, however, of this cathedral, and this *holy* city, are the relics which were saved at the Moorish invasion, and carried away by Pelayus, who, like the pious Æneas, thought more of his penates than his wife:—

" The relics and the written works of saints,
Toledo's treasure, prized beyond [mains,
All wealth, their living and their dead re-
These to the mountain fastnesses he bore."

Those who have not the works of Florez and Morales may consult Southey's ' Don Roderick,' notes, 89, for some particulars as to this grand

" Magazine of ammunition,
Of crosses, relics, crucifixes,
Beads, pictures, rosaries, and pixes,
The tools of working our salvation
By mere mechanic operation."

This superstition is the natural abuse of a yearning placed in every human heart, which therefore was marshalled into the service of a crafty, worldly-wise church. There is an amiable poetical feeling in loving a relic, the all that is left us of a benefactor—a memorial of one lost for ever, and yet to memory dear. These relics are in the *Camara Santa,* or the primitive chapel (repainted, alas!) of *San Miguel,* which is thought to be the second oldest Christian building after the Moorish invasion. It is concealed, for greater security, between the cathedral and its cloisters, and is elevated to preserve the relics from damp : 22 steps ascend to an anteroom with groined roof. Observe the arched way, with foliage and quaint sculpture, which leads to the chapel, 26 ft. by 16. At the end, and two steps lower, is the inner sanctum sanctorum : 12 statues of the apostles, coeval with the building, support the roof, and the mosaic pavement resembles those of Italy of the ninth century, and especially the Norman-Byzantine works in Calabria and Sicily. It was once lighted up by magnificent silver lamps, which were carried off by the French. The devout kneel before a railing while the holy relics are exhibited. Morales thus writes his official report to Philip II. :—" *Estoy escribiendo en la iglesia antes de la reja, y Dios sabe que estoy fuera de mi de temor y reverencia.* Such was the

fear and reverence of this learned man, who trembled before these gold enshrined objects, a fear from which M. Ney, *le brave des braves,* was philosophically exempt.

Printed papers in French, Latin, and Spanish are given to pilgrims, in which the authenticity of each relic is vouched for by the dean and chapter; while Pope Eugenius granted 1004 years and 6 *cuarantenas* (or 40 days) indulgence to all who visit, behold them, and believe that their souls will be saved by the intercession of those whose bones are now bowed down to. The prayer to be recited on the *Fiesta de las Reliquias* runs thus : "Propitiare Domine nobis famulis tuis, per horum sanctorum tuorum, quorum reliquiæ hic continentur, merita gloriosa, et eorum piâ intercessione, ab omnibus semper muniamur adversis" (Morales, 85).

Referring for details to the official statement, these relics were removed from Jerusalem, when it was taken by the Persian Chosraes, to Africa; thence to Cartagena, Seville, Toledo, the Monte Sacro, and Oviedo. They were first kept by the Goths at S°· Toribio, near *Los Escobios de Morcin,* until Alonzo el Casto built the *fortaleza* in 875. They consist of the usual assortments, *e. g.* manna from the desert, a firkin of the marriage of Cana, the bones of Pantaleon, Cucufato, Bachis, Pomposa, and other saints nominated in the paper by the dean, whose very names indicate their antiquity. They have long since been supplanted by more modern and fashionable tutelars, male and female. The relics are quite as old, and the darker the age the bolder the pious fraud. Thus at Glastonbury, once the English Oviedo, they showed the stone which the devil offered to Christ for him to turn into bread, which proved a philosopher's stone to the artful monks.

The Oviedo *Arca,* or chest, is really genuine, and it is made of oak, covered with thin silver plating, with bassi relievi of sacred subjects, and a Latin

2 H 2

inscription round the border, which refers to the contents. Observe particularly the crucifix made by Nicodemus; it is of ivory, about a foot high: the figure exactly resembles the *Cristo de las batallas* of the Cid at Salamanca, which thus fixes its age about the 11th century. The feet are separate, and not nailed one on the other; and as this was made by Nicodemus beyond all question, it is referred to by Spanish theologians as settling a position much questioned. Here is the sandal of St. Peter, and some of the Virgin's milk in a metal box. In another small case is kept the *santo sudario*, or shroud of our Saviour, which is exhibited publicly three times a year, and always on Good Friday, when the bishop preaches: it is then displayed from a balcony which has been harbarously cut out of the staircase of the *Camara Santa* in 1732. The peasants hold up loaves, beads, and other objects, which they are taught and believe do thus acquire a nutritious and medicinal quality. To pry into this arc entailed certain punishment; thus Garibay relates (E. S. xxxix. 122) that in 1550 the bishop, Christobal de Rojas Sandoval, although he had prepared himself by fasting and prayer, on attempting to open it was struck senseless. Thus Eurypylus, at the taking of Troy, obtained an arc, which contained an image of Bacchus made by Vulcan, and given to Dardanus by Jupiter; he attempted to open it, but was deprived of his senses (Paus. vii. 19. 6). So Minerva ordered none to peep into the basket in which she concealed Erichthonius, and all who did went mad and committed suicide (Paus. i. 18. 2): comp. 1 Sam. vi. 19; 1 Chron. xiii. 9.

The identical heaven-wrought *Casulla*, which the Virgin placed herself on the shoulders of San Ildefonso at Toledo, *is said* to be at Oviedo, for the replies to our inquiries were not satisfactory. Another remarkable object is the portable altar used by the apostles: it is shaped like a book,

is encased with silver, and decorated inside with ivory carvings, and certainly is a work of the tenth century. Next comes the cross of Pelayus (*La Cruz de la Victoria*), which fell from heaven at Cangas before his victory, like Virgil's "lapsa ancilia cœlo." It is encased in a magnificent filigree-work made at Gauson, 4 L. from Oviedo. The coeval inscription records that it was given by King Adefonsus et Schemena (Ximena), era 946, A.D. 908. Older still by a century is that which was made by angels, like the cross of Caravaca, although Morales (p. 76) thinks the front only to be their work. This is in the shape of a Maltese cross, enriched with gilt filigree-work, of a Byzantine or Moorish character, and is set with uncut precious stones. The four arms are thus inscribed: "Susceptum placide maneat hoc in honore Dei offert Adefonsus, humilis servus Christi. Hoc signo tuetur pius, hoc signo vincitur inimicus; quisquis auferre presumpserit mihi fulmine divino intereat ipse; nisi libens voluntas dederit mea. Hoc opus perfectum est in era DCCCXLVI, A.D. 808." This cross, therefore, and that at Santiago, are indubitably more than a thousand years old; but neither age nor the threat of the lightning could save *La Cruz de la Victoria* from being seized from the altar by a French soldier, who carried it off, just as the sacrilegious Dionysius stole the pagan *Victoriolas aureas* (Cic. 'N. D.' iii. 34). It was rescued by the canon Alfonzo Sanchez Ahumada by a mere accident, as he told us himself, which hereafter will be cited as a miracle: and that any thing of silver escaped the Gaul is indeed little short of being one.

The fine old library of the cathedral, of which many MSS. really came from Toledo, had long been left by the chapter as food for worms, as Gil Blas' good uncle was a worthy dignitary of these stalls. The register books of deeds, &c., which are kept in most Spanish cathedrals and convents, are here called *Tumbos*, but the usual name is *Libros de Becerro,* from the *calf* binding. (*Becerro* is the diminutive of the Arabic *Baccara,* an ox; unde, *Vaca;* Latinè, *Vacca.*)

Oviedo, as might be expected, contains some of the earliest Christian churches in the Peninsula. They are carefully described by Morales in his ' *Viage,*' by Cean Bermudez (Arch. i. 4), and Widdrington (ii. 102). Their round-headed pillar style, our early Saxon, is here called *obra de Godos,* work of the Goths, in order to distinguish it from the pointed style, which we most improperly call *Gothic,* but which Spaniards with more judgment term *Tudesco,* or Tedesque.

These primeval churches are simple and solid, and usually provided with a projecting shed or roof at the entrance, as a protection against the rainy climate. The best preserved specimens exist on the lofty hill of red sandstone called *La Cuesta de Naranco,* which rises on the opposite side of a valley to the N. of Oviedo. These are among the oldest Christian churches in the Peninsula, and, from being out of the town, have been less exposed to the harpy touch of modernising innovators. They are true types of the Gotho-Hispano temples of the infant monarchy, and so small as to resemble baths or vaulted tombs.

First visit the *Sa. Maria de Naranco,* which is still used as a parish church. The curate lives in a portion of the building, which is contrived by the irregular level of the hill-side. From this point Oviedo, backed by its mountains, is seen to great advantage. The entrance is by a portico. The interior is divided into three parts, the floor of the central portion being the lowest. The main body is about 40 ft. long, by 15 wide, which is large, as Morales says, for a hermitage, but small for a church. The crypt below, says he, was also used as a church, according to the usage of the period. Observe the twisted cable-like pillars, the circular roof, the carved shields, and the three low arches behind the altar. Some of

the columns are said to have been brought from a Roman temple at Lugo. No doubt the early Christians used up the materials of pagan edifices, just as the contemporary Moors did at Cordova and elsewhere (see p. 299). How different, however, the monuments of the two people—how gorgeous and vast the *Mezquita,* compared to these small and simple churches! How strong both are, although composed of different materials, is evinced by their existence after the lapse of twelve centuries.

On the capital of one column is a rude sculpture, which is supposed by the vulgar to refer to the female tribute paid to the Moors by Mauregato, obt. 788. This church, a gem of antiquity, is kept in decent repair by the curate, and at his own expense; for the Oviedo authorities care for none of these things, and even if they had money would not advance a *cuarto* to keep up old stones. The curate, well-meaning but ignorant, has, however, turned out the old font for a spick-and-span new one.

San Miguel de Lino, which stands a little higher up the hill, is of a cruciform shape, and must when perfect have been a miniature church in its proportions, and with all the usual accessories. It is fast going to ruin, being shamefully neglected and desecrated. Observe the windows in the *Crucero,* the short pillars and arches. The vulgar assert that the *ch'ste* Alonzo and his wife Berta had their separate beds in two recesses in the *tribuna :* but these spaces were destined for *objetos de culto,* and the church, according to Morales (Viage, 103), was not built until after their death by Ramiro I. (circa 850): the architect's name was Tioda, or Fioda. Mariana (vii. 13) states that they were defrayed out of the spoil taken at Clavijo, where Santiago fought in person; this side of the hill was then covered with houses, which disappeared when Alonzo el Magno (circa 905) fortified Oviedo. Morales, in 1572, describes the ruined traces of the palace of Ramiro; and fragments are still encased in more modern buildings.

There are two other churches of this period, one about a mile outside the town on the road to Gijon, which was probably built by Tioda, and is dedicated to *San Julian* (Santullano). It has three aisles, and is in good proportion. The character is Byzantine, although Cean Bermudez says Tuscan. Observe the short pillars on each side of the altar, and singular capitals: examine the exterior and the window to the E. The other, *Nᵃ· Sᵃ· de la Vega*, according to Morales, was founded by Doña Gontrodo Perez, obt. 1186, mother of Queen Urraca. She was buried here, and Florez (Rey. Cat., i. 300) has preserved her curious Latin epitaph. See also '*E. S.*,' xxxviii. 151.

Returning to the town, near the cathedral are the remains of *La Corte*, or residence of *El Re Casto*. The *fortaleza* was added by Alonzo III. el Magno, to protect the holy relics from pirates; meaning, no doubt, the Normans, who ravaged the coast in 862 (see p. 240). Morales saw and copied the original inscription. The remains of an old tower have quite the Norman character of the period. This fort, however, and other ancient buildings, were pulled down to make space for the cathedral cloister. Unfortunately, many other of the genuine inscribed stones, mentioned by Sandoval, Florez (E. S. xxxvii. 140), and others, and precious historical evidences, have been allowed to be lost. The *fortaleza* was made into a prison, the usual fate of Spanish alcazares. The date (era 913) was inscribed over the door.

Adjoining the cathedral is another very ancient church, dedicated to *San Tirso;* but it has been sadly modernised. How handsome it once was may be inferred from the description of the Bishop Sebastiano: "Cujus operis pulchritudinem plus præsens potest mirari quam eruditus scriba lauⁱlare." A double arch, with columns in the ex-

terior wall, is all that exists. Of this early period is *San Payo*, close by a church which was originally founded by Alonzo el Casto to the honour of St. John the Baptist, but the dedication was changed when the remains of San Pelayo were placed here by Ferd. I., in 1023 or 1053. This St. Pelayus, the Shant Pelay of the Moorish annalists, was the nephew of a Bishop of Tuy, who, taken prisoner by the Moors at the battle of Junquera, was left at Cordova as a hostage for the prelate, where he was put to death for resisting the kalif in 925. His body was begged as a favour by Sancho El Gordo, who went to Cordova to consult Moorish physicians, and it was removed with great pomp by his son, Ramiro III.

The ecclesiologist will look into the church of *San Juan*, and observe the billet moulding round the front; and near it the huge convent of *San Vicente*, founded in 1281 for Benedictines by the abbot Fromestano. It was a double monastery for monks and nuns. The former portion is now converted into the residence of the gefe politico, and for public *oficinas*, such as the printing, tobacco, and other governmental departments. The cell of Padre Feijoo, one of the brotherhood, is shown. It was he whose critical essays, about a century ago, dispelled some of the crassest popular errors of Spain, which, like mists on hills, have long made the Peninsula their chosen resting-place. The Spanish Benedictines fell off sadly after the death of this Helluo librorum; they never studied much afterwards, because, as their *Feijoo* had read and written enough for the whole world and to the end of the world, they had a fair claim to the benefit of his good works of supererogation. His '*Teatro Critico Universal*,' his '*Cartas Eruditas y Curiosas*,' with replies, rejoinders, &c., "more Hispano," fill 19 vols. 4to., and have gone through many editions: ours, the fifth, was published at Madrid by the heirs of Fⁱᵒ· de Hierro, 1748. Peace to his ashes!

On the wall outside is encased a

monument to Jovellanos, who in our times followed the example of Feijoo: it is placed with much propriety opposite the road to Gijon, the native town of that truly enlightened patriot.

The convent of *San Francisco*, founded it is said by St. Francis himself, is now converted into a hospital. The walk is one of the most beautiful of Oviedo. The view from the stone where criminals are shot is charming, looking over the aqueduct and *San Miguel de Lillo.* Capt. Widdrington describes the fine oak here as the Quercus Pedunculata. This *Paseo* is on holidays frequented by the lower classes, who sing and dance their peculiar circular evolutions: the words of their songs, *viva Pravia,* still refer to Pelayus and his victories over the Moor. Sunday is a grand day for the peasants' dressing and dancing. They assemble on the *Plaza* after mass, where the local costume may be studied. Observe the fair, fresh complexions of these brown-haired daughters of the Goths, whose long locks are plaited in *trensas.* They carry their water-vessels and baskets with the upright gait of a Hebe. The men wear a peculiar skyblue cap or montera, and are fond of an ugly yellow cloth. The convent of *S^{n.} Agustin,* nearly opposite S^{n.} Francisco, is now a *casa de Esposito,* and, as usual, a miserable establishment. (See Seville, p. 271.)

Walk also out on the Santander road, and look back on the imposing jumble which is formed of S^{n.} Vicente, S^{u.} Pelayo, the old tower, and cathedral. The S^{o.} Domingo, on the Leon road, with its groves, has become a hospital. The Asturian mountains, as seen from the *Campo Santo,* are very grand.

The domestic architecture of Oviedo, with projecting roof, is suited to the damp climate. Among the deserted mansions of the nobility may be cited the house of the D. del Parque, now a *fabrica de armas;* that of the M. of Campo Sagrado, a fine square building, in which Gen. Bonnet lived, whose misdeeds are recorded by Toreno (xi.).

Omit not to visit the *Casa Solar* of this historian, whose family is one of the most ancient of the Asturias. The *Calle de la Plateria* has some Prout-like bits. The *Audiencia* has a jurisdiction over 434,600 souls; the number of persons tried in 1844 was 484, giving one in every 865; in Madrid the proportion is one in every 192: so much for the relative morality between this simple highland city and the corrupt capital.

The trout-fishing in the vicinity of Oviedo is capital. Walk out also one afternoon to *Las Caldas,* Calidas, the warm baths, 1 L., which are charmingly situated *en la ribera de abajo.* The buildings were erected in 1731-80, by Manuel Requero Gonzalez. The season is from June 1 to Sept. 30, when they are well attended.

Oviedo, like Lugo, is the centre of many communications. A superb road leads to Leon (R. xcv.). The lateral routes are almost bridle tracks, but extremely picturesque, whether running along the coats or inland. Those which lead to Lugo and Mondoñedo have been described (R. lxxxix. and xc.). To Santander there are two lines, one by the sea-shore, the other by the interior.

ROUTE XCIII.—OVIEDO TO SANTAN-DER.

Venta de Puga	.	.	2
Gijon . .	.	.	2 .. 4
Villa Viciosa .	.	.	4 .. 8
Lastres .	.	.	3 .. 11
Riba de Sella .	.	.	4 .. 15
Llanes . .	.	.	5 .. 20
Columbres	.	.	3 .. 23
S^{a.} Vicente	.	.	2 .. 25
Cumillas .	.	.	1¼ .. 26¼
Santillana	.	.	3 .. 29¼
P^{e.} del Arce .	.	.	3 .. 32¼
Santander .	.	.	3 .. 35¼

There is a daily coach from Oviedo to Gijon.

The 7th edition of the ' Encyclopædia Britannica,' 1842 (see also Escorial), informed mankind, that " *no* coal has yet been discovered in any part of Spain, nor have any indications of the existence of that mineral presented themselves;" but in addition to the long-worked coal-beds of Soria and Seville, the whole of this Gijon district is one coal-field.

The mineralogist will therefore avoid the high road, and make a détour into the *Consejos of Siero* and *Langreo*, ascend the beautiful Nalon to *Sama*, 3½ L., and hence to *Siero*. The Nalon flows through one vast inexhaustible deposit of coal. These beds, like many other buried treasures in Spain, have long been neglected by the apathetic natives; and yet they are destined hereafter to make a great change in their commerce and manufactures. The peasants used to scrape out a little here and there, digging holes after their own rude caprice: a cart-load of the finest coal, and weighing 12 cwt., being worth only 3 reals, or about 8d., at the pit. It used to be carried to Gijon on muleback, where it was worth about 2s., and this in a country where the raw materials, stone for roads, and iron for railroads, iron in juxtaposition with coal, are abundant. Recently, however, a carriage road has been constructed, called *El Carbonero*, which communicates with Gijon. This, in common with most improvements in these parts, was owing to Aguado, who lost his life in the hardships of a journey here over the Pajares in 1842.

This capitalist rose from the dregs of society, and became an *Afrancesado* in 1808. When the French were driven out of Spain by the Duke, he fled with them, and set up a *tienda de Montañes*, or a wine and chocolate shop, in the Rue Jean Jacques Rousseau, at Paris. He managed the 1823 loan for Ferdinand VII., and eventually became ex nihilo a millionaire, a man of *muchas talegas*, of many " purses." The *talega* contains 1000 dollars, and is the Moorish *taleca* or *bidr*, 10,000 dirhems. Aguado was created *Marques de las Marismas* (Swamps): for, among other irons in the fire, he was mixed up in the Guadalquivir company (see R. iii.), and in spite of his *aqueous* name and title, he was *mas agudo que aguado*, and

a shrewd raiser of the wind as well as water. As money and intelligence are the emphatic wants in every Spanish cabinet, whether in Madrid or the Asturias, his death has been a serious blow to this district. He established the chief of the four great companies which are at work here. His apportionment is situated on the Nalon, about 1 L. from Oviedo, and he had secured the monopoly of his new road. Since his death the concern has languished, for in Spain, as in the East, few things are *per autre vie ;* these plans and schemes rise and fall with the individual whose mind and power created and sustained them. There is a truly Spanish difficulty raised in allowing strangers to see the bungling works, the usual effect of ignorance and its concomitant, jealousy. Lower down on the Nalon is the district of the English company. The beds in some places run 13 feet thick, but the average is between 3 and 4. Want of road and means of transport neutralises the abundance of mineral, which is good and of a better quality than most of the French and foreign sulphureous coal: it cannot, however, compete with the English: yet here it lies on the surface, and in a country where the population is swarming, labour is cheap, and man hard-working; where no expensive shafts are necessary, no costly steam-engines required. But the mines are in *Spain*, and not in England.

Sir Robert Peel's duties on the exportation of English coal, gave these mines a spur, and foreign capitalists awakened the Spaniard from his siesta, and taught him, instead of hunting for imaginary lost treasures, to begin to dig up these real sources of wealth. Still they are as yet very imperfectly worked, although the smelting works of Malaga and Cartagena require great supplies. However, in 1841, about 20,000 tons (only) were shipped at Gijon; and such was the paralysing effect of Spanish fiscal laws, tolls, dues, bad roads, and unbusiness-like ways, that 215,000 tons of English coal were imported in 1843 by Murcia alone, although burdened with an export duty of 2*s.* per ton, and a Spanish import duty of 7*s.*

Since Aguado's death, many Asturian mining companies have been set on foot for working these coal and iron ores, and the district has been thoroughly surveyed by practical engineers and geologists. The mines may be safely worked, for this principality, from its geographical position, physical conformation, and the moral character of its inhabitants, has always enjoyed a comparative immunity from the political agitations which have disturbed other parts of the kingdom. The ports of shipment selected by one company are those of *Aviles* and *Riva de Sella.* The former port is capable of admitting vessels of 300 tons burden, whilst the latter boasts of one of the safest and most commodious harbours in the north of Spain. The river Sella, whose embouchure forms the port, can be made navigable, at a comparatively limited cost, for several miles into the interior, and within a short distance of some of the company's most valuable mineral concessions. Those who place confidence in Spanish speculations, and who like to become shareholders, will obtain all particulars at Oviedo, or Baron Morat, or the bankers Rousseaux. The London agents are Messrs. Amory and Co., Throgmorton Street. The Spanish prejudice against coals, as being dirty and unwholesome, must give way when the working of powerful machinery is in question, and as the scanty supplies of wood and charcoal become daily more diminished, and still more if the projected railroad is completed, which will carry coals to Madrid. On quitting Siero we reach La Pola, with a fine but unfinished cinquecento palace. Hence to *Gijon,* Gigia : the Posada is decent. This sea-port is built on a projecting low headland, under the hill Catalina, and although the entrance is bad, yet the anchorage inside is good. The site of *Aras Sestianas* (Pomp. Mela, iii. 1)

has been traced at Cabo de Torres. The Moors destroyed the Roman town, and used it as a quarry to construct Gijon, their frontier defence. The name Gyhon, " valley of grace," is Syrian, and was the place where Solomon was anointed (1 Kings i. 33). Munusa, the Moorish governor, evacuated it in 718, after the loss of the battle of Canicas; and the conqueror, Pelayus, settled in his place, calling himself Conde de Gijon, which he soon made so strong that it beat back the Norman invaders in 844. Henrique II. gave it to his natural son who in it defied Henrique III., by whom it was almost destroyed : it was rebuilt in 1410 by Lucas Bernaldo de Quintana. The bay is pleasant, and the port good for small ships : here the local steamers touch going up and down, and thus those who wish to avoid the rough rides to La Coruña or Santander, can be rapidly conveyed.

Entering at the gate of the Infante Pelayo, the handsome *Calle de la Cruz* leads down to the Mole and port; the fortifications are after the usual neglected style. The town is cheap, clean, and well supplied ; the fish excellent, pop. under 6000. There is not much to be seen. The *Para. de Sn. Pedro* is small ; the statues of the tutelar and of our Saviour are by Ant⁰· Borja. A more suitable church for the growing town was planned by Gaspar Melchior de Jovellanos, who was born here Jan. 5, 1744. He was the benefactor of the town, which he improved morally by his *Instituto Asturiano,* or school of a high order : the building, as usual, is unfinished, for Jovellanos died a miserable persecuted man at Vega, Nov. 27, 1811. Thus Spain rewards those who serve her the best. At Gijon, also, was born Cean Bermudez, the excellent author on Spanish art. Gijon traffics with England in nuts, which come from Villa Viciosa, *el capital de las Avellanas,* and with chesnuts from Colunga. It was from hence that Toreno and the Asturian deputies sailed, May 30, 1808, to implore the aid of England to save them from France. Toreno was a star of the Cadiz Cortes, and one of the few of mortal men who have praised that Bedlamite assemblage, and their impracticable, absurd constitution. He was by birth one of the noblest and richest of the Asturias, and a speaker of much eloquence. As Premier of Spain, he introduced Mendizabal into the loans and finance of Madrid; for results, inquire at the London stock exchange.

Gijon, like Oviedo, was sacked, its warehouses plundered, and its shipping destroyed by the French under Bonnet.

The coast road resembles that to Rivadeo, and is intersected with *rias*, *tinas* or estuaries, cauldrons, and bays. The ascents and descents, the crossing and fording trout streams, are wearisome but picturesque. The coast is infested with *contrabandistas* and *guardas de costa*, or preventive-service men; these firm allies and partners of the smuggler worry the honest traveller, who omits to bribe them. *Villa Viciosa*, with its nuts, may be left to the r.— N.B. Eat chesnuts at *Colunga*. *Riba de Sella* is built on the opposite side of a *ria*, hemmed in by mountains. The Sella comes down from *Infiesta* and *Cangas de Onis;* the fishing higher up, above the junction of the Dobra, near Arriondo, is splendid. The ride to *Sn. Vicente* is intersected by a number of rivers which must be passed, while to the angler these are all that his fondest hopes can desire. First occurs the Agua Mia, near *Pria ;* then the Rio Caliente, near *Rules ;* then the Niembro or Calabres; then the Poa and the Rio de Llanes. *Llanes* is the last town in the Asturias; there are two ancient monasteries, each about three miles distant from Llanes, and about two miles from each other; one is called San *Antolin*, and the other *Celorio*, which is charmingly situated, and has a fine Gothic chapel. *Columbres* is the first town in the *Montañas de Santander*, which are so called to distinguish them from the mountains of *Burgos* and *Rei-*

nosa. From these *Montañas* descend the *Montañeses*, or chandlers, and the celebrated wet-nurses. The vast forest of *Leibana*, between the Peñas de Europa and Reinosa, contains some of the finest timber in the world. See R. cxiv., and the ' *Historia* ' of these districts by Cossio, 4to. Madrid, 1688. The Deva is a noble salmon and trout stream. The angler should ascend into the *Consejo de Cabrales*, and make either *Carreña* or *Arreñas* his head-quarters, where the Cases, coming down from Carmaneña and the Casano, unite and swell the Deva. The next stream is the glorious Nansa, which to the Asturian angler is as the Namsen in Norway.

San Vicente is a miserable place. Here Gen. Sarrut, with 900 dashing Frenchmen, utterly routed 6000 Gallicians, on Nov. 20, 1808. One charge of cavalry was enough to scare the commander-in-chief, who turned, and the troops followed their leader, abandoning all Romana's artillery, and leaving Oviedo open to the spoiler. The Spanish general, Llano Ponté, did not even pause to destroy the boats; worthy of his name, he gave a broad bridge, a pont d'or, not to a retreating but to an advancing foe. (See Schep. ii. 115, and Toreno xi.)

The fine bridge, with thirty-two arches, was built in 1433; the smaller, with eight, in 1779. The panteon of an *inquisidor* is worth looking at; it was sculptured in Genoa. A wellgirt traveller may reach Santander the next day, unless his love for Gil Blas detain him in *Santillana*. This pretty town, the ancient Concana, is placed on the river Besaga, which has excellent fishing all the way up to *Corales*. Santillana is distant about 1 L. from the seaport Suances, Portus Vere-asueca. The *besugos*, a sort of bream, are excellent eating. The Santillans have ceased to quaff the Tartar drink of horses' blood, the luxury of their ancestors (Sil. Ital. iii. 361; Hor. Od. iii. 4, 34).

The name Santillana is the corruption of *Santa Juliana*, as Illan is of St.

Julian, the patron of pilgrims. She is the patroness of the town, to which her body was brought in 1307. Inigo Lopez de Mendoza, the friend of Juan II. and the Mæcenas of Spain, took her name for his title, and gave it to this his city. The arms are, Santa Juliana holding the devil, or Asmodeus in chains. No wonder, therefore, that Le Sage had a partiality to this *native* imp, an " *hijo* " del pueblo. The *Casa Consistorial,* in the *Plaza,* is a fine building, and worthy of a town which really did give birth to the Inigo Jones of Spain, Juan de Herrera. At the *Puente de Arce,* the Pas is passed, which flows down from those healthy mountain districts, where stout single-stick-playing peasants beget those juicy wet-nurses, *Las Pasiegas,* who suckle the sickly children of unhealthy Madrid, and whose rich costume forms a gay feature on the *Prado.* Thence to thriving Santander (see R. cxvii.).

We are now in the country of Gil Blas, and cannot pass by without one word on that charming novel and its author, Le Sage. The lover of Don Quixote and Cervantes may turn to p. 314, and compare the two works and writers : how different, yet both how popular ! Le Sage, a *littéraire de Paris,* who wrote for bread, took for his hero a clever low French-like rogue of a valet, in whom personally we take small interest, for his doings savour of the tricks and tone of the ante-chamber. Cervantes, a soldier and gentleman, chose for his hero the stately old Castilian Hidalgo, for whom, in spite of his monomania, we feel respect and affection. Don Quixote is a *Castellano a las derechas,* a true Spaniard to the backbone of the good old stock ; while Gil Blas is one only in voice, for his hands are the hands of a Frenchman.

It has long been a mooted point who wrote Gil Blas : the work first appeared in French, and was published at different times ; the two first vols. in 1715, a third in 1724, and the fourth and last in 1735. Its success was de-

servedly immediate and extensive; it became European, and a pendant, if not a rival to Don Quixote. It was translated into most languages, and into Spanish about 1783 by the celebrated Padre Isla, the author of ' *Fray Gerundio de Campazas,*' a spiritual Don Quixote, in which the absurd ignorance and superstitions of the mendicant monks were cleverly exposed, although, as usual with Spaniards, the jest was overdone; but they can leave nothing in the inkstand. In spite of his perception of ridicule in others, the Padre Isla boldly asserted that the entire work of Gil Blas was *stolen* by Le Sage from Spain *en bloc,* like the church plate of Cordova, Santiago, &c., by Messrs. Dupont & Co. The Padre, in his translation, retained all the topographical, chronological, and other minor errors, which thick as leaves in Valombrosa, are the straws which show that at least a Frenchman had meddled with the foreign original, just as Mons. Bonnemaison tampered with the transported Raphaels of the Escorial.

Padre Isla's title-page is a choice specimen of the aptitude of *Nosotros* to take *all* the credit to themselves for the labour and industry of others : ' Aventuras de Gil Blas de Santillana *robadas* a España y adoptadas en Francia por M. Le Sage, *restituidas a su patria* y a su lengua nativa por un Espanol celoso, que no sufre *se burlen de su nacion.*' In his fear that the foreigner should make a fool of him, this zealot spoke out the genuine sentiments of *Españolismo;* and it reached beyond the Pyrenees, giving deep offence to the French, in whose character, when national glory and honour are concerned, a liberal acknowledgment of error seldom formed part. Accordingly, in 1818, Mons. Le Compte François de Neufchateau, membre de l'Institut, published a dissertation to prove that Gil Blas *must* be a French work because it was so clever : this plea was demurred to by Llorente, the author of the excellent exposition of the Spanish inquisition, and the quarrel became a very pretty one. The Spaniard had by far the best of the argument, especially as regarded the niceties of national idiom and peculiarities. The substance of his reasoning was put together in a very smart paper in Blackwood, June, 1844, although the printer's devil exhibited throughout it an ignorance of Spanish language, names, and orthography, which would have done credit to M. Le Sage himself. Llorente imagined the author of Gil Blas to have been Antonio Solis, the historian of Mexico, which, however, is a mere conjecture. Others had affirmed that it was written by a nameless Andalucian lawyer, who, about 1654, composed this satire on Spanish ministers, justice, drama, and medicine, which he did not dare to print, and the MS. is supposed to have been obtained by the Mᵃ⋅ de Lionne, a great book collector, who was in Spain in 1656 on the matter of the peace of the Pyrenees. In no country in the world have more works been left in MS. than in Spain, as the expense of printing, the obstacles raised by censors and the Inquisition, and the inadequate remuneration, deterred many authors, who, having gratified their cacoethes scribendi, were content to remain in typeless obscurity. The Marquis bequeathed his library to his grandson, the Abbé de Lionne, the early patron of Le Sage, and his master in the Spanish language. Le Sage certainly never even set his foot in Spain, for, a true Parisian, he adored Paris as much as Socrates loved Athens : his vocation was writing, by which he obtained his living. He began by translating Spanish comedies and novels : he lacked the *invention* of Cervantes, and was an appropriator and embellisher of other men's thunder, nor was he ever held by his contemporaries to be an *original* author, as even Voltaire thought his *Gil Blas* to be pilfered. His genius was synthetical, not creative; he could combine and construct, but not originate. From the

beginning he depended on the sweat of other men's brows : accordingly his mind, from frequent translation, was impregnated with the things of Spain, and his pickings and stealings were not severely visited by his countrymen, who in these matters are not over scrupulous.

It would seem that Le Sage, having all his life avowedly gleaned and paraphrased Spanish books, and having acknowledged that his ' *Bachelier de Salamanque* ' was translated from a Spanish MS. which he never produced, all at once brought forth this ' Gil Blas,' and claimed it for his own. It is, however, admitted by all critics that two-thirds and the best incidents, are certainly of Spanish origin, and Le Sage himself took no pains to conceal the fact. Thus, although the Padre Isla did not know it, he borrowed many of the scenes and characters in ' Gil Blas,' from the ' *Marcos de Obregon*' of Vicente Espinel, from whose preface the opening incident of the student and the buried soul of Pedro Garcias, is taken word for word. So are the scenes of the Posada de Penaflor, of the barber Diego de la Fuente, and the physician's wife; and, as if to whisper whence he stole those sweets, Le Sage actually and honestly gives the name of Marcos de Obregon to the Escudero. He boldly adopted the maxim of Molière, who, like Corneille, borrowed pretty freely from Spanish books : le beau est *mon bien*, et je le reprends où je le retrouve; an appropriation and justification, by the way, from another Spaniard, Seneca, who thus expresses his predaceous principle : "Quicquid bené est dictum ab ullo *meum est.*" (Ep. xvi.)

Probably Le Sage made up his ' Bachelier de Salamanque,' as well as 'Gil Blas,' out of the same Spanish MS., but as the former novel had been seen by others in MS., he did not venture to appropriate that to himself, but proceeded to eviscerate the original, interweaving other stories, and some decidedly his own, which being truly French, mar the Spanish tone and sentiment of the genuine portions.

As he copied from a MS., and not a book in print, partly from the difficulty of deciphering a foreign handwriting in a language which he only understood imperfectly, Le Sage fell into errors of orthography, names, geography, &c., that would have disgraced even a Laborde. Indeed, they are so numerous that the French argue, with great *naïveté*, that this remarkable carelessness and inaccuracy proves that the work *must* have been written by one of themselves. There is, indeed, in 'Gil Blas' a *general* acquaintance with Spain and Spaniards, but it lacks those little nice traits which stamp identity, and mark that intimate acquaintance with τοποι και τροποι, places and manners, which characterizes the genuine picaresque novels of Spaniards; again, the true *Borracha* is often wanting, while occasionally the sewer-smell of Lutetia is substituted. Le Sage, however, when he copied accurately, retained the *Spanish* flavour, becoming French whenever he was original, or assumed that his *ignorance* of a foreign country was *more* correct than a *native's* knowledge: si cela n'est pas l Espagnol, il doit bien l'être. But, Mas sabe el necio en *su* casa, que el cuerdo en la *agena.*

Le Sage published his 'Gil Blas' in mature age, and when a perfect master of that most difficult art, the writing what is agreeable reading : it is his *opus magnum*, and how few mortals ever produce more than one good book. He used his Spanish original as a woof, into which he worked in his own golden threads, which glitter throughout, part indeed of the whole, and yet distinct. Here he poured out the cream of his mind and life ; here he invested the floating capital of his wit, his hoards of memory and biting common sense, observations on men and manners, especially as seen on the low, familiar,

and ludicrous view, sed ridentem dicere verum, quid vetat? All this is his own, and if any proof were wanting of how truly it is French, let them read Padre Isla's version into Spanish, which proves of itself that it is a *translation ;* and, in truth, 'Gil Blas' is too witty for a genuine Spanish work, and the epigrammatic vein is too sustained, too much a thing of composition, than the occasional and more natural flashes, which sparkle like grains of gold in the sand amid the truisms, verbiage, discursive episodes, and *glozas,* in which Spaniards, like Orientals, delight to indulge whether in writing or in talking. Le Sage picked out nothing but plums, winnowing the wheat from the bushels of Spanish chaff; he rejected all common-place on stilts, especially what the natives, who are insensible to bore, and with whom time is of no value, call grave, judicious, and philosophical reflections, *anglicé* twaddle. To Le Sage this merit is due, that he improved on his original ; and if he did occasionally kidnap a Spanish hidalgo, he did not disfigure him like a gipsy, but gave him the polish and amiability of Paris, and at all events never set the stolen gems in lead.

An ignorance of foreign language, inaccuracy of translation, tampering with text, and flavouring every thing up to the tastes and prejudices of Paris, frequently turns out, when Spanish or Oriental literature is in question, to be rather a benefit than an injury to the original; thus how much more pleasant to read are the garbled, incorrect French 'Arabian Nights' of Mons. Galland, than the literal, honest English version of Mr. Lane. However, the tact, cleverness, and brilliancy of a French pen are undeniable; and such writers as Le Sage resemble those revolutionary marshals, who plundered Spain of her heavy church plate and pictures long buried in unvisited convents. Thus the useless bullion was coined into current cash, and many great masters of art, hitherto almost unknown, were introduced to the general acquaintance and admiration of Europe.

The Spaniard is pleased to compare himself to a *tesoro escondido*, to a hidden treasure. Be it so; but it is too bad to turn round and fall foul, like the Padre Isla, on the pains-taking foreigner, who has dug him up like the soul of Pedro Garcias. No doubt, strictly speaking, Le Sage is a plagiarist; but, like Sterne, he is far preferable to scores of less amusing originals, and if he appropriated the *raw* Spanish material, he manufactured it with foreign industry and ingenuity, dovetailing in a rich Mosaic work of his own. Such divers of literature fish up neglected pearls, which they string into a precious necklace, and theirs is the merit of the *callida junctura*, and of that qualified originality which confers a real value on the previously unappreciated, and gives a new life to the dead. Great, indeed, ought the gratitude of Spain to be to M. Le Sage, but not contented with calling him a thief, she filches from him his works and glory.

Let no Englishman deny Le Sage his well-deserved laurel. 'Gil Blas' is inimitable in its line, and is one of the few books which posterity will never let die; it is one of those "little books" which dear Dr. Johnson loved, and which every traveller in Spain should always stow away alongside of his Don Quixote in his *alforjas*. The edition of Evaristo Peña y Marin, Mad. 1828, is very convenient in form.

ROUTE XCIV.—OVIEDO TO SANTANDER.

Siero	.	.	.	.	3	
Infiesto	.	.	.	.	4	7
Cangas de Onis	.	.	.	4	.. 11
Covadonga	.	.	.	.	1¼	.. 12¼
Peñamelera	.	.	.	.	4	.. 16¼
Abandanes	.	.	.	.	2¼	.. 19
Sⁿ. Vicente	.	.	.	.	4	.. 23
Santander.	.	.	.	.	9¼	.. 32¼

The inland road is less fatiguing, because not so much cut up by estuaries as the one by the sea-coast. It threads those mountains which Pelayus

defended, and contains the sites of early churches and battles: it is highly picturesque and Swiss-like, and the fishing is first-rate. None should venture this way except in fine summer weather, taking also a guide, and minding the provend. Leaving *Siero* and its coal beds, and descending to *Infiesto*, the road winds up the pleasant valley of the Sella to *Cangas de Onis*, Canicas (conchas, the shell-like valley), with a good bridge over the confluent Sella and Gueña. The vicinity abounds in game and fish : half a league off is the ancient monastery, *San Pedro de Villanosa*, built about 760 by Alonzo I., who commemorated on an arch the tragical death of his father. Now we enter the glens into which the remnant of the Goth fled after the fatal battle on the Guadalete, in 711. Here Pelayus, Pelayo, whose father Fravila, son of King Chindasvinto, had been murdered by the usurper Witiza, rallied a few brave men, and 7 years afterwards, in 718, gained a victory over the Moors, which delivered Gijon and this nook of Spain from the invader.

Of course the traveller will get a local guide from the *Cura* to take him to Covadonga, La Cueva de Auseva, the cave to which Pelayus fled, like David to that of Adullam, which is distant about 5 miles. This den, from whence the Gothic Lion emerged, lies up the *Rio Bueno*, near the village *Soto*. After ascending the narrow rocky defile of the Deva, now called Rinazo, we reach

" Covadunga el sitio triumfante,
   Cuna *fue en que nació, la insigne España*."

This rocky cradle, which might hold some 300 men, was the Marathon of Spain, where 300,000 Moors are said to have been vanquished, but it is easier to guess an adversary's numbers than to count them like Cocker: see pp. 224, 306. The peasants point out the rivulet which ran red and swelled with the blood of the infidel. The curious old chapel described by Morales (Viage,

63), was burnt in 1775, when Charles III. employed the common-place academical Ventura Rodriguez to erect the present building, which has little in common with Pelayus or the Bishop Oppas. Pelayus became the Dux or Duke of the Goths; he died in 737, having reigned 18 years. He was buried in the small church of *S^a. Eulalia*, which he built half way up a hill, which overlooks the valley and *Bueño :* this simple chapel was afterwards enclosed in a larger pile. The chapel of *Santa Cruz*, so called from the cross of Victory (see p. 700), was built in 735 by Favila in the plain near *Mercado de Cangas*, and Morales has preserved the original inscription. Here it was that Favila killed a bear with his spear, and the *lancia*, a true Iberian weapon and name, still survives in the poles of these mountaineers, who in these localities are great single-stick players. On Sundays piles of poles may be seen *outside* the churches to prevent breaches of the peace before the very altar. They handle their shillelahs with Irish good-will and dexterity, and frequently beat away the bayonets of the troops sent out to put down smuggling.

This victory of Pelayo at Cangas was the first serious blow dealt to the Saracenic invaders, and, in fact, it saved France and Europe from the crescent, as it proved a diversion, and raised up a new enemy in the flank of the advancing Moor, who, now occupied with a resistance at home, could ill spare troops for distant conquests beyond the Pyrenees ; thus the warlike French gained breathing-time and organised resistance, until Charlemagne rolled back the torrent, and planted the cross on the banks of the Ebro itself. Like Bailen in our times, this victory destroyed the supposed invincibility of the infidel invader ; and while it encouraged the victors to persevere on to new resistance, it rendered success easier by disheartening the vanquished. Accordingly, ever after this repulse in the Asturias, the Moor began to be chary of approaching the mountains ; his settlements were formed in the plains, and in the warmer south and eastern coasts ; and when the first violence of the invasion became spent, the located strangers grew attached to their rich properties, and became still more unwilling to undertake distant and dangerous conquests, which, when only poor adventurers, they eagerly followed out.

This signal victory was second in none of its results or prodigies to those crowning mercies of Navas de Tolosa and Salado. According to the B^{p.} Sebastian (E. S. xxxvii. 79), 124,000 Moors were killed in the valley of Covadunga, and 63,000 more drowned under Monte Amosa. According to Paulus Diaconus, "the rest they ran away," into France, where 375,000 were killed ; so Abijah slew 500,000 chosen men (2 Chron. xiii. 17). This Oriental arithmetic formed a model to Buonaparte's *facts, figures,* and bulletins during Moore's campaign. Those who now tread these narrow defiles of Covadunga, will, as at Navas de Tolosa and Salado, see the impossibility of moving, to say nothing of feeding, not 500,000, but 20,000 men ; but the true solution of all these *cuentas* will be to read hundreds instead of thousands. No doubt in these broken localities, as at Bailen, where manœuvring is impracticable, the Spaniards gained the day ; and well would it have been for them if they had always acted on the example of history and the Duke's advice, and kept to their hills, instead of rushing to certain defeat in campal battles. The Moorish annalists treated their conqueror Pelayus with Chinese politeness, calling him a " contemptible barbarian "— " One Belay," who roused the people of Asturish. He was " despised" by the Viceroy, Al-horr, as only commanding 30 men (Moh. D. ii. 34, 260). Pelayus in reality was a true warrior of Spain, *i. e.* a *Guerrillero*, a Sertorius, Cid, or Mina, an Abd-el-Kader Cristiano.

It was on these sites of ancient glory that Ballesteros first emerged into notice, whose subsequent refusal to obey the Duke led to the loss of Madrid, the raising the siege of Burgos, and neutralized the victory of Salamanca. For this disobedience he was only banished to Ceuta, being soon jobbed out again by the anti-English party, of which he was the leader; and now he is the *beau ideal* of a true Spaniard with the Torenos (viii.), Arguelleses (i. 99, 327), and Co., who behold in him the representative of *el orgullo Español*, which will not submit to English dictation (see Peniscola, p. 458).

Ballesteros, by birth an Arragonese, had all the obstinacy and insubordination of his stiff-necked countrymen. He began life as a common soldier in 1804, and was turned out of the ranks for theft. He afterwards was appointed a tobacco registrar in the Asturias, and was busied with his cigars near Covadunga, at the time of the national rising after the butcheries of Murat; then he became, says Toreno, "*entusiasmado*" with the glorious recollections of his "district," and thought himself a second Pelayus; but on May 24, 1810, when the first French detachment came in sight, his tobaccose valour ended in smoke, and he ran at once, never stopping until he reached Potes; and when the French reappeared, started off again to Santander, and leaving his troops in the lurch, rushed with Jose O'Donnell into an open boat, and such was the hurry of the panic of these future heroes, that they forgot even the oars, and rowed away with the butts of muskets.

Ballesteros being a *lechaculo* or toady of the M⁰· of Romana, the commander in these districts, manœuvred into place, and then passed from being the slave to the tyrant. He was by nature impatient of any superior or control; self, indeed, was his only centre, and he fired like a lucifer match at the least opposition. He would not have

obeyed Santiago himself, much less a foreigner.

The Duke soon fathomed this man (see Disp. Feb. 16, Apr. 11, Nov. 15, 1811, and Dec. 18, 1813), and wrote, "He is a mere freebooter, a chief of a disorderly rabble;" "a curse instead of a benefit to the nation which they are employed to defend." "He is not to be depended upon for one moment. Depend upon it he will not co-operate in conjunction with you." Alcaraz and the consequent failure at Burgos proved his truly prophetic intuition of Ballesteros.

This marplot was chosen by Ferd. VII. to be his Minister of War, an art of which, except as a *Guerrillero*, he was ignorant as a child. He poisoned the royal ear with anti-English prejudices, and next, in 1820, betrayed his king, becoming in 1823 his worst persecutor; but no sooner did the French troops appear than, as usual, he was the first to run away. Thus the end of his career was just the same as the beginning. Being caught near Granada by Gen. Molitor in 1823, he saved himself by a dastardly treaty, and died an exile and in disgrace at Paris in 1832.

Covadunga, independently of the religio loci, abounds in interest to the artist, angler, and lover of natural history. Here the traveller may read Southey's Don Roderick, and cull simples with more propriety than the laureate's Pelayo. "Such a bucolic contemplation of nature is very well for a goat-herd (says his friend Wm. Taylor), but where the fate of empires is at stake, the engineer who is sent to reconnoitre is not to lose his time in zoologizing, entomologizing, and botanizing."

On quitting this valley, the *Cordales*, or range of hills is ascended, which overlooks the basin of the Deva, and the opposed Peñas de Europa. *Arenas* is a good fishing quarter. The crystal Cares and Deva unite in the meadow of Alles. Continuing the stream to *Mier*, in its funnel of hills, cross the

Cares, here teeming with trout, and go up the charming valley of *Peñamellera.* At *Cavanzon* we fall in with the Namsa. *Luey* is a good fishing quarter, the weir of Muñorrodero preventing the salmon getting higher up the stream: thence to *Sⁿ. Vicente de la Barquera,* and to Santillana and Santander (see R. cxvi).

ROUTE XCV.—OVIEDO TO LEON.

Mieres.	. . . .	3	
Pola de Lena.	. . .	2	.. 5
Campomanes.	. . .	1	.. 6
La Muela.	. . . .	1¼	.. 7¼
Puerto de Pajares	. .	1¼	.. 9
Buidongo.	. . . .	2	.. 11
Buiza.	. . . . .	2¼	.. 13¼
Robla.	. . . . .	2¼	.. 16
Carbajal	. . . . .	3	.. 19
Leon.	. . . . .	1	.. 20

This is a magnificent carriage and diligence road; no wonder Charles IV., when the enormous cost was reported, asked if it were paved with silver. It is carried up and down descents, is well provided with bridges and parapets, and, as usual with Spanish undertakings, has been conceived on a needless scale of width and grandeur; it is indeed both a *via lata* and a *camino de plata.* The first day's ride will be to the *Puerto de Pajares,* the *portal* of the tremendous mountain wall which divides the Asturias from Leon. Ascending from Oviedo, the look back on this mountain capital is very fine: below in its valleys winds away the charming Nalon, on the banks of which the departing angler has left his heart; here he bids the sweet streams a last farewell, as they "stray by many a winding nook, with willing sport, to the wild ocean." A stone seat near a fountain which gushes from the rock, invites the traveller to repose, and enjoy the panorama. Now we descend to *Olloniego,* with its fine bridge built by Manuel Requera Gonzalez. The older ivy-clad bridge stands high and dry in the meadow, the stream having been untrue to its bed, as at Coria; but Spanish rivers are as classically fickle as the Homeric Scamander and Simois. The artist and angler can

desire nothing more than these sites. Now we ascend a limestone ridge by a zigzag course over the *Pⁿ· de Pudrun,* and next to the charming village *Mieres,* with its bridge. *Santullano* over the Lena, and the whole route, recalls Devonshire. To the r. is the *Monte Sacro* with its hermitage, where the ark of Oviedo rested. The Mieres is soon joined by the Aller. The whole route to Pajares is through an alpine scene of extreme verdure and cultivation: sometimes amid chesnut groves, maize fields, and May meadows; at others, in wild glens of dovetailing hills, where all farther advance seems impossible, where there is just room for the road and its cheerful wayfellow the torrent, "making sweet music with the enamell'd stones," to thread the narrow defile. *Pajares* is a miserable hamlet, but the Posada is tolerable, and the trout excellent. This is the region of clouds and cold; we exchange the verdurous valley for the peeled *Sierra,* whose stony heights seem to defy all further progress. Pillars are now placed to mark the road when covered over in wintry snows: it is, however, seldom quite closed. Among these Aguado caught his death while journeying to Gijon.

On leaving the *Puerto* the road ascends gently through a magnificent chaos of rocks, to the practicable summit, which is a swampy level, surrounded on all sides by barren mountains. This elevated morass, fed by the clouds, is the reservoir from whence tiny streams descending both ways form the rivers of Leon and the Asturias; and here is the boundary of the two provinces. The passage before reaching *Villanueva,* or *Villamani,* becomes so narrow that a torrent barely can flow through, and the road is carried along a superb causeway erected at a vast expense; after this the valleys again open into sun, life, and cultivation. The bridge of *Turio* is placed in a most romantic position. At 4½ L. we pass the poplar-planted *Vega de Gordon;* thence to *Robla.* The beautiful trout-stream La Vernesga skirts the picturesque road, and fills the valley with verdure, soon to be left behind with its flowers and woods; for, after ascending a steepish hill, the eye roams over the interminable plains, and steppes of corn-lands bounded only by the horizon. Adieu mountain, green valley, and crystal stream, soon to be exchanged for dead burnt-up herbage, for the dust and sand of the tawny desert, now doubly odious from the contrast with the fresh highlands. Now we descend over a lonely heath-clad waste to Leon, with its rivers and poplar-planted banks, its ancient walls, and elegant creamy-toned cathedral. (For Leon, see p. 605.)

ROUTE XCVI.—OVIEDO TO LEON.

Beautiful and convenient as was the road just described to the angler and artist, there is a wilder route to the r., which equals it in some, and surpasses it in other respects. It is not easy to give mountain distances in these road-less districts, and the traveller will of course take local guides and attend to the provend. Make, however, for *Grado*, and then ascend the Narcea to romantic *Belmonte*, and thence by the river to *Sⁿ· Andres de Aguera*, and by the Cannedo to picturesque *Pola de Somiedo;* from thence the Puerto of its name is crossed, and we descend through an alpine country to *Carra-scante, Villa Setana*, to *Truovana.* Here flows the noble trout-stream the Luna ; hence to *Las Dueñas*, and 5 L. to Leon, by the valley of the Vernesga.

SECTION XI.

THE CASTILES; OLD AND NEW.

CONTENTS.

The Provinces; the Character of the Country and Natives.

THESE two provinces join each other, and constitute a large portion of the central plateau of Spain, of which they are truly *El coro y Castilla*, the "heart and citadel:" composed chiefly of tertiary formation, they rise at an average about 2000 feet above the sea. This table-land is itself encompassed with mountains, and intersected by diverging ranges: thus the *Montes de Toledo* divide the basins of the Guadiana and Tagus, while the *Sierra de Guadarrama* separates those of the Tagus and Duero; to the east are the *Sierras de Cuenca*, some of the highest mountains of these provinces.

The Castiles, now divided into Old and New, *Castilla vieja y nueva*, formed under the ancients the districts of the Celtiberi, Oretani, and Carpetani. The N.W. portion was called *Bardulia* under the Goths; but this name was changed into that of Castilla so early as 801; the distinction Vetula, *Vieja*, was afterwards added, to mark the difference between it and the *new* and more southern portions which were subsequently wrested from the Moor.

The " canting " name Castilla was taken from the number of castles erected on this frontier of Leon and Asturias, owing to which the Moors called the province *Adhu-l-kilá*, the " Land of the Castles," and also Kashtellah. Of the former number of walled forts in Spain, Livy (xxii. 19), Appian (B. H. 467), and Hirtius (B. H. 8), make mention. These primitive Castilian castles were not the unsubstantial modern *Chateaux en Espagne*, but solid real defences, and held by brave men, and were built in imitation of Roman fortresses, the noble masonry being quite unlike the Oriental *tapia* of the Moorish Alcazares of the south. The Castiles bear for arms, " Gules a castle or."

Castilla la vieja, like Leon, being close to the north-west mountains, from whence the Gotho-Spaniard burst forth against the Moors, was soon wrested from the infidel, and became a petty sovereignty, a *Condado*, or " county," often, however, in some measure subject to the kings of Leon, until declared independent about 762, under the Conde Rodrigo Fruelaz, who was father to the renowned judge, Nuño Rasura, whose descendant, Doña Nuña, twelfth countess, married in 1028 Sancho, King of Navarre; and their son Ferdinand first assumed the title of King of Castile, and of Leon also on his marriage with Sancha, daughter and heiress of Bermudo III. These two kingdoms, separated again for a period, became finally united in the thirteenth century under St. Ferdinand, and were inherited by Isabella, who being *Reina Proprietaria*, or queen in her own right, was married in 1479 to Ferdinand, afterwards King of Arragon, and thus at their deaths the consolidated kingdoms were handed down to their grandson, Charles V. For historical details consult ' *Historia del Condado*,' Diego Gutierez Coronel, 4to. Mad. 1785 ; ' *La Castilla*,' Man. Risco, 4to. Mad. 1792; and the paper by Benito Montejo, ' Mems. Acad. Hist.' iii. 245.

The two Castiles are the largest provinces in Spain, and contain some of the oldest and most interesting cities. The mountains are highly picturesque, abounding in curious botany and geology, and their Swiss-like valleys are watered by trout-streams; they present a perfect contrast to the *parameras*, *tierras de campo y secanos*, the plains and table-lands, which are lonely steppes, bounded only by the horizon, silent, treeless, songless, and without hedges, enclosures, or landmarks, and which look as if belonging to no one, and not worth possessing ; yet the cultivators who are born and die on these spots know whose is every inch, and see with the quick glance of an interested proprietor whatever trespasser passes over the, to him, invisible boundary ; but the stranger's eye vainly attempts to measure the expanse, and the mind gives way to despondency at the sight, where all around, for far and wide, is of equal dreariness (see pp. 47, 307). The Castilians have a singular antipathy to trees, and, like Orientals, they seldom plant any, except those which bear fruit or give shade for their alamedas. *Immediate* profit is their utilitarian standard ; to plant for timber is a thing of foresight and of forethought for others, and is based on a confidence in institutions which will guarantee enjoyment at a distant period. Now person and property seldom have been secure here beyond the moment where might makes right; and misgovernment is either conducted by a *Camerilla* or court martial ; hence the hand-to-mouth system of expedients, each man only thinking for himself and for the day, and exclaiming, " après moi le déluge," *y quien ha visto a Mañana?* The peasants not only do not plant, but recklessly waste those forests which have grown naturally, and seldom even spare the ornamental avenues which the authorities endeavour to form on the road-sides, not because trees are the πρωτη ὕλη, or raw material for gibbets, but because " the spread of their leaves such shelter affords, to those noisy impertinent creatures called birds," who they imagine eat up corn when ripe, forgetting that they are all the rest of the year destroying more destructive grubs. If, however, a tree requires half a century to extend its roots, popular prejudices require ten centuries to have theirs eradicated.

Fuel and timber for domestic purposes are in consequence dear at Madrid, an evil which is daily increasing, and to make matters worse, the soil, exposed to a calcining sun, becomes more and more effete for cultivation, while the rains and dews are absorbed, and the sources of rivers diminished.   Drought is the curse of the earth, as dryness is of the air (see pp. 92, 94); frequently it does not rain for many successive months, and as the peasants do but scratch the ground, their crops are liable to fail, the roots perishing for want of humidity. In summer the air and earth are clouded with a nitrous dust, which irritates the eye, already sickened with the nakedness of the land, and all the discomfort of the desert, without its grand associations.   Water is very scarce, not only for irrigation, but even for domestic uses, and nature and man are alike adust and tawny ; everything is brown, his house, his jacket, his wife, and his ass.

However bald and unpicturesque these plains to every eye but their owners, for the having the fee-simple varnishes up the most hideous landscape, they, like those of Leon, are some of the finest wheat districts in the world.   The *Chamorro* and the *Candeal* are the best and usual sorts of grain, of which, however, there are more than twenty varieties (see Widdrington, i. 423).   *Pan de Candeal*, in Spain, is the term for the finest whitest bread, and is the antithesis of *Pan de Municion*, the *bisoño* fare of the soldier.   These cereal plains might, if tolerably cultivated, be made the granary of Spain and Europe, and even with an agriculture slovenly as that in Barbary, the produce is very great.   However, although there are neither corn-laws nor sliding scales, and subsistence is cheap and abundant, the population decreases in number, and increases in wretchedness : what boots it that bread be low-priced, if wages are still lower ? but Spain is a land of results, not theories.   These plains are also well adapted for the growth of saffron, *Azafran* (Arabicè *Suffrá*, yellow), which enters largely into Spanish cookery and complexion.   The *Garbanzos* also are excellent ; this chich pea, the staple vegetable of the Peninsula (see p. 67), is nutritious, but difficult to digest, and flatulent ; but an unscientific agriculture, combined with difficulties of soil and climate which the national apathy does not combat against, renders the pea genus of much importance, in the absence of artificial winter pasture.   A tolerable red wine is made in some favoured localities. But inadequate roads, canals, and means of transport neutralize these capabilities: the peasant having no market, becomes indifferent, and being without spur or object, he just provides for his rude and animal wants ; of course poverty and ignorance must be the result, as in Estremadura (see p. 516).   There are few isolated farms, since a general insecurity forces men to congregate for mutual protection; the hamlets are scattered few and far between, and the cottages are built of a bad *cob*, mere mud, or of *adobes*, bricks dried in the sun (Arabicè *Attob, tobi*); while the want of glass in the openings called windows adds, according to our ideas, to the look of dilapidation: their hovels are not even picturesque.   Thus, when the invaders tore down the very roofs for their camp fires, the walls, exposed to the winter rain, returned decomposed to their pristine elements, dust to dust.   Now many agricultural families, especially about Ocaña, as near Guadix, burrow in the hill sides, and live in holes fitter for beasts than men.   The labour of the inmates is increased by the distance of their residence from their work : they have to start long before daybreak, and return weary as their cattle after nightfall in truly antique groups—" Fessos vomerem inversum boves, collo trahentes languido." The poor and plain peasants wear the *Paño pardo* and inconvenient *montera*, and eat the bread of affliction earned by the briny sweat of their brow. Some travellers, who merely hurry along the high road, and observe the rustics doing apparently nothing, but loitering in cloaked groups, or resting on their spades to look at them, set all down as idlers or *holgazanes*, which is not the case, for the hand of toil pauses only for the instant when the stranger passes, and then labours on unseen and unceasingly from early dawn to dewy eve; and those who stand still in the market-place are willing to work, but there is none to hire them. Generally speaking, both man, woman, and child are overworked in the fields of Spain, where human bone and sinew supply the want of the commonest machinery ; yet, from knowing no better, the Castilian does not complain, nay, the peasants among themselves are as fond of amusement as children, and full of raillery, mother-wit, and practical joking, and those unamusing unamuseable *Dons* with which untravelled romancers have peopled the Peninsula are certainly not to be found among the lower classes.

The Castilian is *muy honrado y hombre de bien*, an honest right good fellow; but he is well bred rather than polite, and inclined to receive rather than to make advances, being seldom what the French call *prévenant*, but then when once attached he is sincere (see p. 151); his manner is marked by a most practical equality ; for all feel equal to the proudest noble through their common birthright of being Castilians. Treat them, however, as they expect to be treated, and all this ceremony of form and of words, all this nicety of sitting down and getting up, will not be found to extend to deeds. The Castilian, simple and with few wants or vices, lives and dies where he was born, after the fashion and ignorance of his ancestors, and although a creature of routine, and uneducated, he is shrewd and intelligent in his limited scope, and like the peasant Mentor of Horace, " rusticus ab normis sapiens crassâque Minervâ," these Castilians, with their *grammatica parda*, generally take a sounder view of things than their rulers. They have, it is true, no book conversation, but reason rather from instinct, and what they say has a game flavour, albeit sometimes rather strong; but they are neither tame rabbits, nor house-fed lambs; a want of the gentle, the tender, and the conceding marks the character of the Oriental and Castilian; bred and born among difficulties, obstacles, and privations, under a fierce sun, and on a hard soil, the wild weed of strong rank nature grows up harsh and unyielding. Here *man* is to be seen in his unsophisticated, untamed state, in all his native *individual* force; for here everything is personal, and the very antithesis of our social corporate fusing political combinations; as there is no homogeneity, so there is no amalgamation, no compromise, no concession. But to see the Castilian in a genuine condition he must be sought for in the better class of villages at a distance from Madrid, for the capital has exercised no civilizing influence, as under its very walls the peasant is a barbarian, while within them resides the worst *populacho* of the Peninsula ; and it is difficult to say which are there the worst and most uneducated, the highest or the lowest classes. The superior bearing of the manly country *Labrador* over the stinted burgess of Madrid is very remarkable, and in his lowly house and under his smoky rafters, a truer hospitality will be found than in the tapestry halls of the grandee, where most it is pretended ; among themselves the villagers are social and gregarious, their light-hearted confidence contrasting with the suspicious reserve of the higher classes. The homes of the yeomen are cleaner and better furnished than the *posadas;* indeed, as throughout Spain, dirt and discomfort lodge rather at the public inn than in the private dwelling. The interior of the Peninsula is too little travelled by foreigners to make it worth while to consult their whims or wants, and the national accommodation is good enough for the national muleteer and his animals.

The *Castellano* is less addicted to murder and treachery than the irritable native of the south and south-east provinces; he may, indeed, be a less agreeable companion than the Ionian *Andaluz*, or plausible *Valenciano*, but like the Spartan, he is a nobler and more male and trustworthy character; he and his provinces are still Robur Hispaniæ (Flor. ii. 17. 9), and contain the virility, vitality, and heart of the nation, and the sound stuff of which it has to be reconstructed. Meanwhile, the Castilian is not addicted to low degrading vices; although proud, obstinate, ignorant, prejudiced, superstitious, and uncommercial, he is true to his God and king, his religion running often into bigotry, his loyalty into subserviency. These two pivots, these characteristic feelings, still exist, scotched not killed, and the current flows deeply, although silently, under the babble and bubble of recent exotic and most un-Spanish reforms.

Loyal, in the strict meaning of the term *legalis*, he is not, for the law of cities is not the peasant's friend. Their *Justicia*, the very sound of which, like our Chancery, affects every Spaniard high or low with delirium tremens, practically means a denial of justice, and ruin ; it only interferes to punish or oppress; an engine of the strong and rich against weakness and poverty, it never in Spain has been the people's protector ; yet, like many *Cosas de España,* the law itself in theory and on paper is good, and requires little change, the one thing wanting is that it should be *fairly administered by upright, honest judges,* which scarcely can be said to exist throughout the Peninsula.

Therefore the Castilian and Spaniard take the law in their own hands, or rather make a new one which is antagonistic and corrective of that framed by their misrulers ; and they respect their own *private* code quite as much as they disregard the public one, especially in all *personal* offences; hence the wild justice of their revenge (see p. 145). The bulk of the people sympathises with those who break the public law, especially in cases of smuggling ; nevertheless, when not tempted by its all-corrupting profits, the Castilians are moral and well-disposed, and satisfied to leave things as they are; for they have long enjoyed in practice many republican institutions under a nominal despotism ; thus they elect their own alcaldes and officers, who in local Spain are the real rulers, both de jure et facto ; safe in their obscurity, they were indemnified by a liberty of action, which was denied to possessors of rank, wealth, and intellect, who being feared by the king and priest, were accordingly kept down ; and this accounts for the apparent anomaly of the lower classes having opposed those reforms which the higher ones coveted; not that the grandees had any much clearer ideas of real constitutional liberty than a debating club of shop-boys. Meanwhile the people, anxious indeed to see the *derechos de puerta* abolished, and tobacco cheaper and better, cared little for theoretical evils, which were neutralized in practice ; and as the lower classes are by far the best and finest of Spaniards, so are they the happiest; to them equality, liberty, and safety are realities. They indeed may sing on the high roads, who trust for defence to their own good knife. In this land of contradictions the wealthy have few enjoyments from their wealth, and the poor few denials from their poverty (see pp. 278, 433). The rich must depend on institutions for safety, which here too often injure and seldom protect. No wonder, therefore, that these peasants, as Addison said of those in the Georgics, toss about even manure with an air of dignity ; this is the result also of natural instinct even more than of social conventions, since each esteeming himself inferior to none but the king, cares little for the accidents of rank and fortune. Nor does poverty, the great crime never to be pardoned in England, unless it be very grinding, here unfit a person for society, *Pobreza no es vileza:* nor does it destroy personal respectability and independence; indeed, where the majority are poor, the not being rich does not degrade, and an innate gentility of race, which nothing can take away, renders them indifferent to the changes and chances of fickle prosperity, and proud even in rags. The *Castellano*, an old, although decayed gentleman, never forgets, or permits others to forget, what is due to himself; courteous to others, he expects a reciprocity as regards himself, and when once that is conceded, knows well how to give place. As the beggars cover under the stately *capa* their shreds and patches, so he conceals under an outward lofty bearing his inner feelings; he hopes, and his motive is honourable, to divert observation by showing a more swelling port than the family means would grant continuance; hence the struggle between ostentation and want, the *Boato* of the *Bisoño;* but "to boast of the national strength is the national disease." See pp. 172, 203, on this head, and the Oriental resignation with which privations are honourably endured.

The Castilian in *particular* claims to be synonymous with the Spaniard in *general,* pars pro toto he gives his name to the kingdom, nation, and language (see p. 2); and his grand pretension is to be an *old* one, *Castellano viejo y rancio,* and spotless, *sin mancha;* that is, uncontaminated with the black blood of new converts from Moor or Jew. The Cid was the personification of the genuine character of these ancient chatelains of Christendom, and of the spirit of that age: and however degenerated the pigmy aristocracy, the sinewy muscular forms of the brave peasants, true children of the Goth, are no unfitting framework of a vigorous and healthy, although uneducated, mind. Here, indeed, the remark of Burns holds good, that the rank is but the guinea stamp, the man's the gold for all that. "All the force of Europe," said our gallant Peterborough, "would not be sufficient to subdue the Castiles with the people against it; and like him, the Duke, however thwarted by the so-called better classes, never despaired while the "*country was with him.*" He quelled his rising indignation at their juntas, and smothered his contempt of their generals; he collected all his energies to buffet the storm, catching the beams of his coming glory; and, "*cheered by the people's support,*" proved himself, says Napier, " to be a man made to conquer and uphold kingdoms."

The pride and *Españolismo* of the Castilian is naturally immeasurable. No wonder that Coronel, in his preface, modestly asserts, that the sovereignty of Castille is by far the most ancient, noble, and sublime in the world, and so purely Spanish as to proceed from "*divine inspiration ;*" yet foreigners may well think that industrious Catalonia, charming Valencia, and sunny-golden Andalucia, are at least qualified to dispute this precedence with this sluggish, disagreeable, and bald central range. Be that as it may, the *Castellano's* assumption* perpetuates a dogged predilection to self, and prejudices against others, which combined have long kept him in a low stage of civilization: accordingly, these empire provinces are among the most backward, and whatever the fond native may predicate of the superiority of himself and his country, every man who has an acre in England will think this part of the world one of the best that he has ever seen to live *out* of.

The proper periods to visit the Castiles are about the end of the spring, and the

---

* Language and forms of address are exponents of national character, and how superb is the pomp and circumstance of these swelling Orientals; here every beggar addresses a brother mendicant as *Señor, Don,* and *Caballero,* as a lord and knight. As all are peers, all are *Vuestra Merced,* "Your Grace," which when not expressed in words is understood and implied by the very grammar, as the addressing in the third person instead of our curt second one *you,* has reference to this ducal title. (See also p. 155.)

beginning of autumn, as the summers are very hot, and the winters are very cold. The principal objects worth notice are Madrid and the royal *sitios*, Toledo, Cuenca, Avila, Segovia, and Burgos. The scenery in the ranges of the Guadarrama, Avila, and Cuenca mountains is grand, and the geology and fishing, especially near the latter, excellent.

MADRID. The best inns will be found mentioned at page 727, and those who are in a hurry to commence purchases and sight-seeing may turn on to it.

The history of Madrid is soon told. Unlike the many time-honoured capitals of Spain, this is an upstart favourite without merit, and a creation of the caprice of Charles V. The learned compilers of the official *Guia* for 1845, however, state that this is the 2598th year after the foundation of Rome, and the 4014th after that of Madrid, and that this more ancient and nobler city was called by the Romans *Mantua Carpetanorum*, to distinguish it from Mantua in Italy (the real site of this Spanish Mantua being, however, at Ocaña). If Madrid existed at all in the Roman period, which is very doubtful, it probably was the insignificant hamlet Majoritum; at all events *Majorit* was only a Moorish outpost of Toledo when captured in 1083 by Alonzo VI. Enrique IV., about 1461, made some additions to the older town, which was placed on the west eminence over the river, and the narrow streets still contrast with the modern portions which have sprung up to the north-east and south. Madrid was once surrounded with forests, which Argote describes, in 1582, as "*buen monte de puerco y oso*," or good cover for boars and bears, on account of which it was made a royal hunting residence. These woods have long been cut down by the improvident inhabitants, and, like their wild beasts, only exist on the city's shield, the arms of which are a "tree vert with fruit gules, up which a bear is climbing, an orle azure with seven stars argent." This bear, say the heralds, is typified by the *Ursa Major*, and they also call that constellation *El Carro*, because indicating *Carpentum* Mantuanorum. In sober truth, Madrid only began to be a place of importance under Charles V., who, gouty and phlegmatic, felt himself relieved by its brisk and rarefied air; and consulting only his personal comfort, he deserted Valladolid, Seville, Granada, and Toledo, to fix his residence on a spot which Iberian, Roman, Goth, and Moor had all rejected. Declared the court by Philip II. in 1560 (who became more attached to it as the Escorial rose), the city rapidly grew up at the expense of the older and better situated capitals. It is the creation of a century, for it has not increased much since the age of Philip IV.; then, indeed, with reference to London and other European capitals, it really was entitled to rank high, but now, like everything else in ill-fated misgoverned Spain, whose sun has long stood still, it has been outstripped even by our provincial cities.

The gross mistake of a position which has no single advantage except the fancied geographical merit of being in the centre of Spain, was soon felt, and on Philip II.'s death, his son, in 1601, endeavoured to remove the court back again to Valladolid, which, however, was then found to be impracticable, such had been the creation of new interests during the outlay in the preceding reign. Philip II. had neglected the opportunity of making his capital of Lisbon, which is admirably situated on a noble river and the sea; had this been done, Portugal never would or could have revolted, or the Peninsula been thus dissevered, by which the first blow was dealt to Spain's greatness: thus to Madrid, and its Monkish ulcer the Escorial, is the germ of present decay to be traced. Charles III., a wise prince, contemplated a removal to Seville; so also did the intrusive Joseph, but now the disease is chronic and incurable.

Madrid is built on several mangy hills that hang over the Manzanares, which

2 I

being often dry in summer, scarcely can be called a river. The elevation is about 2400 feet above the sea, although in an apparent plain, which, however, is much cut up by gullies that the torrents from the Guadarrama have worn away, and in which some 200 villages pine unseen, concealed in the hollows. This elevation on an open land probably is the reason of the derivation given by some to *Majerit*, which is said to signify in Arabic "a current of fresh air," a *Buenos Ayres*. Sousa, however, derives the name from the Arabic *Maajarit*, "running waters," of which there are scarcely any; for perverse, indeed, has been the ingenuity of its townfolk, who have destroyed both the salubrity of the air and the fertility of the soil; thus destruction of timber has proved alike the curse to Madrid and Rome, the cities of the bear and wolf, and the twin strongholds of the enemy to civil and religious liberty.

The basin of which Madrid is the capital is bounded by the *Sierra* of the Guadarrama and the *Montes* of Toledo and Guadalupe. It consists chiefly of tertiary formations, marl, gypsum, and limestone. The latter, found at *Colmenar de Oreja*, near Aranjuez, is a freshwater deposit, with planorbes; and being of a good colour and substance, is much used in the buildings of Madrid: the common and excellent granite comes from *Colmenar Viejo*, 5 L., near the Escorial. There are many villages of this name near Madrid, which signifies both in Spanish and Arabic "a bee-hive." A curious magnesite, with bones of extinct mammalia, occurs at *Vallecas*, 1½ L. from the capital.

Madrid is as a residence disagreeable and unhealthy, alternating between the extremities of heat and cold, or, according to the adage, three months of winter and nine of hell, *tres meses de invierno y nueve del infierno*. Although, says an accurate writer, Madrid is 10° south of London, the mean annual winter temperature is 43° 7', or only 4° higher than that of our capital; but during every winter a degree of gold is experienced which is very rare in London; in 1830 the thermometer sunk to 9° 5' Fahr., and a great quantity of snow fell, and every year, for several nights, the thermometer descends several degrees below 32°, and the rivers are covered with ice, although it generally disappears in the day. The mean temperature of the three summer months is 76° 2', or 15° higher than London; but during the *Solano*, the south-eastern wind, it frequently rises to 90° or even 100° in the shade, while in the sun the heat and glare are African; to this, as if in mockery of climate, are added the blasts of Siberia, for being placed on a denuded plateau, it is exposed to the keen blasts which sweep down, impregnated with death, from the Æolus cave of the snowy Guadarrama, the nursery of consumption and *pulmonia*. The capital, even if there were no local doctors, would soon cease to be a living city, were it not replenished by the thousands who flock to it from the provinces, for it is the destructive spider which attracts into its web all those who hope to make their fortunes. Yet the natives are loud in its praise, just as weak-minded persons are the proudest of those very errors of which they ought to be most ashamed. The summer is the most dangerous period, when the pores are open, for often, during a N.E. wind. the difference of temperature on one side of a street to the other often reaches 20 degrees, and the incautious stranger turning out of a street which is roasted by the sun, is caught at a corner by Æolus, and incontinently forwarded to the *cemetario*. It was of the *Colico de Madrid*, a peculiar inflammation of the bowels, that Murat sickened in 1808, and the superstitious populace, according to Foy, ascribed it to divine vengeance; but no Nemesis then struck the blow, for the disease is proverbial, and

> " *El aire de Madrid es tan sotil*
> *Que mata a un hombre, y no apaga a un candil*,"—

the subtle air, which will not extinguish a candle, puts out a man's life. Dry, searching, and cutting, this assassin breath of death pierces through flesh and bone to the marrow ; hence the careful way in which the natives cover their mouths, the women with handkerchiefs, the men by muffling themselves up in their cloaks, *embosandose en las capas :* by these unmechanical respirators the lungs are protected, for *el horno se escalienta por la boca,* the oven is heated at the mouth. The average of death at Madrid is as 1 in 28, while in London it is as 1 in 42 : no wonder, according to Salas, that even the healthy live on physic.

> " *Aun las personas mas sanas,*
> *Si son en Madrid nacidas,*
> *Tienen que hacer sus comidas,*
> *De píldolas y tisanas.*"

It is particularly fatal to young children, who during dentition die *como chinches.* The summer scirocco blights vegetation, and by exciting a knife-handling population, fills hospitals with wounded and prisons with murderers. So much for this " Buena *Madre,*" this good mother, from whose tender mercies Moya, on the *delincuente honrado* principle, derives the name of Madrid, *mas bien Madrasta.* The morals of most classes are no better than the climate, as Mesonero calculates that one-fifth of all births are exposed in the *Cuna* (see p. 271) to almost certain death. The wealthier families manage to rear some of their puny children by providing them with healthy wet nurses from the Asturias, and the gorgeous costumes of these aristocratic *Pasiegas* are among the most singular ornaments of the *Prado.*

The townspeople think Madrid the "envy and admiration" of mankind : they talk of it as the capital of *Spain,* i. e. the world, for *Quien dice España dice todo.* There is but one Madrid, *No hay sino un Madrid :* unique, like the phœnix, it is the *only* court on earth, *solo Madrid es corte.* Wherever it is mentioned the world is silent with awe, *Donde está Madrid calle el mundo.* There is but one stage from Madrid to *La Gloria,* or paradise, in which there is a window for angels to look down on this counterpart heaven of earth. The reason why there are no country-houses in the vicinity is seriously accounted for, because no sane person could ever be found to quit this home of supernatural enjoyment even for a day ; nor, indeed, in this hideous, grassless, treeless, colourless, calcined desert, are there many natural temptations ; again, the insecurity of the roads would make the drive in and out to a villa a service of danger, nor would the rusticising *hidalgo* be much securer when arrived, for his house assuredly would be attacked, and his spoons plundered. Were he to surround his domain with a high wall, and guard it with armed retainers, he might take a walk in his garden, and dose about as safely as Hamlet's father in his orchard, in the exact enjoyment of the rural felicity of the mediæval age, when great men lived in garrisoned dungeons ; but all this scarcely comes up to the ideas of 1845, of the air, liberty, and simple nature of a *country* house, or even Clapham. The greatest of punishments to the grandees is to be banished to their distant estates from *La Corte ;* an exile to the Alhambra is equivalent to our Botany Bay . true *courtiers,* at Madrid alone can they live, vegetating everywhere else, thus requiring, as it were, azote instead of oxygen for even existence. This term, *La Corte,* conveys to Spanish ears a meaning which cannot be translated in English. It is like *La Cour* de Louis XIV., the residence of the Sultan, the dispenser of rank and fortune : it is the centre of *Empeños,* jobs, intrigues, titles, decorations, and plunder ; it is the carrion to which flocks the vulture tribe of place-hunters and *pretendientes,* whose name is legion ; yet as a court it is and was at all times a poor representation of real grandeur, and now, compared to others in Europe, it is not much better than a burlesque. It, however, is the curse and bane of Spain, and all well-informed Spaniards declare that the best of their compatriots are ruined by going there, such is its upas-like atmosphere; yet so great is habit, that none desire to escape into a larger, freer air.   The desert comes up to the ignoble mud-walls, and the peasant who scratches the fields beyond them is a barbarian, yet the townsfolk compare these environs to those of Palmyra and Rome : but where are the ancient battlements, palaces, and temples? where is the poetry of those widowed cities of past greatness, to which present loneliness and melancholy form a fitting-frame?   Everything around Madrid is the abomination of a self-created desolation alike without recollections or associations.   Here nature and man seem fitted for each other, for the denuded environs only evince a bad soil and a worse cultivation.

Madrid, this fit capital of a country of anomalies, is not even a city or *Ciudad ;* it is only the chief of *villas.*   It has no cathedral, no bishop; it rises with a cluster of conical, blue, Flemish-looking spires, which, resembling extin-guishers, are no bad types for a town where climate and policy alike conspire to put out life and mind.   Yet this true capital of Spain is, like other rewarded culprits, bedizened with undeserved epithets of honour.   It is " *Imperial, Coro-nado, muy Noble, Leal, y Heroico.*"   All this titulomania sounds well on paper, and suits a city which looks run up by the decree in the Gazeta, signed " *Yo el Rey,*" the ipse dixi et volui of the despot.   This pomp of empty epithet is at once classical and Oriental, it is the Augusta *invicta* of the Roman, the *Kaderah,* " the Victorious" Cairo of the Arab.   But Madrid scarcely existed in the early period of Castilian history, and was built when the age of cathedrals was passed, that age when edifices were raised in harmony with the deep and noble senti-ment within ; hence it has little to interest the antiquarian : it swelled up like a wen, which denotes corruption in the system, and took the form and pressure of the decay of creed and country of which it was the exponent.   It has been calculated that during the 17th and 18th centuries no less than 68 millions sterling were expended in Spain in the building and *decoration of convents,* in-stead of making roads and canals : now the Madrid churches were mostly raised during this fatal period.   Begun chiefly by the Philips III. and IV., continued under the wretched Charles II., fit ruler of a declining power, and perfected under the foreigner, nowhere has the vile Churrigueresque and Rococo of Louis XIV. been carried to greater excesses.   The churches, whitened sepul-chres, are sad specimens of an insatiable greediness for tinsel, and worthy of a period when creed and country alike were starved in realities, while the outside of the platter was made fine, in the vain hope of hiding the rottenness within; again, the Bourbons introduced that particular rage for building and gilding which characterised *Le Grand Monarque,* while Charles III., who wished to be the Augustus of Madrid, unfortunately worked in brick, not marble, and his was the poor age of the commonplace and Royal Academical.   Hence the spiritless, meaningless piles, the long new streets, which present an ostentatious frontage of edifices, run up to flatter the royal eye and the national love for ex-terior show, while behind them are mean, ill-paved, ill-lighted, and ill-drained lanes.   These are the haunts of packs of gaunt, hungry dogs, who, in Spain as in the East, are the busiest and often the only scavengers.   The best houses at Madrid are very lofty, and different families live on different floors or flats, having the staircase in common ; each apartment is protected by a solid door, an " oak," in which there is generally a small wicket, as at a gambling-house, from which the worthy but suspicious inmates inspect visitors before they let them in ; for in this corrupted city nothing and no one is safe.   The interiors, according to our notions, are uncomfortable and unfurnished ; the kitchens, offices, and other necessaries are on the dirtiest and most continental scale.   There is little variety in their parsimonious *puchero,* and, probably, if Asmodeus could

take off the roofs of Madrid at the dining hour, he would see the majority of
the inhabitants wasting their time and appetites over the same *puchero* or pot-luck.
The gastronomy, philosophy, and practice of Spaniards have been touched
upon at p. 160, since dining everywhere forms an important feature in a man's
day, and is a never-failing resource to the traveller: here however the natives of
isolated Castile isolate themselves still more ; they meet in church and on the
Alameda, but not around the mahogany.

It is partly owing to this comparative absence of dinner society that foreign
ministers have less influence here than in any other European court; as the
whole art of diplomacy is centred in the kitchen, it never can come fully into
play in an undining city, where *mecum impransus disquirite* is the axiom of most
men in Spanish office, who seldom thus "lubricate business."

The best dinner and other society is in the houses of the scanty diplomatic
corps, for many powers have not recognized the present state of things; they are
copied by some few of the nobles, rich jobbers, placemen, and contractors, and
those who having emigrated, have discovered that the whole art of cookery is
not condensed, like the imprisoned genius, in an *olla,* or pipkin. The grandees
dine, indeed, with the foreign ministers, but with little reciprocity ; like the
Principes of modern Rome they seldom offer in return even a glass of water :
their hospitality consists in dining with any foreigner who will ask them. Few
of the diplomats after a lengthened residence at Madrid continue much to
invite the natives, as the thankless task is all against the collar. During the
residence of the court at Aranjuez and La Granja rather more intercommunication takes place, but it is of a pic-nic, extemporaneous character, and not
real sustained dinner society ; it is all on a small scale, and a mere child's ball
when compared to the way things are managed in London ; but in truth the
Spaniard, accustomed to his own desultory, free and easy impromptu scrambling
style of dining, is constrained by the order and discipline, the pomp and ceremony, and serious importance of a well-regulated dinner, and their observance
of forms extends only to persons, not to things : so even the *grande* has only a thin
European polish spread over his Gotho-Bedouin dining table ; he lives and eats
surrounded by an humble clique, in his huge ill-furnished barrack-house, without
any elegance, luxury, or even comfort, according to sound trans-pyrenean
notions : few indeed are the kitchens which possess a *cordon bleu,* and fewer are
the masters who really like an orthodox *entrée,* one unpolluted with the heresies of garlic and red pepper : again, whenever their cookery attempts to be
foreign, as in their other imitations, it ends in being a flavourless copy ; but few
things are ever done in Spain in *real style,* which implies forethought and expense. Here everything is a makeshift ; the noble master *reposes* his affairs on
an unjust steward, and dozes away life on this bed of roses, somnolescent over
business and awake only to intrigue ; his numerous ill-conditioned ill-appointed
servidumbre have no idea of discipline or subordination ; you never can calculate
on their laying even the table-cloth, as they prefer idling in the church or *plaza,*
to doing their duty, and would rather starve, and sing, dance, and sleep out of
place and independently, than feast and earn their wages by fair work; nor has
the employer any redress, for if he dismisses them he will only get just such
another set, or even worse.

Few foreigners enjoy much health of mind or body in this unsocial, insalu-
brious city ; nor can foreign plenipotentiaries ever hope for much satisfactory
dealing with a stiffnecked, unbusiness-like government, which imputes to its
innate majesty and real power, a position which, like that of Turkey or Portugal,
is almost upheld by the forbearance, protection, or mutual jealousies of other
and more powerful countries. The Madrid officials have always behaved cava-

lierly towards foreign agents: the Duke, even while saving them, was not "treated as a friend, or even as a gentleman," was "utterly without influence in their councils," for they have a "thorough contempt of," and are "utterly reckless of conduct as regards their foreign allies:" see 'Disp.' Aug. 31, 1809, July 2, 1812, Aug. 25, and Sept. 5, 1813, *et passim.* Small indeed is the redress obtained for gross infractions of treaties and ill-usage of our traders. The man in office, like the cuttle-fish, surrounds himself for protection in an obfuscation of papers: protocol succeeds to protocol, *expediente* to *documento,* until the minister and matter both die a natural death from sheer exhaustion; so it always was. Howell, in Charles I.'s time, describes his pile of unredressed complaints as being "higher than himself." Nor is Spanish expedition always more satisfactory than its procrastination. When the French envoy remonstrated to Philip II. that some of his countrymen had long been kept untried in the prisons of the Inquisition, the king replied that he would cause "good and speedy justice to be shown them," and they were burnt the week afterwards.

Such is Madrid, morally and physically considered; a city in which a lengthened residence withers mind and body. Well might Gongora exclaim, Este es Madrid, mejor dijera *infierno!* and however the *Madrileño* may think it a paradise, the capital has but little hold on the affections of the nation at large. It appeals indeed to their pride and self-interest, but each atomic item which goes up to swell the crowd of fortune-hunters, prefers in his own heart the capital of his native province. Grievously therefore was Buonaparte mistaken when he imagined that the capture of Madrid would ensure the subjugation of the country, which it did in the case of Vienna, Paris, &c.

The aggregate character of the Madrid population, which is formed out of immigrants from every other province, is marked by an assumption of a metropolitan and courtier tone of superiority; there is an affectation of despising the country town and manners, and a departure from national costume: an insincere frivolity, the result of the false intrigues which are carried around on all sides, is also reproached to the *Madrileño.* The females are by no means so attractive, either morally or physically, as those of Valencia and Andalucia: they are more sickly, and their faces are less expressive; they want also much of that natural light-hearted frankness and absence of art which is the Spanish woman's charm. Like the men, they are more *gazmoñas,* or hypocrites; the *populacho,* male and female, is brutal and corrupted; the *Manolo* or *Manola* (words which are abbreviations of Manuel and Manuela) are the best worth the stranger's notice, not however on moral grounds; they are the *Majos y Majas* of Madrid, without however the *gracia* or elegance of the Andalucians, or the simple honesty of the *Charros y Charras* of Leon.

Madrid, since the death of Ferd. VII., has been so much improved as a town, that Spaniards who have recently returned there scarcely know it again. Its first and great benefactor was the M⁵· de Pontejos, who was *gefe politico.* There is also more life and movement in the streets, some of which are better cleaned, paved, and lighted; many of the old names have been changed for democratic and patriotic appellations: these, however, as parties upset each other, are again rechanged; and being liable to alterations at every shift of the political scene, we shall adopt the original nomenclature, with which after all the people are best acquainted. The destruction of convents has opened spaces, and new buildings are erecting everywhere. Again, an unforseen, accidental, and unintentional benefit, has arisen from the recent civil wars and perpetual changes of governments and principles; as each party, when in power, has persecuted its opponents to the death, the leaders of all shades have in their turn been forced to fly for safety either to France or England: thus, while the external fabric was rent, some light has penetrated through the chinks into this long hermetically-sealed country, since the exiles found out that their imagined first of countries was in reality one of the most backward, and each on his return brought back his grain of information. Another source of improvement to Madrid has been the reform of the municipal corporation. Formerly the large revenues were either jobbed and robbed among the members, or wasted in an expensive present to the king, the royal family, or the minion of the hour: now the funds are destined to local improvements. Not that all is done which ought to be, or every abuse entirely abolished; that would be expecting impossibilities: the Augean stable of official corruption, where money is in the case, defies even a Hercules with an Alpheus, that type of a reformer backed by the current of public opinion.

The best points for a panoramic view are from the top of the *S^{a.} Cruz* church tower, or from the mound at the head of the *Buen Retiro* gardens. In shape the town is almost a square with the corners rounded off. Avenues of trees are planted outside the mud-walls, and in the principal approaches on the riverside. Madrid will most please those who have hurried directly into Spain from France, as it is a truly Spanish city, and therefore the costume, *Prado*, and bullfight will strike with all the charm of novelty and strangeness of contrast, which will be wanting to those who arrive from beautiful Valencia, Moorish Granada, or stately Seville. A week will well suffice to see the marvels of the only " court of the world," of which the *Museos* are indeed among the finest in Europe; happy the man who then escapes to Avila, the Escorial and Segovia, or who turns to romantic Cuenca by imperial Toledo and the gardens of Aranjuez; those who the soonest shake the dust off their feet, and remain the shortest time at Madrid, will probably remember it with most satisfaction; for here, love, small like Slender's at the beginning, will marvellously decrease with better acquaintance. The more Madrid is known, the less it will be liked.

> " *Quien te quiere, no te sabe;*
> *Quien te sabe, no te quiere.*"

MADRID.—The hotels until lately were among the very worst in Europe, but the number of new coach companies, by bringing in more travellers, has created a demand for better accommodation; some of these companies have set up inns, or *paradores*, of their own; while many cafés and tolerable *restaurants* have been established, principally by foreigners, as occurs in the East. But those who are travelling with ladies will do well to write beforehand to some friend to secure apartments or private lodgings. Among the best hotels are *La Amistad*, kept by a Frenchman; *La Fonda de Genies; La de Europa*, C^{e.} de Peregrinos; *La del Comercio*, C^{e.} de Alcalá; *La de Paris*, C^{e.} del Carmen, although small is good. These are all well-placed, and in frequented localities.

The celebrated *Fontana de Oro*, long the Hotel of Madrid, and one of the worst in Europe, has been converted into an establishment for baths, lodgings, and reading-rooms.

Those who contemplate making a stay at Madrid, should hire private lodgings, which, although hardly " ready furnished," according to our ideas, are tolerable enough for Spain; some few have *chimineas* or fireplaces. N. B. always select these; for a fire is an unspeakable comfort in fine climates where winter is detestable, as the houses are like hollows of wells, without being always the residences of truth: the hearth, with its cheerful crackle, brings back thoughts of home and England, as a glimpse of the sun does Castile to the Spanish exile in Siberia. The bed is generally placed in a recess, the *Alcoba*, the door to which is glazed; the brick or tiled floors are covered with *Esteras;* the quarters surrounding *La Puerta del Sol* are the best. The traveller will, however, be guided by notices on windows and balconies to those houses in which apartments are placed at his *disposicion.* David Purkiss, *Casa de los Baños*, C⁰· Caballero de Gracia, has good lodgings, with baths, which are much frequented by governmental couriers, and can be recommended. There are several restaurants near *La Puerta del Sol:* one in the *Carrera de S*ⁿ· *Jeronimo* is kept by a Frenchman, and another in the *C⁰· del Principe* is kept by a Piedmontese. You can dine also at the three fondas of Genies, Paris, and El Comercio, from a dollar a head upwards. The cuisine is second-rate, yet, compared to the general gastronomic darkness of Spain, is here considered brilliant. The French cooks of the foreign ministers have done some good, but the *Puchero,* with its stringy savourless beef, *vaca cocido,* and boiled *garbanzo,* is still the staff of Castilian life. This worse than French *Bouilli,* mocks the palate with a show of nutriment: it may be eaten, however, when there is nothing else. Madrid is celebrated for its asparagus, grown at Aranjuez, and the *Hojaldre,* a light puff paste: the confectioners' shops are mostly kept by foreigners, as genuine Spanish pastry, like the buns and tartlets of England, savours of the dark ages, while French *Pâtisserie* is elegant in form, exquisite in material, full of invention, genius, and apricot jam. The *Pasteleria Suiza,* Calle Jacomo Trezo; *Pasteleria Estrangera,* Pª· Sª· Ana; that in the C⁰· del Principe; and the French *Pâtisserie* in Carrera de Sⁿ· Jeronimo, are good. Bottled beer, mixed with lemon juice, is another favourite drink at Madrid, but as might be expected from the ingredients, cannot be recommended to British palates or stomachs.

The common wine, and the best by far, is the rich red Valdepeñas; however, the inferior produce of Arganda is constantly sold for it, and both are adulterated with decoctions of logwood and other abominations. French and foreign wines are dear and bad : the Madrileño, not curious in anything, is very indifferent as to quality ; quantity is his object, and he just drinks the wine which is the cheapest, and grows the nearest. The *Andaluces,* C⁰· de Fuencarral, and *Las delicias de Betica,* C⁰· de las Carretas, deal in Sherries and Malagas, which here are considered as vins de liqueur. Many new and good cafés have been recently established. Among the best are *El de los dos Amigos, El Nuevo, El de Cervantes, De la Aduana,* and *De la Estrella,* all of which are in the C⁰· de Alcalá ; also that of *Lorenzini,* Puerta del Sol, and *El Principe y la Venecia,* C⁰· del Principe. The snows of the Guadarrama chain, if they supply frozen blasts, and be pregnant with consumption, at least during the scorching summer furnish materials for cool drinks and ices in abundance, which are also sold in the streets, and especially by Valencians. The *Agua de Cebada* is very refreshing ; so is the *Orchata de Chufas,* or *Michi michi,* "half and half," being made of barley and pounded *chochos,* the lupines of the old Romans, the Tirmis of the Cairo Arab (Lane ii. 13). These emulsion drinks are very classical, for the *leche de Almendras,* which is prescribed as a panacea by Spanish doctors, is exactly described in Athenæus (ii. 12) Αμυγδαλη—αγαθον φαρμακον. No drink, however, whether medicinal or refrigatory, comes up to the *Agraz* (see p. 69). It cools a man's body and soul, and is delicious when mixed with *Mansanilla* wine.

There are many *Casas de Pupilos.* Among the best are two in the C⁰· de Carretas, two in the C⁰· de Alcalá, and another in the C⁰· del Caballero de Gracia ; but it will be as well in these matters, which change from day to day, to consult your banker or some Madrid friend. The prices in the best for bed, board, and lodging seldom exceed a dollar a-day, which is cheap enough. The society is often good, and, as everywhere in Spain, undeniable as far as manners and high-breeding. Advertisements will also be found as to these and other traveller's wants, in the various daily papers, and *Diarios de Avisos;* in them will also be announced the different sights, religious pageants, theatres, bull-fights, sales, festivals, and scanty popular amusements. The *Gazeta* is the official paper ; and its pages for the last fifty years, the French Moniteur only excepted, are the greatest satire ever deliberately published by any people on itself.

The newspapers of Madrid amounted in 1843 to some forty in number; in 1833, under Ferd. VII., they did not reach half a dozen, and enjoyed a freedom of press similar to that granted by his Holiness at Rome. The sapient Cortes of Cadiz passed from one extreme to another, from the gags of the Inquisition to absolute liberty. The natural consequence of thus arming, without due preparation, a power which England barely can resist, was the raising a new Frankenstein tyrant, worse than all the evils which were overturned : the press became, like an emancipated Caliban, as the Duke so often said, venal, insolent, and licentious. It was bought by parties who rode over the Regency and Cortes (Disp. Jan. 27, 1813); and so it has always been since, when *free, i. e.* the slave of some dominant interest, either of the French, with a view to abuse England ; of the Cuban, to uphold the slave-trade; of the Catalan, to protect smuggling, and write down any tariff or treaty of commerce. Their misstatements work on the national susceptible mind, and obtain prescriptive authority from never being even contradicted by our careless government : well did the Duke suggest " getting hold of one or two of them," not, however, to disseminate falsehood, but to tell the " *truth, the plain truth* " (Disp. Apr. 2, 1813). The masses of the people, from having long been taught

by ruler and priest that others were to think for them, and from not being accustomed to reading or public discussion, believe in the broad sheet, because it is ìn print; they go to it for facts and opinions : hence the editors mislead their dupes, and rise on their shoulders into place and power. Journalism being the ladder of greatness, naturally absorbs the talent of the country, to the detriment of literature in general. The press, thus the organ of the aristocracy of intellect, is not merely a fourth estate, as amongst ourselves, but the *whole state*, as must be the case in all countries unfit for such a liberty. In England journalists have no such social position as they have in Spain or France, simply because the press, although wielding a real political power, reflects and does not lead public opinion : our fixed institutions guarantee *order*, but where that only depends on individuals, the broad sheet becomes the organ of change and revolutions, and those who play best on its stops rise to be personages : thus Gonzalez Bravo passed from editing *El Guirigay,* an Andalucian "*slang*" paper, to be premier. These gentlemen, like Monsieur Thiers, when out of office write historical *romances*, libels, and farces, and when in office plot and plan real tragedies. The circulation of Madrid newspapers is principally confined to the capital; there are few papers in remote inland towns, which vegetate in their usual incurious ignorance. There are many subscription and reading rooms at Madrid ; the best are in the Cᵉ· de la Montera ; and *El Literario*, Cᵉ· del Principe. Those who wish to procure foreign books at Madrid, or when out of Spain to obtain Spanish ones, may apply to *Casimiro Monier,* who has a reading establishment here in the No. 10 Carrera San Jeronimo, and another in Paris, No. 7, Rue de Provence.

Warm baths, the luxury of the Roman and Oriental, have latterly been much increased in the larger towns of Spain. The best are at Purkiss s, those *del Oriente,* Pᵃ· de Isabel II., *La Estrella,* Cᵉ· de Sᵃ· Clara, Sⁿ· *Isidro,* Cᵉ· Mayor, and *La Fontana de Oro.* The *Calle de Alcalá* is the chief rendezvous of the fraternity of the whip; here most of the diligence companies have their " booking offices." Here are to be hired the *Coche de Colleras* and the *Calesa.* The genuine carriages of Spain are still queer concerns, as the drivers are picturesque rogues (see p. 33). A *job* carriage for the day costs from three to four dollars. In the *Calle del Lobo* cabriolets may be hired at 6 reals the hour; in the Cᵉ· *del Infante,* a " glass-coach " is to be had at 56 reals the day, at 28 for a morning, and 30 for an afternoon. There are also strange public omnibuses driven by a *tiro* of mules. There is an open horse-market every Thursday in the Pᵃ· *del Rastro.* The markets for eatables are tolerably well supplied : the best are those of *San Ildefonso,* where the French pulled down a church, and those of *San Felipe Neri* and *La Plaza de Cebada.* The best shops are in the vicinity of the *Puerta del Sol.* And first for booksellers,—the bibliopoles of Spain and their wares have been described at p. 138. Books at Madrid are scarce and dear; those curious in topography and hagiography will find a copious collection in the *Biblioteca nacional,* Plazuela de Oriente. Meanwhile the best *booksellers* are *Ranz,* Cᵉ de la Cour; *Soso, Perez, Sanz,* Cᵉ· de Carretas; *Mijar,* Cᵉ· del Principe; *Dennie y Hidalgo,* Cᵉ· de Montera; and *Dionysio Carriano,* the *Greek* who formerly lived at Seville. For *maps, Lopez,* Cᵉ· del Principe : *tailors, Hernandez,* Pᵃ· del Sol; *Vensilla,* Cᵃ· de Sⁿ· Jeronimo; *Warselet,* Red de Sⁿ· Luis; *Pascual,* Cᵉ· de Fuencarral : *milliners, La Caraset,* Cᵉ· del Principe; *La Vitorina,* Cᵉ· del Carmen; *La Pepita,* Cᵉ· del Olivo. The best *ladies' shops,* or *tiendas de modas,* are *Gines y Narciso,* Garcia Cachera, Cᵉ· del Carmen; *La Francesa,* Cᵉ· de la Montera; and one in the Cᵉ· Mayor, opposite to the Conde de Oñates. At Madrid the traveller will be able to get a laquais de place, an animal which is so much wanted in the inland capitals of Spain ; there is also a sort of club, *El Casino,* to which there is no great difficulty of admission. Foreign money can be changed at the broker's offices in the Cᵉ· Montera and Toledo. It is better to rely in these matters on one's banker ; attend particularly to our advice p. 5.

Madrid contains, according to Caballero, ' *Noticias topografico-estadisticas,*' about 200,000 inhabitants. It is divided into 12 districts, consists of 24 parishes, has 18 hospitals, a *cuna* or *casa de espositos,* a university, 9 academies, 4 public libraries, 3 museums, an armoury, a glorious palace, 3 theatres, a *plaza de toros,* 33 public fountains, and 5 chief gates. Those who wish to know all the rights, prerogatives, and glories of Madrid, are referred to the list of local descriptions appended to the ' *Manual de Madrid,*' which is a good guide-book : the author, Ramon de Mesoneros Romano, has also published a ' *Panorama Matritense,*' 3 vols. 8vo. 1837; this ' Life in Madrid ' gives the picture as seen by a native's fond eye. The collector of Spanish topography will purchase ' *Teatro de Grandezas,*' Gil Gonzalez d'Avila, fo., Mad. 1623 ; ' *Historia de Madrid,*' Gerº· Quintana, fo., Mad. 1629 ; ' *Solo Madrid es Corte,*' Alonzo Nuñez de Castro, 4to., 4th ed. Barcelona, 1698 ; Ponz, ' *Viage I. ;*' and ' *Discurso sobre varias Antigüedades,*' Antº· Pellicer, 8vo., Mad. 1791. Madrid has produced very few great men beyond Lope de Vega, Quevedo, and Calderon. The history of those who have attained mediocrity fills, however, four quartos, ' *Hijos Ilustres,*' Jose Alvarez Baena, Mad. 1790 ; for the *Provincia de Madrid,* the little description by Tomas Lopez, Mad. 1763, is the best. The annual court-guide, ' *Guia de los Forasteros,*' is useful. Mellado, in his 1843 ed. of the ' *Guia del Viagero en España,*' has prefixed a good account of the capital. The best map of Madrid is that published by *Lopez,* Cᵉ· del Principe.

SIGHTS AT MADRID.—Every body must begin with the *Puerta del Sol,* which, like our Temple Bar, is in the centre of the capital, although once the east gate, on which the rising sun shone; now it has been built around on all sides, and the gate is gone, the name only remaining. The small *plaza* is situated in the middle of the long line of streets which run, like porta venas, E. from W., from the *Prado* by the *Calle de Alcala,* and then by the *Cᵉ Mayor* to the river; at this point two other important streets, the *Cᵉ. de la Montera,* and *Cᵗ· de las Carretas,* the Bond Street and Regent Street of Madrid, running N. and S., cross the other two almost at right angles. Thus the *Puerta del Sol* is the heart, where all the greater arteries of circulation meet and diverge, the centre where the stream of Madrid life and the tide of affairs flows and ebbs.

The shops in the streets which branch from it are the most fashionable; their wares, exposed to the eye, speak for themselves. They are mostly closed from one, when nature rings her dinner bell, until three, when the siesta has been dozed out; the scanty carriages have then crept into their coachhouses, and their beasts and drivers into the stalls; even the creak of cart-wheels is mute; the mules and asses, which do the work of parcel-delivering companies, the goats, which do the office of milk-cows, are all sleeping with their masters on the ground on the shady side of the streets: but every where throughout the length and breadth of the land midday heat empties the streets, and increases the languid, monotonous, poco-curante character so common to old inland Spanish towns, where the quiet and want of population mark silent decay and pining atrophy. In Madrid, as being the seat of government, during its waking hours there is a greater semblance of life; but ranked with London, or even Liverpool and Edinburgh, every thing is very second-rate and retail. It will indeed disappoint those who have

listened to the grandiloquent exaggerations of Madrilenians, who on their part will set down the foreigner who is not positively *dazzled* as either envious, malignant, or a fool.

The native really believes in his inflated over-estimate of Madrid, for he is no traveller, and knows of nothing better; and, accustomed to his poverty-stricken inland capitals, imagines this to be what London is, and ancient Rome was, an epitome of the civilised world, της οικουμενης επιτομη. Although the shops cannot at all be compared to ours, which burst with opulence into the streets, yet the rest of the Peninsula considers them to be the magazine, the Pantechnicon of the universe: "You will get it at Madrid," says the semi-Moro shopkeeper of Toledo, Leon, Salamanca, &c., when asked by the foreigner for some article of commonest necessity. Certainly the shops have recently become more European, and there is an improved show of commodities, especially of French millinery and light goods: but everything is a day behind the fair, and articles which are out of fashion, and will no longer sell beyond the Pyrenees, here figure as the last novelties of the season. The shops indicate a limited wealth; little is done on a really grand scale; business is paltry and passive: the people walk about as if they had not much to do, and still less to spend; the generality of native shopkeepers partake of their customers' tobaccose indifferentism; they are without empressement or prévenance, are scarcely civil, and seem to care little, like Orientals, whether you buy of them or not. Even necessaries are dear: Madrid, placed in the centre of Spain, producing and supplying nothing, consumes everything, like an exhausting receiver: as all that enters comes from a distance, the expense is enhanced by transport and heavy duties. If the projected railroads be opened to Barcelona and Aviles, the benefits conferred on the capital will indeed be great.

The real makeshift poverty of Madrid is revealed during the *Feria*, or fair, which begins every Sept. 21, and ends Oct. 4. Then the houses are turned out of doors and their nakedness exposed; then the only " *Corte* " becomes one broker's alley, as every family that has anything to sell exhibits the article in the street. Occasionally a good book, picture, and old Toledan blade might be picked up; but sad is the display—how many are anxious to sell, how few to buy. It is said by veteran fair loungers that the same wares appear every year, just as floating rubbish in a mill-dam keeps coming up and down in one vicious circle; the same results are evident in the *Almonedas*, or sales by private contract, and the auctions, *Subastas*, a term derived from the Roman *Sub Hastá*.

The south side of the *Puerta del Sol* is occupied by the post-office, the *Casa de correos*. This large isolated square edifice was raised in 1768 for Charles III., by one M. Jaime Marquet : the approach and arrangements have been deservedly criticised (see our advice, p. 14). A strong piquet of soldiers is always mounted here, for the building serves also the purposes of a military *post*. Commanding, as it does, the central hotbed of outbreak, the fixed bayonet and ball-cartridge are absolutely necessary, since the very air is poisoned with *asonadas alborotos y ajo*, with treasons, uprisings, and garlic ; indeed, it is said that for a hundred dollars a revolutionary *funcion* may be any day got up here; the very troops are often infected, and fire upon the regular authorities, killing even their own captains-general. Adjoining to the r., at the *Casa de postas*, are the mail and post-horse establishments. Formerly the open *plaza* was disfigured by a *churrigueresque* fountain, the work of the heresiarch Ribera. The statue of *Venus* on it was called by the honest people *Mariblanca* (see Utrera), thus merely changing the name, so inveterate is female worship in Spain; it

has been removed to the *P*ª· *de las Descalzas*.

On the east side is the church *N*ª· *S*ª· *del buen Suceso*, a paltry building with an illuminated clock. Here, in spite of its auspicious name, occurred a sad scene in the annals of Madrid. Murat chose this church and its *patios* for one place of his terrorist butcheries of the *dos de maio*, 1808. Many of his victims are buried here : read the inscriptions, and observe the *Urna* in which repose the ashes of Canon Matias Vinueza, murdered by the pseudo patriots, May 4, 1821. The *Buen Suceso* has the privilege of having mass performed so late as 2 o'clock, P.M., midday being elsewhere the last hour; and accordingly it is the grand place of rendezvous of fine folk, and is much crowded on holidays. But how can *success* fail to a church which so studies the natural wants of its congregation ? Here are convenient hours for good company, music to beguile the service, incense to neutralise bad smells, and excellent light for the display of female dress.

Thus religion, letters, and locality, combine to render the *Puerta del Sol* the real national *Cortes*, or congress, the site of meetings in the marketplace, and the resort of quidnuncs and the many who have nothing to do in a city without trade or industry, and who begin and here end their day : that day, which indeed is of small value, is thus wasted in a lazy routine; but no people better understand the art of killing the enemy time, and each other, and doing that business which the evil one provides for the idle.

Here, therefore, all who wish to study character and costume will never lack subjects for pen or pencil; for the Madrilenian, like the ancient, lives out of doors, *foris* in the *forum*, and wisely prefers the cheerful sun to his own comfortless home, which has no fireside. All this is the classical and Oriental το αγοραϭθαι of the Athenian, who did little else but "either tell or hear some new thing," as it is the *vespertinum forum* of the otiose Horace, who delighted to pick up the last bit of correct intelligence, just as there was "no place in the town," said Addison, " which I so much love as the Royal Exchange." This old-fashioned going out to bring in news, was the occupation of our " Paul's walkers" two centuries ago. Now, in the march of intellect, clubs and morning papers have put an end even to Bond-street lounging, since the newspaper brings to our breakfast in description, all that the ancients and Orientals can only see, hear, and touch bodily, out of doors and abroad. Accordingly, the Spaniard, in whom, as in many other matters, the past and present meet, takes up a position on this *forum* of the *Puerta del Sol*, cloaked like a Roman, while a cigar and the *Gazeta* indicate modern civilization, and soothe him with empty vapour.

The blind are here the usual itinerant vendors of the broad sheet, " second editions," lying bulletins, and flying handbills, *Boletines y hojas volantes.* Indeed, it is quite a proverb to say of one whose vision is going, *Está ya para ir vender gazetas ;* and the blind are the fit guides of those stone blind who believe in the romances which are printed and circulated in this heart and brain of Madrid by those worthy ministers, who, here as beyond the Pyrenees, know well how to pander to the national credulity. And who can doubt the authority of the *religio loci*, the Puerta del *Sol?* Quis solem dicere falsum audeat ? Nor can it be denied, in spite of the clouds of cigars, smoke, and lies, that the shrewd people do, somehow or other, arrive at some truth at last.

Observe the singular groups of sallow, unshorn, hung:y, bandit-looking men, with fierce-flashing eyes and thread-bare shorn capas, which cluster like bees round the reader of some "authentic letter." These form two of the three classes into which a large portion of all who wear long-tailed coats may be divided: first the *Pre-*

tendiente, or place-hunter, who aspires to some situation, a sinecure if possible, his food is hope ; next the *Empleado*, or fortunate youth, who has got into a good birth, whose bliss is the certainty of taking bribes, and the chance of being paid the salary of his appointment ; and lastly, the *Cesante*, or one who, having held some offices, is now turned out, his joys and profits have ceased, his misery is memory, his consolation revenge.

The *Pretendientes y Cesantes* either wear away the thresholds of the minister of the hour, or polish the pavement of the *Puerta del Sol*, with the restlessness of caged wild beasts, for this is the den of the *Empleomanicos*, the victims .of that madness for place which is the peculiar disease of Madrid. Hence this their rendezvous is the mint of scandal, and all who have lived intimately with them know how invariably every one abuses his neighbour behind his back, the lower orders occasionally using a knife, which is sharper even than the tongue. *Self*, in fact, is every where the idol, for no Spaniard can tolerate a rival or superior.

No handbook can detail the " reports of the best informed circles " which are buzzed about on this spot, from the fiery treason to the chilling whisper, the *susurro*, the *se dice en el pueblo*, the frigidus rumor of Horace, the personal abuse, the envenomed calumny, the plausible insinuation ; and all this either dignified by the splendid phraseology of the Castilian idiom, or enlivened by the mocking satire, cutting sarcasm, and epigrammatic wit, in which the dramatic serio-comic Spaniards have few rivals.

Thus these *Empleomanicos* exist, bored and boring, deceiving and deceived, for, true romancers, they are proportionably credulous :

" With them the pleasure is as great
    Of being cheated as to cheat."

The interjection "*Es falso*," "*Mentira*," "*mientes*," is in every one's mouth ; nor is this giving the lie, which in honest

England is *the* deadly insult, often resented. This Asiatic *Doblez* (the Italian *Furberia*), or duplicity, is the more deceptive because it is accompanied by a grave, high-bred manner and plausible apparent frankness which seems honesty itself, and is quite edifying to those who do not know this strange Oriental people; but, as the Duke said, who was truth personified, " It is difficult to understand Spaniards correctly, they are such a mixture of low intrigue coupled with extreme haughtiness of manner" (Disp. Dec. 13, 1810).

The *Puerta del Sol* is also the lounge of the dandies, and those of both sexes whose intrigues are not political. It is also the haunt of beggars; see p. 173 for the specific for this vermin. Here also are held *rifas*, or raffle lotteries, which are common all over Spain. Sometimes the prizes are trinkets for the fair sex, pictures of saints for the devout; at other times a fat pig, or broad ounces of red gold, sure baits, and no mistake, for the bacon appetite and shark-like avarice of those who sigh to become suddenly rich by gambling or jobbing.

Now enter the *C^e. de Alcalá*, which during Espartero's ephemeral rule was called *C^e. del Duque de la Victoria*. Nous avons changé tout cela, says Louis Philippe. It is one of the finest streets in Europe, being placed on a gentle slope, and with just curve enough to be graceful. This great aorta widens like a river, disemboguing its living streams into the *Prado*. The perfect effect is destroyed by the lowness of some of the houses, which are not in proportion to the width which they fringe: the natives, however, are in raptures because it is broad and *foreign*-looking, and therefore a thing not seen in their own older semi-Moro cities; but the glare in summer is terrific, and the M^{s.} de Pontejos deserves well for having planted the acacias. Meanwhile the chill blasts from the snow-capt Guadarrama, piercing the cross-streets, blow out the brief taper of Madrilenian life.

The first edifice to the l. is the fine quadrilong *Aduana* or custom-house, built in 1769; it does credit to Lieut.-Gen. Sabatini, R.A. The east and west fronts are ignoble, but the façade to the street is handsome; the shield and *Famas* are by Michel, and add little to his fame: the *patios* and interior details are so well arranged, that nothing is wanting but commerce; but the fiscal absurdities of Spain, and their corrector, the smuggler, take care that the situation of commissioners should, as elsewhere, be a sinecure and mismanaged. Even the stone satyrs outside smile at the farce of business done within, and the facilities afforded without to fraud. especially since the commerce-strangling decrees and tariff of 1841, by which, virtually, every thing foreign was prohibited from entering Spain except by way of contraband.

Adjoining is the Royal Academy of *Sⁿ. Fernando*, a Bourbon exotic, founded in 1744, and removed here in 1774. Philip IV. had wished to create one, but was prevented by the jealousy, hatred, and uncharitableness of the artists towards each other (Carducho, 'Dial.' 158). Attached to the *Museo* is a collection of natural history; but vainly did Charles III. inscribe over the portal that this was to be the lodging of art *and* nature under one and the same roof: the royal academicians, second-rate imitators of other men's works, not of Nature, have effectually barred the banns. This establishment has too often been the hotbed of jobs, and the nurse of mediocrity. Founded ostensibly with a view of restoring expiring art, it was called in, like Dr. Sangrado, too late; nor was it a humane society which could resuscitate a really and not an apparently dead patient. It came rather to smother the last spark of nationality, then proceeded to hang up its copied inanities as proudly as an undertaker puts up a hatchment. The Academy has never created even a tolerable artist, nor has it infused vitality into itself by incorporating whatever talent may arise elsewhere by individual unaided exertions. The R. A.s have disseminated false canons by their teaching, and encouraged bad taste by their example and the prestige of their rank; for such was the influence of royalty and *La Corte*, that the nation believed it to be in the power of the absolute king, by appointing a dauber to be his *Pintor de Camara*, or his own portrait or historical painter, to convert him into a Titian or Raphael.

The Academy possesses some 300 second-rate pictures, the gleanings from royal private and sequestered collections. About a dozen or so good paintings shine like gold in the dull sand, *rari nantes in gurgite vasto*; a set of small coloured terra-cotta figures, representing the massacre of the Innocents, &c., has recently been added, from the confiscated gallery of Don Carlos, and deserve notice. A printed catalogue of the contents of ten saloons is sold at the door. The gallery is open to the public on Mondays and Fridays, and always to foreigners. There are some reserved rooms upstairs, which however are shown on application, and for a fee: on the ground-floor is a collection of plaster casts made by Mengs, in the hopes of furnishing models from antique sculpture, in which Spain is so very deficient (see p. 107).

The reception pictures of the R. A.s are specimens of a bad Mengs style run mad. The gingerbread throne-room glitters with portraits of the Spanish Bourbons, from the baboon head of Charles III. to the porcine sensuality of Ferdinand VII.; these and their consorts, fit mates, are as fine as feathers, flounces, lace, and diamonds can make them; everything sparkles save their dull eyes, everything is princely save their faces: the originals were made by nature's "journeymen," fiddlers, grooms of the bedchamber, confessors, and so forth, for it is in the power of one woman to taint the blood of Charlemagne; and their portraits were painted by men fit to represent such individuals, by *Los Señores* Lopez, Cruz, Estevé, R.A.s, and some others who are rien, pas même académicien. The oriental natives, who love red gold and diamonds in esse et posse, burst into ecstasies when they behold this dazzle: "Oh wretch!" said Apelles to a dauber of tinsel, "you could not paint Helen *beautiful*, so you have made her *fine*."

Among the best pictures remark in the first saloon "a Christ crucified;" and "a Christ in purple," by Alº· Cano; "a Christ before Pilate," by Morales. The grand Murillo is "*El Tiñoso*," in which Sᵃ· Isabel of Hungary is applying remedies to the scabby head of a pauper urchin; she is full of tenderness, but the sores are too truly painted to be agreeable, for they recall the critique of Pliny (xxxiv. 9) on a similar picture of Leontinus, cujus hulceris dolorem sentire etiam spectantes videntur; but her saint-like charity ennobles these horrors, which a royal hand does not refuse to heal, and how gently; her beautiful, almost divine head contrasts with that of the beggar hag in the foreground. This noble picture was carried off from *La Caridad*, of which in subject it was the appropriate gem, for the Louvre, but Waterloo restored it to Spain, if not to the fair Bætis. It was detained on its passage by the Royal Academy; yet the sainted Isabel, although delivered, had not escaped defilement, having been overcleaned and repainted, especially in the r. corner below.

Next observe a good bronze Minerva. In the second saloon are two superb Murillos, also taken by Soult from *Sᵃ· Maria la Blanca* at Seville, also sent to Paris and rescued, like Sᵃ· Isabel. These glorious pictures represent the legend of the dream of *El Patricio Romano*, which preceded the building the *Sᵃ· Maria la Mayor* at Rome under Pope Liberius, about the year 360: they are semi-circular in shape, to fit the gaps still visible at

Seville. The paintings in the angles are an unfortunate *perfectionnement*, added in France, and distract from the originals, which were both ruthlessly over-cleaned in Paris, and have since been much repainted by one Garcia. The Dream, the best of the two, is an exquisite representation of the sentiment *sleep*. The Roman senator is dressed like a Spanish hidalgo, for the localism and *Españolismo* of Murillo scorned even to borrow costume from the *foreigner*; the patrician has quite a Shakspere look : he is fast asleep at his *siesta*, and no wonder, since he holds a large book, a μεγα κακον, and an undoubted soporific. The Virgin in the air points out the site of the future church. The companion picture, where the dreamer explains his vision to the pontiff, is painted in the *vaporoso* style : the distant procession is admirable.

Observe also a Hercules and Omphale, said to be by Rubens [?]. The bronzes of Charles V. and Philip II. are by Leon Leoni; those of Conde Duque and John of Austria are by Pedro Tacca. In the fourth saloon are some finely painted monks by Zurbaran, especially one of Jeronimo Perez, with a book; the "*Disengaño*," by Antº· de Pereda, is full of sculls and horrors : observe a "*Concepcion*," by Roelas, and a portrait of Antº· Serbas by Frº· Porbus. In the fifth room are portraits of Philip IV. and Maria his wife, by Velazquez [?]. In the seventh are the R. Academical performances. Those who admire Ribera will observe some portraits and pictures painted with his usual fidelity to coarse, ill-selected nature. Some little pictures by Goya are among the best productions of modern Spanish art.

The annual exhibitions of the R.A.s and their compeers take place in these rooms in September, but the spirit of ancient Spanish national art has fled, and painting, which rose with the united monarchy, has shared in its fall, perishing under the foreigner. Now everything is borrowed; there is neither high art nor originality: the best modern painters are but mediocrities. Gutierez is a copier of Murillo, Villamil of our Roberts, but at a most respectful distance. Alonzo, Ribera, Esquivel, look up to Madrazo, who with his R.A.s follows in the wake of Mengs and David, of whom their style is often an exaggeration. They have learnt a mannerism which precludes and defies a return to *nature*, and in the words of the Roman philosopher, " Magistrum respicientes, Naturam ducem sequi desierunt." Accordingly, their art has become a pale copy of other men's ideas and works; under the R. Academical hothouse it pines a sickly forced exotic, and is no longer the vigorous plant of the wild but rich soil of Spain. Not so rose Ribera, Velazquez, or Murillo, whose works bear the impress of the *individual* mind of each great *Spaniard*, who borrowed nothing from the past or foreign, nothing from Apelles or Raphael, from Greece or Italy; nay, they spurned them and their ways, and painted the *Hidalgo* and monachal Christianity or Marianism of Spain; they drew with a local colour subjects which were in correspondence with the national eye and mind, while the mens divinior of Murillo, and the pith and savour of manhood of Velazquez imparted to the commonest subjects their own freshness and fire, as Pygmalión, in that beautiful myth, breathed life into a stone.

In the second floor is the *Gabinete de Ciencias naturales*, which occupies eight rooms, formed by Charles III.: it was pillaged and disorganised by the invaders, but Ferd. VII. did what he could to repair and restore it. It is rich in Spanish minerals and marbles; the light, however, is not good, being excluded, as in so many chapels where there are fine pictures, from a perverse ingenuity, to spite the blessed sun in his chosen land, where the *light is good* as when approved of by the great Creator, and where there are no *blacks*, fog, or window-tax. There is a poor sort of a guide-book, ' *Paseo por el gabinete natural*,' Juan Mieg, 8vo. 1819.

Zoology, ornithology, and natural history have been long neglected in Spain. See Widdrington, i. 40. Latterly, some improvement has taken place; but still in this and other collections they have no one thing complete, and what they have they scarcely know, and, seldom classify scientifically: everything is rather the result of *accident* than of design; but Spaniards seldom can give the commonest information regarding the animal or vegetable productions of their own country, any more than a monk or *cura* can tell the name of the painter or sculptor of the pictures and images in their own chapels. As in the East, what little has been done has chiefly been the work of foreigners, such as Bowles, Lœfling (see p. 190), Boissier, Boutelou, Schultz, Widdrington, &c.; or of Spaniards who have travelled *abroad*, such as Cabanas, Elorza, and others. The *Gabinete* is now under the direction of a Catalan named Graells, from whom better things may be expected. The school of mining is also well managed by Señor Prado. Foreigners have set this branch of immediate profit in action; and Spain being now mining-mad, the demand for intelligent mineralogists is very great (see p. 415).

The specimens of marbles are splendid, and show what treasures yet remain buried in the Peninsula; the ledges of the cabinets are lined with the choicest varieties. Observe the *Verde Antique*, from *el Barranco de Sⁿ. Juan*, near Granada; the brown jaspers, from *Lanjaron;* agates, from *Aracena;* crystallized sulphurs, from *Conil;* lead ores of every tint, from the *Sierra de Gador;* copper, from *Rio tinto;* a lump of virgin gold, from the *Sonora* mine, weighing 16½ lbs.; another of silver, of 250 lbs.; one of copper, of 200 lbs. The grand object of the Spanish gypsies is the large loadstone *La Piedra Iman,* and they are always plotting how to steal this *Bar Lachi,* which they believe to be a love-philtre

and a talisman against policemen, excise officers, and the devil.

The animal kingdom is less rich than the mineral, since the latter is dug out ready, and is a raw material, fit at once for the museum, while the former specimens require art in the stuffing and preparation—things of the practical operative foreigner. Here, however, is *El Megaterio,* the almost unique skeleton of the Mastodon Megalotherion, which was found in 1789, near the river Lujan, 13 L. from Buenos Ayres, and sent home by the viceroy Loreto. It is the largest and most perfect semi-fossil in existence, and the elephant near it looks diminutive. There are also three rooms not shown to the public, which should be inspected: a silver key unlocks the doors. They contain some S. American, Indian, Chinese, Moorish, and mixed curiosities of no great rarity or interest to those accustomed to the better collections of Europe. There are also some anatomical preparations and fœtuses, hidden from an over-susceptible prudery: but let none omit to see the superb collection of about one hundred cinque-cento cups, tazzas, and exquisite jewelled plate. Observe a mermaid with emerald tail, rising out of gold studded with rubies, by Cellini; and a cup supported by a female. Many of these were broken by the invaders, and never have been repaired, for the keepers seem to be entirely unaware of their beauty and rarity.

On the opposite side of the street is *La casa de los Heros,* a great *Almacen de cristales,* and near it the *Deposito Hidrografico* founded by Charles III., and built by Rodriguez, and where there is a tolerable library, and some instruments for nautical and astronomical purposes. In a niche of the *Hospederia de los Cartujos* is the admirable statue of Sⁿ· Bruno, by Mˡ· Pereyra, obiit 1667, which is absolutely a fossil, a petrified monk. His equally fine St. Martin was smashed by the invaders. Lower down on the same side of the street is the house which, since 1814, has been the residence of the English embassy, and in which a more sustained and splendid hospitality has been shown than in any ten houses of any of the grandees. Opposite, at the N. E. corner, is the conspicuous square palace *La Buena Vista*, which was built towards the close of the last century by the extravagant Duchess of Alva. It was bought by the Madrid municipality, and given by them to toady Godoy, then in the height of power. Confiscated in 1808, it was next made the military *Museo*, in which specimens of curious artillery and models of fortresses, &c. were placed. These, when Espartero was regent, and lived here, were removed to the *Buen Retiro*, and they probably will be brought back again. For Espartero see p. 313 and Albacete. The noble mansion contains a magnificent suite of rooms. Here, in 1844, was lodged the Turkish ambassador Fuad Effendi; and, what is not usual in Madrid, *de valde*, or for nothing; thus this land of anomalies provides free quarters for the representative of the hated infidel, the old enemy of most Catholic Spain; and Isabel II. gave to this Moslem the order of her great namesake, whose boast was the having beaten down the crescent.

Continuing our walk is the *Puerta de Alcalá*, built in 1778 for Charles III., by Sabatini. It is the finest gate in Madrid, being merely ornamental; for the walls, a mean girdle to the "only court," are of mud, and might be jumped over by a tolerably active Remus; but they were never intended for defence against any invaders except smuggled cigars; yet although they might be battered down with *garbanzos*, this architectural ornament was mutilated by the invader, whose sportive cannon balls were especially directed at it;—Te saxa loquuntur.

To the l. is the *Plaza de Toros*, which was built in 1749, to support the hospitals and furnish patients. It is about 1100 feet in circumference, and will hold 12,000 spectators. In an architectural point of view this *plaza* of the model court is shabbier than in many provincial towns: there is no attempt at a classical amphitheatre, no adaptation of the Coliseum of Rome: the exterior is bald and plain, as if done so on purpose, while the interior is fitted up with wooden benches, and is scarcely better than a shambles, but for that it was designed, and there is a business-like, murderous intention about it, which marks the Moor, who looked for a sport of blood and death, and not to a display of artistical skill or taste. The bull-fight, a thing of Spain, breathes *Españolismo* from first to last, and rejects even the beautiful of the foreigner as an adulteration. The bull-fights begin in April and continue until November; they generally take place on St. Mondays, and in the afternoon; however, ample notice is given by placards. The *aficionado* will, of course, ride out the previous morning to *El Arroyo de Brinegal*, and see what the *Ganado* is like; he will also secure a ticket on the *shady* side of the *Plaza*, and post himself between the Cᵉ· de Alcalá and the *Plaza* half an hour before the opening the doors to see the arrival of the mob: what a din and dust, what costumes and *calesas*, what wild drivers running outside, what picturesque *manolos* and *manolas* inside; now indeed we are in Spain, and no mistake. The dazzling glare and fierce African sun calcining the heavens and earth, fires up man and beast to madness; now in a raging thirst for blood, seen in flashing eyes and the irritable ready knife, how the passion of the Arab triumphs over the coldness of the Goth: how different is the crowd and noisy hurry from the ordinary still life and monotony of these localities. The horrid excitement fascinates the many, like the tragedy of an execution, for, as a lively Frenchman observes, "*La réalité atroce* is the recreation of the savage, and the sublime of common-place souls." The quadrupeds are as mad as the bipeds, the poor horses excepted, who are worse *baited* than the bulls.

The *toros* for this *plaza* generally come from the pastures of the Jarama: that breed was famous even among the Moors, but every *aficionado* will read the splendid description of one in Gazul's ballad, "*Estando toda la Corte*" (Duran, i. 36). These verses were evidently written by a practical *torero*, and on the spot: they sparkle with daylight and local colour, like a Velazquez, and are as minutely correct as a Paul Potter, while Byron's "Bull-fight" is the invention of a foreign poet, and full of slight inaccuracies.

The bull-fights at Madrid are first-rate, nothing is economised except the horses: this is the national spectacle, and the high salaries paid at "Court" naturally attract, as to our Haymarket, the most distinguished artists. See for tauromaquian details, p. 177.

Opposite are the gardens of the *Buen Retiro*, and their gate *La glorieta.* Returning to the Prado, the view is very striking. The *Prado*, a name familiar to all, is the Hyde-park of Madrid; here, on the winter mornings and summer afternoons, all the rank, beauty, and fashion appear. It is a place to study costume and manners, and to see those antediluvian carriages with ridiculous coachmen and grotesque footmen to match, caricatures which amongst us would be put into the British Museum (see, for details, pp. 33, 157). These lumbering vehicles drive round and round, a routine dull as the Spaniard's and Oriental's monotonous life, where to-day is the reflection of yesterday, and the anticipation of to-morrow. The exceptions are the equipages of the foreign ministers, and of the few grandees and rich upstarts who manage to purchase those of a departing ambassador, or of those who invest their honest gains on the *Bolsa* in a spick-and-span jingling Parisian *equipage.*

The *Prado*, "the meadow," in the time of Philip IV. was a wooded dip renowned for murder and intrigue political and amatory. It was levelled and planted by the Conde de Aranda, under Charles III., and laid out by José Hermonsilla in garden-walks; the length, from the Atocha convent to the Portillo de Recoletos, is 9650 feet; the most frequented portion, "*el Salon,*" extends from the Ce. de Alcalá to the Ce. de Sn. Jeronimo, and is 1450 feet long by 200 wide. The *Salon* terminates with the fountain of Neptune, the work of one Juan de Mena, an individual clearly not connected with the poet. Of the seven other fountains those of Apollo and Cybele are most admired; but these stony things are as nothing to the living groups of all age, colour, and costume, which walk and talk, sit and smoke, like true Orientals, happy to puff away time and life, to smoke and feel 'tis smoke, and think 'tis smoke! The *Prado*, a truly Spanish thing and scene, is unique; and as there is nothing like it in Europe, and oh, wonder! no English on it, it fascinates all who pass the Pyrenees. Its eternal sameness is lost to the guest who tarries but a week, while to the native that very sameness has a charm; for here, as among children and Orientals, custom does not stale; and all prefer an old and the same game to a new one. Where artificial amusements are rare and intellectual pursuits not abundant, when the sun scorches, the shade and a gentle stroll suffice, during which love and love-making becomes an obvious resource and occupation to the young of both sexes; and the appetite for this business grows on what it feeds, until mathematics and political economy seem dry and uninviting pastimes: as the parties get older their life of love is varied with some devotion, a little stabbing, and much tobacco.

Again, it is quite refreshing on the *Prado* to see how united and what good friends all Spaniards *seem* to be. There is no end to compliments and kissings, but deep and deadly are the jealousies and hatreds which lurk beneath; and double-edged are the ideal knives grasped by the murders of the wish, for *muchos besan a manos, que quieren ver cortadas.* However, everything is masked most becomingly, for the Spaniards, like the Moslems, are great in externals both in churches and out; they are most observant of forms and ceremonies, and strictly decent in appearances, and in all that the correct French call *les convenances;* therefore nothing here, or indeed anywhere in Spain, offends the public eye, and one would suppose that Themis sat on every judicial bench, and chaste Diana palisaded every *alcoba* with icicles, so pretty a *mantilla* is thrown over every private intrigue. But everything in short is here most concealed, which is most exposed and "reported" in England, and some think by stripping vice of all its grossness, that half of its deformity is taken away.

The *Prado* is a noisy, dusty scene, as no grass, no continental apology for English lawn grows on this so-called *meadow*, a modest misnomer after the fashion of Les Champs *Elysées* of Parisian paradise. No flowers enamel this *Prado*, save those offered by impertinent daughters of Flora. Fire and water, *Candela Fuego! y quien quiere agua?* resound on every side; since these, long the essential elements for holy purposes, for the furnace of the Inquisition, and the *agua bendita* of the church, are equally necessary to light cigars and put out thirst: accordingly, Murillo-like urchins run about with lighted rope-ends for smokers, *i. e.* for ninety-nine out of one hundred males, while *Aguadores* follow the fire, like engines, with fresh water, for your Spaniard is as adust as his soil, and thirsty as Vesuvius.

Strange as the *Prado* still appears, it is sadly fallen off from the good old times before the fatal invasion and the *nuevo progreso;* every afternoon the march of transpyrenean intellect is crushing some national costume and custom. Oh! the tyranny of English tailors and coachmakers, and of French barbers and *modistes!* Out upon the upper Benjamins and beards *à la Brutus,* which travestie this land of the cloak and Don Whiskerandos. Sad in truth is it to see the *gens togata,* once the models and masters of Europe, casting off their skins and *capas,* to put on the *paletot,* the livery peajacket of the foreigner : but Buonaparte never inflicted more injuries to Spanish man than your little French milliner has done to the daughter of the *saya y mantilla;* nor are even their precious organs of speech safe, their fans or tongues, for they fetter their glorious vernacular, by exchanging it for what they fancy is the idiom of Paris, just as a similar want of judgment was displayed by their foolish ancestors (Strabo, iii. 225 ; and see pp. 79, 199).

On the Prado, the mirror of Madrid, will be seen the lamentable influence of the *foreigner,* for whom in *words* the Spaniards profess* such contempt, but whose *deeds* are indeed at variance with the boast of every mouth, "*Los Españoles sobre todos.*" Here they disenchant the Prado, and do their best to *denationalize* themselves, and to destroy with suicidal hand their greatest merit, which is the being *Spanish;* for Spain's best attractions are those which are characteristic of *herself:* here all that is imitated is poor and second-rate, and displeases the foreigner, who can see the originals much better at home : he crosses the Pyrenees, too weary of the bore, commonplace, and uniformity of ultra civilization, in order to see something new and unEuropean; he hopes

* This also creeps out by the universal anxiety to know the foreigner's opinion of them, and the common deprecatory begging the question anticipatory remarks of, *Los Españoles son muy valientes,* or *las Españolas son muy guapitas.* The serio-comic expression of the speaker while awaiting the verdict of the stranger defies Hogarth ; and never let the individually brave Spaniard be baulked of the courteous assent, *Mas claro, ya se ve.* Again, the volunteer use of the above remarks disarms the men, flatters and wins the women; and as both really deserve the cheap compliment, he indeed is a churl who refuses to pay it.

to find again in Spain, as in the moon of Ariosto, all that has been lost and forgotten elsewhere: hence the never-failing interest which the *lower* classes present. They, by continuing to be national and out-and-out Spanish, are always racy and respectable, and, so far from being ridiculous, like the better classes, are the delight and admiration of the rest of the world. Oh, *fortunati nimium sua si bona norint* (see also p. 384).

The *Prado*, as it approaches the *Pa. de Atocha*, becomes more umbrageous and quiet. This is the favourite site of bores, lovers, and button-holders. Those who remember Spain *when truly Spain* will miss the monks and real *Mantillas*, for the present *Mantilla* is unworthy of the name. Consult on some of these *Prado* particularities, Water-drinking, p. 71; Cigars, p. 193; Costume, p. 196; Walking, pp. 203-212: but the *paso Castellano* cannot be compared to the *aire y meneo* of a Gaditana's gait, nor to the *gracia y piafar* of an Andaluza's amble.

Advancing to the l. is the simple pyramidical monument of the *Dos de Maio*, raised to the manes of the victims of Murat. It was begun in 1814 by the Cortes, but was stopped by Ferd. VII., in whose eyes the senators and heroes of the war of independence found no favour, because of their reforming tendencies. Here a modest Castilian *Leon* puts its paw only on the whole globe. The anniversary of the 2nd of May is celebrated like our 5th of November. The French consider this to be an affront, and offensive to their honneur, and, no doubt, the now dominant Gallo-Cristino faction will discourage the annual solemnity, which, like this monument, is a record and a warning, for the past is the prophet of the future.

These three words, *Dos de Maio,* like our "fifth of November," have a cabalistic meaning, and explain the cause which led to the simultaneous unpremeditated rising of the whole

nation. The sad history is soon told. Murat arrived at Madrid in April, 1808, sent there by Buonaparte, who, wishing to strike a blow of terrorism, knew his instrument. He it was who, with Loison, had massacred the Parisians with grape-shot, Oct. 5, 1795, and therefore was now chosen to re-act that day at Madrid. The forced departure of the king's brothers was resented by the citizens; angry cries were heard. Then Murat ordered the " unarmed groups to be sabred by Gen. Dausmenil, the Poles and Mamelukes distinguishing themselves in carnage" (Toreno, ii.). Thus insult was added to injury, for the Mameluke recalled the former infidel invader. The Spanish authorities now agreed on a truce with Murat, who pledged his honour to observe it; and then, the instant quiet was restored, seized old and young, lay and clergy, and shot them in heaps on the *Prado*, as being the most public place. On the next day he constituted a military commission, headed by Grouchy, when hundreds of Spaniards were put to death. The appalling details are given by Toreno and Blanco White (Lett. xii.), eye-witnesses; see also Foy (iii. 172) and Schepeler (i. 53). But Murat only sought to terrify: "La journée d'hier donne l Espagne à l'Empereur," wrote he. Poor Franconi fool! that day lost even France to his master, while the fate of the two agents satisfied poetical justice. A ball at Pizzo, Oct. 13, 1815, sent " *le beau sabreur* " to his account, executed under the summary provisions of another of his own Draco enactments; and Grouchy is mixed up with the downfall of the prime mover.

Buonaparte, when he discovered that terrorism had only exasperated all Spain, replaced his blundering executioner by Savary, who arrived to command the gallant French army, in spite of their indignation at being placed under a mouchard and one mixed up with the murder of the Duc d'Enghien (Foy, iv. 34). But Buonaparte knew that his tool was fit for any Machiavellianism, and he was right, for Savary soon managed to kidnap Ferd. VII., on whom "sa chaleur et l'air de vérité firent impression." Ferd., ignorant and uneducated, and misled by his pedant tutor Canon Escoiquiz, refused, when warned of the trap, to believe the project. "La seule idée d'une si horrible perfidie était une injure à la grande âme d'un Héros tel que Napoléon," says Foy (iii. 147).

The Spanish heroes of the *dos de maio* were named Jacinto Ruiz, Luis Daoiz, and Pedro Velarte, who are popular because in sympathy with the whole nation, as every true Spaniard in their places would have done the same. These subordinate, or rather insubordinate, officers of artillery refused to obey their commanders, when ordered to surrender their cannon to the French: the two latter perished in the unequal contest. The *philosophy* of the Spanish war of independence was *Españolismo*, *i. e.* impatience under foreign dictation; the *conduct* was accident, impulse of the moment, personal bravery, and contempt of discipline. But who can ever calculate what this volcanic people will do, who never calculate, but whose impromptu actions are guided by passions which are as fierce as the sun in Africa, and as capricious and instantaneous as the hurricane? Here three individuals, with only 3 cannon and 10 cartridges, disobey orders and dare to pit their weakness and want of preparation against the strength of a most military and powerfully organized foe; they had nothing fixed but their great courage and greater hatred of the invader, and they represented their countrymen at large. And although routed, because exposed to unequal chances by their inexperienced chiefs, and left "wanting of every thing in the critical moment" by their miserable *juntas* and governments, yet thousands of humble but brave Spaniards, prodigal of life as Moslems, rose to replace them in this

holy war. The fugitives carried the sad details into the provinces, like blood summons of the East (Judg. xx. 6). The cross of fire passed from hand to hand, its sparks fell on a prepared train, which exploded throughout the land. The flame blazed out in an Ætna eruption, one heart beat in the bosoms of the masses, one cry, "*Mueren los gavachos*," burst from every mouth. They resented the *desprecio* of the foreigner (see p. 604), who assumed to be the regenerator of proud Castile; they spurned his gifts, scouted all prudential motives, and listened to nothing but the clank of his chains. The honest people neither required "fanatic monks nor English gold" to rouse them, as the Buonapartists falsely stated: it was a national instinct, which defied the incubus of their most wretched rulers and leaders: honour therefore eternal is due to the brave and noble *people* of Spain (see our remarks, p. 137).

Turn now to the l. and enter the *Buen Retiro.* This large extent of ruined buildings and pretty gardens was laid out by the Conde Duque de Olivares as a "*pleasant retreat*" for Philip IV., and in order to divert his attention from politics and his country's decay. This *rus* within the walls of the city was devised in order to spare him the pain of quitting the "only court" and terrestrial paradise even for a day. Here was erected a palace and a theatre, in which the plays of Lope de Vega were acted; the former, however, was burnt by accident, when many fine pictures by Titian and Velazquez perished: it was rebuilt by Ferd. VI., and its present desolation is the work of the invaders, who selected this commanding position for a strong military post from whence they could terrorize Madrid: then the theatre, palace, gardens, museo, observatory, were all "vandalized," to use the phrase of Minaño (v. 343).

Entering by the *Pelota* gate, are the remains of the convent of *Sn. Jeronimo*, founded by Henrique IV. in honour of a tournament given there to the English ambassador by Beltran de la Cueva, who was to his master what Godoy was to Charles IV. Ferd. and Isab. added much to the edifice, which was one of the few fine Gothic specimens in Madrid, and its Westminster Abbey, being filled with marble sepulchres of soldiers and statesmen; but everything was smashed to pieces by the invaders. In this convent the *jura*, or swearing allegiance to the kings of Spain, took place at their succession; a ceremony which is equivalent to our coronation. Here in June, 1833, Ferd. VII. summoned a Cortes to ratify the succession of Isabel II.

The *Proceres* or house of peers, created by the *Estamento real* of 1834, sat in *el cason*, or banqueting-room. This, to us a mock house of lords, or rather imitation of a states-general, was soon swept away in the mania for revolution and reform, which mistook innovation for renovation.

The banqueting or ball-room, painted by Giordano in his loose dashing, *Luca fa presto* manner, was much damaged by the French. The *Gabinete Topografico* and *Museo militar* have been moved here from the *Buena Vista*, to which probably they will be taken back: send before for an order of admission, or *Esquela de entrada*. There are two sections: the first, destined to the ordnance department, contains a tolerable collection of matters appertaining to artillery and engineering practice. The second, or *El Gabinete*, is more curious,· and in it are many admirably executed fac-simile models of citadels and ports, especially of Cadiz, Gibraltar, Gerona, and Figueras. Observe particularly the accurate plan of Madrid, the work of Col. Leon Gil Palacio, which conveys a bird's-eye view of the capital. Examine also the original model for the projected palace by Jubara, the cost of which alone would have built a common house.

Near this quarter was *La China*, or royal porcelain manufactory, that was destroyed by the invaders, and made by them into a fortification, which surrendered, with 200 cannon, Aug. 14, 1812, to the Duke. It was blown up Oct. 30, by Lord Hill, when the misconduct of Ballesteros compelled him to evacuate Madrid. Now *La China* is one of the standing Spanish and *afrancesado* calumnies against us, as it is stated that we, the English, destroyed this manufactory from commercial jealousy, because it was a rival to our potteries. "What can be done (as the Duke said) with such libels but despise them. There is no end of the calumnies against me and the army, and I should have no time to do any thing else if I were to begin either to refute or even to notice them " (Disp. Oct. 16, 1813). These china potsherds and similar inventions of the enemy shivered against his iron power of conscious superiority.

The real plain *truth* is this. The French broke the *ollas*, and converted this Sevres of Madrid into a bastile, which, and not the pipkins, was destroyed by the English, who now, so far from dreading any Spanish competition, have actually introduced their system of pottery; and accordingly very fair china is now made at Madrid and Seville, and by English workmen. At the latter place a convent, also converted by Soult into a citadel, is now made a hardware manufactory by our countryman Mr. Pickman. Ferd. VII. ou his restoration recreated *La China*, removing the workshops and warerooms to *La Moncloa*, once a villa of the Alva family on the Manzanares.

Walk now into the pleasant gardens, which were turned into a wilderness by the invaders. Ferd. VII. took great interest in their restoration; he replanted the trees which had been torn up by the destroyers; he cleared out the large pond *El Estanque*, on which he manœuvred his swans and all the navy which French alliances and enmity had left to his country. He also restored the pleasant garden, which hostile ravages had filled with thorns and brambles, and established an aviary and menagerie of wild beasts

Las Fieras : they were favourite pets of his majesty, who delighted in seeing them gnashing their teeth behind the bars, like his subjects in Spanish prisons ; not that the latter were at all so well fed as the former. He also built Chinese pagodas, after the fashion of George IV., and somewhat more apposite, as being near La China, than on the bleak coast of Brighton. At the upper end of the gardens is a mound with a sort of summer-house called *El Belvidere*, and justly, as it commands a good panoramic view of Madrid. Part of these retired and flowery walks are open to the public ; however, the *reservado*, or more retired portion, is *reserved* for the royal family ; but the *administrador* readily grants an *esquela*, or permission to enter, to all respectable applicants, and none should fail to obtain one, for here is one of the finest bronze equestrian statues in Europe. Philip IV. is mounted on his war charger, arrayed as he entered Lérida in triumph. It is a *solid* Velazquez, who painted the picture for it (see Museo, No. 299), which was carved in wood by Montanes, and the model cast in bronze at Florence, in 1640, by Pedro Tacca. The group is 19 feet high, and weighs 180 cwt., yet the horse curvets, supported by the hind legs, and the mane and scarf absolutely float in air. As this fine thing was comparatively lost in the *Retiro*, it was proposed to move it into Madrid ; but the Minister Grimaldi declared that to be too great an honour for any Austrian king, and protested that he would only consent if the head of Philip were cut off, and the baboon, Bourbon one of Charles III. substituted—a pantomimic change worthy of a Grimaldi. There is now some talk of moving it to the *Plaza del Oriente*, when the theatre, &c., are finished.

Return now to the Prado and visit the *Museo ;* there, on the outside, is inscribed " Royal British Artillery, 1 Sept. 1812, A. Ramsay." What a page of history is condensed in that simple record of an *English* private soldier, who marched after Salamanca to the delivery of the capital.

The *Museo* is a huge lumbering commonplace edifice : its heavy granite portico supports nothing, above a heavier cornice rises a paltry, low, unarchitectural upper story. The ill-contrived entrance is not on a level with the building, which is cut up by small square windows, and disfigured by poor crude white statues and medallions. This failure, however, is pronounced by Madrilenians to be a " majestic " work, and one that immortalizes its designer. He was the academical Juan de Villanueva, who raised it for Charles III., as the site of the academy and museum of natural history : left unfinished at his death, it was slowly continued by Charles IV. until the invasion. Then the enemy first gutted the building, and turned it into a barrack ; afterwards they ripped off the lead from the roof, destroyed considerable portions, and left the remainder a ruin ; and so it remained until destined for the picture-gallery, for the establishment of which Ferd. VII. has been fulsomely eulogised by Minaño, Mesoneros, Madrazo, and others, for his love of the arts, about which he cared nothing, and his paternal affection for his people, about whom he cared less, in thus denuding his own private palaces of their finest ornaments, and solely for the public good, the said Ferdinand being about as inæsthetic a Goth as ever smoked tobacco. The real history of the gallery is this. When Ferdinand married his second and best wife La *Portuguesa*, one Monte Allegre, who had been a Spanish consul in France, persuaded him to refurnish the palace with French papers and ormolu clocks and chandeliers—his particular fancy ; thereupon the quaint original and cinque-cento furniture, much of which was of the period even of Charles V. and Philip II., was carted out, and the pictures taken down and stowed away in garrets and corridors exposed to wind, weather, and the usual plundering of Spanish *Custodes.* They were fast perishing and disappearing, when the Marques de Sᵃˑ Cruz, *Mayor Duomo, Mayor* or Lord Steward, and the Duque de Gor, one of the few grandees blessed with a particle of taste or talent (and our authority for this anecdote), persuaded the queen to remove the pictures to the Prado. She advanced 40*l.* a-month towards repairing a few rooms for their reception, and by November, 1819, three saloons were got ready, and 311 pictures exhibited to the public; the extraordinary quality of which, especially of Velazquez, instantly attracted the admiring eye of *foreigners,* who appreciate the merits of the old masters of Spain much better than the natives. Ferd. VII., seeing that renown was to be obtained, now came forward with 240*l.* a-month, and the *Museo* was slowly advanced, one more saloon being opened in 1821. Thus he earned the title of an Augustus, as cheaply as our George IV. has the credit of "presenting to the public" the fine library formed by his father. This he had bargained to sell to Russia, when one of his brothers put in a claim for a share of the proceeds; his majesty thereat having graciously condemned him and the books to a warmer place than St. Petersburg, bundled them off in a huff to Great Russell Street.

The *Museo* is open to the public on Sundays and Mondays, and every day to foreigners on producing their passport. A new catalogue was published in 1843, and is sold at the door, which contains an account of 1833 pictures. Had ten more been described, the number would have tallied with the year. There are more than 2000 pictures got together, for many of which, rooms are not yet prepared, civil wars having consumed the funds destined to advance the fine arts. The glorious pictures formerly in the Escorial were brought to Madrid during the panic of 1837, at the advance of the Carlists under Zariategui, and may be known by having the mark E. attached to them.

Some of the best pictures have been engraved; these are marked C. N., or *Calcografia nacional,* in the Calle Carretas, where they may be purchased. The marks C. L. mean *Calcografia litografica,* and denote those which have been lithographized for the *Colecion,* begun in 1826 by José Madrazo, the president of the Spanish R. Academy, with a letter-press by Cean Bermudez, José Masso y Valiente, and others. Madrazo having obtained from Ferd. VII. a monopoly of lithography in Spain, procured his materials and artists from Paris, but most of them being very second-rate, many of the prints are little better than libels on the originals. Still, as far as it goes, the work is useful, as making known beyond the Pyrenees the subjects, at least, of some of these treasures too long buried in unvisited Spain. Happy the man who sees this glorious assemblage, in this the finest gallery in the world.

No collection was ever begun or continued under greater advantages. Charles V. and Philip II., both real patrons of art, were the leading sovereigns of Europe at the bright period of the *Renaissance,* when fine art was a necessity, and pervaded every relation of life; when churches were decorated by Raphael and Michael Angelo; spoons and salt-cellars carved by Cellini; and plates painted from prints by Marc Antonio. Again, Philip IV. ruled at Naples and in the Low Countries at the second restoration of art, which he truly loved for itself. These three monarchs, like Alexander the Great, took a pleasure in raising their painters to personal intimacy; and nowhere have artists been more highly honoured than Titian, Velazquez, and Rubens, in the palace of Madrid. At a later period, Philip V., the grandson of Louis XIV., added many pictures by the principal French artists of that, their Augustan age.

While the Spanish kings patronised art at home, their viceroys in Italy and the Low Countries collected and sent home the finest specimens of the great

2 κ

artists who flourished from Raphael down to the Carraccis and Claude; and, more than all, these glorious gems *were* preserved pure as when they issued from the studios of their immortal authors. Spain was their last stronghold, for left neglected in a dry conservative climate, at least the incurious Αφιλοκαλια of the natives unintentionally did art good service. "All praise, all *English* gratitude is due," wrote Lawrence to Wilkie, "to this tasteful (? tasteless) indolence of the monks." Hence the pure undisturbed freshness, the unadulterated surface, dirty and cold if you will, and often not even varnished, but not tampered with, but left just as they were when they received their last touches; not things that *were* pictures, like the flayed Correggios at Dresden, or the French-repainted Raphaels. Thus the preserving mantle of neglect, nay, the monkish dirt of the Escorial, *accidentally* (as usual in Spain) preserved Titian, just as the *intentional* mud daubed by the early Christians over the Egyptian hieroglyphics proved a protection to the colours beneath.

The invaders were the first to ravish and then defile these virgin pictures, and, what was worse, they set a bad example and taught lessons of corruption which have since been fearfully carried out. Those pictures which returned demoralized and denationalized, captivated with repainted glitter and varnished faces the native authorities, who, now thinking the rest of their gallery dull-looking and out of fashion, preferred the rouge of a strumpet to the simple blush of a maiden.

The cleanings and restorations done at Paris were at least done by ingenious Frenchmen, and who understood the operative portion of their craft, and were demigods compared to their unmechanical imitators in Spain, where a *Guerra al cuchillo* was proclaimed. The onslaught of the entire gallery having been planned, picture after picture was taken down and ruined. There is scarcely a pure Murillo left

in the whole collection, for on him the cruel experiments were first tried, as *in corpore vili;* the work of havoc goes on, and whenever an empty frame bears the fatal sentence *Está en la restauracion,* the condemned is placed *en Capilla,* and all hope is at an end; it is gone to a purgatory from whence there is no deliverance, no "indulgence;" the last penalty is enforced in underground dissecting-rooms, where the familiars sweep away the lines where beauty lingered, racking and torturing art like their inquisitors did living nature. This record is true : quæque ipse miserrima vidi ! — all remonstrance was useless. When a Spaniard takes anything into his head, however injurious to himself and his country, nothing, as the Duke said, will prevent his carrying it out. The chief executioners were Lopez, Ribera, Bueno, Serafin, Huerta, Garcia, etc. Alas for the fine arts ! thus flayed, scoured, and daubed over. The glazing and last half-tints were effaced, and much became raw and opaque which once was tender and transparent; while new crude colour was *bañado* or spread on, until, in some cases, the outline only of the divine original is left.*

To give a slight notion of the contents of this *Museo,* suffice it to say that there are 27 Bassanos, 49 Breughels, 8 Alonzo Canos, 10 Claudes, 22 Vandykes, 16 Guidos, 55 by Luca Giordano, 13 by Antonio Moro, 46 by Murillo, 3 by Parmigianino, 21 by N. Poussin, 10 by Raphael, 53 by Ribera, 62 by Rubens, 23 by Snyders,

* Spanish pictures ought never to be much cleaned : they are often thinly painted *de primera mano,* or just glazed over with transparent colours, which fatal spirits remove altogether, especially the peculiar *browns* of Velazquez and Murillo, which these artists made themselves from the burnt and pounded beef-bones of their *olla,* hence the name *Negro de hueso.* The olla of Andalucia is the richest and most unctuous in Spain, hence this *local* Sevillian colour. Morales, an Estremaduran, adopted the warmer tone of the local *chorizo,* the rich red-peppered sausage. *Juanes* and *Ribalta* preferred the local *morado,* the purple tint of the there prevalent mulberry juice.

52 by Teniers, 43 by Titian, 27 by Tintoretto, 62 by Velazquez, 24 by Paul Veronese, 10 by Wouvermans, 14 by Zurbaran; with specimens of many other Italian, Flemish, and Spanish artists of eminence.

Like most other Spanish Museos, and indeed things, this is a creature of *accident* rather than of design. There is little order, scientific systematic arrangement, or classification; there is no series of painters marking the chronology, either of art in general, or of any school in particular. It is rather a private than a national collection, and one of chance and caprice. There are none of the beginnings of art: no Byzantine Greek or early Italian specimens of the 14th and 15th centuries, and the reason is obvious; Spain only became a great European power when art was at its apogee in Italy, and her rulers never were antiquarians. Living only for the present day, they took art like everything else, just as it came to hand. Accordingly, the collection is wanting in Fra Bartolomeo, Perugino, M. Angelo, Julio Romano, Ludo· Carracci, Caravaggio, Carlo Dolci, etc. It is also deficient not only in the early Italian and German artists, but even the Spanish: the splendid Valencian and Seville schools (Murillo, Velazquez, and Juanes excepted) are but poorly represented at Madrid: but everything in Spain is local, where painters, like wines and other produce of the soil, are only to be really enjoyed in their own native provinces. Again, Spanish art, like her literature, with few exceptions, scarcely bears translation. See for further details our remarks, p. 114.

We shall follow the numbers of the *catalogo* in briefly pointing out the pearls of greatest price in this galaxy of art: to describe all the pictures would be impossible, nor shall we say much on their subjects or colour, those the reader will *see* before him. He will obtain very little aid from the Spanish *catalogo*, the work of Madrazo.

The former, in Spanish, Italian, and French, were more critical and artistical, having been prepared by an Italian named Eusebi. The present compiler's object seems to have been to give the size of each picture, as if that could possibly interest any one, beyond those who work with line and rule. This merely carpenter criticism has been probably introduced to make size the test of merit, quantity *versus* quality, and thereby enhance the acres of canvas on which his compeers have laboured in vain. ' *Les Musées d'Espagne*,' by Monsr· Viardot, Paris, 1843, is another common guide in the hands of the uninformed, and contains many lively clever *intuitive* and very French criticisms. How much is it to be desired, now that Spain is so easily accessible, that Kugler, Passavant, or some German who really understands art, its history, principles, and practice, should visit the museums of the Peninsula, and at last give to Europe an accurate critical work, on which dependence may be really placed.—Since this sentence was written, the author has heard with pleasure that something of the kind is about to be published by his valued friend Sir Edmund Head, who, as an artist, scholar, and traveller in Spain, is really capable to do justice to his noble subject: meanwhile a humble mite will be offered to the good work in these pages, *El que las sabe mejor, ese tañe las gambetas.*

The opening *Rotunda* contains rubbish: No. 27 is an allegory by J. Ba· Mayno, 1609-1649, an imitator of P. Veronese, and friend of Lope de Vega. On the r. and l. open the saloons appropriated to the old Spanish masters; the centre room, being the post of honour, being given to the modern ones: we will begin there, reserving the good wine for the last. Not that the natives think so, as for one of them who ever looks at Raphael, a score will admire Apariccio: but low commonplace art will always be the most popular with the many, for mankind only sympathises with what it understands: here their director's nonsense suits their nonsense; and not to be able to estimate real excellence, is one sure proof of mediocrity of intellect. Modern Spanish art, the child of corrupt parents, carries from its birth a germ of weakness; see also p. 734. Mengs, the incarnation of the academical mediocre, led the way; then followed David, fit painter of the Revolution, who trampled on the fine arts of cowed Europe. His theatrical scenes à la Corneille, his swaggering, attitudinarian heroes, à la Grand Opéra, combined with a certain Roman severity of drawing and a réchauffé of the antique, bewildered the Spanish R.A.s, already predisposed in his favour by his Mengs-like style. To him, therefore, they turned submissively, in spite of his want of real colour, air, nature, and life the soul of painting; and the disciples, as is common in heresies, outheroded their master. Take for instance 554, by his pupil Apariccio, 1773-1815. When these "ransomed slaves" were exhibited at Rome, Canova, who knew the man, told him, "This is the finest thing in the world, and you are the first of painters." Soon afterwards Thorwaldsen came in and ventured a critique, whereupon the Don indignantly quoted Canova: "Sir, he has been laughing at you," said the honest Dane, to whom Apariccio never spoke again : 577, ditto, "The Glories of Spain." This is the pet picture of the nation, and, like Maldonado's History, is an exponent of Españolismo. Here the Spaniards do the whole work, they alone flutter the French eagles. Observe also, by Apariccio, 584, a Famine at Madrid; this local and national subject is painted in every respect worthy of the Bisoño theme.

Of Madrazo himself, also a pupil of David, observe 564, "Death of Viriatus," transportation is loudly called for : 570, "Ferdinand VII. on Horseback," and worse if possible than the former; alas for Spain, when a countryman of Velazquez, and in the presence of his divine models, should

perpetrate such a wooden tea-board opake inanity : ditto, 570, "Divine and Profane Love," which partakes considerably of the latter quality in conception and execution. All who have studied the works of David, or even of his Italian analogists Benvenuti and Camucini, must be struck with the inferiority of these their Spanish imitators, both in drawing, colour, and composition.

The works of Bayeu and Maella are feeble and commonplace. Goya alone, 1746-1828, shows talent: 551, "Maria Luisa," the Messalina of Spain : 595, ditto, "A Bullfighter." Goya was also an etcher, and published some spirited caricatures, and subjects of low life and free subjects; his unmechanical countrymen, who have had few engravers, think him a combination of Hogarth, Rembrandt, and Callot, which is a slight mistake. The remainder is far better; indeed there are fewer bad pictures (these moderns excepted) than in most public galleries of Europe. Now enter the saloon to the r. Here are the Castellanos viejos y sin mancha, the old masters of Spain, good men and true, free from all infidel and foreign taint, but who now seem to be hung up here as warnings in terrorem, and examples of what modern students should avoid; for, if their directors are artists, then Murillo was a blockhead and Velazquez a dauber.

When we walk up these vast galleries, it seems as if a year were too short to examine the contents : as in the Vatican, a too princely banquet is set before us, and we run the risk either of eating more than we can digest, or of becoming sated with excellence, and loathing the honeycomb; but we soon get fastidious, and the masses simplify themselves; then the planets shine forth, and we reject the modern and rubbish as by instinct. But of one thing, oh beware!—as De Stendhal says, beware of any lassitude of the beautiful; be indeed weary of bores, fly the bad, eschew Madrazo, David, the devil and all his works;

but never, oh never, risk the being tired of the fine and good. Let therefore the visit be repeated often, for picture-seeing is more fatiguing than people think, for one is standing all the while, and with the body the mind is also at exercise in judging, and is exhausted by admiration. In our *brief* notice of "what to observe," we shall chiefly extend our critical remarks to Spanish painters, for those of other schools are sufficiently well understood, and are foreign to this Handbook; we shall also take one master at a time, following the numerical order of the catalogue, which is almost a handbook by itself. By thus confining attention to a single painter, a knowledge of his peculiarities is more likely to be fixed, than by mixing up many artists and subjects together, which fritters and distracts.

The grand masters to observe are Raphael, Titian, Murillo, and still more Velazquez, as the two former may be comprehended equally as well at Rome, Hampton Court, Venice, and Seville; but Madrid is the only home of the mighty Andalucian, for here is almost his entire work. Fortunately for Spain, Buonaparte's generals did not quite understand or appreciate his excellence, and few of his pictures were "transported." Again, from having been exclusively the court painter, his works were monopolized by his royal patron; and being in the palace of Joseph, were tolerably respected even by those who knew their mercantile value. Here, therefore, *alone*, is he to be studied, in all his protean variety of power. For his biography consult Cean Ber. (D. v. 155), and our article in the 'Penny Cyclopædia.' Suffice it here to say that *Diego Velazquez de Silva* was born at Seville in 1599, and died at Madrid, Aug. 7, 1660. He is the Homer of the Spanish school, of which Murillo is the Virgil. Simple, unaffected, and manly, he was emphatically a man and the painter of men, in which he rivalled Timanthes, "artem ipsam

complexus viros pingendi" (Pliny, 'N. H.' xxxv. 10); thus *Las Lanzas*, his finest picture, has no female in it.

Velazquez was equally great in portrait, history, Sujets de Genre, and landskip; he passed at once, without effort or violence, into each, and into every variety of each,—from the epic to the farce, from low life to high, from the old to the young, from the rich to the poor, while he elevated portrait painting to the dignity of history. He was less successful in delineations of female beauty, the ideal, and holy subjects; wherein he was inferior to Murillo. He could draw anything and everything that he could see and touch, then he was master of his subject and never mastered by it; but he could not grapple with the unreal, or comprehend the invisible, thinking with Pliny (N. H. ii. 7), "effigiem Dei formamque quærere *imbecillitatis* humanæ;" and whenever he attempted, which was seldom, any elevated compositions, the unpoetical models from which he studied in youth were always reproduced. "Homo sum," he might well with Cicero exclaim, "et nihil humani a me alienum puto;" and he might have added with Aretino, Il poeta Tosco, when he failed in representing the immortal and divine, "non lo conosco." Yet even in this style, *prose* if you please, but terse, nervous, and Thucydidean, there is no mistake, no doubt, and always so much humanity, truth to nature, and meaning, that we sympathise with transcripts of beings of living flesh and blood, like ourselves. No man, again, Titian not excepted, could draw the minds of men, or paint the very air we breathe better than he: his lineal and aerial perspective is magical; his mastery over his materials, his representation of texture, air, and individual identity, are absolutely startling. His touch was free and firm, uniting perfect precision with the greatest executional facility: he always went directly to the point, knowing what he wanted and when he had got it: he selected the salient features, and omitted the trivial; and as he never touched his canvas without an intention, or ever put one touch too much, his emphatic objects are always effective: again, his subdued tone and slight treatment of accessories conferred a solidity and importance to his leading points, which are all thus brought up and tell. Such a man never can be replaced; his was that high quality of individual genius which only can be itself alone. Having been employed by the king, and not by the usual patrons of art the priest and monk, his pictures are less gloomy than those of Spanish artists who were depressed by the cold shadow of the Inquisition. For *truth* and life-conferring *power* he carries everything before him. Like Shakspere, he took nature for his sole guide. He is by far the greatest painter of the so-called *naturalist* school: hence the sympathy between him and our artists, of whose style he was the anticipation; for similar causes must produce similar effects, allowance being made for the disturbing influence of a different religion, habits, and climate.

Look therefore at every one of his pictures; for, take them for all and all, we "ne'er shall see their like again." Those to be peered into and analysed every day, are 81, portrait of Alonzo Cano; great truth and force: 87, C. L., St. Antonio and St. Paul Hermits. "In breadth," says Wilkie, "and richness unexampled, the beau idéal of landskip, not much detail or imitation, but the very same sun we see, and the air we breathe, the very soul and spirit of nature:" 109 and 114, portraits of Philip IV. and his second wife: 117, a masterly sketch, said to be of the Mᵉ· de Pescara, full of individual identity: 127, C. N., portrait said to be of the corsair Barbaroja, a fine fierce old pirate: 138, C. L., C. N., *Los Bebedores* or *Los Borrachos;* this mock coronation of a drunken group combines the humour of Teniers with the breadth and effect of Caravaggio. The actors may indeed be low in intel-

lectual character, but they are true to the life, and if deficient in elevated sentiment, are rich in meaning, and are transcripts of real man.

Next observe 142, Philip IV. when aged; it is the individual himself, with the Austrian "foolish hanging of the nether lip:" 145, C. L., Fountain at Aranjuez, an exquisite landskip, full of local colour and verdurous freshness and groups which realize the very form and pressure of the period of Philip IV., and are in fact, in *painting*, what the letters of Madᵉ· D'Aunoy are in *description*. Compare it with 540, C. L., another view at Aranjuez. Observe *particularly* all his small bits of landskip, and some studies of architecture done at Rome, others with moonlight effects, and all marvellous gems of art. See 101, 102, 118, 119, 128, 132, 143. Remark No. 155, C. N., *Las Meninas* or *La Teologia;* here we have Velazquez in his own studio. This was called the "Gospel of Art" by Luca Giordano; nor can aerial and lineal perspective, local colour, animal and human life, be represented beyond this. The gradation of tones in lights, shadows, and colours, gives an absolute concavity to the flat surface of the canvas, we look into space as into a room, or as into the reflection of a mirror. The shadows are truly in *chiaro oscuro*, being transparent and diaphanous, and rather a subdued light and less pronounced colour than a dark veil. The picture is remarkable for the chariness of bright colours: an olive greenish tone pervades the background: the accessories are only indicated; indeed of Velazquez it may be also said, as Pliny (N. H. xxxv. 11) observed of Timanthes, "Intelligitur plus semper quam pingitur, et cum ars summa sit, ingenium tamen ultra artem est:" but no painter was ever more *objective;* there is no showing off of the artist; no calling attention to the performer's dexterity: he loved art for itself without one disturbing thought of self.

The scene represents the dull Infanta

Margarita, who is tried to be amused by her pages, while her two dwarfs, Maria Borbolá and Nicolaoio Pertusano, worry a patient dog, which is painted finer than a Snyders; unfortunately these playthings of royal infants, these disports and distorts of nature, then the fashion of the court, are as hideous as Voltaire, *ce bouffon du diable;* and the *Infanta* is mealy-faced and uninteresting, but Velazquez was too honest to flatter even royalty or its fools. These *Enanos* are the *νανοι, Nani* of the ancients, which were the delight of Julia (Plin. ' N. H.' vii. 16) and Tiberius (Suet. in Vit. 61), although Augustus had the good taste to dislike them. Then, as in Spain, the ugliest were the most esteemed, and brought a price proportionate to their oddity, like Scotch terriers, who have their Velazquez in E. Landseer.

Next observe 156, Philip IV., glorious: 177, C. L., C. N., the Conde Duque de Olivares on horseback ; the animal is somewhat large, and his seat is awkwardly forward, but no doubt it was true to life, for Velazquez would not even flatter a prime minister, nor did he stoop even to woo or conciliate the spectator : his practical genius saw everything as it really was, and his hand, that obeyed his eye and intellect, gave the exact form and pressure without much refining. Nothing can be finer than the effects produced with the chary use of gaudy colour in this picture and 155 ; but no man was more sparing of colour; he husbanded his whites and even yellows, which tell up like gold on his undertoned backgrounds, which always represented nature with the intervention of air. Passing now into the saloon to the l., 195, C. L., C. N., the Forge of Vulcan; forcible, but painted from vulgar models. The Apollo has nothing of the deity, while Vulcan is a mere Gallician blacksmith : 198, the Infanta Maria in the court costume of the day. This portrait is interesting, as she was the object of our Charles's romantic visit to Madrid. She was described by

Howell, who was then there, "as a very comely lady, rather of a Flemish complexion than a Spaniard, fair-haired, and carrying a most pure mixture of red and white in her face; she is full and big-lipped, which is held a beauty rather than a blemish, or any excess, in the Austrian family." Afterwards, when the match was off, he speaks with more truth of her being of " fading flaxen hair, big-lipped, and heavy-eyed." His letters, ' *Epistolæ Hoelianæ,*' 4°., London, 1645, give many curious details of Charles and his visit, and what a loss to this series is the portrait of Charles himself, which Velazquez began : pariunt desideria non traditi vultus (Pliny, ' N. H.' xxxv. 2). It would have been interesting to have compared the picture by the Great Spaniard with those which we have by Vandyke, who knew Charles by heart, as well as Velazquez did Philip IV., and as we seem to do so too after visiting this precious *Museo.*

Next observe 200, C. L., Philip IV. in a shooting-dress : 209, a fine Old Lady, in his early forcible style : 230, C. L., C. N., Philip III. on horseback, a marvellous specimen of his effects produced by placing his figure on cool greys; the royal head is full of the individual imbecility of this poor bigot : 245, C. N., an old man called Mænipo : 254, C. N., Esop, finely painted, but more like a cobbler than a philosopher : 255, C. N., a Dwarf, seated as Velazquez saw him, and as no one else could have ventured to paint him : 267, *Un Pretendiente,* or place-hunter, one of the Autochthones of Madrid ; the attitude is admirable: 270, C. L., the young Prince Baltasar, aged six, with his dog and gun. Observe particularly all the numerous sporting portraits of theriomaniac Austrian royalty ; for whether the wearers are dressed for the court or the chase, they wear their clothes with ease and fitness, they are the real everyday garments of living flexible bodies underneath, not stuck on like the fancy masquerade of an imaginative painter, copied from a wooden lay figure: 279, C. N., an admirable full-length portrait of a Dwarf; observe how costume is painted: 284, C. N., *El Niño de Vallecas;* it is wonderful how he could have fixed the attitude: 289, a magnificently-painted portrait; how much effect is produced, with how little detail; how unlike the finished style of Pantoja, yet never was armour better represented; but Velazquez was above all tricks, and never masked poverty of hand and idea under meretricious glitter; with him everything was sober, real, and sterling: 291, C. N., *El Bobo de Coria;* observe the green tones and expression of roguish waggery: 295, the Surprise of Io; nothing can exceed the profound sleep of Argos or the stealthy action of Mercury; the god of thieves is painted in an absolute anticipation of Sir Joshua's style: 299, C. L., C. N., Philip IV., an equestrian portrait; this true Φιλιππος is witching the world with noble horsemanship, the only attitude in which the Monarch of *Caballeros* ought to be painted. This was the picture prepared as a model for the bronze in the *Retiro* (see p. 744). The horse is alive, and knows its rider; how everything tells up on the cool blue and greens in the background; this picture is the antithesis of the Ferd. VII. of the director, being everything that his is not, and nothing that his is: 303, C. N., Queen Isabel, wife of Philip IV., a superb white steed; observe how her costume is painted, and despair; remark also the difference of the horses, those which carry men are fiery and prancing, while those on which women are mounted are gentle and ambling, as if conscious of their timid delicate burden: 319, C. L., the Surrender of Breda, or *Las Lanzas,* is perhaps the finest picture of Velazquez; never were knights, soldiers, or national character better painted, or the heavy Fleming, the intellectual Italian, and the proud Spaniard more nicely marked even to their boots and breeches: the lances of the guards actually vibrate. Observe the contrast of the light-blue delicate

page, with the dark iron-clad General Spinola, who, the model of a high-bred generous warrior, is consoling a gallant but vanquished enemy. He was another of those many foreigners, who, having borne the war-brunt, and gained victories for Spain, have been rewarded with ingratitude. He took Breda, June 2, 1625, and died 5 years afterwards, broken-hearted at Philip IV.s treatment, exclaiming, " *Me han quitado la honra!*" They have robbed me of honour! Velazquez has introduced his own noble head into this picture, which is placed in the corner with a plumed hat. This is indeed a *male* subject, and treated with a *masculine* mind and hand; nor are men aware of how much the sexual undercurrent leads them to admire pictures in which beautiful females are presented : here, where there is no woman whatever, it is the triumph of art by itself.

Observe particularly 332, C. L., C. N., Don Baltasar on horseback ; the child actually gallops out of the frame, and is the anticipation of Edwin Landseer, and his young Highland Chieftains on their wild ponies : 335, C. N., *Las Hilanderas,* the perfection of reality, although taken from ordinary life ; here the artist, feeling at once his power and weakness, has, like Timanthes, turned aside the head of the lady, leaving to the imagination of each spectator to invest her with that quality of beauty which best accords with his peculiar liking: 527, in another saloon, is the portrait of Gongora. The defects of Velazquez, this great *mortal,* for he was not a painter of the ideal, will be seen in 62, C. L., Coronation of the Virgin, who seems a somewhat sulky female, while the Deity is degraded to a toothless monk. But he could not escape from humanity nor soar above into the clouds; he was neither a poet nor an enthusiast, and somewhat deficient in creative power: again, he painted for the court and not for the church ; in a word, Nature was his guide, truth his object, and man his model; no Virgin ever descended into his studio, no cherubs ever hovered round his pallet, no saint came down from heaven to sit for his portrait: hence the neglect and partial failure of his sacred subjects, holy indeed like those of Caravaggio in nothing but name, being groups rather of low life, and that so truly painted as still more to mar the elevated sentiment by a treatment not in harmony with the subject. His Virgin has neither the womanly tenderness of Murillo, the unspotted loveliness of Raphael, or the serenity unruffled by human passions of the antique; he rather lowered heaven to earth, than raised earth to heaven. 63, C. N., the God Mars, is a vulgar Gallician porter: 167, C. L., is in his hard early style, before he was emancipated from the prevalent Ribera peculiarities. So the celebrated Jacob and his Sons, formerly in the Escorial, although a picture of great truth and force, is but a group of Gallicians; yet even when displeased with such repulsive subjects we are forced to submit to the power of master mind displayed in the representation. This *naturalist* picture was painted in the Vatican itself; so little influence had the *foreigners* Raphael and M. Angelo on the local Spaniard, that he dared them with his very failings; such is *Españolismo* (see post, p. 758).

Murillo will naturally come next to Velazquez. He, however, is seen in greater glory at Seville, his native home, where he painted his finest pictures, which have better escaped the fatal *Restauracion.* Referring therefore to p. 263 for some account of Murillo, suffice it to say here that the specimens of this master of female and infantine grace are numerous, but scarcely one has escaped pollution. However, Murillo is so full of subject, so dramatic, and comes so home to, and appeals so to the common sense of mankind, and is recommended by such a magical fascination of colour, that he captivates alike the learned and unlearned, the sure test of undeniable excellence. He has more grace, but far

less of the masculine mind than Velazquez, who compared to him seems somewhat cold and grey in colour, for Murillo painted flesh as he saw it in Andalucia, roasted and bronzed by the glowing sun, and not the pale unripened beauty of the north. Like Titian, his strength lay in ravishing *colour,* none ever rivalled him in the luminous diaphanous streams of golden ether in which his cherubs float·like butterflies; his blending continuity of tints, like those of nature, slide into each other, without a particle of harshness or abruptness; led on by an imperceptible transition, where there is no outline, no drawing, so that it is difficult to say where one tint ends and another begins.

Murillo, moreover, like Velazquez, lacked the highest quality of the Italian ideal; true Spaniards, they were local, and imitated nature as they saw her; thus Murillo's holy subjects are not glorified forms and visions, which compel us to bow the knee and adore, but pleasing scenes of a domestic family, where sports of graceful children attract the delighted attention of affectionate parents. There is neither the awful sublimity of M. Angelo, nor the unearthly purity of Raphael. Again, his *Niños Dios* are not meditative prescient Infant Gods, or his cherubs those angels of heaven from whence Raphael took his types, but simply pretty mortal babes with wings, and not even babes of the world at large, but Spanish ones, nay more. only local Andalucian children; and such also are his male saints, who rose to glory in their old Bætican clothes and bodies.

The stranger will of course look at *all* the Murillos, halting particularly at 43, C. L, a Holy Family; a pretty scene of conjugal and parental happiness. It was cruelly cleaned and repainted at Paris, especially the dog and face of the Virgin; 46, C. L., a fine representation of the Infant Deity: 50, C. L., the Companion Infant Forerunner; the left leg is not pleasing;

observe the contrast of the callous foot hardened by exposure, with the delicate flesh of 46 : 52, Conversion of St. Paul; the thigh of the Apostle and his white horse, cruelly repainted: 54, *La Porciuncula* (see p. 771), overcleaned : 56, C. L., the Annunciation; the Virgin's cheek is repainted; 65, *La Concepcion* (see p. 265), one of those representations of sweet cherubs, and the fair virgin floating in a golden atmosphere, which none could paint like Murillo; and then the gossamer, gauze-like draperies, which play in the air, just veiling human charms, which might suggest thoughts that war with the purity of the Virgin : 82, C. L., a Magdalen, all legs and arms, and in his imitation of Ribera style: 174, Sⁿ· Francisco de Paula, was a magnificent head and beard, before ruined by Bueno : 182, Death of St. Andrew, in his *vaporoso* style, was a glorious picture, but is much disharmonized by the violent white repainting of the horse; the drapery of the Apostle has also been *bañado* and ruined : 189, C. L., Santiago, a vulgar coarse head of rather a Flemish character: 191, C. L., C. N., Adoration of Shepherds in his second style, hovering between Velazquez and Ribera; the drawing is fine and careful; observe the local colouring, and foot of peasant, and how their rich browns give value to the delicate flesh of the Virgin and child : 202, C. L., Infant Saviour and St. John, a rich and delightful picture : 208, C. L., Rebecca at the Well, in his middle style; the females are somewhat Flemish : 211, 2, 6, 7, the Parable of the Prodigal Son; all excellent, but treated both as to costume and conception rather according to a picaresque Spanish novel than Holy Writ : 219, a rich blue Concepcion : 220, St. Augustine; the Virgin, somewhat too far off, gives her milk to a vulgar burly monk in a black robe, with rich red *casulla :* 229, C. L., another *Concepcion,* innocence itself, and beautifully painted ; how rich and juicy the flesh, how full of pulp and throbbing

life : 310, C. L., Sᵃ· Ana teaching the Virgin. The pouting child is admirable, but purely mortal ; the draperies are in imitation of Roelas : 315, C. N., Vision of St. Bernard ; this again shows how closely Murillo observed Roelas ; the draperies of the saint have been repainted; but his head is fine, and the sentiments of gratitude and veneration are admirably expressed. The concealing the feet of the Virgin gives her figure too much height. St. Bernard was a champion of the Virgin, second only to Sⁿ· Buonaventura, the Seraphic Doctor; and both advocated Mariolatry to its wildest extent, substituting her for the Father and the Redeemer. The gift of her milk, so common in Spanish legends, is but a Papal repetition of Juno's suckling Hercules: 326, C. N., the Miracle of the Virgin giving the *Casulla* to Sⁿ· Ildefonso at Toledo, but it is of earth, earthy, and the angels are nothing but milliners, and the saint a monkish tailor: 423, E., is in another saloon. The Virgin, with the rosary, a fine but early picture, in his Ribera manner.

Next observe the paintings of Juan Juanes, the Spanish Raphael, who, however, should be studied in his native Valencia (see p. 445). 73, Visit of Sᵃ· Isabel to the Virgin ; early and hardish, but quite Italian : 75, Death of Sᵃ· Ines, painted like Julio Romano: 150, a Saviour; a subject often treated in this manner by Juanes: 158, ditto, ditto : 165, Christ bearing the Cross; a fine specimen: 169, portrait of Luis de Castelvy, equal to anything of Bronzino : 196, 7, 9, and 336, 7, C. L., subjects from the life of St. Stephen, an Italian-looking series, but the stones (in 196) are too much like dumplings. Observe the delight of the wicked boys ; the faces of the Hebrews, with their hook noses, are somewhat too Jewish for fine art. This remark applies equally to 225, C. L., the Last Supper, for Juanes was rather a mannerist, however ; but the head of Christ is very fine, although it has, unfortunately, been much repainted : 259, the Saviour on the Mount of Olives : 268, Descent from the Cross, one of his best pictures. Juanes, because savouring of a Roman style, and with a harder outline, and more decided drawing, is much admired by many Spaniards, who hate foreign *persons,* but love foreign *things.* Jose Ribera, better known as Spagnoletto (see Xativa, p. 428), may be truly studied at Madrid ; here, this cruel forcible imitator of ordinary nature, riots in hard ascetic monks and blood-boltered subjects, in which this painter of the bigot, inquisitor, and executioner delighted : a power of drawing, a force of colour and effect, a contempt of the ideal, beautiful, and tender, characterize his productions: unpopular in England, his unforgiving repulsiveness and stern harsh character have ranked him among the model-painters of Spain. He was the personal friend of Velazquez, who, like Murillo, studied his style deeply, as may be seen in all their early productions. Ribera was a mannerist, and those who will closely examine half-a-dozen of his pictures, will exhaust the master. Observe 42, C. L., the Martyrdom of St. Bartholomew, a favourite subject of his, and one which few else ever wish to see twice : 44, the Virgin, elderly and haggard ; Raphael would have chosen her young and beautiful : 53, another St. Bartholomew : 72, C. N., the Hermit St. Paul, a repetition of the picture in the cathedral of Granada : 116, C. L., Jacob's Ladder, a fine picture. The general effect is very grand ; the wild broken tree stumps are painted like Sal. Rosa, and the sleep of Jacob (a vulgar brown monk) is admirable : 121, Prometheus, a finely painted picture of gore and bowels, such alone as could be conceived by a bull-fighter, and please a people whose sports are blood and torture ; how different from the same subject by the poetical Titian (see 787): 125, Martyrdom of St. Sebastian : 204, C. L., the Trinity, painted like Caravaggio : 243, C. N., the Magdalen, a hard early picture. There are many

Apostles well painted by Ribera, which we do not enumerate. 285, another St. Bartholomew. In other saloons, observe 415, E., St. Jerome : 419, E., a good portrait of a blind Sculptor. *El Ciego de Gambazo,* in which the sentiment of *touch* is well expressed : 473, St. Jerome : 480, St. Joseph and the Infant Saviour, which is but a transcript of a Spanish carpenter's shop: 484, Ixion at the wheel, or rather a Jew on the rack of the Spanish Inquisition : 542, a Dead Christ lamented ; a powerfully painted group : 545, C. L., two Female Gladiators.

The specimens of other Spanish masters in these two saloons, which best deserve notice, are 40, C. L., St. Peter appearing to St. Peter Nolasco, by F[ro.] Zurbaran, 1598-1662 ; his style is based on Ribera, Domenichino, and Titian ; his best pictures are at Seville ; no one ever painted a Carthusian monk like him ; while the substance, texture, and splendour of his velvets and brocades surpass P. Veronese, having more real stuff in them : 47, portrait of Murillo, by Alonzo Miguel de Tobar, 1678-1758 ; he was Murillo's best pupil : 48, St. Jerome, Mateo Cerezo of Burgos, 1635-1685 ; he was an imitator of Rubens and Vandyke : by him also is 57, C. L., an Assumption : 45, C. L., and 49, a Virgin and Saviour, Luis de Morales, called *El Divino,* who is best to be studied in Estremadura (see p. 524) : 61, C. L., Boys at Play, Pedro Nuñez de Villavicencio of Seville, 1635-1700, a pupil of Murillo and El Calabrese, and this excellent picture proves how well he had studied his first master : 67, C. L., Baptism of Christ, Vicente Carducci, a Florentine naturalized at Madrid : 69, a Flower-piece, Juan de Arellano, 1614-1676 ; he was the Van Huysen of Spain, and is superior to Menendez in fruits and flowers : 79, C. L., View of Zaragoza, Juan B[a.] del Mazo, Madrid, 1630-1687 ; he was a disciple of Velazquez, but his landskips are apt to be too dark : 85, portrait of Wife of Philip IV., Juan Carreño de Miranda, Avilés,

1614-1685; he was the last of the old Spanish painters, and a feeble imitator of Velazquez: 88, C. L., St. John at Patmos, Alonzo Cano, Granada, 1601-1667; a grand picture: 90, ditto, a Gothic King, in feeble imitation of Velazquez: 95, Moses Striking the Rock, Juan de las Roelas, Seville, 1558?-1625; a dark inferior specimen of this truly great man, who only is to be studied at Seville: 96, C. L., Adoration of Shepherds, Pedro Orrente, a Murcian, and imitator of the Bassanos (see Valencia): 100, C. L., a Dead Christ, F$^{ro.}$ de Ribalta, Valencia, 1597-1628; this grand artist, the Annibal Carracci and Seb^n del Piombo of Spain, is only to be really understood at Valencia: 108, Vision of Ezekiel, F$^{ro.}$ Collantes, Madrid, 1599-1656; a horrid subject, and fitter for the monkish cloister than a gallery: 124, Carreño, a Fat Woman: 134, the calling of St. Matthew, Juan de Pareja, Seville, 1606-1670, first the slave and then the pupil of Velazquez; it is truly local and Spanish. The face of the Saviour is most ordinary, while the groups are dressed as in the time of Philip IV.: 146, St. Bernard, Ant$^o.$ Palomino, 1653-1726; he was the Vasari of Spain, but feebler alike with pen and pencil: 151, C. L., the Siege of Cadiz, Eugenio Caxes, Madrid, 1577-1642; this is described in the catalogue as the attack of the English in 1625, by the "Conde de Lest," i. e. Spanish for Essex; the real leader being Lord Wimbleton. The head of Giron, the Spanish general, is fine: 152, C. L., portrait of Don Carlos, son of Philip II., Alonzo Sanchez Coello, a Valencian, ob. 1590; a very interesting historical picture: 153, portrait of Maria of Portugal, first wife of Philip II., Juan Pantoja de la Cruz, Madrid, 1551-1610, pupil of Coello, and, like his master, admirable in painting the rich costumes of the period: 154, portrait of Isabel, the favourite daughter of Philip II., by Coello; the marvellous jewels and ornaments tell up on the dark back ground: 157, Virgin and Child, Morales: 166, C. L., C. N., a

Dead Christ, A. Cano, fine, but stony, and the painting of a sculptor: 170, Virgin and Saints, Blas del Pardo, Toledo, 1497-1557, pupil of Berruguete, and Florentine in style and colour. His conceptions are grand, and partake of Andrea del Sarto, but his colouring is apt to be leaden. The kneeling half figure is Alonzo de Villegas, author of the 'Flos Sanctorum:' 175, Birth of Virgin, and 181, Birth of Christ, are both by Pantoja; he was a hard painter, but excelled in portraits: 188, a Sunset, Mazo.

Now pass into the saloon to the l., 206, Sanchez Coello, portrait, it is said, of the celebrated Ant$^o.$ Perez, the persecuted minister of Philip II. (see Zaragoza): 221, a Magdalen, Jacinto Geronimo de Espinosa, of Valencia, where his best pictures are: 222, Margaret, wife of Philip III., Pantoja; the elaborate finished details are in perfect contrast with the broad handling by Velazquez: 226, C. L., La Divina Pastora, Tobar, cold and poor when compared with Murillo: 227, St. Jerome, Cano: 237 and 8, Apostles by Fra$^{co.}$ Pacheco, Seville, 1571-1654, a feeble painter, but useful author (see p. 115): 277, Pantoja, Philip II. when old, very curious and historical: 283, C. N., Zurbaran, S$^a.$ Casilda: 287, St. Jerome, Ant$^o.$ Pereda, Valladolid, 1599-1669; he imitated Ribera; the cross is well painted: 290, Pantoja, Charles V., aged about 40, in black and gold armour: 297, Naval Combat, Juan de Toledo, Lorca, 1611-1665; he was the Bourgignone of Spain: 305, Mazo, a dark brown view near the Escorial: 307, C. L., Virgin and Dead Christ, Cano; the side of head has been repainted; this is one of his best pictures in this gallery, and of fine rich colour: 314, C. L., Baptism of Christ, Juan Fernandez Navarrete, El Mudo, Logroño, 1526-1579; his finest works are in the chapel of the Escorial: 317, Zurbaran, Sleeping Christ with dark purple drapery, and a fine effect.

Now pass to La Bajada, and observe 357, portrait of the poor creature Charles II., Carreño: 362, Charles IV., an Allegory. Under these two imbeciles Spain and art lost alike their nationality ;—the last daub is by Lopez, *Pintor de Camara !*—368, Charles V. and Philip II., Pereda : 375, a Dead Christ, Domenico Theotocupuli, *El Greco* (see p. 771). Next enter *las Escuelas varias,* which is a collection of different schools, with many fine things from the Escorial ; the grand central gallery is divided into the modern Spanish masters, the old Italians, German, and French. It will be best to take singly Raphael, the Venetians, *i. e.* Giorgione, Titian, Tintoretto, and P. Veronese. Pass therefore up the great gallery, casting only a look on each side at the arrayed gems to 723, C. L., a Holy Family, by Raphael, 1483-1520 ; it is called *del* Agnus Dei, from the inscription carried by St. John, whose body has been very much repainted at Paris, where the exquisite face of the Virgin was rouged. The ruined architecture and landscape, equal to Titian, is said to be by Giovanni da Udina. 726, E., C. N., celebrated *Perla,* which belonged to our Charles I., and was sold with his other pictures by Cromwell. Philip IV. bought so largely at the auction through his ambassador Alonzo de Cardeñas, that 18 mules were laden with the lots, and he was so anxious to get them into Madrid, that he turned out the Lords Clarendon and Cottington, then ambassadors from Charles II., being ashamed to exhibit what once belonged to his old friend and visitor. Clarendon never forgave this, and in 1664, writing to Fanshawe, alludes to the " infamous conduct of Philip in buying so many goods of the crown from the murderers, which they should think in honour of returning before they made any demands on England." When Philip IV. beheld this Raphael, he exclaimed, " This is the Pearl of my pictures," and he was a good judge, and so Kugler considers it to be the most perfect of Raphael's Madonna subjects. Nor was the serious gentleness of the blessed Virgin Mother, her

beauty of form, her purity of soul, ever better portrayed ; the rich Titian-like blue sky, streaked with red, forms a fine background. 741, E., C. N., Tobit and the Fish, *La Virgin del Pez,* a simple grand symmetrical composition, perhaps somewhat too yellow in colour. This was taken to Paris, and was there removed from board to canvas, having been first scrubbed and varnished : 784, Christ bearing the Cross, or *El Pasmo de Sicilia,* and accounted as second only to the Transfiguration by those who look to size, or. are afraid to express an honest dissent when called upon as a matter of course to fall into raptures. This picture underwent even a worse treatment at Paris than the Tobit ; first it was removed from boards to canvas by Monsʳ· Bonnemaison, of whom Passavant (Kunstreise 77) next records this anecdote : Monsʳ· David calling one morning, found him sponging these Raphaels with spirit of turpentine. Even the man of the guillotine was shocked, and ventured to remonstrate, but was answered, " It does no harm, it is nourishing." It was then much repainted ; the tone, in consequence, is hard, brick - dusty, and relackered. Again, however beautiful the Veronica and groups to the r., the principal figure of the soldier in front is somewhat attitudinarian and theatrical.

Next observe 794, E., a sweet Holy Family called *De la Rosa ;* it has, however, been doubted : 798, E., a small Holy Family painted in 1507: 834, E., St. Elizabeth visits the Virgin, a contrast of aged and youthful pregnancy, a subject never over-pleasing. The composition is very simple, with a fine landscape. This also was removed at Paris from board to canvas, and then painted over and extra-varnished. It is inscribed in letters of gold, Raphael Urbinas, F.; Marinus Branconius, F.F.—fecit facere: 901, a portrait, according to some, of Bartolo, the jurisconsult ; according to others, of Andrea Navagiero, ambassador to Charles V., and author of ' *Il Viaggio de Espagna.*' Although somewhat hard and reddish, it is very grand, simple, and effective : 905, C. L., portrait of Cardinal Julio de Medicis, a truly Italian head ; observe the decision in the fine compressed lips and the intellect of the eyes: 909, a portrait thought by some to be that of Agostino Beazano. The Perla and the Tobit cannot be too often studied. Of all the Italian schools, that of Venice is the richest. Titian was the personal friend of Charles V. and Philip II., and (although Kugler doubts it, being evidently unacquainted with the Spanish collections) he came to Madrid in 1532, and remained there until 1535, which accounts for the number and fineness of his works (see Cean Ber. 'D.' v. 30).

Again, of all the Italian schools, that of Venice was the most admired by Velazquez, who candidly stated to Salvator Rosa that he did not at all like Raphael. It was to that city that he went purposely to purchase pictures for Philip IV.; at Madrid, therefore, Titian is to be seen in all his senatorial dignity of portrait and his glorious power of colour—oh magical, ravishing colour! pounded flesh rather, if not rubies and emeralds, and which, in spite of unlearned drawing, carries all before it. Titian was, indeed, a *painter.*

Of Giovanni Bellini, Venice, 1426-1516, observe No. 665, Virgin and Child ; although curious, it is hard, and has been repainted : 414, Jesus giving the Keys to Peter, is a truly early Italian picture; it came from the Escorial, where it was attributed to Giorgione, and was the companion of 792, by that great artist, the Virgin with Saints, and one of the finest pictures in the world: observe the man in armour. Giorgio Barbanelli il Gior-

* See their dialogue, as given by Marco Boschini, ' *Carta del navegar pitoresco,*' Venezia, 1660, p.56. For this interesting and hitherto unnoticed anecdote we are indebted to our friend Mr. Eastlake, R.A., whose intimate knowledge of Italian art and literature needs no eulogium from us.

gione, 1477-1511, died too young, while Titian, his co-pupil, lived too long. His picture, 780, of David killing Goliath, is fine; the cinque-cento costume is interesting, but the proportions between the stripling and the giant are not well observed.

Of Tiziano Vecellio, Cadore, 1477-1576—the immortal Titian—there are 43 pictures, a museum of themselves. 421, E., The Virgin : 428, E., Christ in the Garden, much injured : 437, E., St. Jerome : 465, E., The Virgin: 492, E., St. Jerome: 649, Philip II. : 680, Portrait: 682, Ditto: 685, C. L., Charles V. on Horseback ; this, before its recent restoration, was the finest equestrian picture in the world; it is more sublime and poetical than Velazquez, yet equally true to life; the knight-errant emperor inspires an awe, like the Theodore of Dryden pursuing the perjured Honoria : 695, Titian's own Portrait, venerable and intelligent : 724, a Portrait: 728, C. L., Diana and Actæon ; 729, C. L., Diana and Calisto, two charming sketches, coloured with pounded flesh and turquoise skies; they have been draped and painted over, owing to Spanish prudery ; the drawing is not very accurate, but Titian was 84 years old when these were produced. 740, Portrait : 752, E., the celebrated *Gloria* or apotheosis of Charles V. and Philip II., who, kings on earth, now appear as suppliants before the King of heaven and the angelic court. This, by many considered the masterpiece of Titian, was painted in his best time for Charles V., who directed by his will that it should always be hung where his body was buried : it remained at S[n.] Yuste (see p. 551) until Philip II. moved his father's remains to the Escorial ; and now, because Charles wears the habit of a monk, which, being then the common shroud of Spain, he must do if rising from the grave, M. Viardot (Mus. 42) assumes that this picture was painted *after* Charles's death, and in Titian's eighty-fourth year : setting aside history, only compare the drawing and handling of this with 728, 729.

Next observe 756, The Punishment of Sisyphus : 765, C. L., Charles V. with his Favourite Dog; here one beholds him in his privacy, with his look of care and pain ; but gout in the feet and madness in the brain are the penalties of old blood and high rank : 769, C. L., is his son Philip II.; young, and in armour, rich in costume, delicate in form and feature. These full-lengths are fac-similes of the men; indeed, Titian and Velazquez have so identified the Austrian branch, that we here become as personally acquainted with them as if we had known them alive. 775, E., St. Margaret, very fine, but it has been repainted with false draperies : 776, C. L., Salome with the Head of the Baptist; this exquisite picture is said to be a portrait of Titian's daughter, and if the face be not strictly correct beauty, it is individual : 787, Prometheus; compare the poetical treatment by our Italian with 121, the butcher production of the practical Spaniard Ribera; it is Æschylus contrasted with Torquemada : 801, C. L., Venus and Adonis, glorious; there is an inferior repetition in our National Gallery : seen from a certain distance, when the demitints tell up, all that is flat when one is near then becomes form and meaning : this also is the way to look at Velazquez. 805, E., The Catholic Faith flying for Protection to Spain : 812, Adam and Eve ; observe the *pentimentos* in Adam's head : this was Rubens's favourite, and no wonder, for the forms are more sprawling and the fleshes heavier than is usual in Titian. 813, E., Christ placed in the Sepulchre, fine : 821, the Mᵗⁱ· del Vasto and his Troops, finely coloured, but injured : 822, E., is a repetition of 813 : 851, another St. Margaret; the figure is well relieved by the gloomy rocky background : 852, C. L., Offering to Fecundity, marvellous; but it will shock all Malthusians, for never were

so many or such playful living children better grouped and painted ; unfortunately it has been spotted by retouches : this was the picture which, when at Rome, in the Ludovisi Gallery, was the study and the making of N. Poussin. 854, Victory of Lepanto, painted by Titian when 91 years old; even in his age live his wonted fires; the colouring is rich, the harmonious effect fine, but the composition is feeble; the rows of pillars look like organ-pipes, and the angel seems as if it had been thrown out of window and must break its neck ; Philip II., in his red breeches and yellow boots, places his naked son Fernando somewhat awkwardly on the table: however, as a curiosity of the sustained art of Titian this picture deserves notice. 864, C. L., a Bacchanal ; Ariadne in the Isle of Naxos abandoned by Theseus; this is one of the finest pictures in the world ; joyous mirth and a dance of light never were so coloured ; it is a companion to the inferior Bacchus and Ariadne in our National Gallery. 868, E., Repose in Egypt, a superb landskip; this is the subject engraved by Bonasoni : 878, C. L., Portrait of Isabella, wife of Charles V., superbly painted costume : 882, Adoration of Kings : 915, a magnificent Portrait; observe the effect of the blue sash : 926, Portrait of Alfonzo, Duke of Ferrara ; fine costume.

Jacobo Robusti il Tintoretto, Venice, 1512-1594, worthily sustains his master's style. 490, C. L., a Magdalen, almost naked : 602, Minerva, an allegory : 607, a truly Titianesque Portrait : 626, Ditto : 628, 645, Ditto, very fine : 672, Judith and Holophernes : 679, a singular picture of the Doge seated in Council, in a superb saloon of state, was long ascribed to Tintoretto, it is now ascertained to be by Pietro Malombra, Venice, 1556-1618; it is highly interesting, both as a work of art and local costume. 704, *La Gloria*, the original sketch for the picture in the Doge's palace at Venice, and bought there by Velazquez; it, however, is heavy in colour, and a fricassee of legs and arms; the man with a large head in the corner seems scared and disappointed, as he well might be with such a paradise. 830, St. Jerome: 839, Death of Holophernes: 904, a superb Cardinal: 913, a Venetian Senator: 919, Portrait of Sebastian Veniero.

Pablo Cagliari, Paul Veronese, Verona, 1528-1588, appears in all his gorgeous brocade and splendour of drapery : some of the portraits are very fine; among his pictures notice 453, E., Marriage of Cana; it belonged to our Charles I.: 497, E., Christ at the Column : 625, E., Christ and the Centurion, fine: 661, Rebecca at the Well, rather dark: 691, Moses found in the Nile, a charming gay cabinet picture, ascribed by some to Tintoretto: 710, The Birth of a Prince—celebris mundi Veneris partus; this is an allegory, with too much blue sky and red curtain: 764, Portrait of a Lady: 793, Ditto: 825, E., Christ and the Centurion, fine: 843, C. L., Venus and Adonis, a very fine picture of great repose and effect; the flesh and rich draperies are equal to Titian: 876, C. L., an allegory, Virtue and Vice; neither are very attractive, and the youth is stupid, although finely painted, and the attitudes are very awkward: 896, Cain and his Family, a magnificent composition, a picture of man's despair consoled by a true wife, who will not desert the father of her children : the brown landskip, lowering sky, and breaking halo, are in sombre harmony with the sentiment. 897, E., a Martyrdom of a Saint, fine : 898, C. L., Susanna and the Elders, fine : 899, Christ disputing with the Doctors, finely composed, but somewhat grey, green, and wanting in effect.

Of the Da Pontes, or Bassanos, there are many and fine specimens, but it is tedious to describe these cattle-show pictures of sheep and oxen, for the figures are often only accessories. 615, Leandro, Orpheus, and animals: 620, Jacobo, 1510-1592, Dives and Lazarus:

632, E., The Money-changers in the Temple : 673, Jacobo, Adam and Eve : 675, Francesco, The Last Supper: 701, Leandro, Coppersmiths at Work, a fine specimen : 730, Francesco, Jacob Travelling : 841, Jacobo, his own Portrait : 877, Francesco, Paradise, an excellent specimen of the Master : 880, Leandro, Forge of Vulcan: 910, Leandro, Venice, The Doge Embarking.

Having examined the Spanish school, Raphael, and the Venetians in detail, now take a general view of the rest of the gallery. For the convenience of those who have not looked at any masters separately, an asterisk is placed before those pictures which deserve notice, but which have just been described. In the *Bajada a varias Escuelas*, avoid No. 382, a Christ Buffeted, by the *Director* Sr· Madrazo, which suggests the somewhat irreverent criticism of Alonzo Cano, on being shown a badly executed crucifix, "Forgive them, Lord! for they know not what they do." In the *Escuelas varias* observe No. 407, E., 1577-1640, The Supper at Emmaus, a fine, rich, brown painting, although the Silenus-like figure of "mine host" destroys the dignity of sentiment: 409, an early picture of the Marriage of the Virgin: 414*, Giovanni Bellini: 419*, Ribera: 422,_E., a Concepcion, Rubens, but how inferior in grace to 229 of Murillo: 423*, Murillo: 435, 437*, Titian : 439, E., a Dead Christ, Rubens: 449, 450, E., Philip IV. and his Wife Kneeling, Velazquez: 475, E., a Magdalen, Luis de Carbajal, whose best pictures remain at the Escorial. Those who admire Ribera will find many pictures by him here ; observe especially 484, Ixion: 490*, Tintoretto : 492*, Titian : 496, E., Coronation of Christ with Thorns, Vandyke: 515, Ignacio Iriarte, 1620-1685, a Landskip; Murillo used to say that he was fit to paint scenes in *heaven*, which must be understood as meaning *Andalucia*, the elysium of these local Sevillians: 526 and 532 are other specimens, yet, compared to the Italian, Dutch, and English land-skip-painters, Iriarte is very second-rate; but in Spain, as among the classical ancients, *landskip* was only an accessory, and seldom really treated as a principal either in art or litera-ture: their efforts were vague bald generalities, with no true graphic qua-lity, no precision of touch, no local co-lour, air, sensibility, no individuality. They seldom saw nature with the poet's feeling combined with the painter's eye; the pen and pencil were sculptu-resque rather than picturesque, man being *the* absorbing object. Again, a taste for *landskip* is acquired, and few Orientals or Spaniards have any feeling for nature beyond local associations, or notions of profit and personal enjoy-ment; they love the country, not for itself, but as in relation to themselves: but even some of our gentlemen far-mers are often so blunted by profes-sional habits, as only to be thinking of draining, where Turner would go crazy with delight, and when talking of bullocks which would drive Paul Potter mad, are solely speculating on what per score the carcass will fetch, sinking the offal (see For. Q. Rev. xxxi. 148).

Next observe 530, Sancho Coello, Isabel, third wife of Philip II.: 531, San Hermenegildo, Fro. de Herrera el Mozo, Seville, 1622-1685: 533, Pan-toja, Portrait of Doña Juana: 540*, Velazquez: 543, Magdalen, Antᵒ· An-tolinez, Seville, 1639-1676: 545*, Ribera: 549, Pantoja, Charles V.: 550, Murillo, St. Jerome.

Passing on and passing by the modern Spanish pictures, we enter the magni-ficent Italian gallery, where masters, schools, periods, sizes, and subjects are jumbled together in most Spanish-like confusion and insubordination, each taking its place by accident, like a corps of *guerrilleros.* Where all are good, select, 603, C. L., Giovanni Francᵒ· Barbieri, Il Guercino, 1590-1666, St. Peter in prison: 609, Andres Vaccaro, Naples, 1598 - 1670, San Cayetano,

when a child, offered to the Virgin: 611, Giulio Cesare Procaccini, Bo-logna, 1548-1626, Samson destroying the Philistines: 612, Landskip, Gaspar Poussin; the St. Jerome is by Nicolas: 625*, P. Veronese: 630, Dominico Zampieri, Il Domenichino, Bologna, 1581-1641; St. Jerome visited by An-gels: 633, Christofano Allori, Florence, 1577-1621, portrait of a Lady: 634, Guido Reni, Bologna, 1575-1642, St. Sebastian: 636, ditto, Cleopatra, but somewhat green and slaty: 637, C. L., Federigo Fiori, Baroccio, Urbino, 1559-1613, Birth of the Saviour: 643, St. John preaching, El Caballero Maximo, Massimo Stanzioni, Naples, 1585-1656; his pictures should be examined, as his style much influenced Velaz-quez, who twice visited him and Ri-bera at Naples: 644, Salvator Rosa, Naples, 1615-1673, Isaac and Rebecca: 645, Il Tintoretto: 647, Guercino, the genius of painting in a rich orange drapery: 648, S. Rosa, the Sacrifice of Abraham: 649*, Titian: 651, a curious Venetian portrait of Pejeron, jester to the Conde de Benavente: 653, Gaspar Poussin, landskip and animals: 660, Francesco Albano, Bologna, 1578-1660, Venus at her toilet, very transparent, but the flesh is flat and unprofitable when compared to Titian; and how-ever elegant the cupids, they are con-ventional, and lack the reality of living, child-like joyousness.

Next observe 661*, P. Veronese: 664, C. L., Andrea Vannuchi del Sarto, Florence, 1488-1530, portrait of his wife Lucretia Fede; this once ex-quisite picture was cruelly restored in 1833: 665, G. Bellini: 666, C. L., Leonardo da Vinci, 1452-1519, por-trait of Mona Lisa; there is a repe-tition in the Louvre; this one has been doubted; the drapery is heavy, the cheeks puffy, and the eyes too near the nose: 671, Albano, Judgment of Paris: 672*, Tintoretto: 679*, Pietro Mallombra: 681, C. L., A. del Sarto, Virgin and Saints; compare it with 911: 680 and 682 are two fine por-traits by Titian: 683, landskip, G.

Poussin: 685*, Titian: 689, Sebastian Luciano, Sebastian del Piombo, pupil of Michael Angelo, 1483-1547, Christ bearing the Cross, small, and painted on slate; it has been doubted. These are the pictures on which Morales formed his style. 670, Giov. Bᵃˑ Tiepolo, Venice, 1693-1770, a Concepcion, but far inferior to Spanish treatment; the Virgin's feet are shown: 691*, P. Veronese: 693, Paris Bordone, 1500-1570, portrait of a Lady: 695*, Titian: 704*, Tintoretto: 705, Agostino Carracci, 1558-1601, St. Francis beholding a heavenly Vision; this picture is dark, the saint awkward, and the joined hand of angel to r. common-place; how superior was Murillo's treatment of this subject. 706, Domenichino, Sacrifice of Abraham: 710*, P. Veronese: 711, Cᵒˑ Maximo, Sacrifice to Bacchus; a fine specimen: 721, M. Angelo Buonarotti, 1474-1563, Christ at the Pillar, doubtful: 723*, Raphael: 726*, ditto: 724, a fine Portrait, Titian: 728, 729*, ditto: 730*, F. Bassano: 734, Angiolo Bronzino, 1501-1570, a splendid portrait; a fine pensive character of the high-bred Italian youth: 737, Cᵒˑ Maximo, the Message to Zacharias: 741*, Raphael: 743, C. L., Sal. Rosa, a view in the Bay of Salerno: 751, E., Guido, Virgin on a Throne, a magnificent picture, finely coloured, and grand in expression. In this there is none of his insipid mannerism, and want of real life and personal interest: 752*, La Gloria of Titian: 756*, ditto: 759, E., Sebⁿˑ del Piombo, Christ in Hades; grandly conceived, and a sublime representation of the ghostly mysterious character, which marked all the appearances of the Saviour after the Resurrection. Sebastian was the Dante of painting; who, homeless on earth, made his home more and more in the awful other world.

Next observe 761, Alessandro Allori, 1535-1607, Sᵃˑ Veronica: 765, 769*, Charles V. and Philip II., Titian: 771, Giorgio Vasari, Arezzo, 1512-1574, a Charity, hard and affected,

and merely coloured sculpture: 772, C. L., A. del Sarto, Holy Family, very fine and grand; it belonged to our Charles I., and both Murillo and Mengs must have carefully studied this admirable picture: 774*, Tintoretto: 775, 776*, two superb Titians: 778, E., Holy Family, L. da Vinci, but thought by some to be by Luini: 779, E., Christ bearing his Cross, another very grand Sebastian del Piombo: 780*, Giorgione: 784*, Raphael: 786, Jacobo Palma, an Adoration of Shepherds most richly coloured: 787*, Titian: 788, E., Repose in Egypt, A. del Sarto: 789, Jacobo Carucci da Pontormo, 1493-1558, Holy Family: 790, Cᵒˑ Maximo, the Beheading St. John the Baptist: 792*, Giorgione, glorious: 794*, Raphael: 795, Artemisia Lomi Gentileschi, the Birth of the Baptist; the satiny drapery is painted like Zurbaran: 797, Lorenzo Lotto, a Marriage, said to be between Ferdinand and Isabella, curious for costume: 798*, Raphael: 799, Bernardo Luini, Salome with the Baptist's head; she is a coquettish Italian beauty; it has been cruelly repainted: 801, 805*, Titian: 809, E., Antonio Allegri Correggio, 1494-1534, Jesus and Mary Magdalen. This has been doubted since the false draperies have recently been removed; but Spain is poor in Correggios; those which Godoy had "collected" were re-collected by Murat: two of them purchased from his widow by Lord Londonderry are now in the London National Gallery; the Venus having originally belonged to our unfortunate Charles I.: 814 and 816 are attributed, without reason, to Correggio: 817, Baroccio, a Crucifixion, fine and delicately painted, with much resigned softness in the expression; a view of Urbino forms the background: 821*, Titian: 825*, P. Veronese: 830, Tintoretto, St. Jerome, fine: 833, Luigi Cardi, Il Cigoli, 1559-1613, the Magdalen: 834*, Raphael: 837, A. del Sarto, the Sacrifice of Abraham; curious as being a repetition of the picture sent by the artist to François I., as some atonement for the money which he had embezzled: 839*, Tintoretto: 840 and 844, fine portraits, Duke and Duchess of Tuscany, Bronzino: 843*, P. Veronese, superb: 847, Guercino, a Magdalen, and singularly unpleasing: 849, Giovanni Ant⁰· Licinio Regillo de Pordenone, 1484-1539, the Death of Abel: 851, 852, 854*, by Titian: 855, Guido, a Magdalen: 861, Bronzino, a fine Portrait of a Violin Player: 864*, Titian: 867, Francesco Mazzuoli, Il Parmigianino, 1503-1534, a superb portrait; the silk velvet and fur edging are marvellously painted; the head is full of quiet Italian dignity: 868*, Titian: 871, A. del Sarto, a fine Holy Family; the child looks charmingly at the spectator: 876*, P. Veronese: 879, Parmigianino, C. L., a Holy Family, and a charming specimen: 880*, L. Bassano: 881*, P. Veronese: 882,* Titian: 883, E., An. Carracci, 1560-1609, Assumption of the Virgin: 884, Giovanni Lanfranco, 1581-1647, Funeral of Julius Cæsar, of larger size than merit: 890, Luca Giordano, an Allegory of Peace, of colossal dimensions and diminutive merit: 894, Guercino, Susanna and the Elders, fine, and like Domenichino; her body, however, is rather stony: 896*, P. Veronese, a Grand Specimen: 897, ditto: 898, ditto, fine: 901, 905, and 909*, Portraits by Raphael: 900 and 903, G. Poussin: 904*, Tintoretto, and splendid: 910, L. Bassano, View of Venice, very interesting, although somewhat cold in colour: 911, A. del Sarto, said by some to be by Squazetti: 917*, L. da Vinci?: 920, G. Poussin; this and 916 are superb full-toned specimens, and full of subject: 926*, Titian: 929, Bronzino, a Lady with three Children, grand, but hard and Florentine.

Now examine the German, Flemish, and French schools, which are collected in a circular saloon by themselves, not that they have much in common with each other. The Spaniards have very properly placed Gaspar Poussin, who

was born at Rome, among the Italians, and yet have included Claude and Nicolas Poussin among the French; but Claude left France, aged 12, a pastry-cook's boy, and pies, capital ones no doubt, he would have lived and died making in that paradise of transcendental culinary *artistes.* In beautiful poetical Italy, where there are more altars than ovens, more painters than pastry-cooks, his other dormant capabilities were awaked; then and there the mighty genius imprisoned in a jam-pot burst forth to better things; and the youth having been born artistically again in a new and congenial country, became a great Italian painter: and, like him, Poussin early in life abandoned his unpicturesque country; re-educated at Rome, he could only breathe a classical air; thus, when compelled by Louis XIV. to return to France, he pined, sickened, and would have died, unless restored to a better atmosphere and scenery. Both are essentially Italians as painters, which is their whole attraction; and if this be doubted, compare their style and sentiment to the veritable Frenchmen, whose works are hung near them, to wit, the Jouvenets, Lafosses, Mignards, and Rigauds. As Vandyke was formed by painting English gentlemen and ladies, the noblest and most beautiful models in the creation, so Claude and Poussin were created by the sunny skies, the temples and antiquities of Italy, and they both lived and died at Rome, their adopted country; and their ashes repose on the banks of the classical Tiber, not on those of the commonplace Seine. *Ingrata* patria ne ossa quidem! Their nationality must be decided by their fruit, and they are the golden apples of a garden of Hesperus, and to both may be applied the old adage, non ubi nascitur sed ubi pascitur.

The Poussins, both Gaspar and Nicolas, are first-rate. Observe 942, C. L., Claude Gilee, Lorraine, 1600-1682, Ruins at Rome, with the Coliseum; the figures are by Philipo Laura, as

Claude was acccustomed to say that he *sold* his landskips, but gave away *his* figures. It is doubtful, however, whether even better-drawn figures by another hand really *tell*, either in form or colour, so well as those dashed in by the *landskip* painter himself, who used them not for themselves, but as aids and accessories, which a *figure* painter would forget and convert them into principals. 945, Nicolas Poussin, Normandy, 1594-1665 : 947, C. L., Claude, a Sunset; full of exquisite repose. The figures, except the Shepherd, are by Courtois. 948, N. Poussin, Bacchus and Nymphs, a most classical group, in a splendid landskip : 963, 964, Antonio Rafael Mengs, 1728-1779, Charles IV. and his Wife; both are most truly commonplace : 967, a German picture of the miraculous Hostia at Bolseno : 971, Antº· Watteau, 1684-1721, a Village Wedding : 972, Albert Durer, 1470-1528, his own Portrait, aged 26, signed and inscribed, " Dass malt ich nach meine gestalt, ich war sechs und zwauzig yar alt :" 975, C. L., Claude, Sunset, with a Hermit, doubtful; the figure is by Frº· da Gubbio : 976, C. L., N. Poussin : 982, C. L., N. Poussin, David and Goliath : 983, ditto, a Bacchanal : 988, Claude, Joseph Vernet, 1714-1789, Landskip, with a Cascade : 989, N. Poussin, Mount Parnassus : 991, Watteau, a pretty Scene at St. Cloud : 992, A. Durer, a fine Portrait : 1003, Claude : 1004, 1005, 1025, and 1026, C. L., are small J. van Ostades : 1006, 1020, two curious hunting pictures, by Lucas Cranach, 1472-1552 ; the Elector John of Saxony entertains Charles V., who is to be recognised by his Golden Fleece. The buildings and costume are truly old German; then there is a sea of hartshorn, and a marvellous contempt of perspective. 1009, A. Durer, a Musical Allegory : 1013 and 1014, N. Poussin : 1017, an Allegory, and 1019, a Holy Family, both attributed to A. Durer : 1023, Sª· Cecilia, and 1024, Ancient Rome, both N. Poussin's : 1033, Claude, Ruins,

and St. Anthony being tempted : 1040, Diana, N. Poussin : 1042, Quintin Matsys, 1450-1529, a Village Surgeon : 1044, 1045, and 1047 are three good Vernets : 1049, Claude, a Morning Scene, with the Magdalen : 1050, N. Poussin, Meleager hunting ; a most truly classical composition : 1051, ditto, Silenus : 1057, Mengs, Adoration of Shepherds, an academical, eclectic, and feeble veneering of other men's ideas, especially those of Correggio : 1062, a very fine early Holy Family, with architecture, ascribed to Lucas van Leyden, but it much resembles Fernando Gallegos : 1067 and 1070, N. Poussin : 1069, A. Durer, Adam and Eve : 1080, C. L., Claude, a glorious Italian Sunset, with beautiful water ; the figures of Tobit and the Angel are by Courtois : 1081, C. L., Claude, a superb Sunrise, with sea and architecture ; the groups embarking are by Courtois : 1080, C. L., Claude, a Morning Scene, rather dark, and in an earlier style ; figures by P. Laura : 1086, C. L., Claude, Landskip, with a Ford ; also in an early style, with figures, by P. Laura. These Claudes, when we last saw them, were much in want of lining, but were pure as the day they were painted. These truly *Italian* gems are surrounded by pictures, of whose nationality there can be no mistake; but the clinquant Louis XIV. perriwigs act like foils, by contrasting style ; how the simple feeling of a nature pure and undefiled soars above the theatrical and artificial!

Now pass to the Flemish and Dutch schools. In the *Galeria de Paso* are examples of the Neapolitan and Bolognese artists of the seventeenth century: among them Luca Giordano is remarkable, whose *fa presto* style and hasty presumption led to the utter decline of painting. By him are, 1088, Hercules : 1090, Perseus : 1094, Susanna : 1096, Repentance of St. Peter : 1098, Rinaldo and Armida : 1100, Erminia taking refuge with Shepherds : 1124, Tancredi and Clorinda : 1128, Jacob wrestling with the Angel : 1138,

Turnus conquered by Æneas: 1168, Christ bearing the Cross: 1175, Andromeda: 1186, Flora. These are all on a large scale of canvas; and there are several on a smaller, which are neither worth mention or observation. This master possessed great rapidity of execution; but as little thought and sentiment redeems the masses, we carry nothing away. The visitor may look *en passant* at 1097, P. Veronese, an Adoration: 1105, Lanfranco, Reward of Bravery; and 1114, its companion, Gladiators: 1151, Naval combat; 1160, Consultation at a Sacrifice, are also by Lanfranco, who, like Giordano, was a better painter of fresco ceilings than of easel pictures. By Tintoretto are the small portraits 1112, 1117, 1127, 1139, 1144, and 1180, the Rape of Lucretia.

There is an apartment of state, called *La Sala del descanso,* where the royal family repose after the *fatigue* of visiting the Museo. Here was hung, by order of Ferd. VII., a painting of his landing at *Puerto de Sa. Maria,* by Apariccio: anything so bad never was painted or conceived ; and yet an especial description of this single picture was sold by itself at the entrance of the Museo, which speaks volumes as to the fulsome servility and artistical ignorance of those who then directed the taste of Spain.

The Flemish and Dutch schools come the last in the Catalogue, and, so far as the masters go, the pictures are of the highest quality and very pure. The long connexion between Spain and the Low Countries ensured a constant supply of the best works; and hitherto, from not being valued by Spaniards so much as those of their own and the Italian masters, they have escaped the fatal *restauracion.* The Spaniard, long accustomed to see art the handmaid of religion, or rather the serf, adscriptus ecclesiæ, associates the altar with all painting of a severe and high class; he looks for religious, and especially for monkish and legendary subjects: accordingly, the low, earthy

doings of the Dutch seem to him to be somewhat vulgar, and beneath the dignity of art; while the truth and beauty of their landskip are lost on a nation which is by no means keenly alive to the charms of the country and nature itself.

The best pictures here, of these schools, are those by Rubens, Vandyke, and Antonio Moro. The specimens of Wouvermans are beyond all price, and gems of purest art. Those by Teniers, Snyders, Breughel, P. Neefs, Both, are very fine. Here again, as in the Italian and Spanish schools, the collection is very imperfect. There is little or nothing of such great masters as Rembrandt, Carl du Jardin, Cuyp, Hobbima, Jan Steen, Vandervelt, Mieris, Backhuysen, Vanderneer, Ostade, Ruysdael, Vandervelde, Paul Potter, &c.

To give any particular description of the Ostade class, the dogs, game, kitchenware, and dead drunken Dutchmen, would be tedious as to count the cattle of the Bassans. Yet these pictures are what the "London trade" calls *bank-notes,* since the demand for them is certain, and must be so; for whenever fortunes are made every day, and a picture gallery is thought an appendage of aristocracy, into which, like politics, it gives a sort of introduction, those paintings which give faithful representations of ordinary nature will ever be sought for, since where one person comprehends the ideality of Raphael, the sublimity of M. Angelo, a thousand will relish a true delineation of a flask of beer, and the humour of the boor who drinks it. It is Pickwick and Sam Slick *versus* Dante or Milton. Low art is always the most popular with the many, who receive according to the calibre of the recipient. Again, those who pass from honest industry to become Mæcenases, naturally love to see the business-like item-accuracy and laborious working-out of the matter-of-fact Dutchman, whose artists partook of the commercial character of the country. These pictures, like good names on a bill, speak for themselves, and are understood by your practical men of business and *common* sense, as they make no demand on the imagination; while effects produced by broad masses, indistinct shadowings out, neglect of accessories, and appeals to the mind, positively appear, especially where there is no mind, to be dishonest and unworkmanlike. But an appreciation of all this mechanical detail and *bonâ fide* fulfilment of contract is lost on the Spaniard, who is at best a bungling operative, and one who sometimes promises rather than pays or performs.

Commencing with the saloon to the l., observe 1199, 1205, Rubens, Portrait of Archduke Albert and his wife Isabel; the landskips are ascribed to J. Breughel: 1210, D. Teniers, 1610-1694, a Rustic Festival: 1213, Rubens, Saturn devouring his own Children; this type of revolutions is too infanticidal to be pleasing: 1216, Rubens, the Combat of the Lapithæ; it is full of muscle, movement, and flesh, horse and human: 1217, F. Snyders, 1579-1657, a grand Boar-hunt: 1220, Rubens, a Holy Family, with St. George; very fine: 1229, C. L., Rubens, Rape of Proserpine; grand: 1230 and 1247, Snyders, Dog subjects: 1233, Vandyke, Portrait of the Painter Richart; 1241, Antº· Moro, 1512-1568, a superb Portrait of Catherine, wife of John III. of Portugal: 1242, Vandyke, Portrait of a Cardinal: 1245, C. L., Vandyke, an exquisite Portrait of the Countess of Oxford: 1251, C. L., Rubens, Moses staying the Plague by elevating the Brazen Serpent: 1258, Antº· Moro, full-length Portrait of Doña Juana of Austria; very fine: 1269, 1270, D. Teniers, a Pastoral subject, and a Rural Feast: 1272,1273, Vandyke, Portraits of Henry of Nassau and his wife Amelia: 1274, D. Teniers; the Artist is showing a Picture-Gallery to the Archduke Albert: 1282, Vandyke, Charles I. in armour and on Horseback: 1285, 1288, two fine Game subjects by Snyders: 1292, C. L., Rubens, Adora-

tion of the Magi; it is said that he added the right portion to this picture when at Madrid, and also introduced his own portrait: 1294, C. L., D. Teniers, *La Graciosa Fregatriz;* this is one of his best specimens; here a stealthy, jealous, ill-favoured, feline old wife watches her truant husband like a cat, who is admiring a young and pretty burnisher of saucepans: 1296, D. Teniers, one of his common Temptations of St. Anthony :* 1300, Rubens, the Banquet of Tereus, who, as he well may be, is horrified at seeing the limbs and head of his son, *guisados a la Quesada ;* nor can the talent of the painter unbrutalise the unpleasing subject: 1305,1335, P. Neefs, two of his highly-finished church interiors: 1308, T. Porbus, 1570-1622, a fine portrait of a lady in black : 1314, Vandyke, ditto, ditto: 1320, C. L., Rubens, Mercury and Argos: 1328, 1329, D. Teniers, Monkey Artists: 1330, Rembrandt, 1606-1674, Artemisia about to swallow the Ashes of her Husband : 1336, Ph. Wouvermans, a Mounted Sportsman refreshing at a Venta, capital : 1338, C. L., Rubens, Cadmus and Minerva: 1339, J. Breughel, a large rustic festival, at which the Archduke Albert and his wife are present; a fine speci-

* *San Antonio*, a model of monks, was the first hermit who eschewed the world, its sheets, soaps, and towels, for a den of the desert, in which he worked so many miracles, that hundreds turned anchorites; thereupon the devil worried him day and night under the shape of animals great and small. The sole and bosom friend of the recluse was a pig, for "idem velle atque idem nolle, ea demum firma amicitia," says Sallust: in vain Satan tempted him with beautiful women, the saint remained true to his first love. In the mediæval ages a boar and a sow of this breed were allowed free quarters in towns, being distinguished by a particular mark, and their produce fetched higher prices than ordinary porkers, from the flavour and orthodoxy of their bacon. San Antonio is still the patron of Spanish pigs, mules, and asses, which are blessed and sprinkled on the 17th of January, his day. The hermit has also befriended artists by furnishing both grand and ludicrous subjects taken from his solitudes, penances, and temptations. See Ribad., i. 178.

men: 1344, J. Both, a fine Sunset in a rocky scene, with cowherds: 1345, Rubens, Portrait of Mary of Medicis: 1350, C. L., Rubens, Equestrian Portrait of Ferdinand of Austria; how inferior to Velazquez; 1354, Both, the Passage of the Mountain, fine: 1358, C. L., Rubens, Portrait of a Princess in black costume: 1361, another large Breughel, allegorical figures of Art and Science in a rich gallery: 1373, Rubens, an agreeable picture of a dancing group: 1374, 1375, P. Neefs, fine church interiors; the figures are ascribed to Franck: 1376, Antᵒ· Moro, superb Portrait of Doña Maria, Infanta of Portugal: 1377, Wouvermans, an exquisite hunting scene with ladies and gentlemen on horseback: 1378, Snyders: 1380, D. Teniers, a Rustic Dance: 1382, Antᵒ· Moro, fine Portrait of a Lady: 1383, Wouvermans, a Sporting Party crossing a River; a perfect gem.

Passing now into the saloon to the r., 1392, Vandyke, a fine portrait of Lord Arundel with red scarf: 1393, ditto, a Musician, good fine: 1394, ditto, a Cavalier in black satin, slashed, and very fine: 1400, C. L., Rubens, Philip II. on Horseback, very feebly conceived and drawn both as regards man and beast; the rider's head is too big, and his seat very awkward: 1401, Van-Eyk, 1370-1448, Henry Werlis (for whom this was painted in 1438) Kneeling in his Cell; a curious early picture: 1402, J. Breughel, another of his allegorical pictures like 1361: 1405, Snyders, a fine Lion in a net: 1407, Vandyke, Portraits of himself and the Earl of Bristol, so long minister of Charles I. at Madrid; fine and interesting; 1410, J. Ruysdael, 1640-1681, a small wooded scene: 1418, 1419, P. Neefs, a small pair of church interiors: 1422, 1423, J. Breughel, a large pair of landscapes, with a marketing and junketing: 1425, and the series by D. Teniers, eleven small subjects taken from Tasso, and not over-poetically treated: 1440, Ruysdael, a wooded scene with a lake and ferry:

1442, Rubens, St. George delivering the Damsel from the Dragon: 1443, 1444, J. Breughel, two large Rustic Festivals: 1446, Antᵒ· Moro, a superb portrait of our bloody Queen Mary, which has been well engraved by Vasquez, C. N. The careless, *quien sabe* directors long called this, although the wife of their Philip II., the portrait of an *unknown* person. 1447, Vandyke, Portrait of Liberti, an organist of Antwerp: 1448, D. Teniers, a good Rustic Merry-making; 1449, Rubens, Ulysses discovers Achilles by his grasping a sword: 1451, C. L., D. Teniers, another Temptation of *St.* Anthony: 1457, Both, a mountain and woody scene: 1461, Rubens, Jeremiah in his Cave: 1463, T. Wouvermans, a Party passing a River, a pure gem: 1465, Rubens, Silenus: 1467, T. Wouvermans, Repose after Chase, with horses drinking, a first-rate picture: 1470, C. L., Both, a fine landscape with hermits: 1474, a grand subject of Ceres and Pan, painted by Rubens and Snyders: 1487, J. Breughel, Ladies Gardening: 1488, D. Teniers, Hermits; both these are on a large scale: 1501, D. Teniers, Gipsies telling an old Man his fortune: 1507, Rubens, Mercury; by whom also are the series of Apostles from 1509 to 1514, and from 1531 to 1536, and how tired we get of them: much finer indeed is 1515, C. L., his splendid Portrait of Thomas More; 1528, Rubens, Atalanta and Meleager; 1546, C. L., Vandyke, a fine Pietá: 1551, G. Metzu: 1556, Rubens, Archimedes: 1573, P. Wouvermans, a Departure from an Inn, most beautiful: 1575, C. L., Rubens, Rudolph of Hapsburg places on his Horse a Priest who is bearing the Host: 1576, C. L., Rubens, a very fine picture, with gallants and their ladies, a chef-d œuvre: 1578, Rubens, Vulcan: 1587, ditto, Ganymede: 1588, ditto, Rape of Europa, said to have been copied from Titian by Rubens for our Charles I.; the two masters will bear no comparison except in their exuberance of works, for how coarse, physical, and sensual is the Fleming, compared to the elegant, intellectual voluptuousness of the Italian. 1591, Snyders, a good picture of Quarrelsome Fowls: 1598, M. Coxcis, the Death of the Virgin; this was brought from Sᵃ· Gudula of Bruxelles by Philip II.: 1599, Castle of Emmaus, ascribed by some to Rubens: 1602, a large landscape by Monper, figures by J. Breughel: 1607, C. L., Vandyke, the Treasury of Judas: 1610, C. L., Wouvermans, a charming halt of ladies and gentlemen at a country inn, first-rate: 1615, D. Teniers.

Now descend to the new Flemish saloons on the ground floor. The *bajada* is hung with second-rate miscellaneous pictures. 1620, L. Giordano, a feeble imitation of the Murillo urchins at play: 1623, P. de Cortona, Gladiators, large in size and small in merit; this master, born at the end of real art, was the anticipation of the Mengs and West school: 1625, V. Carducci, a huge head of diminutive intelligence; indeed, size of pictures seems to have been selected here in opposition to quality, *e. g.* 1636, Virtues, &c., by Sⁿ· Bourdon, and 1641, a tremendous Beheading of St. John, with portraits of the period of Philip III.; to say nothing of 1642, a Noah's Ark, by Rosa de Tivoli: 1646 and 1647 are more interesting, as being portraits of Isabella and Ferdinand, copied from Antᵒ· Rincon.

Leaving these acres of painted canvas, we arrive at the new Flemish saloons, where observe, 1654, Rubens, Perseus delivering Andromeda. The armour is finely painted, but the lady is Flemish, flabby, and knock-kneed. 1662, Rubens, Ceres and Pomona: 1666, Rubens, Adam and Eve, finely painted from Titian for our Charles I.: 1670, Flora, a joint work of Rubens and J. Breughel: 1679, 1683, Both, Views of Tivoli: 1681, Rubens, Nymphs surprised by Satyrs, superb: 1685, Vandyke, Diana and Endymion, treated with more elegance than his master: 1686, Rubens, Nymphs and Satyrs; a magnificent picture, and one, like 1681, of those subjects in which he loved to revel, and which none ever painted better: 1689, C. L., Rubens, Orpheus and Eurydice: 1696, C. L., Rubens, the Milky Way, Juno in her Peacock-drawn Car suckling Hercules: 1699, a fine Portrait of a Knight of Santiago: 1704, Rubens, Judgment of Paris, sprawling, flabby, and inelegant: 1710, C. L., Rubens, the Graces, finely painted: 1714, 1717, 1719, all by Antᵒ· Moro, are some fine female portraits: 1716, Rubens, Diana and Calisto, superb colour: 1720, C. L., Rubens, Fortune gliding over the Waters: 1720, Vandyke, St. Francis in Ecstasy, fine: 1727, Rubens, the Infant Saviour with St. John: 1729, Snyders, Dead Game on a Kitchen Table: 1739, Snyders, a Goat suckling a Young Wolf: 1743, 1746, two large landskips, J. Breughel: 1745, 1753, Snyders, Fruit, Live Animals, and Dead Game: 1767, Both, a fine Sunset in a Mountain Scene, St. James baptizes the Eunuch: 1768, Porbus, portrait of Mary of Medicis: 1772, Vandyke, portrait of the Marquesa de Leganés: 1774, Both, a Sunrise, with Cowherds: 1778, Both, Garden at Frascati: 1782, Both, Rocky Scene, with Sᵃ· Rosalin of Palermo: 1784, the Companion with San Bruno: 1786, ditto with Sⁿ· Francisco, figures by P. de Laar: 1788, Swanevelt, 1620-1690, landskip, St. Paul Preaching: 1792, Antᵒ· Moro, full-length portrait of Maria, wife of Maximilian II.: 1803, ditto, Portrait of that Emperor when young: 1793, Swanevelt, a Sunset: 1794, Antᵒ· Moro, a fine portrait of one of the Daughters of Charles V.: 1799, Swanevelt, a fine Sunset: 1804, Antᵒ· Moro, Portrait of a Lady, richly dressed: 1826, Porbus, portrait of a Young Lady: 1827, Both, Landskip, with Cascade and Fishermen, figures by J. Miel.

In the time when Ferdinand VII. was king, certain saloons in this ground-floor were set apart for *La galeria reservada*. This was a sort of Magdalen or penitentiary, into which were banished all peccant pictures whose nudities might corrupt the purity of Madrid; here the Italian and Flemish Ledas, Danaes, and such like improper ladies, blushed unseen, all lumped together, like the naughty epigrams of Martial when collected into one appendix in well-intentioned editions: not that in this harem there was much really offensive, or what in colder climates, and among a less prudish and inflammable people, would have been hidden from public gaze. Again, nudity in art is offensive rather in disposition and intention, than in mere exhibition; thus the nakedness of Milton's Eve causes no shame. All the peccant pictures consigned to the shades below were the works o. foreigners, for, under the censure of the Inquisition, in Spain art took the veil and sculpture the cowl, content to dwell in decencies for ever: see our remarks p. 116. Thus, while much up-stairs was all drapery, more below was all flesh, colour, and sex, gods and goddesses without stays or boddices; here were selected the poetical, voluptuous dreams of mythology, instead of the ascetic legends of vulgar monks and cruel familiars. Several of these paintings, especially those by Rubens, have been emancipated since Ferdinand's death, when freedom was the order of the day; and, indeed, many of the flabby females of Rubens, like drunken Helots, are better calculated to inspire disgust than passion. Among the best by other masters are (see numbers painted on them) 72, 75, by Albert Durer, painted in 1507, Adam and Eve, thin figures, and larger than life: Adonis going to the Chase: Venus and Cupid, A. Carracci, very fine: a clear and transparent Judgment of Paris, by Albano: a group of eight Females drawing Water, Tintoretto, equal to Titian: 192, Poussin, a fine brown Bacchanalian subject: 53, Titian, Woman on Conch, with a Youth playing an Organ: 58, Titian, a Female amusing herself with a Dog; the flesh is wonderfully painted:

a Race of Atalanta, by Guido: 112, Potiphar and Joseph, very spirited: 51, Titian, Danae, a sketch, but a perfect gem, and when seen from a certain distance it is living flesh: Susanna and the Elders, Tintoretto: some copies from Correggio: Leda and the Swan. The picture, a Harper, has been painted over, especially the figure seated on his knee. An Adam and Eve, after Raphael, in chiaro oscuro: 107, a naked Female giving drink to an Eagle in a splendid landscape, like Rubens. These pictures should be particularly inquired after.

The gallery of sculpture is also down stairs, and is very inferior. Spain never possessed much good antique or modern marble sculpture (see our remarks, p. 107). Here again (see pp. 731-48) everything is incomplete, and the work of accident rather than design. There are no specimens of the Berruguetes, Celmas, Darphes, &c., the pupils, contemporaries, and rivals of the M. Angelos, Jean de Bolognas, and Cellinis of Italy, or of other illustrious Spaniards who breathed immortal life into marble, bronze, iron, and silver; there are none of the carved images, *pasos* (see 110), the *barro*, or terra cotta, and painted sculpture, in which Spain stands alone and unrivalled; no sample of that phalanx of mighty men, true *viri* and Barones, *e. g.* Alonzo Cano, Montanes, Juni, Hernandez, Becerra, Forment, &c. In truth, their great names and works are scarcely more unknown at Madrid than in London; they belong to other provinces, and must be sought for in their native localities, where they lie comparatively latitant, among the other lost treasures of this disunited country. It is true that here such sculpture was long held as sacred, from being the representations of the Deity; but the *progreso* has marched over many an altar, and stripped many a niche of its god. And since the lay and profane museums of Seville and Valladolid are stocked with the *sagradas imagenes* of a dethroned Pantheon, surely the capital ought to be able to

2 L

show at least one sample of each name, of which Spain may well be proud, and contain one proof that the chisel of her better days kept entire pace with her glorious pencil. Meanwhile hundreds of foreigners have sojourned in Madrid and departed, without dreaming even of the existence of such things or of those who produced them; and many are the leagues which we have ridden and the hours which we have spent in the search for these gems, which are now in some measure pointed out in our humble pages.

The best of what antique sculpture is here once belonged to Christina of Sweden, and was removed from San Ildefonso. Some of the cinque-cento bronzes and antique heads are good. Observe a small marble Flora, with modern head; a bronze cast of the Hermaphrodite, and some fine *pietre dure* tables; the two seated statues of Charles IV. and his wife Luisa are imbecility coupled with vice; a Castor and Pollux, delicately designed; Isabella, wife of Charles V., in elaborate costume,—it looks like an iron statue; a Grecian colossal head, full of manly beauty,—the original bronze must have been at least 12 feet high; a fine bronze of Charles V. in rich cinque-cento taste; an alabaster bust of Philip II.; a good female torso. But the grand objects of Madrilenian admiration are the works of Señores Sala and Alvarez, especially two figures in boots and pantaloons, called *El grupo de Zaragoza*: this appeals to national glory; and Alvarez, 1768-1826, is popular more from patriotical than artistical reasons, he having refused to make a bust of Buonaparte.

While on the subject of art, it may be as well to take the New Museum, which was opened to the public by Espartero, on the anniversary of the *Dos de Maio*, 1842. It is in the Cᵉ· de Atocha, and is called *Museo de la Trinidad*, because established in the suppressed convent of that name. The edifice, it is said, was designed by Philip II. himself, and was built by

Gaspar Ordoñez; it was first desecrated by the French, who placed here the library of the Escorial. This *Museo* is now in a state of transition, as many alterations and additions are contemplated. Here have been got together from the convents and galleries of Don Carlos and the Infante Sebastian some 1500 pictures, good and bad; for in Spain the finest things frequently disappear, being secured for themselves by the *empleados*, and then reported officially as "missing."

Among the best things, observe the series of pictures representing the sufferings of Carthusian monks, when persecuted by our Henry VIII., and painted by Carducho, for the convent of El Paular. The Miracle of Manna, by Herrera el Viejo; a fine portrait of a *Letrado* with Spectacles, and a *Concepcion*, by Spagnoletto; a Descent from the Cross, by D. Volterra; Misers, by Q. Matzis; some *Caprichos*, by Goya; a portrait of Melendez, by himself; the Abbot Socinas Administering the Sacrament to Sª· Maria Egypciaca, who lived 47 years alone and naked in the desert (see Ribad. i. 557), by Fʳᵒ· Camillo (obt. 1671): this was painted for the Capuchin convent of Alcalá de Henares, and is considered his best work. San Bernardo kneeling before the Virgin, Alonzo Cano; Charles II., by Carreño; a copy of the Transfiguration, by Julio Romano, from the Escorial: a fine picture, by Penni il Fattore; Woman taken in Adultery, Titian; Samson and the Lion; portrait of Archdeacon Albert, Rubens. Observe particularly *El Jubileo de Porciuncula*, a large picture, which *once* was by Murillo. As it is advantageously hung, it still is very striking; its history may be useful to those about to purchase "*undoubted originals*" in Spain (see also our remarks, p. 117). It formerly belonged to the *Capuchinos* at Seville, whose stupid monks exchanged it for some modern daubs to fill their cloisters, with one Bejarano, a bungling picture-restorer. Although much injured from exposure to sun and air, the surface was then pure; Bejarano began by painting it all over, and then offered it to Mr. Williams for £120. The gem being declined by this first-rate connoisseur, it was purchased by Joaquin Cortes (director of the Seville Academy) for Madrazo, for £180 on speculation, who worked much on it himself, and then handed it over to Señor Bueno, one of the most daring of his familiars. Finally, £2000 was asked for the picture, which eventually was bought by the Infante Don Sebastian for £900. Now, except the outline, scarcely one touch is by Murillo. These facts were stated to us by Bejarano, Cortes, and Mr. Williams.

Few Franciscan convents were without their *Porciuncula*, which alludes to their grand jubilee, held every August 1, when all penitents who visited any Franciscan convent, were *ipso facto* whitewashed of all previous sins; hence the jubilee was called "*toties quoties*," for it was an annual benefit. It arose thus:—When St. Francis retired to a cave in the Monte Alverno, five miles from Assisi, he whipped himself all the winter with thorns, and was then visited by the Virgin and Saviour, who brought him red and white roses, which had bloomed from his rods, and granted such an immunity to the spot, that "if a man had killed all the other men in the world, by only entering this grotto he would come out as pure as a newly-baptized infant." Now as in Italy men are largely stabbed, this cave was prodigiously frequented by the perpetrators; soon the revenue derived from their offerings excited the Spanish Franciscans, whose flocks can stab a little, and they induced the Pontiff to concede to each of their convents its imaginary cave, in which the same benefits could be obtained by all who offered pious donations. Accordingly in their grotto chapel a painting of the visit of the Virgin to St. Francis explained the legend to those who could not read.

Among other masters observe the masterpiece of *El Greco.* His name was Domenico Theotocupuli: a Greek by birth, he settled at Toledo about 1577, where he died in 1625. He imitated Titian and Tintoretto, but was very unequal; thus what he did *well*, was excellent, while what he did *ill*, was worse than any body else. He was often more lengthy and extravagant than Fuseli, and as leaden as cholera morbus. He was also a sculptor and an architect. This picture, which shows how well he could paint when he chose, represents the burial of the Conde de Orgaz in 1312. The deceased had repaired a church; thereupon St. Stephen and St. Augustine came from heaven as special undertakers, pour encourager les autres Condes. The black and gold armour is equal to Titian, and the heads of the bystanders, the red brocades and copes of the saints, are admirable : less good are the Virgin, Saviour, and heavenly groups, which are lanky in drawing, and coldly coloured. This grand picture was painted for the church of S⁰· Tomas at Toledo.

There are several good specimens of the Rizi, father and sons, especially of Francesco, who, like Luca Giordano, was one of those who gave the last blow to decaying art. There are others by Pantoja de la Cruz. The series of pictures of the life and passion of our Saviour, painted in 1550 by D. Correa, for the Bernardine monks of Valdeigle-sias, deserve particular notice. This artist studied in Florence. Among other precious things rescued from the infuriate mob are the carvings by Rafael de Leon, wrought in 1561-71, for the aforesaid Bernardines. This *Silla· del Coro*, with much other carving from San Felipe el Real and other suppressed convents, is now stowed away in the magazines of the new university, which is being arranged in what was the Noviciate of Jesuits, in an admirable situation on an eminence above the palace. The sculpture, meanwhile, is seen to great disadvantage; the subjects are the mysteries of the Passion, &c., which are carved in low relief; the ornaments are the usual cinque-cento mixture of the Christian and Pagan. The cariatides are in excellent taste.

Recommencing our walk at the old *Museo*, and continuing up the *Prado*, just beyond the *Museo* to the l. is the *Jardin Botanico*, which is fenced in by a fine iron railing; it was first founded in 1755, by Ferd. VI., and was removed from the Prado to its present site 'in 1781, by the Cᵉ· Florida Blanca. The Linnæan system was adopted, and the plants were scientifically arranged and classified by Cavanilles, the best of the few botanists Spain has ever produced (see our remarks, p. 148). It was full of curious specimens, and an oasis of Flora in the desert of the Castiles. The invaders converted this Eden into a wilderness, uprooting plant and shrub; brambles and thorns were their curse, as at Aranjuez, Abadia, and other gardens of recreation and instruction. When the Duke expelled the destroyers, the face of the earth was renewed, and Art and Nature revived. Now once more it is a charming spot; the garden is kept in excellent order, both in a botanical point of view and one of recreation and delight, and it becomes doubly so as contrasting, like Aranjuez, with the naked environs of Madrid.

Advancing to the Atocha gate, on the eminence Sⁿ· Blas, is the *Campo Santo* or cemetery, and *El Observatorio Astronomico*. The view over Madrid is good. The brick and granite edifice with dome and porticos was built for Charles III., by Juan Villanueva. To the S. is a Corinthian vestibule. The observatory is designed to imitate an Ionic temple. This building of science was entirely gutted by the invaders, who here mounted cannon instead of telescopes. According to their Brillat Savarin, that mortal who discovers a new dish, does more for the happiness of mankind than he who discovers a new star; a gastronomic aphorism which Murat, who had been a waiter in a restaurant, quite under-

stood and acted upon. Ferd. VII. only partially restored the ravages; for astronomy, the delight of the Arab, has never thriven among Spaniards, whose affections are set on things below—of the earth and earthy. Under the hill is the convent of *Atocha*, founded in 1523 for Dominicans, by Hurtado de Mendoza, confessor to Charles V. It was enriched by a succession of pious princes. The ceilings were painted by L. Giordano, and the chapels were filled with vessels of gold and silver. These were all stolen, and everything else desecrated and pillaged by the invaders; and Ferd. VII. on his return employed one Isidro Velazquez (neither a saint nor an artist) to rebuild it. The conventual portion has since been made a barrack.

In the chapel is the celebrated Virgin, the Palladium of Madrid, and especial protectress of the royal family, who always worshipped it every Sunday. Thus Ferd. VII., when he conspired against his parents, first bowed down before the image and craved its assistance. Again, when he was kidnapped by Savary, before starting for Bayonne he took the ribbon of the Immaculate Conception off his breast and hung it on hers. Again, after his restoration, the first thing he did on reaching Madrid was to kneel before it and thank it for having interfered and delivered him. So his ancestor Alonzo VI., in 1083, on the first reconquest of Madrid, laid his banner at her feet. Ferdinand has been laughed at by those who know nothing of Spain and Spaniards for having, during his captivity in France, embroidered for her a petticoat (which he did not do, although his uncle Antonio did). Yet the report came home to the bosom of all the Mariolatrous, who honoured a king the counterpart of themselves. So before this local tutelar his widow Christina bowed, March 23, 1844, previously to entering Madrid, after her return to Spain; not so, however, at Barcelona, where she prayed before Sᵃ· Eulalia, the patroness of that locality.

This Virgin in some degree supplants San Roque, the Spanish Esculapius. She is the Minerva medica, the Ἀθηνη ὑγιεια, who is relied upon by the faculty when the sovereign is dangerously ill, and physicians are in vain—which is peculiarly the case in Madrid. Thus Bassompière, in his dispatch, March 27, 1621, describes the illness of Philip III. : " Les médecins en désespèrent, depuis ce matin que l'on a commencé à user des *remèdes spirituels,* et faire transporter au palais *l'image* de N. D. de Athoche." The patient died three days after the image was called in, ubi incipit theologus desinet medicus.

Convents, indeed, may have been suppressed, but the cloistral spirit being based on the wants and wishes of a credulous southron people, is still deeply rooted in the corruptions of their very nature: still relics are paraded to bring rain and expel disease; still locusts thus are spirited away; still the peasant of Madrid brings his ass to be blessed on St. Anthony's Day.

This Palladium ranks as third in holiness of the myriads in Spain. It is only preceded by those of Zaragoza and Guadalupe. Volumes have been written on it and its miracles; consult, besides the sonnets of Lope de Vega, ' *La Patrona de Madrid,*' Fr⁰· de Pereda, Valladolid, 1604 ; '*Historia de la Santa Imagen,*' Juan de Marieta, Mad. 1604; Ditto, Juan Hurtado Mendoza, 8vo. Mad. 1604; Ditto, Geronimo Quintana, 4to. Mad. 1637.

Some Spanish prelates contend that it was made at Ephesus, in 470, during the Nestorian dispute, and that this " great Diana " was inscribed θεοτοκος, unde *Atocha.* Villafane states that it was either made or, at least, varnished by St. Luke, and that it was taken by Gregory the Great from Antioch, unde *Atocha.* Others are positive that St. Peter brought it with him to Spain; all, however, are quite certain that it was here in the time of the Goths, because it was visited here by Sⁿ· Ildefonso; and say that when the Moors in-

vaded the Castiles, one Garcia Ramirez concealed it so well that he could not find it again; whereupon it revealed itself in some *Baltico* or rye-grass ; or, according to others, in some *Atocha* or bass-weed, whence the name ; but see, on all this, Villafane, ' *Imagenes Aparecidas,*' p. 126.

Ramirez built a hermitage on the spot, and the Moors who endeavoured to prevent him were struck blind. Villafane devotes thirty-three pages to its miracles. It expelled a devil from a boy named Blas, p. 97 (? Gil) ; gave speech to a dumb beggar, who then distinctly said " *De me un cuarto* " (p. 102) ; it raised a cobbler's son from the dead (p. 103) ; it stopped a mason mid-air, who was falling from a roof (p. 111, &c.), but this was a very common miracle in Spain in those times (see Valencia, p. 448), as naturally would be the case, since where convents were being erected on every side, such accidents must constantly happen. The image is very black and old, but the petticoat is brilliant and new ; above and around the heavy altar are hung banners of Spanish victories; all around is a rag fair,—the clothes, crutches, and the votive tablets offered, as among the Pagans, by the cured sick for her daily miraculous intervention in their favour.

The other remarkable images which are worshipped at Madrid are the *Sⁿ· Cristo de la Lluvia,* the Rain Christ, in Sⁿ· Pedro, on its plaza ; the *S⁰· Cristo de la Fé,* in Sⁿ·Sebastian, C⁰·Atocha; the *S⁰· Cristo de las Injurias,* in Sⁿ· Millan, Plª· de la Cebada ; and the *Pasos* or holy images brought out at Easter in the streets, and kept in Sⁿ· Juan de Dios, Plª· de Anton Martin. Other *Pasos* are *N⁰· Sr. de los Azotes,* by Pedro Hermoso ; *N⁰· Sr. en el Sepulcro ; La Soledad,* by Becerra; and *S⁰· Tomas,* by Miguel Rubiales. The church of S⁰· Tomas is a grand *Favissa* or storehouse for wooden saints, sound and damaged (see p. 112).

Continuing our circuit of the city to the r., at the corner of the Cᵉ· de

Atocha, is the huge hospital called *El General*, founded in 1582 by Philip II. It was removed here in 1748 by Ferdinand VI. Like most other hospitals in Spain it is unfinished, for Spanish charity is domestic and dilatory, and what it gives is "nothing to nobody." The medical succour of this *General* somewhat resembles the co-operation of such a *General* as Lapeña, Venegas, &c.; but *Los socorros de España* come proverbially *o tarde o nunca*. The interior of this hospital corresponds with its unfinished exterior. Adjoining is *El Colegio de S*ⁿ: *Carlos*, founded in 1783 by Charles III. as a college of surgeons. Here also neither the building or its intention are quite accomplished. It has an anatomical museum, and some wax preparations chiefly relating to the obstetric art: these the rising Sangrados manipulate just as the nautical students at Seville do models of frigates. But here sailors and surgeons, in travails by sea and land, are taught by the church to call in St. Telmo, San Ramon Nonat, or the *Cinta* of Tortosa, to *deliver* them. Some remarks (see p. 173) have been made on the condition of Spanish hospitals and medical men. They are much deficient, with few exceptions, in all improved mechanical appliances, comforts, and modern discoveries, as is admitted and deplored by all sensible Spaniards. The sanative science does not progress in proportion to the destructive, for the *puñales* of Albacete are better made and more effective than the scalpels; but at no period were Spaniards careful even of their own lives, and much less of those of others, being a people of untender bowels. Familiarity with pain deadens the finer feelings of those employed even in our hospitals, for those who live by the dead have only an undertaker's sympathy for the living, and are as dull to the poetry of innocent health as Mr. Giblet is to a sportive house-fed lamb. Matters are not improved in Spain, where the wounds, blood, and death of the pastime bull-fight, the *muera* mob-

cries, and *pasarle por las armas*, Draco and Durango decrees, and practices of all in power, educate all sexes to indifference to blood, and the fatal knife-stab or surgeon's cut, as *Cosas de España* and things of course.

However, by way of compensation, the saving the *soul** has been made just as primary a consideration in Spain as the curing the *body* has been in England. Here charms and amulets represent our patent medicines; and the wonder is how any one in Great Britain can be condemned to death in this world, or how any one in the Peninsula can be doomed to perdition in the next; possibly the panaceas are in neither case quite specific. Be that as it may, how numerous and well appointed are the churches and convents here compared to the hospitals, how amply provided the *Relicarios* compared to the *Boticas* and anatomical museums; again, what a flock of holy practitioners come forth *after* a *Castellano rancio* has been stabbed, starved, or executed, not one of whom would have stirred a step for an army of his countrymen when alive; and what coppers are not now collected to pay masses to get his soul out of purgatory!

Beware, nevertheless, gentle Protestant reader, of dying in Spain, except in Cadiz or Malaga, where there is snug lying for heretics; and for your life avoid being even sick at Madrid, since if once handed over to the *Cirujanos latinos*, or to the *Cirujanos romancistas*, make thy last testament forthwith, as, if the judgment passed on their own doctors by Spaniards be true, Esculapius cannot save thee from the crows. This low state of medicine has, however, this good effect, that it makes all prudent invalids shun the faculty, and consequently

* The preamble of the law (*Recop.*, lib. iii., tit. xvi., ley 3) expressly states that " the chief object in cases of sickness is to cure the soul," and every physician who fails after his first visit to prescribe confession is liable to a fine of 10,000 maravedis.

many are rescued by the vis medicatrix Nature. Pass therefore, my dear countrymen, through the Peninsula without making the acquaintance of a single medical man, which is not likely if health be attended to, for in this land of anomalies the soldier who sabres takes the highest rank, and he who cures the lowest; here the M.D.s, whom the infallible Pope consults and the autocrat king obeys, are admitted only into the *sick* rooms of good company, which shuts on them the door of their saloons; but the excluded take their revenge on those who morally cut them, and Madrid is indeed *La Corte de la Muerte*, the court of death and *Pulmonia*. The *Descripcion* of the Escorial by Bermejo (p. 153) furnishes the surest evidence of this, in the premature decease of royalty, which may be expected to have the best advice and aid, both medical and theologico-therapeutical, that the capital can afford; but brief is the royal span, especially in the case of females and *infantes*, and the *result* is undeniable in these statistics of death; the cause lies between the climate and the doctor, who, as they aid the other, may fairly be left to settle the question of relative excellence between each other: see on the bills of mortality at Madrid, p. 723.

In Spain, as in the East, all who kill, soldiers excepted, are of low caste, the butcher torero and public executioner for example; the medical man is shunned, not only on this account, and because dangerous, like a rattlesnake, but from prejudices which the church, that abhors blood-shedding and dissection, has always encouraged against a rival profession, which, if well received, might come in for some share of the legacies and power-conferring secrets, obtained easily at deathbeds when mind and body are deprived of strength. Thus the universities, governed by ecclesiastics, persuaded the poor bigot Philip III. to pass a law (*Recop.*, lib. iii. tit. xvi., ley 9) prohibiting the study of any new system of

medicine, and *requiring* Galen, Hippocrates, and Avicena; they scouted the exact sciences and experimental philosophy, which, said they, made every medical man a Tiberius "circa Deos ac religiones negligentior quippe addictus mathematicæ" (Suet.inVit.69); and so they scared the timid Ferd.VII. in 1830, by telling him that the schools of medicine created materialists, heretics, and revolutionists; thereupon the beloved monarch shut up the lecture rooms forthwith (see p. 174). This low social position is very classical: the physicians of Rome, chiefly *liberti*, were only made citizens by Cæsar, who wished to *conciliate* these ministers of the Parcæ when the capital was wanting in population after extreme emigrations(Suet. in Vit.42): an act which may cut two ways; thus Adrian VI. (tutor to the Spanish Charles V.) approved of there being 500 physicians in the eternal city, because otherwise "the *multitude* of living beings would eat each other up." However, when his turn came to be diminished, the grateful people serenaded his surgeon as the "deliverer of the country."

In our days there was only one medical man admitted by the *sangre su* of Seville, when in rude and antiphlebotomical health; and every stranger was informed apologetically by the noble amphitrions that the M.D. was *de casa conocida*, or born of a good family; thus his social introduction was owing to personal, not professional qualifications. And while adventurers of every kind are betitled, the most prodigal dispenser of Spanish honours never dreams of making his doctor even a *titulado*, a rank somewhat equivalent to a pair de France : this aristocratical ban confined doctors much to each other s society, which, as they never take each other's physic, was neither unpleasant nor dangerous, for *entre lobos no se come*. At Seville the medical *tertulia* was held at *Campelos*, *Calle de S*ⁿ· *Pablo*, and a sable *junta* or consultation it was of birds of bad omen, who croaked over the general health with which the city was afflicted, praying, like Sangrado in 'Gil Blas,' that by the blessing of Providence much sickness might speedily ensue. The crowded or deserted state of this rookery was the surest evidence of the hygeian condition of the fair capital of Bætica, and one which we have often anxiously inspected, for whatever be the pleasantries of those in merry health, when sickness brings in the doctor all joking is at an end; then he is made much of even in Spain, from a choice of evils, and for fear of the confessor and undertaker.

Turning S. towards the gate *De los Embajadores*, we enter some bald Champs Elysées-like avenues, which are here grandiloquently called *Las Delicias*, for even heavenly delights are relative. Here is the *Casino* which the Madrid municipality gave to Isabel *La Portuguesa*, the second and best wife of Ferdinand VII. It is a pretty plaything, with pleasant gardens, hothouses, some statues, and a sort of Trianon, once nicely fitted up; the ceilings of the best rooms are painted by Vicente Lopez. This Casino is sometimes called *Las Vacas*, " the Cows," from her majesty's attempt to make butter here.

Three avenues now branch off from the circular plantation above the Casino : the two W. lead to the Manzanares, the Thames of the "only court," and termed by euphuists *Visconde de rios y Duque de Arroyos ;* but this is not the only *Duque* that has been miscreated on its banks : the paltry streamlet, although scarcely furnishing water for the washerwomen, has also fed the dry humour of Spanish wags and satirists from Quevedo, Gongora, and downwards for some centuries. It is entitled a river by courtesy, because it has bridges, which most running waters in Spain have not. The dilemma here has been whether to sell a bridge or buy water. These enormous *Puentes*, about which there is no mistake, are (as at Valencia) not

quite pontes asinorum, since they serve as viaducts across the dip, and sometimes the rain torrents descend from the Guadarrama in such a body, that even their gigantic piers are threatened by the inundations; however, the deluge soon passes away, spent in its own fury ; and whenever it rains, the stranger should run quickly down to see the river before it is gone. In summer the rivulet is scarcely so wide as its name is long, and they say the bed was once *watered* when Ferd. VII. passed it, to prevent his being annoyed by the dust. The dry-shod foot-passenger crosses without knowing it, as in Lucan (ix. 974) :—

" Inscius in sicco serpentem pulvere rivum
Transierat, qui Xanthus erat."

Gongora, besides sundry profane and scurvy jests, likened it to the rich man in flames calling for one drop of water. Tirso de Molina's epigram compares it to the *long vacations* in summer of universities :—

" Como Alcalá y Salamanca,
    Teneis y no suis Colegio,
Vacaciones in Verano
    Y curso solo en Invierno."

The water of this anatomy, which has the form of a river without the circulation, is enticed into holes by naiads, to whom are committed *Los paños menores* of Madrid—quos et venti subeunt et auræ. The lavation, especially under the royal palace, is garrulous and picturesque, for brightly do the parti-coloured garments glitter in the sun. There are also some baths in which the *Madrileños* in summer cool their parched bodies.

The Manzanares rises about 7 L. from Madrid, and enters the Jarama near *Vacia Madrid*. Down stream E. is the unfinished canal, projected in 1668 to connect Madrid with the Tagus, which was begun, as usual, eagerly, and, as usual, soon neglected, and only 2 L. are finished. The stagnant waters are a reservoir of fever ; thus becoming a curse, not a benefit, and adding to the insalubrity of sickly

Madrid : there are a few buildings, and also a chapel for pious bargemen who bring lime to the capital. There are four bridges over the Manzanares : one of wood at the extreme E. end crosses over to the hermitage of *S⁰·* *Isidro del Campo.* The grand pilgrimage (see p. 120) to this male patron of Madrid takes place on May 15, and is a truly curious scene; then all the population is poured forth, and considerable more jollification takes place than devotion, for music and the dance are largely indulged in by the votaries apparently of Bacchus and Venus. Here—and no traveller should fail going there—may be studied most of the costumes, songs, and dances of the provinces, as the natives settled at Madrid congregate in parties with true local spirit, each preserving their own peculiarities. (See for details, p. 190.) It is a truly Spanish and charming scene, far surpassing our Easter Monday at Greenwich, not merely in fun but piety, for this is a religious pilgrimage; thus their wise church renders her acts of devotion sources of enjoyment to its believers, and their flocks, wedded to festivals which suit themselves and their climate, will long prefer them to the dreary Sundays of our purer Protestantism, which has no machinery for canonizing white bait.

Nota bene that this S⁰· Isidro is a very different saint from S⁰· Isidoro, although often confounded by foreigners and heretics. The latter was the learned encyclopædist of the Goths (see Leon, p. 609); the former (like St. Cuthbert, the tutelar of Durham) was an ignorant labourer: hence he is called *El Labrador;* but, as Southey says, "he was a good honest one, and indebted for his apotheosis to the fables which others have invented for him, and not to any roguery of his own." See also the droll ballads of the Laureate (Letters i. 191). Isidro, instead of minding his furrows, passed his time in a siestose consideration of the "egregious doctor" his namesake, he having been born on the very

day that S⁰· Isidoro's body was removed to Leon. Angels during his ecstasies came down from heaven and did his work; hence, say the chroniclers, the still existing miraculous *fertility* of the environs of Madrid. If there were but trees and gardens, S⁰· Isidro would serve for a Pan or Priapus.

Meanwhile the peasants, who plough and pray as those in the Georgics, call upon him to drag their cartwheels out of the ruts, for he is their Hercules Rusticus, and they love to lean in the hour of need and difficulty on any divine or human help rather than on, as the Duke said, "the simple performance every man of his duty." Hence, among a people whose idle day is rounded by a sleep, this lazy advocate of the do-nothing system is truly popular, and he is the Madrilenian St. Monday. Ever since Philip III. was cured of an illness by touching his body, the court *Sangrados,* having great reliance on spiritual remedies, got the Pope to canonize this Isidro, while Lope de Vega wrote a poem in ten cantos, as full of his praise as of scandal against Queen Elizabeth, our *busy* Bess. The Spanish clergy quote S⁰· Isidro as their "*carrière ouverte aux talens.*" Behold, say they, a lowly labourer rising to be the tutelar and patron even of Madrid, *donde está la nobleza del mundo:* but consult Ribadeneyra (ii. 81), from whose pages we extract.

S⁰· Isidro was the son of *Ibn* (the son) de Vargas; he married Maria de la Cabeza, a hind's daughter, and also a saint, but this breed of rustics has since become scarce near Madrid. His miracles naturally were agricultural; thus he found out water-springs, and raised not only corn with, but without ploughing, and horses from the dead (p. 84). The wolves could not eat his oxen (p. 82), which to those accustomed to the beef of Old England will appear no wonder when they see what Spanish Vaca is—*a carne deperro, diente de lobo.* San Isidro, however, managed to eat his own meat, living on such a *puchero* that the angels of

2 L 3

heaven came down to share his hospitality; whereupon his *olla* pot, which he had cleaned out, miraculously replenished itself (p. 83). He died, according to Ribadeneyra, Nov. 28, 973. Gil Davila (p. 21), however, says, on April 1, 1070, a somewhat inauspicious date. When his tomb was opened, the usual miraculous fragrance issued forth, which certainly is a miracle in Spanish rustics, dead or alive (see p. 576). He appeared to Alonzo VIII., in the form of the peasant who showed the path at *Navas de Tolosa* (p. 306). When Isabel *la Catolica*, having been cured by his intervention, went to pray at his tomb, one of her maids of honour, kissing his feet, bit off his second toe as a relic, and forthwith lost her powers of speech; but on ejecting the mouthful recovered her pristine fluency (p. 89). The miracles he every day works are so astounding, that it is a miracle how anybody can ever die at all at Madrid, which they do, *como chinches*. The body of this ploughboy was often placed on the sick-bed of the king, when Sir Henry Halford would have prescribed a warming-pan or a blister; but the natural and medicinal history of relics is too authentic and too clearly understood to require being enlarged on.

Meanwhile as the pagans worshipped St. Triptolemus, because he *invented* the plough, so the Madrilenians adore Sⁿ· Isidro because he *superseded* its use: compare the holy father Matias and his self-acting miraculous cuisine at Salamanca (p. 582). But the standing *miracle* is, how, with these supernatural assistances, the agriculture near Madrid and the cookery at Salamanca should in reality be just the worst in the world. The pagans, instead of Sⁿ· Isidro, had their St. Robigo, and celebrated his *fiesta* on the 7th calends of May, not on the 15th, as at present, but spring time was *the* necessary season, and a few days sooner or later made no difference. The tutelar was fêted, and his priests were

paid, in order to secure success to the corn and drive away blight, the *anublo*: aspera Rubigo parcas cerealibus herbis (Ovid, ' Fast.' iv. 911; and see Pliny, ' N. H.' xviii. 29). The dancings in honour of the wife of Sⁿ· Isidro are the exact ambervalia of the Georgics (i. 343). And, as now at Madrid, these holidays were celebrated *outside* the city, on the Via Nomentana, for the convenience of the *Pagani* or villagers.

Those who wish to know Sⁿ· Isidro's authentic history, as authorised by the church, are referred, in addition to Ribadeneyra and Davila, to his biography by Alonzo de Villegas, 8vo. Mad. 1592; ditto, Jaime Bleda, 4to. Mad. 1622; ditto, Reginal Poc, Perpiñan, 1627; ditto, Gregorio Argaiz, fol. Mad. 1671.

Returning to the Manzanares, pass, without crossing it, the bridge and viaduct *El Puente de Toledo*, which was built in 1735 by Philip V., and is 385 ft. long by 36 wide. Nothing can be in more vile taste, although Sⁿ· Isidro and his wife adorn the scene, looking out for water. The city gate above was begun in 1813 by the Madrid municipality, and finished in 1827 by Antº· Aguado, in honour of Ferd. VII.'s return and the extermination of the French usurpation by the Spanish armies. Here the public executions take place, and generally by the *garrote*, a sort of strangling machine based on the Oriental bowstring; as a more agreeable spectacle, the artist and lover of picturesque peasantry should visit this gate early in the morning, and sketch the groups of market-people, their wares and beasts, who congregate around, awaiting the ceremony of the *derecho de Puertas* (see p. 23). Their indignation at the insolent *Resguardos* gives animation to their eyes and gestures. This *Octroi* was introduced by the French and retained by the government for the sake of the revenue, just as it is at Cairo; and in nothing do the Spaniards and Arabs agree better than in execrating this fiscal scourge of the foreigner.

The next bridge, that *de Segovia,* was designed for Philip II. by Herrera, and is also a huge viaduct, being 695 ft. long, 31 wide. The accumulated sand, which the careless natives never remove, has injured its fine proportions, as at the monuments of Egypt. The truly royal palace rising above now sparkles like white marble on the clear blue sky. The declivities below are left in a most unseemly neglect; they might easily be, and ought to be terraced into hanging gardens, which the slope would suggest to any people except the worshippers of Sⁿ· Isidro, who expect that angels will come and do the work, like Aladdin's slaves of the lamp.

To the l. are the unhealthy enclosures of the *Casa del Campo.* This apology for a country-house was a shooting-box of Charles III., and is connected with the palace by a bridge and a tunnel, which is not quite on the scale of that under the Thames. The house and gardens were ravaged by the invaders, but they were restored by Christina, who here formed a model farm and other rural schemes, which perished, as usual, with the hand that upheld them. The gardens are well supplied with water, and there is a beautiful Italian marble fountain, and a superb equestrian bronze of Philip III. cast by Juan de Bologna, from a drawing made by Pantoja. It was the companion to that of Henry IV. at Paris, which was destroyed at the Revolution. Left unfinished by J. de Bologna, it was completed by Pedro Tacca, whose brother-in-law, Antº· Guidi, brought it to Madrid in 1616. In the *Casa del Campo* horse and hurdle races are given; where the queen's plate is ridden for by the descendants of the iron Alvas and Ponces de Leon, equipped like jockeys: such is the progress of the Anglo-civilization of Castile; but the races and riding are still somewhat inferior to Epsom.

Crossing the Manzanares are the avenues and the *La Florida,* which continue on the road to the Escorial,

and were a very fashionable promenade in the reign of Charles III. Those who like to walk out to the Hermitage of *San Antonio* will see some of his miracles painted by Goya, and some tawdry frescos by the feeble Maella. Another walk ascends to the r. to *Sⁿ· Bernardino,* and hence to the gate of Fuencarral, outside of which is a cemetery. The planted avenues are carried round the shabby walls to the *Prado* by the gates Sⁿ· Fernando, Sª· Barbara, and Los Recoletos, where a fountain, *La Castellana,* has been raised in commemoration of the *Jura* to Isabel II. The space has been laid out in walks and gardens, and a new *Paseo* is in contemplation, to be called *de la Independencia,* which is to occupy the site of the convent of *Recoletos.*

The better plan to avoid this dull walk is to turn out of the Florida at the gate Sⁿ· Vicente, and ascend to the palace. Entering at the *Portillo,* to the l. is the huge *Seminario de Nobles,* built in 1725 by Philip V., in the fond hope that his nobility might be taught something, despairing in which his countrymen invaders converted the school into a barrack. Close by is the fine residence of the Alva family, built by Rodriguez, but injured by frequent fires, and especially by that in 1841. Here was the Correggio Venus teaching Cupid, which once belonged to our Charles I. " Collected " by Murat, it was sold by his widow to Lord Londonderry, and now again has found its way back to London. Among the best pictures which we saw there was a portrait of Columbus, in crimson flowered with gold: Mary Queen of Scots: the great Alva, by Titian: a landskip and battle of Amazons, Rubens: a fine boy in red velvet, Velazquez: a splendid S. Rosa: a Last Supper: and Cupid and a Lion, Titian: Moncada on horseback, Vandyke, very fine; it is engraved by R. Morghen: a Storm, Beerstraten, 1649: Herodias with the head of St. John, Guido: and a noble Florentine cartoon of the Virgin and Child. The university is placed in the C⁴· *Ancha de San Bernardo;* here are some splendid carvings (see p. 771).

Thence to the royal palace, which certainly is one of the most magnificent in the world. It has two open *plazas:* that to the E., *del Oriente,* is a sort of Place de Carousel, for here the invaders demolished eighty-seven houses, and left the space a desert of dust and glare, and impassable in the dog-days. Ferd. VII. removed the ruins, had the locality levelled, and commenced a magnificent theatre and colonnade. The site, indeed, was very convenient for the king, being close to his residence; but is exactly the contrary for the citizens in general, as the place is in a distant angle of the town.

The *Plaza* has rather a French look. It is contemplated, when everything is finished, to remove the fine bronze from the *Retiro,* which will shame the other poor statues of kings and queens. It is also proposed to finish the theatre and make a grand garden, with flowers, fountains, seats, &c., which indeed will be a blessed change; meanwhile, in one of the saloons, *Los Señores diputados* hold their sittings and perform their farce of a pseudo-parliament. The locale is also more appropriately used for public balls and carnival masquerades, where trick and false character are the order of the day, and honestly avowed.

For what a Spanish Cortes was, see p. 214; nor is Spain at present much more fitted for what we think a deliberative assembly than it was then, either as regards materials for a constituency or members. The *Vocales* generally neglect the plain performance of their legislative duties to talk the fluent bombast and nonsense that they love so well. Their debates are "puddles in storms, the ocean into tempest tossed, to waft a feather or to drown a fly." More real business is done, and in a more workmanlike manner, at an English country-parish vestry in a week, than here in a whole session. But Spaniards, in their *collec-*

tive corporate juntas, rarely exhibit the common sense, courage, honourable feelings, or even good manners, in which, as *individuals,* they most certainly are very remarkable (see p. 604). The Spaniard taken singly, and by himself, is indeed a fine fellow, but place him under chiefs, in whom he has no confidence, and whose pre-eminence wounds his self-love, since he holds them cheap as compared to himself—mix him up with colleagues whom he suspects and distrusts, who appropriate to themselves the funds which ought to supply sinews of action in peace or war, then he considers the game as lost and despajrs; and from knowing that all the rest will only consult their *private* interest, he e'en goes with the stream. Hencè there is little union, except to weaken; few dream of making a combined effort for the *public* good; the very idea would be scouted with *carcajadas* of derisive laughter.

Political society cannot be kept together without mutual *concession,* which exists not in the harsh independent character of the Spaniard. Again, parliamentary parties, so necessary for the well-working of the representative system, are here by no means well organized. There is no regular "her majesty's opposition;" everything is personal and accidental. With us a leader of opposition is a minister "in posse;" with them, as in the East, the premier fungus is a thing of the time being only: the rocket shoots up, and falls seldom to rise again. As real power and superiority is derived from office and employment alone, the moment the accidental temporary superiority is withdrawn the holder relapses into his former nothingness, and is forgotten the next week, or *contado con los muertos,* as much as if he were really dead. Rare, rare indeed, is a second appearance on the official stage. And this must long continue to be the condition of ill-fated Spain, until some master-mind appears, who can wield these discordant elements. The noble

PEOPLE of Spain have, indeed, legs, arms, and hearts, but a head is wanting, and then the members disagree, as in the old fable, or like the "trees" in that truly Spanish and Oriental parable, Judges ix. The only abstract Spanish idea of government or sovereignty, either in church or state, as in the East, is that it be despotic (see Durango); even the Inquisition was not really unpopular, and whenever Ferd. VII. committed any extra atrocious act his subjects exclaimed with rapture, *Carajo! es mucho Rey!*" he is indeed a king, ay, every inch! These spoke the whole nation, for all Spaniards felt that, in his place, they would have done exactly the same, and therefore sympathizingly admired. Power expressed by violence flattered their pride, as each atom beheld his own personal greatness represented and reflected in that of his monarch. Despotism, accordingly, if it can only be rendered *enlightened*, or *ilustrado*, as in Prussia, will long prove a real blessing to Spaniards, until their soil is better trenched and prepared for the tree, or rather sapling, of Liberty, for it cannot be transplanted when full grown. Therefore the nation, wearied with civil wars, and a succession of theories and rulers one worse than another, has become apathetic as the burden mule, and turns towards the throne as a refuge from petty tyrants. Thus the governmental incapacity of the Cortes made the *people* rush headlong into the asylum of despotism and Ferdinand (see Daroca); and thus has Narvaez (whose turn too will come) upset so easily the constitution of La Granja.

What is now wanting for Madrid, as indeed for the whole Peninsula, is PEACE and a *strong fixed government*. It is to this craving, this necessity of repose after the excitement of civil wars, and rival parties, that must be attributed the apathy of the shrewd nation, and the well-advised indifference with which it allowed its new charters to be rent by the sword. The country at large was disgusted with the unprincipled adventurers and miserable mediocrity which mocking fortune had floated up from the dregs to the surface. It despised and mistrusted its worthless rulers, and fled from the losing game of *public* politics to *private* and individual interests. Just now the Cortes and constitution are mere words. The elections are a mockery; the *jefes politicos* and their *escribanos* tamper with the registries, intimidate the voters; while opposition candidates are put out of the way, and those who are elected are terrorised by the sword: and the "House" is only fit to commit suicide, and vote away the last securities of its own and the nation's liberty. This, indeed, according to our notions, seems to be adding injury to insult, when the forms and safeguards of free men are prostituted, and made the instruments of lawless autocrats; but true liberty is no child of such revolutions, whose euthanasia is military despotism.

Such is the inevitable consequence of adopting the usages of totally distinct nations, for Spain is little fitted for an English parliament, which has grown slowly with our growth, and in a land of order, peace, and liberty civil and religious. We might as well adopt their bull-fight, as they our House of Commons, much less one of those *paper* constitutions, *plus raisonnées que raisonnables*, which have been imported from the manufactories of Siéyes, Bentham, and other liberty-mongers: it is true such articles pay no duty, or what is the same thing, an ad valorem one.

The royal palace is enormous, and as in that of Aladdin in the East, and in some others in this cognate land, there is more than one window left unfinished; thus it is the fit residence of the sovereign of a people of prouder conception than performance. The square port-holes of the *entresuelos* or *entresols*, those *mezzanini* of Borromini, the corruptor of architecture, and the irregular unsightly chimney-pots mar the elevation, and the untidy, unfinished character of every thing is unsatisfactory; were it not that here is the premier's office, that is the workshop of jobs and *empeños*, the palace would have the deserted, wo-begone, unroyal look of our uninhabited St. James, but the throng of *pretendientes*, *empleados*, *cesantes*, *ojaleteros*, *y demas pordioseros*, gives life to the scene. It occupies the sight of the original Alcazar of the Moors, which Enrique IV. made his residence. This was burnt down on Christmas-eve, 1734, when Philip V. determined to rebuild a rival to Versailles, and Felipe de Jubara, a Sicilian, prepared the model (see p. 743). He judiciously wished to change the site for the Sᵃ· Bernardino hill, but Elizabeth Farnese, the queen, whose ambition it was to advance her children, grudged the expense, and combined *en camarilla* with the minister Patiño; and so many difficulties were made that Jubara died of hope deferred, as most foreigners do who serve Spain. Philip then directed Juan Bᵃ· Sachetti, of Turin, to prepare a smaller and less expensive plan, which, the queen not objecting, was adopted, April 7, 1737.

It is a square of 470 ft. each way, by 100 ft. high. The wings and the hanging gardens are unfinished. The rustic base is of granite; the window work of white stone of Colmenar, which in the bright sun glitters as a fair palace of marble. Visit it also at moonlight; then, in the silent death-like loneliness, the pile looms like a ghostly thing of the enchanter, or a castle of snow. On the heavy balustrade above stood a series of heavier royal statues, which were taken down and sent to Toledo and Burgos, or buried in the vaults, from whence some have been taken out to *adorn* the *Plaza del Oriente*. The principal entrance is to the S., and disappoints; it leads into a huge *patio* of some 240 ft. square, with a glazed upper gallery like a manufactory. Between the arches are several bad statues by de Castro Olivieri, &c., of Spanish Roman emperors — Trajan,

Adrian, Honorius, and Theodosius. The bewigged smirking statue of the baboon-faced Charles III. is no better; it disfigures the grand staircase, which is noble in design and easy of ascent. It is said, when Buonaparte ascended these steps, that he told his brother Joseph, "Vous seriez mieux logé que moi." He laid his hand on one of the white marble lions, exclaiming, "Je la tiens enfin, cette Espagne, si désirée!" So spake Cæsar on landing, "Teneo te, Africa!" But the French, like the Romans, at last discovered that Spain is a morsel easier to be swallowed than digested: "Plus est provinciam retinere quam facere" (Florus, ii. 17. 8). The Duke shortened poor Pepe's tenure: he entered Madrid in triumph after the victory of Salamanca, on the 12th of August, 1812, and was lodged in this palace. "It is impossible," wrote he from it, "to describe the joy manifested by the inhabitants upon our arrival, or their detestation of the French yoke." That yoke, removed by a stranger, was replaced by a native Spaniard, by Ballesteros!

Nothing is more tiresome than a palace, a house of velvet, tapestry, gold and bore: like those who live in it, il n'est pas amusable. Yet this is a truly royal one, in which the most precious marbles are used prodigally in floorings and doorways; the glass chandeliers and the enormous mirrors were cast at San Ildefonso; the ceilings are painted in fresco. Here formerly hung those pictures which Ferd. VII. ejected for French papers. The vaults and store-rooms were filled with fine old furniture; but since his death a gigantic pillage has gone on as regards jewels and every thing of portable value. The chief saloon is called *de los Embajadores*, or the Reception or Throne room, and its decorations are indeed most princely; the crystal chandeliers, colossal looking-glasses, marble tables, crimson velvet and gold, &c., will enchant lovers of fine furniture; here the kings of the Spains when alive received on grand occasions, and when dead are laid out in state. There we beheld the "beloved" Ferd. VII., his face, hideous in life, now purple like a ripe fig, dead and dressed in full uniform, with a cocked hat on his head, and his stick in his hand.

The ceiling is painted by Tiepolo, with the "Majesty of Spain," the virtues of the kings, and the costumes of the provinces, which last at least have some semblance to truth. Mellado (p. 36) lauds these *sublimes rasgos, de sublimes ingenios;* certainly, being on ceilings, they are so far *sublime,* but it is only the sublime of mediocrity, and the genii, or geniuses, were Conrado, Mengs, Maella, Bayeu, Velazquez (no relation to *the* man), de Castro, and Lopez. The most admired ceilings are the apotheosis of Trajan and the Aurora, in the 21st room, by Mengs, whose works are thus described by Wilkie (i. 525), when so anxious to introduce fresco painting into England: "They have given the form and tone, for good or for evil, to modern art. Correggio, with the antique sculpture, and such notions of paintings as may be derived from the relics at Portici, seem the grand models of Mengs' imitation; but Mengs wants both the enthusiasm and the hues of colour of that great painter. The freedom and expression of painting suffer where it reminds one of the antique, even if correctness and purity of form should be attained : this excellence is seen in detached parts and episodes, never in the grandeur of the whole style of composition and ruling sentiment. Mengs has tried to unite, and perhaps it is impossible to unite, the beauties of sculpture and painting, to compound a style of the imaginary excellences of the great pencil, with the real and visible labours of Raphael and Correggio. In examining these frescos, I was less struck with the instances of imitation of what had gone before him, than of those wherein he himself had been imitated by his successors, by artists who

perhaps would shrink from owning it. Not only do we find him in the works of his followers in Italy, but his principles have spread into other countries : in one case weakened by the softness of Angelica Kaufman, and in the other outraged by the severity of David. Even West seems to have been an unconscious imitator of Mengs: and I am not sure that the youthful mind of Reynolds has not been indebted to him for some qualities that he possesses in common with this once great master; having, however, this rare gift, that whatever he borrowed he could improve. It is fresco that Mengs had the merit to revive; but oil-painting he could not revive from the leaden drowsiness in which it lay. Not being a colourist, his works have fallen and paid the penalty of his deficiency; but the system which he reintroduced survives, while he is forgotten. If Mengs has not formed, he has at least given an impulse to the painting of our times; and his success has, I fear, occasioned the opacity and chalkiness which prevail in modern art." There is a 4to. description of these frescos by F^{r.o.} Fabre, Mad., 1829.

The views from the windows which overlook the river are true landskips of the Castilian school; the slopes under the royal eye, are left in ragged mangy deformity ; how the magic wand of the Moor would have clothed the waste with flowers and verdure, and raised hanging gardens and fountains, in imitation of those on the declivity of the Alhambra, which although artificial rival nature herself! Now all is abandoned to filth, rubbish, neglect, and the calcining sun. Below trickles the Manzanares with its great name and scanty stream ; beyond stretch the ragged woods of the *Casa del Campo,* and then the hopeless tawny steppes, bounded by the icy Guadarrama, whose sharp outline cuts the bright sky, and whose snowy heights freeze the gale; all is harsh and torrid, colourless and blanched, but yet not devoid of a certain savage grandeur. A childish Chinese room by one Gasparin is here much admired. The royal chapel lies to the N., and is on a level with the state rooms. Although small, it is splendid. The order is Corinthian, the marbles rich, the stucco gilt. The ceiling was painted by Giaquinto. Here figure S^n. Isidro, the tutelar of Madrid, and Santiago, the patron of Spain. The foundations only of a larger chapel are laid. The traveller should visit the site of the night attack of Oct. 7, 1841, when the Gallo-Christinos endeavoured to carry off the young queen. The plot, planned at Paris, was headed by Pezuela, and Concha the brother-in-law of Espartero, who, when his scheme failed, ran away and hid himself under one of the bridges of the Manzanares, while Diego Leon, a brave sabreur and his tool, was taken and executed. The regent departed from Spanish maxims by pardoning the other criminals, who repaid this unusual mercy by conspiring to his ruin; nay, Concha hunted his benefactor even to the bay of Cadiz, and, had he caught him, assuredly would have put him to death. To complete these *cosas de España*, the regiment *de la Princesa* fired all night at the handful of *Alabarderos*, both sides exhibiting such *prodigios de valor* and bad shooting that four men were killed and wounded between them. Col. Dulce, who beat back the conspirators, was turned out of his place by Christina, and whilst disgracing the defender of her daughter, she smiled on the former bitterest foes and libellers of herself and Señor Muñoz: " C'est une belle alliance, celle de la cour avec la canaille," but " misery makes even royalty acquainted with strange bedfellows." See Widdrington (i. 59), who gives authentic details of this most oriental *transaccion*.

Now visit *La Real Cochera* and *Las Caballerizas*. These enormous coach-houses and stables lie to the N.E.: the latter, once filled with the mules and horses which conveyed the theriomaniac kings to their daily shootings, are now rather empty. The carriages are very amusing ; they are of all forms and ages, from the cumbrous state-coach to the Cupid-bedizened car, from the *coche de colleras* to the *equipage de Paris* and the hearse. The coach-house itself is gigantic, and some of the vehicles are fit for a museum. The hearse made by the Blue-beard Ferd. VII. for his royal wives was found when he died to be too small for his larger coffin, and nothing, as usual, being ready, a *coche de colleras* was taken. The front windows were removed, out of which stuck the foot of the coffin, and a *mayoral* and *zagal*, dressed in the common *calesero* costume, drove it, swearing as usual (see p. 35). They tied up their cloaks and bundles to the holders behind, and so jogged on, smoking their *papelitos*, to the Escorial, the empty hearse following them, for the sake of company and propriety. Monks on sorry hacks led the way, then followed a few ill-appointed soldiers, and grandees, (the Duque de Alagon, as first pimp to his late majesty, riding close to the coffin,) whose nether man was clothed in undertaker black trousers, and upper man in embroidered coats, like Lord Mayor's footmen. Thus we beheld the beloved Ferdinand conveyed to his last home. But public ceremonials in Spain are positively shabby compared to those in England or France, and so it always was (Justin. xliv. 2). So Philip III. was buried with *fort petite cérémonie*, and his son's procession was made " en grande magnificence pour Madrid, mais qui n'esgale point les moindres de celles que l'on fait en France :" as wrote Bassompière to Henri IV., May 16, 1621; now matters are changed for the worse.

The *Biblioteca Nacional* is placed at the corner of the C^e. de la Bola, on the Plaza del Oriente, in a house which once belonged to the Alcañices family, but the handsome fittings-up of walnut and gilt capitals belonged to Godoy. It contains about 200,000 volumes, and is open from 10 until 3. It is very well conducted, and the cool and quiet is truly refreshing after the dust and glare of the Plaza. It is rich in Spanish literature, especially theology and topography, and possesses some cameos, antiquities, and curious MSS. This library has been much increased, *numerically*, since the suppression of convents; the accession, however, has been rather in works of supererogation, ancient books, and monkish lore, and good modern books are here, as in other Spanish libraries, the things needful; but want of funds, as usual, is the cause. This library is well managed, and the *Empleados* are civil and attentive. In *La Sala del Trono* are the coins and medals, which exceed 150,000 in number, and contain very curious specimens of the early Spanish, Gothic, and Moorish mints.

Numismatic science is of Spanish origin, as Alonzo V. of Arragon, in the 15th century, was the first collector for pleasure, and Antonio Agustin, arch. of Tarragona, the first for science, and his work '*Dialogos de las Medallas*,' Tarragona, 1587, has been the model of most others published since. As next to food, coin has long been the thing wanting in Spain, possibly this peculiar rarity and value induced the natives to estimate the currencies of antiquity. Coined money did not exist among the aboriginal Iberians, but was first introduced by the Carthaginians to pay their mercenary Celtiberian troops, who would not take the "leather bank notes" of Carthage, as they distrusted, like their descendants, any payments except those made actually in cash; Murcia and Bætica were mints to the Carthaginians, as Sicily had been before, and hence the quantity of coin still found in these provinces. Under the Romans more than 100 cities between Cadiz and Tarragona had the privilege of a mint, but no gold was ever struck, as the people, like the Germans (Tacit. de Ger. 5), were too poor to require that precious metal: to coin even silver was a prerogative of the Roman governors, and the

subjected Iberians only struck copper. Silver was current in bars as well as coin, and this distinction always occurs in the accounts of the enormous plunder sent to Rome, which was remitted in silver either *επισημον* or *ασημαντον* (App. ' B. H.' 448), terms that the Romans rendered by either *Argentum infectum*, unwrought bars or ingots, or *Bigatum*, coins stamped with the *Biga* or two-horsed chariot. The generic phrase for Spanish coined money was *Argentum oscense, Signatum oscense* (see Livy, xxxiv. 46 ; xl. 43, et passim). This epithet has by some been interpreted as referring to the particular mint of *Osca*, but Florez, '*M.*' ii. 520, justly pointed out the impossibility of one place supplying such enormous quantities, and suggested the true meaning of *Oscensis* to be Oscan or Spanish, the word being a corruption of *Eus-cara*, the national name, whence the still existing term *Basque*. The Iberians broke off pieces of silver bars (Strabo iii. 233), which represented the value of the weight of the fragment; this custom long prevailed among modern Spaniards, who term such fractions *Macuquinos*, and they are still current.

The coins struck by the Romans were frequently bilingual ; having legends in the Latin and *Iberian* character, just as the paper money in Austria is inscribed in the idioms of those among whom it is to be current. The latter character, from its arrow-headed cuneiform letters, has been supposed to be the old Punic, and many Spaniards have attempted to decypher and interpret the writing, which each author reads quite legibly as Hebrew, Phœnician, or Basque, according to his crotchet and the key that he prefers; but Wm. von Humboldt justly deems all these conjectures to be wild and incorrect; and he arrived after much labour to the conclusion that the whole secret has yet to be solved. The early copper coinage is much ruder than the silver; both continued to be current among the Goths until 567, when

Liuva commenced a still ruder substitute, which was used unchanged in form or execution down to Roderick the last of the race; the Gothic coins are small and thin, with the head seen in full face. For all details consult the admirable work of Florez (see p. 133).

The Moorish coinage in gold, silver, and copper is much neater and sharper. The coins are very thin, and are struck out of such pure metal, that they bend easily on pressure. They are inscribed with Arabic characters, which generally denote the name of the petty prince and the place of the mint; see on these inscriptions p. 372. This branch of the Madrid collection has been admirably and scientifically arranged by Gayangos, and is probably the only place in Europe where the subject can be fully understood; not that it possesses much interest, being for the most part the monotonous records of obscure *sheikhs*.

Now return to the S. façade of the palace, and visit *La Armeria real*, which is one of the finest armouries in the world. In order to see it it is necessary to have an *esquela* from the *Caballerizo Mayor*, or Master of the Horse.

The noble gallery, which fronts the S. side of the palace, is 227 ft. long, by 36 wide: it was built in 1565 by Gaspar de la Vega, for Philip II., when he removed the royal armoury from Valladolid. This, as it really contains weapons of all kinds, is a double curiosity, being the best provided arsenal in the land, although, as in other matters, the implements are somewhat behind those used by more advanced nations. It is, moreover, the finest *ancient* armoury in Spain, for many of the others were broken by the people in 1808, when they rose against the French, as then the ill-furnished national arsenals contained nothing; nor had the miserable government means or inclination to procure weapons: they confided in Santa Teresa, and the triple defence of a good cause,—thrice is he *armed* who has his quarrel just. But the less poetical people, before muskets were forwarded from England, broke open the armouries, and thus were equipped with the identical weapons with which their ancestors had fought against their infidel invader. So the Romans were armed after the defeat at Cannæ (Val. Max. vii. 6). The few armouries that escaped the patriots were plundered by the enemy.

A poor catalogue of this *Armeria* was published in 1793 by Ignacio Abadia; and a splendid French work, with engravings, by Gaspar Sensi, at Paris, 1838. The first entrance is very striking, and worthy of this land of chivalry, the Cid and Don Quixote. All down the middle of the saloon are drawn up equestrian figures, while armed knights stand against the walls, surrounded in every direction with implements of war and tournament. Above hang banners taken from the enemy, while the walls are lined with coats of armour; but a Meyrick and Scriblerus would grieve at the overbright polish, for the *Fregatriz* of the Museo (No. 1294) has been here, mistaking the dry rustless climate of Castile for her own Dutch damp land, with pumice and emery, to scrub off the respectable ærugo. The Madrid Murillos are not more overcleaned, nor the coins of the Valencian Peluquero.

Observe the 19 suits of armour of Charles V., chased in fine cinque-cento. On the front of every one is engraved the Virgin, his tutelar, and at the back Santa Barbara—Isis and Astarte. The latter saint is the patroness of Spanish artillery, as Santa Teresa is generalissima of infantry. Santa Barbara is also invoked by all the old women of Spain in thunder-storms, for she directs the artillery both of heaven and of earth. The suits of Philip II. are very splendid, especially those worked in black and gold. Here is the rude litter in which Charles V. was carried when suffering from the gout; it is something between a black coffin-like trunk and a Sclavonian kibitka. Observe his *iron* campaigning plates; how the simple service of this bred and born emperor contrasts with the *golden* nécessaire left behind by the upstart fugitive from Vitoria. Remark the carriage of Juana *La Loca*, and the first ever used in Spain, carved, about 1546, in black wood, in the Berruguete style, with cupids, flowers, and festoons; compare it with a steel vehicle made in Biscay in 1828, and given to Ferd. VII. when he went there meditating to rob them of their *Fueros.* The finest armour is foreign, German and Italian. One suit is inscribed, "Desiderio Colman Cays: May: Harnashmagher ausgemacht in Augusta den 15 Aprilis, 1552," by whom also is a black and gold helmet, dated 1550. The armour of Philip II., when prince, has engraved on it the arms of England, in an escutcheon of pretence for his wife, our Mary. The so-called armour of Philip of Burgundy is inscribed, "Philipus Jacobi et frater Negroli faciebant." A most elegant steel gun is inscribed, "Hizó me en Ricla, Christobal F^r. Isleva, año 1565." Here, as was the case at our Tower, much nonsense is repeated by rote by the keeper regarding sundry helmets of Hannibal and Julius Cæsar : the latter is evidently Italian, and of the 16th century. The armour of the Cid is also fictitious; not so that of Isabella, which she wore at the siege of Granada. The monogram *Isabel* is worked on the visor, and she must have been a portly dame. Ferdinand, her husband, dressed in bran new red breeches, and armed in black and gold armour, is mounted on a war-horse, while S^a. Fernando is kept, as Nelson's wax-work was in Westminster Abbey, in a case. His nether man is altogether apocryphal, notwithstanding which many papal indulgences are granted to all who look with an implicit faith at this cheat: see the affixed notice. This saving one's soul besides gratifying curiosity is an advantage which the *Armeria* of Madrid has over ours at the Tower.

Some of the shields on the walls are superb. Observe one with a Medusa's head; and another studded with cameos, and given to Philip II. by a Duke of Savoy. The armour of the Great Captain is authentic; there are four suits, all richly chased, with a badge of two palm-trees issuing from a coronet. Remark the peculiar coalscuttle helmet of the Rey Chico, and a suit of armour, worked with silver filigree, given to Philip II. by the city of Pamplona. Observe the armour of Guzman el Bueno, of Fernan Cortes, of John of Austria, and worn at Lepanto; of Columbus, black and white, with silver medallions; also a suit of a German elector, heavy, square, and short-legged—there is no mistaking the country of the wearer. The smaller suits, for Infantes and young heroes, are military playthings. The Turkish banners were mostly taken at Lepanto. The collection of guns belonging to Charles III. and Charles IV. is worthy of these royal gamekeepers; many are inlaid with jewels: one was a present from Buonaparte, who soon after *accepted* from his friend his crown and kingdom.

The collection of swords is much more interesting; for this weapon Spain has always been celebrated (see Toledo): many are of undoubted authenticity, although some want confirmation, which is a sad pity, as these are the symbol relics of Spain's heroic and best age; they realise her ballad *Epos,* her best poetry. Shame, as we said at the Alhambra (pp. 368, 379), on the cold sceptic who can believe in St. Ferdinand's plush breeches, and the dull gridiron bar of San Lorenzo, and yet doubt these bright steel blades, and the existence of the stalwart Paladins who wielded them. Look therefore with implicit faith and veneration at the genuine scimitars of those creatures of romance, Bernardo del Carpio and Roldan (Orlando): the sword of the latter is of rich filigree, and no doubt is the identical blade with which he divided the Pyrenees. Observe the equally formidable *Montante,* or double-handed falchion of Garcia de Paredes (see p. 534), with which he kept whole French armies at bay, a class of cutlery not much made just now at Toledo. Then come the swords of St. Ferdinand, of Ferd. and Isab., and of the "Great Captain;" the latter was used when knighthood was conferred on distinguished persons. Next remark those of Charles V., Philip II., Fernan Cortes, and Pizarro, in a steel sheath. In vain the historian will inquire for the sword which François I. surrendered at Pavia; it was *given* to Murat, and, to make the dishonour complete, by the M⁹· de Astorga, whose duty, as *Divisero Mayor de Madrid*, it was to have guarded the relic, as the sword of Goliath was of old (1 Sam. xxi. 9). The implements of tournaments and hunting are extremely curious and complete, as the German love of heraldry and the lists flourished in the congenial soil of the Castiles, the land of personal prowess and the hidalgo and *Paso Honroso* (see p. 604). Observe the halbert of Don Pedro the Cruel, and the *hastas de galiardete*, which were fixed on the walls of captured cities. The saddles and leather shields of the Moors are curious; the latter, or *Adargas*, although light, resisted spear and sword: two hides are cemented together by a mortar composed of herbs and camel-hair; the forms are ovals, and ornamented with three tassels and the *umbo* or knob: they are the unchanged *Cetræ* of the Carthaginians and Iberians (see Sil. Ital. iii. 278; x. 231; Pliny, 'Nat. Hist.' xi. 39; Sⁿ· Isidoro, 'Or.' xviii. 12).

Next visit *La Casa de los Ministerios*, built for the secretaries of state by Sabatini, by order of Charles VI.: it was splendidly fitted up by Godoy, and has a grand staircase and column-supported vestibule. The ante-rooms are thronged with waiters on providence and patient sufferers, emblems of hope and salary deferred, since here are the offices of the Ministers of War, Marine, Justice, and Finance.

The inveterate curse of ill-fated Spain is *misgovernment*. Her ministers, with few exceptions, have for the last two centuries been either incapables or rogues. " The *great want* of this nation," wrote the Duke (Disp. July 20, 1813). " is of men capable of conducting business of any description; and the revolution, as it is called, instead of having caused an improvement in this respect, has rather augmented the evil, by bringing forward into public employments of importance more inexperienced people, and by giving men in general false notions entirely incompatible to their business." Nor have matters much changed, for now *Empleomania*, or madness for place, has infected the nation, for *place*, as in the East, is the source of real power and profit; accordingly, the veriest Jack-in-office, *el villano con poder*, armed with that authority, is sufficient for the oppression of thousands, as the jaw-bone of an ass was in the hands of Samson, since *La Charte* and constitutions are practically but waste paper, through which a *coche de colleras* is driven every day. *Place* gives the holder the key of the public till; *place* enables him to work the telegraph, and thus watch the turn of the stock-market. The object of every official is to make his fortune as quickly as he can, and as he is in a hurry he is not over-scrupulous, for the tenure of possession is brief and uncertain, since countless competitors are trying to oust him and get in themselves. Thus the gorged leech is succeeded by one worse and more hungry, caterpillar follows locust, and the real evils of the state are not only unredressed but increased. Poor Spain, like a dying patient, in vain changes her ministers, turning in her restless bed from one side to another, from one quack to another, for each in his turn becomes the object to be destroyed, and all shout, " Let his days be few, and let another *take* his *office*" (Ps. cix. 8). From 1800 to 1844 there have been 74 ministers of finance, and all with "no effects." Nine ministries have been formed from May, 1843, to May, 1844, and each rather worse than the preceding one, and all soon perishing in the malaria of their own un-popularity and inefficiency.

How can a country be well governed, or any strong government be carried on, where there is no fixity of official tenure, and where, as in the East, in the absence of permanent *institutions*, reliance is placed on *individuals*, on the "happy accident" of the hour? Accordingly, every *pretendiente* pretends to place; his self-love teaches him that he is quite as capable of ruining his country and of benefiting himself as any other man in Spain, just as the Blakes aspired to command armies and lose battles. These incapables, like the clown at Astley's, are all wanting to get up and ride the high horse, jealous as Turks who will bear no rival; so

" All from a government deserve a prize,
Which lives by shuffling and exists by lies."

To put forth manifests, *expedientes* expedients, *documentos* (see p. 137), and the most plausible falsehoods in the most ingenious grandiloquence of state paper style, is *the* great ministerial requisite. Thence the secret of the rise and success of all adventurers, from the Alberonis, Ripperdas, Calomardes, down to the last *Don Fulano Embustero* of the present day. These charlatans, in field and cabinet, have prospered by fooling a generous, self-estimating, imaginative people to the top of their bent; those who have promised to pay the most, who have talked the loudest of national honour, dignity, and strength, have ever been the most popular: nor when the cheat is exposed has the next quack the least difficulty in offering his new nostrum, or the self-same sham wares, in the same language as his predecessor; and thus too long, in peace or war, has the noble people been their victim! What just now is most wanting are *middle classes*, which some hope will in time be supplied among the purchasers of church properties and other vast estates hitherto kept out of the market under the lock of mortmains and entails.

The *Casa de los Consejos*, close by, was built by F^ro. de Mora for the Duque de Aceda. It is a fine Herrera elevation, but the interior, as usual, was never properly finished: the chief façade looks N., and faces the S^a. Maria de la *Almudena*. This church, once a Moorish mosque, retains, like the tower at Tortosa, its name of the Moslem *Mueddin*. It was purified by Alonzo VI., and dedicated to the Virgin : thus the pagan female worship of Astarte, Isis, and Diana is revived under a Mahometan name in a Christian church. The church itself is small, and of no interest; it, however, enjoys the privileges of an *Iglesia Mayor* in this cathedral-less capital. There is a folio volume on the ' *Invention* and Miracles' worked by this graven image, Jose de Vera Tarsis y Villaroel, Mad. 1692.

Now cross the C^e. de Segovia to *Las Vistillas*, long the town residence of the Duques de Infantado, and where Ferd. and Isab. lived. From the windows did Ximenez, when asked by what authority he assumed the Regency, point to his artillery and soldiers in the court below. Nor are matters changed to this day, when might makes right.

Beyond is *S^n. Francisco*, a vast pile, placed in an out-of-the-way locality. The convent is now made a barrack, and the chapel a parish church. It was designed by the monk F^ro. Cabezas, and finished in 1784 by Sabatini. The church, one of the finest in Madrid, is a rotunda, surrounded with chapels : the dome is 163 feet high. The *Jubileo de Porciuncula* (see p. 771) was painted by the feeble Bayeu : the pictures in the chapels by Maella, Calleja, Goya, Velazquez (*not* Diego), and others, are no better.

Proceed next to the *Puerta de los Moros*, and thence to San Andres, which was used by Ferdinand and Isabella as their chapel. Here San Isidro went to mass and was buried; his wooden effigy is curious for costume. The gaudy churrigueresque chapel was raised by Philip IV. and Charles II. The miracles of the tutelar (see p. 777) are painted by Carreño and the Rizzi : his body was removed in 1769 to his new church. Adjoining is *La Capilla del Obispo*, one of the few old Gothic specimens in modern Madrid. It was begun in 1547 by Gutierez de Vargas y Carvajal, Bishop of Placencia. The excellent *Retablo* and Berruguete carvings are by F^ro. Giralte, and painted by Juan de Villondo in 1548, and not by Blas del Pardo, as some state : by Giralte also are the superb plateresque sepulchres of the prelate and his family, and the finest things of the kind in Madrid, the invaders having destroyed those in San Jeronimo. This chapel was injured in 1755 by an earthquake, and repaired in vile taste. There are also some good carvings in the *Sacristia.*

Now visit *La Plaza de Cebada*, the forage, the "hay," the "grass market," and where executions formerly took place. Look at the portal of *La Latina*, or *N^a. S^a. de la Concepcion*, a hospital founded in 1499 by Beatriz Galindo, who taught Queen Isabella Latin. It was built by a Moor named Hazan. Those who wish to see old Madrid and the quarters of the *Manolos* and *Populacho*, may now thread the Calles del D. de Alba, Jesus y Maria, to the *Lavapies*. Those who have no taste for a Castilian St. Giles may pass up by La Latina to S^n. Isidro, in the C^e. de Toledo. This, once a Jesuit's college, was built in 1651, and, now a parish church, is called *La Colegiata :* here bad taste and churriguerismo reign undisputed. This convent was attacked by the Madrid mob, July 17, 1834, who murdered the monks because they had caused the cholera ; enter and look at *the Capilla* Mayor, which was " repaired" by Rodriguez. Here lie S^n. Isidro and his *Santa Esposa :* his statue is by Pereyra. Here are the ashes of Daoiz, Velarde, and some of Murat's victims of the " *Dos de Maio,*" which were removed from the Prado May 2, 1814, with great

pomp. Look into the chapels and sacristies to see to what extent gilt gingerbread Rococo can be carried. The library which once belonged to the Jesuits is still here, and is open to the public.

Turn now to the lt. to the *Plazuela de la Villa*, which is open on one side, to the C^e. Mayor. The " Mansionhouse," or *Casa del Ayuntamiento*, was built in the sixteenth century; the portals are later, and bad. The peristile facing the C^e. de la Almudena was added by Villanueva : the *patio* and staircase inside are simple. At the balcony overlooking the *Platerias*, the Duke, entering Madrid as a conqueror, presented himself to the applause of the delivered citizens : by his side stood *El Empecinado*, " the bemudded."* Thus most truly were England and Spain represented, and each by their best and fitting arm— a general of a *great* war and a leader of a *little* war : the one all plan, foresight, discipline, and organization, the other all accident, impulse, desultory, unprovided and insubordinate. Yet both aiming, and truly to the same end, assisting, and co-operating with each other in a manner which the Blakes, Cuestas, and so-called regular generals never did. For a comparison between one of those " old blockheads" and the Duke, see p. 540.

Opposite, in what was *La Casa de Lujanes*, the tower of which is now used for a telegraph, Francois I. was confined after his defeat at Pavia, until removed Jan. 14, 1526, to the *alcazar.* Here he plighted his word of a king to treaties which, forgetting his chivalrous lament after Pavia, tout est perdu hors l'honneur, he violated the instant he crossed the Bidasoa and touched the sacred soil of France. But this most *Christian* king was absolved from all his oaths by Clement VII. the vicar of Christ; Peter Martyr (Ep. 813) thus

* The Moorish *almogavar*, or frontier partisan soldier, was so called from *Al-Mughab-bar*, the dust with which he was covered in his forays.

wrote prophetically, when François I. was making solemn promises : " Gallum ergo in Matritensem caveam die Aug. 14, Aquila clausit. Quem ex tantâ victoriâ fructum exerpsemus tempus dicet. *Parvum existimo,* quia nimis mitis est Cæsar, Galli *vafri* nimium, in actionibus negociorum :*" and he was right.

Now cross the fine *Calle Mayor* to *S*ⁿ· *Gines,* in the Cᵉ· del Arenal. This church was built about 1358, and injured by fire in 1824. Observe inside the *Paso* of Sᵒ· Cristo, carved by Vergaz, and a painting of " Christ seated and stripped," by Alonzo Cano. Descend to the *Boveda,* or dark vault, where during Lent amateur flagellants whip themselves, the sexton furnishing the cats ; some have nine tails, and are really stained with blood. The penitents being their own judges and executioners, lay on according to their consciences, Γνωθι and scourge Σεαυτον. In the good old times of Philip IV. Spaniards whipt themselves publicly in the streets, and the nice thing was to lay on so stoutly on passing their mistresses, that the blood should spurt on them in a delicate attention which their tender hearts could not resist. The fair sex were only professionally bled, and it was usual that at each venisection the lover should make his *querida* a present, whereby male purses and female arteries were equally exhausted. This gentle self-scourging prevailed among ancient female worshippers ; the self-flagellants of Isis (Herod. ii. 61) set the fashion to the devotees of Bellona at Rome; but when people's religion lies no deeper than the skin they may flagellate themselves with considerable benefit; since the *progreso, Young Spain,* although it still worships female divinities in church and out, whips itself no more, from thinking, like honest Sancho Panza, that the custom is more honoured in the breach than the observance.

Next cross over to the *Plaza mayor,* erected in 1619, by Jⁿ· de Mora. Here the *Autos de Fé* were celebrated ; here

our Charles I. beheld a royal bull-fight, given to him by Philip IV. Here, in one week, at the *Jura* of Isabel in 1833 99 bulls were killed. The locality is well adapted for spectacles ; the space is 434 feet long by 334 wide. By a clause in their leases the inmates of houses are bound on these occasions to give up their front rooms and balconies, which are fitted up as boxes. The royal seat is on the part called *La Panaderia,* the saloons of which, painted by Claudio Coello, were destined by Charles III. to the Academy of History, who have here a tolerable library.

Going out at the S.E. corner is the *Carcel de Corte,* built in 1634, for Philip IV., by Jⁿ· Bª· Crescenti. No Howard has ever visited this home of guilt and misery, the dwelling, as Cervantes says, " of every discomfort, and of every wretched sound." Those who enter, if they have no money, may bid adieu to hope, while judges, jailers, and turnkeys are often accomplices after the fact, with a rich criminal. Since 1808 and the multitudinous changes and chances of political farce and tragedy at Madrid, these dungeons have never wanted a tenant from every shade of opinion; since each party when in power persecutes its opponent. Here Joseph incarcerated the patriots, and the Cortes the *afrancesados.* Here Ferdinand confined the liberals, here the liberals fettered the royalists; here Carlist and Christinist, *Servile, Exaltado,* and *Moderado* have each in their turn tasted the iron of their national *justicia,* particularly since Ferdinand's death, under his even-handed widow, who here shut up the *royalists* in 1836, and the *liberals* in 1844 ; *Cosas de España.* Having observed *effects,* the jurisconsult may next inquire into *causes,* for here are the tribunals of the *Audiencia,* or supreme court of *justice* as it is called. In it every man is assumed to be guilty until he is proved innocent, the judge endeavouring by every means fair and foul to convict the accused ; a Westminster Hall barrister if transported by special retainer to the Rhadamantine court below, would scarcely find himself in a newer practice. Both however err in extremes, since few guiltless escape in Spain, and few guilty are convicted in England; yet our defective laws work well, because fairly administered by able and upright judges, while the better system of Spain works ill, because the ministers are corrupt and unjust. A pure administration of the law, and not a new code, is what is wanting for the peace and welfare of Spaniards.

The jurisdiction of this *Audiencia* extends over 1,022,600 souls ; the number tried in 1844 was 5160, or about 1 in every 200; in the simple mountain Asturias the proportion is as 1 in 898, which offers the best comment on the relative morality of the " only court."

Opposite is the church of *S^a. Cruz ;* from its tower is one of the best views of Madrid. Prison-fanciers may also go to the C^e. de Hortaleza, and visit *Las Recogidas*, or *S^a. Maria Magdalena.* No women can take the benefit of this admirable institution without having duly qualified by undoubted guilt, and none, once admitted, can get out, except to take the veil or marry. Here also is a quarter in which those ladies are confined whose relations think them likely to be benefited by a little restraint; an institution which might be usefully extended to some capitals out of Spain.

In the C^e. de Fuencarral is the *Hospital de S^n. Fernando,* founded in 1688. The facade by the heresiarch Pedro Ribera, 1726, is the pet specimen of the vile taste of the Philip V. period, and certainly entitled the inventor to his admission into any receptacle for criminals or lunatics. It rivals in outrageous churrigueresque the *Retablo* in S^n. Luis, and the *Portada* of S^o. Tomas. In this hospital poor persons of both sexes are received and employed ; their protected work is then disposed of at a low price, and thus, by underselling, does infinite injury to those honest industrious families, who have to provide

materials, besides food and lodging, by their own exertions.

The hospital *S^n. Antonio,* Corredera de S^n. Pablo, was founded in 1606, and has a good oval chapel, with fresco ceilings, by the Rizzi, Carreño, and Giordano. Observe the Sta. Isabel and S^a. Eugracia, painted by Eugenio Caxes, and the statue of the tutelar by Pereyra.

The Foundling Hospital, *La Inclusa,* in the C^e. de los Embajadores, is so called from a much venerated image of the Virgin, which was brought by a Spanish soldier from *Enkuissen* (Enchusen), in Holland ; the very town, by the way, which was the first there to rise in revolt against the practical horrors of the Duke of Alva and the Spanish Inquisition. The influence of the Virgin-Mother is quite lost in this house of crime and suffering : here more than 1200 infants, sinless children of sin, are annually exposed by their unnatural parents, and almost to certain death, from the decreasing funds and increasing misery (see Seville, p. 271). The lying-in asylum for these mothers, in the Calle del Rosal, is called, as if in mockery, N^a. S^a. de *la Esperanza,*— what *hope* is there for their offspring? the more honest vulgar, however, call it *El Pecado mortal,* the deadly sin: here unmarried women are *confined* in both senses of the word, and papal bulls of dispensation obtained, being first duly paid for.

The Poor-house, or mendicity asylum, was founded in 1834, outside the gate S^n. Bernardino, in order to provide for the increasing misery, the result of the constitutions and civil wars; here a sort of existence and occupation is scantily eked out to the destitute. It was the plan of the M^s. de Pontejos, by whom was founded, in 1839, the *Caja de Ahorros,* or savings-bank, an institution quite new in Oriental Spain, under whose life-giving sun every plant grows rapidly save confidence; here, where few ever trust each other, and especially when cash is concerned, the common investment is mother earth, into whose bosom their dumb dollars are deposited

New Castile.

MADRID.—SPANISH STOCKS.

793

(see p. 5). Spain, however, is the land of the unexpected; and, contrary to all calculations, this establishment has not worked ill: 4 per cent. is paid to all depositors, which is more than Spanish talents buried in the Peninsular earth usually produce.

The *Imprenta Real* is in the Cᵉ· de Carretas. This heavy building, by one Turillo, contains the royal printing and engraving establishment. From this press have issued many splendid specimens of typography; here may be obtained impressions of those pictures in the Museo which have been engraved; but they are second-rate, for Spaniards have never excelled in the burin, which requires too much patience, and is too mechanical; at first they employed foreigners, Flemings and Italians, and latterly Frenchmen. Very few Spanish artists have ever etched, for Ribera was, in fact, a Neapolitan; and in no country have illustrated works been less produced. The Bourbons introduced a taste for engraving portraits, and some plates by Celma and Carmona are tolerable.

The *Casa de Moneda*, or mint, is in the Cᵉ· de Segovia: the coinage is slovenly, the machinery foreign, the dies ill cut and worse worked. For Spanish money, see p. 4.

A Stock Exchange, or *Bolsa de Comercio*, was established in 1831, and as all men in power use their official knowledge in taking advantage of the turn of the market, the *Bolsa* divides with the court and army, the moving influence of every *situacion*, or crisis of the moment: clever as are the ministers of Paris, they are mere scholars when compared to their colleagues of Madrid in the arts of working the telegraph, gazette, etc., and thereby feathering their own nests.

The public exchange is held in San Martin, from 10 to 3 o'clock, where those who like Spanish 5 per cents. may buy them as cheap as stinking mackerel. The stocks are numerous, and suited to all tastes and pockets, whether those funded by Aguado,

Ardouin, Toreno, or Mendizabal, "all honourable men:" in some the principal is consolidated, in others, the interest is deferred; the grand financial principle in all having been to receive as much as possible, and pay back in an inverse ratio. As in measuring out money and oil, a little will stick to the cleanest fingers, the ministers and contractors made fortunes and actually " did " the Hebrews of London. But from Philip II. downwards, theologians have never been wanting to prove the religious, however painful, duty of bankruptcy, and particularly in contracts with usurious heretics. The stranger, when shown over the Madrid bank, had better evince no impertinent curiosity to see the " Dividend *pay* office," as it might give offence. Whatever be our reader's pursuit in the Peninsula, let him

" Neither a borrower or lender be,
For loan oft loseth both itself and friend."

Beware of Spanish stock, for in spite of official reports, *documentos*, and arithmetical mazes, which, intricate as an arabesque pattern, look well on paper, without being intelligible; in spite of ingenious conversions, fundings of interest, &c., the thimblerig is always the same; and this is the question, since national credit depends on national good faith and surplus income, how can a country pay interest on debts, whose revenues have long been and now are miserably insufficient for the ordinary expenses of government. You cannot get blood from a stone.

Mr. Macgregor's report on Spain, March, 1844, is a truthful exposition of commercial ignorance, habitual disregard of treaties and violation of contracts. At p. 84, he describes her public *securities*, past and present. Certainly they had very imposing names, *Juros, Vales reales*, &c.; but no oaths can attach real value to dishonoured paper. According to some financiers, her public debts, previously to 1808, amounted to 83,763,966*l.*, which have since been increased to 279,083,089*l.*, farthings

2 M

omitted: this possibly may be exaggerated, but at all events, Spain is over
head and ears in debt, and irremediably
insolvent. And yet few countries, if
we regard the fertility of her soil, her
golden possessions at home and abroad,
her frugal temperate population, ought
to have been less embarrassed than
Spain; but Santiago has granted her
every blessing, except a good and honest government.

The national bank, called *de San
Fernando*, was founded in 1827, and is
in the C⁹· de la Montera. It issues
notes for 500 and 1000 reals, which
will not pass out of Madrid, for all
who are not *Madrileños* wisely prefer
local dollars to court paper: the circulation is about 120,000l. These notes
are cashed every day from ten to one,
and we advise our readers to lose no
time in changing theirs. The history
of this bank of San Fernando is characteristic. Previously there existed that
of San Carlos, founded in 1782, with
exclusive privileges of receiving deposits, and a monopoly of issuing paper;
but, in spite of charters and solemn
pledges, Ferd. VII., July 9, 1829, created this rival, in favour of some capitalists who advanced him money. The
natural consequence was that the older
establishment failed; but the rule of its
destroyer was brief, for its turn arrived
in the usual cycle of *mala fe*, and, in
spite of Ferdinand's solemn guarantee
and especial charter for its monopoly,
an opposition bank, under the title of
Isabel II., has recently been set up,
which, at least, had the modesty not to
assume a *sainted* name. However, this
breach of faith has not this time broken
the older bank; nay, it has rather done
it good, for the sleeping partners were
roused from their bed of protected monopoly, and forced by competition into
habits of business, which of course have
increased their profits.

A general Life and House Insurance
Company (C⁹· del Prado, No. 42) was
only founded in 1842: so new here is
any security for person or property,
long doubly hazardous. In the C⁹·

Sⁿ· Juan is the *Platería*, established by
Charles III., who sent Auᵗᵒ· Martinez
to Paris and London for ideas and
machinery: the work-room is fine; but
not much plate is now made in Spain,
whose gold and silver ages are past.
Recently several literary and artistical
societies have been formed, such as *El
Ateneo*, a kind of club; *El Liceo ar-
tístico y literario*, a sort of Royal Institution for lectures and meetings every
Thursday; a Philharmonic Academy;
a *Conservatorio de Artes*, C⁹· del Turco,
with a few mechanical models, and library on those subjects; the *Conservatorio de Musica* was founded in 1830 by
Christina, in order to force Italian notes
down Spanish *gargantas*. The pupils
hitherto have not attained mediocrity:
Spaniards are musical without being
harmonious, as those who read Sil. Ital.
(iii. 346) must know; and as those
who do not, may learn of any muleteer,
or in any of the national operas, the
Venta.

There are three theatres at Madrid.
Al *El Teatro del Circo*, which has recently been erected, a pale attempt at
an Italian *opera* and French *ballet* is occasionally made. The grand new theatre in the *Plaza del Oriente* is unfinished, and the two others, and older,
are the mean and unworthy cradles of
the modern drama of Europe. The
original theatre for which Calderon,
Cervantes, and Lope de Vega wrote for
Philip IV., was burnt by the French.
The present *Teatro de la Cruz*, the Theatre of the Cross! which will hold about
1300 persons, is badly contrived; it was
built in 1737, by Ribera, who exercised
his genius, fertile in absurdities, in
making such an edifice, that no subsequent efforts, short of pulling it down,
can ever render it tolerable: the architect, like a Cuesta or Blake, made such
dispositions as rendered failure a certainty, in acting and actions. The other theatre, called *Del Principe*, was built by
Villanueva, in 1806, and will contain
only 1200 spectators. It need not be
said, that the smell of the continent
fully pervades these confined houses,

during whose spectacles no neutralizing incense is used, as is done by the wise clergy. If the atmosphere were analized by Faraday, it would be found to contain equal portions of stale cigar smoke and fresh garlic fume. The lighting, except on those rare occasions when the theatre is *iluminado*, is just intended to make darkness visible, and there is no seeing into the *palcos* or the *gallinero*, that henroost towards which the eyes and glasses of the Reynards, who sit in the *Lunetas* or stalls, are vainly elevated.

Spanish tragedy is wearisome: the language is stilty, the declamation ranting, French, and unnatural; passion is torn to rags. The *sainetes*, or farces, are broad, but amusing, and perfectly well acted ; these, indeed, are the true vehicles of the love for sarcasm, satire, and intrigue, the mirth and mother-wit, for which Spaniards are so remarkable; and no people are more essentially serio-comic and dramatic than they are, whether in *Venta*, *Plaza*, or church. The *Sainete* is deserving of its name, which signifies the tit-bit, the *brain* of the quarry, with which the sportsman rewarded his hawk.

The *Bolero*, of course, is the *Salsa de la Comedia, on n'écoute que le ballet ;* there women cease even to talk, and men to expectorate. For the Spanish Theatre, etc., see p. 185.

Very few of the palaces of the Grandees contain anything worth notice. They were plundered by the invaders, and their owners are not overgifted with taste; nor are the rooms much better furnished than the heads or cellars of the proprietors. Spain, indeed, is a shadow of departed greatness, and of all shadows none are more unsubstantial, with few exceptions, than the present holders of the time-honoured titles of her heroic age. The poor descendants of those real men who rendered great names glorious, still flutter in the faint reflection of a past effulgence, their present insignificance being heightened by the former importance of those whom they misrepresent: they

have grown with the growth and declined with the decline of their country. Living ruins without the dignity of antiquity, they are degenerate alike in body, mind, and estate; their close intermarriages, by breeding in-and-in, have perpetuated physical and moral insignificance as their birthright ; they set the laws of organic nature at defiance, and hence their stinted forms and defective brains. To be a *Grande* it almost now seems necessary to be *chico*, or small in person and intellect. This pigmy proportion of body and brain is in an inverse ratio to magnitude of rank and wealth, as if it would seem that Providence created them in order to show how little importance it attached to these gifts, so coveted by mortals. The *Grandes*, again, from never allying themselves with the commonalty, stand alone like barren palm-trees and on the surface ; they have no deep roots intertwined with the social system, nor the education or talent to carve out for themselves a position. They rarely reach mediocrity, for the few *Duques* who have held office or scribbled, would not in England be admitted into an annual, or appointed on the committee of a country book-club ; no wonder, then, that these *Hijos de algo* are ousted in political power by *novi homines* either *Hijos de se y de sus obras*, or by upstart adventurers, lampooners, stock-jobbers, small littérateurs, and soldiers of fortune. Uneducated and untravelled these popinjay butterflies are fit only to swell the levees, the *Besamanos* of the court, where, true *Palaciegos*, the insects glitter in embroidery and decoration. Madrid is indeed *the* court of fine names, gilt gingerbread, and trappings of honour, as the *forms* of real strength are resorted to, in order to raise the apparent splendour of a faded country, to mask the absence of living spirit by the symbol, to cover the mean heart under a brilliant star: nowhere, not even at cognate Naples, is there a greater prodigality of utterly undeserved titles and decorations. The badge confers, indeed, small honour,

but not to have it is a disgrace. Formerly, said the shrewd *Populacho*,
rogues were hung on crosses, now crosses are hung on rogues : for these matters, see Quart. Rev., cxxiii. 110.

The largest of the Grandees' houses,
and a real *poor* house, is that of the Duque de Medinaceli, Cᵃ· de Sⁿ· Geronimo : it looks like ten houses taken from
Baker Street. The plate and armoury
were appropriated by the invaders.
Here are kept, in scandalous neglect,
some antiques which were brought from
the *Casa de Pilatus* at Seville (see p.
260). They are not of high art: observe a fawn, a Mercury, and Apollo.
Here are two very early cannon (see
Baza, p. 408): the library, once open
to the public, is now food for worms.
The Conde de Oñate has also a good
house; so has the Duque de Hijar, and
the Mᵃ· de Astorga.

Charles I., when at Madrid, lived
in the *Casa de las siete Chemineas*. It
is in the south-east corner of a small
plaza, into which the last street on the
l. hand of the Cᵉ· de Alcalá leads, just
opposite the British embassy. This is
the house which the Venetian envoy
held so long, and even against Philip
IV., and our minister Fanshaw. See
his Letters, ii. 129.

Pursuing that street, is *Las Salesas
viejas*. This enormous nunnery, a
second Escorial, was built in 1758, by
one Carlier, for Barbara, queen of
Ferd. VI., in imitation of Madᵉ· de
Maintenon's St. Cyr, as a place of retreat for herself, and a seminary for
young noble females. The size, enormous cost, and vile taste, led the critics
to exclaim, " *Barbara Reina, barbara
obra, barbaro gusto, barbaro gasto.*"
Barbara, besides meaning *barbarous*,
has, in Spanish, the secondary signification of immense, outrageous. Over
the façade is a bas-relief of the *Nᵃ·
Señora de la Visitacion*, to which mystery the building is dedicated. The
imposing Corinthian chapel is now
converted into a parish church. The
king and queen are buried here: their
tombs were designed by Sabatini, and

executed by Gutierez. They are composed of the finest materials, but the
figures of Plenty and Justice (raræ aves
in Hispaniâ) are after the taste and
truth of the grand epitaphs *composed* by
the *poet* Juan de Iriarte. The marbles
of the high altar are truly magnificent:
the green pillars were brought from the
quarries of San Juan near Granada.
The handsomest façade of the *Palacio*,
so called because the residence of
Queen Barbara, looks to the garden.

The *Descalzas Reales* in its *plaza*
was founded by Juana, daughter of
Charles V. Observe her kneeling
effigy placed on her tomb, and wrought
in marble by P. Leoni. The frescos
were painted in 1756, by Velazquez
(*not* Diego). The *Retablo* of the high
altar is by Becerra. The abbess of this
convent ranked as a grandee.

There are very few interesting tombs
in modern Madrid, as the finest in the
Sⁿ· Geronimo and *Sⁿ· Martin* were destroyed by the invaders. *Herrera*, the
architect, was buried in San Nicolas;
Lope de Vega in Sⁿ· Sebastian : he died
Aug. 27, 1637, at No. 11, Cᵉ· Francos.
Velazquez, who died Aug. 7, 1660, was
buried in San Juan. It was pulled
down in 1811, in the time of the
French, and his ashes scattered to the
winds, as they had treated those of
Murillo (see p. 260). So were scattered
those of Cervantes: he died April 23,
1616, in the Cᵉ· del Leon, No. 20, Man-
zana, 228, and was buried in the Trini-
tarias Descalzas, Cᵉ· del Humilladero,
and when the nuns moved to the Calle
de Cantarranas, the site was forgotten,
and his remains are now left unhonour-
ed. In that convent the daughters both
of Cervantes and Lope de Vega took
the veil.

Spain, having denied bread to Cervantes when alive, has recently given
him a stone ; a monument has been
raised in the Pⁿ· Sⁿ· Catalina, with his
statue modelled by Antᵒ· Sola of Barcelona, and cast in bronze by a Prus-
sian named Hofgarten. He is dressed
in the old Spanish costume, and hides
under his cloak his arm mutilated at

Lepanto, which he never did in life, it being the great pride of his existence. The reliefs on the pedestal of Don Quixote's adventures were designed by one Piguer; the cost was defrayed out of the *Bula de Cruzada*. thus Cervantes, who when alive was ransomed from Algiers by the monks of Merced, now owes to a religious fund this tardy monument. The street in which he lived is now called C⁰· de Cervantes. The bones of *Calderon de la Barca* were moved April 19, 1841, from La Calatrava nunnery, and interred in the *Campo Santo de San Andrea.*

The celebrated Padre Henrique Florez, whose works we so often quote (see p. 133), died, aged 71, May 5, 1773, in his convent *San Felipe el Real*, near the *Puerta del Sol*, and was buried in the fine chapel: now all is swept away. Here was preserved his splendid library and his extraordinary collection of notes and papers for the continuation of the '*España Sagrada*,' and for the preservation of which he obtained from Clement XIII. a bull excommunicating all who should remove or injure them. This however proved a *brutum fulmen* against the invader, as Gen¹· Belliard, in 1808, turned the beautiful church into a stable, and used up those MSS. and books of Florez which were not burnt for camp kettles to make beds of for the troops: thus perished antiquarian researches that never can be replaced, as most of the original documents afterwards met with the same fate from the same destroyers: hence the present difficulty in continuing the '*España Sagrada :*' see for details Risco's preface, '*E. S.*' xliii. ix. (compare Simancas, p. 622). For particulars of the life of Florez, see '*Noticias de la Vida*,' by Francisco Mendez, Mad. 1780, his companion and learned author of the '*Typographia Española*,' see p. 138.

Sᵒ· Domingo el Real was founded in 1217. The portal and coro were added by Herrera for Philip II. in 1599, whose son Don Carlos was buried here, until removed to the Escorial. Ob-

serve the kneeling effigy of Don Pedro. There are so very few churches worth visiting at Madrid that the ecclesiologist had better hasten to imperial Toledo, the seat of the primate of Spain. *San Ildefonso* was rebuilt in 1827, the French having destroyed the former church. *San Marcos*, Cᵉ de Sⁿ· Leouardo, was erected by Ventura Rodriguez, who lies buried in it. In *San Pedro* is an image, much appealed to when rain is wanted, and therefore called *El Santissimo Cristo de la Lluvia*. In *San Sebastian*, Cᵉ· de Atocha, is another *Paso* carved by Monasterio, and called *El Santissimo Cristo de la Fe :* here Lope de Vega was buried. *San Luis*, in the Cᵉ· de la Montera, is a choice specimen of Madrilenian *churrigueresque*. In *San Milan*, Pᵃ· de la Cebada, is an image, *El Sᵒ· Cristo de las injurias*, much adored by the peasants of the market. *Sᵒ· Tomas*, Cᵉ· de Atocha, is full of churrigueresque architecture and *Pasos* by Rubiales, others of which may be seen in the *San Juan de Dios*, Pᵃ· Anton Martin. For *Pasos* see p. 109.

The immediate environs of Madrid offer small attraction, as the city of pride and pretension stands alone in its desert solitude. There are no daughter suburbs, no Belgrave Squares, no Nouvelle Athenes ; few are the villas, the *rures in urbe*, which tempt the citizens beyond the mud walls of their paradise. The rare exceptions are mostly royal property ; one of the prettiest is *la Moncloa*, on the r. of the road to the Escorial, and overlooking the bed of the Manzanares. It once belonged to the Alva family ; it was purchased by Ferd. VII., who removed to it the porcelain manufactory after the French had destroyed *La China* (see p. 743). Here his Majesty made some bad, coarse, and very dear pots and pans.

El Pardo is a royal *sitio* or shooting-box, distant 2 L. on the Manzanares. It was built by Charles V., and added to by Charles III., whose favourite preserve it was : the covers extend to

15 L. in circumference. The royal apartments are commodious, with some of the ceilings painted in fresco by Galvez and Ribera. Some of the glass chandeliers are large and fine. There is a small theatre in the building.

The *Alameda* is a villa erected on the road to Guadalajara by the late Duchess Countess of Osuna, at an enormous expense, and to produce an enormous failure. On the evenings of summer holidays the citizens venture outside the gate of Alcalá to *La Quinta del Espiritu Santo*, the " farm of the Holy Ghost!" or to *Chamberi*, outside the gate of Bilbao, where they refresh themselves in second-rate public-houses with cheap adulterated wines. On a hill about ¾ of a L. on the road to Toledo is *Caravanchel*, or rather the *Caravancheles*, for the two villages close adjoin each other, being distinguished by the epithets upper and lower, *de arriba y de abajo*. They are to Madrid what Highgate and Hampstead are to London; and here the *Madrileños* recreate themselves on holidays in bad taverns, and in what they fancy is the country. Their celebrated

Star and Garter, *La Vista Alegre*, was so called from the *cheerful* view over the nakedness of the land. Here Christina created a villa, where royal and rural fêtes are given, and the courtiers amused amazingly, in the want of food and drink, by countesses tumbling into fish-ponds, and by grandees* falling off whirligig St. Bartholomew Fair wooden horses; oh, what a falling off was there, from the Cid and his Babieca! Christina, although bred and born at beautiful Naples, was so fond of this villa, that she took the title of *Condeza de Vista Alegre*, on departing quasi incognita from Valencia, after her abdication, and when her throne and children were left behind : but the classical and national denomination of the "rueful countenance," would better have suited the sadness of the occasion and her own forced errantry. In Spain, however, words and titles are given to conceal thoughts and deeds ; so it is now said that Señor Muñoz is to be created Prince of *Vista Alegre*, and then this Spanish Belvedere Apollo will rival his predecessor Godoy, the Prince of the Peace.

COMMUNICATIONS FROM MADRID.

Before quitting the capital remember to get the passport *en règle*, and do not put off the obtaining all necessary *visés* to the last moment. The official subalterns in the " only court," are not more to be hurried than masters of our Court of Chancery, and a day is soon lost in loitering in the ante-rooms, where real business *festinat lenté* and moves *con pies de plomo*.

Madrid, being placed like a spider in the middle of the Peninsular web, may justly be termed the heart in which the grand arteries of the circulation centre. Just now there is much talk of *railroads*, and splendid official and other *documentos* are issued, by which the " whole country is to be intersected (on paper) with a net-work of rapid and bowling-green communications," which are to create a " perfect homogeneity among Spaniards ;" for great as have been the labours of Herculean steam, this amalmagation of the Iberian rope of sand has properly been reserved for the crowning performance.

The following are the grand railway lines in contemplation :—Madrid to Bilbao, Madrid to Aviles by Valladolid and Leon, by an English company ; Madrid to Barcelona by Zaragoza and Lérida, by an English company ; Madrid to Alicante, by a Spanish company ; Madrid to Cadiz, by an English company; Madrid to Badajoz, by an English company. Minor and lateral branches are

* The last summerset was performed this Spring by the *Duque de Castro-Terreno*, Lieut. Gen. in the Catholic armies, and Knight of the Golden Fleece.

also contemplated to run from Merida to Lisbon and Seville, from Barcelona to Tortosa and Mataró, from Reinosa to Santander, and from Madrid to Aranjuez : most of this is to be effected by the iron and gold of England, that fond and foolish ally who fights and pays for all. As this Hand-book is solely destined for the service of Englishmen, our speculators will do well to reflect, that Spain is a land which never yet has been able to construct or support even a sufficient number of common roads or canals for her poor and passive commerce and circulation. The distances are far too great, and the traffic far too small, to call yet for the rail, while the geological formation of the country offers difficulties which, if met with even in England, would baffle the colossal science and extravagance of our first rate engineers. Spain is a land of mountains, which rise everywhere in alpine barriers, walling off province from province, and district from district. These mighty cloud-capped *sierras* are solid masses of hard stone, and any tunnels which ever perforate their ranges, will reduce that at Box to the delving of the poor mole. You might as well cover Switzerland and the Tyrol with a network of *level* lines, as all simpletons caught in the aforesaid net will soon discover to their cost. The outlay will be in an inverse ratio to the remuneration, for the one will be enormous, and the other paltry. The parturient mountains will assuredly only produce a most musipular interest.

Spain again is a land of *dehesas y despoblados :* in these wild unpeopled wastes, next to travellers, commerce and cash are what is scarce, while even Madrid, the capital, is a city without industry or resources, and poorer than many of our provincial cities. The Spaniard, a creature of routine and foe to innovations, is not a locomotive animal ; local, and a fixture by nature, he hates moving like a Turk, and has a particular horror of being hurried ; long, therefore, has an ambling mule here answered all the purposes of transporting man and his goods. Who again is to do the work even if England will pay the wages? The native, next to disliking regular sustained labour himself, abhors seeing the foreigner toiling even in his service, and wasting his gold and sinews in the thankless task. The villagers, as they always have done (see p. 291), will rise against the stranger and heretic who comes to " suck the wealth of Spain;" supposing, however, by the aid of Santiago and Brunel, that the work were possible and were completed, how is it to be secured against the fierce action of the sun, and the fiercer violence of popular ignorance. The first cholera that visits Spain will be set down as a passenger per rail by the dispossessed muleteer, who now performs the functions of coach and steam. He, the *arriero*, constitutes one of the most numerous and finest classes in Spain. He is the legitimate channel of the semi-oriental caravan system, and will never permit the bread to be taken out of his mouth by this Lutheran locomotive; deprived of means of earning his livelihood, he, like the smuggler, will take to the road in another line, and both will become either robbers or patriots. Many, long, and lonely, are the leagues which separate town from town in the wide deserts of thinly-peopled Spain, nor will any preventive service be sufficient to guard the rail against the *Guerrilla* that will then be waged. A handful of opponents in any cistus-overgrown waste, may at any time, in five minutes,break up the road, stop the train, stick the stoker, and burn the engines in their own fire, particularly smashing the luggage train. What again has ever been the recompense which the foreigner has met with from Spain but breach of promise and ingratitude? he will be used, as in the East, until the native thinks that he has mastered his arts, and then he will be cast out and trodden under foot ; and who then will keep up and repair the costly artificial undertaking? certainly not the Spaniard, on whose pericranium the organ bumps of operative skill and mechanical construction have yet to be developed.

The lines which are the least sure of failure will be those which are the shortest, and pass through a level country of some natural productions, such as from Cadiz to Seville through the wine and oil districts; from Barcelona to Mataró, from Reinosa to Santander, and from Oviedo to Aviles, through the coal country; certainly, if the rail can be laid down in Spain by the gold and science of England, the gift, like that of steam, will be worthy of the ocean's queen, and of the world's real leader of peace, order, liberty, good faith, commerce, and civilization; and what a change will then come over the spirit of the Peninsula! how the siesta of torpid man vegetation, will be disturbed by the shrill whistle and panting snort of the monster engine! how the seals of this long hermetically shut-up land will be broken! how the cloistered obscure, and dreams of treasures in heaven will be enlightened by this flashing fire-demon of the wide-awake money worshipper! what owls will be vexed, what bats dispossessed, what drones, *Maragatos*, mules, *Ojalateros*, and asses, will be scared, run over, and annihilated. Those who love Spain, and pray, like the author, daily for her prosperity, must indeed hope to see this " net-work of rails " concluded, but will take especial care at the same time not to invest one *Cuarto* in the imposing speculation.

Meanwhile as diligences, *coches de colleras*, and quadrupeds, do the road work until these wonderful rails are laid down, and as sometimes Spanish performance does not keep pace with the promise, the following communications from Madrid have been and will be described for the information of travellers :—

Madrid to Andalucia by Bailen, R. viii.
Madrid to Murcia by Albacete, R. xxx.
Madrid to Valencia by Almansa, R. ciii.
Madrid to Valencia by Cuenca, R. civ.
Madrid to Teruel by Calatayud, R. cx.
Madrid to Zaragoza by Calatayud, R. cxii.
Madrid to Burgos by Lerma, R. cxiii.
Madrid to Valladolid by Segovia, R. xcix.
Madrid to Salamanca by Avila, R. xcvii. and lxvi.
Madrid to Lisbon by Badajoz, R. lv. and liv.
Madrid to Toledo, R. ci.

One word before starting. Hurry across the Castiles and central provinces by day and night in swift coaches, by extra post and mails, until the rails can convey you quicker; above all things beware of walking or riding journeys, especially in winter or summer : preferable even is the mud, wet, and cold of the former, to the calcining heats of the latter, which bake the mortal clay until it is more brittle than an *olla*, and more combustible than a cigar. Those " rayes," to use the words of old Howell, " that do but warm you in England, do half roast you here; those beams that irradiate onely, and gild your honeysuckled fields, do here scorch and parch the chinky gaping soyle, and put too many wrinkles upon the face of your common mother." Then, when the heavens and earth are on fire, and the sun drinks up rivers at one draught, when one burnt sienna tone pervades the tawny ground, and the green herb is shrivelled up into black gunpowder tea or souchong, and the rare pale ashy olive-trees are blanched into the livery of the desert ; then, when the heat and harshness make even the salamander muleteers swear doubly as they toil along like demons in an ignited salitrose dust, then, indeed, will an Englishman discover that he is made of the same material, only drier, and learn to estimate water; but a good thirst is too serious an evil in Spain to be made, like an appetite, a matter of congratulation ; for when all fluids evaporate, and the blood thickens into currant jelly, and the nerves tighten up into the catgut of an overstrung fiddle, getting attuned to the porcupinal irritability of the tension of the mind, how the parched soul sighs for the comfort of a Scotch mist, and fondly turns back to the uvula-relaxing damps of Devon;—then, in the Hagar-like thirst of the wilderness, every mummy hag rushing from a reed hut, with a porous cup of brackish water, is changed by the mirage into a Hebe, bearing the nectar of the immortals; then how one longs for the most wretched *Venta*, which heat and thirst convert into the Clarendon, since in it at least will be found water and shade, and an escape from the god of fire.   Well may Spanish historians boast, that his orb at the creation first shone over Toledo, and never since has set on the dominions of the great king, who, as we are assured by Berni (*Creacion*, p. 82), "has the sun for his hat,"—*tiene al sol por su sombrero;* but humbler mortals who are not grandees of this solar system, and to whom a *coup de soleil* is neither a joke nor a metaphor, should double up sheets of brown paper in the crown of their beavers.   Sic nos servavit Apollo.   And oh! ye our fair readers, who value complexion, take for heaven's sake a parasol.

EXCURSIONS ROUND MADRID.

Every one of course will visit *Los sitios reales*, or the "royal seats" of the Escorial, San Ildefonso, and Aranjuez: in order to economise time, these may be included in other routes; thus those about to travel from Madrid to the S. or E. may first take Toledo and Aranjuez, and then journey on, if to Valencia, by Cuenca, and if to Andalucia, by the Sierra Morena.   Those proceeding from Madrid to France may pass by Avila, the Escorial, Sⁿ· Ildefonso to Segovia, and thence to Valladolid and Burgos.   Those going from Madrid to Vigo, may proceed by Segovia, San Ildefonso, the Escorial, Avila, and Salamanca.

ROUTE XCVII.—MADRID TO AVILA.

Boadilla	2¾	
Brunete	2¼ ..	5
Chapinera	3 ..	8
Val de Iglesias	2 ..	10
Guisando	1 ..	11
Tiemblo	1 ..	12
Berraco	2 ..	14
Avila	2 ..	16

There is a sort of *coche* to Avila, which starts from the *Meson de los Huevos*, Cᵉ· de la Concepcion Geronima.   Avila by the direct Villacastin road is about 20 L. from Madrid: the shortest road is by the Escorial, 16 L. (see R. xcviii., xcix.); but an asbestic antiquarian may hire horses and a guide and ride across by *Guisando*.

Quitting the capital, after crossing the Manzanares, the road strikes into a desert-like country.   On passing the rivers Guadarrama and Alberche, we enter Old Castile and soon reach *Val de Iglesias*, once celebrated for its carvings (see p. 771).   The Escorial lies to the r. distant about 2 L.; the intervening farm *del Guexijar*, produces the rich full-bodied wine, called *el vino santo*, so relished by the holy monks of the Escorial, who were οινοβιοι rather than κοινοβιοι.   Formerly all the windows of that convent with a sunny aspect· were lined with portly bottles exposed to the mellowing rays, after the Horatian maxim—Massica si cœlo, &c.   Such was the wine of the Græcian priests (Od. ix. 196), the *Vinum Dominicum* of the Romans (Pet. Arb. 31).

In the Parroquia at *Robledo de Chavela* is, or now perhaps *was*, a *retablo* with 17 pictures of the life of the Virgin, by Rincon, court painter to Ferd. and Isabella : yet being thus *arrinconado*, or buried in an out-of-the-way corner, possibly they still exist.   On reaching the Geronimite convent of *Guisando*, observe in the vineyard some of the strange animals of granite called *Toros* by tauromachian Spaniards, who ought to have known better what a bull was like and what he was not; to us they seemed rather of the hippopotamus or rhinoceros breed.   These sculptures have been injured both by man and time, and the inscriptions on one plinth are not coeval with the animal. Some consider them to refer to victories gained by Cæsar over the sons of Pompey. These *Toros* were once very numerous in the central regions of Spain; thus Gil de Avila, writing in 1598, enumerates 63 of them, while Somorrostro, in 1820, only 37, so rapidly are these unexplained relics of antiquity disappearing. Interesting as our Druidical cromlechs, they are used up by barbarians to mend roads and repair pigsties. Much ink has been expended in discussing their origin and object: some contend that they were set up by Hercules, *i. e.* the Phœnicians, in commemoration of the bull Apis; but Tyre never would have selected an Egyptian symbol, even supposing that her merchants ever penetrated so far into the interior of Spain, which they did not. Others maintain that Hannibal made these *landmarks* in the shape of his elephants; others, and perhaps correctly, hold them to be the rude idols of the aborigines, whose god, *Neton* or Mars, was the sun adored at Heliopolis under the form of a bull, the "golden calf" of the Israelites (Macrob. 'Sat.' i. 19, 21). All, however, is mere conjecture, whereat in derision Cervantes makes his knight of the wood weigh one of these *Toros*. Now Young Spain cares little for anything beyond the present, and one live bull in the *plaza* in her eyes is worth a hecatomb of these brutes in granite. Consult ' *Declaracion del Toro,*' Gil de Avila, 4to., Salamanca, 1597; ' *Viage artistico,*' Bosarte, 32; ' *Noticias*' de Florez, 133.

It was at Guisando Sept. 9, 1468, that the memorable meeting took place between Henrique IV. and Isabella: then the impotent king declared his sister as his heir, but while signing the deed with one hand, he plotted with the other its non-execution; *Cosas de España:* see Prescott, ' Ferd. and Isab.,' chr. iii.

Turning up the Alberche, an excellent trout-stream, cross over to *Berraco*, amid pine-clad hills. Observe the costume of the women. Soon the road enters the rugged districts of Avila; and passing over the *Puerto*, the pleasant *vega* opens, watered by the Adaja, with the lines of walls and towers of the mountain city. The distant appearance is imposing; the city has a fortified feudal look, to which the colour of the granite material contributes: inside, the streets are narrow and gloomy; in the suburbs, however, are some pleasant *alamedas*. The walls are nearly two miles in circumference; they once had 88 towers, and were built in 1090 98, by the architects Casandro and Florin de Pituenga, for Don Ramon, son-in-law of Alonzo VI., by whom Avila was repeopled.

Avila is the capital of its cold mountainous province, but the *parameras* or plains are fertile, and many sweet valleys are enclosed in the spurs of the hills, and watered by trout-streams. There is also good shooting in the *Montes y dehesas*. The peasantry are very poor, and much land remains uncultivated. The laws of mortmain, and manorial and feudal rights, have here been peculiarly oppressive (consult Minaño, i. 328, and ' *Estadistica, etc. de Avila,*' Bernardo de Borjas y Tarrius, Mad., 1804; and for the city itself, ' *Grandezas de Avila,*' Luis Ariz, fol., Alcalá de Henares, 1607). This book contains some curious pedigrees; indeed, from the number of knightly families, the town was entitled *Avila de los Caballeros*. Avila, say the Spaniards, was originally called *Abula*, after the mother of Hercules, by whom the place was founded, but the word in Hebrew signifies "fruitful."

The Inns are very bad: the least bad is at *La Mingoriana*, on the *plaza*, and *La del Empecinado*, Puerta del rastro. The Madrid *galerus* put up at the *Meson del Huevo*. Avila is the see of a bishop suffragan to Santiago, and has a university. Pop[n.] under 5000. It is a dull decaying place, and never has recovered the hostile occupation of Gen. Hugo.

The Gothic cathedral was built in 1107, by Alvar Garcia de Estrella: the principal entrance is enriched with work of an early period. First examine the exterior with its castellated machicolations, half church, half fortress; a cross marks the spot where the loyal citizens elevated Alonzo VIII. for their king, when only a child of four years old, and hence called *El Rey Niño*. They defended him against his usurping uncle, Ferd. II. of Leon, who wished to profit by the civil feuds between the Laras and de Castros, the former having taken offence at the child's father, who died in 1158, having appointed their rivals as his guardians. Avila defended Alonzo until he was eleven years old, and hence received the title of *Avila del Rey*, and for armorial bearings, a tower with the royal figure at the window. If the loyal townsfolk could uphold, so they could degrade their sovereigns: here, June 5, 1465, the effigy of the weak Henrique IV. was placed on a throne, clad in royal robes; sceptre, crown, and other attributes were then taken away one by one by the grandees, headed by Alonzo Carrillo, archbishop of Toledo, and the denuded statue was kicked off the throne, and his brother Alonzo proclaimed in his stead: see Prescott, ' Ferd. and Isab.,' chr. iii.

The interior of the cathedral is simple. Observe the circular absis behind the high altar. The *Retablo* is of the time of Ferd. and Isabella: the pictures are by Santos Cruz, Pedro Berruguete, and Juan de Borgoña; painted in 1508, they are among the oldest specimens in Spain. The transept was finished in 1350, by Bishop Sancho de Avila; the painted glass is very fine; much of it was executed in 1498, by Juan de Santillana. Observe the St. John the Baptist, the *Santas* Inez, Cristina, and Cecilia, and those in the *Capilla del Cardenal;* the latter windows were painted in 1520 by Alberto de Hollanda. The *Silla. del Coro* was

carved in 1536-47 by Cornelis, with an infinity of saints and small figures. The backs are inlaid with a dark wood called *Texa*, which grows on the neighbouring hills of *Las Navas*. In the *trascoro* remark, among some fine reliefs, an Adoration of the Kings, a Flight into Egypt, a San Joaquin and Sᵃ· Ana.

Observe particularly the tomb of the learned *Alfonzo Tostado de Madrigal*, bishop of Avila in 1449, and hence called *El Abulense*. Clad in pontificalibus, he is in the act of writing, which was the joy and business of his life: obiit 1455, aged 55. He was the Solomon of his age, and wrote de rebus cunctis et quibusdum aliis, or, as his epitaph has it, " Hic stupor est mundi, qui scibile discutit omne." The inscription, among other necrological information, states that he lived and died a virgin, and "wrote for certain three sheets per day, every day of his life, and that his enlightened doctrines caused the blind to see." Ponz (*Viage*, xii. 306) calculates that his pen covered 60,225 pages with " *Sana catolica y verdadera doctrina*." Tostado, this *burro cargado de letras*, was in fact a heavy pedantic polemical commentator, who "never reconciled divinity with wit." His books, quantity versus quality, undeniable, unmitigated prose, and dissertations on broomsticks, are now fortunately food, or rather poison for worms. For his biography, consult his Life by Gil de Avila, 4to., Salamanca, 1611. Look also at the ancient *retablos* in the chapel of San Antolin: that of *San Segundo*, a tutelar of Avila, and attached to the cathedral, was built in 1595 by Frᵒ· de Mora, one of Herrera's best pupils ; the fine stone came from the quarries of *Cardenosa*. The cloisters are simple, but deserve notice. In the town the church of *San Salvador* is of the same period as the cathedral.

The great glory of Avila is, however, a female, one superior in erudition and sanctity to Tostado himself, and like him a virgin, whose corrected appellation is *Nuestra Serafica Madre Sa. Teresa de Jesus:* born here, March 28, 1515, of noble parents, Alonzo de Cepeda, and Beatriz de Ahumada, when only seven years old, she longed to go to Africa to be martyrized by the Moors; at twenty she took the veil, and soon after was carried up into heaven, and was shown the plan of reformed nunneries, which on her return to earth she carried out, founding herself seventeen convents of bare-footed Carmelites. It was soon revealed to her that conversation with ordinary men was criminal, and she passed twenty years in intimate connexion with angels, who visited her, probably, in the form of monks. At last she became the "spouse of the Saviour," and took his name; as her whole constitutional temperament was towards love, her religious development naturally was modified by that tender bias. According to her, the pains of the damned in hell consisted in their incapacity of loving and being loved. Teresa is a great favourite with Spanish artists, who generally represent her as dying away while an angel touches her heart with a fire-tipped arrow. The 27th of August is kept all over the Peninsula as the holy day sacred to this mystery, which is called *La trans-verberacion del corazon de Sᵃ. Teresa de Jesus;* a name longer even than *transubstancion.* Spanish monks, however, were quite as combustible; thus San Luis de Gonzaga is always painted so inflamed with love, that fire issues from his breast. Teresa is at other times drawn "writing at a table, while a dove at her ear whispers 'Newes from her spouse.'"

She was a voluminous author: the best edition of her revelations is that of Madrid, 1793! '*Obras y Cartas,*' 6 vols. 4to. Philip II. collected her manuscripts, like Sibylline books, which are preserved in the Escorial, and were shown by the monks as gems, to which ancient and Arabic MS. were as dirt: her handwriting was as vile and straggling as that of Philip him-self. For details of her compositions, see Antonio (Bib. Nov. ii. 295), in which, published at Madrid in 1783! they are treated as " inspired writings;" but she in truth was a mere tool of the Jesuits, and especially of Fʳᵒ· de Borja, while her writings were *edited* by two crafty Dominicans, named Ibañez and Garcia, who knowing how strong in man is the tendency to believe in some revelation, put forth these cheats, which their dupes swallowed greedily. " A wonderful and horrible thing is committed in the land;· the prophets prophesy falsely, and the *priests have rule* by their means, and the *people love to have it so* " (Jer. v. 31): compare also Isaiah viii. 19 with Acts xvi. 16; and the damsel possessed with a spirit of divination, which brought her masters *much gain* by soothsaying. Philip II. upheld Teresa, who in her turn was as ready εs το φιλιππιζειν, and support his bigotry, as the Pythia of old was to act in collusion with his name-sake of Macedon (Cic. ' De Div.' ii. 57).

Sᵃ· Teresa died at Avila Oct. 4, 1582, 10,000 martyrs assisting at her bed-side, and the Saviour coming down in person to convey his bride to heaven. This sort of " *sound* Catholic and *true* doctrine " fills 18 pages of Ribadeneyra (iii. 252). Consult also the work of Diego de Yepes, Mad. 1599; the 4to. of Fʳᵒ· de Ribera (her confessor and manager), Mad. 1602. This volume, from its authenticity, has often been translated. Read also the poem in 8vo. by Pablo Verdugo, Mad. 1615, and *La Amazona Christiana,* Barᵗᵉ· de Segovia, 8vo. Mad. 1619; and her life by Miguel Bᵃ· de Lanuza (a great biographer of the Spanish saints), folio, Zaragoza, 1657.

Sᵃ· Teresa has now superseded the mediæval goddesses, the Eulalias, Leocadias, &c., for she was declared by the silly Philip III. to be the lady patroness of Spain, as Juno was of Carthage, and Minerva of Athens; Santiago remaining the male Hercules. On March 12, 1622, Gregory XV., bribed by the gold of Philip IV., placed this love-sick nun in the calendar of Romish saintesses, instead of in Bedlam ; and now Avila is termed "a precious shell which contains a pearl of great price," to wit, her fragrant uncorrupted miracle-working body ; and to this the Cadiz Cortes, the collected wisdom of Spain, turned in their hour of need, and having refused command to the Duke, appointed her *Generalisima* of the Spanish armies—*Dux fœmina facti ;* and the first act of the war minister in 1844 was to promote Queen Christina to be a Colonel of Chasseurs, whose uniform, as a delicate compliment to her virtue, was white and blue, the colours of the *immaculate* conception.

Sᴬ· Teresa is buried in San Jose, which she founded herself. Visit the nunnery : her statue sanctifies the portal. The chapel is a very holy place, and frequented by pilgrims, in smaller numbers, however, than heretofore. The nuns never presume to sit on the seats in the *Coro,* but only on the steps, because the former were occupied by angels whenever Sᴬ· Teresa attended mass, and the carving, at all events, is worthy of such occupants. The nuns show, besides the tomb, many inestimable relics of their founder, which are not worth notice. Among other tombs observe that of her brother, Lorenzo de Cepeda, obiit 1580 ; and a kneeling prelate, Alvaro de Mendoza, obiit 1586 : also two superb sepulchres under niches, with Corinthian pilasters, and kneeling statues by Fʳᵒ· Velazquez, 1630. The trees of *La Encarnacion* are said to have been planted by Sᵃ· Teresa.

Spanish priests and monks have never shown much invention in their legends or miracles, which they either imported from other countries ready made, or went to Paganism for materials. Sᵃ· Teresa is an imitation of St. Bridget of Sweden, who also was the "spouse of Christ," as also the revealer of his wishes, and *Embajadrix del Cielo,* also a founder of convents, a

tool in the hands of her crafty confessors, Peter and Mattias, and also canonized.

Again, these Santas Teresas and Catherines of Sienna, &c., were but the Pythonesses and Sibyls of old, reproduced under new names. The Circes and Sirens changed men into beasts just as these *santas* made them fools ; but so it has ever been since the father of all lies selected the first woman to beguile the first man, and father of all men ; for when a lady is in the case, bird-lime is never wanting for the wicked one to catch male souls. Their persuasive eloquence, which requires small fuel of facts, added to sexual influence, is irresistible, nor is nonsense any objection. The sayings of Sᵃ· Teresa, like those of San Tiresias of old, either came true or did not. But solemn humbug always captivates the many, who estimate as magnificent whatever they do not understand ; so the spirit-moved Teresa of the Æneid (vi. 50) spoke the unknown tongue, "nec mortale sonans," and her influence, of course, was unbounded ; indeed, the sane Pagans reasonably derived the term Μαντεις, απο τον μαινεσθαι, from the decided symptoms of loss of intellect. A want of common sense has never in Spain been an objection in a ruler or leader, male or female ; nay, some of their most venerable saints have been selected from the most ignorant monks and nuns. Thus Ribadeneyra, the grand hagiographical authority, quotes largely from the writings of *el Sapientisimo Idiota,* who wrote worthily of his name. So the Moors respect their idiots, and call them *Santons,* thinking, because they are fools on earth, that their sainted minds are wandering in heaven : "Hæc et alia generis ejusdem, ita defenditis, ut ii qui ista finxerunt, non modo non insani, sed etiam fuisse *sapientes* videantur" (Cicero, ' N. D.' iii. 24). The Pagan philosophers attributed much of all this to wind and flatulence, and when these ravings were belched forth, afflata est numine quando, termed the

performers Εγγαστριμνθαι or ventrilo-
quists. These the priests of Delphi
put on a tripod, and the Spaniards
crowned with an aureola, when in
England a straight waistcoat would be
called for, except in real cases, such as
Johanna Southcot. Again, how Pagan
and Oriental are all the minor details
of Sᵃ· Teresa. Mahomet fed a tame
pigeon from his ear, and persuaded
true believers that it communicated
to him the Koran; long before, however, Herodotus (ii. 55) had noticed
the doves of Dodona, and the word
πελεια, in Thessalian, signified both an
old woman and a pigeon. As to marriages with the Deity, the Pythoness
Dione was allowed to cohabit with
Jupiter (Strabo vii. 506), who was also
thought by a Roman *beata* to be in
love with her; and St. Augustine,
justly indignant at these blasphemies,
remarks, "Si *verum* attendamus, dete-
riora sunt templa ubi hæc *aguntur*,
quam theatra ubi *finguntur*" (De Civ.
Dei, vi. 10). In Spain, where the passions are fierce, the monks, victims of
unnatural celibacy, fell in love with
the paintings and images of the Virgin,
as the Pagans did with those of Venus
(compare Pliny, ' N. H.' xxxvi. 5;
with Palomino, ' *Mus. Pit.*' ii. 139,
and Carducho, ' *Dialogos*,' 121). The
nuns, unwilling brides of heaven, more
than adored beautiful male saints, and
especially Sⁿ· Sebastian, the Romanist
Apollo; but as Pliny observed (N. H.
ii. 7), the alliances with the Pantheon
never were prolific. Cupid and Psyche,
Bacchus and Ariadne, &c., are all
types of these "sponses." (See also
Bayle's article on St. Catherine of
Sienna, and Bochart's *Hierozoicon*, ii.
chr. 49.)

The finest monument in Avila is that
in the Dominican convent erected to
Prince Juan, only son of Ferd. and
Isab. He died at Salamanca in 1497,
aged only 19, for the young bride-
groom, like Raphael, was killed by
ignorant *sangrados*, who mistook the
causes of his momentary exhaustion.
His death created a national grief,
equal to that of our Princess Charlotte.
He was a prince of infinite promise,
and his loss entailed the ruin of Spain,
which his parents had raised to its
really greatest position. The crown
passed to the *foreigner*, for Charles V.,
a Fleming by birth, was an Austrian
in heart, and wasted on German politics the blood and gold of Spain. This
beautiful tomb, the masterpiece of
Micer Domenico, of Florence, was
raised by the prince's treasurer, Juan
Velasquez, who added a short but
pathetic epitaph. It is placed under
an elliptical arch, and resembles the
exquisite royal sepulchres at Granada.
In the *Capilla de Sⁿ· Luis Beltran*, is
another fine monument to Juan Davila
and Juana Velasquez, attendants on
the prince. The *Sillᵃ· del Coro* is most
elaborate. Some have attributed the
paintings in the *Retablo* to Fernando
Gallegos.

Next visit *San Vicente*, an extramural church, built in 313, and, according to the inscription, by a converted Jew, who is buried here. Observe the enriched principal and lateral entrances. This St. Vincent, like
his namesake of the Cape, was martyrized by Dacian; born at Evora or
Talavera, when brought before an image
of Jupiter, he stamped upon the altar,
which instantly received the impressions of his feet. He was executed,
Oct. 27, 303, and his body cast to the
dogs, but a serpent watched over it; a
notion taken from the *draco*, which
guarded the tomb of Scipio Africanus
(Pliny, ' N. H.' xvi. 44; and see Cicero, ' de Div.' i. 33). The reptile flew
at a *rich* Jew, who came to mock the
corpse, and who in his fright vowed, if
he escaped, to build and endow a
church, which he did. (See Ribad.
iii. 308; Morales, ' *Cor. Gen.*' x. 362;
and Ariz, 30.) The possession of St.
Vincent's body is said to " *ensure*" to
Avila *gracia y ventura, para hacerse
entre todas mas dichosa*, and yet with
Tostado and Teresa to boot, few places
are more miserable. The hole out of
which the snake came, *El bujo* (im-

properly called *El Herrojo de Sn. Vicente*), was one of the three sites of adjuration. (Compare Sa. Gadea of Burgos, and Sn. Isidoro of Leon, p. 609). The prelate who succeeded Tostado, one Martin Vilches, wished about the year 1458 to ascertain whether the saint's body was really below the stone. He put his arm into the hole, and drew it out quickly, bitten and bleeding, possibly by the snake. A board, marked with his blood, was long shown as evidence, and a relic for the edification of the pious. The bishop, to make amends, raised the present tomb, to which many devotees contributed, whose arms are thereon. After that the populace, and all who wished to make a solemn adjuration, put their fingers into the hole, as the populace at Rome does into that of the Bocca de la Veritá, until the ceremony was prohibited by Isabella. "Tango aras et numina testor" (Æn. xii. 201). Primitive religion was connected with law and government: stones, enduring types of judgment seats, formed the symbol of Bethel, Gilgal, and Mispech. Such were the Druidical cromlechs, such the "black stone" of Iona, adjuration to which settled all disputes, like the black stone of the Caaba at Mecca. Ophic superstitions pervade all the legends of antiquity. Compare the serpent of Esculapius, the avenging snakes of Laocoon, and those in the temple of Jupiter (Livy xxviii. 11).

The artist and architect will find much to study in Avila. Among the ancient mansions, observe those of the *Condes de Polentinos*, with an enriched portal of armed men, and an elegant but dilapidated *patio;* the *Casa de Colmenares*, and the noble courtyard in the house of the *Ms. de Velada.* In Avila are some of the *Toros* of the Guisando breed. For communications with Salamanca, see R. lxvi.

ROUTE XCVIII.—AVILA TO THE ESCORIAL AND SEGOVIA.

Urraca	2½	
Las Navas del Marques	3	5½
Al Escorial	3	8½
Guadarrama	2	10½
Va. de Cercedilla	2	12½
Castrejones	2	14½
Sn. Ildefonso	2	16½
Segovia	2	18½

This rough mountain ride is often snowed up from November to April. The hilly crest overlooks the *parameras* of Avila, and the valley of the Alberche, with the dreary environs of Madrid sweeping to the horizon. In the cold elevations near *Las Navas* grows the texa, amantes frigora taxi, whose dark wood resembles mahogany. The cream, or curds, *la nata*, is celebrated at Madrid, but would not do in Devonshire. *Nata*, in Arabic, signifies "whatever rises to the top;" *Manteca*, butter, is also Arabic, the "pith or marrow." *Las Navas* contains 3000 inhabitants; it lies in a damp hollow, fenced in by mountains. After crossing a tributary of the Alberche, and ascending a spur of the *Sierra*, the vasty grey Escorial looms in view.

ROUTE XCIX.—MADRID TO THE ESCORIAL AND SEGOVIA.

Alas Rosas	3	
Puente del Retamar	2	5
Galapagar	1½	6½
Al Escorial	2	8½
Segovia	8	16½

There is a diligence; the office is at 26, Ce. de Alcalá. The road is unnecessarily magnificent, but Spaniards, whenever they finish anything, do it in Roman style; and no expense was grudged on this *Camino real*, which, although of little use to commerce or the public, led to the covers and convent of the king, whether monk, gamekeeper, or both, as the Austrians and Bourbons mostly were. Leaving Madrid by the planted banks of the Manzanares, pleasant when there is any water in the river, to the r. is *Moncloa* (see p. 797). On passing the *Pa. de Hierro*, the toll-house, and huge bridge, soon the desert environs of Madrid are entered. In summer time, when the heavens are on fire and the earth tawny and toasted, nothing is wanting but the plague to make the Oriental picture perfect. The contrast of leaving a crowded city increases the forlorn loneliness and dilapidation, which, as in the East, is the character of Spain, where villages are in decay, lands uncultivated, and living mortals are either veiled or cloaked. There is nothing *riant* or verdurous; few are the smiles on the face either of man or nature; here everything is harsh, and devoid of the tender and love, however full of fire and passion; silence and nudity prevail, and yet there is wanting the melancholy grandeur of the perfect solitude of the desert; here there is just population enough to show how scanty it is, and yet to disenchant the poetry of utter loneliness and uninhabited abandonment. Again, the desertlike features offend here, because out of place when so near a royal court, while the bungling partial cultivation which roots up the wild flower of this Campagna can indeed destroy its sentiment, without being able to gladden the eye by rich produce, and fields laughing with corn and wine; here the wheat wrestles with the thistle and weed for its very existence.

The whole route to the Escorial continues thus barren, desolate, and without grandeur; the soil is poor, and the boor who scratches it is almost a savage: yet this wilderness, which disfigures Madrid, forms no bad approach to the gloomy pile, which, at the fifth L., is seen under the jagged, sullen *Sierra*. The fascination increases as we draw closer within the power of this magnet's attraction; curiosity rises to fever heat, and the edifice itself seems as we approach to grow in size as well as interest; it looms so large, that it is not lost even among the mountains. The E. end of the chapel, and the projecting handle of the gridiron, mar the elevation; but as a whole it rises grandly from the gardens and terraces, embosomed in plantations, which fringe the edge of the desert; all around, on either side, from roseless *Las Rosas*, and

Galapagar, is *dehesa y despoblado.* Here and there long lines of walls enclose the now deserted dwarf covers of *El Pardo* and *La Zarzuela*, and other preserves of theriomaniac royalty. On passing a boulder granite stone, a cross indicates the former dominion of the cowl; hence, through poplars and pollarded elms, the road ascends to the wind-blown hamlet, which looks paltry when compared to the single edifice, whose size is increased by the insignificance of so many smaller buildings.

The *Escorial* is placed by some geographers in Old Castile, but the division of the provinces is carried on the crest of the *Sierra*, which rises behind it. The best *Posadas* are *La Fontana*, *La de los Milaneses*, *La del Correo*. The best guide is Cornelio, a blind man who leads the blind, but he sees clearly with his " mind's eye," knows every corner, and particularly points out the finest views. The convent being in strict *Clausura*, a permission from the pope's nuncio at Madrid used to be necessary for all females who wished to pry into the *penetralia monastica.* The Escorial is now a shadow of the past, for the shell has lost its living monks, and those revenues whereby they lived. The enormous pile, exposed to the hurricane and mountain snows, was only to be kept in repair at a great outlay. In the five years after the sequestrations of Mendizabal, more injury ensued than during the preceding two centuries. The rains penetrated through the damaged roof, and damp, sad destroyer, crept into the untenanted chambers. The eighth marvel of the world, which cost millions, was perishing for the sake of a few hundreds, until Arguelles, in 1842, destined a pittance out of the queen's privy purse, and stayed the immediate ruin; these outlays have been continued since royalty has resumed her rights; nor will those who know Spain be even surprised to see the monk once more reappear and claim his own; and he is almost necessary for the foreground of this picture, as for him the pile was reared, and without his return its ruin sooner or later is certain. Vast and useless as the pyramids, the Escorial is too big to be moved even by the slaves of the lamp, even had they been imps of Spain. Out of the way, it is fit only for a convent. It might, indeed, supposing it were three times as large, be made the new poor-law union of the Peninsula. It has also been stripped of its gold by the invaders, and recently of its fine art; for above 100 of the best pictures were brought to Madrid in July, 1837, when the Carlists, under Zariategui, advanced on Segovia.

For the Escorial as it was, consult the excellent *Historia de la Orden de Sⁿ· Geronymo,*' José de Siguenza, fol. 4 vols. Mad. 1600-5. This learned man, an eye-witness of its building, was its first prior: ' *Descripcion...del Escorial,*' Fr^{o.} de los Santos, fol. Mad. 1657; of this there is a meagre translation in 4to. London, 1671, by a servant of Lord Sandwich, who in his title-page tells us that "the Escurial had lately been consumed by fire!" ' *Le reali grandezze del Escuriale,*' Ilario Mazzolari de Cremona, 4to. Bologna, 1648: ' *Descripcion,*' &c., Andres Ximenez, fol. Mad. 1764. These describe its splendid condition before the French invasion. The best subsequent guide is the ' *Descripcion Artistica,*' Damien Bermejo, duo. Mad. 1820, which is to be had in the village. There is a set of accurate views by Tomas Lope Enquidanos, sold at the Madrid *Imprenta real.* Herrera published himself a list of his original plans and elevations, ' *Sumario de los diseños,*' duo. Mad. 1589.

The correct title of the edifice is *El real sitio de Sⁿ· Lorenzo el real del Escorial.* The latter name is derived by some from *Escoriæ,* the *dross* of mines, which do not exist here, an etymology mean as that of the *tiles* of the Tuilleries. Casiri (Bib. Arab. Es., i. 20, ii. 61) reads in the name the Arabic " a

place of rocks;" others prefer " Æsculetum," a place of scrub oaks, Quercus Quejigo, which are the weed of the locality. The edifice is a combined palace, convent, and tomb, and for these purposes was it reared by Philip II., who is called by the monks " the holy founder," and by others *El Escorialense.* His ostensible object was to carry out the will of his father in constructing a royal burial-place, and to fulfil a panic-inspired vow made during the battle of St. Quintin, when he implored the aid of San Lorenzo, on whose day it was fought. Thus, in doubtful conflict, the Pagan Fulvius Flaccus bribed Jupiter by vowing a temple (Livy xl. 40); so, says the same author (x. 19), did Appius Claudius; and Cæsar himself before Pharsalia promised a shrine to Venus Victrix (Plut. *in Pomp.*).

San Lorenzo, the Hercules of this most ultra-Catholic Philip, was a native of Huesca, and like a true Arragonese stood fire better than the holy founder. He was broiled by Valentianus, Aug. 10, 261, on a slow fire, and not quickly done, *à la bifstec.* He bore the operation with great sang froid, for Prudentius (Peri. ii. 401) relates that he directed the cooks to turn him, when one side was burnt, " converte partem corporis, satis crematum,'' then " ludibundus " he jocosely invited them to eat him and see whether he was most savoury, if welldone or underdone.

" Tunc ille : coctum est, devora
Et experimentum cape
Sit crudum an assum suavius."

So Justin, xliv. 2, describes an Iberian, qui inter tormenta risu exultavit, serenâque lætitiâ crudelitatem torquentium vicit: compare the bakings of San Cucufat, p. 489.

The battle of St. Quintin was fought Aug. 10, 1557. The whole glory, as at Pavia, Lepanto, Bailen, the Peninsular war, &c., is now claimed by the Spaniards for themselves, but, like many others, it was won by a *foreign* commander, by Philibert of Savoy, who was ably seconded by D Egmont, with Flemish infantry and German cavalry, and better still by 8000 English, under Lord Pembroke. The French were completely routed, and lost 3000 men, 4000 prisoners, colours, baggage, and artillery. Had Philip II. pressed on, he might have captured Paris as easily as the Duke did after Waterloo;* but he wanted means of moving, like Castaños, and like him (see Bailen) was not even on the field of *his* victory. He passed his time between two confessors, vowing convents, and swearing, if once safe, never to conquer twice. And this colossal pile is proportionate to his piety and fears, for celui qui faisait un si grand vœu, said the Duke of Braganza, doit avoir eu grand peur; and, in truth, it is the only *benefit* which Spain derived from that important victory. Philip, tired of war's alarms, reposed under *his* borrowed laurels, and took to building, for which he was really fitted, being a man of taste and a true patron of artists. As he was of a shy phlegmatic temperament, he, like Tiberius, made the dedication of this temple his excuse to escape from the publicity of Madrid, certus procul ab urbe degere (Tac. ' An.' iv. 57). The first stone was laid April 23, 1563, by Jⁿ· Bª· de Toledo, whose great pupil, Juan de Herrera, finished the pile Sept. 13, 1584 ; yet now, in the seventh edition of the ' Encyclopædia Britannica ' (iii. 427), among the gross errors of most of its Spanish articles (e. g. Gijon p. 703), it is gravely asserted, " that the Spaniards, less patriotic than the French, have, for their greatest works, employed the architects of France and Italy ; so that *of course* the country can boast of no peculiarity of style redounding to its own credit ; the palace of the Escurial being by a *French architect*, and

* According to De Thou (xix.), the real obstacle was the withdrawal of the English troops in disgust at the arrogance and bad faith of the Spaniards. The moment they retired victory departed with them (compare Navarrete).

abounding with deformities of the French and Italian schools, cannot be cited in favour of Spain." This mistake arose from the audacious assertion of a common French mason, one Louis Foix, who having carried a hod there, said, on his return to France, that he had " built the Escorial." This, possibly a joke, was believed by Colmenar and Voltaire, for what will not vanity gulp down or dishonesty misstate; thus *La Tour de Corduan*, a pepper-box-domed lighthouse, raised near the mouth of the Gironde in 1611, is ascribed to this Foix, as " an architect of the Escorial." But the name *Foy*, notwithstanding its apparent meaning, is one which scarcely implies the absolute authority of good faith in French versions of facts and events in Spain ; tali fronti nulla fides.

On the same 13th of Sept., 1598, did Philip II. die here, having lived in his vast convent 14 years, half-king, half-monk, and boasting that from the foot of a mountain he governed half the world, old and new, with two inches of paper. The holy founder is compared to Solomon, who reared the temple, which was not permitted to men of blood, like David and Charles V. But the yoke of building kings is grievous, and as Judah and Israel divided under Rehoboam, so Portugal was lost to Spain under Philip IV. The Escorial altogether was a mistake, for the selection as a site for state business was ill chosen, while to raise a convent when monks had done their work as pioneers of civilization was an anachronism : again, the enormous expense absorbed sums which would have covered the Peninsula with a net-work of roads and canals, of which there were just as too few as there were of convents too many. The Escorial also tended to fix the residence of the court at Madrid, the bane of Spain. Thus injurious from the beginning to the end, this useless colossal pile totters to its fall, a thing to point a moral and adorn a tale : Non in aliâ re *damnosior* quam ædificando was the just remark of Suetonius (in vit. 30), when reflecting on the sad results of the Golden Palace of Nero.

The Escorial will disappoint at first sight, for expectations have been too highly raised; but this is the penalty which the credulous hope of travellers must pay, who will go on expecting too much in spite of illusion-dispelling experience. Yet happy the frame of mind which always hopes, and woe unto that traveller who comes into the Castiles without some poetry, some romance, to gild the harshness and discomforts which here too often characterize the reality.

The edifice has nothing in form or colour which is either royal, religious, or ancient. The clean granite, blue slates, and leaden roofs, look new, as if built yesterday. It has the air of an overgrown barrack or manufactory. The multitude of bald windows (they say that there are 11,000, in compliment to the Cologne Virgins), the green shutters and chickets are offensive; the windows of the entresols look like portholes, and, from the thickness of the walls they might be made real embrazures for cannon. The windows are too small, but had they been planned in proportion to the facades, the rooms lighted by them would have been too lofty, and thus external appearance was sacrificed for internal accommodation: now they are spots which cut up breadth and interfere with the sentiment of solidity. Bigoted, indeed, was Philip when he could sacrifice an opportunity of building a perfect palace, to an idle legend of a gridiron; and poor Herrera, forced to lower his genius to a plan worthy of the Beefsteak Club or Cobbett's register, was indeed the real martyr. The redeeming qualities are size, simplicity, and situation. It stands about 2700 feet above the level of the sea, and is part and parcel of the mountain out of which it has been constructed: it is so large that it looks, not a wart upon Olympus, but grand even amid the mighty buttresses of nature, which

form an appropriate background to the severe picture. The ashy pile looms like the palace of Death, who hence sends forth his blasts of consumption, which descend from these peeled Sierras to sweep human and vegetable life from the desert of Madrid. Cold as the grey eye and granite heart of its founder, this monument of fear and superstition would have been out of keeping, amid the flowers and sunshine of a happy valley.

The edifice is a rectangular parallelogram, measuring 744 feet from N. to S., and 580 from E. to W., but let us not measure it, for the sentiment of vastness is independent of actual size; it is chiefly built in the Doric order. The interior is divided into courts, which represent the intersections of the bars of a gridiron, while the handle forms the royal residence; the feet are supplied by the four towers at the corners. The N. and W. sides, which front the village and mountains, have a fine paved *Lonja* or platform: to the E. and S. terraces look over formal hanging gardens and fishponds. The slopes below are well planted, especially *La Herreria* and *La Fresneda*: the elms, according to Evelyn, were brought by Philip II. from England. The W. or grand façade faces the Sierra, and we stumble upon it, for the convent turns its back on Madrid, as if to show that the inmates ought to renounce its earthly doings and intrigues. On the north *Lonja* is a subterranean gallery 180 ft. long, 10 high, and 7 broad, tunnelled in 1770 by the monk Pontones, in order to afford a communication during the winter hurricanes, which the guides say once hoisted an ambassador, coach and all, into the air, to say nothing of the petticoats of monks and women blown up like balloons, and lords of the bedchamber by the score whirled round and round like dead leaves. By this passage, if fame do not wrong the holy celibates, many fair visitors were introduced who were not provided with a passport from or for the nonce. The convent, on account of the winds, is not placed according " to the cardinal points;" their violence is disarmed by its being set a little out of the square.

The guides know by rote all the proportions. They repeat that the square of the building covers 3002 ft.; that in the centre is the chapel, surmounted by a dome; that there are 63 fountains, 12 cloisters, 80 staircases, 16 court-yards, and 3000 ft. of painted fresco. It was at once a temple, a palace, a treasury, a tomb house, and a museum; "exceeding magnifical, of fame and glory throughout all countries." But in Dec., 1808, the French, under La Houssaye, arrived and sacked a pile, which recorded their former defeat at St. Quintin. See the deplorable details in Minaño (iii. 381). The Escorial never recovered this, which he justly terms " the ferocious vandalism of an accursed warfare leagued with plundering avarice." Ferd. VII., however, did what he could to repair his birthplace, and hence has been called the *second* founder.

The grand *Porteria* or entrance is on the N. façade, but it is seldom used; so after hunting about for an entrance, you at last discover to the W. a mean kitchen door, over which a San Lorenzo, 15 ft. high, is judiciously placed, with a proportionate gridiron, pour encourager les bifstecs. Two jaw-bones of a whale, caught off Valencia in 1574, complete this *bodegon*, or *tableau de cuisine*. This monster of the deep could have swallowed San Lorenzo, done or undone, and these relics are fit emblems of monastic maws and powers of deglutition. But now, alas! the monks are swept away, and the picture is incomplete. These Jeronimites, as usual with this order, were great agriculturists, or rather bailiffs, for they only superintended the working labourers, who, like Job's oxen, " were *ploughing*, and the asses *feeding* by them." The many windows of the convent were garnished with portly

bottles of *vino santo* (see p. 801), and when strangers arrived, the anchorites, smoking their *cigaritos*, peered out from between them, looking down on the vain world which they had renounced, their black heads and fleecy robes resembling sleek maggots in filberts, for few of the monastic order were fatter, and a gaunt Jeronimite was rarer than a plump Spanish soldier, but beasts of prey never attain the good condition of farinaceously fed animals. Here experiments were tried on the elasticity of the human skin, and how much stretching it would stand without bursting. The prize monks rejoiced in their fat, like the white-teethed swine of Homer, θαλιθοντς αλοιφη; now the lean kine of reformers have eaten them up, peace to their bones!

The grand central Doric and Ionic portal is never opened, save to admit royalty, either alive or dead. The first *Patio* is called de los *Reyes*, from the statues of " the Kings" of Judah, connected with the Temple of Jerusalem. They are 17 ft. high, and were all cut by Jⁿ· Bᵃ· Monegro, out of one granite block, of which enough still remains to make up the dozen. The hands and heads are of marble, the crowns of gilt bronze, but the figures are lanky and without merit; the least bad is that of Solomon. The court is 320 ft. deep by 230 wide, and is too crowded, being all roof, with no less than 275 windows: again, the pediment over the entrance into the church is too high and heavy. This court was the last finished. On the south side is the library, and opposite the students' college.

Hence by a dark passage to the grand chapel, *El templo*, which was begun in 1563 and completed in 1586: observe the construction of the flat roof, over which is the quire or *coro alto*. The interior of the chapel, as seen from under this sombre grotto-like arch, is the triumph of architecture: it takes away the breath of the beholder from its majestic simplicity. All is quiet, solemn, and unadorned;

no tinsel statues or tawdry gildings mar the perfect proportion of the chaste temple; the religious sentiment pervades the whole of this house of God; everything mean and trivial is forgotten. An awe, *der schauer des erhaben*, creeps over mortal man, who feels that the Holy of Holies overshadows him.

The chapel is a Greek cross, with 3 naves, 320 ft. long, 230 wide, and 320 high to the top of the cupola, but the secret of its grandeur is in the conception and proportion. The black and white pavement is serious and decorous. 8 of the compartments of the vaulted roof are all painted in fresco (blue predominating), by Luca Giordano. The *Retablo* of the high altar is superb, and is ascended to by a flight of red-veined marble steps. The screen, 93 ft. high by 43 wide, employed the artist, Giacomo Trezzo, of Milan, 7 years, and it is composed of the 4 orders. The dividing columns are jasper, with bronze gilt bases and capitals, and the roof is painted in fresco by Luca Cangiagi. The pictures in the *Retablo*, of the Adoration and Nativity, by Pelegrino Tibaldi, are very cold; while his San Lorenzo, "non satis crematus" puts out the gridiron fire from sheer rawness. Again the martyr is so gigantic that he might have eaten up the disproportionate Romans as easily as Capt. Gulliver routed the Lillyputians. The Saviour at the Column and bearing the Cross, and the Assumption of the Virgin are by F⁰· Zuccaro. The bronze medallions, the holy rood, and 15 gilt statues, are by Pompeio Leoni and his son. A wooden tabernacle replaces that of a splendid gilt bronze, which was designed by Herrera, and executed by Trezzo, and was one of the finest works of art in Spain, or indeed in the world; the older writers talk of it as a "specimen of the altar ornaments of heaven." This glorious work of art, which took 7 years to be made, was destroyed in five minutes, by the long bearded pioneers of La Houssaye, who broke it, thinking that it was silver gilt, and being disappointed, he cast it away as *Nehustan*, or *worthless* brass, not that he was a Hezekiah.

On each side of the high altar are low chambers or oratories for the royal family, while above are placed bronze-gilt and painted kneeling effigies. *Al lado del Evangelio*, is Charles V., his wife Isabel, his daughter Maria, and his sisters Eleonora and Maria. The epitaph challenges future kings to outdo him, and until then to cede the post of honour. Opposite kneel Philip II., Anna his fourth wife, mother of Philip III.; Isabel his third wife, and Maria his first, at whose side is her son Don Carlos. These statues are portraits, and the costume and heraldic decorations are very remarkable. Philip II. died in a small chamber near the oratory, below his figure. The minor altars are more than 40 in number; some of them, and the piers, are decorated with magnificent pictures by Juan Fernandez Navarrete *el Mudo*, the Dumb, but who spoke by his pencil with the bravura of Rubens, without his coarseness, and with a richness of colour often rivalling even Titian. The light is bad for seeing them, but the monks under the glorious sun of Castile cared nothing for *art*, they only looked to making it serve their *obscurantismo*. They are full-length figures of saints and apostles, and among the finest are Sⁿ· Felipe and Santiago: observe the way the drapery is painted. Sⁿ· Juan and Sⁿ· Mateo are equal to Tintoretto; S⁰· Tomas, Sⁿ· Barnabe, and Sⁿ· Andres are very grandiose. Other of the altars are by the Zuccaros, Luca Cangiagi, Alonzo Sanchez, Luis de Carabajal, both imitators of *el Mudo*, and Pelegrino Tibaldi.

The *relicario* is to the r. of the high altar, in the transept; when the doors are open the contents appear arranged on shelves, like an anatomical museum, although few Spanish surgeries possess so splendid an assortment. Philip II. was a *relicomaniac*, and collected bones, &c. more eagerly than

Titians; accordingly all who wished to curry favour with him, sent him a well authenticated tooth, toe, &c., which he encased in gold and silver, cumulatque altaria donis. There were 7421 specimens preserved in 515 shrines of Cellini-like plate, but La Houssaye took all the bullion, and left the relics on the floor. These, when he departed, the monks collected in baskets, but in the confusion many of their labels got undocketed, so that the separate items cannot now be identified with that scrupulous accuracy and regard to truth which every one knows is observed in all *Relicarios ;* yet, as far as public adoration and benefit are concerned, the *aggregate* amount is the same. The French also took more than 100 sacred vessels of silver and gold, besides the gold and jewelled *custodia,* the silver female image called *La Mecina,* the silver full-length statue of San Lorenzo, which weighed 4½ cwts., and held in its hand one of the real bars of his gridiron, set in gold, which La Houssaye stripped off, leaving the iron for the consolation of the monks, just as the aurivorous Dionysius left the statue of the Epidaurian Esculapius, simply removing his beard, which was made of gold (Cic. *de N. D.* iii. 34). This inestimable bar was found in the tomb of San Lorenzo, at Tivoli, by St. Gregory himself, and is here valued as highly as the scythe at Corcyra, with which Saturn mutilated his father (Apoll. Arg. iv. 985). Just now iron rails are more esteemed ; but relics have had their hour, and the dry bones of holy monks will no longer satisfy the belly or knife and fork question of to-day; yet before " *Navies*" worked miracles and moved mountains, the cathedral of Exeter had the felicity to possess some of the real coals on which St. Lawrence was broiled, and a bit of his body (Dugdale, ' *Monast.*' Ed. 1655, p. 226). La Houssaye also carried off the splendid silver lamps, which Ferd. VII. replaced in a baser metal ; as Rehoboam did after the temple had

been plundered by Shishak (1 Kings xiv. 27); by him also were made those trumpery pulpits which mar the simplicity of the chapel.

Next descend into the *Panteon,* the *Pagan* term given by the *Catholic* Spaniards to a *Christian* burial vault. This is placed under the high altar, in order that the celebrant, when he elevates the host, may do so exactly above the dead. Philip, although he built the Escorial as a tomb-house for his father, prepared nothing but a plain vault, which, like that of Frederick the Great at Potzdam, by the absence of tinsel pomp, becomes at once impressive and instructive, from the moral which such a change in such a monarch must suggest. Philip III., his silly son, began the present gorgeous chamber, which Philip IV. completed in 1654, moving in the royal bodies on the 17th of March. The entrance, with its gilt ornaments and variegated marbles, has nothing in common with the sepulchral sentiment. Descending observe the portrait of the monk Nicolas, who remedied a land-spring which is heard trickling behind the masonry. Observe now the portal, read the inscription, *Natura occidit,* &c. Descending again by a jasper-lined staircase, at the bottom is the *Panteon,* an octagon of 36 ft. in diameter, by 38 ft. high. The materials are richest marbles and gilt bronze; the Angels are by Antº· Ceroni of Milan ; the tawdry chandelier by Virgilio Francli of Genoa ; the crucifix is by Pedro Tacca. There are 26 niches hollowed in the 8 sides, with black marble urnas ; those which are filled are inscribed with the name of the occupant. None are buried here save kings and the mothers of kings ; for etiquette and precedence in Spain survive the grave ; and to preserve propriety the males are placed separately and opposite to the females. The royal bodies are really deposited in their *Urnas,* as Philip IV., in 1654, opened that of Charles V., which was found to be perfectly preserved ; and

Ferd. VII., at his restoration, had the others examined, fearing that the republican invader might have rifled them, as elsewhere either to insult dead royalty, or procure lead to destroy the living.

Ferdinand VII., as well as his worthy mother, had a morbid passion for descending to this bed of death, and looking at the identical urns, for all are occupied by rotation, which then empty, were yawning hungrily for them; but neither took much moral benefit from this memento mori, or the lesson, how history treats royalty when defunct. The divinity that doth hedge kings is here at an end; all to their wormy beds are gone—the ambition of Charles V., the bigotry of Philip II., the imbecility of Carlos II., the adulteries of Maria Luisa, the ingratitude of Ferdinand. Dust to dust, expende Hannibalem! How little remains of those for whom the world was too small. Now all distinctions are over, the game is played out, whether tragedy or farce. *Shiek mat,* "the king is dead," and the pieces are huddled indiscriminately into the box. Who can now distinguish, as Diogenes said, the scull of Philip from that of a peasant?

Generally speaking, when the party of visitors is numerous, each carries a taper, which, by lighting up this chamber of death, injures its impressiveness. It then becomes a mere show-room, where fritter and glitter ill accord with the lesson which this finale of pomp and power ought to suggest. The native, who has little feeling for the tender or retrospective, glories in this magnificence which mocks the dead: the red gold captivates his mind, and he thinks for such a tomb as this that kings must wish to die.

Visit rather this sepulchre alone, and when the tempest howls outside, and the passages are chilling as death, when the reverberating slam of doors, the distant organ-peal and chaunt, and the melancholy water-trickle is heard between the thunder-claps, when the silent monk shrinks closer into his cowl, and his flickering taper scarcely renders the darkness visible; then, as the gaudy gilding fades away, the true sentiment swells up, until the heart runs over. Royalty struggles even with nothingness, and the dead but sceptered emperor rules over our spirit from his grave; now extinguish the brief taper and depart; the iron door grates its hinges ere it be locked, and the dead left again alone in cold obstructious apathy. Those who, like ourselves, have often descended into this vault, and after long intervals, must be struck with its unchanged, unchangeable state; however altered those who revisit them, they remain the same, nor heed the chances of the living; they sleep soundly, life's fitful fever over, where the wicked have ceased to trouble, and the weary ones are at rest.

Ascending from the *panteon,* at the first break or *descanso* in the staircase a door leads to what is called *El Panteon de los Infantes,* a sort of catacomb into which the "rest of the royal family" is lumped together, as in our toasts: it is commonly called *El Podridero,* the putrifying place, and is an exact pagan *Puticolus, Puteus,* quasi *ab putescere.* Bermejo (p. 153) gives a list of the deceased, the shortness of whose lives is remarkable. Among them lies the body of Don Carlos,* the son of Philip II., and the body exists, according to M. Bory, who examined the coffin from *pure historical* research, as he says (Guide, p. 18). Few strangers ever visit this *Podridero,* nor are the contents or name very inviting.

Next visit the *Anti-Sacristia,* with

* All the stories of this Prince's love for his father's wife, and his consequent murder, are pure fictions of poets, the Schillers, Alfieris, etc. Raumur has demonstrated that Carlos, weak from his birth in mind and body, was much injured by a fall, May 15, 1562. Subject to fits and fevers he hated his father, and was at no pains to conceal it. He was very properly arrested, January 18, 1568, and by April 13th, one writing from the spot remarks, "there is now as little talk upon the subject as if he had been dead ten years." Both he and the queen died natural deaths, and not the slightest love affair ever took place between them.

fine arabesque ceilings, and pass on to the *Sacristia*, a noble room 108 ft. long by 23 wide. The ceilings are painted by Granelo and Fabricio. Above the presses, in which the dresses of the clergy were stowed, once hung the Perla of Raphael, and some of the finest pictures in the world. At the S. end is the *Retablo de la S*ᵃ. *Forma*, so called because in it is kept the miraculous wafer which bled at Gorcum in 1525, when trampled on by Zuinglian heretics. Rudolph II. of Germany gave it to Philip II., an event represented in a bas relief. Charles II., in 1684, erected the gorgeous altar, which is inscribed, "En magni operis miraculum, intra miraculum mundi, cœli miraculum consecratum." When the French soldiers entered the Escorial the monks hid the wafer in the cellar, and the spoilers, busy with emptying the casks, passed it by, and Ferd. VII. restored it in great pomp, Oct. 28, 1814. The *Forma* is exhibited for adoration, or "*manifestada*," every Sept. 29 and Oct. 28, on which occasions the picture, which usually is hung before it as a curtain, is lowered down, and has consequently been much injured. This, the masterpiece of Claudio Cuello, the last of good Spanish painters, is the real relic; it is full of marvellous reality. The scene represented is the apotheosis of this wafer in this very *Sacristia*. The cunning priest watches the glorification of the *Forma*, and the triumph of his trick ; upright, he looks down with a dry satirical expression on the kneeling imbecile Charles II. and his lubberly lords of the bedchamber. The painting of the priests, monks, and dresses is admirable. This *Forma* is never shown to heretics. On these matters see Daroca.

Behind the altar is the *Camarin*, erected in 1692 by José del Olmo and Frᵒ· Rici. It is a gem of precious marbles. La Houssaye carried off the lamps, the sacramental services, the splendid *viril sobredorado*, the gift of Leopold II., and in short everything either gold or silver.

Now visit the cloisters or courtyards, and first the two large ones, the upper and under. The *claustro principal bajo* is a square of 212 ft. each side. The walls are painted in raw fresco, with sprawling figures by L. Carabajal, Miguel Barroso, L. Cangiagi, and P. Tibaldi: some are faded by exposure to the damp air, and others were defaced by the French. The central *Patio de los Evangelistas*, a square of 176 ft., with its ponds and formal box-fringed gardens, was so called from the statues of the Apostles, wrought by Jⁿ· Bª· Monegro. Hence we pass to rooms once filled with pictures. *Las Salas de los capitulos* are three in number, that called *El Vicarial* being to the r., and *El Prioral* to the l. Here hung the St. Jerome of Titian, and the Jacob of Velazquez; all that now remain are the fine landskips of nature, those views from the windows which none can take away. Hence to the *Iglesia vieja*, which was used as a chapel while the *templo* was building. Here hung the Tobit of Raphael ; while in the adjoining refectory the Last Supper of Titian flaps in its frame, left to perish in the stony room, like hatchments in our damp country churches.

The grand staircase, that feature in which modern architecture triumphs over the ancients, leads to an upper *claustro :* it was designed by Jⁿ· Bª· Castello, and lies to the W. It is painted in fresco by L. Cangiagi, L. Giordano, and P. Pelegrino. Here is the battle of St. Quintin, and the capture of the Constable Montmorency ; while to the E. Philip II. is seen planning the Escorial with his architects. On the ceiling is *La Gloria*, the apotheosis or ascending into Heaven of Sⁿ· Lorenzo with saints and the blessed, and among them Charles V. and Philip II. All this space was thus covered in seven months by Giordano, too truly *Luca fa presto*, and his fatal facility and want of thought dealt the last blow to falling Italian art.

In the upper cloister 50 pictures

formerly were arranged. To the N.E. is the *Aula del Moral;* here hung the Gloria of Titian. Adjoining is the *Camarin,* once filled with cabinet pictures and the most precious relics, such as the black and gold portable altar of Charles V., a marriage firkin from Cana, a skeleton of one of the innocents massacred by Herod, a bar of Lorenzo's gridiron, much MS. of Sᵃ· Teresa (N.B. Read her legend, Avila, p. 804), together with one of her pens. Mr. Beckford (ii. Lett. xi.) describes another " quill from Gabriel's wing, a most glorious specimen of celestial plumage, full three feet long, of a blushing hue, more soft and delicate than the loveliest rose." Truth, however, which is so essential in these matters, compels us to add that in our times this relic was not shown.

The *cella prioral,* fitted up with good marqueterie, overlooks the fishpools and gardens. Here hung the fine portrait of Jose de Siguenza, the first prior, by Alonzo Sanchez Coello. The eight smaller cloisters or courts resemble one another. Now that they are untenanted, these long passages seem to lead to nothing, and we miss the monk, fit inmate of the cold granite pile, stealing along as he was wont with noiseless tread and Schidoni look. Spain, however, is the land of the unexpected, and nothing would surprise us less than the restoration of the cowled brotherhood to the Escorial; and in truth the building without them is like a frame without its picture.

Passing, therefore, to the *Coro alto,* the ceilings of the *ante coros* are painted by L. Giordano. Here are kept *Los libros de Coro,* or splendid choral books of gigantic parchment, and illuminated by Andres de Leon : they were 218 in number. The quire looks down on the chapel. To the N. is the royal seat into which Philip II. glided with his brother monks, like his father and so many of his ancestors (see pp. 477, 497, 614); and here he

was kneeling when * he received the news of the victory of Lepanto, which saved Europe from the Turks : his joy was damped by jealousy of his natural brother, Don John of Austria, who commanded the Christian allied fleet. The Spaniards claim the whole glory for themselves, but, like the triumphs at Almeria and Tortosa, the real brunt was borne by the Genoese under Doria and the Venetians under Barbarigo.

The dark rich stalls of the *Coro* are carved in the Corinthian order, out of seven sorts of wood; observe the huge *Facistol,* which nevertheless moves round with a touch. The lateral frescos, by Romulo Cincinato, represent the Martyrdom of San Lorenzo, the tutelar of the convent, and the history of St. Jerome, the head of the order; the others are by L. Cangiagi, and of no merit. The invaders smashed the original and splendid crystal chandelier; the present one, with birds, etc., is truly contemptible ; the crucifix is made of fragments of a finer one, which the French also knocked to pieces : the wood is called *angelico,* because marked with the five wounds of the Saviour— of this Philip II. ordered his coffin to be constructed : the grand organs are carved in Cuenca pine : behind the seat of the prior is the celebrated white marble Christ, which was given to Philip II. by the Grand Duke Cosimo, and was brought from Barcelona on men's shoulders ; the anatomy is fine, but the expression of the face is ordinary, and the space between the nose and lips too great, which is destructive of classical beauty : it is inscribed "Benvenutus Cellini, Civis Florent : faciebat 1562," and is described by him in his autobiography. The figure was quite originally naked, but Philip II. thereupon covered the loins with

* The easy defeat of the *Invincible* Armada of Philip was announced to Elizabeth when *dining* on a bird always beloved by Britons (Pliny, ' N. H.' x. 22), and a fitter fare for our thrifty busy Bess than the olla of her fasting bankrupt rival, for

" He who eats goose on Mich'mas day,
   Shall ne'er want cash his debts to pay."

2 N

his handkerchief, which was long pre-served as a relic.

The great library is placed above the porch of the *Patio de los Reyes;* over the entrance is the common excommu-nication by the pope of all who should steal the books, to which the invaders paid small attention. The arched room runs from N. to S., and is 194 ft. long, 32 wide, and 36 high; the pavement is marble, and the bookcases were exe-cuted by Jose Flecha, from Doric de-signs by Herrera. There are ample tables of marble and porphyry provided for the use of readers, were there any; the ceilings are painted in fresco, blues and yellows over predominate, and the colours are too gaudy for the sober books, while the figures being too co-lossal, injure relative proportions; but these errors pervade the ambitious works of Tibaldi, who out-heroded M. Angelo, without possessing a tithe of his gran-deur or originality. Other frescos are by B. Carducho, and of subjects analo-gous to a library, and the personifica-tion of those liberal sciences which Philip II. and his Inquisition all but extinguished practically. First, Philo-sophy shows the globe to Socrates, and others; below is the School of Athens; then follows the Confusion of Tongues, Nebuchadonezzor instituting the first Grammar School; Rhetoric surrounded by Cicero, Demosthenes, and others. Further on we see Dialectics, Arith-metic, Music, Geometry, Astronomy, and Theology, with appropriate groups and attributes; but nothing is so tire-some as allegory. On the walls hung portraits of Herrera, the architect of the Escorial, and of Arias Montano its librarian, and the still more striking one of their master, Philip II., when old; it is full of identity and individuality; here we see him in the flesh and spirit, with his wan, dejected look, marked with the melancholy taint of his grand-mother, and his bigot, grey eye, cold as frozen drops of morning dew : the sus-picious scared bigot seemed to walk out of the frame into his own library. The books have their edges, not backs, turned

to the spectator; thus they were origin-ally arranged by Montano, and things do not readily change in Spain, nor did the monks trouble the repose of the vo-lumes. The library in 1808, before the invasion, contained 30,000 printed, and 4300 MS. volumes. Joseph re-moved them all to Madrid, but Ferd. VII. sent them back again, minus some 10,000; and among them the catalogue, which was most judiciously purloined. Thus what is lost will never be known, and certainly never be missed. The rarities usually shown are a fine Alcoran, a New Testament of the Emperor Conrad, 1039, etc.; but books are made to be read, not looked at. The upper library, which is not public, contains codes, missals, and Arabic MSS., of which a catalogue was published by Miguel Casiri, a Syrian : *Bibliotheca Arabica-Hispana Escurialensis,* folio, 2 vols., Madrid, 1760-70, a work, however, which teems with inaccuracies, for Casiri was care-less and reckless, and utterly ignorant of the Augustan age of the Arabic lite-rature of Cordova. But Arabic lite-rature has been much neglected in Spain, where, primâ facie, it might best have been cultivated, for Spa-niards are no philologists, and a rem-nant of hatred against the Moor long prevailed, and Moorish books were burnt by the clergy on the absurd sup-position that all were Korans; see Conde's Preface to Xerif Aledris (Madrid, 1799). Thus thousands of precious volumes of Arab art and science were irreparably lost, as those of antiquity were from the holocausts of Omar and Gregory VII. The present Arabic MSS. were obtained by *accident :* the prime founder of Spanish Museos, one Pedro de Lara, a captain of Philip III., captured near Sallee a Moorish ship, containing 3000 volumes, the library of king Zidan, who offered 60,000 ducats for their ransom; but a civil war in Morocco intervening, Philip III. carted them off to the Escorial; of what *acci-dent* gave, *accident* took much away, as many were burnt in 1671, by a casual fire; nor has any one ever looked at them except Conde, who garbled many of his extracts. Being an *Afrancesado*, he was employed by the invaders to select the best things for Paris; and he did not forget himself. Thus when his library was sold in London in 1824, the MS. *Cancionero of Johan de Baena*, written for Juan II., and the missing gem of the Escorial, reappeared. Mr. Heber bought it for 131*l.*; it is now in the Bibliothèque du Roi, at Paris. The librarian of the Escorial is professedly ignorant of Arabic: such things, however, occur in other museums and universities. Spain now possesses a first-rate Arabic scholar, in our excellent friend Don Pascual Gayangos, who should explore the Escorial. The superb collection of medals formed by Anᵗᵒ· Agustin, Archbishop of Tarragona (see p. 785), and subsequently much increased, were all swept away by the enemy, who seldom overlooked anything in the shape of a coin.

The grand kitchen of the Escorial deserves the gastronome's inspection, who will grieve at the fireless grates, on which San Lorenzo might have been broiled: alas! no smoke now issues from the chimneys. This department was once worthy of 200 monks, who had little else to do but to eat. In the medical dispensary, or *La Botica*, was a fine Raphael-ware cistern, painted with the judgment of Solomon. The *Colegio* is not worth visiting, although there is a whispering gallery which amuses silly folk, just like that under the Alhambra. From the kitchen to the royal residence the transition is easy, especially as it is placed in the handle of the gridiron, *el mango de la parrilla*. Here the Catholic kings, whose life was one dull routine, spent six weeks every year, after leaving their summer quarter of Sⁿ· Ildefonso. They thus became the real handle of the man of the cowl, who had access to the despot at his first rising and at his last folding the arms to sleep. The courtiers, however, even in the time of Philip II., thought of nothing but feastings and intrigues amatory and poli-

tical; thus mixing up the frivolities of a most profligate court with the outward show of monastic austerities. Walk through the royal suite of rooms, which are very meanly furnished. In the *Sala de las Batallas*, observe the fresco of Granelo and Fabricio, the battle of Higueruela, where John II. and Alvaro de Luna defeated the Moors: the costume is most curious: this was copied for Philip II. from an original chiaroscuro roll 150 ft. long, which was found in the Alcazar of Segovia: between the windows are the battle of St. Quentin and others in Flanders: the ceilings are decorated with arabesques.

In a room adjoining Ferd. VII. was born, Oct. 14, 1784; and here, Oct. 29, 1807, he was nearly sacrificed by his own mother, and her minion Godoy; Charles, his father, consenting to his own shame and their crimes. The prince was arrested for high treason, when he, coward-like, betrayed his advisers, and this act, which would have ensured his and their ruin, saved them all, for the dreaded name of Buonaparte was found mixed up in the secret correspondence, and the craven court hushed the matter up.

Visit also the humble apartments in which Philip II. lived, half a monk, as he reserved all his magnificence for the temple; and then descend into the small room in which he died, having been carried there in order that his last glance might be directed to the altar; his lingering end was terrific, for then he was haunted with doubts whether his bloody bigotry, the merit of his life, was not in truth a damning crime. His ambition was then over, and a ray of common sense taught him to distrust the efficacy of relics in securing salvation, and to fear that a Moloch persecution breathed little of the true spirit of Christianity. (2 Thess. iii. 15.) But he was a type of Spain in the sixteenth century, a despot in politics and polemics: he was the impersonation of Romanism, then threatened by the Reformation; his religion was modified by the genius of the man

2 N 2

and his country ; thus his idiosyncracy was cold, phlegmatic, suspicious, timid, and arbitrary, while that of Spaniards breathed the fierce intolerance and propagandism by the sword of the Moslem ; a sincere believer, he accounted it rather as a favour done to his victims if by torturing or burning their mortal bodies he could save their souls ; he was reckless of worldly consequences, and preferred to have no subjects at all, rather than millions who should be heretics.

Philip was of a delicate constitution, naturally indolent, and without any inclination for bodily exercise or martial deeds : he lacked the great king qualities of his father : weak in body and timid in mind, in exterior a Fleming, in haughty deportment a Spaniard, his suspicions and averseness to being seen grew upon him as he waxed older, then he became more and more silent, priding himself on concealing his thoughts ; he rarely laughed, and never so heartily as on receiving the news of the St. Bartholomew massacre ; he had much application, and loved doing business himself, but seldom made real progress, as he shrank from decisions, and thought that when he had gained time he had gained everything ; yet his great boast was that he at the foot of a mountain and with a bit of paper could make himself obeyed in the old world and the new. As a political personage he was a failure ; under him Spain lost her invincible armada and the Low Countries : yet what a position was his, had he felt and been equal to the moment! Ferdinand and Isabella had beaten down the Moor at home, while Charles V. had humbled France and was master of Lombardy ; in quiet possession of peace and power, Philip might have been a legislator and a benefactor to his country : he might have given Spain a code of laws, covered her with a net-work of roads and canals, and fixed the capital at Lisbon. All of this he sacrificed to fight the battles of the Vatican and build a convent : but whatever his faults, which partly

were the result of his political position and the spirit of his age, he at least was a true patron of art and artists ; he discovered or created talent to execute his mighty works ; thus Augustus raised up a Horace and Virgil. Much light has been thrown on his private history by Raumur, who has published authentic contemporary documents ; nevertheless, his biography, attempted by Watson, has yet to be really written, and it occupies at this moment the pen of Mr. Prescott, who assuredly will do justice to his splendid subject.

Before leaving the Escorial, clamber up to the *Sill*^{a.} *del Rey*, the eminence from whence Philip II. used to contemplate the progress of his buildings. Visit also the parks and plantations, which contrast agreeably with the desert beyond them. Enter the *Casa del Campo*, a miniature country house, too small indeed to live in and yet too large to wear at a watch-chain : it was built by Juan de Villanueva for Charles IV. when prince, and like that at Aranjuez, is the plaything of a spoilt infant. It is expensively ornamented with marble, marqueterie, arabesques, and with poor portraits of the ignoble-looking Spanish Bourbons. Ferd. VII. refitted it up with modern furniture from Paris ; the gardens are pretty and full of water. The cabinet pictures are second-rate ; they were formed for the rising Mæcenas by his French and Italian valets! tel maître tel valet.

A noble road winds from the Escorial over the Guadarrama chain (see p. 644) amid immemorial pines and firs to *San Ildefonso*. It was constructed at a reckless expense, for the personal convenience of the King : it is occasionally blocked up by winter snows. After passing the *puerto*, we descend into the village, which has some 3500 inhabitants, who have suffered much from the discontinuance of the visits of the court, which formerly always passed the hot months of June, July, and September in these cool altitudes. This true castle in the air is, say the Castilians, a worthy *château* of the king of Spain; as he is the loftiest of all earthly sovereigns, so his abode soars nearest to heaven, of which Madrid is the counterpart: at all events the elevation cannot be doubted; as the palace is placed on the N.W. range of the Sierra, 3840 ft. above the level of the sea, and thus, in the same latitude as Naples, stands higher than the crater of Mount Vesuvius. The localities are truly alpine; around on all sides are rocks, forests, and crystal streams, and above towers *La Peñalera*, rising, according to some, above 8500 feet. While *nature* is truly Spanish, here *art* is entirely French: for the one-idead founder Philip V. could conceive no other excellence but that of Marly and Versailles. In reserve and bigotry a Philip II., his hippochondriac shyness drove him into retirement, wanting nothing but his mass-book and wife, and thus becoming a puppet in her and her confessor's hands. He was no sooner fixed on the Spanish throne than he meditated its abdication, always harbouring, like Henry II. in Poland, a secret wish to return and reign in France: it chanced that while hunting at Valsain in 1722 he observed this *granja*, then a *grange* or farmhouse of the Segovian monks of *La Parral*, of whom he bought the site; and here he died, July 9, 1746, and here he is buried, carrying his hatred to Austrian recollections even to the grave. He would not associate with them even in the Panteon of the Escurial, a building which in common with every thing Spanish he slighted. His was the fatal reign when nationalism was effaced by French opinions, language, customs, and alliances. Never, as Foy justly remarks (ii. 160), was Spain so isolated as under the rule of Philip V.; in the days of her native sovereigns she mingled with Europe and brought back art and civilization; now she became a vast convent, and her people became the monks and recluses of the world, with the Inquisition standing as a sentinel to prevent the entrance of truth.

First visit the *Colegiata*, built from a design of Teodoro Artemans, in the form of a Latin cross. On each side are the royal pews or *tribunas*, enclosed with glass. The dome is painted in fresco by those twins of common-place, Bayeu and Maella: the white stucco is picked out with gilding; the *Retablo* is composed of fine jaspers with red pillars from Cabra. The altar was made at Naples by Solimena. The tabernacle is of rich *Lapis Lazuli*. Observe the tomb of Philip V. and his wife Isabella Farnese, with their medallions, and Fame, Charity, and other ornaments in the worst taste, and the work of Messrs. Pitué and Dumandré; "awful in simplicity," however, according to M. Bourgoin. Joseph Buonaparte, nevertheless, closed the *colegiata* July 14, 1810. The palace, a thing of the foreigner, looks as if it had been moved by the slaves of the lamp from the bald levels of the Seine to a wild Spanish sierra; it is a sensual, theatrical, French château, and the antithesis of the proud, gloomy Escorial, on which it turns its back. A portion of the old *Granja* is still preserved near the *Fuente*, for the building is a thing of expedients and patchwork, and so far a thing of Spain. A long line of railing, like that of the Carrousel at Paris, divides three sides of a square. The centre body is destined to the royal family, and the wings to their suites. The façade fronts the garden, and is cheerful, although over-windowed and looking like a long Corinthian conservatory. The saloons above and below were once filled with paintings and antiques, among which were the marbles of Christina of Sweden, purchased for Spain by Camillo Rusconi. After having been long neglected, they were carted out to Madrid by Ferd. VII., when he refurnished the palace with his favorite modern trumpery; and then many of the finest things of course disappeared. The royal apartments are light, airy, and agreeable, without being magnificent, and in them strange events have taken place.

Here, in Jan. 1724, Philip V. abdicated the crown, which he resumed in the next August at the death of his son, having been urged to become once more a king by his wife, who was very soon weary of private life: here in 1783 Charles III. received the Count d'Artois (Charles X.) when on his way to *take* Gibraltar, which he did *not* do.

Here Ferd. VII., Sept. 18, 1832, revoked the decree by which he had abolished the Salic law, and declared his daughter Isabel, born Oct. 10, 1830, to be heiress to the crown, an act which cursed his ever ill-fated country with civil wars and a disputed succession. The secret history is as follows: *Don Carlos*, his brother and heir presumptive, was married to a Portuguese princess, between whom and her sister *La Beira*, a deadly palace war was waged by *Carlota*, the wife of *Don Francisco de Paula*, a younger brother of the king, a man of more good nature than sense, and completely ruled by his intriguing consort. When Ferdinand married Christina, the Neapolitan coterie gained so much on the Portuguese one, that on the queen's pregnancy being declared, her sister induced Tadeo Calomarde, the minister of justice, to suggest this change to the uxorious king, and the decree was smuggled through the royal closet without the knowledge of the other ministers: thus Ferdinand deprived his brother Carlos of his birthright, that brother who had been the friend of his youth and the companion of his French captivity, and who had refused in 1827 to assist in his dethronement.

In the autumn of 1832 Ferd. fell dangerously ill in this same palace, and his death during an attack of lethargy was actually announced to the Emperor of Russia by Monsieur D'Oubril, his plenipotentiary; the succession of Carlos was then quite certain; his reign might indeed have been leaden and that of a King Log, but it would have been one of slow yet certain improvement, for all the non-

sense about his restoring the Inquisition, &c. was a thing of unscrupulous party tirade. Carlos, although devoid of common talent, and fitter to lose than win a crown, was at least a man of honour and principle, rare qualities in a Spanish court. Christina at this crisis had no party whatever, and she herself drew up a revocation of the decree, which was signed Sept. 18, by the guided hand of the unconscious testator; this second act was managed by the royal confessor and Alcudia, the principal mover being Calomarde, who now undid his former work, in his terror at the certain *venganza* which the Portuguese faction would have taken; and Antonini, the Neapolitan ambassador, confirmed his statement and urged Christina to save herself. Ferdinand two days afterwards recovered by a miracle, for Carlos had not caused him to be smothered as Tiberius was. Carlota, who was at Seville, on hearing of the revocation hurried back day and night, and welcomed Calomarde with blows and Billingsgate. As the king regained strength, the queen recovered courage, until on Oct. 31 the revocation was revoked, Christina throwing the whole blame of the past on Calomarde, who was forthwith turned out of office and Spain. The king, still weak, now delegated his authority to his wife, who had nursed him most tenderly, and she instantly created a party by displacing all ultra Royalists and Carlists, or by substituting men favourable to moderate reforms. Ferd. died Sept. 29, 1833; then ensued the terrible civil wars which have rent and impoverished poor Spain.

This self-same palace, as if by poetical justice, became the theatre of another tragedy by which Christina in her turn was deprived of her royal rights: here, Aug. 12, 1836, intimidated by rude soldiery, headed by one Garcia, a serjeant, she was compelled to proclaim the democratical constitution of 1812. The secret underplot of this intrigue was to bring about a change of the conservative ministry into one ultra-radical, and the final result, as might be expected, was the downfall and exile of the queen regent, and the present restoration of things as they were.

The gardens of the palace are among the finest in Spain; the grand walk in front, called the *parterre*, for everything in name and style is French, looks over flowers, water, and mountains; here the fruits of Spring ripen in Autumn: as everything is artificial, the cost was enormous, reaching to 45 million piastres, the precise sum in which Philip V. died indebted; thus those palaces in Spain which the Austrian kings began are unfinished, while those which their Bourbon successors raised are not paid for. To form these gardens rocks were levelled and hollowed to admit pipes of fountains and roots of trees, whose soil was brought up from the plains. It requires to be constantly renewed, and even then the vegetation is dwarf-like; but despots delight in enriching favourites without merit, and their outlay contrasts with the people's misery. The yoke of building kings is grievous, and especially when, as St. Simon said of Louis XIV. and his Versailles—Il se plut à tyranniser la nature. Thus Nero, in the words of Tacitus (An. xv. 42), *usus et patriæ ruinis,* employing architects, quibus ingenium et audacia erat, etiam quæ natura denegavisset per artem tentare. San Ildefonso after all was but an imitation, and Delille, in praising its gardens, justly remarked, " Philippe défiait son ayeul et retracait la France." Although smaller, these gardens are far more real than their type; water is their charm, which here is no turbid puddle forced up by a wooden waterwork, but a crystal distillation, fresh from a mountain alembic; the *Cascada* is a grand falling sheet, which under the sun of Castile glitters like melted silver; it is supplied from a reservoir above, which, as at Aranjuez, is modestly termed *El Mar*, the ocean; but Spaniards lose nothing for want of

large words, and this pond is but that of Nero, Stagnum *maris* instar (Suet. 31). In honest old England, where people have a notion what the sea is, and call things by their right names, this pond might be stretched into a lake.

The gardens in which art rivals nature are divided into high and low; they are laid out in a formal style, being planted in avenues and decked with marble statuary; there are 26 fountains, the finest are those called *Los Baños, La Latona* or *Ranas, El Canastilo, Los Vientos, La Andromeda, La Pomona,* and *El Neptuno,* at which, says Mons. Bourgoin, genius presides, and where he read Virgil and quoted " Quos ego." The *Fama* is the most famous, and shoots up water 130 feet high(?). The fountains play on the first Sundays of June, July, August, and September, days on which the traveller should visit this spot. The chief statues are the Apollo and Daphne, Lucretia, Bacchus, America, Ceres, and Milon; they are more admired by Spaniards, who have very little fine marble sculpture, than they deserve; possibly because the work of foreigners, to wit, Messrs. Carlier, Pitué, Dumandré, Bousseau, and others not worth naming. Consult for details the guide book by Santos Martinez Sedeño, Mad. 1825. This palace and gardens, like the other royal sitios, suffered much during the civil wars; some repairs were however made in 1842, by Arguelles, which have been continued.

Charles III. came every year to *La Granja* to fish and shoot, and as his second hobby was the forcing manufactures, he here set up *La Calandria,* to make linen, and *La fabrica de Cristales,* to make glass and pottery: these exotics, like the trees in the gardens, have never flourished in an artificial soil, and the less as everything was conducted on a royal scale of loss (compare Guadalajara). It was a Bourbon plaything, a hotbed of jobbing and robbing, in which directors *made* their fortunes out of the public purse.

This establishment was founded simply because one Thevart in 1688 had formed a similar one at Versailles: meanwhile here even the sand has to be brought from Segovia, while the expense of transport and breakage of mirrors alone consumed every chance of profit.

Excursions may be made to the nursery gardens of *Robledo* and *Colmenar*, and to the *Quinta de quita pesares*, the Sans Souci of Christina, an anodyne for *sorrow*, which buttermaking contributed to *banish*. Visit also *Valsain*, Val Sabin, the vale of Savins, distant 1 L. This, an ancient hunting-seat of the crown, was inhabited by Philip V. during the building of *La Granja ;* but now it is almost a ruin, having been left unrepaired since a fire. The trout in the Eresma are excellent : 2 L. on is *Rio Frio*, where Isabel widow of Philip V. began a palace, which she neither finished nor paid for. It is a fine architectural shell, with a noble staircase and granite pillars.

Those returning to Madrid on horseback should, after seeing Segovia, make an excursion to *El Paular*, the once wealthy Carthusian convent on the opposite side of the Guadarrama. It is 2 L. from La Granja by *El Reventon*, " the cleft," a pass which crosses directly over the glorious ridge, with the grand *Peñalera* rising to the r. about 8500 feet: when this route is snowed up, there is a circuitous one to the convent, which overlooks the pleasant valley of the trout-stream Lozoya. The edifice was raised by John I. to carry out a vow made by his father, Henry II., while campaigning in France. The *Capilla de los Reyes* was built in 1390, by Alonzo Rodrigo, and the church in 1433-40 by a Segovian Moor named Abderahman ; since its suppression, the paintings by Carducho have been removed to the new *Museo* at Madrid. The exquisite *Retablo* was wrought at Genoa, and of the same period was the *Sillª. del Coro.* There is a fine sepulchre of one of the

Frias family, and an outrageous churrigueresque *trasparente* erected in 1724. The ceilings are painted by the feeble Palomino. The Paular is no longer what it was (see Ponz, x. 69), when the monks, lords of all around, were paper-makers and breeders of sheep on a large scale, and their hospitality was commensurate, as all strangers were lodged, fed, and welcomed ; now their kitchen fire is put out, and their gardens of fruit and flowers encumbered with weeds. From thence follow the river, and rejoin the high road at *Biutrago* (see R. cxiii).

Descending from La Granja into the plains, we soon reach the ancient city of Segovia : the least bad of the bad inns is *El meson grande* on the Plaza, and *El cafe nuevo* in the Calle real. SEGOVIA is of Iberian name and origin, *seca* and *sego* being a common prefix, while *Briga*, " town," is a still commoner termination : consult for historical details ' *El glorioso San Frutos*' (the tutelar of the city), Lorenzo Calvete, Valladolid, 1610 ; ' *Historia*,' &c., Diego Colmenares, fol., Mad. 1640 ; ' *Viaje artistico*,' Isidoro Bosarte, 8vo., Mad. 1804 ; ' *El Acueducto*,' Andrez Gomez de Somorrostro, fol., Mad., 1820 ; ' E. S.' viii. and Ponz, ' *Viage*,' x.

The long city with its narrow irregular streets stands on a rocky knoll which rises E. and W. in a valley, with the Alcazar perched on the W. point. It is girdled to the N. by the trout stream Eresma, which is joined below the Alcazar by the *clamorous* rivulet El Clamores ; the banks of these streams are wooded and pretty, and contrast with the bleak and barren hills. The strong town is encircled by walls with round towers, built by Alonzo VI., which are seen to great advantage from the hill of the Calvario ; it is altogether a good specimen of an old-fashioned Castilian city, with quaint houses, balconies, and a Proutlike *plaza*. It is sadly decayed and decaying, the population, once exceeding 30,000, having dwindled to less than 9000. It is still the see of a bishop, suffragan to Toledo. The climate is miserably cold, and the environs bleak and uninteresting.

According to Colmenares Tubal first peopled Spain, then Hercules founded Segovia, for which Hispan erected the *bridge*, as they call the aqueduct, although it brings water over men, not men over water. The city bears " *El Puente*" on its shield, with one of the heads of Pompey's sons looking over it. This Roman work, from its resemblance to the masonry of Alcantara and Merida, was probably erected by Trajan, but neither Segovia nor its aqueduct are mentioned by the ancients, with whom such mighty works seem to have been things of course. As the steep-banked rivers below are difficult of access and their waters not very wholesome, the pure stream of the *Rio Frio* was thus brought from the *Sierra Fonfria*, distant 3 L. The aqueduct begins near Sⁿ· Gabriel, and makes many bends in its progress, but of course every traveller will walk its whole length. It runs 216 feet to the first angle, then 462 feet to the second at *La Concepcion*, then 925 feet to the third at *Sⁿ· Francisco*, and then 937 feet to the city wall. Some portions are comparatively modern, although they are so admirably repaired, that it is not easy to distinguish the new work from the old. This aqueduct was respected by the Goths, but broken down in 1071 by the Moors of Toledo, who sacked Segovia and destroyed 35 arches. It remained in ruin until Aug. 26, 1483, when Isabella employed a monk of the Parral convent, one Juan Escovedo, who, born in the Asturias, about 1457, and the son of a mere carpenter, had the good taste to imitate the model before him, and therefore was the first to restore the Græco-Romano style in Spain; when he went to Seville to report the completion of the repairs. Isabella gave him for his fee all the wood work of the scaffoldings; see for curious particulars ' *Historia de la Orden de*

San Geronymo,' Jose de Siguenza, iv. 40

The new work is intermixed with the old, and occurs chiefly near the angles of *La Concepcion* and *San Francisco*. Escovedo also built the bridges over the Eresma.

The aqueduct commences with single arches which rise higher as the dip of the ground deepens, until they become double. Those of the upper tier are uniform in height; the three central are the highest, being 102 feet. This noble work is constructed of granite without cement or mortar; and like other similar erections of the Romans, unites simplicity, proportion, solidity, and utility, and its grandeur is rather the result of these qualities than the intention of the architect. (See Merida, p. 530, and Alcantara, p. 547.) An inscription formerly ran between the tiers of the central arches, and the learned strive in vain to make out what the words were, guessing from the holes which remain for the pins of the bronze letters which have been extracted. The niche here above, which is supposed to have held a statue of Trajan, is now filled with a decayed image of a saint which looks like a putrifying corpse. According to some antiquarians the aqueduct was built by one *Licinius*, but the unlearned people call it *El Puente del Diablo*, " the devil's bridge," because his Satanic majesty was in love with a *Segoviana*, and offered his services for her favours, when she, tired of going up and down hill to fetch water, promised to consent, provided he would build an aqueduct in one night, which he did. One stone, however, having been found wanting, the church decided the contract to be void, and so the hard-working devil was done, as is generally the case with the foreigners and heretics who labour in vain in this orthodox land of ingratitude. The Spaniards, however, think the devil very clever, and *Sabe mucho, un punto mas del Diablo* is a delicate compliment. It is in vain to talk to them about Trajan, &c.; they prefer the devil, and especially as a Pontifex maximus. (See Tarragona, p. 473, and again p. 493.) But whatever surpasses the limited means and knowledge of the vulgar is attributed to supernatural agency and called a miracle: compare *Los Milagros* of Merida (p. 530): so the Arabs hold the pyramids to be the work of genii, the jin (*Ionios*) (Conde, i. 46), and thus in England the author of evil gets the credit of works of public utility, bridges, dykes, punch bowls, and bowling-greens: but if history is to be credited, churchmen have ever been the true pontifices, and this bridge might also be called *El puente del Monje* (Juan Escovedo), as that in Cardigan has a second name of *Pont y monach*. Thus an option is given to travellers to choose a monk or devil according to their tastes.

The aqueduct, be its author who it may, is well seen from *S*ⁿ· *Juan*, in its beautiful perspective, overtopping the pigmy town. The grandest point is from the corner of the *Calle de gascos*, but the stones have suffered from houses having been built up against the arches, and have been discoloured by chimney smoke and drips from *Cerbatanas*, or gutters and pipes. A plan was in vain proposed in 1803 to Charles IV. to remove all these unsightly causes of injury. However, in Sept. 1806, the carriage of the pregnant ambassadress of Sweden having upset by these encroachments, whereby she had a miscarriage, the king ordered the arches to be cleared (compare the similar good results of an *accident*, the moving power of Spain, which happened to the Nuncio at Aranjuez). It was intended to have opened the whole of the *Plaza del Azoquejo*, and thus to have made a grand square with the aqueduct on one side, exposed in all its unveiled majesty. The French invasion marred the scheme of questionable artificial amelioration, for the very irregularity and meanness of the buildings around render the aqueduct the

emphatic feature, as it soars larger and nobler by the force of contrast.

Older than the aqueduct is a 'rude statue either of Hercules or of a lunatic with a boar's head, which is imbedded in the staircase wall of a tower in *S*ᵒ· *Domingo el real.* This convent, once called *la Casa de Hercules,* was given the nuns in 1513. The antique has been white-washed, and is despised. Nothing more is known of its origin, than of two of the *Toros de Guisando* breed (see p. 801), which remained exposed to street injury. The larger was called *El Marrano* de Piedra, the smaller La *Marrana* or sow, the sex being assumed. *Marrano* is a corruption of the Arabic *Barrani,* a small pig.

Next visit the cathedral, a noble florid Gothic pile, which is seen to great advantage from the *plaza.* The square tower, crowned with a cupola, rises 330 feet high, having been lowered 22 feet from fears of lightning. Ascend it, as the panorama over the city, gardens, convents, gigantic aqueduct, and mountain distances, is superb. This cathedral was the last built in Spain in the Gothic style, the previous one having been almost destroyed by the reformers or *Comuneros* in May 1520. These *Commoners* commenced business by pulling down churches, hanging the authorities, plundering the rich, and burning houses for the public good. A few relics were saved in the *Alcazar,* which beat off the mob; and after the rebellion was put down, the bones of San Frutos were brought out, whereupon La *Modorilla,* or loss of common sense, an epidemic generated by the popular excesses, ceased.

The new cathedral was begun in 1525 by Juan Gil de Ontañon and his son Rodrigo, their beautiful cathedral at Salamanca (see p. 574) having been chosen as a model, and the interior of this copy, although less decorated, is also light and cheerful. The great *Retablo,* composed of precious marbles, was put up for Charles III. by Sabatini. The *trascoro* is enriched with the salmon-colored marbles of which the beautiful diamond-formed pavement is partly composed. The ancient sepulchral tombs were carted out and lumbered up near the entrance with sad indecency. Among them is the last memorial to Rodrigo Gil, obt. 1577. Near the gate of San Frutos is a magnificent Retablo by Juni in all his daring manner of 1571. The figures are larger than life, and the sentiment is the profound and terrible grief of the Virgin.

The cheerful Gothic cloisters belonged to the former cathedral; they were taken down, and put up again by Juan Campero in 1524, a triumph of art. Among the sepulchres observe that of Diego de Covarrubias, obt. 1576. The fine prelate with closed eyes and clasped hands is arrayed in pontificalibus. Remark also the tomb of the Infante Don Pedro, son of Henrique II. He was let fall from the window of the Alcazar in 1366 by his nurse. Judging from his statue, he must have been a fine baby for nine years old; but Spanish infants sometimes remain children to a great age. "I cannot be afraid," said our bold Bess, "of a Prince (Philip III.) who was 12 years learning his alphabet." Here also lies Maria Saltos, a frail beautiful Jewess by creed, but Christian in heart; she was about to be cast from a rock (see p. 828) for adultery, when she invoked the Virgin, who visibly appeared and let her down gently. She was then baptized Maria del *Salto* of the *Leap*, became a saint, and died in 1237. See Colmenares, chr. 21.

The Alcazar in which Gil Blas *was* confined, for Le Sage like Cervantes has given an historical and local habitation to the airy nothings of fancy, rises like the prow of Segovia over the waters-meet below. The great keep is studded with those angular turrets which are so common in Castilian castles, but the slate and French-like roofs in other portions mar the effect. The building was originally Moorish, and was mag-

nificently repaired in 1452–58 by Henrique IV., who resided and kept his treasures in it. At his death the governor André de Cabrera, husband of Beatrice de Bobadilla, the early friend of Isabella, held the fortress and money for her, and thereby much contributed to her accession. From this Alcazar Dec. 13, 1474, she proceeded in state and was proclaimed Queen of Castile. In 1476 the Segovian mob rose against this Cabrera, when the queen rode out among them alone, like our Richard II. from the Tower, and at once awed the Jack Cades by her presence of mind and majesty. Charles V. pleased with the Alcazar's resistance to the *Comuneros* in 1520, kept it up, and his son Philip II. redecorated the saloons. The tower was converted into a state prison by Philip V., who confined in it the Dutch charlatan Ripperda, who had risen from nothing to be premier, *cosas de España.* The Alcazar was ceded to the crown in 1764 by the hereditary *Alcaide*, the Conde de Chincon, whose ancestor had so hospitably welcomed in it our Charles I. He lodged there Wednesday 13 Sept. 1623, and supped, says the record, on "certaine trouts of extraordinary greatnesse," bigger than that which poor Gil Blas had at Peñaflor. The castle palace was at last made into an artillery college, and as it is one of the few in Spain which the French did not destroy, remains as a specimen of what so many others were before their invasion. The general character is Gotho-Moorish: the ceilings and cornices are splendidly gilt; the inscriptions in one room give the names of many kings and queens from Catalina, 1412, down to Philip II., 1592, whose shield quarters the arms of England in right of his wife, our bloody Mary. In the *Sala de los Reyes* (from the window of which the *infante* was let fall) are some singular statues of Spanish kings, which were begun by Alonzo IX., continued in 1442 by Henrique IV., and added to in 1587 by Philip II. The inscriptions were prepared by Garibay the historian, in 1595, Philip himself correcting the rough copies. The *Pieza del cordon* is a singular trunk-headed saloon, in which Alonzo *El Sabio* rashly ventured to doubt the sun's moving round the earth, whereupon his astronomical studies were interrupted by a flash of lightning, in memorial of which, and as a warning for the future, the rope of St. Francis was modelled and put up. The king had worn it as a penance and also as a conductor, for like the pagan laurel it disarms the electric flash, having been cast round the earth at its creation by St. Francis, who thus preserved the globe from Satan. The chapel contains some fine arabesques: the views from the windows are striking, although not quite so floral and picturesque as represented to Gil Blas by the governor, who somewhat overcoloured things for the honour of Castile.

Descend we now to the Eresma by *Puerta Castellana*, look up at the quaint Alcazar from the *Fuencisla*, near the *Clamores*, now doubly clamorous from chattering washerwomen, the Naiades of the rustling stream. The cliff above *Fuencisla*, Fons stillans, was called La Peña *grajera*, because the crows nestled there to pick the bodies of criminals cast down from this Tarpeian rock. The cypress opposite the *Carmelitas descalzas* marks the *exact* spot where Maria Saltos (see p. 827) lighted unhurt; and in the chapel is the identical image of the Virgin which saved her. The image was miraculously concealed during the time the Moors possessed Segovia, but reappeared on this site when the Christians recovered the town, and thereupon the convent was built and richly endowed.

Now turn to the l. up the valley of the Eresma to the *Casa de Moneda*, or mint, which was founded by Alonzo VII, rebuilt by Henrique IV. in 1455, and repaired and fitted with German machinery by Philip II. in 1586. Formerly all the national coinage was struck here, as the river afforded water-power, and the adjoining *Alcazar* was the treasury : in 1730 the gold and silver coinage was transferred to Madrid; now nothing is struck but copper, and for this Segovia is ill selected, as the distance is so great to Rio Tinto, from whence the metal is brought. Adjoining on a slope is *La Vera Cruz*, a very curious church, built in 1204 by the Templars, but now going to ruin : observe the octagon forms and the square tower.

Higher up is the *Parral*, a once wealthy Jeronomite, which nestles amid *vines* and *gardens*, under a barren rock, hence its name and the proverb, *Las huertas del Parral paraiso terrenal.* The judicious monks, indeed, loved to shelter their devotion from the cold, but now their paradise is cursed with weeds and brambles. The convent was built in 1494, by Juan Gallego : observe the portal ; the superb *Coro* was raised in 1494, by Juan de Ruesga ; the walnut *Silleria* was elaborately carved in 1526, by Bart[e.] Fernandez; the *Retablo Mayor* was painted in 1526, by Diego de Urbina, for the Pacheco family. The superb sepulchres of Juan and his wife Maria, kneeling with an attendant, have been barbarously whitewashed. The cloister and ceilings of the library and refectory are worth notice; the tower was raised 29 ft. in 1529, by Juan Campero.

If the projected *Museo* of Segovia be complete, of course the traveller will visit it, and see the wrecks saved from these and other devastations. Segovia abounds in artistical subjects. The *S[a.] Cruz*, or Dominican convent, was founded by Ferd. and Isab., as the *tanto monta* motto indicates ; the *reja* and *retablo* were given in 1557, by Philip II. In *S[n.] Juan* are the tombs of many of the Segovian *Conquistadores* of Madrid ; *e. g.* Diez Sanz, Fernan Garcia, etc. Here also lies the historian of Segovia, Colmenares, ob. Jan. 29, 1651. The portal of *San Martin* is curious; observe the tombs of Gonzalo Herrera and of his wife :

the architect may look at a pretty *aximez* window in the *Casa de Segovia*, at the bishop's palace, with granite front and figures of Hercules : observe also the tower in the *Plaza de S^n. Esteban*, with the Saxon arches, capacious capitals, and open *corredor*, in the church in which Juan Sanchez de Zuazo is buried (see p. 217). The *Puerta de Santiago* is Moorish ; the granite portals and peculiar Toledan ball ornaments prevail in Segovia.

The wretched city has never recovered the fatal day of June 7, 1808, when the invaders first entered it under Gen. Frere; who, notwithstanding no sort of resistance was made, sacked it, *à la Medellin ;* for he too, like his model,Victor, began life as a drummer boy. See, for sad details, Schepeler, i. 424. Then again, as in the time of the *Comuneros*, the altars were desecrated and plundered. The former prosperity of Segovia depended on its staple, wool, but then the flocks were eaten up by the wolf, and now only a few poor cloth manufactories languish in the suburb *S^n· Lorenzo.* In 1829 some improved machinery was introduced, which the hand-loom weavers destroyed. The *Cabañas*, or sheep-flocks of Segovia, furnished the fleeces, and the Eresma, a peculiar water for washing the wool : for *Merinos* and the *Mesta*, see p. 517. The sheep washings and shearings, once grand festivals, were held much after the Oriental fashion of Nabal, 1 Sam. xxv.

The vast flocks of the monks of the Escorial, el Paular, and other proprietors, were driven in May into large *Esquileos*, or quadrangles of two stories, over which a " *Factor* " presided. First, the sheep went into the *Sudadero*, and when well sweated had their legs tied by *Ligadores*, who handed them over to the shearers, each of whom could clip from 8 to 10 sheep a day. When shorn, the animals next were taken to the *Empegadero*, to be tarred and branded ; after which the whole lot were looked over by the *Capatazes*, or head shepherds, when the old and use-

less were selected for the butcher ; the spared were carefully attended to, as being liable to take cold after the shearing, and die. During all these processes, food and drink were plentifully carried about to all employed, by persons called *Echavinos*. The wool is sorted by *Recibidores*, and the bad, *las Cardas*, set aside. The *Pila*, or produce, if sold at once, is then weighed, or if destined to be washed is sent to the *Lavadero*. There are 3 different classes of wool, which are determined by an appraiser, the *Apartador*, of whom there is a guild at *Segovia*. The value has fallen off since the invasion, as from 8 to 3 ; then too, many barns and buildings were destroyed, which, from want of capital, have never been restored ; the subsequent loss of S. America completed the ruin. The common cloth made here was coarse, but strong; a little, however, of a finer sort, called *Bicuña* from an American goat, was made for the rich clergy, with a soft nap; now those customers have ceased. The extent, however, of the former boasted commerce must be somewhat discounted (see *Rio Seco*, p. 616), for the real staples were coarse *Xergas* (Arabicé Xercas), serges and *Paños pardos :* these, in the time of Juan II., sold only for 40 maravedis the yard, while cloth of Florence fetched 167, and fine scarlet of London 400 ; in fact, the home manufactures were only used by the poor, and for liveries, while the rich, as now, imported everything of a better quality from abroad. Yet anti-manufacturing Spain prides herself in the order of the Golden *Fleece*, forgetting that it was established by the good Duke of Burgundy, to mark his preference for his rich, manufacturing, intelligent towns, over a poor, proud, indolent and ignorant feudal nobility— a feeling diametrically opposed to genuine Spanish notions. *Pecus*, unde *Pecunia*, was the secret of the power of Bruges and Ghent, and the *Golden Fleece*, the symbol of the commercial Argonauts, became, like our *Woolsack*, the " canting " charge of a woollen staple. Again, strictly speaking, Spain has no right to this order, which passed with the Low Countries to Austria. Nevertheless, having lost the substance she clings to the form, for neither nations or individuals like to relinquish even the semblance of title or power. There is a direct road from Madrid to Segovia by *San Rafael*, 17 L., which leaves the Escorial to the l. ; it is often impassable during winter from the snow, but in summer a diligence runs backwards and forwards, starting from *El Meson* de los Huevos.

Those who wish to visit *El Paular* may rejoin the high road to Madrid at *Buitrago*, a very ancient walled town on the Lozoya, where the trout are excellent: pop^n· about 400. 5 L. from hence, on the road to *Guadalajara*, is *Uceda*, another most ancient but now decayed walled town on the Jarama, pop^n· 700, where also there is excellent trout-fishing. Uceda was once an important city, and its castle has been the prison of eminent men; in it Ximenez was confined by Carrillo, Archbishop of Toledo, who resented his acceptation of the arch-priesthood of Uceda, given him at Rome in 1473 by Paul II. Ximenez refused to succumb, and after six years' resistance succeeded in keeping the benefice. Here again the Great Duke of Alva, after his failure in the Low Countries, was banished by Philip II. until his services were required to conquer Portugal. Near *Uceda*, in a mountain defile, is the hamlet *Patones*, in which during the Moorish dominion a Christian population lived unmolested, secure in their obscurity. They elected among themselves a sovereign, or rather a sheikh, and the title of *Rey de Patones*, " king of big ducks," became hereditary in the family of Prieto; but when the real monarch came to live at Madrid, the Patonese, from a sense of the ludicrous contrast, dethroned their titular, and simply entitled him *Justicia*, "the Justice." Near Prieto is a stalactitical grotto called *La Cueva de Requerillo*.

This route is altogether uninteresting. *Sepulveda*, one of the most ancient of Castilian towns, is now much decayed : pop^n· under 1600. It is pleasantly placed on the confluence of the Duraton and Castillo, under the hills, with gardens, *alamedas*, and pastures. It was recovered from the Moors by the Conde Fernan Gonzalez in 913, who granted it municipal rights. These *Fueros de Sepulveda*, from their well-considered provisions and precedence in point of time, became the models of many of the earliest charters of Spanish cities.

For Aranda del Duero, see R. cxiii.

Those who are going to France from Madrid will do well to take R. lxxvii.

EXCURSIONS FROM MADRID—*continued*.

None should fail to visit *Toledo*, the imperial capital of the Goths, and *Aranjuez*, the happy valley of Castile. Those who are going to Valencia should thence pass on to *Cuenca* and *Albarracin ;* and even those who return to Madrid, if they have time, are advised to make the detour by *Cuenca*, Teruel, the baths of Sacedon and Guadalajara (see Index).

ROUTE CI.—MADRID TO TOLEDO.

Getafe	2	
Venta de Torrejon . .	2 ..	4
Illescas	2 ..	6
Yunco	1 ..	7
Cabañas	2 ..	9
Olias	1 ..	10
Toledo	2 ..	12

A diligence starts from the *Plaza del Progreso*, No. 10. The road, if road it can be called, is often only a cart-track carried over desert-like plains, which in summer are clouded with dust, and in winter are ankle-deep in mud. Toledo, because not visited by the King, was never noticed by Spanish way-wardens. It would seem that in Levitical Toledo, as at Santiago, the clergy were so intent on smoothing the ways to a better world, that they quite overlooked the unimportant ones in this.

Leaving Madrid by the bridge of Toledo, after passing *Caravanchel de arriba* (see p. 798), we reach *Getafe*: pop^{n.} 2500. This miserable specimen of a Castilian country town has a grand *Parroquia*, which contains some pictures. *Illescas*, illic *non* quiescas, say creeping things, is an equally wretched place. The *S^{a.} Maria* has a fine Moorish belfry, which the natives have disfigured with a modern pointed roof. The once superb Franciscan convent was gutted by the invaders, who must have thought, when they compared the pomp of the masonry-built churches to the mud hovels around, that Spanish laymen were only created to support priests. Illescas possesses a miraculous Virgin, called *La de la Caridad*, whose handsome chapel in the hospital has some pictures by El Greco. *Olias* resembles the preceding places in poverty and discomfort: here also is a hospital for those who sicken by the dreary way.

TOLEDO.—The best inns are *Parador del Arzobispo, La Caridad, P^{da.} del Mirador*, on the E. entrance, and in the town *Fonda de los Caballeros*, which is a large clean house. Toledo is the capital of its district, whose hilly portions, *La Sierra* or *Los Montes de Toledo*, which divide the basins of the Tagus and Guadiana, extend over 40 L., and were once covered with timber, which has been cut for building and fuel for Madrid, and never replanted. Full details will be found in the '*Memorias*' of Eugenio Larruga, vols. 5 to 10.

Toledo, now slighted for upstart Madrid, was the chosen city of the early annalists and antiquarians. The best works to consult are, '*Summi templi Toletani Descriptio*,' Blas Ortiz, duo., Tol^{o.} 1549; '*Historia y Descripcion*,' Pedro de Alcocer, fol., Tol^{n.} 1554;

'*Descripcion de Toledo*,' by F^{ro.} de Pisa, but edited by Tomas Tamaio de Vargas, fol., Tol^{o.} 1617; '*La Primacia de Toledo*,' Diego de Castejon Fonseca, fol., 2 vols. Mad. 1645; '*Los Santos de Toledo*,' Ant^{o.} de Quintana Duenas, fol., Tol^{o.} 1651; '*Historia de Toledo*,' Pedro de Rojas, Conde de Mora, fol., 2 vols., Mad. 1654-63; '*Los Reyes Nuevos de Toledo*,' Christobal Lozano, 4to., 1667, or the later edition, 4to., Mad. 1764; '*Esp. Sag.*' v. vi.; and Ponz, '*Viage*,' i.

Imperial Toledo, the navel of the Peninsula, " the crown of Spain, the light of the whole world, free from the time of the mighty Goths," as its son Padilla addressed it, is a city of the past. When seen from afar, nothing can be more imposing, but there is rottenness in the core. This Durham of a once golden hierarchy is in perfect contrast with the modern capital, for here everything is solid, venerable, and antique. Toledo has not been run up by academicians to please the hurry of a king's caprice, but is built like a rock, and on a rock. Like Rome, it stands on seven hills, and is about 2400 ft. above the level of the sea. The Tagus, boiling through the rent or *Tajo* of the mountain, hems it around, just leaving one approach by the land side, which is defended by Moorish towers and walls. Inside, the streets, or rather lanes, are steep and tortuous; but such intricacy however rendered them easy to defend when attacked, and kept them cool in summer. Some indeed are so narrow that no sun can enter, while a small strip of blue sky above just answers Virgil's question (Ecl. iii. 104): " Dic quibus in terris—tres pateat cœli spatium non amplius ulnas?" The streetology is difficult, for of these winding *wynds*, irregular as *guerrilleros*, none run in a parallel or straight course, but twist and turn each after its own fancy, coming to most illogical conclusions. The houses are massive and Moorish-like; each family lives in its own secluded castle, and not in flats or apartments as at Madrid. Here again we find the Oriental *patio*, over which awnings are drawn in summer, as at Seville. Their areas are kept very clean, as the rain-water is collected from them for domestic uses. Toledo, although deficient in water, is a clean town. It is bitter cold in winter and hot in summer. The hills reflect back the sun's rays, but the river-meadows are pleasant; and the Tagus is indeed a river, and not a dry ditch like the Manzanares. The Toledans, like their houses, are solid and trustworthy rancid Castilians, and *muy hombres de bien*. Here the glorious *Castellano* is spoken in all its purity of grammar and pronunciation.

In the heart of the city towers the cathedral, around which clusters multitudinous churches and convents, many now silent as tombs. Even Salamanca, a city of learning, was scarcely more hardly treated by the invaders than Toledo, the see of the primate and great Levitical city of Spain. What the foreign foe began, the domestic reformer completed, as by the appropriation of ecclesiastical revenues, the means were taken away by which this priestly capital existed; now they are partly restored, but the die is cast, and Toledo will decay and become a Thebes, in which the untenanted temples alone remain. Formerly it contained, besides the cathedral, 20 parish and 6 Musarabic churches, 9 chapels, 3 colleges, 14 convents, 23 nunneries, 9 hospitals for males, 1 for females, and 9 chapels, a tolerable spiritual provision for a population now dwindled down from 200,000 to 15,000, *Cosas de España*, and very different from our Stockport, where three churches suffice for 60,000 busy souls, whose real divinity is *capital*. Let no cottonocrat, no mere man of money or pleasure, visit this gloomy, silent, and inert city, which is without trade, industry, credit, or manufactures; but to the painter, poet, and antiquarian, this widowed capital of two dynasties is truly interesting, as it carries us away from the present; it is a living ruin, a semblance

of life struggling with decay, where the grand erections of former prosperity seem now a mockery and insult.

The foundation of Toledo is of course ascribed to Hercules, *i. e.* the Phœnicians; others, however, prefer Tubal, who built it 143 years to a day after the deluge; nor have its townsfolk yet forgiven the Abbé de Vayrac for saying that they boasted that "Adam was the first king of Toledo, and the newly created sun rose over this spot, because the centre and throne of the world." Be that as it may, Toledo when taken by Marius Fulvius, U. C. 561, 193 B.C., was "urbs parva sed loco munita" (Livy, xxxv. 22). The name has been derived from *Toledoth*, the Hebrew "city of generations," as having been their place of refuge when Jerusalem was taken by Nebuchadnezzar. No doubt many Jews did fly to "Tarshish," to the "uttermost parts of the earth," in order to escape the calamities in Palestine; and certainly when Toledo was first taken by the Moors it was filled with Hebrews, or, as they called them, "Amalekites," who, resenting the Gothic persecution, facilitated the progress of the Berbers, who themselves were half Jews and half Pagans. The extraordinary spoil, as detailed in ' Moh. D.' ii. 7, and Conde, i. 38, proves how rich the city then was. Among the precious items was the table of Solomon, for which Musa immediately inquired and carried off, just as the French generals, with the guide books of Ponz and Cean, demanded and removed church plate and pictures.

Conde interprets Toledo, quasi Tolaitola, "alturâ perfectum," or *atalaya* grande, from the Arabic *attalah*, a place of look-out, and to this day the *Alcazar* towers nobly over the city, its beacon and sentinel. Leovigildo, under whom the Gothic monarchy was consolidated, removed his court from Seville, and made Toledo the capital of Spain. His successor, Recaredo, brought the kingdom entirely into the Christian fold, and hence were held here so many of those important councils * which give such insight into the spirit and condition of that age, for they in reality were convocations and parliaments, as the sacerdotal aristocracy imitated social and civil supremacy. The Goths, who have been unjustly stigmatised as destructive barbarians, repaired and improved the city, bridges, and Roman walls, portions of which exist, for Toledo was one of the few towns exempted from the decree of Witiza, by which so many others were simultaneously dismantled, as if to render conquest easier to the invader. But history in Spain is always reproducing itself; compare the similar policy of Cato (App. ' B. H.' 467; Livy, xxxiv. 17).

Wamba was the benefactor of Toledo, as is recorded in the inscription over the great gate, " Erexit fautore Deo rex inclytus urbem, Wamba." This is indeed " a long time ago," for Wamba is the Japetus of Spain, and the phrase *en el tiempo del Rey Wamba* proverbially denotes a date beyond legal memory, as " old as the hills," *au temps où la Reine Berthe filait.* Wamba was half poisoned in 687 by Ervigius, and when supposed to be dead, was clad as usual in a monk's dress for burial; and, therefore, when he recovered, was compelled to continue the cowl. The quarrels between the usurper and rightful heirs weakened the Gothic government, and enabled the Moors, in 714, to subdue the divided kingdom, just as afterwards, in 1492, the dissensions of the Moslems paved the way to their final defeat by Ferdinand and Isabella. The Jews of Toledo, when their Moorish friends seized their money, turned to the avenging Christian, and facilitated the

* Some works on these councils have been mentioned at p. 361. The best edition is far is '*Collectio Maxima*,' José Saenz de Aguirre, folio, 4 vol. Roma, 1693-4; or the new edition, folio, 6 vol. Roma, Jos. Catalani, 1753.

conquest of the city in 1085, by Alonzo VI., who thereupon took the title of Emperor of Toledo, giving " himself seated on an imperial throne" for the bearing on its shield, and naming the Cid as its first *Alcaide*. Toledo, honoured by the sovereign and made the primacy of a rich clergy, was always loyal ; thus when Burgos disputed its new precedence in Cortes, Alonzo XI. exclaimed, " let Burgos speak first, I will speak for Toledo, which will do what I wish."

First walk round this most picturesque old city, beginning at the north-eastern land approach; descend to the *Puerta del Sol,* a rich Moorish gate of granite horseshoe arches, with upper intersecting ones of red brick, and follow the old road which winds down by the church of *Santiago ;* observe its courtyard, portico, and absis ; thence pass on to the *Puerta de Visagra,* now blocked up, and therefore called la Puerta *lodada.* With regard to the walls there are two circumvallations ; the inner, built by Wamba, runs up from the bridge of Alcantara under the Alcazar to the gates of *Sa. Cruz* and *Cambron,* and thence to the bridge of S$^{n.}$ Martin; while the outer line, built in 1109 by Alonzo VI., which also begins at the Alcantara bridge, keeps in the hollow by *Las Covachuelas* to the present new gate; continuing thence to the *Pa. Lodada,* and then joining the old wall near *El Nuncio,* and thus inclosing the former Moorish gate. The name *Visagra,* said by some to be *Via sacra,* the road by which Alonzo entered in triumph, is simply *Bib-Sahara,* the Arabic " gate of the country ;" and the rich cereal and pastoral district between Illescas and Aranjuez is still called *La Sagra,* Arabicé "the support." Others read in it the Hebrew *Sahar,* " bright," as being the E. gate on which the rising sun would shine, and through which " those who went out early," *Saharaim,* would pass.

The new gate was built in 1575 by Philip II., who adorned it with the eagle and shield of Charles V., the guardian St. Michael, and statues by Berruguete. Read the inscription which records how Philip restored the "Divos patronos urbis, and destroyed Moorish impieties. Wamba, at least, ascribed his buildings to the assistance of God, Fautore Deo; compare Philip's Christian Latin, with a genuine Pagan dedication found here (Cean, ' Sumº·'119). Herculi patrono, Endoval Tol. [Diro Toletano], V. V.   Osca deis tutel. &c. The use of Latin of itself gives a Pagan turn to this sort of inscriptions, even if the purport were not so similar. Observe also the image of San Eugenio, one of the Divi of Philip: he was sent by St. Denis to Spain, A.D. 65, and became Bᵖ· of Toledo; but going back to France, was murdered at St. Denis. His body, however, was discovered by Ramon, a Frenchman, and second archbᵖ· of Toledo, who brought the right arm here in 1156, and Philip II. obtained the rest from Charles IX. Thus the parts were reunited Nov. 18, 1565, after 1468 years of separation (see Pisa, 84, and ' E. S.' v. 224; and for an ancient parallel see Leon, p. 609).

The Alameda outside this gate was planted in 1826 by the Corregidor Navarro, who laid out the gardens and plazuela de Marchan, but the statues of Toledan kings are bad and heavy. In the suburb, Las Covachuelas, are some degraded Roman remains. Close by is the Hospital de Afuera, built by Bartolomé Bustamente in 1542, for the Card. Primate Juan de Tavera, whose life is written by Salazar de Mendoza. The magnificence led the envious to reverse the remark of their prototypes in Matthew xxvi. 8, and say, " Why is so much given to the poor ?" The façade is unfurnished, for, although the founder left the hospital his heir, he could not bequeath his spirit of beneficence, and his executors, whose charity began at home, pocketed the funds; the interior and arrangements are most wretched. Enter the noble patio, and proceed by a colonnade to

the chapel, whose Retablo was designed and painted by El Greco in 1509. Here lies the founder on a noble cinque cento Urna, guarded by the cardinal virtues, to which few cardinals were ever better entitled. The details of the whole are infinite, and this was the last, but not the best work of Berruguete, who died in 1561 in the room under the clock.

Turn now to the r., and observe the slits for arrows in the Puerta Lodada, and the horse-shoe arches above : this gate was built by Moorish workmen for Alonzo VI. A fine outline of convents and palaces, all ruined by the invader, crests the hill running by the lunatic hospital, El Nuncio, to the pinnacled gate of Cambron. Below to the r. the remains of a circus can just be traced : adjoining to them was the prætorian temple, which was converted into a church by Sisebuto in 621; it is now called El Cristo de la Vega. Examine well this curious but much degraded basilica, with its absis and external round-headed sunken archwork. In it were buried the tutelars of Toledo, San Ildefonso and Sᵃ· Leocadia, the events of whose lives have been so much illustrated by Spanish artists and authors. Leocadia, born in 306, was cast down from the rocks above by Dacian : a chapel was raised on the site of her fall, in which councils were held, during one of which, in 660, angels appeared and removed the stone from her sepulchre, when she arose " clad in a mantilla," and informed the president, Sᵃ· Ildefonso, that " her mistress lived through him." He had written a mariolatrous treatise. The author was so pleased that he took the knife of the king Redecivintus, and cut off a corner of her veil, which was shown to Philip II. in 1587; the body, according to some historians, ascended to heaven, while others have proved that when the Moors invaded Toledo, a Fleming carried it off to Flanders, which, indeed, was an act of great piety; for few braves Belges, when about to run away for 1200 miles, would select such a portable valuable as a dead woman (see Florez, 'E. S.' vi. 308, quoting Pisa). The corpse was rediscovered at S^{n.} Gislem, in 1500, when Philip I. obtained a portion of it for the chapter of Toledo, and the rest was removed by Philip II. when fearful that the heretics would conquer the low countries. He received the remains at the cathedral in person, April 26, 1587. All this translation, the expenses of which were enormous, was managed by a clever Jesuit, one Miguel Hernandez, who published an octavo life of Leocadia at Toledo, in 1591. Consult also her biography in Pisa, and in 'E. S.' v. 507, in which is printed an account of the council scene, written in 775 by Cixila, archb^{p.} of Toledo. The 26th of April is still a grand holiday in honour of this santa.

Above to the l., and growing, as it were, out of the rock, rise the remains of the palace castle, built by Wamba in 674, in order to command the W. approach of the city : the masonry is truly Cyclopean. Below, on the river bank, is a Moorish arched *alcoba*, with an Arabic inscription, which is called by the vulgar *Los Baños de Florinda—de Cava*, who is said to have been bathing here, when Roderick most orientally beheld from his terrace above the charms of this Gothic Bathsheba. The sad results are matters of history (see also our remarks, pp. 349, 353). The bridge of S^{n.} Martin below binds rock to rock, and completes the picture. Now turn back, and ascend to the *Puerta del Cambron*, and enter Toledo; in the inside niche of this gate is a statue of Leocadia by Berruguete, which is Florentine in style, tender and beautiful in form, and sweet, gentle, and serious in expression.

Advancing are the remains of the once splendid Franciscan convent, called *San Juan de los Reyes*, because dedicated to their tutelar saint (see p. 386) by Ferd. and Isab., who built it in commemoration of the decisive victory at Toro. The site is well chosen, being truly royal and commanding.

Observe their badges and symbols (see p. 130), and the votive chains suspended outside by captives delivered from the infidel by the intervention of the Virgin ; Catenam ex voto Laribus. The portal, an exquisite gem, was finished by Alonzo de Covarrubias for Philip II. This convent, which was one of the finest specimens of Gothic art in the world, was all but demolished by the invaders, who entirely gutted and burnt the quarters of the monks. The splendid chapel escaped somewhat better, having been used as a stable for horses; but the troops, whiled away their leisure by smashing the storied painted glass, and mutilating the religious and heraldic ornaments, whose richness was once past all description, as those specimens which were out of reach evince. Observe the shields, eagles, badges, cyphers, coronets, and the fringing inscription, so common at this period. The cloisters, with fine pointed Gothic arches, deserve notice ; a few vile repairs have been done here by plastering up arches, and making more hideous the previous Vandalism : the space, which once was a pretty garden, is now cursed with weeds, fit companions to the ruin all around. Opposite to this convent was the grand palace of the great Cardinal Ximenez, which the invaders first pillaged and then destroyed.

Turn now to the l., and descend by narrow lanes to the former *Juderia*, or Jews' quarter, in which two most singular synagogues yet remain, although sadly degraded. The first, now called *La S^{a.} Maria la Blanca*, was built in the ninth century ; but in 1454, when San Vicente de Ferrer goaded the mob on against the Jews, it was converted into a church, and so remained until the French degraded it into a storehouse. The architecture deserves much notice ; observe the three aisles divided by polygonal pillars, which support horseshoe arches, springing from bastard Gothic capitals ; remark the circular patterns in the spandrils, the stars, chequer-work, and engrailed Moorish arches. The building is somewhat too high in proportion with width; the ceiling is said to be made from beams of the cedars of Lebanon.

The other synagogue, although less ancient, is finer and better preserved; it is called *El transitu* from a picture of the death of the Virgin, which has disappeared during recent reforms. It was built by Levi, treasurer to Don Pedro the Cruel, for the Spaniards were then ruled by the intelligent, but by them despised Jew, just as the Moorish Kaid of Tetuan Hash-Hash was governed, when we were there, by his Hebrew Chancellor of the Exchequer Levi. A peculiar talent for money concerns always has marked the children of Israel, especially when in a strange land; thus Joseph became treasurer to Pharaoh, Daniel to Nebuchadnezzar, and Mordecai to Artaxerxes. Don Pedro, however, in 1360, being in want of cash, and knowing the value of a Jew's eye, tortured and killed poor Levi, and then seized his money-bags. (See for a curious picture of Hispano - Oriental manners, chapters 7, 15, and 30 of the ' *Chronica de Don Pedro*'). He had previously patronised the Jews, who soon became so rich and numerous that the former synagogue was too small, and this splendid "place of congregation," συναγογη, the *Jama* or Mosque of the Moor, was built in a mixture of the Gothic, Moorish, and Hebrew style, which must indeed have once been gorgeous, but the Spaniards have disfigured the E. end with a trumpery gilt *retablo* that conceals the lace-like embroidery; the upper parts, being out of reach, have escaped better, so observe the honey-comb cornice, the rows of engrailed Moorish arches, and the superb *artesonado* roof. A broad band with foliage contains the arms of Leon and Castile, and is edged with a Hebrew inscription, which is translated by Juan José Heydeck in the ' *Memorias de la Ac. Hist.*' (iii. 31). Isabella in 1494 gave the building to the order of Calatrava, when the holy of holies was converted into an archive, and the galleries of the Jewesses into a dwelling of the animal who is called *El custodio* or *conserje*.

There is a history of the *Sepharaim* or Spanish Jews, by James Finn, 1841, which by no means exhausts the subject. They were of a very high caste; and although persecuted by Goth, Moor, and Spaniard, by followers of creeds both alike daughters of the old Testament, they clung closely to their faith. Strange religionists, who turned, when the only depositaries of the real word of God, to every idolatry, worshipping a golden calf (and probably because it was *golden*), even under the thunders of Mount Sinai, and yet when the true Messiah came, to supersede the old law, then they clung doggedly to what they before abandoned. Spain (Tarshish) was always the favored locality of the Jew when forced from Palestine. Being men of peace and money, they were always persecuted by the men of war, who seldom can live on their pay. Such was the *Judaicus Fiscus* of Domitian (Suet. 12), such the policy of Tiberius, who banished all Jews from Italy who would not abjure their creed (Tac. ' An.' ii. 85), for the purification of religion was always made the pretext of appropriating avarice. The Christian Goths, equally fond of money as the Romans, had the additional accusation of the guilt of the crucifixion. In 694, by the 17th council of Toledo, the Jews were ordered to be cut off with the " scythe of revenge," for corresponding with the " Filistins " of Barbary. It was then, when driven by persecutions, that they called in the avenging Moors, and opened the gates of *Toledo*, it is said, on Palm Sunday, when the Christian garrison was worshipping at the tomb of Sᵃ Leocadia. For this service they at first were favored by the Moslem, and being left in peace again soon became so rich, that their heresies began to stink in Mohammedan nostrils, and they were either strangled or robbed. In this dilemma they turned to the avenging Christians, and let in Alonzo VI., who also for a time encouraged and protected them. As they sided with Don Pedro (because they had lent him money) in the civil wars of 1369, they were treated as traitors by the successful Henrique II., who confiscated their cash. Then ensued the ferocious crusades of San Vicente de Ferrer (see p. 448), who halloed on a fanatic mob to robbery and murder, by representing these atrocious crimes as meritorious acts of religion. The great modern master of Jewish persecution was the perfidious *Philippe le Bel* of France, son of Saint Louis and murderer of two popes. The Spanish Jews, having been long hunted like beasts and impoverished, were finally expelled from Spain by Isabella in 1492, who therefore is called *Jesebel* in their chronicles. Vast numbers settled on the Mohammedan shores of the Mediterranean, where their descendants still speak Spanish. Many, however, remained behind, professing to be Christians, but in secret following their own religion and mammon. And some still exist, a curious fact discovered by Borrow and quite unknown to Spaniards. These Jews are quiet and in easy circumstances, trafficking in wool and *longanizas*, which they sell but do not eat, as pork enters largely into this excellent sausage. Although the Spaniards are unaware of their existence, the name Jew, *Judio*, is still the *maledictio pessima*, the *Nimreseth*, the insult never to be forgiven, *anathema maranatha.* Spaniards even in this century were taught to think all foreigners to be heretics and Jews. The cry of *Judiada* is still a prelude to certain murder (see p. 596). " I hate oppression in every shape," said a Valencian *Liberal* to Lord Carnarvon, " I am a friend to the human race; if indeed there be a Jew among us, burn him, I say, burn him alive."

Next visit the adjoining church of *Sⁿ. Tomé*, with a Moorish brick tower. Here long was preserved the masterpiece of *El Greco*, the burial of *el*

conde de Orgaz (see p. 771). Near Sⁿ. Tome is a vacant space, on which stood the house of Juan de Padilla and of his noble wife Maria, the leaders of the *comunero* insurrection ; this Charles V. ordered to be razed in 1522, when a granite pillar with a branding inscription was placed on the site ; a memorial which in its turn has been destroyed by modern reformers. Descend now to the Moorish bridge of *Sⁿ. Martin*, which was broken in 1368 by Henry of Trastamara, and repaired by Archbishop Tenorio, a kinsman of "Don Juan," and a celebrated pontifex maximus. Observe in the tower a statue of *San Julian* by Berruguete. The bridge is narrow and elevated on account of the occasional swellings of the river, which rushes down from a rocky gorge, on the r. crest of which towers the toppling city. The river, pleased to escape from its prison, meanders away amid *las Huertas del Rey*. Below all is repose, and the green meadow woos the lingering stream (compare Ronda, p. 331). On the hills are the *cigarrales* of Toledan villas, not so called from the multitudinous *cigars* smoked therein, but from the Arabic *Zigarr*, *Cegarra*, " a place of trees." The correct Castilian term is *Casa del Campo* or *quinto*, Arabicé *Chennat chint*, " a garden." In Gallicia, they are called *Aldeas*, Arabicé *Aldaiâ*, " a small place ;" in Aragon *Torres ;* in Andalucia *Haciendas ;* in Granada *Carmenes*, Arabicé *Karm*, " a vine."

The wild and melancholy Tagus (see p. 547) rises in the *Albarracin* mountains, and disembogues into the sea at Lisbon, having flowed 375 miles in Spain, of which nature destined it to be the aorta. The Toledan chroniclers derive the name from Tagus 5th king of Iberia, but Bochart traces it to *Dag*, Dagon, a fish, as, besides being considered auriferous,

* *Orgaz* lies about 5 L. S. of Toledo, near the spurs of the *Montes*, popⁿ. 2500. The parish church, Sⁿ. Tomé, although unfinished, is a superb specimen of the designs and masonry of Herrera. The ruined castle of the Condes is picturesque.

both Strabo and Martial pronounced it to be piscatory, Πολυιχθυς, *piscosus.* The best trout-fishing is to be found near the source. Grains of gold are indeed found, but barely enough to support a poet, by amphibious paupers, called *Artesilleros* from their baskets, in which they collect the sand, which is passed through a sieve.

The Tagus might easily be made navigable to the sea, and then with the Xarama connect Madrid and Lisbon, and facilitate importation of colonial produce, and exportation of wine and grain. Such an act would confer more benefits upon Spain than ten thousand *charters* or paper constitutions. The performance has been contemplated by many *foreigners*, the Toledans looking lazily on; thus in 1581, Antonelli, a Neapolitan, and Juanelo Turriano, a Milanese, suggested the scheme to Philip II., then master of Portugal; but money was wanting—the old story—for his revenues were wasted in relic-removing and in building the useless Escorial, and nothing was made except water parties, and odes to the "wise and great king" who *was* to do the deed, " *I'll do, I'll do, I'll do*," for here the future is preferred to the present tense. The project dosed until 1641, when two other *foreigners*, Julio Martelli and Luigi Carduchi, in vain roused Philip IV., who soon after losing Portugal itself, forthwith forgot the Tagus. Another century glided away, when Richard Wall, an Irishman, took the thing up in 1755, but Charles III., busy in waging French wars against England, wanted cash. The Tagus has ever since, as it roared over its rocky bed, like an untamed barb, laughed at the Toledan who dreamily angles for impossibilities on the bank, invoking Brunel, Hercules, and Rothschild, instead of putting his own shoulder to the water-wheel. In 1808, the scheme was revived by Fro. Xavier de Cabanas, who had studied in England our system of canals and coaches. He introduced diligences into Spain,

and published a survey of the whole river; this folio ' *Memoria sobre la navigacion del Tajo*,' Mad. 1829, reads like the blue book of one discovering the source of the Niger, so desert-like are the unpeopled, uncultivated districts between Toledo and Abrantes. Ferd. VII. thereupon issued an approving *paper* decree ; and so there the thing ended. His decrees amount to eighteen thick volumes, although Cabanes had engaged with Messrs. Wallis and Mason for the machinery, &c.; for recently the project has been renewed by our friend Bermudez de Castro, an intelligent gentleman, who from long residence in England, has imbibed the schemes and energy of the foreigner. *Verémos!* for hope is a good breakfast but a bad supper, says Bacon.

Now cross the bridge of Sⁿ· Martin and ascend the steeps to the l.; soon town and river are lost in a valley of rocks; above is the blue sky and below a rivulet where damsels wash their linens, colour the grey stones with sparkling patches, and cheer the loneliness with songs. Follow the stream to the Tagus, and having looked at the Moorish mills, reascend into a scene made for Salvator Rosa, until on reaching a chapel Toledo reappears with its emphatic *Alcazar* towering over rock, ruins, and river; then clamber up to the shattered castle of Cervantes, a name which has nothing to do with the author of ' Don Quixote,' but is a corruption of *San Servando,* and it *guards* the approach to the bridge below, and commands a most glorious view of Toledo. To the r. below is the rose-planted *Alameda* laid out at the head of the road to Aranjuez. The meadow opposite is a field of romance: here Alonzo held a *cortes* when the Cid complained of his vile sons-in-law the Counts of Carrion ; here some much degraded ruins are still called *Las Casas de la Reina,* being the supposed remains of a fabulous castle in the air, which Galafre, a king who never ruled, built for his daughter

Galiana, when courted by Charles Martel, who never was in Spain, who slew in her presence his rival Bradabante, who never existed : for the true history of this Moorish villa see Gayangos (Moh. D. ii. 383). The ruins are not worth walking out to, which we did.

The bridge, like others over the Tagus, is called by pleonasm *El puente de Alcantara*, the "bridge of the bridge," for the Spaniards did not even understand the *name* of a *thing* which the Moors made for them. Here the Romans were the first to build one, which was repaired in 687 by the Goth Sala : destroyed by an inundation, it was rebuilt in 871 by the Alcaide Halaf, repaired in 1258 by Alonzo el Sabio, restored by Archb. Tenorio about 1380, and fortified in 1484 by Andres Manrique. Examine the towers and tête du pont, and the statue by Berruguete of San Ildefonso, who is the *Divus tutelaris* to whom Philip II. dedicated the bridge, as is stated in an inscription. From this point the walls diverge, running to the r. in double line, the upper one being that built by Wamba, the under that of Alonzo VI. Ascend the hill to the l. and rest for a moment to look down on the roofless *Ingenio*, the water-work engine, whose ruin seems made for artists. Toledo, built on a lofty rock, was badly supplied with water, whereupon the Romans stemmed the defile with a gigantic viaduct and aqueduct, which ran from the *Puerto de Yevenes*, distant 7 L. Some remains may be traced near *Los Siete cantos* and under the convents Sⁿ· Sisla and Santiago, and the line is still called *El Camino de Plata*, the "road of silver," a common Spanish corruption of via *lata*. When the Moors conquered Toledo there was also an enormous Nàúrah, *Noria* or water wheel, 90 cubits high, which forced up water by pipes, a work of the Jews, who introduced the hydraulics of the East, where water is the blood of the earth and the element of fertility : no people

ever exercised greater power over this element than the Spanish Moors (see p. 430). The amphibious Moslem loved cool water, for ablutions inside and outside are both pleasant and religious under a torrid sun ; so where a Greek put up a statue, and a Christian a crucifix, he constructed a fountain or dug a well. The Toledan Moors were first-rate hydraulists (see ' Moh. D.' ii. 262) : their king Al-mámun, Ibn Dhia-nún, or Jahya, had a lake in his palace, and in the middle a kiosk, from whence water descended on each side, thus enclosing him in the coolest of summer-houses, exactly as is the Kasr Dubarra now existing at Cairo. Here also were made the *clepsydræ* or water clocks for the astronomical calculations of Alonzo el Sabio, to study which Daniel Merlac came all the way from Oxford in 1185. Charles V., who delighted in mechanics, in 1565 caused some Greeks to descend at Toledo in a diving-bell, and the same year brought from Cremona a watch-maker named Juanelo Turriano, to repair the original *Noria*, which in 1568 forced up 600,000 buckets of water daily. Disputes however arose between the crown and the corporation as "conservators of the river," between whom the Turriano family, being foreigners, were cheated, and died beggars. Soon after the indignant Tagus damaged the engine, which the natives could not repair, and thereupon applied to an English company, who declined, disliking the security offered for payment, since when the ruin has been complete, and Toledo, the "light of the world," obtains its water by the primitive machinery of donkeys, which are driven up and down by bipeds whose quality of mechanical intellect is cognate : see for curious details Cean Ber. ' A.' ii. 100.

Next visit the Alcazar, the *Atalaya* of Tolaitola, the Mount Zion, or palace and fortress, and the emphatic feature of a city which it once defended and now adorns. It was the Amalekite *Kassabah*, to which additions were made in 1085 by Alonzo VI.: the oldest portions overlook the Tagus, as the castle of Presburg does the Danube. It was much improved by Alvaro de Luna, and by Charles V. in 1548, who employed Henrique de Egas and Alonzo de Covarrubias to add the fine façade and staircase, which Herrera completed for Philip II. The whole was burnt in the war of succession, not by the English, as Cean Bermudez states, but by the Portuguese general Atalaya, who vented his hatred for Spanish things on his namesake city and castle : the ruins were repaired by Cardinal Lorenzana, the last of the great and good primates of Toledo, ultimus Romanorum ; he converted them into a *Casa de Caridad*, in which paupers were employed in silk-weaving. His whole life and income were devoted to good works ; he supported the French exiled clergy, and when the Pope was insulted at Rome by the armed republicans, hastened there to offer comfort, which the tormentors refused to permit. Torn from his spiritual chief, Lorenzana resigned his primacy, and died in 1804. But the French never forgave his assistance to their priests, and when they entered Toledo especially persecuted his works, as he was beyond their reach. They ejected the paupers, seized the funds, converted the asylum into a barrack, which was burnt as a last legacy by Soult's troops when evacuating the half ruined city. The crumbling walls of the quarters in which the soldiers lodged were, when we were last there, still defiled with the most obscene writings and drawings.

The ruins are impressive, and things of Toledo, a place of palaces without princes, convents without monks, and *exclaustrados* without bread. Observe the Berruguete façade, windows, the *patio* with granite pillars, the fine stair-case, and upper gallery decked with heraldic ornaments, which the invaders mutilated. In the saloons overlooking the river the widow of Philip IV., the queen regent, was con-

fined during the minority of Charles II. ; her mode of life has been graphically described by Mad$^{e.}$ D'Aunoy, and Dunlop, ii. 123. She was first the tool of the low adventurer Nithard and then of her base paramour Valenzuela; but there is nothing *new* in Spanish history past or present.

Now proceed to the *Zocodover*, a name which to readers of Lazarillo de Tormes and Cervantes recalls the haunt of rogues and of those proud and poor Don Whiskerandos who swaggered and starved. *Suk* in Arabic, *Zocco* in Spanish, and *Soke* in English, signify a "market-place" and vicinity to cathedrals, for commerce and religion went hand in hand ; the shrine attracted multitudes and "money changers," while its sanctity protected commerce. This *plaza* is most Moorish, with its irregular windows, balconies, blacksmiths, and picturesque peasantry : now a long and almost the only widish street in Toledo leads to the Gothic cathedral, whose exterior is neither beautiful nor symmetrical, while the N. entrance is blocked up: the best points of view are to the N. W., either from the *Plaza del Ayuntamiento* or *de S^{n}. Yuste ;* one tower is finished and rises in a thin spire, encircled as with crowns of thorns.

The church chronicles state that this temple was built to the Virgin while she was alive, and that she often came down from heaven to it, accompanied by St. Peter, St. Paul, and Santiago. Converted by the Moors into their grand mosque, Alonzo VI. guaranteed it to them, with that ample toleration which the infidel always observed to their Christian subjects, but which the Spanish Christians never respected with the Moors ; thus Ximenez broke the treaty of Granada ere the ink was dry, and so now Bernardo, the first archbishop, backed by Alonzo's queen, Constanza, a native of France like himself, the moment the king was absent, seized the mosque and dispossessed the Moors; then the *Alfaqui*, foreseeing that resistance was useless, interceded with Alonzo, and the building was pulled down in 1226 by St. Ferdinand, who himself laid the first stone of the present cathedral: designed by Pedro Perez, it was completed in 1492, plundered in 1521 by Padilla's mob, and again in 1808 by La Houssaye. Previously it was a mine of wealth and art; thus Cean Bermudez enumerates 149 artists, who, during six centuries, were employed by the richest prelates of Spain to make a temple worthy of the primacy, a dighity which was long held by the master mind of the day, for the religious profession was not then a bar to office, but a recommendation; not a burden to politicians, a governmental difficulty, but a binding bond: now, indeed, religion is but a mere fragment of what it was, when all in all in everything, and when the same intellect that ruled the church sustained and governed the state. The older archbishops of Toledo were great alike in peace and war; the *Rodrigos* headed victorious armies, the *Tenorios* built bridges, the *Fonsecas* founded colleges, the *Mendozas* and *Ximenez* were third kings and regents, they founded universities, while the *Taveras* and *Lorenzanas* raised houses of charity and hospitals. These, indeed, have been swept away by rude hands, foreign and domestic, but their memory abides, nor will the new lay appropriators easily either repair the outrages, or rival those works of piety and science, those offerings which the consecrated hands of old had laid on the altar. The prelates of Spain's chivalrous and mediæval period were bred in the cloister, then the only asylum of peace, learning, and the arts which humanize. They had "leisure," without which, says the wisest of men, none can become wise. The church was the best school for ministers of state and men of business, as the great laity then thought of nothing but war, or the chace, its mimic pursuit. But now the service of God disqualifies its professors from serving their Queen and country; and so far from being ministers of state, they are degraded to be

mere *ministri* of the altar, while even their paltry wages were unpaid.

The primate of Toledo have for suffragans, Cordova, Jaen, Cartagena, Cuenca, Sigüenza, Segovia, Osma, and Valladolid: the chapter was truly imperial, and consisted of nearly 100 dignitaries and prebendaries. Here, as at Leon and Burgos, the king was always a canon; so the priesthood of the Paphian Venus was held by a Prince of the Blood, for thus the prestige and power of royalty was enlisted in the *service* of the church; and to show its power, the monarch was always fined for non-attendance in *coro* on St. John's Day.

Before entering, examine the exterior and gates. *La puerta de los Leones* is so called from the lions with shields on pillars. The deeply-recessed portal with Gothic figures and niche work, was wrought by El Maestre Egas, in 1459, in a beautiful white stone, which, soft at first, hardens with time; the upper works were restored in bad taste in 1776, by Mariano Salvatierra, by whom is the "Assumption of the Virgin." The exterior of the Michael Angelesque bronze doors were cast in 1545 by Frᵒ· de Villalpando, and the insides were finely carved in wood in 1541 by Diego Copin, of Holland; but the tournaments, centaurs, &c., are scarcely suited for a Christian temple's entrance: the modern Ionic gate is equally out of keeping with the Gothic style of the cathedral. The *Puerta del Reloj*, or *de la Feria*, is much blocked up by buildings, and is also disfigured by some modern red and gilt wood-work, which ill accords with the Gotho-Tedesque stone carvings; the bronze doors were cast to match those of the opposite gate; that to the l. is by Antonio Turreno 1713, that to the r. by Antᵒ· Dominguez. They are also ornamented with carvings inside, which are older in date and better in style; the *Puerta del Perdon* has six niches on each side, which are carried all up round the arch.

The interior, although fine, is infe-

2 o

rior to the cathedral at Seville both in form and height. Here the lateral naves are somewhat low and crowded with piers, and fatal whitewash has been unsparingly laid on; the general style of the Gothic is simple and pointed. The painted windows are superb; look at them about sunset, when as the aisles darken these storied panes brighten up like rubies and emeralds. The recent spoliations and appropriations have tended to dim the former magnificence of this splendid temple, which now lacks the spirit and movement of life, for here solitude and melancholy brood enshrined, and sad is the livery of Toledo. The pomp and ceremonies used to be remarkable even in Spain, where a really *divine* service was performed; then the vast space was crowded with ant-like myriads, and the city of the sleeper awoke as by a touch of the wand, and filled its streets, changing into stir and crowds its usual death-like monotony.

Proceeding to details, there are five naves, supported by 84 piers; the length is 404 ft., the width 204; the central nave is the highest, rising to 160 ft. The cloisters lie to the N. near the *Sagrario* and *Salas*, which contain the relics and pictures. The windows, the reds and blues of which are matchless, were painted chiefly by foreigners (see p. 252), by Alberto de Holanda, Maestro Christobal, Dolphin, Juan Campa, Luis, Pedro Frances, and Vasco de Troya. The subjects are taken from the Bible and legends of local saints, interspersed with the shields of the donors.

The *coro*, as usual, is placed in the heart of the central nave, but as the rich *trascoro* is not very high, the eye sweeps over it: the coro is a museum of sculpture; the under stalls, carved in 1495, by El Maestre Rodrigo, and enriched with grotesque tedesque ornaments, represent the campaigns of Ferd. and Isab. Observe, in these authentic contemporary records of places and costume, the surrender of the Alhambra. The upper stalls are in a perfect clas-

sical contrast, being embroidered with a prodigality of ornament; above them, in alabaster, is the genealogy of Christ, while the niches are divided by candelabra pillars resting on heads of cherubs. The seats are separated by red marble columns; the inscription placed here by Card. Tavera in 1543 tells the truth. "Signa tum marmorea tum ligna cælavere hinc Philippus Burgundio, ex adverso Berruguetus Hispanus; certaverunt tum artificum ingenia, certabunt semper spectatorum judicia," and in passing judgment, it is not easy to distinguish the works of one master from those of the other; of the 70 stalls the 35 on the *Lado de la Epistola* are by Vigarny, who died here in 1543, and was buried near his works; but when the pavement was afterwards repaired his grave-stone was cast out among the rubbish by the chapter, alike devoid of good taste or gratitude. In criticising the two great sculptors it may be observed that Vigarny is simple and grand in draperies and expressions, while Berruguete is more elegant and Italianlike. The latter artist also carved the Primate's Throne, and the Transfiguration over it, a subject which from its very nature is ill adapted for solid materials. In the *coro* observe the exquisite *Atriles* of gilt metal, wrought with scriptural bas-relief, divided by female figures, a truly Florentine-like masterpiece of Villalpando. The *Facistol* or *Lettern*, an Eagle on a Gothic Tower, with statues in niches, is excellent. The black wooden image of the Virgin before it is very ancient, and the petticoat modern and splendid. The *Reja*, the gilt pillars which support the curtains, and the candelabra, are of the cinque-cento taste, and are by Donmigo de Cespedes. The modern organs are churrigueresque, and out of harmony with the works of the giants of old.

Passing the *Entre los dos Coros*, observe the two pulpits of metal gilt, and placed on short marble columns; these, worthy of Cellini, were made from the bronze tomb raised for him-was wanting, the church was robbed without consulting Gregory XVI., who was never appealed to until satisfied lewdness, superstitious fears, and yearnings for despotism, required him to do the work of the Palace at Madrid.

The Musarabic ritual was that of the Spanish Goths, which, free from the modern inventions of Rome, was the oldest in Christendom, and the nearest approaching to the Apostolical primitive form which was once delivered to the Saints ; it is to Spain what the Rito Ambrogiano is to the Milanese : the original text was first tampered with in 633 by Sⁿ· Isidoro and Sᵃ· Leandro, who are compared to Ezra who remodelled the Books of the Old Testament : the new version was enjoined by the 4th council of Toledo, being principally directed against the Arian heresies, which denied the divinity of the Son ; it was preserved by the Christians, who, under the tolerant rule of the Moor, here retained six churches, which still exist on the same sites, and should be visited ; they are Sᵃ· Eulalia, Sⁿ· Torcato, Sⁿ· Sebastian, Sⁿ· Marcos, Sⁿ· Lucas, and Sᵃ· Justa, and their names are the best tests of their antiquity. The features of this ritual are its simplicity and earnest tone of devotion, and absence of auricular confession. The prayers and collects are so beautiful that many have been adopted in our Prayer Book ; the host was divided into nine parts, which represent the Incarnation, Epiphany, Nativity, Circumcision, Passion, Death, Resurrection, Ascension, and Eternal Kingdom.

The term *Mozarabe Muzarab* has been erroneously derived from Musa and his Arabs, and from *mixti-Arabes*, presuming that the Moors spoke Latin, and thus called the Christians who lived mixed with them ; but the Arabic *Must-Arab* means men who have lived with and tried to imitate the Arab, and who were not *Arab-al-Araba* like the Hebrew of the Hebrews (Moh. D. i. 420). The discontinuance of the Gothic ritual was the work of the French, who

denationalised Spain by the introduction of ultra Romanism ; for Bernardo, not content with dispossessing the Moslem, next assailed the Christians, and worked on his weak countrywoman, Queen Costanza, until she perverted her husband ; thus " *strange* wives" seduced Solomon, as the Tyrian Jezebel had Ahab, into gross superstitions. Alonzo, however, had much difficulty in substituting the Gregorian mass-book in the place of the Gothic and national one ; for his independent subjects, who abhorred foreign dictation and innovation, clung to their primitive ritual, distinguishing its rival as *el rito galico*, an epithet since given to other benefits derived from France : at last the change was effected by judicial combat, for the sword was then appealed to in all Gordian knots, both of law and theology ; a solemn trial by battle was held, each ritual having its armed champion ; but when the Gothic defender, Juan Ruiz, defeated his Gallo-Papal opponent, the perfidious Bernardo refused to abide by the award of his self-sought trial, and then appealed to the test of fire, when the two volumes were placed on a burning pile, when the Gothic one remained unconsumed, while the Gallo-Romano leapt out. In spite, however, of these two verdicts the French fashion prevailed, and the antagonist rituals first were allowed a concurrent usage, until Rome, by bribes and force, finally trampled down its rival ; hence the proverb, *Donde quieren Reyes ahi van leyes*, or, " might makes right." The Gregorian mass was first chaunted at Toledo, Oct. 5, 1086. Thus the little wedge was introduced and carried out in Spain, the darling object of Gregory VII. and of the fiery Hildebrand ; thus the *Roman* ritual, drawn up in a tongue which the people did not understand, became established, to the exclusion of the Musarabic, and the centralization of the Vatican broke down religious national independence. Ximenez printed the original ritual at Alcalá de Henares in 1500 ; as the edition became self by Alvaro de Luna, and broken up by Henry, Infante of Arragon, when soured by his defeat at Olmedo, whereupon Alvaro sent him a copy of verses on this paltry revenge, while Juan de Mena (Cop. 264) condemns the uncivilized Vandals whose "hearts were harder than the bronze;" what would he have said of those of this century? The glorious *reja* was wrought in 1548 by Villalpando. The *Capilla Mayor* was enlarged by Card¹· Ximenez, but the rich Gothic work at the sides is older, and is part of the original work of Tenorio. The lofty *Retablo*, with five divisions, contains carvings of the life of the Saviour and Virgin, executed about 1500, by Juan de Borgoña, Fernando Rincon, el Maestre Felipe, and others under Pedro Gumiel (*el honrado*, see Index). The whole is *estofado*, or painted and gilt. Here are the tombs of the *ancient* kings, *los Reyes Viejos;* to wit, Alonzo VII., Sancho *el Deseado*, Sancho *el Bravo*, and the *Infante* Don Pedro. Here also lies buried the Card¹· Mendoza, ob. 1495; this high-born and great prelate of sacerdocracy almost shared the sovereignty with Ferd. and Isab., whence he was called Tertius Rex, and indeed he united religious with ministerial power, and his decrees ran like those in the East, "Saul *and* Samuel" (1 Sam. xi. 7). This was the Ego et Rex meus which our Wolsey imitated; and now, a king in life, he lies interred in death among kings, the rare privilege of Jehoiada (2 Chr. xxiv. 16). His tomb, heightened with white and gold, is the work of Henrique de Egas, and is worthy of this glorious high altar, where all around, front and sides, is most elaborate; observe the infinite details of pinnacles, winged angels, and statues in niches, and among them the Shepherd (*San Isidro*, see p. 306) who led the Christians to victory at *Navas de Tolosa*, and of the " good Alfaqui," who interceded with the treaty-breaking Bernardo (see p. 840).

Next observe the sober Gothic *Respaldos del Coro*, erected by Archb.

Tenorio in the 14th century, which contrast with the *Trasparente*, an abomination of the 18th century, but which is the boast of the Toledans, to their disgrace. This was wrought by Narciso Tome, a heresiarch of churriguerism, who here tortured *solid* material into clouds, rays of light, and into everything most aërial; this fricasee of marble cost 200,000 ducats. The Archbp. Porto Carrero imported quarries from Italy, and ought to have been called *Porto Carrera*; he was the prime mover of Philip V.'s succession; this king-maker lies buried near the C⁴· del Sagrario, with the epitaph "Pulvis et umbra nihil," which cannot be said of this *trasparente*, as it is so very huge and so white that it cannot be hid, but arrests the eye to the detriment of finer objects; it is the style of Louis XIV. gone mad, yet it was inaugurated with bull-fights, sermons, and sonnets. A monk, one Fʳº· Galan, wrote a poem on this " *Octava Maravilla;*" in spite, however, of its absurdities, it evinces much depraved invention, and great workmanship and mastery over material; unfortunately a fine old *Retablo* and pictures were destroyed, as at Leon, to make room for this monstrosity in marble.

Next visit the chapel of *Santiago*, erected in 1442 by that great imp of fame, the Constable Alvaro de Luna, as his family burial-place; and as he was master of Santiago, the *Veneras* or scallop-shells abound, as also do his *canting* arms, "gules party azure, a crescent (Luna) reversed argent." The original bronze tombs were converted into pulpits, and the present ones of alabaster were sculptured by Pablo Ortiz in 1489, and erected by Maria, daughter of Alvaro. The armed *Maestre*, who was executed at Valladolid, in 1451, by his ungrateful sovereign, lies with his sword between his legs, while knights in hauberk mail kneel beside; near him is the *urna* of his wife, Juana de Pimentel, ob. 1489, for the repose of whose soul nuns are praying; the portraits of the deceased being near the altar. Observe also the once gilt tomb of Juan de Zerezuela, Archbp. of Toledo, ob. 1442; he was half brother to the Constable, and whole brother to Benedict XIII.; the head is very fine.

Next visit the most beautiful *Capilla de los Reyes nuevos*, the chapel of the *new* or later kings, as compared to those buried near the high altar; it was planned in 1531 for Card. Tavera, by Alonzo de Covarrubias, and executed by Alvaro Monegro; heralds marshal the stranger into this chamber of departed royalty, where under white and gold niches of Cellini plateresque embroidery, repose Henrique II. ob. 1379, his wife Juana ob. 1381, their son Juan I. ob. 1390, his wife Leonora ob. 1382 (their effigies knelt at the *Presbiterio*), Henrique III. ob. 1407, his wife Catalina (daughter of our John of Gaunt), ob. 1419. Juan II., by whose orders this chapel was built, is buried at Miraflores, but his statue is placed here among his ancestors.

Every other chapel must be visited, although to describe them would fill a volume. In *Sⁿ· Eugenio* are some remains of the old mosque, with Cufic inscriptions, and an arch and tomb of elaborate *Tarkish* work. In the *Sᵃ· Lucia* are some ancient monuments and inscriptions of the 13th century, a good painting of the martyrdom of St. Peter, and outside to the l. another of St. John with a lamb, and full of effect. In the *Cᵃ· de la Antigua*, observe the rich Gothic work of the deeprecessed niche of the Virgin's image. In *la Adoracion de los Santos Reyes*, observe the stone portal painted in red, blue, and gold; the *Retablo*, the *reja* with twisted bars, and the picture of the dead Saviour. The *Cᵃ· de Sⁿ· Pedro* is used as the Parroquia of the Cathedral.

The chapel of *San Ildefonso* contains splendid tombs; first, that of the primate Gil de Albornoz, ob. 1350, which is a masterpiece of Gothic niche and statue work; then that of his nephew Alonzo, Bp. of Avila, ob. 1514, which is a charming cinque-cento, with a raised work of birds, fruit, &c. picked out in white and gold, which canopies the *urna* on which the prelate lies. Near in a niche is the sepulchre of Inigo Lopez, who died in 1491 at the siege of Granada; the head is wreathed with leaves almost like a turban. Near is the tomb of Juan de Contreras and of Card. Gaspar Borja, ob. 1645. This noble Gothic chapel is also illustrated with sculpture relating to the tutelar Sⁿ· Ildefonso, whose legend has given subjects to Murillo and the best Spanish artists. He was born at Toledo in 690, became chaplain to Sⁿ· Isidoro, and took great part in the establishment of mariolatry, having written a book in defence of the perpetual virginity, of the αιει παρθενος, which some French heretics had questioned; his sermon on this text is still extant (see ' E. S.' v. 493), but some of the arguments, however fitted for a congregation of Goths, cannot well be here repeated. One morning the Virgin came down from heaven, and attended at matins in the cathedral, sitting in her champion's seat, as she did in Teresa's at Avila (p. 805), and as the gods of Greece did, who, however, preferred meat to mass (Od. vi. 203; Il. i. 424). No person has ever since occupied her seat since Sisibertus, who trying to do so, was instantly expelled by angels. The Virgin next, when she had chaunted the service, placed on her defender's shoulders *La Casulla* or cassock, and then speaking like the Veian Juno's statue (Livy, v. 22), told him that "it came from the treasures of her son." The original narrative, drawn up by Cixila in 780, was republished and confirmed by the Spanish church in 1750 (see ' E. S.' v. 509). At the Moorish invasion this cassock was carried into the Asturias, and is said to be in the chest of Oviedo, invisible indeed to mortal eyes (see p. 700); nor could it be worn by any mortal save Ildefonso, for when his successor put it on it nearly strangled him, like the maddening shirt given by Deianira.

" *Prisóle la garganta como cadena dura*
Fue luego enfogado por su gran locura."

The female deities of the Pagans were equally liberal in their gifts, which also were articles of dress, like the *Peplum* of Minerva, or the *Cistus* of Venus. (Compare the Cinta given at Tortosa by the Virgin.)

San Ildefonso (whose grand festival here is Jan. 22) became primate of Toledo, where he died in 617, and was buried at the feet of Sª. Leocadia; his body at the Moorish invasion was also carried off, and also was long lost, until it turned up after this wise. About the year 1270 a Toledan shepherd was caught in the cathedral at Zamora, and suspected of being a thief, but he replied, " San Ildefonso appearing in person, led me here and vanished ;" thereupon Alonzo VIII. dug the site, the usual sweet smell arose, a body was found, and a chapel was built, to which rich pilgrims made offerings, and miracles were daily worked; see the authentic details in Ortiz (Chr. xiv.). As Zaragoza claimed the primacy of Arragon because the Virgin had come down from heaven to visit Santiago there, so Toledo owes its elevation in Castile to the similar compliment paid to San Ildefonso; accordingly Card. Rojas erected a shrine over the exact spot, which rises in a pyramidal pile of carved Gothic work; observe his arms and portrait. The beautiful basso-relievos by Vigarny represent Sª. Ildefonso preaching his remarkable sermon, and his receiving the *Casulla ;* behind is the real slab on which the Virgin's feet really alighted ; encased in red marble, this object of universal adoration is railed off, and inscribed, " Adorabimus in loco ubi steterunt pedes ejus." The older motto according to Ortiz (67) ran thus—

" *Quando la Reina del cielo,*
Pusó los pies en el suelo
En esta piedra los pusó
De besarla tened uso
Para mas vuestro consuelo."

The multitude thus taught by the church the comfort of kissing have ac-

tually worn away the stone, as at Zaragoza and Santiago : the friction of pious lips rivals that which the idols of antiquity could not resist; but such is the nature of things, as Lucretius observes, *de Rerum Natura*, i. 317—

Tum portas propter ahenas
Signa manus dextras ostendunt attenuari
Sæpe salutantum tactu.

Thus also the *footsteps of the Goddess* were kissed, according to Apuleius (Met. xi. 251), exosculatis deæ vestigiis. But adamant itself cannot resist this continual wear and tear, or as Hudibras says, of

The marble statues rubbed in pieces
With gallantry and pilgrims' kisses.

For the comforts of this osculation, see pp. 124. Near this chapel are two fine pictures of Saint Anthony and Vincent Ferrer.

Next visit the *Capilla Mozarabe,* the Musarabic chapel under the unfinished tower ; the *Retablo* is of the date 1508. This peculiar ritual was re-established here in 1512, by Ximenez, to give the Vatican a hint that Spain had not forgotten her former spiritual independence ; in fact, however ultra-Romanist the policy and practice of Spaniards has apparently been, they have always resisted the *real* dominion of the *foreign* pontiff' ; they hoisted his creed and dogma alike in opposition to the *Koran* of the invading Moslem as against the *Bible* of the Reformation ; but the Catholic king was the champion of the Pope for his own Spanish purposes; thus, so long as Rome stimulated his armies, and sustained his ambition and inquisition, he was the eldest and most dutiful son of the church, but when the *Italian* wanted to force on Spaniards *Italian* schemes and persons, then *Españolismo* took offence. So the Iberian bribed his gods when favours were wanted and granted, being ready, if rejected, to resort to defiance and ill-treatment; Clement VII. was imprisoned by Charles V., and the city sacked by his troops, worse even than by Gaul, ancient or modern : again, in our times, when money very rare, it was reprinted by Lorenzana, in 1760, at *Puebla de los Angeles*, in Mexico, and again, by him, at Rome, in 1785-1804 ; consult for details his prefaces, also Ortiz, chapter 41, the life of Ximenez, by Eugenio Roblez, 4to., Toledo, 1604, and '*History of the Reformation in Spain*,' by M'Crie. The walls of this chapel were painted in fresco by Juan de Borgoña, in 1514, and represent the campaign of Oran, which was planned, defrayed, and headed by Ximenez in person ; hence the saying, "*Pluma, Purpura, y Espada, solo en Cisneros se halla.*" On the day that Oran was taken, May 18, 1508, the sun stood still ; thus the whole system of the heavenly spheres was deranged, in order that a ferocious sack might be prolonged under the eyes of the Cardinal, who blessed the soldiers while rioting in blood and lust. These solar miracles, however, were always very common in Spain and Africa (see p. 290) ; so before Scipio's expedition the latter, two suns shone out, but the historian (Livy, xxix. 14) attributed the belief to superstition, for men were then " proni et ad nuncianda et credenda prodigia."

Next visit *La Sala Capitular de Invierno*, the winter chapter house : the ante-room is very Moorish. The square portal was executed by Bernardino Bonifacio, and the door-way by Antonio Gutierez, in 1504, after designs of Ant°. Rodriguez ; the superb *artesonado* ceiling was painted by Fr°. Lara. Observe particularly the elaborate carvings on the oldest wardrobes, which were wrought for the Archbishop Siliceo, in 1549-51, by Gregorio Pardo, a pupil of Berruguete, to whom they are erroneously attributed. On entering the *sala* first look up and down at the pavement and glorious ceiling. The walls are decorated with a series of paintings, executed in 1511, for Card. Ximenez, by Juan de Borgoño, and which much resemble Pietro Perugino in style. The best are The Nativity of the Virgin—Her meeting St. Elizabeth in a rocky scene—The

Gift of the *Casulla*—and a pretty " Holy Family " near the throne. Above the seats are hung portraits of the Primates, which, from Ximenez downwards, are genuine ; the earlier are good and true men of master mind, but the church kept pace with the degradation of country and art, and the bathos is complete in the booby baboon *infante* Luis, who is the personification of mitred imbecility.

Now visit the portion of the cathedral which contains the pictures, relics, &c., that are kept in the *Sacristia*, *Sagrario*, *Ochavo*, and other saloons which were undertaken in 1616 for Card. Rojas by J⁰. B⁰. Monegro and others, and finished by Archbᵖ. Moscoso in 1652-8. The Rojas family lie buried in the chapel of S⁰. *Marina*. The ceiling of the *Salon de la Sacristia* is painted by Luca Giordano, with the standing miracle of the *Casulla* : observe the artist's own portrait near the window to the l. of the altar. Among the best pictures are a Venetian-like Martyrdom of S⁰. Leocadia by Orrente, with a fine figure in black near a pillar—*El Calvario*, or Christ bearing his cross ; *El Greco*, somewhat hard ; also by him a Nativity and an Adoration. Inquire particularly for a small S⁰. *Francisco*, a carved image of about 2½ ft. high, by Alonzo Cano, which is a masterpiece of cadaverous extatic sentiment. In the *Vestuario* are other pictures, and among them a Julio II. equal to Vandyke ; a Nativity and a Circumcision by Bassano ; a sketch by Rubens of St. George and the Holy Family ; an Entombment, Bellino. The *ochavo* is an octagon completed in 1630 by a son of *El Greco*, with most precious marbles and a painted dome. This is the *Donarium* or treasure-house of the Virgin (compare Apuleius, ' Met.' ix. 183) ; here are kept her splendid dresses and the most efficacious relics ; the church plate was once a mine of Peru : the chief articles were removed to Cadiz at the invasion, just as the Toledans eleven centuries before sent away to the Asturias their penates and property, which thus escaped the infidel spoiler. The French however gleaned pretty well, having taken about 23 cwt. of silver from this cathedral, not leaving even enough for the celebration of their own professed religion. The admirer of old plate will inquire for the silver gilt urnas, made for the bodies of Sⁿ· Eugenio and Sᵃ· Leocadia for Philip II., by Fʳᵒ· Merino, 1566-87; a statue of Sᵗ· Ferdinand in silver; a Gothic Custodia, a master-piece of Henrique de Arphe (see p. 632); the identical cross of Card. Mendoza, which was hoisted in 1492 on the captured Alhambra; the sword of Alonzo VI., the conqueror of Toledo—these two last are indeed historical relics; an *Incensario* (the precise antique θυμιαματηριον Thuribulum) made in the shape of a ship (navis, nave, *nief*); a Gothic spire-shaped *Relicario*, which branches out like an épergne and holds some well preserved relics; a precious vessel, encased (like the ancient crysendela) with antique gems, &c., among which is a priapic subject, but Millin (Mon. Ant. i. 262) had before observed a *Ciboire*, the receptacle of the *host, i. e.* Christ locally and corporeally present, in which phallic medallions were set. Inquire for the allegorical silver figures of the four quarters of the globe. The regular showman however will point out the chief items of the precious relics and quaint old silver work yet surviving, which are arranged in a combination of the sideboard and an anatomical museum. Toledo, in the Gothic age, was so renowned for her goldsmiths that the ornaments of the mosque of Mecca were made here; it was also a city of relics (see Oviedo, p. 699), and still possesses, besides the Virgin's milk, and thorns of the Saviour's crown, specimens of almost every thing and person mentioned in the old and new Testaments: an exact inventory is given by Ortiz (chr. 25), a chapter which a thousand years hence will itself be a curious relic of dark ages.

But the Virgin is here the queen and "great Diana;" her image graven in black wood, to which the text (Song of Sol. i. 5) "nigra sum sed formosa" is applied, is seated on a throne, under a silver gilt canopy supported by pillars; her crown, worthy of the Empress of Heaven and Earth, is a mass of jewellery, with a remarkable emerald and dove of pearl, hanging under a diamond cross; her wardrobe, kept in a smaller *Sacristia,* rivalled those of Monserrat, Zaragoza, and Guadalupe (see Index). On grand occasions she is arrayed in brocade, stiff with gold, pearls, and barbaric magnificence, in order to display which, the petticoat is widened out at the base, terminating in a point with her crown : her rings, necklaces, and trinkets are countless. Sad, indeed, would be the lament of the blessed Virgin, whose sweet charm was her lowly simplicity, could she come down once, visit this cathedral, and see all this worldly pomp of female dress and vanity.

Next visit the elegant Gothic cloisters, which, full of sunshine and flowers, were erected by Archb. Tenorio in 1389, on the site of the Jews' market, whose smell (see p. 295) offended the Primate's nose and whose vicinity grieved his piety. As they would not sell the ground, he instigated the mob in his sermons to burn the houses of the unbelievers, and then raised this beautiful enclosure on their foundations. He caused the walls to be painted in fresco, in the style of Giotto, with subjects which are described by Ortiz (ch. 52), who particularly specifies groups of heretics burning, no doubt those Jew marketers, whose obstinate souls were then doomed to the same flames by which their dwellings on earth were consumed. These extraordinary and almost unique specimens of art in the 14th century, were all effaced in 1775 by the barbarian chapter, who employed the feeble Bayeu and Maella to cover the spaces with their commonplace academical inanities, whose raw modern tones mar the sober Gothic all around. These daubs represent the miracles and legends of *S⁰·ᵉ Eugenio*, *Sᵃ· Leocadia*, and other local *Divi et Divæ*. Opposite to that in which Philip II. translates Eugenio's body, is a most interesting Gothic inscription let into the wall, which was found in 1581, in digging the foundations for *San Juan de la Penitencia;* this early record of Spanish mariolatry runs thus, " In nomine Dni consecrata est, Ecclesia Scte Marie, in catolico die primo idus Aprilis, anno feliciter primo regni Dni nostri gloriosissimi Fˡ· Recaredi Regis Era 625," *i. e.* A.D. 587. Leaving this first of April date, proceed to the beautiful plateresque gate *del Niño perdido,* "of the lost child," which was erected in 1565 by Toribio Rodriguez. This little Cupid of Toledan mythology has been the theme of many a pen and pencil ; consult therefore the church-authorized '*Histories*' by Rodrigo de Yepes, 4to. Mad. 1583 ; by Juan Marieta, 8vo. Mad. 1604; by Sebastian de Hieve, and also by Pisa (see p. 215). The Toledan clergy, in order to infuriate the fanatical mob, used to accuse the *rich* Jews of crucifying a Christian boy at their Passovers, and of putting his heart into a *hostia,* as a charm against the *holy* Inquisition ; thus in 1490 they gave out that a boy of Guardia, *El Niño de Guardia,* named Juan Passamonte, was stolen and murdered ; hence Cervantes, with a secret sneer, bestowed the name of Passamonte to his choice trickster. These accusations are an old Oriental story, for such were the sacrifice to Moloch, and such the boy Simon of the council of Trent in 1472. One of the earliest calumnies of the Jews against the Christians had been that they killed a Pagan child in order to dip in his blood the bread of their sacrament (Justin Mart. 'Dial.' 227) ; and to this day in the East, whenever the pious Moslem wishes to plunder the wealthy Jew, this crime of child murder is mooted : thus, in a just retribution, the children of those once persecuted by the Jews retaliate the same charge against the descendants

of the accusers of their forefathers. As *Heresy*, a question of opinion, is too nice for mobs, social crimes, which they can understand, must be imputed in order to inflame their passions ; thus infamous offences have been imputed, and superstitious, which secret rites and closed Passovers rendered credible, for omne ignotum pro nefando est, as mystery implies atrocious guilt. Child murder is one of the oldest charges, because the most successful, as rousing mothers against the offender, and converting the fair sex, man's ruler, into furies.

In the corner of the cloisters is a grand picture of the Virgin and Sⁿ· Blas, with the armed Infante Don Fernando, painted in 1584 by Luis de Velasco, by whom is the Incarnation of our Saviour, over the door. Observe the fine tombs of the prelate Arias, and of the founder Tenorio, obt. 1399, the latter being wrought by Fernan Gonzalez. The upper portion of these cloisters was completed by Ximenez. A door to the E. leads to the *Sala Capitular de Verano,* the summer chapter house, in which are three excellent pictures, called *La Espada, El Pujaro,* and *El Pez,* which were painted in 1584 by Velasco, although they have long been erroneously attributed to Blas del Pardo.

Next visit the chapter library, a treasure which, as in some Protestant cathedrals, is buried in a napkin, as it is not open to the public, but left to the banquet of moths, *arcedianos,* and worms. In the ante-room are 6 fine pictures, of which the Judith and Goliath are the best. The library, a noble saloon, is fresh, clean, and free from dust; little indeed ever enters save the light and air of heaven. It contains a good collection of Greek, Latin, and Arabic MSS.; a Bible of San Isidoro ; the works of Sᵗ· Gregory, in 7 vols., of the 13th century; a fine Talmud and Koran ; a Greek Bible of the 10th century; an Esther, in Hebrew; some MSS. of the time of Dante; an illuminated Bible, given by Sᵗ· Louis, and many missals of the age of Leo X. The printed books *are said* to exceed 7000 in number, and were given by Lorenzana; but nothing is more unsatisfactory than a hurried *looking* at books (which are meant to be read at leisure), and especially when a hungry or siestose canon is yawning at your elbow, and repenting of having unlocked the prison-door.

In the W. plaza of the cathedral is the archbishop's palace, the portal of which was made by Tavera for his *Hospital de Afuera*, but was appropriated by his successor, whose charity began at home. The adjoining *Casa del Ayuntamiento* or mansion house was built by Domenico Greco. On the fine staircase are some verses addressed to the municipality so perfect on paper and in theory, which are a satire on every junta's practice, *desechad las aficiones, codicias, amor y miedo*, a useful but somewhat neglected caution. The architect will have much to observe in Toledo ; one peculiarity is the arrangement of the house portals, the soffits, projecting door posts, lintels, and cannon ball ornaments. Visit *La Casa de Vargas*, which overlooks the *Vega*, and was built for the secretary of Philip II. by Vergara, as richly as a piece of Cellini plate. Observe the ruined façade, *patio*, and staircase. It had long been abandoned by its unworthy owner, the Conde de Mora, a μωρος, although a descendant of Toledo's historian, yet time had used it gently until the invader came, who having pillaged the interior, burnt and destroyed the rest: le temps, qui détruit tout, a été moins cruel que vous.

Near the *Zocodover* is the *Hospital de la Cruz*, founded by the great Mendoza Card. de Santa Croce. The position over the Tagus *is* glorious, and the building *was* one of the gems of the world, nor can any chasing of Cellini surpass the elegant portal, over which the Invention of the Cross is placed. The general style of the edifice is in the transition from florid Gothic to the classical and renaissance.

It was finished in 1514 by Henrique de Egas, for whose exquisite chiselings the creamy stone, *La piedra blanca*, seems to have been created. A superb *patio* is enriched with the arms of the proud Mendoza, and their *Ave Maria gratia plena* motto. Observe particularly the staircase, which, with its ceilings, balustrades, &c. baffles description. The chapel, one fine long nave, is unfinished, nor is the altar placed where it was originally intended. There are some bad pictures by L. Giordano, and a portrait of the founder. This dilapidated building is now used as a *Casa de Espositos*, a subject which we have already inflicted on our readers, p. 271, ex uno disce omnes.

In adjoining *El Carmen* are the Berruguete noble tombs of Pedro Lopez de Ayala, obt. 1444, and of another Don Pedro, obt. 1599. In the *Calle de las Tornarias* is a beautiful but degraded Moorish house, called *El Taller*. Observe the *artesonado* woodwork, the *Lienzo* and inscriptions in the *Colegio de Sᵃ. Catalina*. Visit the forbidden and fabulous cave of Hercules, now made a reality by Scott and Southey (see his Roderick, note 54), into which Don Roderick descended and saw the vision of the invader. The entrance lies near Sⁿ. Gines, and was opened in 1546 by ArchbP. Siliceo, but it has never since been properly investigated.

In the *Calle de Cristo de la Luz* is a very curious Moorish mosque, which was afterwards given to the Templars : the roof is supported by four low square pillars, each having different capitals, from whence spring double arches, like those at Cordova. The ceiling is divided into 9 compartments, with domes or *medias naranjas ;* the suspended shield, " gules a cross or," was left, *se dice*, here by Alonzo VI., who paused to say mass when he entered Toledo as its conqueror. In the same street is a gloomy pile with gratings, which was the prison of the penitents of the Inquisition, and the corner house was the " Refugium parturentium," a lying-in asylum for the unmarried mothers, an institution once very necessary in this city of rich levitical celibates. Navagiero (p. 8) thus sketches clerical life at Toledo in the time of Charles V. : "I Padroni di Toledo e delle donne precipue sono i preti, li quali hanno bonissime case e trionfano dandose la miglior vida del mondo, senza che alcuno li reprenda." No wonder that Cortes cautioned Charles V. *not* to send out such prelates and dignitaries to the New World, fearing that their *example* might bring Christianity into disrepute even among the untutored Indian savages. The *Bisoño* gentry, continues Navagiero (p. 10), had no "ducats," "ma in loco de quella suppliscono con superbia, o come dicono loro con fantasia, della qual sono si *ricchi* che si fussero equali le faculta no bastaria il mundo contra loro :" nor in regard to pretension and poverty has much change taken place.

The ecclesiologist should inquire for the beautiful Ionic chapel in the Bernardine convent *Los Silos*, and the fine Assumption of the Virgin by El Greco. In *San Roman* is much Moorish work, with singular arches and ancient pillars, and near it, at *San Clemente*, is a fine cinque-cento gate. In *San Pedro Martire* are some good statues of Faith and Charity, and one in black and white marble of the Dominican Martyr. Let none fail to visit *San Juan de la Penitencia*, founded by Ximenez in 1511; for the chapel is of the richest florid Gothic, with a dash of the Moorish style: observe the projecting roof at the entrance, the *Azulejos*, the *Lienzos* and shutters, the high altar and superb *Reja*. Here also is the fine tomb of F^{ro.} Ruiz, Bishop of Avila, a friend of Ximenez, and by whom the edifice was completed. The hair perhaps of the seated females is faulty, but the curtain raised by angels throws a fine sepulchral shadow over the prelate's effigy. The pillared *Retablo* is filled with tedesque paintings. The *artesonado* ceiling, with honeycomb dropping corners, and rich lo-

zenge work, is worthy of the Alhambra. In *La Concepcion* is some Moorish work, but it is not easily seen, as the nunnery is *en clausura*. The nunnery of *Santiago*, which commands a splendid view over the Tagus, has two pretty patios, enriched with pillars and porcelain tiles : the chapel is elaborately decorated, but, as usual, the interior can only be imperfectly seen through the grating. In the *Sala Capitular* are some pictures, and a dead Christ, attributed to Alonzo Cano.

The *Hospital de los Locos*, or so-called *asylum* for lunatics (*Locoa*, Arabicé, mad), is, like the *Morostan* of Cairo (*Maρos*) and most similar establishment in Spain and the East, no honour to science and humanity. Insanity seems to derange both the intellects of the patients and to harden the bowels of their attendants, while the usual misappropriation of the scanty funds has produced a truly reckless, make-shift, wretched result. There is no attempt at *classification*, which indeed is no thing of Spain. The inmates are either crowded together,—the monomaniac, the insane, the raving mad,—in one confusion of dirt and misery, where they howl at each other, chained like wild beasts, and treated even worse than criminals, for the passions of those the most furious are infuriated by the savage lash. There is not even a curtain to conceal the sad necessities of these human beings, now reduced to animals: everything is public even unto death, whose last groan is mingled with the frantic laugh of the surviving spectators. In some rare cases the bodies of those whose minds are a void are confined in solitary cells, with no other companions save affliction. Of these many when first sent here, to be put out of the way by friends and relations, were *not* mad, soon indeed to become so, as solitude, sorrow, and the iron enter their brain. This establishment, one which the Toledan ought to hide in shame, is usually among the first lions which he forces on the stranger, and especially on the Englishman, since, holding our worthy countrymen to be all *Locos*, he naturally imagines that they will be quite at home; but the sight is a sad one, and alike disgraceful to the sane as degrading to the insane native. The wild maniacs implore a "loan" from the foreigner, for from their own countrymen they have received a stone. A sort of madness is indeed seldom wanting to the frantic energy and intense eagerness of all Spanish mendicants, and here, albeit the reasoning faculties are gone, the national propensity to beg and borrow survives the wreck of intellect, and in fact it is the indestructible "common sense" of the country. The fittest inmates would be those who have advanced money on Spanish securities, be they what they may.

There is generally some particular patient whose aggravated misery makes him or her the especial object of cruel curiosity. Thus, in 1843, the *keepers* (fit wild beast term) always conducted strangers to the cage or den of the wife of a celebrated Captain-General of Catalonia, an officer superior in power to our Lord-Lieutenant of Ireland. She was permitted to wallow in naked filth, and be made a public show. The Moors, at least, do not confine their harmless female maniacs, who wander naked through the streets, while the men are honoured as saints, whose minds are supposed to be wandering in heaven (see p. 805). The old Iberians (infants in medicine) at least professed to cure madness with the herb *vettonica*, and hydrophobia with decoction of the *cynorrhodon* or *dog*-rose-*water*, as doubly unpalateable to the rabid canine species (see Pliny, 'N. H.' viii. 41; xxvi. 11).

The celebrated *Fabrica de armas*, or manufactory of Toledan swords, is placed on the banks of the Tagus, about two miles S. W. of the city. The huge building was raised for Charles III. by Sabatini, and is well provided with forges, &c.; but life is now wanting, friget non fervet opus,

and the sword of Spain herself, alas! is blunted. The few blades which are still made here are of a fine temper and polish, and so elastic that they are sometimes sold in boxes curled up like the mainspring of a watch, or "compassed," as Falstaff says, "like a good Bilbao, in the circumference of a peck, hilt to point, heel to head." Arms were the joy and life of the aboriginal Spaniards, nay dearer than life, for when they were taken from them the disarmed committed suicide (Livy, xxxiv. 17; Sil. Ital. iii. 330; Justin, xliv. 2, 5). They then as now, always went armed, and this being provided with means of defence and aggression, fostered that reliance on self, on personal prowess and independence, which has at every period been their characteristic. Hence also as the weapon was always at hand, their tendencies to *guerrillas* and murders. This custom of always carrying cold steel, το σιδηροφορεισθαι, unusual among the civilized Greeks and Romans, was stigmatized by Thucydides (i. 5) as an evidence of barbarism and insecurity of person and property. The ancient Germans always went armed; thus the-Goths brought their habit into a congenial soil. With the Gotho-Spaniard the hand was for the sword, and the heel for the spur.

The swords of Spain were so excellent, that they were adopted by the military Romans, who retained the *epithet* Spanish. Polybius distinguishes between them and those of Gaul, while Dio. Siculus (v. 356) enlarges on their merits and mode of manufacture. No wonder that Hannibal, a true soldier, should see their efficiency, and arm his troops with them. Sil. Ital. (ii. 397) describes the splendid suit of armour wrought in Gallicia as a present for this great captain. The Romans, fighting him with his own weapons, provided their *velites* or light troops with the Spanish sword, which were made both for cutting and thrusting (Polyb. iii. 114).

Their double edge was no less fatal than the genuine Iberian dirk, the prototype of the modern *cuchillo*, which Cicero calls *pugiunculus Hispaniensis*, but the vernacular name was *daga* (dagger), which the Greeks rendered by βραχυ, ξιφις βραχυτερη, from its shortness. Thus our " rare Ben Jonson" speaks of the modern rapier " as the *long* sword, the *father* of swords," an idea followed out by Hudibras,—

" This sword a dagger had, its page,
That was but little for its age."

From thus *attending* on the long sword, it was also termed παραξιφις and εγχειριδιον, a little *handy* thing. The Spanish word *broquel* is derived from βραχυ, and the helpmate was never permitted to be divorced from its liege master. Thus the *hidalgo* was ordered by Philip II., in 1564, only to appear with his *espada* (spatha) and his *broquel;* the use of the latter was to cut meat and despatch a prostrate foe; and it was worn by the Iberians in their girdles as the *cuchillo* is now in the *fajas* (Livy, vii. 10). As the bayonet is *the* English weapon which decides her *great* victories, so this dagger and the *cuchillo* are the deadly tools of the *guerrilla*, and settle the little warfare. With this the Iberians slaughtered their enemies at Cannæ (App. ' B. An.' 562), as the Spaniards in our times massacred thousands of French stragglers and wounded. This again was the *sica*, the arm of the *Sicarii* or cut-throats of antiquity, as it was of the Miquelites of Cæsar Borgia, and is to this day the formidable weapon of the wild Berber Moors in the Ereefe mountains, and of the Spaniard from the Bidasoa to the Straits. On the Iberian Pugio see Mart. xiv. 33 ; Strabo, iii. 231; and Diod. Siculus, v. 356. For Spanish knives see p. 858.
The identical mines worked by the ancients still produce the finest ores, for the soil of Spain is iron-pregnant. Those near Calatayud on the Jalon, the " steel tempering " Bilbilis, rival

the metals of the Basque provinces and the iron mountains (Pliny, ' N. H.' xxxiv. 14) of *Somorrostro* and *Mondragon ;* and the unmechanical Spaniards still work their mines exactly as the rude Iberians did, for their smithies, *ferrarias*, are the unchanged *ferraria*, which brought so much cash to Cato (Livy, xxxiv. 21). The old Spaniards buried the steel in the earth in order that the baser portions might rust away. The finest ones are those of *Mondragon*, which are found in a red clay ; this is the *hierro helado*, the frozen iron, the precise effect of the Jalon, qui ferrum gelat, to which Martial alludes (i. 50. 12). Accordingly the steel was tempered in winter, and the blade when red-hot was whirled round in the cold air, and when reduced to a *cherry* heat (the *cerezado* of present practice) was put into oil or grease and then into boiling water (see Mondragon, R. cxviii.).
The military Romans kept up the Iberian processes and manufactories, which were continued by the Goths, as San Isidoro (Or. xvi. 20) particularly praises the steel of the Bilbilis and Taranzona. The Moors introduced their Damascene system of additional ornament and tempering, and so early as 852, this identical *fabrica* at Toledo in work under Abd-r-rahman Ben Alhakem (Conde, i. 285). The Moors introduced a large double-handed double-edged sword (Conde, i. 456), which became the model of the mediæval *montante*. The best marks are those of *El Morillo, el Moro de Zaragoza* (on these brands see Left. 13 of ' Dillon's Travels in Spain'). The next best were made by Italians, by Andre Ferrara, who settled at Zaragoza, and by whom were furnished those splendid blades which Ferdinand sent to Henry VIII. on his marriage with his daughter Catherine. These " trenchant swords were the Toledos trusty," of which, says Mercutio, " a soldier dreams." These were the weapons which Othello the Moor " kept in his chamber" like a treasure,

"a sword of Spain *the ice-brook's temper*, a better never did itself sustain upon a soldier's thigh." Other good marks are *la loba*, and *el perrillo*, the little dog ; thus Don Quixote in his adventure of the lion observes that his " blade was not a *perrillo*."

The finest collection of historical swords in the world is at Madrid (see p. 787). The sword, the type and arm of chivalry, has always been honoured in Spain. The Moors petted and named them like children ; Mahomet called his the "sword of God," Kaled ben Walid ; the *Tisona*, " the sparkling brand," and *Colada* of the Cid were his spolia opima from Moorish kings. These were his *queridas prendas, caras prendas,* which he loved better than his wife and daughters, and which figure so much in his *Romancero* (Duran, v. 154). Thus Charlemagne had his *Gaudicoso ;* Roland his *Durandal ;* Arthur his *Excalibur,* which Richard Cœur de Lion exchanged in Sicily with Tancredi for an entire fleet. Many of the mediæval Spanish swords have mottos indicative of the fine old Castilian, e. g. *no me saques sin razon, no me envaines sin honor,* do not draw me without *cause,* do not sheath me without *honour.* The introduction of firearms dealt the first blow to Toledan swords, which then became the arm of cavalry, in which the Spaniards do not excel. The last blow was the fashion of the smaller French sword, which dispossessed the Spanish rapier : but even under the Goths we find that the arms of the warlike French were popular : they were called *Franciscas* (Sᵃ· Isid. ' Or.' xviii. 6). The student may refer to the essay on ancient Spanish arms, the Lancea, Gæsum, Olosideron, &c. (' *Historia literaria,*' Mohedano, iii. 336).

This transition from old swords to old castles is easy ; many fine specimens abound near Toledo, especially at *Orgaz, Montalban, Escalonilla,* and *Torrijos* on the road to Maqueda (see p. 543).

Villamejor. 3
Aranjuez . . . . . . 3 .. 6

This, the carriageable road made by Cardinal Lorenzana, is taken by the diligence, and ascends the basin of the Tagus, which flows on the l., sometimes near, sometimes at a distance, through the valley of *La Sagra* (see p. 833). Its green banks mark its course, winding like a snake in the desert. The villagers between the river and Madrid are genuine rancid old Castilians, and have been drawn to the life by Borrow. Here exist the Arab love of tribe and hatred of neighbour, for *Vargas* and *Villaseca* hold no communion (compare p. 422). The peasants are purely tillers of earth and breeders of asses.

Villa *mejor* was made a much *worse* hamlet by the invaders, who sacked it and ravaged the fine establishments raised there by Charles III. *Aranjuez* is approached by the *Campo Flamenco,* for here all is foreign. This oasis shows what might be done elsewhere by common sense and water. The diligence inns are the best : that *de las cuatro naciones,* kept by an Englishman, is not distinguished either by civil treatment or moderate charges.

ARANJUEZ — ara jovis—originally the summer residence of Lorenzo Suarez de Figuerra, *Maestre de Santiago,* became a royal property when the mastership was merged in the crown under Ferd. and Isab. Charles V., in 1536, made it a shooting villa, and Philip II. employed Herrera to construct additional buildings, all which were taken down in 1739 by the Bourbon Philip V., who substituted a French château. There the court resided every spring until June, when the place ceases to be pleasant or healthy, as the heats act upon the waters, and fill the air with fever and ague ; then royalty departed, leaving the villages to dullness and pestilence. During the recent troubles and consequent absence of the court, by which alone this fictitious place prospered, ruin and weeds threatened palaces, gardens, and cottage. Then, indeed, did Aranjuez excite pity rather than admiration, for loneliness and poverty are exactly what ought not to exist in the residence of a monarch. A something was done in 1843 by Arguelles towards staying the deterioration, and no doubt, if peace is preserved, the court will fall back into its ancient routine, to the benefit at least of this spot.

Meanwhile, according to the people of Madrid, the valley of Aranjuez is a Tempe, and while the *Escorial* is the triumph of art, this is of nature; and certainly to those born amid the silent, treeless, arid Castiles, this place of water brooks, gardens, singing birds, and verdure, is a happy change, where the contrast heightens the enjoyment of *real* country, of which otherwise they have only an abstract notion; but every thing is by comparison, and in England Aranjuez would be no great matter. Its charm consists more in what nature has done than man, for here the coolness suspends the irritation of the desert, and soothes the disgust of the Castiles. Now, as if in a spirit of contradiction, while at Madrid there is a fine palace without a garden, here there is a fine garden without a palace, as the edifice is contemptible, and with small pretensions either to royal magnificence or common comfort. The gardens were laid out by Philip II., and are such as Velazquez painted (see Museo, Nos. 145, 540); but the *Château* was completed by Charles IV., the most drivelling of Spanish Bourbons : again, it was frequently plundered by Soult, Victor, and others, for whose " vandalic devastations " see Minaño, i. 238. They converted the gardens into a wilderness, and the palace into a home for owls, yet our Duke, even when far away, at Villatoro, wrote immediately to Hill, who was about to occupy Aranjuez, " *Take care* that the officers and troops *respect* the king's houses and gardens " (Disp.

Sept. 20, 1812). So Marlborough, when advancing a conqueror into France after Malplaquet, " ordered Fenelon's house to be spared."

Aranjuez, during the *Jornada* or royal season, used to contain 20,000 persons in a crowded and expensive discomfort ; but when the court was absent, it dwindled down to 4000, and was dull as a theatre after the play is played out, and the spectators and actors gone. Then it resembles Sans Souci, Versailles, and other untenanted whims of despots. In olden times the accommodations were iniquitous, for even the deipnosophist diplomats lived in troglodyte houses burrowed in the hill sides, after the local rabbit-like style of these wretched localities (see p. 310). At a subterraneous dinner, however, given by the Nuncio, a cart broke through and announced itself as an *entrée* for the nonce, whereupon the Italian Grimaldi, minister to Charles III., who had before been at the Hague, planned a sort of Dutch town, with avenues in the street, and thus changed the village, as his celebrated namesake, the clown, would have done in a pantomime. Thus diplomacy has given Spain another good turn, as at Segovia (p. 826).

There is not much to be seen or done at Aranjuez, since even the gaieties of the season were dull without being decent, intrigue, political and otherwise, being the engrossing business, and Mammon and Venus the idols. Here the Evil One always found something to do for the idlest, most ignorant, and most profligate courtiers of Europe. Here, as the French lady said of Versailles, " Outre la passion, je n'ai jamais vu de chose plus triste." " Que ne puisse-je vous donner (wrote Madᵉ· de Maintenon) une idée des grands! de l'ennui qui les dévore—de la peine qu'ils ont à remplir leur journées." If that could be predicated of the brilliant society of Louis XIV., how much truer must it be of dull routine of the unsocial Spanish court! *Escotes* or picnics occasionally flourished, in which the grandees, appropriately mounted on asses, performed *Borricadas* in the woods, occasionally after Don Quixote's fashion; for when a *Madrileño* on pleasure bent gets among real trees, he goes as mad as a March hare—dulce est desipere in luco. Aranjuez has a noble *plaza de Toros*, a tolerable theatre, and a telegraph, which was set up to amuse Ferd. VII., whose passion·was to hear something new. It is said that the first message which he sent to the grave council of Castile at Madrid, was "a nun has been brought to bed of twins;" the immediate answer was, "Had it been a monk, that would have been news." On a hill to the l. going to Ocaña is a pond, here called, as usual (see p. 823), the *sea, El mar de Ontigola*, but Spanish geese are all swans in their magnificent misnomers : however, *no todos son ruiseñores*, as Calderon says.

The beloved Ferdinand did not by any means renounce the good old recreations of his royal ancestors, for he never missed *Herradura*, to which he took his delicate Christina and maids of honour, just as Philip IV. did his. The cream of the *funcion* was seeing an operation performed on young bulls, which fitted them for the plough. The term *Herradura* is derived from the branding cattle with a hot iron, *Ferradura à ferro*, which is of Oriental origin, and was introduced by the Saracens into France, and is still called *La Ferrade* at Camargue near Arles. It also prevailed in Spain among the Goths (Sᵃ· Isid. ' Or.' xx. 16). The royal breeding establishments near Aranjuez, like those near Cordova, were all destroyed by the invaders, but restored by Ferd. VII. The *garañones*, or the asses of Don Carlos, in size and capabilities, did honour to their patron. These and every thing were upset during the civil troubles : however, in 1842, Arguelles partially restored the establishment, sending to England for stallions.

The palace scarcely deserves a visit; it is placed near the Tagus, at the Ma-

drid end of the village, or rather the "metropolis of Flora," as the natives say. A bald *Plaza de San Antonio*, a sort of French *place du Carrousel*, with a *corredor* and iron railing, affords space for dust and glare. The interior of the palace contains some bad pictures, and fresco ceilings by Conrado Bayeu and others, which are no better. There is some good marqueterie carving, and the look-out on the gardens over the *parterre, isla*, and cascade is charming. Here all the trees in Castile seem collected as a salon for a Cortes of all the nightingales of Spain, and how sweet, after the songless, arid desert, is "the melodious noise of birds among the spreading branches, and the pleasing fall of water running violently." These nightingales sing alike whether the court be there or not; these feathered choristers of nature care as little for a human audience, as does their mistress for such spectators, who is busiest about her greatest works in the deepest solitudes, when she most unveils her greatest charms. How mellow sounded the rich notes of sad Philomela, when last we wandered in these groves. Yet why sad ? what has *he* to be sorry for who cheers his tender mate during her long incubation with his sympathy, congratulation, and best marital melody?

There is a description of the palace and gardens by Alvarez de Quindos, 4to. Mad. 1804, and a guide published in 1824 by Manuel de Aleas. There are also some engraved plans and views by Domingo de Aguirre. The gardener will take the visitor round the lions of the *Isla*, the last fountain of which was painted by Velazquez. The best objects to observe are La Puerta del Sol, the Fountain of the Swan, *La Cascada*, Neptune, and the Tritons; in a word, here Nereids, Naiads, and Dryads might sport, while Flora and Pomona looked on. The elms brought from England by Philip II. grow magnificently under this combined heat and moisture.

The *Casa del Labrador*, or labourer's

cottage, is another plaything of that silly Charles IV. (see p. 820); however, if imperial Madrid can select a ploughman for her patron (see p. 777), her monarch, with equal good sense and taste, may prefer a hovel to a palace. But all this is a sham, and a thing of mock-humility—a foolish toy fitted up for the spoiled children of fortune, in which great expense and little taste are combined to produce a thing which is perfectly useless, without being over-ornamental. The *Florera* or *Jardin Ingles*, the *English* garden, as all foreigners call any irregular place without order and with weeds, was laid out by Richard Wall, an *Irishman.*

It was at Aranjuez, March 19, 1808, that Charles IV., in order to save his wife's minion, Godoy, abdicated the crown. Toreno prints all the disgraceful letters written by him and his wife, the proud monarchs of Castile! to Murat, their "very dear brother!" to Murat, who a few years before had been a waiter, and who in six weeks afterwards, deluged their capital with Spanish blood. Godoy, a tool of Buonaparte, was thus saved, in order to consummate his guilt and folly, by signing with Duroc, at Bayonne, the transfer of Spain to France, stipulating only, mean to the last, for filthy lucre and pensions. The celebrated insurrection of Aranjuez, which placed Ferd. VII. on the throne, was, like most things in Spain, the result of chance and *accident*, the usual moving power; and Schepeler (i. 23) justly remarks, that the people and actors were all "sans plan, sans conduite, comme poussés par le même instinct;" and in this sentence is combined the whole history and philosophy of Spain and Spaniards, from the days of the Iberian down to last Saturday.

For the road to Madrid see p. 312, and for the communications south see R. viii. Those who have leisure will do well to strike off to Ocaña and Tarrancon, 8 L., and thence make for *Cuenca*, returning to Madrid by any of the routes, which will be pointed out in their places.

MADRID TO VALENCIA.

There are two routes; one, which is very circuitous, passes by *Albacete* and *Almansa*, while the other runs directly through *Cuenca.* The former is that taken by the mails and diligences. The coach-offices are in the *Ce. de Alcalá*, No. 15 and No. 21. The latter is scarcely carriageable throughout, although the road-makers have long been at work, and especially latterly, near *Las Cabrillas.* The former, or the *Camino real*, branches off at Albacete for *Murcia*, and at Almansa for Alicante, and is for the greater portion dull and uninteresting, while the excursion to Cuenca, although few travellers ever make it, abounds with every thing that the artist, antiquarian, angler, and geologist, can desire.

ROUTE CIII.—MADRID TO VALENCIA.

Angeles	2	
Espartinas	3	5½
Aranjuez	2½	8
Ocaña	2	10
Villatobas	2½	12½
Corral de Almaguer	3	15½
Quintanar de la Orden	3½	19
Mota del Cuervo	2	21
Pedernoso	1½	22½
Pedroñeras	1	23½
Provencio	2	25½
Venta del Pinar	2	27½
Minaya	2	29½
Roda	2½	32
Gineta	2½	34½
Albacete	2½	37
Pozo de la Peña	2½	39½
Villar	3	42½
Bonete	2½	45
Almansa	3½	48½
Venta del Puerto	2	50½
Venta de Mojente	3	53½
Venta del Rey	3	56½
Alberique	2	58½
Alcudia	1½	60
Alginete	1	61
Catarroja	3	64
Valencia	1	65

These 65 leagues are equivalent to 76½ post ones. To *Ocaña*, see R. viii., after which the high road branches off to the l., continuing almost to *Almansa* over a dreary, treeless, salitrose, poverty-stricken country of corn and saffron. *El Corral* contains some 4000 hard-working agriculturists : soon the *Rianzares* is crossed, from which Señor Muñoz takes his ducal title, and then the *Jiguela*, both being tributaries of the Guadiana. Now we quit New Castile, and enter into equally dreary *La Mancha* (see p. 307). To the r. of *Quintanar* lies *Toboso*, and the country of Dulcinea, and those bald steeps which genius has clothed with immortal interest. The swampy plains between *Minaya* and *Albacete*, were drained by Charles IV., who employed one John Smith, a gentleman not easily identified, as his engineer. Thus the air is rendered less unwholesome, and the marshes more fertile, but all these improvements ceased when the French arrived, and the districts were mercilessly ravaged both by Moncey and Caulaincourt. Just before reaching *Gineta*, a corner of Murcia is entered (see p. 405).

Albacete, Abula, owing to its central position, from whence roads branch to Murcia, Valencia, and Madrid, is a place of great traffic, and a town of locomotives from the dilly to the donkey. The *Fonda de la diligencia* is the best inn : the *Paradores* and *Mesones* are numerous and large, for the bipeds, quadrupeds, and wheel carriages that rest here are countless. The name *Albacete* signifies in the Arabic "a vast plain," and of such it is the busy capital ; pop^n. above 11,000. The environs are fertile, being irrigated by a canal, which tends to the increase of corn and saffron, while the undrained swamps produce fevers, agues, and mosquitos. Another element of prosperity is its *audiencia*, or high court of appeal, which was carved in 1835 out of the once monopolizing *chancelleria* of Granada : the jurisdiction extends over 986,000 souls ; the number tried in 1844 were 3332, being an average of one in every 330.

Albacete is called the Sheffield of Spain, as Chatelherault is in France ;

but every thing is by comparison, and the coarse cutlery in each, at whose make and material an English artisan sneers, perfectly answers native ideas and wants. The object of a Spanish knife is to "chip bread and kill a man," and our readers are advised to have as little to do with them as may be. The *cuchillo*, like the fan of the high-bred Andaluza, is part and parcel of all Spaniards of the lower class, who never are without the weapon of offence and defence, which is fashioned like a woman's tongue, being long, sharp, and pointed. The test of a bad knife is, that it won't cut a stick, but will cut a finger, *Cuchillo malo, corta al dado y no al palo.*

This knife, the precise *daga* of the Iberians (for details see Toledo, p. 853), is the national weapon : hence *Guerra al Cuchillo* is the modern warcry which has supplanted the old *algarada* of *Santiago y Cierra España!* Now Castile expects that every knife this day will do its duty, and such was the truly Spanish war defiance which Palafox at Zaragoza returned to the French summons to capitulate. This "long double-edged" tool is either stuck, as the old dagger used to be, in the sash, or worn in the breeches' side-pocket, where our carpenters carry their rule, like the Greek heroes did their παραμηρια. Such, however, was the Oriental fashion, down the "right thigh" (Judges iii. 16); and so the anelace in Chaucer bare "a Shefeld thwitel in his hose," just as the *Manolas*, or Amazons of Madrid, conceal a small knife in their garters by way of "steel traps set here." This trinket is also called a *puñaleco* and *higuela*, which, strictly speaking, means a "petticoat bustle ;" and all these weapons are akin to the Mattucashlash dirk, which the Scotch Highlanders carried in their arm-pits : a feminine *puñaleco* now before us has the motto, *Sirbo à una Dama,* I serve a lady— Ich Dien. Gentlemen's knives have also what Shakspere calls their "cutler poetry," and it is a Moorish custom, for our friend Gayangos has traced in what appeared to be a mere scrolly ornament, on a modern Albacete *cuchillo*, these Arabic words, " With the help of Allah! I hope to kill my enemy." Thus the Spanish manufacturers have many centuries worked after the same pattern, and for the same beneficent object, each operative copying his model by a certain instinct, without even understanding the meaning of what he is rudely scratching on the blade. The mottos of the Toledan rapiers were superb (see p. 854), and those on the knives follow at a humbler pace ; e. g., *Soy de mi Dueño y Señor*, " I am the thing of my lord and master." So Nero's poignard was inscribed " *Jovi Vindici* " (Tac. 'An.' xv. 74). When the *Sistema*, or *constitution* of 1820, was put down, royalist knives were inscribed *Peleo á gusto matando negros*, and on the reverse, *Muero por mi Rey*, " I die for my king; killing blacks is my delight." The words *Negros* and *Carboneros* have long been applied in Spain to political *black*guards, who are whipped and hung with as little scruple in benighted despotised Spain as niggers are in free and enlightened America.

The term *Navaja* means any blade which shuts into a handle, from a razor to a penknife: the *Navajas* of Guadix, which rival the *Puñales* of Albacete, have frequently a *molde muelle* or catch, by which the long pointed blade is fixed, and thus becomes a dagger or hand bayonet. The click which the cold steel makes when sharply caught in its catch, produces on Spanish ears the same pleasing sensation which the cocking a pistol does on ours. The gipsies being great hole-in-*corner* men and *cut*purses, *Rinconetes y Cortadillos*, and patrons of slang and flash men, have furnished many *cant* names to knife, e. g. *glandi*, *chulo*, *churri*, *La Serdanie*, *Cachas dos puñales a una vez ;* the Catalans call it *El gavinete*. It is termed in playful metaphor *La tia*, my aunt ; *Corta pluma*, a penknife; *Monda dientes*, a tooth-pick ; and the Spaniards are quite as learned in its

make and cut. Thus Sancho Panza, when he hears that Montesinos had pierced a heart with a puñal, exclaims at once, " Then it was made by Ramon Hozes of Seville."

However unskilled the regular *Sangrados* may be in anatomy and use of the scalpel, the universal people know exactly how to use their knife, and where to plant its blow ; nor is there any mistake, for the wound, although not so deep as a well, nor so wide as a church door, " 'twill serve." It is uusally .given after the treacherous fashion of their Oriental and Iberian ancestors, and if possible by a stab behind, of which the ancients were so fearful, "impacatos a tergo horrebis Iberos" (Geor. iii. 408), and " under the fifth rib," and " one blow " is enough (2 Sam. xx. 10). The blade, like the cognate Arkansas or Bowie knife of the Yankees, will "rip up a man right away," or drill him until a surgeon can see through his body. As practice makes perfect, a true *Baratero* is able to jerk his *navaja* into a door across the room, as surely and quickly as a rifle ball; a Spaniard, when armed with his *cuchillo* for attack, and with his *capa* for defence, is truly formidable and classical (see p. 202, 276). Many of the murders in Spain must be attributed to the *readiness* of the weapon, which is always at hand when the blood is on fire : thus where an unarmed Englishman *closes* his fist, a Spaniard *opens* his knife. This rascally instrument, a true *puñalada de picaro*, becomes fatal in jealous broils, when the lower classes light their anger at the torch of the furies, and prefer using to speaking daggers: then the thrust goes home, vitamque in vulnere ponit. The numbers killed on great festivals exceeds those of most Spanish battles in the field, yet the occurrence is scarcely noticed in the newspapers, so much is it a matter of course; but crimes which call forth a second edition and double sheet in our papers, are slurred over on the continent, for foreigners conceal what we most display. In minor cases of flirtation, where capital punishment is not called for, the offended party just gashes the cheek of the peccant one, and suiting the word to the action observes, "*ya estas senalaā ;*" "Now you are marked ;" again, "*Mira que te pego, mira que te mato,*" are playful fondling expressions of a *Muja* to a *Majo*. When this particular mark is only threatened, the Seville phrase was "*Mira que te pinto un jabeque ;*" "take care that I don't draw you a xebeck" (the sharp Mediterranean felucca). "They jest at wounds who never felt a scar," but whenever this *jabeque* has really been inflicted, the patient, ashamed of the stigma, is naturally anxious to recover a good character and skin, which only one cosmetic can effect; this in Philip IV.'s time was cat's grease, which then removed such superfluous marks,

—— El sebo unto de gato,
Que en cara defienda los señales.

In process of time, as science advanced, this was superseded by *Unto del Ombre*, or man's grease. Our estimable friend Don Nicolas Molero, a surgeon in high practice at Seville, assured us that previously to the French invasion, he had often prepared this cataleptic specific, which used to be sold for its weight in gold; but having been adulterated with spermaceti by unprincipled empirics, it fell into disrepute. The receipt of the Alabastrum which Venus gave to Phaon, has puzzled the learned Burmann no less than that of the balsam of Fierabras has the modern commentators of Don Quixote. The kindness of Don Nicolas furnished us with the ingredients of this *pommade divine*, or rather *mortale*. "Take a man in full health who has been just killed, the fresher the better, pare off the fat round the heart, melt it over a slow fire, clarify, and put it in a cool place for use." The number of religious festivals in Spain, combined with the sun, wine, and women, have always ensured a supply of fine subjects.

Albacete, from its central position, was occupied in 1843 by Espartero, who hoped thereby at once to menace Murcia and Valencia, protect Madrid, and secure a retreat to Andalucia, but he succeeded only in the latter. His fall, like his rise (see p. 313), was a *Cosa de España ;* no sooner was he in power than his place was envied, and he became unpopular among rivals, whose self-love was wounded by his superiority, and the fickle "many," especially if of Oriental origin, pass readily from shouts of Hosanna to cries for blood. Again, his talents, never more than mediocre, had been exaggerated, Nanum, Atlanta vocamus, just as in the reaction they were equally underrated, and the Duque *de Victoria* passed by an easy transition into a *Duque de Nada*, a nothing and nobody. Personally brave and honest, his grand error was a wish to govern according to the *Constitution*, in which even Hercules could not have succeeded ; his next blunder was choosing for his minister one Becerra, a member of the senate, whereby the lower house was affronted ; then followed his rejection of the Amnesty bill, which under the pretence of "*Union* and *Oblivion* among Spaniards," things utterly impossible, was in reality an invention of his enemies to bring back his exiled opponents. Again, Espartero, like an honest Spaniard, abhorred the French yoke, and turned to England as the true deliverer of his country, and accordingly had been taken up as an *individual* by our foreign office ; thereupon, as might have been conjectured, Paris became a hotbed of plots and intrigues, and every unfair means was resorted to which French double-dealing backed by Italian Machiavelianism could devise, while a venal press was bribed to work on the impressionable *Españolismo*, by falsely representing the regent as *L'Agent de l'Anglais*, which the smugglers of Catalonia re-echoed, who dreaded a treaty of commerce.

Thus Espartero had all the odium of being an *Anglo-Ayacucho*, without the support of England, by whom he was *morally* abandoned, first because a

Tory government saw the evident impolicy of espousing the cause of a mere *individual*, and one moreover a radical and church appropriator, who never in the long run could be popular with the essentially loyal and religious Spaniard; and secondly because our government is either too honest or too indifferent ever to fight its unscrupulous *friends* and enemies by their own weapons. Again, the regent was opposed by all the spiritual influence of Rome backed by an army of despoiled and starving priests and monks. Nor was money wanting from beyond the Pyrenees to foment an outbreak which always may be got up in any Spanish town for about £100; as everywhere there are plenty of patriots and *Cesantes*, to whom order is annihilation, and who batten in disturbance, since, the moment authority is put down, they step in to rob the public till, to smuggle and work the telegraph. The first explosions were the simultaneous *pronunciamientos* of Lugo and Malaga, towns the antipodes of each other, so effective was the cry against the *Foreigner;* the Spaniards now rose against English dictation, and in defence of national independence as guaranteed by France, oh perversion of terms and truth! Thus Guizot, a Protestant and prime minister of a Roi citoyen, succeeded, with the cry of civil and religious liberty in their mouths, in again effecting (see p. 846) the restoration of despotism and ultra Romanism.

When the tug of war arrived, Espartero, *more Hispano*, "was found wanting in everything at the critical moment;" devoid of all the sinews of war, he had neither talent nor energy in himself to supply them. Now he had no Col. Wylde as at Bilboa, no traitor Maroto as at Vergara, to do the work; nay, as rats leave a falling house, he was deserted in his hour of need by those whom he had raised. Zabala, his own familiar friend, who had eaten his bread, was the first to betray his master at Valencia, while Seoane and Zurbano in the N. allowed Narvaez to

march on Madrid by Teruel; but even then, had Espartero fought his enemies with their own weapons, had he crushed them down with a rod of iron, and shed, as Narvaez threatened, "oceans of vile black blood," he might have prolonged the struggle; but he was afflicted, incredible as it may appear, with the monomania of governing according to *constitutional law!* instead of adopting the only Spanish system of might making right, as those who dethroned him most wisely did, for all conciliation, compromise, or concession, is imputed by Spaniards and Orientals to "fear and weakness." Thus the regent remained smoking and slumbering over "parchment charters" at Madrid, when his daring, active, and unscrupulous opponents were up and about, and instead of being brief when traitors took the field, he seemed only to wish to give his enemies time to collect, and his friends opportunities to separate. He only left Madrid June 21, to linger at Albacete until July 7, too long and doing nothing; then, when the game was thrown away, he retreated to the bay of Cadiz, to take refuge on board an English man-of-war, like Buonaparte, of whom he is the caricature. His fall appeared strange to those who judge of the things of Spain by those of Europe, but among Spaniards his exit created neither surprise nor sympathy. There, as in the East, the parvenu pacha bubble rises, swells, and bursts, to be heard of no more; and ere a week was past, Espartero was *contado con los muertos*, and forgotten as if really in his grave. Again foreigners "*wondered*" that a nation of such African passions and Gothic determination should only exhibit a passive lethargy when the new dictator rent with a sword the precious charters of his predecessor; but in all these scene-shiftings, the chords to which the hearts of Spaniards alone will respond remained untouched. The deed was done by a Spaniard, and neither assailed their faith nor throne. The masses care no more for a *constitution* than the Berber or Oriental; with them this thing of parchment is no reality, but a mere abstraction, which they neither understand nor estimate. The people do not want their laws to be changed, but to have them fairly administered; the laws are good in theory, although worm-eaten in *practice* by bribery and corruption. Confer a spick-and-span patent Benthamite *constitution* on Spaniards, and they will take it without thanks; annul it, and they will respond by a patient shrug. Their only idea of government is *despotism*, and under such they have always lived, nor, however odious in *theory*, did it ever press harshly on the nation in *practice*. But Spain is the land of contradictions. See on these matters Madrid pp. 733, 788, Daroca and Durango.

After leaving Albacete the road branches from *Pozo de la Peña* to Murcia (see R. xxx.), continuing on to Valencia, over an undulating country. At Chinchilla another road (R. xxxiii.) branches down to Alicante, through the hills of Villena, which gladden the eye of the plain-sick traveller. *Almansa* is well-built and tolerably flourishing, pop. 7000. The *Vega* is irrigated, and many of the ague-breeding swamps have been drained, especially those of *Salahar* and *Sⁿ. Benito.* The *Pantano* of *Alfera* is a fine reservoir of water, here an element of incredible fertility under this almost African sun. Near Almansa was decided, April 25, 1707, *one* of the few battles in which the French have ever beaten the English; and here, as at Fontenoi, traitors fought against their country and for its enemy. The French were commanded by an *Englishman*, by Berwick, natural son of James II., and nephew to Marlborough, and therefore of a good soldier breed; while the English were commanded by a *Frenchman*, one Henri de Ruvigny, an adventurer, created Earl of Galway by William III. This type of a Cuesta or

Blake was personally brave, but a "child in the art of war," always "eager to fight campal battles," and never doing so except to be beaten. The English at the critical moment were deserted by their Spanish allies, who, as at Barrosa, Albuera, Talavera, &c., left them to bear the whole brunt. *Socorros de España,* whose assistance is best expressed by the French word *assister,* which means being present without taking any part. Again the battle, like that of Albuera, ought never to have been fought at all, for even Peterborough, whose whole system was daring and aggressive, had now urged a Fabian defensive campaign; but he was opposed by Stanhope, who was talked over by the Spaniard Mˢ· de las Minas, just as Beresford was by Castaños. The allies numbered only 12,000 foot and 5000 cavalry; the French exceeded 30,000, and they moreover were fresh and ready, while the English were "marched and counter-marched," as at Barrosa, and brought to the field weary and starving. The day was chiefly lost by the cowardice of the Portuguese General Atalaya. The French victory was complete, but their laurels were stained by the ferocious sack of Xativa and breach of every plighted capitulation. Orleans, afterwards the Regent, arrived too late for the battle, and thus lost a chance of wiping out his disgraces before Turin in 1706. A short mile from Almansa is a paltry obelisk, which marks the site of this most important battle, and is commensurate with Spanish governmental ingratitude; and small indeed is the mention made by Paez and Co. of the brave French who did the work, as the glory is claimed for *Nosotros.*

Crossing the *Puerto* we descend to the pleasant Valencian coast by charming defiles. Passing *Mogente* to the l. and Xativa to the r. the villages increase; the heaven and earth are changed; all is gay and genial; it is one continued garden of graceful rice-plant and palm-tree. *Alberique* is proverbial for a fertility that knows no repose, it is a *Tierra de Dios—trigo ayer y hoy arroz*, a land of God where rice to-day, succeeds to the corn of yesterday. Now we turn our backs on the bald, central, table-lands, on the dull *Paño pardo, Montera*, and mud cottage, and welcome the sparkling Valentian, with his oriental and parti-coloured garment, gaudy and glittering as the sun and flowers of his province. *Alberique* is surrounded with *acequias*, canals, by which the rivers are drained. The *grand acequia del Rey* crosses the road into the Albufera, and isolates with the Jucar and its tributaries a remarkable rice-tract. The raised causeway passes on through sunken irrigated plots of ground, which teems with plenty, agues, and mosquitos (see for Valencian details, p. 429). There are several routes from Madrid to Cuenca, one runs by the plains (R. cviii.), another by the mineral baths and mountains (R. cvii.), and another which communicates with Valencia, which we now proceed to describe.

ROUTE CIV. — MADRID TO VALENCIA BY CUENCA.

Bacia Madrid	3	
Perales de Tajuña	3	6
Fuente dueña	3½	9½
Tarancon	3	12½
Huelbes	2	14½
Carrascosa	2	16½
Horcajada	2	18½
Cabrejás	3	21½
Albaladejito	3	24½
Cuenca	1	25½
Fuentes	3	28½
Reillo	2	30½
Arguisuelas	2	32½
Cardenete	2½	35
Camporobres	3	38
Utiel	3	41
Requena	2	43
Siete aguas	3	46
Venta de Buñol	2	48
Chiva	2	50
Venta de Pozos	2	52
Valencia	3	55

The country to *Cuenca*, in common with the central table-land of the Peninsula, although uninteresting, produces much corn and saffron. After leaving Bacia Madrid, the Jarama is crossed, a little above its junction with the Manzanares. The dreary character of the vicinity of Madrid begins to diminish near *Arganda*, with its olives, vines, and corn-fields; the red wine is excellent. *Perales* lies in a rich valley watered by the *Tajuna*, which, coming down from the Sierra de Solorio, joins the Henares. Crossing it we enter Villarejo, which has a fine ruined castle, and the parish church contains some pictures by Pedro Orrente; thence crossing the Tagus over a desolate country to *Fuente Dueña*, with its Moorish castle, another monotonous track, with here and there some of Don Quixote's windmills, leads to *Tarancon*, a town of some traffic, from being in the middle of many cross communications. The W. façade of the fine parish church retains its ancient and minute Gothic ornaments, but the N. was modernized into the Ionic order in the time of Philip II. The country now resumes its desolation, and the villages are scanty, and the population ill clad, over-worked, and poverty-stricken.

Ucles (popn. about 1500) lies 2 L. from Tarancon, amid its gardens and *Alamedas*, which are watered by the Bedija; on a hill above towers the once magnificent convent belonging to the order of Santiago, of which Ucles was the first *encomienda*, and the abbot was mitred; it was founded in 1174, on the site of a Moorish *alcazar*, of which *La torre Albazana* and a portion was annexed to the new edifice; the chapel was built in 1600, in the simple Herrera style. Ucles is a fatal site in all Spanish annals, for here, in 1100, Sancho the son of Alonzo VI. was defeated and killed by the infidel, whereby his father's heart was broken; see the affecting account in Mariana (x. 5): again, here, Jan. 13, 1809, Victor routed the miserable Venegas, who had advanced from *Tarancon* to *surprise* the French, who to his surprise turned on him, whereupon he fled at once to *Ucles*, and occupied the strong hill;

but no sooner did the daring enemy begin to ascend it, than, as at Somosierra and elsewhere, the Spanish army, left half fed and half armed, and discouraged by their unworthy chiefs, turned and ran, Venegas setting the example, and surviving for fresh disgraces at *Almonacid;* then Victor treated Ucles *à la Medellin*—he harassed the clergy and respectable inhabitants, and made them drag up the hill, like beasts of burden, whatever articles of their property could not be carried off, in order to make a "*feu de joie*" for his victory; next sixty prisoners were slaughtered on the shambles, which was *facetiously* selected for the appropriate butchery. Victor then marched the survivors to Madrid, having all who dropped on the road from hunger or fatigue, shot on the spot. Toreno (viii.), Southey (xviii.), and Schepeler (ii. 151), enter into appalling details; the latter compares Victor to Tamerlane, "sorti au berceau avec le signe du sang." The amiable Monsr. de Rocca honestly records and laments the horrors which he then witnessed.

Near Ucles, at *Cabeza del Griego,* are some Roman remains, the supposed site of ancient Munda and Cartima (for details, with plans, see 'Mem. Acad. His.' iii. 170; and 'E. S.,' xlii. 332).

Quitting *Tarancon,* the elevated table-land, broken, however, by undulations with swamps in the hollows, continues to *Horcajada,* a true *hanging* place. Now the hills are covered with pines and oaks, and we ascend a *puerto* or pass over the highest ridge, from whence the waters descend E. and W. Crossing the Jucar after *Albaladejito,* the country becomes picturesque; and after threading a planted defile, rock-built scrambling *Cuenca* is entered over its ancient bridge; the Posada is only tolerable; when the road over *Las Cabrillas* is completed, no doubt a *Parador de las Diligencias* will be set up.

CUENCA, a word derived either from *Concha,* ' a shell,' or from the Ara-

bic *Cuemcom,* "a pitcher," is indeed a hill-girt shell, and the capital of its mountainous district, being itself about 3400 feet above the level of the sea. The chains to the N.E. are continuations of the Cantabrian range, which serpentines through Spain by Burgos, Oca, Montcayo, Molino de Aragon, and Albarracin. The fine forests called *los Pinarios de Cuenca* are proverbial, and rival those of Soria. The scenery in these immemorial woods and rocks is Salvator Rosa-like, while the lakes and streams—virgin waters in which fly is seldom thrown—teem with trout; the hills abound in curious botany and geology, which have yet to be investigated.

Cuenca, in the fifteenth and sixteenth centuries, was densely peopled with busy rich traders in its staple, wool, but now all is desolate and poverty-stricken; the district is one of the most thinly-populated in the Peninsula, having scarcely 300 souls to the square league; while Cuenca, its capital, barely contains 3000 inhabitants. The mountains, *montes orospedani,* were the fastnesses of the brave Celtiberians, who waged a desperate *Guerrilla* contest against the Romans, just as Juan de Zerecedo did in the War of the Succession, and the *Empecinado* in our times, against the French; hence the many sackings of Cuenca; the first and most fatal was by Caulaincourt, who was sent by Savary to relieve Moncey, after his failure before Valencia. The invaders entered July 3, 1808; the clergy, who came out in their sacred dresses to welcome them, with flags of truce, were fired on and butchered; for the details, which exceeded, says Schepeler, "les horreurs *ordinaires,*" see his history (i. 148). Caulaincourt's private spoil in church plate was enormous, for he had the glorious *custodia* moved to his quarters, and there broken up into portable pieces; nevertheless he was afterwards made by Buonaparte *gouverneur de ses pages;* this Mentor having taught their young ideas to shoot, was sent to his account by a bullet at Moscua, Sept. 7, 1812. Cuenca was again sacked by Gen. Hugo (the ravager of Avila) June 17, 1810, and again April 22, 1811, by La Houssaye, the spoiler of Escorial and Toledo; nor has the impoverished city ever recovered. It was once celebrated for its splendid silver-work, and the family of the Becerriles were here what the d'Arphes were to Leon, or as in Italy, Foppa (Caradosso) of Milan was to Cellini of Florence; Alonzo and F^{ro.} Becerril both lived at Cuenca, early in 1500, and by them was wrought the once glorious Custodia, or church plate (see pp. 125, 632). Martyriço details the splendid crosses, chalices, etc. which were taken by Caulaincourt, whose wholesale sacrilege created such a national indignation that Joseph, the very day on which he entered Madrid, decreed their replacement at the cost of the government. It need not be said that nothing was ever done: but the paper read well; nay, Joseph, while penning it, was himself busy with Ferdinand's plate chests, which he soon carried off (see Toreno, iv.).

Cuenca is romantically situated, about half-way between Madrid and Valencia, on the confluence of the Jucar and Huecar, and between the heights San Cristobal and Socorro; for details consult ' La Historia,' Juan Pablo Martyriço, folio, Mad. 1629, a curious volume, which also contains portraits of the Mendozas, long its governors. According to this author the city was founded on the very same day and at the very same hour that Rome was. In honest truth, however, it is purely Moorish, and like Ronda, Albama, and Alarcon, is built on a river isolated rock. It was given in 1106 by Ben Abet, king of Seville, as part of the portion of Zaida his daughter, and wife of Alonzo VI. The inhabitants, however, rebelled, and the city was retaken by Alonzo VIII. Sept. 26, 1177. The truly Spanish campaign is detailed by Mariana (xi. 14); Alonzo VIII. was, as usual, in want of everything at the critical mo-

ment: the site of his camp of starvation is still shown at *Fuentes del Rey.* The town was captured at last by a stratagem, devised by a Christian slave inside, one Martin Alhaxa (*buena alhaja de criado*), who led out his Moorish master's *merinos*, as if to pasture, but then gave them to his hungry countrymen, who, having eaten them up, put on sheep's clothing, and were led back on all fours, being let into Cuenca by a small still-existing postern in the walls; from this strange flock sprang most of the *hidalgo* families of Cuenca, *e. g.* the Albornoz, Alarcon, Cabrera, Carrillo, Salazar, &c.

Cuenca, once celebrated alike for its arts, literature, and manufactories, is now only a shadow of the past; its prosperity was blighted by the French invasion. It now only retains its picturesque position, which could not be destroyed; still the beautiful Huesca and Jucar (*sucro*, the sweet waters, *aguas dulces*), come down through defiles planted with charming walks, and spanned with bridges, placed there for the artist; above topples the eagle's-nest town, with its old walls and towers, and houses hanging over the precipices and barren rocks, which enhance the charm of the fertile valleys below. From the suburb the town rises in terraces, as it were of roof above roof, up to the Plaza and Cathedral, which occupy almost the only level space, for the streets are steep and narrow; among the bridges, observe that *de San Pablo* over the Huecar, which connects the town with the Dominican convent; worthy of the Romans, it rivals in height and solidity the arches of Merida, Alcantara, and Segovia, and rises 150 feet, connecting the broken rocks. It is reared on colossal piers, and was built in 1523 by F^{ro.} de Luna, at the cost of the Canon Juan de Pozo, for the convenience of the monks. The façade of *San Pablo* has unfortunately been modernized, but inside is the extraordinary carved *Retablo* of the date 1447, which originally belonged to the high altar of the cathedral; before it

2 P

lay the recumbent figure of Juan de Pozo, the founder.

The Cathedral is one of the most remarkable in Spain, being a museum of fine art; the first stone was laid in 1177 by Alonzo VIII., who removed to the new bishopric the ancient sees of Valera and Arcos; the style of the edifice is simple and severe Gothic with a semicircular E. termination. The façade fronting the Plaza was modernised in 1664-9 by a blunderer named Josef Arroyo, by order of the chapter, which once was very rich in cash, although miserably poor in good taste. The barbarians have done their worst to modernise and disfigure their venerable church; they painted the interior in black and white like a mosque at Cairo, although it was done in imitation of the cathedral at Siena, and in compliment to Diego de Mendoza, a Cuencan, who then ruled so long a despot, and who now is buried in this cathedral. Of his great family was Don Garcia Hurtado de Mendoza, fourth M⁵· of Cañete, the hero of the Araucanian war, which forms the subject of *the* Epic of Spain by Ercilla. See ' *Los Hechos*,' &c. by Suarez de Figueroa, 4to., Mad. 1613.

Walk to the transept, and look around, and especially at the fine painted windows and the circular sweep; the arches are semi-Moorish and semi-Gothic, and spring from a bold cornice, which projects beyond the heads of the lower columns. The ornate semi-Moorish arch which forms the entrance to the high altar, and is beyond praise, springs from corbels placed in the lateral walls; and a similar oriental form is preserved in the arches at the W. end of the cathedral, but they spring from the heads of the piers in the usual plan of Gothic construction. The Coro, placed as usual in the centre, was unfortunately modernised and spoilt by Bp. Florez, of whose vile period are the organs and jasper pulpit; the splendid *reja*, however, and the eagle lettern, or *facistol*, are of the olden time, and masterpieces

of Hernando de Arenas, 1557. The original *Retablo* was removed in the last century to San Pablo in order to make place for the present high altar, which is indeed as fine as jaspers can make it; although classical in style, it is stamped with the academical commonplace of its designer Ventura Rodriguez, obt. 1785. The statue of the Virgin was sculptured in Genoa; the *trasparente*, the boast of Cuenca, is dedicated to San Julian, who, with San Onorato, are the honoured tutelars of this city. The jaspers are very rich, and the bronze capitals costly; the green columns were brought from the *Barranco de San Juan* at Granada, and rival those in the cathedral there, and at the *Salesas* of Madrid. The *urna,* with the statues of Faith, Hope, and Charity, were wrought at Carrara, in 1758, by Fr°· Vergara, a Valencian settled in Italy. The cost of transport from Alicante was enormous: but they are academical inanities without life, soul, or sentiment. As Cuenca is placed in a jasper district, the cathedral is naturally adorned with this costly material; all the chapels deserve notice. Beginning, therefore, at the r., observe the portal and *reja* of the glorious *Capilla de los Apostoles*, which is built in rich Gothic with a beautiful stone from the neighbouring quarries of Arcos. Passing the classical Retablo, observe a smaller altar of the time of Philip II., with a much venerated image of *La Virgen de la Salud,* a Minerva medica; advancing near the gate to the bishop's palace is the *Cª· de Sⁿ· Martin*, with a good altar and carvings, and four remarkable sepulchres of the early prelates, Juan Fanez, a descendant of the Cid, Lopez, Pedro Lorenzo, and Garcia. Few things can surpass the plateresque entrance into the cloisters, which rises 28 feet high, and was wrought in Arcos stone by Xamete in 1546-50, as is inscribed on labels, at the cost of the Bp. Sebastian Ramirez. Some suppose this Xamete to have been a Moor, inferring so from the name *Xamete,* "bicolor;" at all events he must have studied in the Cellini schools of Italy, and is a worthy rival of Berruguete and Damien Forment; to see this arch alone would repay the journey to Cuenca, for. it cannot be described, being a thing of the age when the revived arts of paganism wrestled even in the churches with Christianity; here we have saints and harpies, lions, virgins, tritons, vases, flowers, allegorical virtues, &c. all jumbled together, but forming in the aggregate, a whole of unexampled richness and cinque-cento effect.

The cloisters are in a different style, having been built in 1577-83 by Juan Andrea Rodi, with the fine stone from the neighbouring quarries of *La Hoz*. The simple *Doric* of Herrera was then in vogue, which contrasts with the plateresque frieze at the E. end, which is the work of another hand and period. Next observe the burial chapel of the Mendozas, in form a Greek cross with a cupola, while the Corinthian high altar is adorned with paintings and sculpture : the monuments enriched with jaspers and arched niches are ranged around; observe that with marble columns of Doña Inez, and that of Diego Hurtado, viceroy of Siena, obt. 1566. From the cloisters you may ascend to the *Secretaria*.

Next visit *La Capilla de Nª. Sª. del Sagrario*, with its superb jaspers, and observe the miraculous image which aided Alonzo VIII. in his victories. The façade to the *Salar Capitular* is worthy of Xamete; the walnut doors carved with St. Peter, St. Paul, and adoration of the kings, are attributed to Berruguete, but the Transfiguration is by an inferior hand; the walnut *Silleria* is also excellent. The chapel of *Sⁿ. Juan* was founded by the Canon Juan de Barreda, and has a fine Corinthian *Reja*, with cherubs and armorial shields. The *Cª. de Sª. Elena* opposite the *trasparente* has a beautiful portal and good walnut *Retablo*. On the l. side of the cathedral are the chapels of *Sⁿ. Juan el Bautista*, with

paintings in the *Retablo* by Christobal Garcia Salmeron, who, born in 1603, became pupil of Orrente, and adopted Bassan s style, especially in his Nativity and the Baptist preaching. Observe the *Reja* in the chapel of the Muñoz family. The *Cª. de los Caballeros*, so called from the tombs of the Albornoz family, although it somewhat encumbers the body of the cathedral, is very remarkable; the door is such as becomes the entrance of a chamber of death, being *ornamented* with a celebrated stone skeleton. The *Reja* is excellent, so likewise are the windows, which are richly painted and decorated with armorial blazons. The fine pictures in the Retablo were given by the Prothonotary Gomez Carrillo de Albornoz, who had lived long in Italy; they are painted by Hernando Yanez, an able artist whose works are very rare in Spain; he is said to have been a pupil of Raphael, but his style is more Florentine than Roman.

Among the many grand sepulchres observe that of the great Cardinal, Gil Carillo Albornoz, whose life has been written by Baltazar Parreño; observe also the tomb of his mother, Teresa de Luna, and the fine military figure to the l. of the high altar. There are other works by Xamete in the chapels of Sⁿ. Fabian, Sⁿ. Sebastian, Sⁿ. Mateo, and Sⁿ. Lorenzo.

Near the Cathedral is the bishop's palace, with a portal of mixed Gothic, and a fine saloon inside, called *El de Sⁿ. Julian*, all of which the French pillaged completely. Many of the oldest parish churches are built on the walls, and thereby add to their irregular and picturesque effect. The interiors have for the most part been sadly modernised by the once rich clergy, who tortured their fine woods into churrigueresque and gilt gingerbread; in that dedicated to *San Juan Bautista* are the tombs of the Montemayors : one dates 1462, another is in the plateresque taste, 1523, with the

2 p 2

recumbent figure of Don Juan in sacerdotal costume.

The curious old *Casas Solares*, or
family mansions of the *Conquistadores,*
are now desolate, and their armorials
remain over the portal-like hatchments
of the dead : the interiors were gutted
by the invaders. Many of these houses
are picturesquely built over the declivities, such as the Alcazar of the *Mendozas*, which towers over the Jucar :
observe the houses of the Priego and
Carrillo families, and some in the *Calle
de Correduria.* The mint, now un-
used (for there is no bullion to coin),
was built in 1664, by Josef de Arroyo. The Franciscan Convent was
erected in the 12th century by the
Templars. The position of the *Carmelitas Descalzas* over rock and river is
fine, so also is that of *Sⁿ. Pedro de
Alcantara*, which is placed near the
Jucar outside the town. Cuenca once
was remarkable for its colleges, print-
ing-presses, manufactories, arts, science,
and industry, all of which was so utterly swept away by the French as to
make the detailer, Toreno (xx.), in-
nocently wonder how a nation so civilized and humane could select for de
struction the works of Spanish piety
and learning. What would he say of
the ruins of Toledo and Salamanca?

Cuenca, in its good old times, produced great men of varied excellence.
Among her worthies may be named
Mendoza and Gil Albornoz, generals
and prelates; the artists Becerril, Xamete, Yanez, and Mora, the best pupil
of Herrera. Here were born Figueroa,
the poet, and Alonzo de Ojeda, the
friend of Columbus; and last, not
least, Lope de Barrientos, the book
burner (see p. 582). The city bears
for arms " Gules, a sacramental chalice, with a star of eight rays argent."
For excursions and lateral routes see
next page.

Continuing the route from Madrid
to Valencia from p. 864 we reach
Fuentes, or Fountains, which lies in a
dip much subject to inundations of the
Rio de las Moscas; that, as its name

implies, will delight *Fly* fishers. *Reillo,*
of Roman foundation, has a ruined
castle on the heights. *Cardenete,* a
larger hamlet, stands near the Guarzun
and Cabriel, which flow under the
ridge that divides this basin from
that of the Jucar. It has an old castle,
built by one of the great Moya family,
whose marquisite lay to the N. between
the rivers Cabriel and Alfambra.
Utiel communicates with the extraordinary salt mines at Minglanilla through
Caudete, the route passing over the
Contreras ridge, a wild, broken, and
pine-clad country abounding in game.
Requena is a large town, pleasantly
situated in a well irrigated *Vega.*
Population 1000. A diligence runs
from hence to Valencia. The parish
churches *Sⁿ. Salvador* and *Sᵃ. Maria*
have good Gothic façades. The road
now enters the *Cabreras* or *Cabrillas*
range, which separates Castile from
Valencia. The heights are broken
and pine-clad, the valleys watered by
clear streams, of which the rivulets of
Buñol, Yatoba, and Macastre flow into
the Requena, itself a tributary of the
Jucar. Near the *Venta de Siete aguas*
we enter the charming province of
Valencia, by a broken defile of ascents
and descents, and intersected by
streams. From the heights of the *Cabrillas* the sunny plains open, studded
with sparkling farms and villages,
placed in a scene of fertility without
rival ; in the distance are the hills
above Denia, and the blue sea girdle.
Not far from *Buñol*, which lies under
the *Cabrillas*, are some stalactitical
caves, called *Las Maravillas,* or the
Marvels. *Chiva* is noted for *mala gente,*
and the robbers lurk in hiding-places
which seem made for them. They are
notorious for cruelty, often ill-using
their victims, and stripping them to the
skin, *dejandoles en cueros,* very much
after the ancient Oriental thieves near
Jericho. Emerging from the hills and
passing the wooded plain *del Quart,* a
change comes over vegetation, and we
behold the carob, pistachio, the mulberry, the drooping palm, and tall

whispering canes. We now enter the *Huerta* of Valencia, the paradise of the Moors; thus passing from the desert óf the hills into a land of promise, overflowing with oil and wine (see p. 429).

ROUTE CV.—CUENCA TO VALENCIA
BY MINGLANILLA.

Valera de Arriba . .	3		
Valera de Abajo . .	1	..	4
Bonache de Alarcon .	2	..	6
Alarcon	3	..	9
Villanueva de la Jara	3	..	12
Iniesta	3	..	15
Minglanilla . . .	2	..	17
Villa Gordo . . .	3	..	20
Requena	5	..	25
Valencia	12	..	37

This wild bridle road—attend to the provend—is full of interest to the artist, angler, and geologist. *Alarcon*, pop. 800, a truly Moorish fortress city, is built like a miniature Toledo, on a craggy peninsula, which is hemmed around by the Jucar. It can only be entered from a narrow neck of land which has been likened to the handle of a frying-pan, a comparison more apposite than elegant. The land approach is still guarded by Moorish towers and an *Alcazar ;* while the painter-like gates and bridges, the steep ascent into the town, with the gardens, water-mills, defiles, and river below, recall Ronda. This now decayed, but once important town, still contains five parish churches. The S⁺ *Maria* has a façade of the time of Charles V. with a Gothic interior. The *Sⁿ. Juan* has a Doric front, and has or had a splendid Custodia, made by Christobal Becerril, 1575. The façade of the *Trinidad* is ornamented with arms and scroll-work of the best time of Ferdinand and Isabella. *Alarcon* was taken from the Moors in 1177, by Fernan Martinez Zevallos, whose descendants hence bore the title of *Señores de Alarcon;* and it was to Hernando, one of them, that François I. was delivered in charge after Pavia. His commentaries, '*Los Hechos,*' etc., folio, Mad. 1665, are truly chivalrous and interesting. This city, in July 1195, was the scene of a tremendous

battle between the Moors and Alonzo VIII. of Castile, and the year became a date among the former, *Amu-l-Alark.*

Villanueva de la *Jara* is placed, as its name implies, in a region of *cistus : Iniesta* (broom) indicates a similar botanical position. Indeed these desolate districts are covered with rich aromatic underwood, in which the bee and *feræ naturæ* delight and multiply : the *Parroquia* at Iniesta is fine. The celebrated salt mines lie about two miles E. of *Minglanilla.* Pop. about 1500. Descend into the galleries, which, when lighted, resemble Aladdin caverns of jewels. It is rather a quarry of salt than a mine, for the mineral is a pure deposit ; it may be compared on a smaller scale to the salt mines at Wieliczka near Cracow. It seems to be inexhaustible ; the working affords occupation to the neighbourhood. The miners seen in crystal vaults look like kinsmen of Lot's wife, after her saline transformation (compare Cardona, p. 500). Now the road crosses over the wild *Contreras* ridges into a wooded game country, and so on to the Cabriel, which joins the river Jucar near *Cofruentes* (confluentes-Coblenz) : thence to *Requena ;* among its pines and rocks occur bits of scenery worthy of Salvator Rosa.

Those who having made the Cuenca tour wish to visit Murcia before going to Valencia must regain the high Madrid road at Almansa, and then proceed S. by Route xxx.

ROUTE CVI.—CUENCA TO SAN CLE-
MENTE.

Valdeganga	3		
Valverde	3	..	6
Cañavete	3	..	9
Sⁿ. Clemente . . .	3	..	12

The route is uninteresting, the villages ruined, the districts thinly peopled and poverty stricken, for few portions of Spain were more often or more cruelly ravaged by the invaders, especially under La Fontaine, Victor, and Frere. See, for sad details, Schep. iii. 118.

EXCURSIONS NEAR CUENCA.

These are numerous and full of attraction for the geologist and angler. At *Bonache* is the singular *Cueva del Judio*, and at *Ballesteros*, S. of Cuenca, is a black loch called *La Laguna Negra*, which is said to have a subterranean communication with that of *Fuentes*, some cattle drowned in one having reappeared in the other. Another lake, called *el Poço Ayron*, distant 1 L. from *Almarcha*, is said to be bottomless. There a Don Buesso, according to legend, threw in twenty-four of his mistresses stark naked, one of whom pulled him in after her. Near *Montalvo*, five L. from Cuenca, is another lake, which however has a bottom, and is shallow; the winter wild-fowl shooting on it is first-rate. Visit the stalactitical cave called *la Cueva de Petro Cotillas*, taking torches, which lies about three L. up the delicious valley of the Huecar, near *La Cierva*, where fine violet jaspers are found. The Huecar is smaller than the Jucar, but its waters possess a peculiarly fertilizing quality, as its garden fringes evince. The whole route to *Palomera*, two L., is ever verdurous from perennial *fountains*, by which Cuenca is well supplied with water; and possessed an excellent hydraulist in 1538, named Juan Velez. *The Fuente del Frayle*, near Palomera, is more worthy of an Egeria than an illote friar. The mills on these streams, the pines and rocks covered with wild flowers, are truly picturesque.

The botanist and angler will on another day ascend the Jucar. The valley soon widens and becomes quite Swiss-like; about a mile up are the *Fuentes del Rey*, where Alonzo was encamped; above this, a clear trout-stream waters the plain, having issued from its mountain sources. 2 L. on is the *Valde Cabras*, famous for pines, which floated down the Tagus to Aranjuez in order to supply Madrid with building timber. The *Pinus Halepensis*, called *Alvar* by the woodmen, is very abundant. 1½ L. higher up is *Una*, with its trout-stocked *Laguna*, or lake, on which is a movable island (?). Near here are some coal-mines, and one of a fine jet or *Azabache*. Those who wish to extend their geological or piscatory pursuits into the mountains and return to Madrid, may take the following line:—

ROUTE CVII.—CUENCA TO MADRID BY SACEDON.

Buenache de la Sierra	2	
Beamud	3	.. 5
Tragacete	3	.. 8
Checa	5	.. 13
Peralejos	2½	.. 15½
Cueva del Hierro . .	2	.. 17½
Beteta	1	.. 18½
Canizares	2	.. 20½
Priego	2	.. 22½
Val de Olivas . . .	2	.. 24½
Alcocer	2	.. 26½
Sacedon	2	.. 28½
Auñon	2	.. 30½
Tendilla	3½	.. 34
La Armilla	2	.. 36
Santorcaz	3½	.. 39½
Los Hueros	2½	.. 42
Puente de Viveros . .	1	.. 43
Madrid	3	.. 46

The mountain portion of this route is a wild bridle road, and almost without accommodation, especially the first 13 L.; take, therefore, a guide, and attend to the provend. At *Bonache* the purple jaspers vie with those of yellow and purple which are found at the *Hoya de Machado*, 2½ L. E. of Cuenca, where visit the *Cueva del Judio*.

Tragacete, pop. about 900, and the only halting-place for the first night, lies in a valley girt with hills, and watered by the Jucar, which rises near it; here are found rock crystals. The next day's ride plunges into the gnarled and tangled *Sierras* of *Albarracin* and *Molina de Aragon;* crossing the *cerro de San Felipe* at *Fuente Garcia*, which is their nucleus, the Tagus rises in its snow-girt cradle from a small fountain, *El pie isquierdo :* the situation is romantic. The valley is hemmed in with the mountains and the *Muela de San Juan*, or the jaw of St. John, on the heights of which snow remains for eight months of the year. The Tagus flows W., whilst on the opposite ridge rises the Cabriel, a tributary of the Jucar, both excellent trout-streams. These central mountain alembics furnish many other rivers. The *Turia* or Guadalaviar, *Wada-l-abyadh*, "the white river," rises in the *Muela de S^{n.} Juan* and flows to Valencia ; the *Mesa*, a fine trout-stream, rises opposite in the *Fuentes de Jarava* and flows into *Molina de Aragon*, and then into the Tagus. Among other good fishing rivers are the *Escabas*, which rises in the *Cerro Canales*, near Tragacete, and flows by Priego to join the Guadiela. The evidences of volcanic action are everywhere manifest, for many lakes are formed out of previous craters, such as those of Barbagada, Mintrosa, Cabdete, and Valmoro.

Leaving *Tragacete*, cross the *Cerro de S^{n.} Felipe* into the pine woods of *Checa*, which is prettily situated on the *Cabrilla* ; thence to Tremedal, which lies to the r. near Orihuela, and has long been famous for "its high place" and heaven-descended Palladium, to which pilgrimages are made. The French, under Henriod, sacked Orihuela, Nov. 25, 1809, and blew up the sanctuary, but the image was concealed by a peasant, and after the destroyers retired, was brought back in pomp, and its escape has ever since been considered a new miracle (Toreno x.). *Peralejos de las truchas*, a name which makes the trout-fisher's mouth water, is a good halting-place. Now we enter the mineral-water district : when at *Beteta*, visit *La Cueva de los Griegos*, whose dripping waters have a petrifying quality ; at *Los Baños de Rosal* is a warm ferrugineous spring, with a fountain of sweet water, which issues from underneath the hermitage of this virgin of the *rosebush*. The waters have been analized : see ' *Noticias*,' 4to., Domingo Garcia Fernandez, Mad. 1787.

Beteta—Arabice "Splendid "—still preserves portions of its Moorish walls and alcazar. The chief baths are at *Solan de Cabras*, now called a *real sitio*, as it has been visited by Charles IV.

and Ferd. VII., for whose accommodation a road was made up the rugged valley. The locality is oval in form and enclosed by pine-clad hills and watered by the *Cuervo*, a good trout-stream and tributary to the Guadiela. The mineral spring rises under the hill *Rebollar*, and the baths are close by ; that patronised by Royalty is dedicated to San Joaquin. Early in the 16th century some shepherds observed their goats, *Cabras*, dipping themselves when afflicted with cutaneous complaints, and by following their beasts' example, discovered the secret. The bathing season is from June 15 to Sept. 15, when waters are used both internally and externally : their taste is subacid, with a mean heat of 17° above zero, Réaumur. They are slightly unctuous to the touch, as containing petroleum, and also hydro-chlorates of soda, and magnesia, combined with carbonic acid gas. From these baths there is a carriageable road to Madrid ; they may also be approached from Cuenca by a shorter route than this just described, for it is only 10 L., and runs through *Priego*, where there is a large and tolerable *posada*, pop. about 1100. The place is beautifully situated on an eminence above the excellent trout-stream, the *Escabas*, near which are also many *montes y dehesas*, that abound with game, especially the district near the truly sequestered *Desierto*, a convent founded by Charles III. *Priego*, seated at the foot of the Sierra, combines the productions of hill and plain, and is a good quarter for the angler. The bread, mutton, and wines are excellent and cheap, but the peasantry are poverty-stricken amid this plenty. It has a ruined castle, an old Gothic church, and a new one begun with a rustic belfry in the Brunelleschi style by Miguel Lopez. The botany is highly interesting ; near it the beautiful trout-stream *Trabaque* flows into the Guadiela, when the united clear sea-green waters wind into the Tagus through red sandstone rocks, with charming artistical bridges and mills.

After passing decayed *Alcocer* the country alters in character, and we quit the basin of the Guadiela, and strike across to *Sacedon*, which, with a pop. of 2500, is placed in a picturesque hill-girt valley. The warm baths, the ancient Thermida, are much frequented in the season from June to Sept. by the sickly *Madrileños*, when a diligence of the Carsi y Ferrer Company goes backwards and forwards. The waters were analysed in 1801, and are described in a treatise published that year at Madrid by Villalpanda. The principal ingredients are muriate of chalk and magnesia; the mineralogy in the vicinity is curious. Certain crystals are found here marked with oxides of iron, and called *Piedras de San Isidro* after the ploughman patron of Madrid. Ferdinand VII. created a small bathing-town near the spring, which is now called *El Real Sitio de Isabel.*

South of Sacedon, on the opposite side of the Guadiela, is *Almonacid*, where Sebastiani routed Venegas, Aug. 15, 1809. This man commanded 27,000 men, and was to have co-operated with Cuesta and the Duke at Talavera (see p. 542), but he kept away in consequence of secret instructions from the traitor *Junta* of Seville. Left single-handed, his whole conduct exhibited a gross ignorance of his profession; for on the 10th he ought to have attacked the French, who were far inferior in number; but he delayed until their reserves had arrived; and then, when he ought to have avoided a combat, courted one, and was utterly and instantaneously defeated, one gallant French charge sufficing to put his whole army to flight, he himself leading the way, which his ill-equipped dispirited troops could but follow. This miserable man was thereupon rewarded by being made governor of Cadiz, and was afterwards created Marques de la *Reunion* by Ferd. VII. Can the mockery of misnomer go beyond this? Thus the title of a *Belle Alliance* was conferred on

the very *delincuente honrado* by whose failure of junction the allied cause was exposed at Talavera to such imminent peril. To complete these *Cosas de España*, Toreno (ix.) imputes the disaster of Almonacid to one Zolina, another regular Spanish general, who declined fighting in consequence of the bad omen of his horse having stumbled in the advance. According to Schepeler, this man always had a chaplain at his side, and in battle never drew his sword, but told his rosary; and on another occasion refused to cross a murmuring brook, because it spake heaven's warning against the attempt. Can it then be wondered at that the Spanish armies should have everywhere been scattered like sheep before the French, who were led by capital officers? What availed the individual bravery of the Spanish troops when thus exposed to shame by traitors and incapables in battle, while before and after the contest they were left wanting in everything that alone can constitute a soldier, by their infamous *juntas* and governments?

Four L. from Almonacid is *Huete*, a town of ill-fame, since the proverb says, *Huete miralo y vete*, look at it and begone; and here, in 1706, the baggage of Lord Peterborough was plundered by the worthy villagers, who also butchered some English prisoners; thereupon our general took the place, but, in spite of just provocation, mercy being the badge of true nobility, he neither burnt it nor ravaged the plain, *à la Medellen* or *Ucles*. He merely ascended to the convent into which all the women had taken refuge from our doubly gallant countryman's apprehended vengeance, having gone up there on the pretence of making a fortification, but "really only to have a peep at the cowering covey." Peterborough after this retired from Spain, disgusted at her thankless government: his irritated feelings were thus tersely but harshly expressed in a letter to "old Sarah." "The most disagreeable country in the world is Spain, her officers the greatest robbers, her soldiers the greatest cowards. The only tolerable thing is your sex, and that is attended with the greatest dangers" (Mahon v. 214).

Quitting *Sacedon* we enter some wild pine-clad defiles, and then emerge into the gorge of the Tagus, which is crossed at the *Puente de Auñon;* thence through oak-underwooded table-land, into a deep valley with a sweetly situated convent, to *Tendilla,* now decayed, but once the stronghold of the mighty Mendozas, whose ruined Alcazar still frowns above. The first *Alcaide* of the Alhambra took his title from this town. Madrid lies 13 L. distant. Those who have not seen *Guadalajara* and *Alcalá de Henares* may return by R. cxi. There is a shorter route from Cuenca to Madrid by the plains and over a wild upland and woodland country, abounding in game.

ROUTE CVIII.—CUENCA TO MADRID.

Either Albacete }
  or Canaveras } · · 6
Priego · · · · · 2 (see p. 871).
Madrid · · · · · 8

Those who are proceeding from Cuenca either to Valencia or Zaragoza, and wish to visit portions of these geological mountains and piscatory valleys, should make for *Teruel,* from whence roads diverge into Arragon and Valencia, which, although they do not strictly come into this section, may for convenience sake be now described.

ROUTE CIX.—CUENCA TO TERUEL.

Buenache. · · · · · 3
Tragacete · · · · 5 · · 8
Frias . · · · · · 3¼ · · 11¾
Albarracin · · · · 3 · · 14¾
Va. de Falantre . · · 2¼ · · 17
Teruel · · · · · 2¼ · · 19¾

Attend to the provend, and take a local guide, for the country is wild, and the roads rough and intricate, but they lead into districts the joy of the angler and geologist. For the route to *Tragacete,* see p. 870. *Albarracin* is a wild mountain town—popⁿ· under 2000—and built beneath an eminence

on which the older city stood, as its walls and ruins denote. The broken *Barranco* of the Guadalaviar is picturesque; here the winter's snows and cold are severe. The districts are thinly peopled with a pastoral peasantry, who breed sheep of a small size, but which furnish good wool and excellent cutlets. The pine woods provide fuel for numerous *ferrarias* or smithies, in which the abundant iron ores are as rudely smelted as in the days of the Celtiberians; however, if the soil be uncultivated, and man be driven by vicious institutions into poverty and idleness, nature, ever active, has clothed the wastes with aromatic herbs, and like her the bee is ever busy. Here the air is scented far and wide with the perfume of wild flowers—the advertisements by which Flora attracts her tiny-winged customers alone, for no biped botanist has ever investigated these neglected sweets. The honey is delicious, and *Moya,* with the hills near the Cabriel, are the Hymettus of Spain; from hence probably came the mel excellente hispanicum, which is lauded by Petr. Arbiter (66).

Teruel, situated in Arragon, is the chief town of its partido: popⁿ· about 7500: the *Posada* is only tolerable. Seen from afar, with its old walls, gates, and Arragonese towers, the city has an imposing look, rising above its well-wooded *Vega* on the Turia, which is here joined by the Alfambra, both fine fishing streams. The interior is solid and gloomy. The cathedral, raised to a see in 1577, is dark and much disfigured by stucco and churrigueresque. The Corinthian stalls in the quire are good, and still better is the cinque-cento *Retablo,* a noble work by Gabriel Yoli, a French sculptor, who flourished here about 1538. Observe also the portal and columns of the splendid *Capilla de la Epifania;* to the r. of the transept is a picture of the Eleven thousand Virgins, by Antº· Bisquert, a rare Valencian artist.

The bishop's palace has a grand *Patio,* although the upper *corredor* offends

2 P 3

from having more pillars than the
under ones, which thus are placed on
crowns of the arches. In the *Parroquia
de S. Pedro* is another fine *Retablo* by
Yoli, with pictures of the tutelars Sᵃ·
Joaquin and Sᵃ· Teresa, by Bisquert.
All those whose hearts have ever been
touched by the tender flame, should
visit the cloisters, in which are preserved the remains of the " lovers of
Teruel," so familiar to readers of
Spanish plays. The names of these
Peninsular Heloïse and Abelard were
Isabel de Segura and Juan Diego
Martinez de Marcilla. They died in
1217, and their skeletons were brought
here in 1708. See ' *Los Amantes de
Teruel*,' by Perez de Montalban. In
the church of *Santiago* is a fine dead
Christ by Bisquert, who evidently
formed his style on Ribalta, the Carraccis, and Sebⁿ· del Piombo: Bisquert died in 1646 of grief that Frᵒ·
Ximenez should have been chosen iⁿ-
stead of himself to paint the " Adoration of the Kings" in the cathedral.
His works are very rare, scarcely
known in Spain, and absolutely unknown out of it.

The former *Colegio de Jesuitas*, and
now the *Seminario Auxiliar*, is a fine
building. Look by all means carefully at the aqueduct *Los Arcos de
Teruel*, which is worthy of the Romans
in form, intention, and solidity. It
was raised in 1555-60 by a most skilful French architect named Pierres
Bedel. Teruel bears for arms, its
river, a Bull (*Toro*, Teruel), and a star
above it. We are now in the centre
of the volcano-disturbed nucleus. At
Caudete and *Concud*, 1 L., are some of
the largest bone deposits in Europe,
which, as they have only been mea-
gerly mentioned by Bowles, now clamour loudly for Dr. Buckland. The
bones are found in every possible state,
fossil and otherwise, and it has been
conjectured from the number of human
remains, that some great battle must
have been fought here: the *Cueva
Rubia*, a Kirkdale on a large scale,
deserves particular investigation. The

town and all the districts were sacked
by Suchet, who spared neither church
nor cottage, age nor sex.

ROUTE CX.—TERUEL TO CALATAYUD.

Caudéte	2	
Villarquemado . . .	2	.. 4
Torremocha	2	.. 6
Villafranca del Campo .	2	.. 8
Monreal del Campo. .	2	.. 10
Camin real	1	.. 11
Calamocha	2	.. 13
Vaguena	3	.. 16
Daroca.	2	.. 18
Retascon	1	.. 19
Miedes.	3	.. 22
Belmonte.	2	.. 24
Calatayud.	2	.. 26

This is the road to Zaragoza, and
that by which Ferd. VII. came down
to Valencia on his return from his
captivity in France. It was at *Daroca*
that he heard of the downfall of Buonaparte, and forthwith meditated up-
setting the Cortes, an act to which, had
he been anything loth, he was
not, the nation itself would have driven
him. Sick of the incapacity and pro-
fligacy of its misrulers, and desponding
in all their nostrums, it rushed headlong into the arms of a legitimate chief,
and, flying from petty tyrants, welcomed even a despotism, in which it
saw *power*, and hoped to find peace
and protection; but such ever has been
and will be the tabula post naufragium,
the great rock in a weary land. It is
but the χειροκρατια, which Polybius (iv.
46) considered the consequence and
Euthanasia of democracy. Spain, in
welcoming back the Bourbons, resembled Rome when leaping into the
absolutism of Tiberius, who, like Ferdinand, despised his slaves, " Oh homines ad servitutem paratos" (Tacit.
' An.' iii. 65). The grandees set the
example of putting on legitimate chains
—all hastened, to use the words of the
same philosopher (An. i. 2, 7), " ruere
in servitium; consules, patres, eques,
quanto quis inlustrior, tanto magis falsi
ac festinantes,—lacrimas, gaudium,
questus, adulationes miscebant."

This was a reaction, which " won-
derers," who knew nothing of Spain and

Spaniards, have never got over, nor ceased to denounce Ferd. as a Nero and monster; but to all who know this country and people, it was an event which could not fail to occur, and in which the king was only the head of the serpent, whose progress is forced by its tail. The intuitive Duke long foresaw the whole, and, writing in Sept. 5, 1813 (Disp.), remarked, "If the king should return, he will overturn the whole fabric if he has any spirit," and he did.

After crossing the bone and fossil district, the road follows the Jiloca, which rises near *Celda*, a hamlet, whose *Parroquia* contains an excellent plateresque *Retablo. Monreal* was founded in 1120 by Alonzo I. of Arragon, as a check upon Daroca, which he did not take from the Moors until two years after. *Daroca*—popⁿ· 500—has a decent *Posada.* The name *Dar-Auca* indicates that it was once the *Douar* or residence of the tribe of *Auca*, now it is the chief place of the fertile basin of the Jiloca, and of a district abounding in corn and wine. The position is very picturesque, placed in a hill-girt valley, around which rise eminences defended by Moorish walls and towers, which, as at Jaen, follow the irregular declivities, and command charming views from above. Daroca, lying as it were in a funnel, is much liable to inundations; hence a *Mina* or tunnel has been cut, by which an outlet is afforded to the swollen waters; the passage, when dry, is used also as a *Rambla*, or road. This work of truly Roman utility and magnificence was executed in 1560 by Pierres Bedel, the same able Frenchman who raised the Teruel aqueduct. The tunnel is 2340 ft. long, 24 ft. wide, and 24 ft. high.

But Daroca boasts of far greater marvels than this. First comes *La Rueda*, or miraculous mill-wheel, which during an inundation at night of the 14th of July, 1575, rolled away of its own accord, and broke open the city gates, thereby letting out the waters and saving the townsfolk, for the watch-men and wardens were as usual fast asleep. This piece of *good luck* happened very appropriately on the day of San *Buenaventura*, whereupon the wheel was enclosed as a relic in the *Calle Mayor*, and placed under a picture of this *fortuna bona virilis.* The second marvel is the stone man, not the *Convidado de Piedra* of Don Juan, but the petrified body of one Pedro Bisagra, which was placed in *La Trinidad*, with a basket on its arm. This fossil, when alive, was in the habit of stealing grapes, and being once caught, flagrante delicto, denied the fact, adding, that he hoped, if he told a lie, that *Los Santos Corporales* would turn him into stone, which they forthwith did, and the culprit in the saxeous change lost two-thirds of his original height, contracting like a shut-up telescope. The geologist, after looking at the bone fossils at *Caudete*, should report on this rare specimen, which the naturalist may compare with the water man at *Lierganes.* The third and greatest marvel, and that which the Darocan considers superior to all the wonders of the world past and present, is *Los Santos Corporales*, or, as they are here called, *El Santo Misterio ;* they are preserved in the *Colegiata.* This fine Gothic church, built by Juan II. of Arragon, who died in 1479, was altered in 1587 by Juan Marrón, who wrought the Corinthian portal and the bas-relief of the *misterio.* The tower is much older, having been raised in 1441 by the queen of Alonzo V. The chapel in which the relics are preserved has a cinque-cento *Retablo*, with black marble Salominic columns, and an Ascension of the Virgin sculptured in 1682 by Frᵒ· Franco. The legend has been authorised by many Popes, and is hallowed by innumerable indulgences still granted to faithful believers. The reader who wishes for all the authentic details must consult ' *La Historia de los Corporales*,' 8vo., Gaspar Miguel de la Cueva, Zaragoza, 1590. The ' *Rasgo*' of Moya, p. 113, ' *Coronica de España*,' Beuter, Valencia, 1604, ii. 42. There is also a local

876   ROUTE CX.—DAROCA.—LOS CORPORALES.   Sect. XI·

history of Daroca, '*Antigüedades,*' 4to.,
Nuñez y Quiles, Zaragoza, 1691; the
facts briefly stated are as follows. In
1239, one Don Berenguer Dentenza
was besieging the castle of Chio, near
Bellus, in Valencia, when 20,000
Moors came to its relief, whereupon
this Spanish Dentatus sallied forth with
five knights to drive them back. The
curate of Daroca had previously consecrated six *hostias,* but before the party
could communicate the infidels attacked them; thereupon the priest,
whose vocation was pacific, ran away
at once, but first he wrapped the six
wafers up in their *Corporales,* or nap-
kins (Anglicé, *Corporax*), and threw
them into some bushes. The six Spaniards, as was usual in those days of
miracles, instantly and easily defeated
the 20,000 Moors, and when the coast
was clear, the curate reappeared, looked for and found his *Corporales,* which
now contained, instead of six wafers,
six bits of bleeding flesh : thus transubstantiation was incontestibly proved.
But now the six knights wanted each
to secure the treasure, and the question
was thus decided :—They were put in
a box, and placed on the curate's mule,
it being agreed that wherever the beast
halted, there the *Corporales* should remain. The mule returned alone to
Daroca, although more than 100 miles
off, and over mountains without roads,
and knelt down at the curate's *Parroquia* (compare San Ramon Nonat, p.
501). From that moment offerings
poured in, whereby many souls were
saved, and the church much enriched.
This miracle by a happy coincidence
occurred much about the time that a
Hostia bled at Viterbo, whereby Urban
VI. was induced, in 1263, to institute
the festival of Corpus Christi, whose
presence thus locally and corporeally
in the wafer was doubly proved, and
no Christian country has offered more
wonderful evidences of the fact than
Spain ; thus at *Ivorra,* near *Castelfolit,*
the grand relic is called *Lo Sant dupte,*
the holy *doubt,* not *dupe,* because in the
12th century the curate having con-

secrated the wafer, *doubted* whether it
contained mortal blood, whereupon so
much gushed out that the altar was
inundated, and the cloth by which it
was wiped up became relics (see Ponz,
xiv. 152). Again, at Valencia, when
a church was burnt down, it was found
that a *Corporax* remained quite unconsumed, and the asbestic relic naturally became an object of universal
veneration.

If our readers will turn to Leon, p.
610: to Lugo, p. 650; to the Escorial,
p. 815; they will see how great is the
worship and adoration paid in Spain
to the *Santa Forma,* or consecrated
host; but to those who sincerely believe in transubstantiation, this adoration must be the necessary consequence;
for here the Saviour is locally present
in the flesh, and not in his glorified
body, in which alone, as being an immortal Spirit, he truly exists, and in
such a glory, as at the transfiguration
and calling of St. Paul, mortal eye
may not behold.

The doctrine of transubstantiation
was first invented in 831 by a French
monk, one Pascacius Radbertus, but
it soon died away, until the eleventh
century, when it was revived, and
finally established in 1215 at the fourth
Lateran council, from which all Protestants, and with perfect reason, dissent.
Thus the very institution which the
divine founder of Christianity meant
to be the symbol of common member-
ship with him, and a religious fellow-
ship of all mankind among each other,
has been perverted by Rome into the
test and touchstone of religious separation. It is impossible to understand
Spanish fine art and customs, without
some notion of the manner in which
the Gospel record of the Sacrament is
here systematically set at nought. Here
spirituality has been altogether corpo-
realised, and the letter and meaning of
the institution departed from. First
of all no "*bread is broken,*" but a
stamped wafer substituted; next, the
cup of which "*drink ye all*" was the
command, is denied to the laity. The

Saviour, in the institution of this solemn memorial, replaced, as every one of his words demonstrate, the pasqual lamb of the Passover of the old law by a more touching memorial, in remembrance of himself, when the new perfect revelation was complete. The Spaniard, however, prefers using the consecrated elements in the old Pagan acceptation of *Hostia*, a living victim offered in *sacrifice*, which contradicts the evidence of our senses, and would lead even a poor Pagan to exclaim again, "Ecquam tam amentem esse putas qui illud quo vescatur Deum esse credat?" (Cicero, 'N. D.' iii. 16).

It is obvious, if the people can be made to believe that the priest has the power, at his own good pleasure, to call down the Deity from heaven and carry him in his hands, that this invocator and minister must rise above common humanity. Accordingly, when all kneel to the elevated host, they in reality kneel to the priest, who, standing on the raised altar, looks indeed down on the inferior flock beneath him; and, in order to rivet this pre-eminence outside of the church as well as inside, the law of John I., 1387, declares that all persons shall kneel at its presence, even Jews or Moors (see lib. i. tit. 1. ley 2). The wafer is spoken of, and treated as God himself, as "*Su Majestad*," and its presence is announced by a bell, at which all must kneel, as we have often seen done at Seville, even when a river so wide as the Guadalquivir flowed between, and also during dinner at a captain-general's, when all rose and knelt at the balconies. The populace, on hearing the ringing, cry out, "*Dios Dios*," and uncover; hence the proverb, "*Al Rey viendolo, a Dios oyendolo.*" This homage is paid to the king on *seeing* him —to God on *hearing* him; but the Protestant traveller will do well never to offend the weaker brethren, by refusing to join in the universal bowing to that name at which all may well bow; indeed, a few years ago a recu-

sant would have been torn to pieces by the mob. It is usual whenever the host is being carried to a dying person, that the persons in the first carriage it meets should descend and make room for the priest, a custom to which royalty ostentatiously conforms. Again on every Easter Monday the host is taken in a magnificent procession to the houses of those sick, *los impedidos*, who had been *hindered* from communicating in the church; then the streets are tapestried as if for the passage of the sovereign, while the priest, bearing the *Viril*, rides in triumph in a gilt coach, attended by the chief inhabitants, and looks out complacently on the multitude, who kneel on each side, crossing themselves and beating their breasts most orientally (Herod. ii 40, Larcher's note, and Luke xviii. 13).

The abuses and profanation to which this *transubstantiation* daily leads in Spain can scarcely be alluded to. First a credence table is ready to *test* God's blood, as by it the Dominicans poisoned the emperor, Henry III., whence the Pontiff himself drinks it through a reed. Again, at every bull-fight the priest attends with the consecrated wafer, in case it may be required for any fatally wounded, being taken away again if not wanted. Again, the lord mayor's show procession of the wafer on Corpus Christi Day is *the* sight of many towns; and as such is brought out at other times to amuse royalty (see p. 434). These remarks might be infinitely extended, but the subject is one which Protestants scarcely can venture to approach, however much familiarity and the lowering tendencies of materializing the spiritual may have accustomed Spaniards to behold, and even jest at such lamentable desecrations.

Daroca blazons on its shield "*six Hostias*," thus eclipsing Gallicia and Lugo, its former honourable distinction having been six geese, the canting *Ocas*: the town has also six other parish churches. Visit *Santiago*, whose façade is handsome, while inside is a picture of the battle of *Clavijo*, by Ambrosio Plano, a native artist. Daroca and the whole district were dreadfully ravaged in Nov. 1809, by the invaders under Clopicki ; and yet Ferd. VII., when restored by England, selected this place to give a hurried proof of his gratitude, even before he reached Madrid, and issued a decree directing the day of *S^n. José* to be particularly celebrated, in order to "*purify*" immaculate Spain from the taint of heretics, meaning his English deliverers ; and, not contented with this, he soon re-established the "Holy Tribunal" professedly for the same reasons and object.

The botanist in these parts will find a wide and hitherto uninvestigated field ; the fruit is excellent, especially the pears called *Pera pan* and *Cuero de Dama* and the *camuesa* apple. South of Daroca is the plain of *Bello* with its brackish lake *la gallocanta*, near which barrilla, saxifrage, and other salitrose plants abound ; beyond it lies *Villar del Saz*, where there are iron-mines which furnish for Calatayud (see R. cxii.) a mineral of immemorial celebrity. Those who do not wish to go to *Calatayud* may cut across 16 L. by *Cariñeña*, in whose cereal *campo* the fine wines *El ojo de gallo* and *Blanco imperial* are grown, which form the usual beverages of Zaragoza. Those who are pressed for time may leave out Daroca altogether, by turning off at *Lechago*.

Molina de Aragon lies 9 L. S.W. of Daroca ; pop^n· 3500. It is the capital of its *Señorio*, and became incorporated with the Castilian crown by the marriage of the heiress Maria with Sancho el Bravo, in 1293. The city lies with a S aspect on a slope over the Gallo, an excellent trout-stream, and is protected by its walls and Alcazar from the N. winds. The whole of this district was ravaged by the invaders in Nov. 1810, when three parts of the unhappy city were burnt, and all the neighbouring villages sacked, for the French remembered and revenged the ancient

hatred of these districts to their ancestors. This country was ceded to Du Guesclin and his "*compagnies des pillards*" (see Navarrete), by Henrique II., in recompense for their services in enabling him to dethrone his brother ; but, impatient of a foreign dictation, the people rose against their new masters, and implored the aid of Pedro IV. of Arragon. There is a good local '*Historia*' by Diego de Castrejon y Fonseca, duo. Mad. 1641.

ROUTE CXI.—TERUEL TO VALENCIA.

Puebla de Valverde	.	3	
Sarrion	.	2¼	.. 5¼
Barracas . . .	.	3¼	.. 9
Jerica . . .	.	3	.. 12
Segorbe . . .	.	2	.. 14
Torres torres. .	.	3	.. 17
Murviedro . .	.	2	.. 19
Albalat . . .	.	2	.. 21
Valencia. . .	.	2	.. 23

Valverde, placed on an eminence, contains 1000 souls. The Ionic portal to the Parroquia is of the date 1591. Sarrion has a mineral fountain, *La Escareluera*. Crossing the rugged Javalambre chain, leaving the *Peña golosa* to the l. is *Alventoso* on its rocky *wind*-blown knoll, placed over a dip well watered by the confluents of the Mijares ; thence over a wild rough country to the province of Valencia at *Barracas*, whose hills as well as those of *La Pina* abound in game. Soon descending into the pleasant fertile *Huertas* of Jerica, cold Arragon is exchanged for genial Valencia. Jerica (Jericho), pop^n· 3000, is placed under a slope crowned with a ruined castle on the banks of the Palancia, which is here crossed by a good bridge, built in 1570 by Juan de Muñatones, bishop of Segorbe. Many Roman inscriptions are found in this district. The *Parroquia* has an elaborate stone portal ; hence to *Segorbe* (see p. 453).

ROUTE CXII.—MADRID TO ZARAGOZA.

Puente de Viveros	. .	3	
Alcalá de Henares .	. .	2¼	.. 5
Venta de Meco .	. .	1¼	.. 7
Guadalajara . .	. .	3	.. 10

Torija	3	.. 13
Grajanejos	3	.. 16
Almadrones	2¼	.. 18¼
Torremocha	3	.. 21¼
Bujarrabal	2¼	.. 24
Lodares	2¼	.. 26¼
Arcos de Medinaceli	2¼	.. 29
Huerta	2	.. 31
Monreal de Arizar	1	.. 32
Cetina	2	.. 34
Alama	1	.. 35
Bubierca	1	.. 36
Ateca	2	.. 38
Calatayud	2	.. 40
Frasno	3	.. 43
Almunia	3	.. 46
Venta de la Ramera	3	.. 49
Muela	2	.. 51
Garrapinillos	2	.. 53
Zaragoza	2	.. 55

There is some talk of a railroad between Madrid and Zaragoza, which is to be carried on to Barcelona; meanwhile the old *camino real* is taken by the diligence, and most uninteresting it is. There are also minor branch diligences, which run from Madrid to *Alcalá* and *Guadalajara*, the two places the most worth seeing; the traveller therefore might visit them first, having previously secured a place in the Zaragozan diligence, to be taken up at Guadalajara; the *Paradores de las diligencias* are throughout the best inns. Those who have leisure might visit *Sigüenza* and *Medinaceli*, diverging from Guadalajara, and taking up the Zaragozan at *Huerta*. After leaving Madrid, and before crossing the Jarama, to the l. is *La Alameda*, one of the few attempts at a villa near this capital, where the late Condeza Duqueza de Osuna expended *un dineral* in the vain attempt to create an oasis in the desert. Crossing the Jarama, to the r. is *Torrejon de Ardoz*, where Don Hernardo Muñoz was born, his father keeping an *Estanco* or tobacco shop; this fortunate youth served in the body-guard of Ferd. VII., where his black whiskers attracted the gracious notice of the fair Christina, who, at her royal husband's death, raised him to her bed, and created him Duke of Rianzares : *intrepido es amor y de todo sale vencedor.*

Again, at Ardoz, in July 1843, the eventful drama of Espartero's career was brought to a conclusion, and a Spanish Waterloo struck down the regent adventurer and caricature of Buonaparte; here the *valientes* of Narvaez encountered the *valientes* of Zurbano, and having smoked prodigies of cigars at each other, " fraternised," and sheathed their terrific swords. This bargain battle finished what the traitor convention of Vergara began ; and now Narvaez became the dictator, and ruled in his stead — more fortunate than Cæsar, because raised without any loss of precious life, at least on the field of battle, for " black" blood was copiously enough shed on the scaffold. The conqueror was raised to the title of Duque de Ardoz. In estimating *ducal* titles on the other side of the British channel, the safe rule will be to adopt the meaning attached to other conventional words ; take, for example, the phrase " worth a million :" that signifies, in England, of pounds sterling ; in France, of francs (9½d.); and in Spain, where the bathos is complete, *reales*, of which one hundred go to our pound ; and so with dukes, which Ferdinand and his successors made by the dozen, and Buonaparte and the Bourbons by scores at a time ; while England, the unconquered by sea or land, only created two in a century and a half—Marlborough and Wellington. So Nelson, who triumphed at the Nile, *died* a viscount, while M. Decres, who was beaten there, and fled, lived to be a *Duc et Pair.*

A bald dreary country continues to *Alcalá de Henares,* " the castle of the river ;" Arabicé, *El Nahr,* which this once flourishing university bears on its shield for arms. The place looks imposing when seen from afar, from its walls and towers, but inside all is decay. The old city *Alcalá el viejo,* was built on the *Cerro de S. Julian del Viso,* and was called *Complutum,* quasi *confluvium,* from the junction of rivers. It was taken by Alonzo VI., who was encouraged by a vision of the Cross in the air, which was seen by the Archbp.

Bernardo, to whom the monarch granted all the lands near the site of his opportune vision; hence the prosperity of the place, which grew under the fostering protection of the Toledan primate. Bernardo built a hermitage on the hill of *La vera Cruz*, " the true cross," to which a *Retablo* was given in 1492 by Pedro Gumiel, an architect of *Alcalá*, who is generally called *El honrado*, because his works never exceeded his estimates ; and all who to their cost have dabbled in brick and mortar, raw materials of ruination, will visit this good man's memorial, since, take him for all in all, they ne'er will see his like again in Spain or out of it. Even Solomon, the wisest of men and greatest of builders, was out in his reckoning to the tune of 720,000*l*., which he borrowed of a friend (1 Kings ix. 11). The Archbp. Tenorio erected the wall and bridge in 1389; but the great benefactor was Cardinal Ximenez, who, having been educated here, remembered in his day of power the school of his youth, and raised it in 1510 to be a university, as Wolsey, imitating him, did Ipswich. It once had 19 colleges and 38 churches, and was so amply provided that Erasmus perpetrated a pun on *Complutum* by calling it Πανπλουτον, from the abundance of wealth, and the " *cumplimiento*" of all learning ; and here at least were born Cervantes and Antonio Solis, the historian of S. America.

Ximenez, disgusted at Ferdinand's suspicious ingratitude, retired here after the conquest of Oran, and devoted his time and income to his new buildings. During his regency he amassed much treasure, with all of which, when Charles V. reached Spain, he endowed his university, saying, " Had an angel asked me for it before my sovereign's arrival, I should have thought him a devil ; and should he ask me again for it now, I should think so still." Alcalá became to Salamanca what Cambridge is to Oxford ; and François I., who, when a prisoner, spent here three days of continual festival, being welcomed by 11,000 students, remarked that " one Spanish monk had done what it would have taken a line of kings in France to accomplish." The celebrated Polyglot Bible was printed here, hence it is called the Complutensian, in 6 vols. folio, 1514-15. Ximenez its projector, like Ptolemy Philadelphus with the Septuagint, spared neither pains nor cost. In 1502, he began to collect materials and editors, and lived to see the last sheet in type; but after his death Leo X., warned by Cardinal Pole of the danger to the Papacy, in circulating the Book of *Truth*, " the light shining in a dark place," delayed the publication until 1522, and then limited it to 600 copies. The expense of the edition exceeded the then most enormous sum of 52,000 ducats ; three copies only were printed on vellum, one for the Vatican and one for Alcalá; the third was bought by Mr. Standish for 522*l*., and bequeathed to Louis Philippe; the text is in Hebrew, Greek, Latin, and Chaldaic, but is not highly esteemed by Biblical critics; the MSS. have come to a sad end. In 1784 Professor Moldenhauer went to Alcalá to consult one of the early Gospels, for which he in vain inquired of the heads of colleges and fellows, who, like their brethren at Salamanca, were contented to suck their alma mater, in lazy enjoyment of undisputed possession, and knew nothing about manuscripts, and not much more about anything else. Here, books were destined, according to them, to support worms, whose bellies may well fatten on exploded nonsense, for the *Index expurgatorius* had taken pretty good care to keep out of Spanish libraries all the works which were really worth reading.

At last Moldenhauer discovered that the librarian, about thirty-five years before, when wanting room for some modern trash, had sold the parchments to one *Toryo*, a sad radical and fire-work maker, who used them up for rocket cases. The sale was entered in the official accounts, " como membranas *inutiles*," and the quantity sold was so great that it was paid for at separate times. So, recently, during the civil wars, cart-loads of conventual deeds and medieval parchments have been sold to the glue-makers, who looked to this source for a supply of raw material. Thus the only adhesive element in unamalgamating Spain is obtained at the cost of her literature and antiquities.

Yet this land of anomalies and contradictions was among the first to translate the Bible, which now its churchmen the most forbid, as, since they have departed from its letter and spirit, the book condemns them. They pretend, imitating the Moslem's refusal to *print* the Koran, that the rendering it thus common would derogate from its sanctity. Borrow, in his graphic 'Bible in Spain,' has shown the deadly hostility of the priests to the inspired volume, which they burn as the Pagan pontiffs of old Rome did the rituals of antagonist creeds (Livy, xxxix. 16). So the lies of man are substituted for the truth of God.

Inspect, as we have so often done, any Spanish religious library, or open any of the books of devotion furnished by confessors to women and the many, they will mostly be found·to be either mariolatrous fallacies, idle legends, and lives of monks, false alike in history, chronology, and geography, as in morals and religion; but "woe unto them that call evil good, and good evil; that put darkness for light, and light for darkness; that put bitter for sweet, and sweet for bitter" (Isa. v. 20). Can it be wondered at, since the truth has so long been systematically withheld, and Spaniards forbidden and unable to "search the Scriptures," that at present there should only be two classes, either *infidels*, who live in a cold negation of all religious truth, and reason, with Voltaire, that in order to be really enlightened it is necessary to believe nothing—or *bigots* who swallow greedily the stones that have been given them for bread? The former class are on the increase among the upper and middling ranks, for, as Aristotle said, errors when exploded and falling into contempt, drag truth down with them; since men, when they discover the cheats of what has been long practised on them, in resentment against the abuses of superstition, war against real religion, and doubt everything; nor have they anything better to fall back on than this dreary, heartless infidelity, as there is no *via media*, no Protestantism, no Bible in Spain.

Alcalá is now a poor and ignorant place; for the removal of the university to Madrid has completed its ruin, and, like Salamanca, it is a shadow of the past. Visit the *Colegio mayor de S^n· Ildefonso*, which Ximenez began in *Tapia ;* and when Ferdinand objected to the humble material, replied, that it became him, a creature of dust, to leave marble for his successors. Hence the inscription, "Olim lutea nunc marmorea." It was finished in 1533 by Rodrigo Gil. There are three *patios ;* one is in the Doric, Ionic, and Berruguete style: that called *El Trilingue* was completed in 1557. The chapel, built by Gil de Ontañon, is magnificent; here the rich Gothic is tinctured with Moorish decoration, *azulejos y lienzos.* Observe the fretted arches under a matchless *artesonado* ceiling, with ribbed pannels and alhambra stars. The founder lies buried before the elaborate *Retablo ;* his effigy reposes on a most superb raised *Urna,* the master-piece of Dominico el Fiorentino : the *Reja* is by the Vergaras, father and son, 1566-73. The rich cinque-cento ornaments present the usual struggle between Pagan and Christian devices: the *Paranimfo,* or hall of former ceremonials, is adorned with exquisite plateresque upper galleries; the lacunares of the *artesonado* roof are very rich. Ximenez died at Roa, near Valladolid, Nov. 8, 1517, in his eighty-first year, broken-hearted at the ingratitude which Charles V. showed, like his grandfather, towards an old and faithful minister. So died Columbus, Cortes, and Gonzalo de

Cordova. Ximenez was a stern reformer, and bigoted persecutor of Jew and Moor; but none can doubt his honesty of purpose,' however mistaken his policy. His nobly planned palace is still unfinished : the windows of the first *patio* resemble those by Berruguete in the *alcazar* of Toledo; the second *patio* is plateresque, and was built by the primates Fonseca and Tavera : the staircase and façade to the garden deserve notice. Alcalá was repeatedly sacked by the invaders; hence the churches and convents are now plateless, pictureless, and desolate. In the *San Diego* is the grand sepulchre and recumbent statue of the primate Alonzo de Carrillo, obt. 1482. The principal church, *el Magistral*, is Gothic, with an excellent *Reja* by Juan Frances, and elaborate *Silla. del Coro;* here lies Pedro Gumiel, *el honrado,* now forgotten and dishonoured.

The glory and safeguard of Alcalá is the altar of the tutelar saints, *Justo y Pastor;* these Gemini, like the Fratres Helenæ, are συνναιοι, and keep house together. They were sons of a Gothic gentleman, says Pius V., and when aged seven and nine years, were going to school on Aug. 6, 306, to learn their alphabet, or "*primeras letras*," when Dacian put them to death, whence Sⁿ· Isidoro calls Pastor a lamb. The stone on which they were executed still bears the impression of their knees, and is worshipped by the peasants at *El Paredon del Milagro,* about two miles from the town. When the Moors invaded Alcalá the martyr bones were carried off to Huesca, and were brought back in pomp by Philip II. as the most appropriate patrons of a place where the young idea is or was taught to shoot. Ribadeneyra (ii. 444) gives fuller details; see also Prudentius (Per. iv. 41). Alcalá has a theatre, a *Plaza de Toros,* and two pretty *Alamedas* called *el Sal* and *el Chorillo.* Many changes have taken place since the suppression of convents, some of which are now schools for cavalry education; cedant togæ

armis. There is a local history by Portillo y Esquivel.

Two L. S. is *Loeches,* with the Dominican convent to which the Conde Duque retired when disgraced by Philip IV.; here he wrote, under the signature of Nicandro, that famous vindication of his policy, which being unanswerable, completed his ruin, for he was banished to Toro, where he died in 1643, haunted, as he thought, by a spectre; say rather by the ghost of Spain, whose greatness he had murdered : he was buried in this convent's chapel, which he had adorned with ten pictures by Rubens, but which disappeared after this wise : In 1807, Mr. Buchanan having commissioned Mr. Wallis to make purchases of paintings for him in Spain, the agent bargained with the nuns for six of these pictures at 600*l.*, but before they were handed over, Buonaparte's troops reached Madrid, and Mr. Wallis being taken for one of them, narrowly escaped being hanged at Loeches. After this compliment he applied to Sebastiani to assist him, who, as Mr. B. informed us, offered his bayonets, provided he had the choice of two of the pictures for his fee : accordingly they were all removed by force, when Sebastiani took the two finest as the lion's share : one of them, the Triumph of Religion, certainly not of the eighth commandment, is now in the Louvre, sold by him for 30,000 francs to the French government. The four other pictures soon caused a breach of another commandment, viz. the tenth; or, to use the polite periphrasis of Mr. Buchanan, "attracted the attention of the government of Buonaparte," and were placed by Wallis for protection in the house of M. Bourke, the Danish minister, who unluckily was himself a dealer in virtú, and by whom they sold for 10,000*l.* to Lord Grosvenor: thus Mr. B. lost both cash and pictures (see his ' *Memoirs of Painting,*' ii. 222, which give curious details how collections were formed with English gold, Corsican brass, and French iron). Sebastiani, in 1814, when matters looked rather awkward, offered to an English gentleman to sell his *Collection* of seventy-three pictures for 11,000*L*, and they were proposed to George IV., who was unable to buy them, from having spent all his loose cash in feasting the allied sovereigns: thereupon many were then purchased by Messrs. Watson Taylor and Alex. Baring.

To the r. of Loeches, and about 2 L. from Alcalá, is *Corpa*, famed for its hunger-provoking waters. Morales (*Ant. de España*, 57) relates how a labourer sat down one fine Monday with his week's provision of bread, and forthwith ate his daily loaf, and then washed it down at the spring; but the more he drank the more he ate, until the seven loaves were gone; hence it is called *La fuente de siete hogazas.* Other divines say that the rustic had eaten all his seven loaves at once, and feeling considerably distended, drank of the waters, and immediately digested the whole mass. Read this, ye aldermen of London, with what appetite ye may. These provocative fluids are, alas! sad streams of supererogation in these hungry localities, where food, not digestion, is wanted.

Leaving Alcalá the bald plains continue to *Guadalajara (Wádd-l-hajarah)*, "the river of stones," which are more liberally bestowed in these cereal plains than loaves. This river, the Henares, is crossed by a bridge, built in 1758, on Roman foundations. The town, especially when seen from Sᵃ· Antonio, outside the walls, rises in a fine jagged outline with crumbling battlements, while the gardens of the Mendoza palace hang over a wild ravine. Inside, however, it is dull and poverty-stricken; and so it always was; therefore Archbishop Fonseca used to say that "although only 4 L. from Alcalá, it really was 140 off in wealth and learning," but now both are on a par in both poverty and ignorance: popⁿ· about 6700. The *posadas* are bad; that of the diligence is the least so.

Guadalajara was reconquered from

the Moors by Alvar Fañez de Minaya, whose mounted effigy the city bears for its arms. The readers of old ballads will be familiar with this relative and fidus Achates of the Cid, to whom he gave his precious swords (Duran, v. 154). Alvar was a fierce *guerrillero* of that exterminating age, and, like his master, spared neither age nor sex, hewing the infidel to pieces. No wonder that the Moorish annalists never mention the name Albarhanis without adding, " May God destroy him" (Moh. D., ii., ap. 32). The great lords of Guadalajara were the Mendozas, the Mecenas family of the Peninsula. The façade of their curious but dilapidated palace is studded with projecting knobs, while an ample armorial shield with satyrs for supporters crowns the portal: high above runs an elegant row of Moorish windows, from whence François I. beheld the tournament given him by the D. de Infantado, whose magnificent hospitality is described by eye-witnesses (see ' Hechos de Alarcon,' x. 302, fol., Mad., 1665; and ' Historia de Pescara,' viii., ch. 3, Zaragoza, 1562). The Mendoza lived here in almost royal state; his retinue, body-guard, &c. are detailed by Navagiero (p. 7). On entering the house the *Patio* is singularly rich and quaint; over the arcades are strange sculptured lions, with heads like hedgehogs, and a profusion of scrolls and shields. All is now the abomination of desolation: the rooms of state are partitioned with *tapique*, and dwarfed down to the wants of the degenerate inmates. It is melancholy to walk through this palace, which is a thing of the country,where past splendour struggles with present decay. The splendid *artesonado* ceilings being out of reach, mock with their gilded magnificence the indigent misery of the walls below, and the azulejos retain their Primaticcio designs. In a room upstairs some portraits of the grim Mendozas frown flapping in their frames at this neglect of their descendant the Osuna and richest grandee in Spain. Observe the ceilings in a saloon which overlooks the weed-encumbered garden, and another which bears the arms of England, with the Tudor badges and supporters. The *Sala de Linajes*, once the saloon of the genealogies of the proud Mendoza, has been converted into a magazine! Observe the chimney pieces, and especially that in the long gallery. This palace was completely gutted by the republican invaders, who resented the hospitality shown to even their *own king* in his hour of need.

Next visit *S*ⁿ· *Francisco*, and observe in the *Capilla de los Davalos*, a sweet statue of a sleeping female, holding the cordon of the tutelar; here youth and beauty have met with an untimely end, cut off in their prime: che sciagura! had she been eighty-two years old, and ugly, none would have cared dos reales about her.

Now descend into the *Panteon*, where reposed the ashes of the Mendozas, the brave, the pious, the learned, and the magnificent. The sepulchre, worthy of their goodness and greatness, rivalled in rich marbles those of the Medici at Florence and the Escorial, and was begun in 1696, and finished in 1720, at the then enormous cost of 180,000l.: it contained twenty-eight tombs, and among them that of the duke who had befriended François I., but his ashes, in 1809, were cast to the wind by the invaders, who made bullets out of the leaden coffins, and then broke the precious marbles into pieces. Infantado after their expulsion long left the vault purposely unrestored, as a mute but eloquent record of revolutionary philanthropy. The Duque was personally obnoxious to the French because a true Spanish patriot. He was appointed commander-in-chief at this place Dec. 2, 1808, after La Peña had been defeated before the town, which was then dreadfully sacked by Bessières.

Near the Mendoza palace is a pseudo-Moorish brick building, which was converted by the invaders into a bat-tery, and since into a prison : opposite is the royal manufactory, a French scheme of Philip V., who wished to force Spain, a naturally agricultural country, into making bad and dear wares. Here all the merino fleeces of Spain were to be wrought into cloth for nothing less than the supply of the whole world; but all this ended in more cry than wool : *mucho ruido y pocas nueces*. Bolstered up from 1757 to 1784 by Charles III., at an enormous loss, it became such a hotbed of robbery, jobbery, disorder, and mismanagement, that the minister Wall, an Irishman, contrived to decoy over one Thomas Bevan, from Melksham in Wiltshire, to set the machinery and matters to right, just as the Orientals do, then leaving the poor foreigner, when his task was accomplished, to die of a broken heart at the failure of every grand promise which had been made to him : *Cosas de España* (compare pp. 279, 839). This establishment was gutted and ruined by the invaders, who so far, but quite unintentionally, conferred a benefit, for " Multi etiam cum obesse vellent profuerunt, et cum prodesse obfuerunt (Cic. ' N. D.,' iii. 28). Ferd. VII.,˙ on his restoration, restored this ruinous concern, as he did the Inquisition, for deep indeed have the Colbert maxims sunk into every Bourbon heart ; everywhere, in defiance of sounder principles, they will force their royal hobby manufactures by premiums, &c., which are so many taxes on their own consumers. Thus millions on millions have been misspent, which might better have been laid out in roads, canals, or agricultural improvements.

Next visit the *Plaza de S*ᵃ· *Maria*, and observe the picturesque arcades and the former mosque of *S*ⁿ· *Miguel*, with its colonnaded entrance, round buttress pillars with pointed heads, horse-shoe arches, machicolations, and herring-bone patterns under the roof. The church of *S*ⁿ· *Esteban* has the Toledan circular absis and rows of arches on the exterior. There is a history of Guadalajara, by Fernando Pecha, a Jesuit, but published under the name of Ant° Nuñez de Castro, fol., Mad., 1653. About 2 L. E. of *Torija* are the plains of *Briguega*, or the *Alcarria*, Arabicé a place of farms or *Alquerias*. This fine pastoral and wheat district was originally a vast lake, which was separated by the Guadarrama chain from the similar one, now the *Tierra de Campos* in Old Castile. The fresh-water basin is composed of rich red marl and loam, and is irrigated by streams which flow into the Tajuna. The district is elevated some 4200 ft. above the level of the sea. The aromatic shrubs of the hills render the honey very fine, while the wines of *Poyos* are excellent. Guadalajara is the chief town.

Briguega, Centobriga, is an old and once walled city of 4800 souls. Here, Dec. 9, 1710, Vendôme defeated Stanhope, whose victories over the French at Almenara and Zaragoza had recovered Madrid, as Salamanca did in our times. His heavy German allies having, however, neglected to secure the communications between Portugal by Alcaraz, Vendôme seized the opening, and with the characteristic decision and rapidity of his countrymen, advanced from Talavera on Madrid with greatly superior forces, just as Soult did from Hellin. Thus the Allies were forced to fall back on Catalonia, as the Duke was on Portugal. The selfish Austrian, Charles, led the retreat, carrying off all the cavalry with him as his escort, and thereby depriving the army of all means of obtaining intelligence and watching the enemy. The Allies divided into three bodies, the Portuguese taking the centre, the Germans the r., and the English the l. The Allies proceeded over-leisurely, and were pounced upon quite unawares by the dashing Vendôme, who wisely made his first attack against the little English band, which then, as in our times, was, to use Stanhope's words, " the salt which seasoned the whole." Vendôme had more than

20,000 men, while Stanhope had scarcely 5500, with no cavalry and very scanty ammunition. He instantly sent off to Staremberg, who, although distant only a five hours' march, now, when minutes were winged with destinies, was two days in coming up, thus occasioning his ally and himself to be defeated in detail. Stanhope resisted the French as long as his powder lasted ; he then capitulated on most honourable terms, which Vendôme stained his great glory by shamefully violating. The next morning, that is, the day after the fair, the lumbering Staremberg reached *Villaviciosa*, distant about 1 L., with 13,000 men, and fought so gallantly that Vendôme at one time meditated a retreat on Torija : thus had these slow allies only marched a little quicker and joined Stanhope, the French must have been destroyed. Night came on, leaving the battle undecided; then it was that Vendôme prepared for Philip V. in his bivouack that truly victor bed, one made of the captured flags of the enemy. Next morning Staremberg retreated, and reached Barcelona with only 7000 men. Charles soon after became Emperor of Germany, and Bolingbroke by selling England and Spain to France secured the crown to Philip V.: so ended the War of Succession, of which Lord Mahon has given us so excellent an history.

Four L. from Briguega through *Solanillos*, is *Trillo*, a town of 800 inhabitants, near the Tagus and *Cifuentes ;* it possesses excellent mineral baths, which are much frequented from June 15 to September 15 by the sickly Madrileños. A diligence runs backwards and forwards during the season from Madrid, through Guadalajara; the baths are situated about a mile from *Trillo*, by a pretty planted walk ; one, called *La Piscina*, is destined for lepers, and there is also a hospital in which the poor are received—and most poorly. The equally frequented baths of *Sacedon* lie a few L. S. of Trillo.

At *Almadrones*, the road branches

to the l. to *Sigüenza* in Old Castile, 4 L.; few visit this city, which, however, contains a cathedral full of magnificent art. Pop. about 5000. It is the chief town of its district, which, possessing fine plains and plenty of water, might be made the granary of Spain. *Sigüenza* was built, it is said, by fugitives from Saguntum. The site of the Celtiberian *Segontia* Seguncia is distant about 2 miles, and is still called *Villa Vieja*. This, once an important frontier town of Castile and Arragon, was reconquered in 1086 by Alonzo VI., and still retains portions of its ancient walls and gates. As it is built in the shape of an amphitheatre on the side of a hill, sloping down the valley of the Henares, the upper town is steep, with the height crowned by the episcopal palace or *Alcazar*, for the bishop was once señor or lord of Sigüenza. The Gothic cathedral, a very fine substantial edifice, has a simple façade between two towers, with a medallion of the Virgin giving the *Casulla* to Sⁿ· Ildefonso over the central portal; descending into the interior, the 24 noble clustered piers which support the middle and highest of the three naves are striking. The much admired *Trascoro*, with red and black marbles, was raised in 1685 by Bishop Bravo, to receive a graven image of the Virgin which had been miraculously preserved from the Moors. The rich Gothic *silleria del coro* was carved in 1490; the huge organs are of much later date. The simple and classical *Retablo* of the high altar is composed of three tiers of the Ionic, Corinthian, and Composite orders, and was with the bas-reliefs raised in 1613 by Bishop Mateo de Burgos. The statues of Faith, Hope, and Charity deserve notice. Among the many tombs of prelates in the *Presbiterio*, remark, near the door of the *Sagrario*, the recumbent effigy of the first bishop, the Frenchman Bernardo, who afterwards became the celebrated Primate of Toledo; he was killed in a battle near the Tagus, and however indifferent to truth or the

distinctions of meum and tuum, was at least a gallant soldier. The portion of the transept in which are the relics of Sⁿ· *Librada*, the patroness of the city, is elaborately architectural. Observe the details of the *Retablo* and the niche in which her body reposes; above is a sculpture in which she ascends to heaven, and nothing that minute labour and gilding can effect has been spared. The founder, the Bishop Fadrique of Portugal, kneels in a highly-wrought niche near his work.

The chapel of Sª· *Catalina* is near the door which opens to the market-place. Observe a delicate plateresque portal and *reja*, and some superb sepulchres with recumbent figures; *e. g.* of Martin Vasquez de Sosa; Sancha, his wife; Martin Vasquez de Arce, 1486, and a fine armed knight of Santiago. Above all notice that of the bishop of Canaria, Fernando de Arce, obiit 1522, by whom some of the others to his ancestors were raised, for it is truly Berruguete, with statues of children, shields, and cinque-cento decoration, amid which the prelate lies at full-length on the *Urna*. Another sepulchre of older date fills the centre of this extraordinary assemblage of monumental art. How impressive, how Christian is the sentiment here! There is no aping the pagan costume of antiquity, but everything speaks Spain and the period, the gallant crusader, the pious prelate, lie stretched on the bed of death, yet the clasped hands, now that sword and crosier are laid aside, indicate hope, faith, and confidence in another life. The *Retablo* is churrigueresque, but the original one is put up in the *Sacristia* with an excellent but much injured Florentine picture of the Crucifixion. The adjoining *Capilla de* Sⁿ· *Fro.* *Xavier* has also a plateresque portal, and in the semicircular chapel is the tomb of Bishop Bravo, with a fine crucifix. The portal to the *Sacristia* or *Sagrario*, is in best plateresque, and in the same style is the wood carving inside, while the *Relicario* is filled with statuary and minute sculpture, and the *reja* is excellent. The glorious church plate disappeared during the war of the invasion. The Gothic cloisters, with delicate windows and enrichments, were finished in 1507 by Cardinal Bernardo Carvajal, and were paved in the last century by Bishop Bullon, who disfigured the general character with his coats of arms. Examine, however, the doors and contiguous chapels.

The Geronomite *Colegio* was founded by one of the Medinaceli family, who lies buried in the transept, obiit 1488. Observe the tomb of Bishop Barte· de Risova, obiit 1657, and the classical cloister of Tuscan and Doric. Sigüenza has pleasant walks on the river banks, which were laid out by Bishop Diaz de la Guerra, for the bishops have been signal benefactors to their city. They raised the aqueduct, which crosses a glen below their palace, and supplies the town, and is a work of truly Roman intention, solidity, utility, and grandeur. It was at Sigüenza, Nov. 30, 1808, that Castaños, after his defeat at Tudela, surrendered his command to La Peña of Barrosa infamy; then the hero of Bailen, who never had but that accident to win a victory, from being the idol of Spain, became at once an object of popular scorn.

The road to Zaragoza may be rejoined at *Lodares*, passing first to *Medinaceli*, 4 L. This is not a " city of heaven," either metaphorically or really, but simply the "city of Selim," and once the strong frontier hold of a Moor of that name, and, accordingly, the scene of many conflicts between both the Moors against themselves and against the Christians. Here, on Monday, Aug. 7, 1002, died the celebrated Al-Mansúr, " the victorious," the Cid of the Moors, and the most terrible enemy of the Christians. Mohammed Ibn Abi was born Oct. 28, 938, near Algeciras; he was first a letter-writer at the gate of the palace at Cordova, then the secretary of Sobha, the mother of Hishem II., whose *Amir* he rose to be by a long tissue of Oriental and

Spanish intrigues, treacheries, and murders, and became the *Hageb*, or Maire du Palais, and in reality the master of the puppet Sultan. He waged deadly war against the Christians, proclaiming a " holy crusade," or *Algihad*, every year, when his raids or *talas*, eatings up and razzias of Gallicia, even exceeded those of modern invaders. He also took authors, his Borys and Pelets, with him to vilify his opponents, and glorify his own honour, mercy, and goodness. He was defeated in 997 at *Calatanazor*, and sickening, as some say, in consequence; nay, others pretend that he killed himself (see 'E. S.' xxxiv. 309): but suicide is not an Oriental or Spanish resource, being altogether opposed to their singular resignation and fatalism. Al-Mansúr in reality died a natural death, and, weeping at the anticipation of the falling to pieces of a power which he had consolidated, and which in Spain, as in the East, solely depended on the individual support of its founder. He was buried in the dust of fifty campaigns, for after every battle, a true Almogavar (see p. 790), this *conqueror* by name and deed, used to shake off the soil from his garments into a chest which he carried about with him for that purpose: so *victorious* Nelson sleeps in a coffin made from a captured enemy's battle-ship. Al-Mansúr's sad anticipations were soon verified, for after his death his army disbanded after a true Oriental manner, each man to his home; and with its support fell the Kalifate of Cordova; the binding hoop was removed, and it split into petty disunions, and was broken by the Christians in detail (consult ' Moh. Dyn.' ii. lib. vi.). Mons. Viardot, ' Essai sur les Mores en Espagne ' (i. 110), has made of Al-Mansúr a hero of a novel, as Florian did of Gonzalo de Cordova and Chateaubriand of the Abencerrage. Reinaud (Inv. des Sarrasins, p. 217), a critical writer, cautions his readers against M. Viardot's ultra-French polish.

Medinaceli, now the chilly home of some 1600 mortals, is built on a steep eminence over the trout-stream *Jalon*, and gives the ducal title to the great family of Cerdas, the rightful heir to the crown, for Fernando, called *de la Cerda* from a peculiar tuft or bristle, the eldest son of Alonzo el Sabio, died during his father's lifetime, leaving two children by Blanche of Bourbon, who were dispossessed in 1284 by their uncle Sancho el Bravo (Mariana, xiv. 7). The Spanish historian was not aware how ancient an Iberian custom was this succession of brothers to the exclusion of nephews (see Livy, xxviii. 21). It was introduced into Spain in all probability by the Carthaginians, as the rule prevailed in Numidia (Livy, xxix. 29). The dispossessed dukes of Medinaceli long continued at every new coronation to claim the crown and to be fined a small sum pro formâ. Their petty capital has a *Colegiata*, a dilapidated palace with a good Doric courtyard, and the remains of a Roman arch. The city was taken from the Moors in 1083, by Alvar Fañez de Minaya (see p. 883), whose mounted effigy it blazons for its arms.

At *Arcos*, we cross the *Jalon*, and soon entering Arragon bid adieu to the Castiles at *Huerta*, which is a poor town, nipped and chilled by the winds of the bleak *Moncayo* mountains; however, it possesses one of the finest Bernardine monasteries in all Spain, built on the site of a palace of Alonzo VIII. in 1142-7; it has been altered from time to time and much injured by modern bad taste. There are 2 *Patios*, that with a double colonnade is most elegant; the pointed Gothic below contrasts with the round arches above. This convent was the burial-place of many ancient knights of the 13th and 14th centuries, who died fighting the Moor, *e. g.* the Finajosas, Perez, Martinez, Manriques, Montuengas, Muñoz, and others, whose Froissart epitaphs are preserved by Ponz (xiii. 54), soon to be swept away. The *Silla. del Coro*,

full of Berruguete and cinque-cento caprice, is most elegant; observe the stall of the abbot. Near the high altar lies Rodrigo Ximenez de Rada, the warlike primate who fought at *Las Navas de Tolosa*. The church was formerly painted with representations of that decisive victory. The once excellent library has shared the fate of most in Spain. Among the remarkable personages buried here is the *San Sacerdote*, Martin de Finajoia; also many of the French legionaries who came to aid Henrique II. against Don Pedro. This monastery deserves a careful inspection.

Arragon (see Sect. xiii.) is entered at *Ariza*, a name said to be derived from the Basque *Ari*-za, abundance of sheep. It is a miserable place, retaining some of its former mud walls and fortifications. Hence following the Jalon, is Alhama, placed under a noble rock above the river; distant 2 L. are the baths, the Roman Aquæ Bilbilitanæ, which are frequented from June to September. Thence passing *Bubierca*, Voberca, to *Ateca*, a town of 3000 souls, which was conquered from the Moors by the Cid, and a tower on the Valeucian road still bears his name. About 10 miles off, at the monastery of *Piedra* are some grand cascades; that called *La Cola del Caballo*, " the horse's tail," is 300 feet high.

Calatayud is the second town of Arragon. The diligence inn is the best, but the *Parador de Llover* is decent. Pop. about 16,000. The city has an imposing look, imbedded among rocks and with a noble castle. The hills are grey, hungry, barren, scaly, and crumbling, as are the ruined edifices which are built out of them and among them, for the whole place is dilapidated and dull. It is of Moorish origin, as the name implies, being the " Castle of Ayub," Job, the nephew of Musa, who to construct his new frontier town, used up the remains of ancient *Bilbilis* as a quarry; that old Iberian city lay about 2 miles E. at *Bambola*, and was celebrated for being the birth-place of

Martial and the site of a victory gained v. c. 680, by Quintus Metellus over Sertorius. It was also renowned for its superior steel and streams, *"Aquis* et armis nobilem"* (Mart. i. 50. 4), for Equis is an incorrect reading. These waters were those of the *Jalon,* "Armorum *Salo* temperator" (Mart. iv. 55. 11). See also Justin (xliv. 2), and Pliny (N. H. xxxiv. 14), and for Spanish swords, Toledo, p. 852. The fourteen medals coined at Bilbilis are enumerated by Florez (M. i. 169). Modern Calatayud must closely resemble ancient Bilbilis as described by Martial (x. 103) ; it is cold and cheerless, being exposed to the blasts of the dreaded *Moncayo,* mons Caunus, *calvus.* This *bald* Sierra, a peeled mass of red sandstone and limestone, divides the basins of the Ebro and Duero, and being detached, catches the clouds and is the dwelling of Æolus and *Pulmonia,* as in the days of Martial (i. 50. 5), who dreaded "sterilem Caunum cum nivibus."

Martial himself, although an Arragonese by birth, was in truth rather an *Andaluz gracioso.* He went to Rome, where he neglected business and took to writing epigrams like Salas, and *Seguidillas* like Quevedo. The characteristics of his style are well summed up by his friend Pliny in his 'Epistles' (iii. 21), as partaking *salis et fellis,* of salt *sal andaluza* and gall, and he might have added of dirt; but ancient ballad-mongers were frank and open in their expressions, nor was there then any inquisidor to force them into decency and an outward observance of *les convenances.* What the ancient *Seguidillas were* may be inferred from that quoted by Suetonius (Cæs. 49), *Gallias Cæsar subegit,* etc. ; but those who will look into the ' *Cancionero de burlas, Madrid, por Luis Sanchez,*' i. e. printed in London, by Pickering, will see the Spanish muse in tolerable déshabille. Martial toadied Domitian when alive, by whom he was knighted, but abused him when dead. He took disgust at being neglected by Trajan, his

paisano, and returned to Spain after 35 years' absence, from whence he wrote an account of his mode of life to Juvenal, and which, rude as it was compared to the luxuries of Rome, he preferred, like a true Spaniard, sic me vivere, sic juvat perire (xii. 18).

Calatayud is a genuine Arragonese city; and now the peculiar soffits and carved projecting rafters of roofs commence, and the Castilian *Quinta* gives place to the *Torre,* and the dully *Paño pardo* for blue and yellow velveteens. The town is cheap, as the environs, being well irrigated by the Jalon and Jiloca, are full of pastures, fruit, and vegetables ; the hemp is equal to that of Granada. The city has also a theatre, a *plaza de toros,* and some pretty Alamedas.

There are two *Colegiatas.* One, *El S⁰. Sepulcro,* was built in 1141, and originally belonged to the Templars; the altar of the *sepulcro* is made of marbles of the province. The second, *La de S⁰. Maria,* has a most elegant cinquecento portal, erected in 1528, but the interior is less good, having been disfigured with stucco work of bad taste. There are a few second-rate pictures by Arragonese artists. The pavement, put down in 1639, is of a marble called Claroboya, which resembles the Parian; the belfry is octangular, as is common in Arragon and Catalonia. The Dominican convent has a glorious *patio* with three galleries rising one above another: observe a portion of the exterior enriched with pseudo Moorish work like the prisons at Guadalajara, although, when closely examined, it is defective in design and execution; seen, however, from afar it is rich and striking. The city arms are truly Celtiberian, "a man mounted without stirrups, and armed with a lance :" such a charge occurs constantly on the old coins. A cross has been placed in his other hand, and the motto "Bilbilis Augusta" subjoined. Consult the local histories, ' *Tratado,*' Miguel Marquez del Villar, 4to., Zaragoza, 1598; and another by Jero-

2 Q

nimo Escuela, 1661. Near Calatayud and *el camino de la Soledad* are some curious stalactitical caves. For the country towards Teruel, and communications with Valencia and Cuenca, see R. cviii. cx.

Leaving Calatayud the vineyards commence; the wines made in the *campo de Cariñena*, which lies some 10 L. to the N.E., are among the best in Arragon. *Almunia* is prettily placed amid gardens, cypresses, and olives, with a richly ornamented octangular belfry. Now the fine road continues over dreary plains and chalky mountains to *Muela*, whence Zaragoza, with its thin lofty *torres*, forms the emphatic feature of a magnificent panorama, backed by the shadowy Pyrenees, and sweet is the prospect, the gardens, olive groves, and vineyards, after the wilderness left behind: for Zaragoza and Arragon, see Sect. xiii.

ROUTE CXIII.—MADRID TO BURGOS.

Fuencarral	1	
Alcobendas	2 ..	3
San Agustin	3½ ..	6½
Cabanillas	3 ..	9½
Lozoyuela	2½ ..	12
Biutrago	1½ ..	13½
Somosierra	3 ..	16½
Castillejo	3 ..	19½
Fresnillo	2½ ..	22
Onrubia	2½ ..	24½
Aranda de Duero . .	3½ ..	28
Gumiel de Izan . .	2 ..	30
Bahabon	2 ..	32
Lerma	3 ..	35
Madrigalejo	2½ ..	37½
Sarracin	3 ..	40½
Burgos.	2 ..	42½

This being the grand route to France, is the one the most travelled in Spain; and those who are forced to travel on it in their own carriages (see p. 15) will find relays of post horses at the different *paradas*. The journey is also performed by many mails, diligences, and public conveyances. The route is most wearisome, as the road is out of repair, and the towns miserable; the *Posadas* of the diligences are, however, very tolerable. The *Sillas Correo* or mail is the best mode of travelling, because the quickest; happy the man who can sleep, dislocating ruts permitting, from Madrid to Burgos, after which the country gets more interesting. We strongly advise all who have not seen the Escorial, Segovia, and Valladolid, to make for Burgos by going through those places by Routes cix., lxxix., and lxxvii.

The desert begins on quitting the mud walls of Madrid, and the miserable people and country look as if they were all in Chancery. At windblown *Fuencarral*, to the r. of *Chanmartin*, is an old mansion of the Mendoza family, in which Buonaparte lodged from Dec. 2, 1808, until Dec. 22, and here, Dec. 3, he received the Madrid deputation headed by the traitor Morla, for a fear of dying by the Spanish knife, retaliatory of the *Dos de Maio*, made him shy of living in the capital.

San Agustin, although among the last stages to a city which its townsfolk consider to be the first stage to heaven, is no *Civitas Dei* of the ancient father whose name it bears. Like Medinaceli, this *delincuente honrado* is a wretched place, and never has recovered from the ill-usage of the French after Dupont's defeat at Bailen. The whole line of road to Burgos was then ravaged, "harvests of wheat were eaten up, flocks and herds, vines and fig-trees, and the fenced cities impoverished;" nothing escaped them, for they robbed even beggars, and those Spanish beggars. The unarmed villagers in vain applied to Marshal Moncey for protection; he forbade them to extinguish the flames with which he burned their homes, and they were left to water the ashes with their tears (Schep. i. 448). Savary escaped the popular fury disguised as a servant, following the respectable example of Nero (Suet. 48), and setting one to Buonaparte at Orgon. Joseph made off among the first, he who the day only before the battle of Bailen had entered Madrid as its sovereign, thus creeping like a moth into the ermine of Castile; now he fled, "oh, vice of kings! oh, cutpurse of the empire!" having first plundered Ferdinand's plate chests (Toreno, iv.), as he did his galleries at his subsequent flight. In the same July, thirty-seven years afterwards, he died an exile at Florence, leaving sundry millions of francs; but his Imperial Majesty began life as the clerk of a pettifogger, and at a time when

" L'on a vu des commis, mis
  Comme des princes,
  Qui d'hier sont venus, nus,
  De leurs provinces."

Dreary now becomes the face of nature, and the heat in summer is terrific (see p. 800); green as a colour, and water as a liquid are curiosities; it is just the place to send a patient to who is afflicted with hydrophobia: however, at *Cabrenillas* and *Lozoyuela*, the spurs of the Somosierra and range commence, and are cooler, but the passes are often infested with robbers; the peasants, now few and poor, are clad in *paño pardo*, their waistcoats are cut open at the chest, and they wear *monteras* as in *La Mancha ;* the women on holidays put on picturesque boddices laced in front; their children are swathed up like mummies. For *Biutrago, Uceda,* the trout fishing, and *Patones,* see p. 830. The pass or *Puerto* over the Somosierra is the natural gate and defence of Madrid, and was strongly occupied by the patriots with 16 cannon, Nov. 30, 1808. " Their misconduct," says Napier (iv. 2), " can hardly be paralleled in the annals of war; it is indeed almost incredible to those acquainted with Spanish armies, that a position in itself nearly impregnable, and defended by 12,000 men, should, without any panic, but merely from a deliberate sense of danger, be abandoned at the wild charge of a few squadrons, which two companies of good infantry would have effectually stopped; the charge of the Poles, viewed as a simple military operation, was extravagantly foolish,

but taken as the result of Buonaparte's sagacious estimate of the real value of Spanish troops, was a felicitous example of intuitive genius. The Spaniards ran in every direction. The appearance of a French patrole terrified the vile cowards, who halted near Segovia, and the multitude fled again to Talavera, and there consummated their intolerable villany by murdering San Juan, their unfortunate general, and fixing his mangled body to a tree, after which, dispersing, they carried dishonour and fear into their respective provinces." To murder* unsuccessful generals is an old Punic and Iberian habit, and frequently torture was added (App. 'B. H.' 309, 312; Justin, xxii. 7). Similar examples occurred constantly during the Peninsular and recent civil wars, and were the wild justice, the revenge taken by the ill-used soldier for long years of misgovernment and deception. The *Juntas* and generals in their stilty speeches and bombast proclamations held out to their troops that they were invincible; no wonder, therefore,when the day of battle and the first charge of the tremendous French dissipated the illusion, that the half-starving, ill-equipped soldiers, embittered by disappointment and defeat, should attribute the, to them, astounding reverse, to their chiefs, and put them to death as having purposely sold and betrayed everything to the enemy. Certainly, as Napier says, the *collective* misconduct of the regular armies of Spain was in painful contradiction to the valour of the *individuals* of whom they consisted, and scarcely a battle was fought during the whole war in which this sad fact was not demonstrated; but truth and justice also require that the real culprits should bear the blame and dishonour, and not the *people of Spain*

* The Spanish Goths used this *dulcem vim* in order to make their chiefs take, not relinquish, command, Thus Wamba was informed, " Nisi consensurum te nobis modo promittas, gladii modo mucrone truncandum te scias."—' E. S.' vi. 535.

or the *nation at large*, and we have always in common fairness pointed out this important distinction: see particularly our remarks on the personal bravery and nice feeling of honour of the *individual*, pp. 137, 604. We have also shown that the real incubus was a vile government and unworthy chiefs: see Ocaña, p. 310, and Almonacid, p. 872. " Always bear in mind," writes the just Duke (Disp. April 16, 1813), " their total inefficiency, their total want of everything that can keep them together as armies." Had the Spaniards been placed like the Portuguese under English officers, and also well clothed and armed, with his " pocket and belly " wants provided for, they, too, would have become the " fighting cocks of the army." " Our own troops," says the Duke, " *always fight*, but the influence of regular pay is seriously felt on their conduct, their health, and their efficiency ; *as for the French troops, it is notorious that they will do nothing unless regularly paid and fed* " (Disp. July 25, 1813); and yet the Spaniards, when half naked, half armed, and starving, always courted the unequal combat even to rashness, " such was their insatiable desire," says the Duke, " to fight pitched battles with undisciplined troops." That indeed might show a military ignorance of the chances of success, but certainly was no trait of cowardice. Look again at the conduct of the *guerrilleros*, who waged the true warfare of Iberia, each man for himself in a personal desultory combat; what energy was not exhibited, what rapidity of movement, what skill in plans, what spirit in execution, what privation under fatigue and hardship, what valour, insomuch that their deeds seemed rather things of romance than of reality. The Spaniards, as a people, at all times showed a determination to face the enemy, being as ready for the encounter after defeat as before it; for never, as Polybius said (xxxv. 1), did one battle determine the fate of Spain, as a Jena or Waterloo did of Prussia

or France ; nor was it ever easy, even when the regular armies were beaten, to hold the conquest (Florus ii. 17. 7). The inveterate weakness of Spaniards has been their want of union, or " of putting their shields together " (Strabo, iii. 238). Thus the miserable *pobrecitos*, who by the sport of mocking fortune were raised to power and command, never would act cordially for the common good (see what Polybius said of them, *Rio Seco*, p. 618); nor, puffed up with conceit, would they allow a *foreigner* to take their place (see *Penis-cola*, p. 558). So it always was, and a foreigner was the more hated if successful, because his merit enhanced their worthlessness (Polyb. i. 36). Thus their Carthaginian ancestors, having been led to victory by Xantippus, a Lacedemonian, professed to honour him in public, but gave secret instructions to have him put to death, which he was (App. ' B. P.' 6).

Again, the self-love of each individual Spaniard leads him to undervalue and mistrust every one else; nor were many of their leaders calculated to neutralise this national tendency, which their " ignorance of their profession " and invariable defeats strengthened rather than weakened; witness the incapacity of such men, spoilt children of disgrace, as Blake, Cuesta, Venegas, La Peña, Areizaga, Mendizabal, &c., and the whole war never produced even mediocrity in a Spanish general, for those modern heroes, Castaños and Friere, were but poor creatures and " children in the art of war;" the one never gained any battle except *Bailen*, which was an accident, while the other was beaten everywhere except at *San Marcial*, where he was supported by the English. *Despondency* as regards public affairs of all kinds is a marked feature in the national mind. Spaniards, who have seen that all attempts to cure political evils only make matters worse, despair altogether, and just let things take their course, and take care of their individual selves—sauve qui peut.

Accordingly at this rout of Somosierra the French made few prisoners. " Velocitas genti pernix," says Justin (xliv. 2). The sinewy Spaniard has *buenos jarretes;* thus Musa reported (Conde, i. 59) " cuando quedan vencidos son *cabras en escapar* a los montes, que no vean la tierra que pisan." The whole army disappeared from the face of the earth, as is usual in the East and in Spain (see p. 311). Buonaparte reached Madrid without encountering a single opponent, and little did the bulk of Spaniards care for its loss. The Spanish official version of *Somosierra* is characteristic; according to Paez (i. 354), here "a body or corps of Spaniards *combated* the *entire* French army commanded by Napoleon in person;" that is, 12,000 men ran at the sound of the horseshoes of a few hundred Polish lancers led by Krasinski.

The high road over the *Puerto* is often blocked up with winter snows, but a commodious *Parador* or *Venta de la Juanilla* has recently been built here by the diligence company. The pass is placed on the dorsal spine which divides the two Castiles. Now we descend into a hideous country, rich, however, in corn and wine, and thence to *Aranda* on the Duero amid its vineyards. The poplar-fringed river is crossed by a good bridge, and the overhanging, balconied houses are picturesque. The bishop's palace was gutted by the French. Popⁿ· about 4500. Visit the irregular market where the peasants group together like Sancho Panza, with their *alforjas* on their shoulder. The women now wear red stockings and petticoats of thick serge green and blue.

The S. portal of the chief church is the fine Gothic of Ferd. and Isab., whose badges are mingled with the shields of the Enriquez, admirals of Castile: observe the scale-form stone-work over the door, which has good carved pannels, and rich niches and statuary, with three alto relievos, the Bearing the Cross, the Crucifixion, and Resur-

rection. The *Retablo* inside is good, and contains subjects from the life of the Virgin. The Doric and Ionic portal of the Dominican Convent is classical. Here is (or was) the fine *Retablo* and sepulchre wrought by Juan de Juni for his patron Alvarez de Acosta, Bp. of Osma. The pulpit is made up of sculpture taken by barbarians from this tomb. Aranda, now a miserable place, was once inhabited by kings: for its past glories, consult ' *Obispado de Osma,*' Lopez Loperraez, p. 174.

The communications with Arragon and Navarre by Soria, and the E. portions of Castile will be found at R. cxxix.

At *Gumiel,* observe the Corinthian portal of the parish church erected in 1627, and enriched with apostles, cardinal virtues, and the Assumption and Coronation of the Virgin. Distant ½ L. is the ancient monastery of *Sⁿ· Pedro de Izan,* which contains some remarkable sepulchres; the dreary, lifeless, treeless, waterless country continues to *Lerma,* a decayed place of some 1300 souls, and built on the Arlanza, a fine trout-stream ; the shooting also near it at *El Bordal* is good. This place gave the ducal title to the premier of that bigot imbecile Philip III. as all readers of ' Gil Blas' know; he was a fit minister of the rapid decline of Spain's short-lived greatness, and his worthy principles were hypocrisy masking avarice ; thus while founding convents, he plundered the public. Philip IV., on his father's death, squeezed out this full sponge, and then beheaded his agent Rodrigo Calderon, just as Henry VIII. did the Empsons of his father. At Lerma, in 1604, the minister raised a vast palace, designed by Frᵒ de Mora, the best pupil of Herrera, and in the style of *Las casas de oficios* at the Escorial; the *Patio,* a noble staircase, and colonnade show what it was before the French invasion, when everything was pillaged, and the edifice turned into a barrack. *La Colegiata* was also built by this Duke :

the *Retablo* is in vile taste, but the tabernacle, with fine marbles and bronze angels, is better. The superb monument to the Cardinal Lermas has been attributed to Pompeio Leoni.

To the r. of Lerma, about 1 L. from *Covarubias*, is the ancient monastery of *San Pedro de Arlanza*, which existed in the time of the Goths, as in it Wamba took the cowl; it was restored in 912 by the Conde Fernau Gonzalez, in gratitude for his signal victory at Cascajares: here was guarded the wonderful cross which was sent him by Pope John XI., which rivalled those of Oviedo and Caravaca, as a sure remedy against hail-storms; its virtue was tested in 1488 by the Bp. Luis de Acuña, who put it into a fire, whereupon the flames were instantly extinguished (see Sandoval's 'Idacio,' p. 336). Here also was kept *La Virgen de las Batallas*, a bronze goddess of war, a Bellona, which was coeval with that of the Cid (see p. 575). The count died in 968 and was buried here; he indeed was the founder of the Castilian monarchy, and a perfect hero of romance, being always up to his elbows in adventures; his grand deeds were the defeats of the infidel at Lara, Osma, and Piedrahita; his escape from prison and other spirit-stirring incidents are told in some charming old ballads: see Duran, v. 27

Leaving Lerma, the weary traveller gladly beholds the walls of Burgos, with its domineering castle and splendid cathedral rising nobly above the plantations on the banks of the Arlanzon. The best inns are *El Parador de Diez; El Parador de Badals*, C^e de Cantaranas; *El Parador del Dorado*, C^{e.} de la Pescaderia, where the mail stops. There are also good quarters in the Plaza in which is the bronze fountain of Flora. Few travellers halt at Burgos, as they are either in a hurry to get on to Madrid, or in a greater hurry to get out of the Castiles; yet here the antiquarian and artist may well spend a couple of days: for its history, con-

sult '*Historia de Castilla*,' Diego Gutierez Coronel, 4to., Mad. 1785; the paper by Benito Montejo in the '*Mem. de la Acad. de Hist.*' iii. 245; '*Viaje Artistico*,' Isidoro Bosarte, 8vo., Mad. 1804; and Florez, 'E. S.' xxv. xxvi.

BURGOS, a name connected by some with the Iberian *Briga*, at all events means a "fortified eminence," and is akin to Πυργος, Burgus, Burgh, Borough, Bury, &c. Lying near the *Montañas*, from whence so early as 874 the hardy highlanders turned against the Moors, the city was founded in 884 by Diego de Porcelos, and became the capital of the infant monarchy; it bears for arms, "gules, a half-length figure of the king, with an orle of 16 castles or." It was at first subject in some degree to the kings of Leon, when Fruela II., about the year 926, invited the chief rulers to a feast, and then put them to death after a proceeding common enough in Iberian, Punic, Oriental, and Spanish policy (see *Estella*). The citizens of Burgos thereupon elected *judges* to govern them, just as the Moors of Seville chose Mohammed Abu'-l'-Kasim to be their *Kadi-l-jamah* or chief judge, when the Ummeyah dynasty was destroyed. The most celebrated of these magistrates were *Nuño Rasura, Lain Calvo*, and others who figure in old historical ballads. At length Fernan Gonzalez shook off the yoke of Leon, and in him the title of "*Conde de Castilla*" became hereditary, and a "Count" was then equivalent to an independent sovereign. Thus as among the Jews the age of the law preceded the age of the monarchy. His granddaughter Nuña married Sancho el Mayor of Navarre, whose son, Ferdinand I. of Castile, united in 1067 the kingdoms of Leon and Castile, by marrying Sancha, sole daughter of Bermudo III. See 'E. S.' xxvi. 63.

When Alonzo VI., in 1085, raised Toledo to the rank of capital, disputes of precedence arose between Burgos and its rival, which were only compromised in 1349 by Alonzo XI., who directed Burgos to speak first in Cortes, saying that he would speak for Toledo. The kings of Castile, by removing their court from Burgos, cut away the sources of its prosperity, which the invasion completed. The population has decayed from 50,000 to 12,000 ; but still Burgos is venerable-looking, dull, damp, and cold, with a true character about it of a genuine old Gothic Castilian city, and those who dwell in it are also *Castellanos rancios y viejos* (see p. 720). Its chief support arises from the traffic of travellers going to Madrid. It contains 14 parishes, and is placed on the Arlanzon, over which there are three stone bridges. A smaller stream, *El Pico*, which is divided into water-courses, here called *Esquevas*, traverses the streets, which are thus cleansed and freshened. Burgos has an *audiencia* which was carved in 1835, out of the *chancilleria* of Valladolid, a public library, *museo*, theatre, and wretched *cuna*. Its cheese, the *quesu de Burgos*, is very much renowned in Spain, but those who know Stilton and Parmesan will think it better suited to hungry Sancho Panza's taste than to theirs.

The French entered Burgos for the first time Nov. 10, 1808, which is the epoch of its ruin : the whole Spanish army, which unfortunately was placed under the incompetent Belveder, having turned and fled at the opening charge of the bold invaders, who did not lose 50 men. Now this dedecus ingens, and one of the common instances of the evil results of bad chiefs, is put forth as the *great glory* of Burgos by all modern Spanish writers, from Minaño (ii. 201), down to Mellado in 1842 (p. 133). The unresisting city was then sacked by Bessières, *a la Rio Seco ;* here, however, he was only the agent of Buonaparte in person, who wished, by an early example of terror, to intimidate all future resistance. Such was the barbarous Roman policy in Spain, where even Scipio, at the taking of Carthagena, ordered his troops to kill every living being, Καταπληξεως χαριν, in order that his

name might be a "stupifying terror" (Polyb. x. 15). Buonaparte's views were so perfectly carried out, that he thought it prudent to lament in a bulletin to be read at Paris, the "horrors which made him shudder," but which one little word *spoken* by him on the spot would have prevented. Here he remained 12 days beating the English with the paper pellets of his brain.

Burgos is the see of an archbishop having for suffragans, Pamplona, Palencia, Santander, and Tudela. The king, as *Señor de Vizcaya*, was one of the canons of the chapter, as at Leon and Toledo. Amongst those members who have risen to the tiara, are Rodrigo Borgia, Alexander VI. (see p. 427), who was archdeacon of Burgos. The cathedral, one of the finest in Spain, is unfortunately much blocked up by mean buildings ; but seen from afar, when towering over its incumbrances, it rises a superb pile of florid Gothic, with clustering filigree pinnacles. It was begun July 20, 1221, by the Bishop Mauricio, a friend of St. Ferdinand. The grand or W. entrance is placed between two towers that are crowned by spires of most delicate open stone-work, which indeed looks so much like lace, that one wonders how it has not been blown away in this stormy climate. The three portals which correspond with the three aisles, are unfortunately out of keeping ; as, in a fatal rage for modernising, some barbarian chapter removed the former deep-recessed Gothic doorways. The central one is called *de Sᵃ. Maria*, for to her this temple is dedicated ; *her* motto is worked above in the balustrade, while *her* Conception and *her* Assumption and *her* Coronation are sculptured over the entrances ; but all, whether in heaven or earth, is *hers* in this mariolatrous creed. Observe particularly the beautiful rose window, and the niche work and finials. The ground at this front is very uneven, but not unpicturesque. Look at the singular fountain and the flight of steps, as the whole jumble forms a picture by Roberts. The gate to the N. is some 30 feet above the pavement of the cathedral. This *Puerta alta* is also enriched with a recessed doorway, and ranges of statues in niches. Inside it is ascended from the transept by a highly novel and elaborate staircase, designed by Diego de Siloe, in whose details Paganism struggles with Christianity, and hippogryphs with canonised saints. Observe also the door called *La Pellegeria*, and inside, the tomb of Bernardino Gutierez, which is ascribed by some to Torregiano, and the foliage and children are truly graceful: the opposite gate is adorned with pillars and Gothic work. Observe the St. Peter, St. Paul, the Virgin and Child, and a kneeling Prelate.

The interior is, as usual, blocked up by the *Coro*, and its massy *Reja*; but the *Cimborio* is a noble octagon, rising 180 ft. from circular buttresses, and adorned with imperial and archiepiscopal arms. Felipe de Borgoña, the architect, lies buried near this his grand elevation. Si monumentum quæras circumspice. It was completed Dec. 4, 1567, at the expense of the Archb. Juan Alvarez de Toledo, son of the Duke of Alva, the original transept having fallen in March 4, 1539. The fine organs are by Juan de Argete. The walnut *Silla·del Coro* is of different periods and artists: observe the archbishop's throne. The first tier of stalls is carved from the Old Testament, but the backs are more modern. The lower tier are in the Berruguete style, and some of the figures are quite Italian. The elaborate *Reja*, the work of Jⁿ·Bᵃ·de Celma, was given in 1602, by Cardl. Zapata; and there is good Gothic work on the *Respaldos del Coro*, but the *Trascoro* has been modernised with incongruous Corinthian, and in the same bad taste; a Gothic portal was removed, and one of a Greek character substituted. The *Reja* of the transept was wrought in 1723 for the Archb. M. F. Navarrete,

by a lay monk named Pedro Martinez; but these railings, beautiful in themselves, over-imprison the cathedral. The high altar ranks as a *Capilla Real*, because here lie buried some royal corpses. Observe the figure of Doña Beatriz holding a tablet. The *Retablo* is composed of the classical orders, with the Salominic or twisted spiral pillars, and was put up by Archb. Vela in 1575: the carved figures are somewhat lengthy. The emphatic image, that of the Virgin, was wrought by Miguel de Ancheta of Pamplona. This grand *Skreen* is the work of the brothers Rodrigo and Martin de la Aya or Haya, 1577-93. Observe tree of the Saviour's genealogy, which winds up like ivy. Unfortunately many of the figures have been mutilated, and replaced by inferior hands. The magnificent silver *custodia* was plundered by the French: still, however, there exist six candelabra of the finest plateresque art, which on grand occasions are placed before the high altar. Inquire also for *La Cruz grande de las Processiones*, a superb work of Enrique de Arphe.

The various chapels of this cathedral deserve close inspection, as being full of good sculpture, tombs, and painted glass. The grandest of all is that *del Condestable*, which was erected as the burial-place of the Velasco family, the hereditary Constables of Castile. This rich Gothic *Capilla* is as large as some churches, and is admirable inside and outside; indeed its pinnacles or *agujas* form a charming cluster, and correspond with the spires. The entrance is very striking. First observe the solid buttress, piers, and wreathed pillars, enriched with niche work, and children supporting carvings under glorious canopies. The white stone forms an admirable material for admirable sculpture. The subjects are the Agony of the Saviour; the Bearing the Cross; the Crucifixion, which is the best; the Resurrection and Ascension. The engrailed edges of the archway form a rich lace-like frame, under which the light, simple, and cheerful chapel is seen, with its tombs and heraldic decorations. Before the *Retablo* reposes the founder Pedro Hernandez de Velasco, obt. 1492, and his wife Maria Lopez de Mendoza, obt. 1500, at whose feet lies a dog, emblem of her fidelity. These fine tombs were sculptured in Italy in 1540, the costumes, armour, lace-work, and details deserve inspection. Next observe the lofty and superb *reja*, which is crowned on high by Santiago. This railing is indeed a masterpiece of Christobal de Andino, 1523, a native of Burgos; now, alas! it is dimmed by age and neglect, but what must it have been in all its freshness, when first revealing to Burgos the glories of the *Renaissance.* Observe the lock and the kneeling figures holding a shield, which are quite à l'antique. Among other precious objects are a block of polished jasper weighing 200 cwt; a beautiful *Purificacion* in the *Retablo;* but the statues of *San Sebastian* and Sⁿ⁻ Jeronimo, said to be by Becerra, are more admired than they deserve. The carved stalls are good. The much lauded picture of the Magdalen with auburn hair is here erroneously ascribed to Leonardo de Vinci; at all events it is a good Lombard picture. The *Sacristia* which adjoins contains some old church plate, *e. g. cetros* or silver staves, pixes, incensaries, a good chalice and cross by Juan D'Arphe (see on these matters pp. 125, 632). Observe also a Virgin in ivory and ebony in a pearl-ornamented niche. To the l. of this chapel is the grand tomb of Juan de Orteaga Velasco, abbot of Sⁿ⁻ Quirce, obt. 1559. Observe the Cherubs, Caryatides, Conception of the Virgin, and Baptism in the Jordan. Among other sepulchres in the chapel *Sᵃ⁻ Ana,* is that of Archb. Luis de Acuña Osorio, who finished one of the towers; the effigy is a portrait. Observe the statues of the cardinal virtues. The altar is excellent Gothic. The *Retᵒ⁻* contains the meeting of Sⁿ⁻ Joaquin and Sᵃ⁻ Ana, the parents of

the Virgin. Observe an elaborate genealogy, and a fine Florentine picture of the Madonna with a child on her knee attended by St. John and St. Joseph.

The chapel of Santiago is the *parroquia* of the cathedral, and the *Retᵒ⁻* with the mounted tutelar is good: in its *Sacristia* are two superb cinquecento sepulchres of the Archbᵖ⁻ Juan Cabeza de Vaca, 1512, and of his brother Don Pedro. In the centre of the chapel lies the Archbᵖ⁻ Juan de Villacreeses, arrayed in pontificalibus. Observe the costume of the two recumbent figures of the Escalona family, and of the Lesmes de Astudilla, with the sculpture representing the Presentation of the Virgin, Sᵗ⁻ John, and Santiago. In the adjoining *Cᵃ⁻ de Sⁿ⁻ Enrique* is a magnificent Italian marble sepulchre, with a kneeling figure in bronze of the prelate and founder Enrique de Paralta y Cardeñas, 1679. Observe the carving of the stalls, the *Atril* and bronze eagle. In the *Cᵃ⁻ de la Visitacion* lies Alonzo de Cartagena, who in 1435 succeeded his father as archbishop; also San Juan de Sahagun, clad as a monk, with a book at his feet; an admirable piece of minute art. In this chapel are six pictures of the life of Christ, by an old German artist. Inquire for the image of Nᵃ⁻ Sᵃ⁻ de Oca, on a throne, with the child holding an apple, as this is the group carried about for public adoration. On page 125 of the *Puerta del Perdon* are 2 grand statues of the Saviour conceived like Sebⁿ⁻ del Piombo, with the legend, "Ego sum principium et finis; alpha et omega:" by him also is the picture in the *Cᵃ⁻ de la Presentacion,* the second to the r. on entering from the W., and one of the finest paintings in Old Castile. In it the Virgin, larger than life and full length, is seated with the Infant, who gives benediction : the child is somewhat hard and stiff. This masterpiece is here erroneously ascribed to Michael Angelo. It was presented to the chapel by the founder, a Florentine named

Moci. The old *Retablos* are concealed by modern trumpery; observe, however, the figures of Sᵃ· Casilda, and a saint on horseback. Here is the tomb of Jacobo de Bilbao, the first chaplain of the chapel; his head is fine; the other details are in a truly plateresque and Berruguete style: equally rich is the door of the *Sacristia*. Observe also the organ and balustrade, and the tomb of Alonzo Diaz de Lerma, nephew to Moci; the head drapery and sarcophagus are finely sculptured: the medallions on the sepulchre of Gonzalo Diaz de Lerma are not so good. The window of this chapel is large and grandiose. In the next capilla *La del Cristo en agonia* is a Crucifixion by Mateo Cerezo, the Vandyke of Spain, but the colouring is brown and foxy, a common fault with this master. The *Capilla de Sᵃ· Tecla* offers a grand specimen of churrigueresque to lovers of gilt gingerbread.

Next visit the *Sala Capitular*, which has some bad pictures, but a good *artesonado* roof. In the Pieza de Juan "*El Cuchiller*," the carver, is the armed effigy of that gallant knight who pawned his clothes to procure a supper for Henrique III., who had no money to buy one, and this while the Archbishop of Toledo was giving a grand supper, at which the king went in disguise: see for particulars Mariana xix. 14. But a makeshift menage distinguishes every house in Spain, from the venta to the palace, in which, among the other necessaries wanting, that of a well-stocked larder is the foremost. The queen, like all her subjects, lives from day to day and from hand to mouth, for when night sets in nothing but a glass of water is ever to be found under royal or pauper roof. *Cosas de España :* Σπανια, *i. e.* want, hunger, destitution. The adjoining *Sacristia* is churrigueresque, with a ceiling coloured like a china dish. Inquire for a fine Florentine table of *Pietre Commesse*, and particularly for *El Cofre del Cid*, the worm-eaten old chest, which, *como cuenta la historia* (see

his ' *Cronica*,' chr. xc.), he filled with sand, and then telling the Jews Rachel and Bidas that it contained gold and jewels, raised a loan on the truly Spanish security. Now matters are entirely reversed, and unless universal fame wrongs Señor Mendizabal, a Spanish Jew premier "does" the Christian money lenders. But the honest *Cid* did not repudiate; he, incredible as it may now seem, actually repaid both principal and interest. Oh, *rare* Cid! *Honra de España*. He moreover was grieved at being reduced to such shifts by his king's ingratitude.

> *Oh necesidad infame*
> *A cuantos honrados fuerças*
> *A que por salir de ti*
> *Hagan mil cosas mal hechas!*

The *Sacristia vieja* contains poor portraits of prelates of this cathedral, with quaint *letreros* or labels; here also are some good walnut carvings of Pedro Martinez, 1723. This place is used as a *Favissa* or store-room for the damaged carved images of gods and goddesses. Now pass into the beautiful cloisters, which, like the chapel of Sᵃ· Catalina, are placed on an irregular level. Observe particularly the curious old pointed work at the entrance, and a grand doorway carved in oak, with a noble pannel of a crowned king. The head of a monk, from which the outer rim of the arch springs, is said to be the bust of San Francisco, and at all events is a fine thing. In the cloisters observe the windows, staircases, and the tomb of Diego de Santander, obt. 1533, which has an exquisite alto relievo of the Virgin and Child; remark also the sepulchres of Gaspar de Illescas and Pedro Sar de Ruilobo, with a dead Saviour. Observe a group of four crowned figures on the corner shaft, near the tomb of Francisco de Mena, and the *Urna* of Gonzalo de Burgos, an eminent lawyer, and the curious *Retᵒ·* in the corner, dedicated to Sⁿ· Geronimo, with mediæval sculpture. The dates of the tombs range from the 14th to the 16th century.

Next ascend the castle hill, looking on the way at the ancient church of *Sa. Gadea* (Agueda), which was one of the three *Iglesias Juraderas*, or churches of purgation by adjuration (see *Leon,* p. 609, and *Avila,* p. 806). The touchstone of truth is a lock *el cerrojo,* which is called *del* Cid, because on it he obliged Alonzo VI. to swear twice that he had no hand in his brother Sancho's assassination at *Zamora* (see p. 586), which the king never forgave. So Callipus was made to purge himself by oath in the temple of Ceres and Proserpine, when suspected of having plotted the life of Dion (Plut. in Dion.). When this practice was abolished in Spain by Isabella, in the *Leyes de Toro,* the Bp. Pascual de Ampudia caused the lock to be affixed up out of reach, either to preserve it as an antiquity, or to nail it, in terrorem, as a forged coin is on a counter. All who wished to clear themselves used to *touch* it, *tango* aras et numina testor (Æn. xii. 201), and then kiss their thumb (see our remarks, p. 124). Something of this form exists in the Spanish complimentary phrase, *Beso a Vmd.* la mano. The lower classes now, when taking an oath, often close their hand and raise the thumb, which they kiss. Such is the import of the old Highland song, " There's *my thumb,* I'll ne'er beguile thee."

The interior of S*a.* Gadea has been plundered, and was abominably modernized in 1832, when the old *Retablos,* &c. were carted out. Observe, however, the baptismal font, the tomb of the chantor Alonzo Delgadillo, and the statues of the Virgin and St. Peter.

Hence ascending the hill we reach the triumphant arch erected by Philip II. to Fernan Gonzalez, in the Doric style, with ball-tipped pyramids : this " High Street," or *Calle Alta,* as being nearest to the protecting castle, was the first inhabited when Burgos became a city, and here the aristocracy lived. The site of the Cid's house was cleared in 1771, and is now marked

by pillars ; it is a small space for so great a man, but his glory fills the world : now all is neglected and going fast to ruin, for the heroic ages of Spain are past, and such memorials of these genuine Old Castilians shame the modern mediocrities. The streets of the ancient parish of S*u.* Martin, higher up, were entirely rased by the invader, whose quiver here was indeed an open sepulchre, for now a *Campo Santo* or public cemetery has been laid out, where graves replace houses once warm with life. An old gate preserves its Moorish arch. Above, the hill of the castle comes to a point, and beneath it nestles the closely packed town. The view from the heights is extensive ; now the pinnacled cathedral is really seen ; beyond in the distances, to the N., are the monasteries of *Miraflores* and *Cerdeña,* while to the E., outside the town, rises the royal convent of *Las Huelgas,* with the green *Isla* and *Vega* stretching beyond.

The positions which the Duke occupied were on the opposite hill, beginning at S*n.* Miguel, on the l. of the road to Vitoria, and extending to S*n.* Pedro. The castle was the original palace of the early kings, and here took place the bridal of the Cid, and that of our Edward I. with Eleanor of Castile ; in it also Don Pedro the Cruel was born. Now paltry and hors de combat, in those days it was a true Moorish *Alcazor,* and was much improved by Isabella, Charles V., and Philip II. The state-rooms were destroyed by an accidental fire in 1736, which was allowed to burn out, not a creature in Burgos even attempting to extinguish it. The ruins, beautiful even in decay, were used up by the French to erect fortifications, which they themselves destroyed when Reille retired, June 14, 1813, before the advancing Duke. Then the enemy mined the cathedral, which only escaped, like the Alhambra, by accident, from the train having failed, while by a premature explosion many hundreds of the engineers were " hoisted into the air by their own petards," in the sport of a retributive Nemesis.

This castle is memorable for the Duke's repulse in 1812, after his victory of Salamanca, which had driven Soult out of Seville, and Joseph out of Madrid, when their conqueror would have pursued them into Valencia, had not the "service been stinted and neglected" by both English and Spanish governments. Everybody who was to have co-operated with him failed: Gen¹· Maitland was sent to the eastern coast too late, and then did nothing, while the Spaniards were routed at Castalla. Thus his plans were deranged, and it now only remained to him, by taking Burgos, to open communications with Gallicia: he divided his army, and leaving Hill at Madrid, ordered Ballasteros to place himself at Alcaraz, between the French and the capital ; but this worthy co-operator, by refusing to obey a *foreigner*, left the flank open to Soult, who advanced on Madrid with such overwhelming numbers, that Hill was obliged to evacuate Madrid, and the Duke to raise the siege of Burgos. Thus were the results of the British campaign sacrificed to a vicious *Espa‑ ñolismo* (see p. 458). Previously the Duke had been forced to sue the citadel, as at Badajoz, "in formâ pauperis," "beseeching, not breaching," as Picton said. "What can be done?" as he wrote before setting out (Disp. Aug. 23, 1812); "what can be done for this *lost nation?* as for raising men or supplies, or taking one measure to enable them to carry on the war, *that is out of the question.* I shudder when I reflect on the enormity of the task which I have undertaken, with inadequate powers myself to do anything, and without assistance of any kind from the Spaniards, or, I may say, from any *individual* of the Spanish *nation*," even nation, "for the enthusiasm of the people spent itself in vain boasting" (Disp. Dec. 24, 1811). Yet he did not despair: no time was now to be lost. He marched for Burgos Sept. 1, 1812,

expecting to be joined by the Gallician army under Castaños, which, 35,000 strong on paper, arrived, after infinite delays, only 11,000, weak, "and wanting in everything, at the critical moment," while Madrid would not furnish the means of moving one gun ; and such was the neglect of our home government, that the Duke arrived at Burgos on the 19th with only three eighteen-pounders, and scarcely any ammunition. A few guns were sent him *after* the siege was raised! The Spaniards also had deceived him by reporting that the castle was very weak, but the first glance revealed to him its formidable strength, and it was defended by a splendid garrison under the gallant Dubreton. "This most difficult job is not one to be carried by any trifling means," said the Duke: he, however, gained the heights of *Sⁿ. Miguel* by assault, and on the 22nd could and ought to have taken the castle at the breach below the church *Sᵃ. Maria la Blanca*, had the field‑officer obeyed his instructions. The attack of the 28th, on the side of *San Pedro*, having also failed, he was reduced to sap and mine ; but on hearing of Soult's advance, he seized the nick of time, and instantly, Oct. 21, filed off by night, along the Arlanzon, under the guns of the castle, and thus gained a day's march on the French, and brought his army safely to Ciudad Rodrigo, the enemy, in spite of his vast superiority of numbers, never venturing to attack him (see Rueda, 621). Now Señor Toreno criticizes his operations, as the pedant Phormio lectured Hannibal on the art of war; blinking at the same time the misconduct of Ballesteros, the *real* author of the failure (Disp. Nov. 2, 1812): call ye that backing your friends ?

Burgos is shaped in an irregular semi-circle, with large portions of the old walls remaining on the river front. The grand gate *de Sᵃ. Maria*, for here everything breathes female worship, is massy and battlemented, and her image crowns the pile. Charles V. added the statues of Burgalese Worthies, which are grouped around his own, to wit, Don Diego Porcelos, Fernan Gonzalez, the Cid, Nuño Rasura, and Lain Calvo. The river Arlanzon flows through planted walks to the *Isla*, where the French built a stone bridge, which the patriotic natives destroyed after the evacuation, because the work of an enemy (see San Lucar, p. 229). The river flows down to the *Vega*, while higher up is the *Espolon* or Esplanada, which with its gardens were laid out by the Mˢ· de Villena. The heavy statues of Fernan Gonzalez, Alonzo III., Henrique III., and Ferdinand I., were placed there by Charles III. The modern row of houses on the Espolon contrasts with the gloomy half fortress mansions in the Calle-alta, San Lorenzo, Avellanos, Sⁿ· Juan, and older quarters. The architect may select as good specimens of the earlier mansions, La Casa del Cordon, the house of the Constable, with its towers, arms, and the rope over the portal. Observe the enormous armorial sculpture of this powerful family at the back of their chapel in the ca-' thedral. Their palace was gutted by the invaders, by whom almost all the family portraits, once the most complete series in Spain, were destroyed, and ever since dilapidation has prevailed. Those *Azulejos* and *Artesonados* which escaped show that the whole edifice originally must have had a Moorish character. The *patio*, with its galleries, and arms of Feria, Mendoza, and Haro, is still striking. To the l. of the *Puerta del Sarmental*, and opposite the cathedral-cloister, is the archiepiscopal palace; look at the portals of No. 34, *La Llana de afuera:* No. 4, *Cᵉ· Avellanos :* No. 7, *Cᵉ· Sⁿ· Lorenzo;* observe the cornice under the roof. In the *Cᵉ· de la Calera* is the Casa de Miranda, with superb *Patio*. The windows, portals, and cornices of these old Burgalese residences deserve notice. The irregular brick-built *Plaza Mayor* was designed by Ventura Rodriguez in 1783. Some poor shops are ranged under the arcades, into which penniless loungers, cloaked in thread-bare *Capas*, look wistfully. In the centre is a bronze statue of Charles III., by one Domingo Urquiza, who has metamorphosed the princely Bourbon into a perriwigged baboon. Visit the Town Hall, or *Casa del Ayuntamiento*, not for the poor portraits of judges, kings, queens, or a straddling one of the Cid, but because his ashes were moved from their original resting-place, and placed here in a walnut tea-urn in a paltry chapel! where also is a sort of *concepcion*, attributed of course to Murillo.

Among the churches visit the Gothic *San Esteban*, with a rich façade. Inside the elegant arch with gallery above it, the rose window, the monuments, pulpit, and bas reliefs of the Last Supper, form an artistical group. The Dominician *Sⁿ· Pablo* has a noble cloister, with tombs in the Berruguete style, and the Gothic arches of the transept are fine; here were the sepulchres of the Gallos, 1560-93; of the Maluendas, 1562-74; of the Bishop Pablo de Sᵃ· Maria, his wife and children, he himself having been a converted Jew. A married Roman Catholic Bishop, and one of Jewish origin, is certainly not a thing of Spain, whatever our Protestant Dr. Alexander may be at Jerusalem. The Gothic Benedictine *Sⁿ· Juan* contained fine tombs of the Torquemada and Castro Mogica families.

Burgos, like Valencia, p. 449, has a miraculous self-navigating crucifix, called *El Cristo de Burgos*. According to the '*España Sagrada*' (xxvii. 495), a Burgalese merchant found the figure steering itself, like Santiago (see p. 662), in the Bay of Biscay; being placed in a convent it worked so many miracles, and attracted so many offerings, that the Archb. wished to move it to the cathedral. It raised ten men at once from the dead, and extended its arms to Queen Isabella, just as the polite statue of Memnon bowed to Sabina, wife of Adrian. Previously to the invasion the chaplain used to tell the populace that its beard grew as regularly as his own. Dii te Dama-sippe Deæque *vérum* ob consilium do-nent tonsore! A French Bishop bit off its toe, which he carried home as a relic, just as that of Pyrrhus was kept as a cure for the spleen (Pliny, 'N. H.' vii. 2). Marshal Bessières, bred a barber boy, laughed at the beard, but respected the remaining toes, for he only carried off a crown of gold which had been offered by the C⁰· de Ureña, just as Dionysius only relieved Escu-lapius of his golden beard. Long be-fore, the unpretending Burgalese image had shaken the diadem off its head, which was placed in consequence at its feet, like the golden pateræ of Juno (Livy vi. 4; Cicero de N. Div. i. 34); and like others "removed" by the aforesaid Dionysius (Cic. de N. D. iii. 34). This crucifix was carved by Nicodemus, out of supernatural ma-terials; and so none could tell of what wood the Lycæan Apollo was wrought (Paus. ii. 9. 7). To us the former appeared, after close inspection, to be graven out of Sorian pine, and either by Becerra or Hernandez: still the Burgos connoisseurs prefer Nicodemus. Be this as it may, as a work of art it is admirable, and the expression of suf-fering in the head drooping over the shoulder is very fine; nor will the lace petticoat displease our fair readers. When we last were shown this cruci-fix it was covered with curtains as at Valencia (see p. 443).

Burgos was very rich in these mi-raculous images, being so near Val-ladolid, the great school of Castilian sculpture. Florez (E. S. xxvii. 518) describes one in *La Trinidad*, a church which the mob were damaging in 1366, when a stone fell and struck the figure's nose, which bled copiously: so in ancient days four images at Cassena *sweated* blood for 24 hours without ceasing; so did the Cumæan Apollo (Cic. de Div. i. 43).

The Franciscan convent *was* a most exquisite pile. It was founded in 1256 by Ramon Bonifaz, the French admiral who broke the bridge of boats at Seville; but his tomb and his works were demolished by his invad-ing countrymen, who did not even re-spect that *rara avis inter Gallos*, a vic-torious sailor. They also destroyed the glorious Gothic *Trinitarios*, just, however, leaving one fragment alone, as a specimen of former beauty, which since has been pulled down by the Spaniards. In *Sᵃ· Ana* are some fine tombs of bishops, especially one under an elegant niche or arch, and another which is an isolated sarcophagus. The church *Sⁿ· Gil* is full of Gothic sepulchres; observe that of the De Cas-tros, 1529. In the *Calle de Sⁿ· Juan*, once the residence of grandees and now of paupers, is the *Hospicio*. Ob-serve the façade and porches, also the machicolated gate of Sⁿ· Juan, to the l. In *San Nicolas* are the tombs of the Polanco family, 1412-1503, by whom the high altar and skreen were given. In *San Lesmes* is a good re-tablo in the *Capilla Mayor*, with ex-cellent sculpture, relating to Sᵃ· Isabel and Sⁿ· Juan, inscribed MRS, *i. e.* Martines, by whom it was executed in 1560, as well as the tomb of Juan de S. Martin.

Near the *Isla*, a short walk below Burgos, is the celebrated Cistertian nunnery of *Santa Maria la Real*, com-monly called *Las Huelgas*, because built in some "Gardens of Recreation" which belonged to Alonzo VIII., who founded it to gratify the wish of his wife Leonora, daughter of our Henry II. The pious work was begun in 1180, and was rewarded by the victory of Las Navas de Tolosa. It presents a wall-enclosed aggregate of ignoble buildings of different periods, granges, offices, &c., which cluster around and block up the convent. This, once a museum of art and wealth, was ravaged by the invaders; and recently a hospital attached to it, and destined for sick pilgrims going to Compostella, has been suppressed. The abbess was a princess palatinate, and styled by "the

Grace of God," and the nunnery was nullius diocesis, possessing more than fifty villages. Passing through many *patios* to the chapel, observe the Gothic front, with a statue of the Conception, raised by Ferd. and Isabella: here also are ranged many old sepulchres. Inside there are two cloisters, which resemble those of Amalfi and Calabria, in the form of the round-headed arches, *obra de los Godos,* and the grouped pillars and Norman-like capitals. In the *Coro* of the chapel is the tomb of the founder, but this and other monuments are imperfectly seen through the gratings, as the interior is in strict *clausura,* and no males are allowed to enter. This was the Sᵗ· George's chapel of the early kings of Spain, and here Sᵗ· Ferdinand knighted himself; here his son Alonzo El Sabio conferred, in 1254, that honour on our Edward I.; here the gallant Alonzo XI. kept his vigil, and knighted and crowned himself; here was the articulated statue of Santiago, which, on some occasions, placed the crown on the head of Spanish monarchs. Night and day solemn services were chanted over royal ashes, until the invaders converted the chapel into a stable, when a portion only of the superb carvings of the quire escaped. Observe a curious old painting of the victory at *las Navas de Tolosa,* and a gilt pulpit. In the interior is the chapel of *Belem* (Bethelem), which is built in a transition style, between the Gothic and Moorish; indeed the arches and *lienzos* might belong to the mosque of Cordova. Now this Escorial of Old Castile is hastening to decay: for past glories consult ' E. S.' xxvii. 574, and ' Ponz,' xii. 61.

Burgos, being a town of passage, was constantly made the quarters of advancing or retiring armies, hence the dilapidation of sacred edifices, and, what is worse, by Roman Catholics; for our Protestant Duke directed, by a general order, that " churches were not to be used by troops without permission of the inhabitants and clergy, and when used the utmost care to be taken of the

sacred vessels and those articles which serve for religious purposes; neither horses nor other animals were to be put into churches, on any account whatever."

EXCURSIONS NEAR BURGOS.

Every one should devote a day to a pilgrimage to *Miraflores,* and the tomb of the Cid. Crossing the river and turning to the l., the road soon ascends the hills, and the Carthusian convent is seen at a distance of two miles, rising, with its nave and buttresses, like Eton College Chapel. It was built in 1441, on the site of a palace of Henrique III. by his son Juan II., for a royal burial-place; having been accidentally burnt in 1452, it was restored by Henrique IV., and finished in 1488 by Isabella, after designs of Juan de Colonia, in the finest style of the florid Gothic: she also raised the magnificent *Retablo,* the *Coro* and the sepulchre of her parents, which are unequalled in Spain or elsewhere. The artist was *El Maestro Gil,* father of the celebrated Diego de Siloe; he was employed for four years on the work, which was completed in 1493, and well might Philip II.—a good judge of art —exclaim when he saw it, " *We* have done nothing at the Escorial." Here lie Juan II. and his second wife Isabella, with his son the Infante Alonzo; their alabaster sepulchres baffle pen and pencil alike. Nothing can surpass the execution of the superb costumes, animals, ornaments, enriched sides, saints, evangelists, etc. The royal effigies were placed on each side of the Retablo, which was richly decorated with subjects from our Saviour's life. It is truly grievous to behold the wanton mutilations of the invading soldiery. The *Silleria del Coro* was carved by Martin Sanchez, in 1480; the chapel, as usual in *Cartuja* convents, is divided into three portions—the outer one for the people, the middle for the lay monks, *Legos,* and the innermost for the *Sacerdotes.* The painted glass is of the fifteenth century; the walls were framed with Berruguete shells, and festoons for pictures of the life of the Virgin. The splendid oratory of Juan II., given him by Martin V., was carried off by the invaders, together with all the fine Florentine pictures, and those relating to the life of San Bruno, by Diego de Leyva, who died here a monk, in 1637. They next proceeded to ravage the gardens and burial-ground; now a few cypresses, sad mourners, remain in the weed-encumbered cloister, while in the angles are the frames from whence the paintings were torn.

Continuing the ride over bald downs, *San Pedro de Cerdeña* appears in a wooded dell, enclosed by long walks. The façade was modernised in 1739. Over the portal the Cid, mounted on Babieca, cuts down Moors *à la Santiago;* the gallant war steed was honoured in life and death, like Copenhagen, the Waterloo charger of our Cid, for none ever rode Babieca after her master departed; and when she followed him her grave was prepared before the entrance of the monastery by Gil Diaz, one of the Campeador's most faithful followers.

The French arrived here Aug. 10, 1808, and gutted the buildings, and burnt one of the most curious archives and libraries of Spain; fortunately, many of the old muniments had been printed by a monk of this convent, whose work is now of such authority as to be admitted as evidence in courts of law. Let every book collector secure the ' *Antigüedades de España*,' Fro. de Berganza, 2 vols. folio, Mad. 1719-21. This monastery was the first ever founded in Spain for the Benedictine order, and was raised by the Princess Sancha, in 537, in memorial of her son Theodoric, who died while out hunting, at the fountain *Cara digna,* whence the name *Cerdeña.* The convent was sacked by the Moor Zephe, in 872, who killed 200 monks; but it was restored in 899 by Alonzo II. of Leon, and the blood of the murdered friars always issued out every year at the anniversary of their martyrdom quite fresh and miraculous, like that of San Januario at Naples; and all this was pronounced to be perfectly correct by Sixtus IV., in 1473; this flux, however, ceased in 1492, when their manes were satisfied by the final downthrow of the infidel.

Then, however, by way of compensation, the body of Sⁿ· Sisebuto, twenty-ninth abbot, began to work such miracles that the peasants prayed to him as their intercessor with God, and also offered money at his sepulchre, at which cripples were regularly cured (Florez, ' E. S.,' xxvii. 238). The ravages during the war were partially restored by a monk named Bernardo Zubia Ur, of Bilbao. The singular register book *el Libro Becerro,* of the date 1092, was saved by a monk named Miguel Garcia, who happened to be consulting it when the invaders arrived (comp. p. 551). The Benedictines, in 1823, unfortunately restored the chapel with tawdry reds and yellows, and picked out the pillars in black and white. Among the few inscriptions that escaped the French was that on the tomb of Sancha, obiit æra 580; they however mutilated the sepulchre of Theodoric. The old cloisters have also been modernised, but some of the original short pillars and capitals may be traced, and a slab still marks the spot where the 200 monks bled annually.

One word on the Cid, now we stand near his grave. Rodrigo Ruy Diaz, of Vibar, where he was born in 1026, is the Prince, the Champion of Spain, *El Cid Campeador,* and the Achilles and Æneas of Gotho-Spanish epos, for no incident of his Condottieri *Guerrillero* life is unrecorded in song, that form of primitive history; thus, as Schlegel says, he is worth a whole library for the understanding the spirit of his age and the character of the old *Castellano,* the chatelain and champion of Christendom, of whom this doughty Palatine was the personification, as he felt himself to be to the backbone, *Soy Don*

Rodrigo de Vibar, Castellano à las derechas. Cast in the stern mould of a disputed creed and hostile invasion, when men fought for their God and their fatherland, for all they had or hoped for in this world and the next, the Cid possessed the virtues and vices of the mediæval Spaniard, and combined the daring personal valour, the cool determination and perseverance of the sledgehammering, crushing Northman, engrafted on the subtle perfidy and brilliant chivalry of the Oriental. Like an Alaric or Tamerlane, he was terrible to his enemies, kind and generous to his friends, charitable to the poor, liberal and submissive to the priest, and thus presented that strange mixture, which still marks Spanish and Arab character, of harshness and benevolence, cruelty and generosity, rapacity and munificence : for darker traits we must consult the Moorish annalists, since the early Spanish *histories*, being compiled exclusively by clergymen, naturally painted in a couleur de rose, not of blood, their champion, by whom infidel kings were destroyed and their temples overturned, while Christian altars were endowed with the spoil.

The '*Poema del Cid*' was written in the twelfth century ; and this, the epic of Spain, is thus, like the ' Iliad,' at once the earliest and finest work in the language, and is stamped with a poetry of heroism. Even then its Achilles, the Cid was spoken of with pride and affection, being already, like Nelson, the property of his whole nation, El mio Cid, *my* Cid. " He who was born in a *good* hour "—" he who in an auspicious moment girded on sword ;" and he feels himself to be the honour of his country, " *Soy el Cid, Honra de España*," which he is always ready to prove by his good sword. The leading events of his life have been handed down in an unbroken series of Spanish and Moorish writers ; Alonzo el Sabio, in the thirteenth century, speaks of him as already the hero of many early ballads. Conde and Gayangos find the

Arabic authors tallying exactly with the Spanish in dates and facts : they paint him, as he was to them, a fierce, perfidious, and merciless enemy. The type of the Cid is Oriental, and Biblical history abounds in parallel chiefs who raised themselves to power ; such were Jephthah, Rezin, David, &c. And as the latter was persecuted by Saul, so the Cid was by Alonzo : and both being compelled to carve out their fortunes with their own good sword, gathered around them " vain and light persons" (Judges ix. 4), " people in debt and discontented " (1 Sam. xxii. 2) ; and just the sort of desperate characters with nothing to lose and everything to gain, who are so well described by Sallust (B.C. 14) as forming the recruits of the radical patriot Catiline.

Again, in semi-barbarous nations and periods agriculture and war are the only professions which do not degrade. The Iberian of old, like the Pindarree of Hindostan, loved the joys of battle, the excitement of the *raid*, and the possession of red gold ; while the chase, that mimic war, with love, the guitar, and personal decoration filled up his brief hours of peace. These elements still exist, and form the basis of Spanish character : thus to this day they are personally brave, fond of adventure, and prodigal of life ; and never has a Sertorius, a Hafssun, a Cid, wanted gallant followers. So in our times the Minas and Zumalacarreguys have enacted deeds which only require the distance of centuries to appear almost equally fabulous ; but these very qualities, admirable for predatory forays, ambuscades, and a desultory irregular *petty war*, have always incapacitated Spain from producing a really great general, for the Great Captain is the exception, which only proves the rule (see p. 215).

There is nothing in the Cid's rise or career more strange or eventful than in those of Jephthah or David. He too was superstitious and reckless of the rights of property and the life and happiness of men : but true to his faith and king, as the Lord's anointed, while a halo of power gilded over his misdeeds. Thus during the invasion church and palace plunder, if committed by armed marshals, is to be overlooked; while, had private men done the same, it would have justly been stigmatized as robbery and sacrilege; but in those unprincipled and semi-civilized days, no disgrace was attached to bold violence, for those got who had the power, and those kept who could. Thus the conduct of David towards the people of his protector Achish is recorded but not condemned by Samuel (1, xxvii. 8), nor is the ferocity combined with perfidy of the Cid stigmatized by his clerical chroniclers. There is no doubt as to the accuracy of their general although flattering statements: thus Niebuhr, the decided sceptic of old history, considers the Cid to be a real character, and cites his ballad memoirs as early instances of records based on truth, yet hovering on the verge of fabulous times. Masdeu, however, thought fit to doubt his very existence ; but this arose from a secret pique against Florez and Risco, his rival antiquarians : and in our times Dr. Lardner, in his cyclopediac compilations, has repeated these absurd *Patrañas.* Our readers will do better to refer to the ' *Chronica del Cid,*' fol. Burgos, 1593 ; to ' *La Castilla,*' Manuel Risco, 4to., Mad.,1792 ; to the '*Romancero del Cid,*' Juan Müller, duo., Francfort, 1828, which is well fitted for the *alforjas* of the traveller. In his library at home the best place should be given to the new edition of the ' *Chronica del Cid,*' by Herr von Huber, Marburg, 1844. This, our estimated friend and able Spanish scholar, is the author of the ' *Skitzen aus Spanien,*' one of the best sketches of this original people and country. The Cid again is *the* hero of Spanish ballad poetry, the most convenient edition of which is that published in five volumes at Madrid, 1828-32, by Agustin Duran: Depping also, in 1817, printed at Leipzig a good selection,'*Samlung der besten alten*

Spanischen Romancen,' and his countryman Nicolas Böhl y Faber edited at Hamburg an excellent ' *Floresta.*' Mr. Murray's superb edition of our honoured master Lockhart's spirited translations is justly eulogized in two papers on this subject in the 'Edinburgh Review,' No. cxlvi., and 'Westminster Review,' No. lxv., in which these subjects are considered. The Cid has recently been rendered familiar to English readers in the lively volume of our friend Mr. Dennis, duo., 1845.

Suffice it now to state that the Cid, out of favour at court, was thrown on his own resources: and as the rich lands of the infidels in those days were considered fair game by the Christians, he assembled an army of bold adventurers and captured Valencia, where he ruled on his own account, and died in 1099. His body was then brought to Cerdeña, mounted on Babieca, and was placed armed on a throne, with *Tisona,* " the sparkling brand," in his hand, with which, according to legends, he soon knocked down a Jew, whose valour plucked the dead lion by the beard. Ximena, his widow, in order to keep him quiet, had him then put under ground. The still existing tomb was raised in 1272, by Alonzo el Sabio, who composed the now scarcely legible epitaph—

Belliger, invictus, famosus marte triumphis, Clauditur hoc tumulo magnus Didaci Rodericus.

The original sepulchre was erected in the site of honour, near the high altar ; but when the chapel was remodelled in 1447, the abbot, Pedro de Burgo, moved it into the *sacristia,* from whence it was turned out in 1541 ; thereupon the garrison of Burgos complained to Charles V.,who ordered the good Cid's tomb back into the chapel,whence Feb. 5, 1736, it was moved into the chapel of San Sisebuto, which was fitted up in a semi-theatrical manner, with trumpery shields, &c. Around him were interred his faithful Ximena, his two daughters, Maria Sol, queen of

Arragon, and Elvira, queen of Navarre, with their husbands; his only son, who was killed at the battle of Consuegra, together with Martin Antolinez, Pero Bermudez, and others his staunch and faithful companions, among whom was Alvar Fañez Minaya, his first cousin and fidus Achates, or, as he used to call him, his " right arm;" for he was to the Cid what Lord Hill was to the Duke. The Cid blazoned on his shield two swords crossed, Tisona and Colada, with a cross between them, enclosed with a chain.

Paltry as was this chamber of death, the Cid was not permitted to rest in it after so many movements alive and dead, for in 1808, when the French invaded Spain, " their curiosity," says Southey (Chr. of Cid, 432) was excited by nothing until they came to Burgos, and heard that *Chimene* (Ximena) was buried at Cerdeña, from which time parties were daily made to visit her tomb, and spouted passages from " Corneille," or rather from what Corneille had adapted from Spanish authors, who were to him almost what Menander was to Terence. His ' Cid ' was made up from ' *Las Mocedades del Cid* ' of Guillem de Castro, and the ' *El honrador de su Padre,*' of the Jeronomite monk J[n.] B[a.] Diamante; so the critics of the day, encouraged by the jealousy of Cardinal Richelieu, apostrophised the plagiarist by raising de Castro's ghost to reclaim his borrowed plumes. Corneille also misplaced the scene at Seville, then and for more than two centuries after in the possession of the Moors, and made the Cid always talk of Granada, a city not begun to be built for one hundred and fifty years after his death. Corneille, however, only borrowed *ideas*, and if he was a plagiarist, like Le Sage (see p. 707), he, like him, never set a Spanish gem in dross, Nihil non tetigit quod non ornavit; and thus, out of neglected or rude materials, founded the tragedy of his country among whose many illustrious names

his own shines out, and lives justly immortal.

Some of his armed compatriots, notwithstanding the high moral of the poetry which they quoted, borrowed all the church plate, while a certain M. de Salm-dyk " visita l'église dévastée," and carried off the breast-bone of the Cid and thigh-bone of " Sa Chimene" (Schep. ii. 255). The invaders next removed the old sepulchre itself to decorate their new promenade at Burgos, a theatrical affair which made even a French " *apothicaire* " sick ; what, ho, apothecary ! who in his amusing ' *Mémoires* ' (ch. 42) administers a brisk cathartic to General Thibeault, who, in the hopes, as he says, of linking his insignificance with the immortality of Rodrigo, had inscribed his name on the tomb as perpetrator of the transportation. But *El gran Lor* avenged *El mio Cid,* and fell in with this Thibeault (whom he had before trounced at Vimiero), and gave him his quietus at Aldea de Puente, Sep. 29, 1811. The Cid's sepulchre was taken back to Cerdeña in great pomp July 30, 1826; but the ashes were again to be disturbed by the march of intellect; then, when convents were sequestered, they were put into a walnut tea-urn and conveyed to the mansion-house of Burgos, a motion which does honour to the absolute wisdom of Spanish mayors and the proverbial taste of municipal corporations : requiescant in pace!

COMMUNICATIONS WITH BURGOS.

Those who arrive coming from France are advised to go to Madrid by Valladolid, Segovia, and the Escorial (see R. lxxiii., lxxv.), and thus avoid the most dreary line (R. cxiii.) through Aranda. Burgos being a central point has many diligence communications with Madrid, Valladolid, Santander, Vitoria, Logroño, and thence to Tudela, Pamplona, Zaragoza, and Barcelona.

ROUTE CXIV.—BURGOS TO
SANTANDER.

Quintaña Dueñas	.	½	
Huermeces	. . .	3	.. 4
Urbel del Castillo	. .	2½	.. 6½
Basconcillos	. . .	3	.. 9½
Llanillo	. . . .	1½	.. 11
Canduela	. . . .	2½	.. 13½
Fuenvellida	. . .	2½	.. 16
Reinosa	. . . .	1½	.. 17½
Barcena pia de concha	.	3	.. 20½
Molledo	. . . .	1	.. 21½
Cartes	. . . .	3½	.. 25
Arce	. . . . .	2	.. 27
Santander	. . .	3	.. 30

The *Catalanes* company have a diligence, and they include all the outgoings in the fare. This will take the angler into some of the finest salmon and trout fishing in Spain, as from Santander he may either turn to Bilbao and the Basque provinces, or strike to the l. to Oviedo, Lugo, and the Vierzo.

Leaving Burgos the road enters the valley of the river Urbel. *Vibar*, where the Cid was born, lies to the r., and the hills of Villadiego on the l. Next we ascend to *Urbel del Castillo*, built on La Pinza, over its trout stream. This decayed place was originally the seat of the see of Burgos; hence by the range which divides the basins of the Ebro and Pisuerga to Canduela and Reinosa. The latter is the chief town of its district. The mountains around are very lofty, and often covered with snow. This is the nucleus whence *Las Montañas de Santander* and those *de Burgos* diverge. They abound in natural, neglected, or ill-used forests of oak and chesnut. The botanist and angler should make for the environs of *Leibana*. *Potes* will be a good head quarter; it stands in the centre of four charming Swiss-like valleys, the *Val de Prado*, *Cereceda*, *Val de Baro*, and *Cillorigo*. The fishing in the Deva, Nansa, and Sal, is excellent. Potes was one of the first towns entered by Soult, who, with the Parisian guards, was welcomed with palms, but the place was forthwith sacked, and the inhabitants butchered (Schepeler, ii. 116).

The forests of Leibana are magnifi-

cent and neglected as usual, for nature supplies the Spaniard with every *raw* material, but little is the additional value conferred by his art or industry; nay, oftener the unappropriated produce is left to rot on the soil, nor are even those who would turn it to better account, allowed permission. Thus, in 1843, a proposition was made to the Minister of Marine by Messrs. Septimius Arabin and Co., for the purchase or working of the forests of Asturias for a term of 20 years. The company engaged to furnish to the State all the building timber necessary for the navy, and undertook to build whatever vessels might be required from models furnished by the minister. In order to cover their expenses, the company required a grant to be made to them of 500,000 trees. The following was the reply of the minister:—" The Spanish people duly appreciate the importance of their forests. The company desire to receive two trees for one which they will cut down for the interest of Spain; so that for the acquisition of one ship, Spain will give two to a foreign nation. The Spanish government has still the means of improving and increasing her navy without destroying her forests. The government is, however, grateful for the interest shown by the English house for the Spanish navy, and is not surprised at the feeling. Spain has for a long time had multiplied reasons to believe that a great number of nations feel an ardent wish for the diminution of the Spanish navy. As long as the present minister shall remain at the head of the Marine department, he can never listen to a proposition which can give rise to an idea similar to that which in his opinion has dictated the proposition." Meanwhile the forests of Leibana will remain in their primæval repose and natural decay, while *El Ferrol* cannot supply a spar for a cockboat; but " to boast of his strength is the national disease" of a Spanish misminister, whose words are greater than his ideas, and who will repose under his laurels, having thus proudly rejected the *foreigner*. This amusing state paper did credit to a cabinet, of which the ci-devant editor of the Madrid ' Slang' was *premier :* risum teneatis? *Reinosa* is the chief place of its mountainous district. Some of the passes to the N. W. slopes are very high : the *Portillo de Bedore* rises 3800 ft., and that de Lunada 3400 ft. above the sea level. The Ebro rises in Fontibre or Fuentes de Ebro, from a wild and rocky source. It flows 342 miles through the Rioja, and divides Arragon. *Reinosa* is a tidy hill town, with a good street and bridge: Pop^n. 1500. It is a busy place frequented by carriers, who convey across the *Puerto* the corn and wine of the plains, and bring back the iron and fish from the coasts. Santander may be called the sea-port of Madrid: many projects have been formed on *paper* to facilitate this important communication. Thus the grand canal of Castile, which was begun in 1753, and is not yet finished (see p. 640), was to connect Segovia and Burgos; next a new and shorter road was to be opened to Burgos, and now the Castile canal company and municipality of Santander propose to construct a railroad from the latter town to Reinosa, which, *if* they accomplish, will be a great benefit to central Spain (see, however, p. 779).

The fairs of July 25 and Sept. 21 at *Reinosa*, are attended by most picturesque peasants and *Pasiegas*. There is good shooting in the hills, especially in the *Montes* and *Breñas*, near Val de Arroyo, and the Dominican convent *Monte Claros*. This naturally almost impregnable country, which might have been made the Torres Vedras of Gallicia, was absurdly abandoned in 1808 by Blake, who quitted it to court defeat at Espinosa. Then Reinosa was so wantonly and dreadfully sacked by Soult, that Schepeler (ii. 39) imagined the invaders wished to leave it as a monument of the greatest horrors which they could by any means perpetrate.

Crossing the noble mountain *Puerto*, we descend, with the trout-stream, the *Besaya*. This lofty range extends about 12 leagues, and is one of the coldest in Spain. The hard rocks will, however, offer fine opportunities for English engineers to exhibit their skill in tunneling and circumventing, and afford an admirable means of sinking some of the superabundant gold of *la perfide Albion*. *Somaoz*, in the valley of *Buelna*, lies half-way between Reinosa and Santander, and the country is truly Swiss-like and alpine. The Pas is soon crossed, where the Santillana and Oviedo road joins in (see p. 707). This is the healthy country of *Las Pasiegas*, who, bursting with mountain juices, suckle the puny children of the better classes in sickly Madrid. For Santander, see R. cxvii.

ROUTE CXV.—BURGOS TO LOGROÑO.

There is a diligence over this road, which communicates with Tudela, and thence to Pamplona and Zaragoza and Barcelona. The hilly broken country continues to *Velorado*, over the mountains of Oca. In the valley Atapuerca, near Zalduendo, was fought, in 1053, the battle between Ferd. I. of Castile and his brother Garcia of Navarre, who was killed and buried at Najera: thus Rioja was annexed to Castile. Mariana (ix. 4) details the punic perfidy and Iberian strategics of these fratricidal princes.

The district of *la Rioja* lies between Burgos, Soria, and Alava, and is so called from its river La Ojʼa, El Rio Ojʼa, which rises in the bills of San Lorenzo. The rich valley is in the shape of an S, being some 24 L. in length, with an unequal breadth, varying from 8 to 10 L. It is divided into high, *alta*, and low, *baja*. The former runs from Villafranca de Montes de Oca to Logroño, and the latter from Logroño to Agreda, and are divided by the chain which separates the basins of the Ebro and Duero. The whole extent is about 270 square leagues, with a pop^{n.} of 25,000. The soil is fertile, but most slovenly cultivated; and this district, devoid alike of pleasure or interest, may fairly be blotted out of every traveller's map. Consult for details ' *Memorias Politicas*,' Eugenio Larruga, vol. xxvii. 206; and ' *La Descripcion de la Rioja*,' Juan Josef de Salazar.

S⁰. Domingo de la Calzada, of the " causeway," stands on the Oca, and contains some 5000 souls, and shares with *Calahorra* in the dignity of a bishopric, like Jaen and Baeza, and our Bath and Wells. The cathedral, of a simple, massy, early Gothic, was begun in 1180 by Alonzo VIII., and finished in 1235, but was much injured by fire in 1825. The *Coro*, high altar, and chapel of the tutelar, are in the Berruguete style. This St. Domenick was not the bloody inquisidor, but an Italian, who was sent to Spain in 1050 by Pope Damaso II., as an exorciser, at the request of the peasants, who were eaten up by locusts. These rapacious visitors he drove into the lands of the infidel, and then liking the fertile locality himself, settled there instead. He next paved the road for pilgrims to Compostella, and worked more miracles after his death than even during his lifetime (see Ribad. ii. 68). His crowning feat is charged on the city arms, which are " Argent, a tree vert, with a sickle, a cross, a cock and hen proper." Southey made a droll ballad on the legend, which Moya (Rasgo, 283) had gravely illustrated in prose. The sickle and tree represent the forest which the saint first mowed down, and then set up a *Venta*, the Maritornes of which fell in love with a handsome pilgrim, who resisted; whereupon, smarting under the *spretæ injuria formæ*, she hid some spoons in this Joseph's *Al-*

forjas, who was taken up by the Alcalde, and forthwith hanged. But his parents some time afterwards passed under the body, which told them that he was innocent, alive, and well, and all by the intercession of St. Domenick; thereupon they proceeded forthwith to the truculent Alcalde, who was going to dine off two roasted fowls, and, on hearing their report, remarked, You might as well tell me that this cock, pointing to his rôti, would crow; whereupon it did crow, and was taken with its hen to the cathedral, and two chicks were regularly hatched every year from these respectable parents, of which a travelling ornithologist should secure one for the Zoological Garden. The cock and hen were duly kept near the high altar, and their white feathers were worn by pilgrims in their caps. Prudent writers will, however, without minding S⁰· Domingo, put a couple of ordinary roast fowls into their " provend," for hungry is the road to *Logroño*. The saint's other miracles are detailed in the works of Luis de Vega, 4to. Burgos, 1606; and Andrea de Salazar, 4to. Pamplona, 1624. The scholar may compare these portentous pullets with the pagan *pulli*, by which the aruspices enlightened the ancients, and they too were kept in caveæ; their revelations were so clear, that even Bœotian augurs could interpret the crowings of their *Gallos Gallinaceos* (Cic. 'de Div.' i. 34): Livy (xxxi. 1) records that a cock and hen changed sexes. But fowls have long figured in mythologies; witness the cock of Esculapius, the doves of Venus and S^{a·} Teresa. Jupiter at least had an eagle; but those who reflect on the dog of S⁰· Domingo, and the pig of San Antonio, will ask, like Cicero (N. D. iii. 17) how low you are to descend in this bathos? " Si dii sunt, suntne etiam nymphæ deæ? si nymphæ, Panisci et Satyri. Tum Charon tum Cerberus dii putandi;" but such things, as the Roman philosopher observed, are the invention of poets. Much as Spaniards have neglected ornithological science, they have always excelled in the miraculous investigation of the plumed tribe: thus, Lampridius, praising Alexander Severus, says that he beat even the augurs of Spain.

Najera, now a decayed place of 3000 souls, was once the court of Navarre, and here St. Ferdinand was crowned. In the Benedictine *Sᵃ· Maria* lie interred 35 bodies of the royal families of Castile and Navarre. The elaborate Gothic *Coro* was carved by El Maestro Andres and Nicolas in 1495, and the cloister was filled with statues by A. Gallego, 1542-46. The convent is, or was, adorned with a superb portrait of Ruiz Perez de Ribera, by Pantoja, 1596. Observe the *Retablos* of Juan Vascardo and Pedro Margoledo, 1631, and the early painting of Maestro Luiz, 1442. It was between Najera and Navarrete that the Black Prince replaced on his throne the perfidious, cruel, and ungrateful Don Pedro, just as the Duke, at the not distant *Vitoria,* did the beloved Ferdinand VII.; and striking is the parallel throughout, for thus the past is the prophet of the future, and the present vouches for the past. Then, as in our times, the Peninsula was made the arena for the war between rival giants, between England and France; then · the Black Prince, in despite of inferior forces, everywhere defeated the skilful and brave Du Guesclins, just as the Duke did the Soults; then, as recently, the single-handed Spaniards, led by unworthy chiefs and "wanting in everything," were easily defeated by the highly-organised French; then, as now, the Spanish juntas and rulers were proud, obstinate, and self-confident when danger was distant, but craven and clamorous for aid when it drew near: insolent and sanguinary in the hour of prosperity, when the *foreigner* had done their work, they treated him ungratefully, violated every promise, and robbed him even of his glory.

The French were valorous, chivalrous, and soldierlike, but not over-respectful of the rights of property or the sufferings of man. The English were brave in battle and honest in word and deed : they, as in our times, never took up a position which they did not hold, and never attacked an enemy's which they did not carry. They were only subdued by climate, starvation, and wine, ever their worst of foes : they duly appreciated the gallant French " as the only troops worth fighting against," and the French, like Buonaparte, felt that "the English alone were to be dreaded." The Spaniards resented this inferred *menosprecio,* and hated friends and foes alike, using and abusing them alternately—" a plague on both your houses." So the beloved Ferdinand wished to see his English allies *Los Borrachos,* hung up *con las entrañas* of his French enemies *los gavachos,* just as a good Moor s prayer runs, *Ensara fee senara, le houd fee sefood,* the Christian to the hook, the Jew to the spit.

Froissart has graphically painted the campaign; begin at ch. 230. Unamalgamating Spain was torn and weakened by civil dissensions. Then Pedro, the king, was opposed by his natural brother Henrique de Trastamara, an ally of France, which put forward Pedro's ill-usage of his wife, Blanche of Bourbon, as the pretext for invasion, while the real object was to combat English influence, and give employment to her revolutionary legions, *Les pillards, les compagnies,* whose trade was war, and who, by the peace with England, were left without employment. Then these blest hirelings, who living might have proved their country's shame, were vomited forth into unhappy Spain, where glory and plunder baited grave-traps were laid. Don Pedro, far away at Seville, at first "swelled and soared in the air, boasted of his strength," and, "reposing under his laurels," made ho sort of preparation for defence; but when the French advanced with their usual tremendous rapidity and power, he, like the juntas of 1810 and 1823, crouched into the mire, and ran at once to beg the aid of Edward III., as in our times the Torenos did of George III. The Black Prince crossed the Pyrenees in Feb. 1367; he arrived at Logroño " enduring the greatest anguish of mind," from want of food and every promised co-operation of Pedro's worthless ministers. Such anguish, and from the same causes, was endured by our Duke after Talavera; but neither despaired, being sufficient in themselves. The morn of April 2 beheld 30,000 English (Mariana, xvii. 10, says 20,000) opposed at Navarrete to 80,000 French and Spaniards, enough, as our Duke said at Rueda, to " eat him up." The Spaniards despised the foot-sore English, who were shrewdly out of M. Foy's "beef and rum." They were only afraid that we should run away before they could catch us all in a net; so thought the Cuestas when " hunting" the French (see p. 541).

In vain the brave and skilful Du Guesclin, who remembered Poictiers, spoke of prudence, and counselled, like Soult on the Tormes, a Fabian defence, " Let them starve in hungry Navarre, and rot on the marshes of the Ebro." His words, like those of our Duke before Ocaña, were lost on the Spanish chiefs, who cried, " We are double their number, we will outgeneral and beat them." The French opened the battle with one of their characteristic tremendous en avant attacks, but the English stood firm and silent, receiving the head of the column with an iron sleet of arrowy shower. Then the foe wavered; then "up, guards, and at them :" then followed the "sauve qui peut." The French were sacrificed by their allies; for Don Telmo, who before the battle had been the greatest boaster, like his type Gaal (Judges ix.), now ran ere it commenced, and thus exposed the flank of his allies, who were left to bear the whole brunt, to do the work; just as the

Cuestas, La Peñas, and Blakes did at Talavera, Barrosa, and Albuera. Don Telmo next himself set the example of flight, like the Areizagas and Venegases at Ocaña and Almonacid.

The victory was settled before twelve o'clock, the English having lost, according to even Froissart, a French author, only 40 men, their opponents 17,500. The Spanish army disbanded "each man to his own city." The sanguinary Pedro now proceeded, after the Oriental fashion, to butcher his prisoners, and was with difficulty restrained by the indignant English general, as Cuesta was by the Duke after Talavera, for sweet mercy is nobility's true badge, and humanity in the hour of victory is an older English adage than even immortal Nelson thought. Don Pedro next claimed all the glory for himself, and quitted the army to butcher opponents, burning even women alive. Active in "vile, black blood-shedding," he neither repaid one farthing of the loans, nor furnished his quota to the expense of the war, but violated every treaty and every pledge. At length the Black Prince, bright mirror of English good faith and chivalry, quitted Spain in disgust, exclaiming that " the Castilian had shamefully and dishonourably failed in his engagements" (compare St. Quintin, p. 810); and so the Duke retired after Talavera : and so again when he had replaced Ferdinand on the throne, " Le gouvernement ayant manqué à tous les engagements faits avec moi, j'ai donné ma démission" (Disp. Oct. 30, 1813). No sooner were the English withdrawn than the French reappeared; and now having only the ill-equipped Spaniards to deal with, overran the Peninsula at a hand gallop : thus the promenade militaire of the stout Du Guesclin in 1369 was but the prototype of that of the puny Angoulême in 1823.

Navarrete was the Vitoria of the age, as it cleared Spain of the invaders, while their redoubtable general fell a prisoner into the hands of the Black

Prince, who knew well how to honour a brave opponent, having, according to M. Villeneuve (B. U., xii. 175), saved him from the ferocious Pedro. But no satire can be more severe on *Las Cosas de España* than the account of Mariana himself, who by the way calls Du Guesclin, Bertran Claquin. Henrique II., when enabled to dethrone his brother by this *foreign* general, granted to him his own previous title of *Conde de Trastamara*, and also made him *Duque de Molina :* thus introducing the ducal title for the first time in Spain. But he was robbed of his appanages by insurrections fostered at the Spanish court, just as Pedro, having granted the *Señorio* of Biscay to the Black Prince, sent secret orders to impede his taking possession. Such has been the reward which *foreign* generals have often received from Spanish kings; and so their ancestors the Carthaginians, having been saved by Xantippus, a Lacedemonian, covered him *publicly* with honours, but had him *privately* drowned (App. ' B. P.,' 6).

Nowadays Spanish historians simply talk of a "decisive battle between Don Pedro and his brother," the part of Hamlet being left out. And so Mellado blinks our great Duke's victories, while, to complete the traits of national character, Mons. Foy (i. 205) ingeniously ascribes this victory, *not* to the English, but the "Normans and *Gascons*" who served under the Black Prince. Well done, Gascons! See also Roncesvalles.

For Logroño and its communications, see R. cxxxiv.

ROUTE CXVI.—BURGOS TO VITORIA.

Quintanapalla	.	.	.	3	
Castel de Peones	.	.	.	3	.. 6
Briviesca	.	.	.	.	2	.. 8
Cubo	.	.	.	.	.	3	.. 11
Pancorbo	.	.	.	.	2	.. 13
Miranda del Ebro	.	.	3¼	.. 16¼
Puebla de Argamon	.	3	.. 19¼
Vitoria	.	.	.	.	.	3	.. 22¼

This is the great line from Madrid to France, and travelled by mails and diligences; the road is very good, and runs through a hilly but well-cultivated and agreeable country. *Briviesca,* Virovesca, is a square regularly-built town on the Oca, and Isabella took it as a model for Santa Fè, near Granada. In the *Colegiata,* in the *Retablo* of Sᵃ Casilda, are images of St. Peter and St. Paul, by Becerra. The Gothic high altar and *Retablo* of Sᵃ· Clara are fine. It was at Briviesca in 1388, that Juan I. held a Cortes, in which he gave to his eldest son the title of Prince of the Asturias, in imitation of our Prince of Wales, and at the express desire of John of Gaunt, whose daughter was married to the heir apparent. The angler, artist, and antiquarian should make an excursion to the celebrated Benedictine convent at Oña, which stands in its hamlet near the Ebro, about 4 L. from Briviesca; for details consult Florez (' E. S.,' xxvii. 250) and Berganza (i. 30). It is dedicated to *San Salvador,* and once lorded over its rich hill-encompassed valley, watered by the sweet rivers the Vesga, Omino, Oca, and Bureba; the gardens and fish-ponds were delightful. The perennial fountain Sagredo gushes out, like that of Vaucluse, in a torrent of crystal water. The whole *merindad* of *Valdevielso* is truly Swiss and pastoral. The mills are very artistical. About 1 L. from Oña is *La Horadada,* a lofty bridge of one arch thrown over the Ebro, and thought to be Roman. The convent, now, alas, going to ruin, was founded in 1011, by the Conde Don Sancho for his burial-place; he died Feb. 5, 1017 ; his epitaph, in a Leonine versification and play upon words, records his deeds and worth. *Oña* has been derived from Maiona, the count's mother, who, fearing her son was about to marry a Moorish princess, gave him poison in a cup, which he managed to make her drink, and then raised the monastery in expiation; but the mother's real name was Abba or Ava. The ladies' names, however, in those days were quaint; thus the first abbess, the count's daughter, was called Tigritia. Mariana (viii. 2) states that the

2 R

custom of women drinking before men arose from this maternal malice. The exterior of the convent is ancient, simple, and severe; the interior was formerly *duplex*, that is, conveniently arranged for monks and nuns under the same roof — abuses which were reformed in 1032. The Gothic chapel was begun in 1470; the cloisters were finished in 1503, and are most airy and elegant. Observe the slim windows, pinnacles, and shields, and among the lay sepulchres those of the Bureva, Sandoval, and Salvador families; the royal tombs in the chapel consist of four rich *urnas;* here repose the Infante Garcia. Sancho de Navarra and his wife, and Sancho II., who was assassinated at Zamora. Observe the old paintings and shrine-work canopies. The prosody of Sancho's epitaph would perplex Porson : " Sanctus formâ Paris, et ferox Hector in armis," etc. It was on the high altar here that St. Ferdinand was placed by his mother, until the Virgin cured him of the worms; on this miracle Alonzo el Sabio wrote a ' *Romance*.' This convent was pillaged by the invaders, who burnt the fine library; again in 1835 it was made a barrack by Cordova, who used the cloisters as a stable, while his troopers added new injuries to the already mutilated sepulchres. Cordova's halt was during one of his absurd " marchings and counter-marchings " over mountains higher, as he said, than eagles ever soared, in order to tire his unfortunate troops, which he *did,* and to assist Gen. Evans, which he did *not,* as he left his brave ally in the lurch in the hour of danger. There is a finely engineered road from Oña to *Villacayo,* 6 L. over the heights.

After quitting Briviesca the road continues to *Pancorbo,* Porta Augusta, the picturesque pass between the defiles of the mountains of Oca and the Pyrenean spurs; the river Oroncillo and the road have scarcely room to thread the narrow gorge or *garganta,* in the middle of which is a chapel to N^a. S^a. del *Camino,* our Holy Lady who super-

intends *the way* and protects travellers from avalanches, for all around arise fantastic rocks which hem in this natural portal and barrier of Castile, and in which the old Spaniards defied the Moorish advance, and the modern ones ran away frightened even at the name of Buonaparte. Above is a ruined castle, which commands a fine view of the Rioja; in it Roderick is said to have seduced the ill-omened Cava, *ay! de España perdita por un gusto.* This castle was strengthened by the invaders in 1810, and dismantled in 1823 by Angoulême, who, although then the ally to Spain, was glad to destroy a barrier to future invasions. Now all is *hors de combat,* except the Moorish caverns or *Algibes ;* not even the guns spiked by the French, nor the shot and shells rolled down the rocky crevices, were removed when last we were there.

Leaving Pancorbo, soon the Bilbao road branches off to the l.; the Ebro is passed at *Miranda* by a fine bridge; here we leave the dreary Castiles and enter *Alava* and the Basque provinces (see heading to Sect. xii.). Nature becomes fresher, the population increases, and the towns have more trees and gardens near them; the face of man is ruddier, but poverty is still here. The open belfry of the churches now is changed for a square tower. *Miranda* contains 25,000 souls, and is utterly uninteresting. Here are placed the custom-house offices, as this is the fiscal frontier of Castile, whose system does not obtain in the Basque provinces which we now enter. After these visitations the road continues to be excellent. The Ebro is a geographical and vegetable line of demarkation; soon maize becomes the staple food, and the cereal region is left behind. *Miranda del Ebro* has an ancient church with the porch in front, the common protection against weather in these damp N.W. provinces. *Logroño* lies 10 L. from Miranda del Ebro; the first three to Haro are picturesque, as following the windings of the river.

La Puebla de Arganzon is placed.

in the defile of the *Morillas* hills, and is the gorge by which the waters of the basin of Vitoria, once a lake, made their exit. The road and the Zadorra run through this pass into the plains at the head of which Vitoria rises in the distance. This undulating basin is about 12 miles in length by 10 in width, and is cut up by the Zadorra, which serpentines down the portion to the l.; it is interspersed with woods, villages, and broken ground, which offered strong positions of defence to the French against the English attack.

On the 20th of June, 1813, our army bivouacked on the Bayas, a mountain stream which flows to the l. of the road, and occupied *Tuto, Subijana de Morales* (the Duke's head-quarters), *Zuazo, Vitoriano,* and *Marquina.* The enemy, commanded by Joseph and Jourdan, was strongly posted in front, at the opening of the pass; their right was at *Tres Puentes,* and their left at *Subijana de Alava,* with the hill of *Arinez* in their centre, not far from which is a height called *Inglesmendi,* the "English mound," where five centuries before they had defeated the French. On the 21st the Duke ordered Hill to open the ball; he, with Murillo, scaled the elevations to the r., where the gallant Col. Cameron fell, who begged to be so placed that he might die happy at the sight of the foe in flight, and his last wish was gratified, for the French under Gazan and Darricau were forthwith driven down. Meanwhile Graham, who had been sent with 20,000 men from *Marquina,* the extreme left, to sweep round to the Bilbao road, routed Reille at every point, Lonja and the Spaniards holding *Gamarra menor,* and the English turning the enemy at *Gamarra mayor* and *Abechuco,* and thus depriving them of the possibility of retreating by the Irun road. While these two distinct battles and victories were being gained, the Duke led the centre and struck the heart of his opponents. He threaded the defile by *Nanclares,* Kempt at the same time, with the light

division, crossing the *Zadorra* at *Tres Puentes,* and bursting into the French position, of which the *Mamario de Arinez* was the key, Joseph wavered and detached Villate to Gomecha in his rear; the Duke saw the moment, and with the intuitive decision of genius, ordered a general charge. The rush at the hill of *Arinez* was splendid. Old Picton leading on his "invincible division," encouraging them kindly as he was wont, "forward, ye fighting villains!" and they followed their brave leader to a man. The French resisted like good and stout soldiers, but as at Salamanca now this division, in the words of their leader, "although opposed to five times their numbers and to 50 cannon, bore everything down before them, with the eyes of the whole army beholding them." At last their lines gave way, Joseph leading the flight, just as at Cressy, where, says old Aleyn, " the kinge turned head and so soon his men turned tayle." The enemy, says Southey, "were beaten before the town, in the town, through the town, out of the town, behind the town, and all about the town." They fled, leaving behind them baggage, eagles, 6000 killed and wounded, 150 cannon, and even their plunder. The battle was soon over, for as at Salamanca, the numbers being nearly equal, the Duke took the aggressive ; yet not two-thirds of his army were British, and the returns separate the wheat from the chaff, for our loss was 3308, the Portuguese 1049, the Spanish 553 ; now the latter claim most of the glory, and Mellado in his, the last published, guide, does not even name the English ; and prints are engraved representing the Spaniards under Alava alone driving the French out of Vitoria. The Cortes indeed, July 3,1813, directed a monument to be here elevated to the Duke, which is cited by Arguelles (Hist. i. 20) as a proof of official gratitude ; but it need not be said that nothing ever was done except on paper; however, the victory was complete, and Clausel escaped by a miracle to Huesca, as Joseph did to

2 R 2

Roncesvalles. Then the Duke having engrafted on the stem of noble birth the distinction of personal nobility, pressed on in his pursuit of the fugitives to the Pyrenees, and on their summits, says Napier, " emerging from the chaos of the Peninsular struggle, he stood a recognised conqueror; then, on those lofty pinnacles the clangor of his trumpets pealed clear and loud, and his splendor appeared as a flaming beacon to warring nations." Vitoria not only cleared Spain of the invader, but cheered Europe at large, for the recoil shook Buonaparte at Dresden, as Salamanca had in Russia ; it induced the Allies to refuse the armistice, fixed the wavering adhesion of Austria, and thus was the harbinger of glorious Leipzig. Mons. Bory (Laborde, i. 132), describing this battle, after severely criticising the *mollesse* of the English attack, continues thus : " les braves, débandés par le découragement des chefs, se jetèrent vers les Pyrénées, tandis que Lord Wellington, qui *se crut* vainqueur de Vitoria, s'arrêta paisiblement avec toutes ses forces dans une ville sans importance (which he did not), au lieu de marcher vivement sur Bayonne. Sans avoir vaincu *selon la signification du mot*, les Anglais demeurèrent en possession de quatre-vingt pièces de canon au moins (*i. e.* 151). La France n'eut pas à regretter plus de cent braves (*i. e.* 6000) tués ou blessés qui restèrent sur le champ de bataille." The comparative smallness of the French loss arose first, because, as at Oudenarde and Ramillies, they were beaten too quickly ; and secondly, because, as at Salamanca, their fugitives threw away arms, etc.—all that constitutes a soldier, but impedes celerity of movement.

Again, the enormous booty which they left behind was a temptation which our troops could not resist ; they who defied the steel of the enemy were vanquished by his gold. And yet these were fair battle prizes, won from strong men by stronger, and after a well-fought field, not the pillage of

unresisting citizens. Now five millions of dollars were taken by the English troops, but thereby all " order and discipline were annihilated," as the indignant Duke said, who, as a gentleman and soldier, hated the sound of pillage : "je suis assez long temps soldat pour savoir," wrote he in his nervous Anglo-français, " que les *pillards* et ceux que les encouragent *ne valent rien devant l'ennemi* (Disp. Dec. 23, 1813, March 5, 1814, June 27, 1815). The English wearied themselves in searching for booty rather than in following up their victory, and thus stooping to pick up gold, they lost, like Atalanta, the race of honour. The old curse of the *Aurum Tolosanum* pursued both conquerors and the conquered. Here, as at Bailen (see p. 304), the French movements were hampered, for behind the town were collected in nearly 2000 carriages and vehicles the aggregate plunder of the whole Peninsula during five years, and a desire to secure this " butin infame " damped all eagerness for combat, while the waggons, &c. impeded their retreat. Our Duke, whose policy was English honesty in word and deed, and who, like the heroes of antiquity, preferred bright honour to filthy lucre, whose motto was τιμη μαλλον η κρηματα, whose pursuit was " gloriam ingentem, divitias honestas," never contaminated his golden mind with the dross of peculation or pillage ; he never sold his large glory " for what might be graspt thus." His shrine of renown, like that of Gustavus Adolphus, was only to be approached through the temple of virtue, and he trusted to a grateful country to provide means for the support of a dignity which he carved out with an untarnished soldier-sword. Such also is our *sailor's* maxim. " Corsica," writes Nelson (Disp. June 27, 1794), " in respect to prizes, produces nothing, but *honour far above wealth*. Had I attended less to the service of my country, I might have made some money too : however, I trust my name will stand on record when the money-makers will be forgot." Southey has most graphically described the extent and variety of the French collections, the church plate and pictures, the delicate eatables, the mistresses, the poodles, parrots, and monkeys. The Duke treated the women with the chivalrous courtesy of a Scipio or Peterborough, by protecting them from all insult, and sending them in their own carriages with a flag of truce to Pamplona. Joseph narrowly escaped with his life, but his carriage was taken, like that of his brother at Waterloo, and it was filled, says Toreno (xxii.), with pickings and stealings and obscene objects imported from France, while Marshal Jourdan's *Bâton* was found in his *fourgon de comestibles;* this, with the colours of the 100th regiment, was "laid by the Duke at the Prince Regent's feet," who, with great good taste, repaid the compliment by returning the staff of an English field-marshal to the captor. The enemy's losses were so complete as to furnish jokes to themselves. Thus *L'Apothicaire,* in his clever '*Mémoires*' (chr. 42), consoled his friends so cleaned out by this Wellington purge by quoting Horace, "You all of you came into Spain thinner than weasels, and now as thin you must go out." The French soldiers also derided their general, who before had been beaten at Talavera, and exclaimed irreverently, "the sea fled, and Jordan was driven back."

The *Spolia opima* of Vitoria were found in the imperial of Joseph's carriage, for his Royal and Imperial Majesty had there stowed away many of Ferdinand's choicest cabinet pictures, which now worthily ornament Apsley House, fair battle-won trophies, not the free gift of bayonet-threatened chapters nor the fee of bribed violence (see p. 253). Nay, no sooner had the Duke learnt that the pictures were more valuable than he thought, than he wrote to express his desire to "restore" them to Ferdinand, suspecting that they might have been "*robbed by Joseph*" from the royal palaces (Disp. March 16, 1814).

Mons. Bory attributed the loss of Vitoria to the French soldiers' want of confidence in their chiefs, yet Sallust (B. C. i.) dated the decay of Roman arms to the misconduct of the Syllas in Asia, who then first collected "tabulas pictas—vasa cælata," and never scrupled "ea privatim ac publice rapere, delubra spoliare, sacra profanaque omnia polluere;" but there is nothing new under the sun. Another prize, more precious for the sacred cause of truth and history than plate or paintings, was also taken here in the usurper's carriage, namely, the official and confidential correspondence between Madrid and Paris, and which reveals some secrets of Buonaparte's prisonhouse and lifts up a corner of his mantle of ruse doublée de force; these thoughts, shot from his innermost quiver, give the best contradiction to his *public bulletins* and statements, that poison with which he fed his subjects instead of bread. These *private* papers, never destined for the Moniteur, fully corroborate the Duke's *public* dispatches, for the noble mind will dare do all but lie. That Buonaparte was a first-rate general and a meteor genius none can deny, and least of all the English, of whose steel he was a worthy foe; nor was one leaf of his large chaplet earned at their expense, and those who unjustly seek to curtail its fair proportions deprive our sailors and soldiers, who cropt his garlands for their crest, of half their glory: but the truth was not in him. Who can fail to apply to this wonderful man, one of true Italian intellect and Machiavellianism, what Livy (xxi. 4) so unjustly predicated of the mighty Hannibal?—"Has tantas viri virtutes, ingentia vitia equabant, inhumana crudelitas, perfidia plusquam punica, nihil veri, nihil sancti, nullus Deûm metus, nullum jus jurandum, nulla religio." For Vitoria, see p. 928.

ROUTE CXVII.—VITORIA TO SANTANDER.

Miranda del Ebro . .	6	
Ameyugo.	2¼	.. 8¼

Valderama	.	.	.	.	4	..	12½
Frias	.	.	.	.	.	1½	..	14
Trespaderne	.	.	.	2	..	16
Monco	.	.	.	.	2½	..	16½
Villarcayo	.	.	.	.	2	..	20½
Espinosa	.	.	.	.	.	3	..	21½
Salcedillo	.	.	.	.	1	..	22½
San Roque	.	.	.	2½	..	25
Lierganes	.	.	.	.	2	..	27½
Santander	.	.	.	.	3	..	30½

Retracing our steps to *Miranda del Ebro*, we soon turn off from the high road to *Frias*, a dilapidated old town on the Ebro, with a bridge said to be of Roman foundation; from the ruined castle of this place the great Velasco family derive their ducal title. At *Villarcayo* the Burgos road branches down and crosses the Ebro at *Puente de Arenas*, by which the Duke, June 14, 1813, marched his army; thus by a masterly manœuvre he turned the French position at Pancorbo, and the first-fruits were the evacuation of Santoña and Bilbao by the enemy, which enabled the English fleet and stores to move up from Portugal, and thereby supply the army in the unfriendly Basque provinces. Napier (xx. 7) thus heroically describes the English advance through these alpine localities: " The glories of twelve victories playing about their bayonets, the French flying like sheep before wolves, all their combinations baffled, rivers dried up, ravines levelled by the genius of him who was soon to annihilate them." The Duke poured his men through the intricate passes between Frias and Orduña, in which they toiled for six days, and then " trickling from the mountains like raging streams from every defile went foaming into the basin of Vitoria," to victory. This splendid advance is described even by Mons. Savary " as a movement which none would have dared to execute before an active and manœuvring enemy," but which was now accomplished without the firing of a single gun, like a quiet march in the time of peace, and this in defiance of a first-rate French marshal and his magnificent soldiers, "such (in the words of the Duke, who never

denied to his gallant opponents their great and well-deserved military merit) as the Austrians and Russians have not yet had to deal with " (Disp. Dec. 21, 1813).

Not far from Villarcayo, on the road to Bilbao, is the Old Castilian city of *Medina de Pomar*, pop. 1200. It is pleasantly placed on the excellent trout-streams the Trueba and Nela, and has a good bridge, a fine fountain on the *Plaza*, and some grand tombs of the Velasco family in *Sᵃ· Clara*. One Duke of Frias lies clad in armour, with his wife near him; observe the animals at their feet.

From Villarcayo to Santander there are two roads, one by *Soncillo*, 3½, and hence 12 by the *Camino real de la Rioja*, and the other a bridle and shorter, by Cabada and Espinosa. Espinosa lies in a pleasant valley watered by the Trueba, which, with the Nela, soon joins the Ebro. The inhabitants had the privilege of *mounting* guard over the King's person at night; hence it is called *Espinosa de los Monteros*. This honour was granted in reward of the valour of Sancho Montero, by whom the Conde Sancho's life was saved in 1113. Consult ' *Origen de los Monteros*,' Pedro de Guevara, 4to., Mad. 1632.

Espinosa witnessed, Nov. 10 and 11, 1808, a crushing instance of the ignorance of Blake, Mahy, and Mendizabal in the art of war. When posted on strong heights they were surprised by Victor and dislodged, when the whole dispirited army followed their unworthy leaders' example of flight, and this just at the moment when Castaños was losing the battle of Tudela; thus Moore, who had advanced into the Castiles relying on the broken reed of Spanish co-operation, was left with his handful of Britons to bear the whole brunt. Blake and Mahy, when out of breath, halted at *Reinosa*, from whence and its almost impregnable passes they again fled at the mere report of the French approach, leaving Santander to its fate, which was utterly sacked. Then all the stores sent by England for Spain's defence fell into the enemy's hands, to be used against the very ally who had furnished them; and to complete the farce, now Paez (i. 345) describes the handicap at Espinosa as *una vigorosa resistencia.*

Lierganes lies on the Miera, a delicious trout-stream; here in the 16th century were established some iron foundries by a Flemish company, and the hamlet still sends forth itinerant blacksmiths and needy knife-grinders into central Spain. Here was born, in 1660, Fro· de la Vega Caz, the Spanish merman, or *Hombre pez.* This man-fish took to the sea in 1674, and was caught in some fishermen's nets near Cadiz, in 1679, whereupon Señor Caz, on being hauled out, exclaimed, " *Pan, vino, tabaco,*" bread, wine, tobacco; on hearing which the sailors saw at once that he was a countryman and Christian; and as he afterwards said " Lierganes," they identified his locality. However, this amphibious mountaineer, like a true seaman, soon got sick of land, and disappeared again among the fishes. His house was long the lion of Lierganes, archbishops, and even Feijoo, the refuter of popular fallacies, believing in all this nonsense: see the whole *critical* account, ' Teatro Critico,' vi. Dis. 8; and compare the stone man of Daroca. This miraculous seaman would have made a good match with the marvellous land-man Tages, who, when ploughed up, so much amazed the beholders of antiquity (Cic. ' de Div.' ii. 23). Now we enter the iron district, and the best mines are those of Pamanes, Vizmaya, Montecillo; but Somorrostro, the finest of all, is distant 12 L. The forests of oak and beech furnish a bad fuel for the furnaces; yet the port of Gijon could supply coal to any amount. At *La Cabala,* on the Miera, Charles III. established an artillery foundry.

Santander, Portus Blendium, has decent inns, *Las Fondas de Boggio, De Criston,* and *El Parador de Moral,* Calle de Becedo. The town is well placed on the S. tongue of a headland,

and is protected to the N. by a hill; the harbour is accessible and sheltered, and the anchorage good. Pop. above 13,000. It is a thriving place, having risen at the expense of Bilbao, for during the civil wars the merchants removed their establishments to this less disturbed district. Santander has a theatre, *Liceo,* and baths; however, it is a purely commercial place, and devoid of objects of art or interest. The fine quay and newly-built houses of the chief merchants have rather a French than a Spanish look, and the shops abound with Parisian *colifichets* and poor hagiographical engravings. The busy quay, with its bales, sugars, flour barrels, and bustle, contrasts with the fishy poverty of the older town, especially the quarter of San Pedro: what a change from busy industry and prosperity to crime, indolence, and sickly mendicancy! Here porters' work, as in Bilbao, is done by women, if these androgynous epicene Amazons can so be called. The local carts are coffin-looking concerns, built after the Affghan waggon with solid *creaking* wheels (see p. 588). The fresh-aired walks on the hill command pretty views over the *Ria,* the *Muelle de los Naos,* the Crowded with Shipping, and the battery *de San Felipe:* the *Alamedas de Becedo* and *de los Barcos* are the fashionable walks. The hospital, *cuna,* and prison do little credit to science and humanity. Santander is a cheap and well-provided place; the fish both of sea and fresh water is plentiful and excellent. The green valleys of the Pas supply butter, which is brought in by Swiss-like *Pasiegas,* who carry baskets fastened with straps, and by which they are bent double; however, when the weight is removed, they spring up straight like a bent cane. The Vin du pays is a poor cidery chacoli, nor is the water good, but there is a mineral spring called *La Salud* about two miles off, which is much frequented for visceral disorders from June to October; and about 20 miles off, at *Ontaneda*, there are baths, with a large and decent *Parador*.

Santander is the residence of the provincial authorities, and the see of a bishop, suffragan to Burgos, which was founded in 1174 by Alonzo IX.: the cathedral is one of the most unimportant in Spain; the bay and port were much esteemed in the early periods of Spanish history. From hence, in 1248, St. Ferdinand's fleet sailed to blockade Seville, which is commemorated on the city's shield. It afterwards decayed into a mere fishing town, but rose when made a *puerto habilitado*, or port entitled to trade with S. America, and it still supplies Cuba with corn from the Castiles, bringing back colonial produce; and as it is in fact the seaport of Madrid, whenever the canal of Castile or the railroad to Reinosa be finished, it must necessarily profit largely—pero Dios sabe *cuando*.

Here Charles V. landed, July 16, 1522, to take possession of Spain; and from the same quay our Charles embarked to quit Spain after his romantic visit to Madrid; he arrived here on the 11th of Sept., 1623 (old style, *i. e.* on St. Matthew's, the 21st), and was nearly drowned on Friday the 12th when going to visit his ship; he sailed, however, on the 17th, and arrived safely at Portsmouth on Sunday, October 5, to the inexpressible joy of the whole nation, which 26 years afterwards almost as gladly saw him beheaded.

Santander was ferociously sacked by Soult, Nov. 16, 1808, and yet no place during the war exhibited more selfish localism or greater unfriendliness to our delivering armies. The Junta having clamoured for our aid, turned round like Berbers when it was granted, abusing and ill-using its defenders; the citizens refused even to lodge the Duke's couriers, although paid for by England and for Spanish purposes. They placed his wounded in quarantine, and in the most offensive manner (Disp. Jan. 14, 1814). "The town of Santander," wrote he, "has at one stroke virtually cut off the supplies of the allied armies of every description, and has thereby done that which the enemy has never been able to effect." Again, Oct. 14, 1813, he notices the "bad temper shown by Santander to the English, which he had not observed in any other part of Spain." Again, when Evans landed with his legion, the citizens refused to contribute to the bare necessities of those brave men whose assistance had been implored. The capital fishing districts extending westwards towards Oviedo have been described in Routes cxii. and cxiii. There are diligences from Santander to Burgos, R. cxiv., and to Valladolid, R. lxxvi., in the summer; a coasting steamer occasionally communicates up and down between San Sebastian and Cadiz. For the land route to Bilbao, see R. cxxiii.

SECTION XII

THE BASQUE PROVINCES.
ALAVA; VIZCAYA; GUIPUZCOA.

CONTENTS.

The Provinces; the *Fueros;* Character of Natives and Country; Manners and
Language.

Las Provincias Vascongadas consist of the three united provinces of *Alava, Vizcaya,*
and *Guipuzcoa.* *Vizcaya,* the largest, contains about 106 square leagues; *Gui-*
puzcoa, the smallest, only 52; it is, however, the most densely peopled, and at the
rate of 2000 inhabitants to the square league; *Alava,* containing about 90 square
leagues, lies between *Guipuzcoa* and Navarre. These provinces, forming the mountainous triangle of the N.W. of the Peninsula, are the *Cantabria* of the ancients,
a name derived by some from *Kent-Aber,* which they interpret the " Corner of
the Water." This corner of the land, like our Wales, is the home of the remnant of the aboriginal inhabitants, the αυτοχθονες, who, whenever pressed
upon by foreign invaders, have taken refuge in its rugged retreats, in which
they could not be conquered by a small army, and where a large one would
starve. Thus unsubdued, the character of an unadulterated primitive race
remains strongly marked in language and nationality. The nominal Roman,
Gothic,* and Moorish yokes were too short-lived to have left evidences of impression. These highlanders, bred on metal-pregnant mountains, and nursed im-

* The Goths could not subdue these rebellious highlanders, although Recared, as Sᵘ.
Isidoro tells us, used especially to send his troops there to keep his soldiers' hands in
fighting condition—quasi in palæstri ludo (Chron. Era 585).

2 R 3

amid storms in a cradle indomitable as themselves, have always known how to forge their iron into arms, and to wield them in defence of their independence ; and what sword equals that one which is moulded from the ploughshare? This *sufficiency in self* is the meaning which *Perochegui* reads in the Basque name, which he derives from *Bayascogara*, "somos bastantes." The Basque of this day is the unchanged Cantaber : impatient of foreign rule, *indoctus juga ferre nostra*, he clings to his immemorial liberty, and looks down on even the old Castilian as a new and secondary formation. A sense of separate weakness has kept these provinces together, and has taught the secret of *union*, the one thing wanting to unamalgamating sectional Spain. The binding ties are a common council of representatives, and a common alliance against all that is not Basque. This federal association is expressed in their national symbol of three hands joined together, with the motto " *Irurac Bat*," which is equivalent to the tria juncta in uno of the Bath order of our *united* kingdoms. The armorial shield is " argent, the tree of guernica vert, two wolves gules, with an orle eight crosses or."

The Basques have been less successful in resisting invasions by sea, for they were partly overcome about the year 870 by a fair-haired Northman, named Zuria, an adventurer either from Norway or Scotland; and to this foreign admixture their fair complexions and immemorial representative government have been traced. These provinces, when the descendants of the Goths began to gain ground on the Moorish invaders, formed themselves into a confederation of small detached tribes or republics, placed under a nominal Lord or *Señor*, until at length, in the 14th century, Nuña, the 19th Lord, died, leaving two daughters, one of whom having married Juan of Arragon, Pedro the Cruel seized the opportunity, put her husband to death, and annexed the *lordship* to the crown of Castile; soon afterwards he ceded it to the Black Prince, in reward for his assistance at Navarrete; however, private instructions were given to the Basques not to allow the *foreigner* to take possession, which he never did : and considering the Punic character of Don Pedro *el cruel*, his deliverer was fortunate to escape even with life; and compare p. 913.

The Basques have not forgotten their double-dealing monarch's hint, and have turned his own arm against his successors; thus, whenever they have issued decrees militating against their *fueros*, they have been received with lip obedience, and treated like waste paper—*obedecido pero no complido*, obeyed but not carried out. Although incorporated with the Castilian monarchy, the national *fueros* were rigidly retained; and these the kings of Spain, as *Señores* only of Biscay, always swore on their accessions to maintain, and as regularly endeavoured to subvert, as Ferdinand VII. would have done, had not the French revolution in 1830 nipped his project. The Basques, accordingly, are always on their guard, and justly dread the modern doctrines of centralization, by which local liberties are undermined; and their fears were prophetic, for the first impolitic act of Castanon, after Ferdinand's death, was to abolish these *fueros*, which threw the Basques into the cause of Don Carlos, in whom they beheld a non-innovating principle; their cry was, " *Conservar intactos la Fé, y las costumbres antiguas ;*" and they fought *his* battle more for *their* own independehce than from any love for his person or claim. These Basque *fueros* were regularly digested for the first time in 1526, by a native commission appointed by Charles V., and were printed in 1527. The political economists of Madrid have always considered these privileges to be obsolete inventions of mediæval necessity, and now injurious not only to the kingdom at large, but to the Basque provinces themselves; and in practice they breathe a paltry parochial isolation, a rigid monopoly, and detestation of free trade ; each *Partido* or district treating its neighbours as rivals, and seldom even purchasing anything from them until all raised at home be first consumed; but men will bear and glory in any chains provided they be self-imposed, and in local self-government national character and fitness for liberty is formed; therefore the Basques, who take the good with the bad, and who have been happy and free under their chartered rights, cling to them as guarantees of future vitality and prosperity; and their shadows of liberties, as we English may think them, were as bright lights shining in the circumambient darkness. The *fueros* of the Peninsula have survived many a change and chance, and have resisted many a foe domestic and foreign; they have continued to exist when little Spanish existed save the fertile soil and the noble hearts of the honest people; they kept Spain Spanish, because such institutions were congenial to national character, which, essentially local, abhors a foreign centralizing system. They again have grown with the country's growth, and have become part and parcel of the constitution; and although not perhaps abstractedly the best, yet are the only ones which it has been possible to obtain and maintain. Sooner or later, however, the Basque *fueros* must be abolished whenever a really strong government can be formed; meanwhile the policy of imperium in imperio continues, by which the *alcalde* is the Sheikh, and the *cura* the Pope of their particular village, and these they rule in temporals and spirituals, indifferent to the orders or wishes of those who are their nominal superiors, whose commands they either evade or disobey. The religious independence secured by the *fueros* presents a strange anomaly in prelatical Spain; here the episcopal office is unknown, and the parish priest is exempt from all diocesan control. The amount of taxes, again, is determined by the popularly elected representatives, and the supply is called *Donativo*, a gift, not a tribute or *service*, as in Navarre. They are free also from the *quinta*, or accursed conscription, that *contribucion de sangre*, as Spaniards, who do not mince words, call this blood tax, the fit invention of a Revolution which, like Saturn, devoured its own children. Each *partido* here raises its own *tercios* or militia, who are not compellable to serve beyond their respective provinces; hence the difficulty which Don Carlos had to get his Basques to advance into Arragon or the Castiles. Again, they are exempt from the burdensome *papel sellado* and stamps and taxes of Castile, as well as from governmental *Escribanos*, who, as a class, are the greatest *picaros* or rogues in Spain or out, as their duty it is to take depositions, which they colour or weaken according to the amount of the bribe. Again, these provinces are free from the fiscal scourge of Spanish custom-houses and their officers; accordingly the Spanish line of the inspecting and preventive services was not placed on the Bidasoa, the real frontier of the Peninsula, but on the Ebro; and these provinces, lying between France and Old Castile, became a neutral ground and paradise for smugglers, whose great gains were made at the expense of the treasury of Spain. Espartero, when angered by the plots hatched against him at Paris, moved up the commercial frontier to its geographical one at the Pyrenees, which struck at once at this contraband trade; but this sound policy was upset in the changes which succeeded, and in the shifts and expedients of the day, when the inconsistent Christinists re-opened the question of the Basque *fueros* in 1844, which they had been the first to abolish in 1833.

Other details will scarcely interest an English reader; one privilege is universal nobility, which is secured to all by the mere fact of being born in these provinces. Sons of old and good Christians, free from all Jewish and Moorish taint, they represent the "Hebrew of the Hebrews," and are the *most* Gothic gentlemen of Spain, and are consequently all *Caballeros hijos de algo*. It is true that where all are so noble, the distinction is of small importance; nevertheless, like other highlanders, these Basques are grievously afflicted with genealogy and goître. Perochegui (Origen. p. 96) thus modestly eulogises his beloved Cantaberria: " *Hidalga in abstracto, rio caudaloso de Nobleza, solar indicativo y demonstrativo de Nobleza, antiquisimo seminario de la nobleza de España.*" It would be better if there were a few more modern and ordinary seminaries.

Peppery as the Welsh, proud as Lucifer, and combustible as his matches, these pauper peers fire up when their pedigree is questioned. Here pride of birth (no element of meanness in itself) is carried to an abuse, and when coupled with *poverty*, that magnum opprobrium, justifies the remark of Juvenal (iii. 152) of its making men ridiculous; and well did Don Quixote know how to annoy a Biscayan by telling him that " he was no gentleman." Basque gentility often consists rather in blood than manners; better born than bred, the Cantabrian is not always courteous nor overquick in rendering honour to whom honour is due; like a wild ass of the desert, he considers a sort of boorishness to indicate a republican independence, and thinks the deference which one well-conditioned person pays to another (and the surest security for reciprocity) to be a degradation to his noble birthright; the treatment which our soldiers have met with from the Basques, from the Black Prince down to Sir de Lacy Evans, has always been the reverse of friendly, even while fighting their battles. The Duke never found an enemy among the honest PEOPLE of Spain until he entered these provinces, when the Basques, saved from the invaders by him alone, rose in his rear, as in olden time, " impacatos a tergo horrebis Iberos" (Georg. iii. 408); so they repaid Charlemagne, whom they had called in to assist them. From such allies well might the Duke pray to be delivered; from all enemies in front he could protect himself; and at last, when a conqueror on the Pyrenees, ever prescient, he warned the ministry at home to prepare for a war with that very country which without him would have remained a province of Buonaparte's, who had been welcomed by the Basques with arches of triumph, inscribed, " à l'héros invaincu, les Cantabres invaincus."

The modern Basques, however brave and active as individuals, form very bad *regular* soldiers, as they are too obstinate and self-opinionated to tolerate drill and discipline; again, they can only be managed, and that imperfectly, by one of themselves; hence Gonzalo de Cordova affirmed that he would rather be a keeper of wild beasts than a commander of Basques. As *Guerrilleros* they are excellent, since their active mountain and smuggling habits educate them for a desultory war of frontier ambuscade, foray, and bush-fighting. In the wild sierras of *Guipuzcoa* bands were raised by the shepherd Gaspar Jauregui, which were always a thorn in the path of the invader.

In time of peace, commerce and fishing form the occupations of those who dwell on the sea-board; the ores of the iron-pregnant hills are also worked at smithies rude as in the days of the Iberians, the Basque not being a contriving operative. The limited attractions offered to strangers are chiefly those of nature, for the towns are without social, historical, or artistical attraction, while the villages have been almost all ravaged during the civil wars: first, because without walls; and secondly, because the male population was away in the armies. Nevertheless there is much less of squalid poverty and ragged misery in them than in the mendicant mud hamlets of Castile, where the sun dries up the earth and exhausts even human industry. The chief towns have few charms except to commercial travellers, for the republican inmates have neither palaces nor picture galleries: nor have these non-episcopalians cathedrals; and since wealthy prelates and chapters have been wanting, there are few churches of architectural pretension. The towns are Swiss-like, surrounded with green hills and enlivened by clear trout-streams; the streets are often drawn in straight lines, which intersect each other at right angles; the *Alamedas* are pretty; a *Juego de Pelota*, or fives court, and a public *Plaza*, are seldom wanting : the defences and walls are solid, for stone and iron abound, and the climate is damp.   When it rains it does so " contrary to all reason and experience," κατα δοξως, which we take to be the true etymon of our " cats and dogs." The sombre-looking balconied dwellings are so solidly built that they look like fortresses; here every gentleman's house is indeed his castle: they also resemble prisons from the iron *rejas* with which they are barred and blockaded.   The soffits which support the projecting eaves are often richly carved; these, indeed, protect the houses from the rains, but deluge passengers with shower-baths.   To this state of insecurity is added a pomp of heraldry, as armorial shields, as large as the pride of the owners, are sculptured over the portals, and contain more quarterings than there are chairs in the drawing-rooms or eatables in the larder; but pride and poverty put out the kitchen fire.

Agriculture, as being the occupation of Adam, the first gentleman who bore arms, is not held to degrade these peasant peers.   Their *Hidalgos*, or better classes, are something between our small squires and substantial yeomen, and their rank on the score of nobility is much higher than on intellectual grounds, since whole coveys of them would never make a Cervantes or a Velazquez; but how can he get wisdom that only holdeth the plough, and whose talk is only of bullocks?

As these provinces were not wrested in one campaign from the Moors, like Murcia, &c., grants of wide districts were never made to great nobles; property accordingly is much subdivided into freeholds, with peculiar entails.   Capital and knowledge being scarce, even agriculture is imperfectly conducted; nor is artificial pasture much known, although there is a rumour of turnips; human thews and sinews supply the office of machinery; women and children toil in the fields *machinas de Sangre*, and overworked as among the Arabs; but this is their hard fate along all these north-western provinces.   There is a struggle for land, and in a dense, competing population, all must labour early and late or starve.   Thus, in spite of these provinces having been so long the scene of the recent murderous civil wars, the numbers killed are not missed; the gap is filled up by the superabundant swarm.   The Basque farms are small, many not exceeding four or five acres, or so much land as a man, his wife, and family can labour; cultivation with the spade is much in vogue, or rather with a sort of prong-fork or mattock called *Laya*.   In spite of hard work the agriculturalists are in general tolerably well off.   Meanwhile the peasantry are the best portion of the Basques, and if kindly treated are civil and hospitable as far as their humble means allow.   They are simple, hardy, and patient, having the virtues and vices of highlanders; nor, from knowing no better, do they repine at their lot, but feeling strongly the attaching power of a mountain home, they love their rocks and Alps, and are wretched when torn from them.

" Dear is the shed to which their souls conform,
    And dear the hills which lift them to the storm."

These provinces are made up of mountain and valley, with a sea-board line. The elevated slopes are covered with oak and chesnut trees; the produce of the latter is exported to England, and enters into the diet of the frugal natives, *Calientes y Gordas*.   As this pastoral country is akin to portions of the Asturias and Gallicia, refer to the introductory observations of Sections ix. and x. Corn only ripens in favoured localities; maize is the staple "bread-stuff;" good milk, bad cheese, and fine apples are plentiful as in the Georgics.

——Sunt nobis mitia Poma
Castaneæ molles, et pressi *copia* lactis.

Here also is made a poor wine called *chacolí* (see Bowles, 305), Arabicè *cha-calel*, weakness, thinness; and the drink justifies the derivation, since it is far inferior to good Devonshire cider, and resembles those very *ordinaire* French wines *de Surenne* and *de Brie.* The Basques, from having nothing better, drink it copiously, and from habit have even got to like it; however, it disagrees with the palate and stomach of foreigners, who have not the dura Bascorum ilia; but the bowels, digestion, and endurance of the Cantabrian are inherited by the Basques, who are still "hiemisque æstusque famisque invicti" (Sil. Ital. iii. 326). The lower classes, as in the East, are frugal rather from poverty than will, temperate from necessity, not choice. Where meat and drink are set before them, they will consume any *given* quantity, and lay in a provision for at least 24 hours, being always uncertain of getting a similar supply. The way to their heart lies through their belly, and their blessing on the hospitable stranger is connected with "savoury meat."

The Basque, as being the head of the Iberian family, is naturally prejudiced in favour of his country and himself; ultra local, hates even his parish, and therefore overrates his own ignorance as much as he underrates the intelligence of others. If the *Castellano* sees double in his own favour, the Basque sees quadruple, and his power of vision is keen in all that concerns himself and his interests, for in his limited scope *self* forms the foreground and emphatic feature of his parochial picture ; but *self* being placed so near, stands forward in too large a scale and in too bright colour, and as his eye for perspective is as defective as it is for proportion, every thing and person beyond his boundary appears too diminutive and subordinate.

Sunday is the day to observe the costume and amusements of the peasantry ; it is still called *Astartea*, or the feast dedicated to Astarte, who is practically replaced by the Virgin. But thus our *Easter* is but Eostre (Vesta ?), an Anglo-Saxon goddess worshipped in April; so the break-of-day drum-roll in Spain is still called *la Diana.*

The Basque holidays are celebrated with the song, dance, single-stick, and broken heads, which they love like their neighbours the Asturians, whom they hate. Their songs resemble those of the Gallicians, whom otherwise they abhor. Their so-called musical instruments, like the *chillo* (see p. 588) of the solid heavy wheels of their light carts, are worthy to accompany such harsh voices and melancholy melodies ; but these teeth-on-edge-setting squeaks and creaks afford infinite delight to the grave oxen and their patient drivers. The instruments consist of the Moorish *Pandero* and *Gaita*, or bagpipe, which seems to have some sympathetic attraction for all long and highland ears. *Gayt* in Arabic signifies the long neck of the ostrich, and hence its secondary meaning of a pipe. The Basque dances are Salic and singular ; the *Zortico*, or "evolution of eight," consists of two parts, *La danza real*, the opening, and the *Arrin arrin*, or the conclusion. This is largely capered at Azpeitia to the sounds of rude fifes, tambourines, and a sort of flageolet, *el silbato*, which resembles those of the Pifferari at Rome, and is probably equally antique. The *Carrica* is a dance performed in the streets ; the *Espata danza* is a remnant of the primitive *Tripudium* of the Iberians (see p. 189). The leathern-eared Basques delight in every other sort of atrocious noises, and especially in firing off guns at weddings. Their costume is not becoming, their shocking bad hats are quite Irish. These hirsute and galligaskined rustics wear brogues, *Abarcas espadillos*, made of skins and tied loosely with thongs (see note, p. 34); thus the water and mud ooze out. In dry weather they prefer the sandal *Alpargata*, which, however, will not stand much wet. Shoes are a rarity, whether of leather or of wood, *Madreñas*, the French *sabots.* The women wear their hair in long plaited tresses *trensas*, and cover their heads with a hood or *capuz*, which is more convenient than picturesque. The Basques are much given to pilgrimages to hill tops (see p. 120), where the *chacoli* and *shillelah* are devoutly used ; and how well chosen are these *"high places!"* How the fresh air exhilarates, how the views delight, how as we ascend is the earth left below, while we mount as it were to heaven, and then with what an appetite do all descend, and how sweet is sleep when the conscience is at rest and the frame is weary from this combination of devotion and exercise!

Among other antique customs corn and bread are offered to the manes of the deceased on the anniversary of death ; these oblations are called *Robos*, from an Arragonese measure taken from the Moorish *Arroba*. Compare the " Sparsæ fruges" of Ovid (Fasti, ii. 538), and the barley offered to the Polian Jupiter (Paus. i. 24. 4). The Basques, as becomes a people sui generis, have a language of their own, which few but themselves can understand ; nor is it worth the trouble of learning, as it is without a written literature, while the conversation of the natives is scarcely of that high intellectual quality which repays the study. The enunciation is not easy, at least, if the Andalucian's joke be true, who says "that the Basque writes Solomon and pronounces it Nebuchadnezzor." The fine-eared fastidiousness of the ancients rejected as barbarous these Basque words, spellings, and sounds ; they could neither be written nor spoken from their το ανδις της γραφης (Strabo, iii. 234 ; see also Pliny, ' N. H.' iii. 3, and Martial, iv. 55-9). Pomponius Mela (iii. 1) goes farther :—" Quorum nomina nostro ore concipi nequeant." After such authorities we too protest against being held responsible for the spelling or meaning of any Basque word which we may be compelled to use.

Again, our readers are cautioned against the wild theories and treatises of Basque antiquarians, which rival those of Ireland. Humboldt, a critical German, and free from national prejudices and predilections, is the safest guide. He considers the Basque to have been formerly spoken all over the Peninsula, as is evidenced in the nomenclature of localities and other things which are not subject to changes.

The Basques call themselves *Euscaldunac*, their country *Euscaleria*, and their language *Euscara*. They have no F, and no word beginning with an R. This *Eusc* is the old Osc, Vesc, Vasq, of Italy and Iberia. According to Perochegui, Adam, the first gentleman, spoke Basque, as being the language of angels, which seems strange ; it was, moreover, brought pure into Spain, by Tubal, long before the confusion of tongues at Babel. Angelic or not, it is so difficult that the devil, who is no fool, is said to have studied seven years in the Bilboes, and to have learnt only three words. The grammar and declensions, as may be supposed, are very intricate. The language is distinct from the Irish, Celtic, and Welsh, with which it has been often supposed to be a sister idiom. Our friend Borrow, one of the Polyglots of the day, assures us that it is of a Tartar origin, resembling in structure the Manchou and the Mongolian, with a decided Sanscrit element (see for Basque grammars and dictionaries p. 86).

The best works to consult on these provinces are ' *Averiguaciones da Cantabria*,' Gabriel de Henao, fol. Sal^a· 1689 ; ' *La Cantabria*,' Florez, 4to. Mad. 1768; ' *Historia de Alava*,' Landazuri, 4to. Vitoria, 1798; ' *Noticias Historicas de Alava, &c.*,' Juan Ant^o· Llorente, 4to., 5 vols., Mad. 1806-8 ; and the excellent ' *Diccionario Geographico de la Academia*,' De Travia, 4to., 2 vols., Mad., 1802.

VITORIA is a busy, flourishing *coach* town, and being on the high road between France and Madrid, is full of diligences and decent inns; *El Parador Viejo* and *El Parador Nuevo* are the best, and indeed some of the best in the Peninsula, being more European than Spanish, and possessing carpets, papered rooms, and even bells. *Vitoria*, pop. about 12,000, is the capital of Alava: it is placed on a gentle eminence above *its plain*, for such the word *Beturia* signifies in Basque. The city was much improved about 1181 by Sancho *El Sabio* of Navarre, to commemorate a *Victory* gained here over the Moors. That name the Duke has confirmed and fixed for ever (for *the* victory see p. 915). The town is divided into the old and new portions, which contrast with each other; the former, with its curious *plaza*, its dark tortuous streets, being in perfect contrast with the latter, which is all line and rule. Vitoria has a *Colegiata*, which Adrian VI., who in this place received the intelligence of his having been elected Pope, promised to elevate to a see, but which he did *not*.

The public *Alamedas* are charming, especially *La Florida* and *El Prado*, outside the town, where under leafy avenues the lower classes meet and dance. There is, moreover, a theatre and a *Liceo*. The climate is temperate, the living cheap and abundant, the fruits and vegetables much like those in the West of England. The fine modern *Plaza*, like that at Salamanca, which was its model, is an arcaded square of 220 ft., and was built in 1791 from designs of Justo Ant. de Olaquibel. Here idlers in the market-place resort to hear something new, while industrious labourers stand for hire, and Hebe-like maidens come for water and gossip. The *Casa Consistorial* is a fine edifice. There is little to be seen else. Visit the hospital with its classical façade, designed in 1630 by the Capuchin Lorenzo Jordanes: the dark stone from the quarries of Anda

adds to the grandiose character. The interior arrangements are not what they ought to be. Ascend the belfry of *Sa. Maria ;* the vast plain is studded with some 168 villages. Observe the porch under this tower, with niche-work and statuary; before the high altar widows prostrate themselves the anniversary of their husbands' death on a black cloth, lighted with yellow tapers. In the *Sacristia* is or was an injured "Dead Christ" by Ribera, 1645, and in *El Noviciado* up-stairs a "St. Peter and St. Paul," by the same painter, and fine.

Look at the *Retablos* in the churches of *Sn. Vicente* and *Sn. Miguel;* the latter is by Hernandez; the statue of the Concepcion is excellent. Vitoria bears for arms "a castle supported by two lions," like other Basque towns. The inhabitants denied all assistance to our wounded, although the army expended in it most of the money and booty wrested from the invaders, thus enriching a place which the enemy had impoverished. Here, as at Talavera, was denied to an ally's gold what an invader obtained by iron; but in Spain, as in the East, force seems necessary to obtain supplies. The authorities refused to our commissaries even the use of empty convents and churches which had been gutted when Vitoria was sacked by Verdier, June 5, 1808. Here again Gen. Evans and his legion were left to rot like dogs in damp vaults, unaided and not even pitied by those who ruled in Vitoria. There is a local '*Historia*' by Landazuri, 4to., 2 vols., Mad., 1780.

There are diligence communications with Irun, R. cxviii.; Burgos, R. cxvi.; Madrid, R. cxiii. ; Pamplona, R. cxix.; and Bilbao, R. cxx.

ROUTE CXVIII.—VITORIA TO IRUN.

Arrazabe	2	
Salinas de Leniz . .	2¼ ..	4¼
Escoriaza	1 ..	5¼
Mondragon	1 ..	6¼
Vergara	2 ..	8¼
Villareal	2¼ ..	11¼

Villafranca	3	.. 14
Tolosa	3	.. 17
Andoain	2	.. 19
Astigarraga	2	.. 21
Oyarzun	2¼	.. 23¾
Irun	2¼	.. 26

Quitting Vitoria, we soon enter the Welsh-like hills with green copses, maize crops, and pretty villages perched on the eminences, amid chesnut groves. Now the Irish-looking hat gives place to the low blue cap or *Bereta*. The legs of the peasants are swathed up to the knees with Moorish bandages, and their feet encased in Iberian *abarcas*, brogues. The women toil at their hard tasks, and look old and broken; were it not for their white handkerchiefs, sex (the very young only excepted) would be obliterated by their thus doing the work of men (see our remarks p. 647). The architect will now remark the pepper-pot belfry-domes of the churches, the carved coats of arms over the portals of the manor or *family* mansions, *las casas solares*, and the solidly built houses, with projecting cornices, and protecting roofs. Here rain and damp are the enemies of the climate, while stone and iron are the drugs of the soil.

Soon we ascend the ridge of *Adrian*. At *Arlaban*, May 25, 1811, the *Guerrillero* Mina surprised Col. Lafitte, who was convoying Masséna's plunder after Santarem had settled his pretensions to soldiership. Mina spared his captives, but Masséna he meant to have hung, had he not escaped by accident, from having loitered behind in the stews of Vitoria. The enormous booty became, says Toreno (xv.), a powerful incentive to new recruits, who swelled the roving bands, confirming thereby Napier's assertion that much of this sort of patriotism was grafted on the stock of pillage—a remark which, because true, gave such dire offence to Arguelles, who, like Maldonado (ii., 442), beheld in these semi-bandits the personifications of purity and patriotism, and the real and sole deliverers of Spain. That they were a most formid-

able *nuisance* to the invaders cannot be doubted, and none more cheerfully acknowledged the value of their co-operation than the Duke; but great military armies, like the French, are never to be subdued by such desultory antagonists, however brave or active: for the *Guerrillero* see Index, and Sect. xiv.

After descending the ridge of *Salinas* the province of *Guipuzcoa* is entered. *Escoriaza*, a fine hamlet of 1600 souls, has a parish church, with a good nave and transept, and a hospital founded in the 15th century by Juan de Mondragon, and now abandoned, the funds, as usual, having been misapplied. Observe the bridge and arch over the Deva, a charming trout-stream.

Mondragon, a walled town, is also well placed on this beautiful river, and the Aramoyano; pop. 2500, and chiefly blacksmiths. The isolated *El Campanzar* may, in the words of Pliny (N. H., xxxiv. 14), be termed "a hill of iron." Here is a mine of most remote antiquity; the ore is found in a reddish clay, and yields at least 40 per cent. of the finest metal. Very fine iron is also procured from *La Mina de hierro helado*, "the ice-brook's temper," and from *La Cueva de Udala*. Consult Bowles, 337, and our remarks, Toledo (p. 853).

Vergara, which lies 2 L. out of the road from *Mondragon*, is a Swiss-like town on the banks of the Deva, whose pleasant basin is girdled by mountains. There is a decent *Posada*. Pop. about 4000. The *Plaza* has a good *casa consistorial;* there is, as usual, a capital fives-court. Here was concluded, after much parley, the famous or infamous traitor convention or Carlist capitulation of Aug. 31, 1839, between Maroto and Espartero, whereby the former, reeking with the blood of his comrades whom he had executed at Estella, consummated his career by betraying his king and master. Thus were sold those mountain posts which, defended by stout highlanders, long had defied alike the Christinos and Legionaries. The secret history of this *transaccion*,

with much curious and Spanish detail, is to be found in the work called
'*El Campo y la Corte de Don Carlos,*'
with an appendix of '*El convenio de
Vergara,*' 3rd edit., Madrid, 1840.
Dissensions prevailed in the camp of
Don Carlos, who himself was fitter to
lose than to win a crown, for had he
evinced a particle of talent or spirit, he
long before must have been at Madrid;
at last even the wearied and impoverished Basques were anxious to *fra-
ternise.* The site of the Judas *kiss* is
called *El Campo del Abrazo;* but *Ardoz* paid off *Vergara,* and then Espartero in his turn was bought and sold,
and the first then to abandon him was
the very Zabala who here had been his
go-between with Maroto, who soon fell
into universal disgrace, and obtained
permission to exile himself to Cuba:
" 'tis sport to see the engineer hoist
with his own petard." Spaniards, like
the Orientals, have no horror of treachery in the abstract, but they dislike
the traitor, *la traicion aplace pero no el
que la hace:* had Zimri peace who slew
his master? If the treachery fails, then
they turn on their base agent, threatening sword and "fire" (compare Judges
xiv. 15).

Passing *Villareal* is *Ormaiztequi,*
where Zumalacarreguy, the excellent
Guerrillero chieftain of Don Carlos,
was born Dec. 29, 1788; now a ridge
is crossed which separates the valleys
irrigated by the Deva and Orio. *Villafranca* is a solid, well-built town; on
the heights of *Descarga,* Zumalacarreguy entirely routed Espartero, driving
with his wild guerrilleros the regular
troops before him into Vergara. Passing a Swiss-like country, intersected
by trout-streams, we reach *Tolosa,* with
a decent diligence *Parador.* Tolosa
Ituriza (Ituria in Basque means "a
fountain") is one of the best towns of
Guipuzcoa, of which it is the central
place, and therefore has been made the
capital, to the infinite disgust of *S^n.
Sebastian;* accordingly no love is lost
between the two cities. It is built on
the Oria and Arages, under the mountains Ernio to the W., and Loaza to
the E. Pop. under 5000. The town
consists of six streets, which are intersected by three others; the fine old
gates were defaced by the French.
There is the usual fives-court on the
new *Plaza.* The church S^a. *Maria*
has a good portico between its towers:
the original *Retablo* was built in 1781;
the present one, of a simple classical
elevation, is enriched with different
local marbles. Tolosa abounds in the
casas solares, the family houses of men
of ancient pedigree, among whom Mi-
ñaño mentions that of *Andia,* in whom
he erroneously states that our order of
the Garter is *hereditary,* it having been
conferred on their ancestor Domenjou
Gonzalez, Aug. 20, 1471, by Edward
IV., in compliment to the aid rendered
to him by a legion sent from *Guipuzcoa*
to meddle in English civil wars. The
records of our Garter are missing from
the 7th to the 12th year of Edward IV.
(Anstis, ii. 184); and possibly this
Basque member may have been decorated in that disturbed interval; at all
events England has returned the favour
by despatching Sir de Lacy Evans,
G.C.B., to interfere in Cantabrian
squabbles. During the Peninsular war,
the authorities of Tolosa not only refused assistance to our soldiers, but
" positively ordered the inhabitants not
to give it for payment;" they plundered even our magazines, and refused
to give up their pillage when discovered
(Disp., Nov. 27, 1813).

From Tolosa there are diligences to
S^n. Sebastian, distant 4½ L.; but the
traveller, if he be bound for that sea-
place, had better by far make the
détour by Azpeitia (see R. cxxv).
There is also a diligence to Pamplona
(R. cxxxvii.).

The road continues through an excellent fishing country, and crossing
the rivers Oria and Leizaran, ascends
by the strong defences of *Andoain* to
Hernani, a long narrowish street, which
is built under the fortified hill S^a. Barbara on the river Urumea: it has a
good town-house and fives-court, with

pretty walks outside the gates. Pop. about 2500. Here the Legion, under Gen. Evans, almost as soon as they had landed, Aug. 29, 1835, made a needless reconnaissance, which ended in a repulse, trifling however compared to their total defeat on the same ground, March 16, 1837, when Evans, relying on being assisted from the Lecumberri side by the Christinos under Sarsfield, sallied forth from Sⁿ· Sebastian, distant about 1½ L., to assault the strong Carlist lines both here and on Sᵃ· Barbara to the l.; but in the moment of danger he was left by his allies to bear the whole brunt, for Sarsfield, scared by "a snow-storm!" marched *not* to the field of battle, but back to Pamplona, and that without giving Evans proper notice; *Socorros de España:* but the "sluggard is wiser in his own conceit than seven wise men who can render a reason" (Prov. xxvi. 16). Thus unsupported, the false position of the Legionaries was completed by the withdrawal of the 450 royal marines, who, by a widish interpretation of the laws of non-intervention and the rules of sea-service, had been marched inland: this regular force once withdrawn, nothing could impede the Carlist advance, and the Legion turned and fled (see Evans's '*Memoranda,*' 8). Sarsfield was soon afterwards murdered by his own troops, a rather common finale to unsuccessful generals in Spain (see p. 596).

The road continues hence to *Astigarraga* amid dove-tailing mountains; thence crossing a crystal stream, the *Chaparrea,* into picturesque *Oyarzun,* with its square tower rising over the defile: the arcades indicate the constant rain and necessity for shelter. It has a pretty *alameda* and the usual fives-court. The Pyrenees now soar to the r., while to the l. lies rock-built *San Sebastian* and the land-locked bay of *Pasages.* This line of broken country was taken by General Foy when retreating from Bilbao after the battle of Vitoria, when he made for France with such extraordinary rapidity that even

our gallant fox-hunter Graham could not catch him.

ROUTE CXIX.—VITORIA TO PAMPLONA.

Guevara	.	.	.	2¼	
Salvatierra	.	.	.	1¼	.. 4
Aranaz	.	.	.	5	.. 9
Irurzun	.	.	.	3¼	.. 12¼
Pamplona	.	.	.	3	.. 15¼

This is the line by which the Black Prince advanced in 1367 to victory, and that by which Marshal Jourdan retreated in 1813 after his defeat at Vitoria. The rich country or basin lies between the *Sierras* of Sⁿ· Adrian and Andia, and the scenery is fresh and full of fruit and cultivation. *Guevara,* on the Zadorra, was one of the strongholds of the Carlists; the castle on the hill was meant to be an imitation of that of St. Angelo at Rome. Observe in the town the *Casa solar* or *Casa fuerte* of the Ladrones de Guevara, an illustrious house; the name *Ladron,* "robber,"was given as an augmentation of *honour, a good* thief, to Sancho de Guevara, in the tenth century. In the year 885, Garci Iniquez, king of Navarre, was surprised at St. Juan de la Peña by the Moors, who having killed him and his queen, left their bodies naked on the plain, after which Sancho riding by perceived a hand issuing from the female corpse, which he delivered of a boy, and after bringing up the orphan, ultimately presented him to the people, having thus *robbed* death of their king. His descendant Gen. Santos Ladron was the first victim of the recent civil war, having been executed by the Christino Castanon within a short time after Ferdinand's death. The *Ladrones* of Spain are no doubt indigenous; they are scattered over the length and breadth of the land, and are to be found sometimes on the high roads, and always in the offices and treasuries of cities. *Good* thieves being scarce are proportionally estimated; thus San Dimas is universally worshipped as El *buen Ladron,* but the patron of the light-fingered and unprincipled is *S^{n.} Nicolas*, our "old Nick," who is also the sea-god of modern Greek pirates. The lady patroness in Spain of rogues is *N^{a.} Señora del Carmel*, who is generally represented with a large crowd of kings and monks, &c., who creep under her capacious petticoat.

Salvatierra, safe ground, a name which Joseph, resting for the first time after his flight from Vitoria, must have thought very appropriate, is the chief place of its *Hermandad*. Pop. about 1500. It stands near the Zadorra, on the spurs of the hills, overlooking a rich plain, which its agricultural inhabitants cultivate: the stone walls are still good; the gates were repaired by Charles V. Passing hence to the valley of *Borunda*, are the villages *Alzazua* and others, the scenes of *petty wars* between the Carlists and Christinos. The road in some parts enters Old Castile and then Navarre through a pleasant farm-studded country to its capital Pamplona.

Vitoria to *Bilbao*. There are several routes; those who love a mountain ride may bid adieu to wheels and scale the heights of *Altubi*, and then thread the valleys of *Orosco*.

ROUTE CXX.—VITORIA TO BILBAO.

Murguia	3	
Barambio	2	5
Orosco	2	7
Areta	1	8
Bilbao	3	11

Another road strikes up the Swiss-like valley of Orduña, starting from Miranda del Ebro.

ROUTE CXXI.—VITORIA TO BILBAO.

Miranda del Ebro	6	
Berquendo	2½	8½
Berberena	3	11½
Orduña	2½	14
Llodio	3	17
Areta	3	20
Bilbao	3	23

At *Berberana* there is an old castle and a large new posada. The road to Orduña over *La peña sobre Orduña* is finely engineered, while from the eminences the panoramas are noble. *Orduña*, from its position with *Amurrio* on the road to Bilbao, is of great military importance; the latter spot, as commanding four roads, was strongly fortified by Espartero, and became to Bilbao what Ramales is to Santander, the inner or land-side outwork. It was for taking Ramales that Espartero was made the Duke of Victory. Orduña, one of the last towns of Old Castile, is placed on its beautiful plain, near the Nervion, which flows hence to Bilbao. Pop. 3400, and principally agricultural. The town preserves its ancient walls and towers; it has a good *plaza*, with arcades and shops under them, and a handsome fountain raised in 1745: the principal streets communicate with this square. The climate is damp, the fruit excellent, and the trout-fishing capital. Ancient *Orduña* was built nearer to its celebrated Alp *La peña de Orduña*, which formed the mountain barrier frontier of the refugee Iberians; the peaks are covered with sand the greater part of the year. The road now follows the Nervion river through a charming cultivated country, with an air of industry, comfort, and rural prosperity, more like England than the forlorn, desolate, and poverty-stricken districts of the central Castiles. From *Orduña* Gomez started in June, 1836, on his military tour of Spain, and passed unmolested through the length and breadth of the land, frightening Christino towns and armies out of their propriety. He was pursued by Espartero and Narvaez, but these great generals were always just too late, arriving, as their bulletins stated, after the "bandit had fled in terror from their victorious veterans."

ROUTE CXXII.—VITORIA TO BILBAO.

Luco	2½	
Ochandiano	3	5½
Durango	3	8½
Zornoza	1½	10
Bilbao	3	13

This, the diligence road, is well engineered and generally in good condition; leaving Vitoria, it passes through the villages *Gamarra menor y mayor* and the sites where Graham dislodged and beat Reille during the battle of Vitoria, thereby turning the French position and forcing them to abandon the Irun high road and retreat by Salvatierra. *Durango* is a Swiss-like old town, placed on its river of the same name; pop. about 3000. Here are the usual *Alamedas* and fives-court. The altar in the church of *Sᵃ. Ana* was raised in 1774 by Ventura Rodriguez. *Durango*, the capital of its *Merindad*, from the central position is an important military point. It was between it and *Elorio*, at the hermitage of *Sⁿ·* Antolin, that Maroto met Espartero, Aug. 25, 1839, to plan the betrayal of Don Carlos, who, instead of boldly advancing with his Castilian battalions and seizing his traitor-general, fled to *Villareal,* and thus encouraged defection.

It was from Durango that he had before issued his famous, or rather infamous, decree, that all *foreigners* taken in arms against him should be put to death without trial; an Oriental and Draco proceeding, which, however disgusting to Europe, was in perfect accordance with all the immemorial and still existing laws and feelings of Spaniards, among whom it was and is of an every-day occurrence, being simply one of the common form, almost stereotyped *Bandos* which every Spanish man armed with brief authority issues at once, and acts upon without mercy or remorse; witness the wholesale executions, without form or trial, of the Españas, Eguias, Minas, Rodils, Zurbanos, &c., for their name is legion: or cross the Atlantic, and observe the identical policy and practice carried out by the cognate Oribés, Rosas, Sᵃ· Anas, &c. Here and there they are so completely *cosas de España,* or matters of course, that they create neither surprise nor pain; and this Durango decree, like the similar *bando* and executions at Malaga of Moreno, only attracted European notice because some *foreigners* were its victims.

By some wiseacres it has been ascribed to the personal cruelty of Don Carlos, who has been stigmatised as a monster on the ground that he was the inventor of such a summary process; but such accusers are either biassed by political prejudices or ignorant of the history and philosophy of Spain and Spaniards, when they thus argue about the matter as if it had taken place in England. Don Carlos, whatever may have been his faults, which were rather those of head than heart, was a man of strict honour, and by no means of a sanguinary or unforgiving disposition : he merely acted as his cabinet advised him, and exactly as ninety-nine out of one hundred Spaniards always have done before him, and always will do. There, as in the East, a policy of perfidy and death has always been pursued against enemies, and especially if they be intermeddling foreigners; there war assumes a personal character, and becomes one of petty hatred and revenge rather than a general contest for great principles; there life has never at any time been valued; in the prevailing indifference or fatalism, all know that they owe nature a death, and fancy that the moment is predetermined, which no forethought or precaution of theirs either can advance or retard when the fatal hour is come; and this is one of the secrets of the valour of the individual Spaniard and Oriental. In Spain life is staked every day, and all parties stand the hazard of the die; those who win exacting the whole pound of flesh, and those who lose paying the forfeit as a matter of course: to beg for or grant pardon would alike degrade the petitioner and sparer, as strength is estimated by the blows struck, not by those that are withheld. Mercy to a foe when down is thought imbecility or treachery; the slightest forbearance, concession, conciliation, or hesitation would be imputed, not to kindly principles, but to weakness and timidity (see the Duke's notions how to deal with Spaniards, p. 347). Fair play and equity are motives which would be received with incredulity or shouts of derisive laughter; for here, as in the East, wherever there is power it is used without scruple, and submitted to even to injustice, as each and every individual Spaniard feels that he in similar circumstances would have done the same; and to this day, had Espartero not been afflicted with the mania of trying to govern according to foreign practices and constitutions, but had adhered to the ways of Spain, crushing his opponents with the sword, bullet, and bowstring, shedding "vile black blood" as in a Roman proscription, he would still have been regent, and strong and respected. To attempt to conciliate those who are not to be conciliated is holding out a premium to agitation; and whenever a people from *inherent vices of race* are unfit for self-government, and have no control from *within*, they must have it forced upon them from *without*.

A real Spanish authority prides itself on a stern, harsh inexorability, and adopts what have been blandly termed "prudent and vigorous" measures, a "salutary intimidation," by just lopping off opponents' heads, as Tarquin did those of the sweet lilies. Political antagonists, and much more, if foreign ones, are presumed to be guilty, and, if identified, are shot on the spot, without trial, just as the "prudent and vigorous" viceroy of Ireland executed the *foreign* Spaniards of the Armada when wrecked on the coast. However frigid and dilatory the government on all questions of domestic improvement, when traitors take the field, it is indeed brief—off with their heads: nor on these occasions does it ever become unpopular with Spaniards, who, like Orientals, have no other abstract notion of sovereignty except a despotism (see p. 781); and the really strong and civilized alone can afford to be generous, while the weak resort to cruelty which is proportionate to their previous terror.

To defraud, ill-use, and abuse the foreigner is the essence of *Españolismo*,

against whom the Iberians waged a war of fire πυρινος, one *al cuchillo*, to the knife, and without quarter or treaty ασπονδος (Polyb., xxxv. 1, i. 65). In the East prisoners have always been killed almost as a matter of course (see 1 Sam. xi. 34; 1 Sam. xv.; Isa. xiii. 6). And as Amaziah cast down ten thousand at once from a rock (ii. Chr. xxv. 12), so Hannibal cut the throats of five thousand Romans; ίνα μη εν τω κινδυνω νεωτερισειαν (App. 'An.' 556), or *que no haya novedad*, as a modern Spaniard would say while starving them or doing the same thing : and the common phrase of the day is *assegurarles*, to make sure of them; just as the soldiers proposed to do with St. Paul (Acts xxvii. 42). Mercy is held to be expensive, while death is economical, and saves rations, which are scarce in Spain. The manner in which the Spaniards massacred the French prisoners during the war is well known, and in justification it may be stated that such reprisals were a natural retaliation for the wholesale executions of the terrorist *Victors*, who first taught the lesson, and were only compelled to lean to mercy by having their own measure of death dealt out to them. In vain the Duke counselled amnesties towards the *Afrancesados* (Disp. June 11, 1813): in vain again did he send Lord Eliot to stay the fratricidal bloodshed. The Spanish premier, for only listening to the proposal, was hurled from office amid the *mueras* of Madrid. A copious "shedding of vile black blood" is the ancient uninterrupted panacea of all military *Sangrados*, whatever their shade of politics. Amnesties, &c. have always been scouted as the base inventions of the foreigner and enemy; therefore when the Spaniard, whether Carlist or Christinist, perused the diatribes in the English press against the decree of Durango, they only smiled at the writer's total ignorance of Spanish common sense and customs, and murdered on, unchecked by the public opinion of Europe, of which they are either entirely ignorant, or for which they have a profound scorn and contempt. Those therefore who prefer the practice of Westminster Hall to the summary proceedings of *cuatro tiros*, *pasale por las armas*, and the bowstring garrote, should not interpose in the domestic quarrels either of Spain or Barbary. The foreign adventurers moreover sought the penalties of the decree of Durango, of which they came forewarned, for it was passed before they landed; nor, had even a Christino packed jury been assembled, would it have found Don Carlos guilty, as regarded these foreigners, of infringing the laws of Spain, or of doing anything repugnant to the feelings of the nation. Those who measure Spaniards by a European standard, and condemn their *things* because differing from ours, certainly prove that they have better hearts than heads, and a clearer perception of the laws of humanity and justice than of logical reasoning, or of the usages of this Oriental country and people.

Approaching Bilbao is *Arrigorriga*, where Espartero and Gen. Evans were defeated by the Carlists, Sept. 11, 1835. The *ponte nuevo*, near the scene of battle, is made for the artist. *Bilbao.*—The best inn is the *San Nicolas*. Bilbao (Bello vas, "the beautiful bay or ford"), the capital of Vizcaya, is placed on the Nervion, which divides the old town from the new: the river disembogues at *Portugalete*, distant about six miles, and has a dangerous bar. The name in Basque is *Ibaizabel*, and this is the "narrow river,' whose windings are "the *Bilboes*," where in steam-tugless days our ancient mariners feared to be caught, and to which Beaumont and Fletcher (Wild Goose Chase, i. 2) compared being married. Bilbao being situated in a gorge of hills is damp, and pulmonary diseases are prevalent; pop[n.] about 15,000 : the city is purely mercantile, and possesses no fine art; many of its older churches and convents were destroyed during the recent sieges, or since suppressed. The principal streets are straight and

well built, the houses lofty and substantial; the roofs project, forming penthouses and protections against sun and rain. Bilbao is well supplied with fish, flesh, fowl, and green herbs, and the foreign merchants are hospitable. The *Café Suisso* is a favourite resort, where the Biscayans eat ices, play at dominos and at *Mûs*, a game of cards, and grimace. There is very little to be seen. The *Campo Santo*, or new burial-ground, is admired by judges of cemeteries. The *Arenal*, or "Strand," is the favourite *Alameda* and public walk. The Nervion is crossed by a new iron suspension-bridge, which is thought by the Basques to be the eighth marvel of the world; but the old bridge is much more artistical, and was also once the boast of Bilbao, and still forms the charge of the city arms with two wolves, the cognizance of Diego Lopez (Lupus) de Haro, Lord of Biscay, who built it circa 1356. The Tuscan *carneceria*, or shambles, is also considered to be a lion, second only to the cemetery—pleasant sights! The streets are clean and the town quiet, for no carts or carriages are allowed to enter, and goods are drawn about on trucks. The hospital, commenced in 1818, is unfinished. The walk to the Punta de Banderas, whence the merchants telegraph arriving ships, is agreeable, being enlivened with gardens, mountains, and sea. There the river presents a considerable show of business : Santander, however, has risen at the expense of Bilbao; for during the recent sieges many merchants removed their establishments to a city free from warlike interruptions, which are fatal to peace-loving commerce. The women in Bilbao do porters' work, just as in the fields they do that of men and horses. For the river and coast, see p. 937.

The Bilbaoese during the Peninsular war refused even the use of the convents which the French had gutted for the wounded English, who at Vitoria had delivered their city (Disp., Aug. 19, 1813). Again, they opposed the landing of English stores for the Duke when advancing a conqueror into France (Disp., Oct. 14, 1813); and yet Bilbao had been sacked without remorse by Gen. Merlin, who boasted in his bulletin that "he had extinguished the insurrection in the blood of 1200 men " (Toreno, v.). This *conjurer*, like Victor at Talavera, obtained all he wanted by a wand of iron, while everything was denied to the gold of a merciful ally.

Bilbao, in the recent civil wars, was twice exposed to destructive sieges; the dilapidations have, however, been much repaired. Don Carlos, in the first case, had absurdly ordered Zumalacarreguy to attack this place, instead of at once pushing on to Madrid, which must have surrendered, such was the prestige of the *Guerrillero's* victories over the Rodils, Quesadas, Osmas, and other regular Christino generals; thus in the War of the Succession the archduke Charles forced Peterborough to besiege Barcelona, instead of pouncing on the dispirited capital, and these sieges lost to both these Charleses the crown of Spain. Bilbao was defended by Mirasol, a personally brave man, but "a child in the art of war," who selected a line of defence beginning at the rise Larrinaga, on to Sᵃ· Cruz, and down to the Zendeja, thus actually leaving to the enemy the heights Morro and Artagan, which commanded his position and the town. On the 10th of June, 1835, Zumalacarreguy, having routed Espartero at Descarga, came to Bilbao and seized the church and *Palacio de Begoña*, which Mirasol had left undefended, almost as if to assist his assailants. This point enfiladed the town, which must have capitulated had not a ball struck *El Tio Tomas* in the calf of his right leg, while standing in the balcony. The Basque surgeons did the rest, and in spite of the advice of Mr. Burgess, sent their patient to his grave at Segana on the Orrio, June 25; with him died the Carlist cause, for Eraso raised the siege on the 1st of the ensuing July. The conduct of Mira-

sol inside and of Alaix outside was, in the words of even their partisan, Mr. Bacon, "a burlesque on war," for both did everything that they ought not to have done, and nothing that they ought to have done; the real work was performed by the English sailors, under Capts. Ebsworth, Lapidge, Henry, and Lord John Hay; they defended the trenches, they supplied arms and food, for the Christinos were in "want of everything at the critical moment," the poor soldiers having been neglected as usual by their pauper government. Bilbao, relieved by others, now called itself a modern Saguntum, a *Ciudad invicta*, and, reposing under its laurels, made no sort of preparation against future attack, although warned of its approach; thus when the Carlists re-appeared, October 23rd, they at once carried all the undefended positions on the right bank of the Nervion, from Sⁿ· Agustin to *Los Capuchinos*, the Christino general Sⁿ· Miguel abandoning everything without a struggle; and then, had the Carlist Eguia occupied, as he ought to have done, the Begoña hill and the opposite Miravilla, the *Ciudad invicta* would have been conquered at once. Nay more, Sⁿ·Miguel had even omitted to secure the convent *Mames* and the church *Abando*, the keys of his defence. Those who wish to see these sites will obtain an excellent view from *Los Capuchinos*. But now the English blue jackets, under Lord John Hay, came again to the rescue; his sailors beat Eguia from *El Desierto*, and held Portugalete. Meanwhile Espartero, either from want of means or talent, was busy doing nothing but "marching and counter-marching" his poor soldiers, and issuing orders, counter-orders, and dis-orders; he wasted fourteen precious days in moving from Balmaceda, distant only twenty miles, and that never would have been done had not every sort of supply been furnished by the English; such, indeed, was the destitution of this army that its officers—Espartero being almost the only exception — wished orientally to retire "each man to his own home," and leave Bilbao and Christina to their fate, *Sócorros de España*. Then it was that Capt. Lapidge and Col. Wylde pointed out the true line of relief by crossing the river, which they persuaded Espartero to do on the 24th, having, it is said, used a gentle violence with "his Grace;" then English sailors prepared rafts, which the fire of English artillery protected, and so the Nervion was first passed, and next the Asua at Luchana, and thus Bilbao was relieved after a sixty days' siege, on which the whole question of the war turned; and one short day more would have exhausted both the townsfolk and their enemies, who were equally reduced to the last extremities of destitution, and the weather was terrific. The Carlists made a very feeble resistance against the Christinists, who advanced in a snow storm, and bivouacked that night without food and half naked, on the ground, with true Spanish endurance of hardships. The garrison in Bilbao in the meanwhile offered no sort of cooperation by way of sortie, such was the incredible ignorance or want of vigilance on the part of their commanders. Espartero, although in bad health, displayed much courage under fire, while the besieged and besiegers, during the desultory contests, fought with all the desperate personal valour and individual implacability of local hatreds, hand to hand, knife to knife. The emphatic want on both sides, when everything was alike wanting, was a *head* to plan the war greatly and carry it out worthily. *Cosas de España*, the best Carlist account is Henningsen's "Twelve Months' Campaign with Zumalacarreguy;" for Christinist details consult the lively "*Scenes and Adventures*" of *Poco Mas*, in which Mr. Moore, a hearty partisan, while "reporting" the glories of "his Grace," proves beyond doubt that Wylde, Hay, and the English did the work. Again Mr. Bacon, an equally staunch and honest partisan, admits, in his "*Six Years in Biscay*," that "no satire can

be written equal to the official bulletins" of the Christinos. But the Castilian is such a sonorous sesquipedalian language that it seems to be made for *Valientes* who trumpet forth their own *prodigios de valor*, their own "*glorias y fatigas*." Espartero was only compared, on this 24th of December, to our Saviour! The Madrid government responded with equal eloquence; cheap ribbons, thanks, and odes, in short every reward was given except money; and now Mellado, writing in 1843, does not even allude to the English; thus the stout Legion was done not only out of its glory, but its pay. However, there is nothing new in all this, and the Black Prince fared no better (see *Navarrete*, p. 912). And when will our worthy countrymen, who fight and pay for all, consult Spanish history, that old almanac, but in every page of which it stands thus recorded, for the benefit of *foreigners*—

Those who in our "things" interpose,
Will only get a bloody nose.

There is some talk of a railroad from Bilbao to Madrid; and as Gen. Cordova boasted that he led his troops to victory over these mountains "higher than the eagles soar," no doubt Spanish engineers will do as much.

ROUTE CXXIII.—SANTANDER TO BILBAO.

Langre	. . . .	2	
Meruelo	. . . .	3	.. 5
Santoña	. . . .	2	.. 7
Laredo	. . . .	1	.. 8
Islares	. . . .	2	.. 10
Castro Urdiales	. .	2	.. 12
Somorrostro	. . .	2	.. 14
Bilbao.	. . . .	3½	.. 17½

For Santander see p. 919. This bridle road is much cut up by the bays and rivers of a hilly and indented coast; an occasional steam communication in summer offers a shorter and more convenient passage by sea. If the weather be fair cross the *Rio* to Langre, thus avoiding the land circuit. Nothing of interest, however, occurs before Santoña and Laredo, which rise

2 s

opposite each other on their excellent bay; but neither need be entered, as they can be passed by on the l. *Santoña* is the Gibraltar of Cantabria. The *Monte*, under which it is built, is severed by the Isthmus *el Arenal de Berria*, which intervenes between the hills *Brusco* and *Groma*, and the isolated Ano, just as the neutral ground does between the " Rock " and *San Roque:* the bay contracts opposite *Santoña*, and is crossed at the passage, *Pasage de Salue.* The Franciscan convent, higher up on the *Canal de Ano*, is pleasantly situated. From Santoña the corn of Castile and iron of Biscay are largely exported. The storms off the coast are sometimes terrific; and here, in October 1810, a British squadron was wrecked. Santoña was fortified by the French, who were regularly supplied from France by *sea*. See the indignant Lesaca correspondence of the Duke to Lord Melville. Santoña capitulated in March 1814; but the Duke refused to ratify the treaty in consequence of the breach of all faith shown by the French garrison of Jaca (Disp. April 1, 1814). *Laredo* is also protected by its headland *El Rastillar*, which defends the s. side of the bay. The lands gain on the coast; and this port, which under the Romans contained 14,000 souls, now has dwindled to 3000. Part of the Moorish chain of the Seville bridge was long hung up in the Sª· Maria here, having been broken by a Laredo ship, and it forms the charge of the city's shield. *Castro Urdiales*, of which the Black Prince was *Señor*, has also its bay, headland, rocks, castle, and hermitage of *Sa· Ana.* The place was sacked by Foy, May 11, 1813, on quitting it to retreat to France, when, says Southey (Chr. 43), " He butchered men and women, sparing none, and inflicting upon them cruelties which none but a devilish nature could devise." The ravaged town has since been rebuilt, and is now clean and regular. The port is so beloved by the sailors of the storm-tossed Bay of Biscay, that they

say " *A Castro o al Cielo*." On this iron-bound coast the mighty Atlantic is first repelled, and the volume of waters thrown back on the fresh incoming waves, and thus a boiling race is created. At *San Anton* near the town is a ruined convent of the Templars; the fish is excellent, especially the *besugo* and *bonito*, a sort of tunny and bream. The rocky hills are terraced with vines, which produce a poor *Chacoli*. The *Somorrostro* district has been immemorially celebrated for iron; the ore occurs abundantly in beds from 3 to 10 feet deep, in a calcareous earth, and when taken up and wetted, sometimes it is of a blood colour. It yields from 30 to 35 per cent. metal; about 6000 tons of iron are made annually in these districts, which are worth in bar from 20*l.* to 27*l.* per ton; but it could not compete with English iron, without heavy protecting duties, which thus secure to Spain a dear and bad article, as it is softer and with a longer fibre than ours, which is attributed to its being smelted with charcoal, not coal; the mining and smithies are primitively rude; foreigners, however, are slowly introducing more scientific methods; the steel for swords was better made, a manufacture in which the warlike Spaniards have always excelled immemorially (see Toledo, p. 855); the " good Bilbos " of Falstaff were wrought from the produce of the hill *Triano.*

All this district affords much occupation to the mineralogist and geologist, as the *Monte Serrantes* was once a volcano; leaving it to the r., and crossing the *Concha de Bilbao*, is *Portugalete*, placed on the neck of the Nervion, with a dangerous bar; six pleasant miles lead to Bilbao; to the l. is the convent *El desierto*, now indeed a desert, but once a monastic paradise, for the wily monks hid from the world their real comforts under an austere name; thus the Franciscans, by a vow of poverty, amassed wealth; near the *Desierto*, which is placed on the confluence of the Galindo and Nervion, was the roadstead of the English *non-intervening* squadron, by which alone Bilbao was twice relieved, and Don Carlos twice defeated. Proceeding onwards on the r. bank is *Luchana*, from whence Espartero took his title of *Conde*, ascending per saltum to that of *Duque*; but once pass over from Dover, and military strawberry leaves are plentiful as blackberries, while England in two centuries has created only Marlborough and Wellington; but as to relative *value*, see p. 879. Those who cross the river will enter Bilbao by the upper road through *Deusto*; those who continue on the l. bank will pass the *Cadagua*, and continuing under the ridge of *Castrojana*, enter the old town under the fort of *Miravilla*.

ROUTE CXXIV.—BILBAO TO SAN SEBASTIAN.

Algorta	2		
Plencia	2	..	4
Baguio	2	..	6
Bermeo	2	..	8
Guernica	2	..	10
Elancobe	2	..	12
Lequeitio	2	..	14
Ondarrea	2	..	16
Motrico	1¼	..	17¼
Deva	1	..	18¼
Venta de Ibarrieta .	2	..	20¼
Orio	2	..	22¼
San Sebastian . . .	2¼	..	25

The steam communication is preferable to the bridle-road; those who adventure by land, after crossing the *Asua* will reach the fishing town *Algorta*, and thence turning to the r. *Plencia* with its bridge, and *Villano* with its signal *Atalaya;* thence leaving the headland *Machichaco* to the l. on to *Bermeo*, Flavio Briga, which has a good harbour and free from any bar. This busy fishing town contains some 4000 amphibious inhabitants. Here was born Alonzo de Ercilla, the soldier epic poet of Spain, whose best authors have been men of the sword, and this hero wrote his finest stanzas on the pommel of his saddle. At *Mundaca*, famous for tunnies, the road to *Guer-*

nica follows the l. bank of the river Mundaca.

Guernica, as its Basque name signifies, is placed on the "slope of a hill," below which is a "reedy flat" called *El Juncal*, which is much subject to inundations, but full of snipes and wild fowl in winter. At Guernica was held the Parliament of Basque senators. This *Witenagemote* originally sat under the overspreading canopy of an ancient oak, which the town still bears on its shield. Among rude primitive people, before temples were raised by the hand, a noble tree inspired a reverential awe, and was dedicated to the Deity (Pliny, N. H. xii. 1). Groves also were afterwards planted as marks of sites dedicated to worship and covenant (Gen. xxi. 33). Joshua (xxiv. 26) placed the book of the law under an oak, "by the sanctuary." Such, again, was the sacred Δρυς of the Druids; such were the *Ygdraisel* or consecrated trees, under which were seated the twelve deified judges of the Norwegians. The association of religion with trees and groves long survived after the erection of temples. St. Bridget of Ireland formed her "chapel" out of an oak, her *kill* Dara. So our Fairlop oak, like the terebinth tree of Abraham, is an example of the admixture of religion and traffic which always characterized these silvan sanctuaries.

The *Casas consistoriales*, and more than half the town of Guernica, were burnt in 1808 by the French republicans, the preachers of universal freedom and philanthropy. These theorists, who planted sham trees of liberty and real guillotines at home, cut down the true oak of the free Basques, one which was very old even in 1334 (see Mariana, xvi. 3), one "Religione patrum longos servata per annos," and under whose venerable canopy Ferd. and Isab. swore in 1476 to uphold the Basque *Fueros*, as their grandson Charles V. did again, April 5, 1526. When the English cleared Spain, an oak sapling was planted to replace the original tree, but even that tender plant was hewed down by Armildez de Toledo, a general of the then liberal Christina.

The oak of Guernica, like the altar of *N^{a.} Senora de Begoña*, near Bilbao, was a place of refuge for debtors. It was also a sort of place of *habeas corpus* return, or a court of appeal, as no Basque could be arrested without a summons to appear under it, and learn the charge against him, and thus prepare his defence. The word rendered *grove* in our Bible (Gen. xxi. 33) is read by Parkhurst as *Asel*, oak, and he conjectures that the *Asylum*, or sanctuary of Romulus, which was placed between two oaks, may be derived from it.

Those who have read Wordsworth's plaintive sonnet, and have pictured to themselves a wide shadowing oak, under whose boughs mossed with age, and high top bald with dry antiquity, silver-haired men sat in council, just as one reads of in Telemaque, and other equally true delineations of society as it is, will find to their horror that the *Casa de Juntas* is a huge, ungainly, new mass of stone of passing pretension, and a sort of Corinthian summer-house, while Basque senators, in French pea-jackets, complete the ruin of all national, primitive, and picturesque associations.

About a mile from the town is a Roman encampment, which is not worth visiting. Returning to the coast at *Lequeiteó*, a post strong by nature and art, and placed on its river, girdled by the *Lumencha* and *Otoya* hills, we enter the easily defended country which all the way up to *Guetaria* was abandoned to the Carlists in 1836 by Iriarte and Cordova. *Ondarroa*, the "mouth of Sand," has a snug but not a deep port, a decent church built on piles, and a good bridge over its river. Now we quit Vizcaya and enter Guipuzcoa. *Motrico, tucio-turbolico*, whence much fish (quere *turbot?*) is sent to Madrid, in the Basque signifies a hedge-hog, *Tricu*, which the rock is *said* to resemble. This pretty port is surrounded

with wooded hills; the land teems with fruit and vines which are trellised over the fishermens cottages. Here is produced a red *Chacoli*, which the natives think equal to Bordeaux, but they know no better. In the church *were* a Crucifixion, attributed to Murillo, and a S^{a.} Catherine by Johan Boechorst, 1663 : enquire for them. *Deva* is charming, and contains some 3000 piscatose souls: here the orange and olive ripen. It was proposed on paper to make this place the port, which by means of a canal, and the rivers Zadorra and Ebro, *were* to connect the Atlantic with the Mediterranean, and still the sheltered secure bay is the outport of Vitoria and Mondragon. The square town, with streets intersecting each other at right angles, lies below the slope of the *Iciar*. It has two *Plazas*. The parish church is one of the finest in these provinces, and near it is the mansion-house with portico and clock-tower. The panorama from the summit of the *Izarraiz* is magnificent, and the wide expanse of ocean contrasts with the mountain jumble of the land. At *Zumaya* we cross the excellent salmon and trout stream *Urola* (*Ur*, water, *ola*, smithy, *Ferreria*), then the *Oria*, which rising near the *Puerto S^{a.} Adrian*, finishes its beautiful course, separated by a ridge from the basin of the *Deva*: both riversare precious to the angler. Thence to *S^{n.} Sebastian*, rising on its conical rocky knoll (see R. cxxv.).

In briefly describing the route from Bayonne to Irun, we refer for all details, which do not touch on English or Spanish interests, to Mr. Murray's excellent ' Hand-book for France' (R. lxxvi.). And first we strongly advise all entering Spain for the first time to run over our 207 preliminary pages.

ROUTE CXXIV. A.—BAYONNE TO IRUN.

	Posts.	
Bayonne		
Bidart.	1¼ ..	
St. Jean de Luz . .	1¼ ..	3
Urugne	2¼ ..	4¼
Irun	2 ..	6¼

Bayonne (hotel de S^{a.} Etienne), the

Basque *Bay-o-na*, " the good port," is placed on the Nive and Adour (Ur, ὕδωρ, *Duero*, the Sussex Adur). The strong citadel, fortified by Vauban, was the key of Soult's position in 1814, and the scene of one of the last most murderous and unnecessary conflicts between the French and English. Buonaparte's abdication on the 7th of April, 1814, was known to Soult on the 12th, and a suspension of arms had been proposed by the Duke; accordingly, our troops were off their guard, when before daylight of the 14th a sortie was made by the French, which was signally beaten back; but this tragical episode to the war cost the lives of 2000 brave men. Here the *bayonet* finished the work, and on the spot where it was first used by some Basques, who stuck their knives in their muskets' muzzles: now it is *the* English weapon, which no foe ever has dared to face twice.

In the old castle of Bayonne, opposite the Prefecture, in 1563, did Catherine de Medicis, an Italian Machiavelli, meet Alva, a Spanish man of blood and bigotry, and plan the massacre of St. Bartholomew, which was executed Aug. 24, 1572, to the joy of the Vatican and the Escorial, for Philip II. never laughed heartily but that once.

There are plenty of mails and diligences from Bayonne to Burgos and Madrid; the traveller reaches Burgos the third day, as Tolosa and Vitoria are made halting places at night. Those who are not hurried should stop at Irun, and take up the Vitoria road after making a détour through *San Sebastian* (R. cxxv.). At Bayonne the bother of passports must be attended to, from which no honest men are exempt, except robbers and smugglers. The document must be *vised* by the Spanish and English consuls, the latter charging 3 francs for his permit. Bayonne is quitted by the *Porte d'Espagne:* soon to the l. is the *Château Marrac,* whose dishonourable recollections long will survive those ruined walls, in which Buonaparte embraced

his decoyed guest Ferdinand VII., and then sent him from his table to a dungeon : here also, soon after, did Godoy sign away with Duroc that crown which British valour replaced on a thankless head. To the r., about 5 miles from Bayonne, is *Biaritz*, from whose cliff-built Phare the rocky, ironbound coast of hard Iberia looms in view. This first glance of a new land and people relieves the dull monotony of the commonplace *Landes* which extend to Bordeaux, and which lack the desolate poetry of the deserts of Castile. Now what a change awaits those who love surprises and comparisons! It is the passing into a new planet, or like crossing from Dover to Calais, both so near indeed to France, and yet so widely, so irrevocably apart from antipathetic French ways and things.

At *Bidart* the Basque country is entered, and the peasantry are at least cognate with those on each side of the *Bidasoa,* but theirs is a neutral ground, and they are Basques, that is, neither French nor Spaniards (read our heading to this Section). *St. Jean de Luz*— inn La Poste—placed on the Nivelle, like Irun, is a Basque misnomer, for it is not a " city of light," a Gades or lucis domus, but of " mud," and a Lutetia, or lucus a non lucendo. Here, in 1660, Louis XIV. was married to Maria Teresa, daughter of Philip IV., and higher up to the l. are the heights of *Ainhoüe,* where, Nov. 10, 1813, the Duke routed Soult and Foy, driving them headlong from their tremendous fortifications and capturing 51 cannon. Here, again, the Duke long had his head-quarters, winning golden opinions from his very foes by protecting them from the plunder not only of the Spaniards, but of their own countrymen. " Je suis assez long-temps soldat pour savoir que les pillards et ceux qui les encouragent ne valent rien devant l'ennemi" (Disp., June 27, 1815). How truly English is the sentiment, as well as the language in which it is expressed ; for the Duke created a new Anglo-French dialect, which his Dispatches have rendered classical. The gallant French estimated the worth and valour of their generous foe as the Carthaginians did of Scipio, exclaiming that "one like the gods had come among them who overcame all alike by his goodness as by his arms" (Livy, xxvi. 50). The authorities everywhere presented addresses to him, which the modest hero, who did good by stealth and blushed to find it fame, begged Lord Bathurst *not* to publish (Disp., Nov. 21, 1813 ; April 12, 1814). Like the old Roman, he never trumpeted forth his own prodigies of valour—that he left to others : " optimus quisque *facere*, quam dicere, et sua ab *aliis* benefacta laudari malebat" (Sall. B. C. 8). The French offered prayers to heaven to long preserve "un héros aussi grand que sage," and they were heard, serus in cœlum redeat. They also proved by their actions that a brave enemy can become a noble friend, for here did the Duke receive " repeated intelligence and warning from the *French* of acts of treachery meditated by the Spaniards " (Disp., Jan. 13, 1814).

Urugne, the last post station in France, is in the spurs of the mountain range, which, called the *Pyrenean* (see Index), extends from the Mediterranean to the mouth of the Miño in Gallicia. The French custom-house is at *Behobia,* a small village with a poor inn, *La Poste,* which prepares the traveller for a Spanish *Posada.* Here the baggage of those coming from Spain is severely searched by the semi-soldier *Douanier,* who thus wages war in peace-time ; nor are the persons even of ladies always respected, but on both sides of the Bidasoa a straight waistcoat seems to be put on all fair, free, commercial enterprise, to the benefit of the smuggler and inconvenience of the honest merchant and uncommercial traveller. The objects most searched for are tobacco and sealed letters. Coined money is not allowed to be taken *out* of Spain; you may bring *into* it as much as you please, but " no

money *is* ever returned" here : beware therefore of having anything contraband, and make a full declaration of whatever is doubtful (read also our remarks, p. 205), and begrudge not a compliment to the well-known *politesse* of *la Grande Nation,* which softens even a Douanier's heart ; that of a Spanish *Resguardo* is better assailed by a dollar : at all events be patient and good-tempered, for these detentions and scrutinies, so inexpressibly odious to freeborn Englishmen and the curse of continental travelling, cannot be escaped and must be endured. Those who proceed from Spain to Bayonne are advised to have their luggage *plombé,* paying for each package a sous, as the leaden seal keeps off the harpies, like that of Solomon did the devil.

A wooden bridge painted with a dingy red, which, although the colour of the guillotine, is a very favourite one for shutters, &c. on the French side, crosses the *Bidasoa,* which flows like the British Channel between the two antipathetic nations. The name means in Basque either the "way to the west," or *vida,* "two," and *osoa,* "streams," because composed of two streams flowing one from *Elisondo* and the other from the *Baztan.* The length of the Bidasoa is about 45 miles, forming for the last 12 the boundary. In olden times Spain claimed not only the whole river, but so much of the French bank as its waters covered at high tide. These questions, long matters of *rivality,* were settled by the French republic and Charles IV., by each country retaining its own shore. The river widens below the bridge into a tidal *rio* or estuary, and the embouchure is guarded on the Spanish side by *Fuenterrabiá,* which looks strong at a distance, which it is not : it faces *Andaye,* a French village celebrated for its brandy. Between the bridge and the sea are some fords which are practicable at low water, being covered at least 14 ft. at high tide : these were made known to the Duke by a Basque fisherman, and thus, as at Oporto, he was enabled again to surprise and defeat Soult. At the close of a thunder-storm, Oct. 7, 1813, our troops, at a given signal, wound slowly like serpents across the sands, effected a passage, dashed up the *Montagne d'Arrhune*, and carried by sheer daring the rugged, natural frontier of France, which skilful engineers had been fortifying for three months.

Standing on the bridge and looking up the river to the l., in front rises the celebrated hill of *Sⁿˑ Marcial* (see p. 945), and on the flats below the bridge are the huts set up by the Spanish authorities as *Lazaretos*, or quarantine houses during the cholera of 1833. Anything more uncomfortable or less suited to sanatory purposes never was contrived in the East, for they are fitted to breed rather than to prevent a plague. Looking down the stream is an ignoble patch in the waters dignified by the name of *La Isla de los faisanes*, the island of pheasants, which are just as plentiful here as phœnixes or birds of paradise in the Champs Elysées at Paris. On this neutral ground, in 1463, Louis XI. had an interview with Henrique IV. The perfidious award of the former led to the formation of the Spanish league and deposition of the latter (Prescott, ch. iii.). Mariana (xxiii. 5) and Comines (ch. 36) have given the curious details of this meeting. The mean appearance of Louis offended the Spaniards, who always visit in grand costume, while the French satirically laughed at the Don's *Boato*, so the two kings embraced, and then, like the devils in Asmodeus, hated each other ever afterwards. Here again, in 1660, Cardinal Mazarin met Louis de Haro and arranged the marriage between the daughter of Philip IV. and Louis XIV. (see for details E. S. xxxii. 118). The singular mutual suspicions and etiquette are accurately described by Dunlop (Memoirs, ch. xi.). It was in fitting up the saloon of conference that Velazquez sickened of a tertian fever, of which he soon after died at Madrid.

Thus Spain's greatest artist was sacrificed on the altar of upholstery: for the particulars of his death, see Palomino, (Mus. Pit. ii. 521). This Spanish Vasari gives us a full-length portrait of the magnificent costume worn by Velazquez on the occasion, who eclipsed the lords of the bedchamber as much in the sparkle of his diamonds as in the brilliancy of his intellect.

Louis XIV., *Le Grand Monarque*, lived to afterwards deprive the Catalonians of their liberties, which he then pledged his honour to uphold, and placed his grandson on the throne of Spain, which he had guaranteed never to do at his marriage with the daughter of Philip IV.: thus the weaker kingdom became locked in the embrace of the stronger one, and from that fatal moment has been alternately her dupe or victim. The Spanish policy of Louis XIV. has now become a French axiom of state, whether France be ruled by a Bourbon or Buonaparte, and Foy (ii. 211) candidly remarks, " *La soumission absolue*, et avec une garantie stable de l'Espagne, n'était elle pas la conséquence naturelle et nécessaire de l'extension de la France au-delà des Alpes et du Rhin, ses limites naturelles?" He proceeds to term these views *saines et politiques*, as undoubtedly they are for *one* party, since the Pyrenean boundary, says the Duke, is "the most vulnerable frontier of France, probably the only vulnerable frontier" (Disp., Dec. 21, 1813). Accordingly France has always endeavoured to dismantle the Spanish defences and to foster insurrections and *pronunciamentos* in Catalonia, for Spain's infirmity is her opportunity, and therefore the "sound policy" of the rest of Europe is to see Spain strong, independent, and able to hold her own Pyrenean key.

The Bidasoa once crossed, the Basque provinces are entered, and although they are cognate with those on the r. bank, yet the change of country is striking. Now, as on passing the lines at Gibraltar, we step from a highly organised power to one where nothing is *réglementaire*, where nothing is done in real style—a lazy, Oriental, unbusiness, make-shift character pervades every civil and military department of this misgoverned land, where even the regimental bands do not keep tune nor the troops march in time ; but here *uniformity* in dress or deeds is not. The authorities seem to have put Spain and Spaniards into our Chancery, such is the dilapidation of things real and personal. If, however, the neglected soldiers, &c., be such as Falstaff would not march through Coventry with, each individual is a fine, brave, temperate, and patient fellow, and for a picturesque foreground group in your first sketch of Spain are worth a dozen French marshals: attend to our advice (p. 9) in matters of pen and pencil, for here, as in the East, even the best intentioned may be taken up for spies and not well treated (2 Sam. x. 3). Our experience leads us to coincide with that of our friend Capt. Widdrington (ii. 202), who loves Spain and Spaniards so well and understands them so perfectly, he "never visited barracks at all ;" he never " attempted anything of that sort even in the most quiet times," as all have here a " paltry and contemptible feeling of jealousy which is highly discreditable." Nor is much lost by restraining curiosity as regards citadels, arsenals, hospitals, &c., which generally, as in Moorish Barbary, are full of nothingness, and " wanting in everything at the most critical moment;" a state of things which arises partly from the poverty, and more from the bad management and apathy, of those rogues or incapables who too generally misgovern these fine but ill-fated lands.

The first sight and welcome of Spain scarcely will inspire first love ; but the noble PEOPLE and their wild, racy, original country improve on better acquaintance, and the more as we advance into the sunny, Oriental east and south. Now all around breathes *ajo y Españolismo*, and however lacking in surface and sensual civilization, MAN is here the vigorous plant of a strong soil ;

here he stands erect, full of personal dignity and individual worth and independence : the members, indeed, are strong in masculine virility and vitality, although a head be wanting. Yet the Spanish people are still unbroken in despite of Austrian and Bourbon, who have failed to dwarf their high spirit and character, and sacrifice their worth, valour, and intelligence to advance the personal intrigues of unworthy rulers in church, camp, and cabinet.

IRUN, the first Spanish town, rises conspicuously in front on its hill ; the *Posada de las diligencias* is decent, and Ramon, " mine host," obliging. As he combines also a little coach-office managing, with " neat accommodation for travellers," conciliate him with a cigar, and consult with him as to getting on to Burgos, having made the tour to Tolosa via San Sebastian.

Irun, *Irunia*, signifies in Basque the " *good* town,' and thus, opening Spain with a misnomer, gives a hint to strangers not always to translate Spanish words or titles in a too literal meaning ; here at least the reverse is nearer the mark, for to speak in truth, and not in irony, this is but a bad and good-for-nothing place, peopled with some 4000 paupers, who live on the crumbs of those who come and those who depart ; placed, however, as at the entrance of Spain, and on the high road to Madrid, it at least is a *good* coach town, and means of escape are plentiful. Few travellers remain here long; they are either in a hurry to get into the Castiles, or in a far greater hurry to get out again. Mails and diligences start for Madrid by *Vitoria* (R. cxviii.), and thence by *Burgos* (R. cxvi.), or *Valladolid* (R. lxxvii.), which *we strongly recommend as the most interesting line ;* to *Pamplona* (R. cxxxviii.), and hence by *Tudela* (R. cxxxii.) to *Zaragoza*, from whence diligences run to Barcelona (R. cxxvi.). Another mode of reaching the capital of Arragon is by the diligence to Tudela, which branches off at *Tolosa* (R. cxviii.), and then passes on to *Pamplona* (R. cxxxv.) and to Tudela (R. cxxxii.). Spanish inns and diligences have already been described (at pp. 17-21); the latter will be found when coming from France to be good, cheap, and expeditious, and the fatigue is lightened by a few hours allowed every night for repose. The inns are decent; clean water and towels greet the dusty, thirsty passenger; a tolerable dinner is provided for those who can stand oil and garlic; the beds also offer to the very tired means of snatching the few hours' repose which the *mayoral* and *voltigeurs* winged and creeping permit. Some delicate travellers, however, have compared the mattresses to sacks of walnuts or potatoes. At early dawn a cup or *jixara* of good chocolate and some roasted or fried bread is ready. N.B. Drink water after this cup, oh ye bilious ones. The prices for these comforts are moderate, and moreover fixed; thus the stranger is protected from roguish *venteros*, if he cannot from their vermin. The average expense at Spanish *posadas* for a day's board and lodging may be taken at from a dollar to a dollar and a half, which is cheap enough. On some roads small guidebooks, or *Manuales de Diligencia*, are sold for a trifle, and are well worth the purchase. *Robbery* on the road is very rare, and in nothing indeed has Spain been more misrepresented. The coach proprietors generally take proper precautions, or pay black mail.

Those going to Madrid, who are not pressed for time, are recommended, instead of pursuing the direct but dull diligence line through Burgos and Lerma, first to visit *San Sebastian* (R. cxxv.), and branch off from *Burgos* (R. lxxvii.) to *Valladolid*, and thence by *Segovia* and the *Escorial* to the capital.

The military man, while his first *puchero* is stewing at *Irun*, may walk out to the hill of *San Marcial*, the site of noble deeds of Spanish arms. Seated on the knoll near the hermitage, a stone covers the ashes of the brave who

died here; and a cannon on the anniversary fires salvos in their honour, sounds unpleasing to the echoes of opposed heights. The hill is so called after an obscure saint, on whose day, in 1522, Beltran de la Cueva here defeated the French under Bonnivet, who had invaded Spain, in the hopes of reversing their previous disasters at Logroño; and now, Aug. 30, 1813, Soult, making an ill-conceived, ill-executed, but desperate attempt to relieve San Sebastian, ordered Reille to cross the Bidasoa and attack the Spaniards, who, under the nominal command of Freire, were posted on San Marcial. At that moment the Duke rode up, and his presence produced the cheering influence which that of Hercules and Santiago did in olden times (see Zubiri). Now the Spaniards felt that they were worthily commanded, and worthily did they do their duty, proving to Europe that those qualities yet remained uninjured which once rendered their infantry the terror of the world. Eighteen thousand French, with their usual tremendous advance, scaled the *Monte de los lobos ;* but now 12,000 *Merinos,* who knew that their true shepherd was near, turned upon the *wolves*, charging them manfully with the bayonet, and driving them back headlong. " Their conduct," says the Duke, " was equal to that of any troops I have ever seen engaged.'' Every repeated French " attack was defeated with the same gallantry and determination.'' Thus the last battle fought on the soil of Spain, like Bailen the first, added a laurel to the national chaplet; and to these, the Alpha and Omega of the Peninsular war, the Spanish annalists turn proudly, nor let any one begrudge their well earned glory. To these two days their Maldonados mainly ascribe the deliverance of their country and of Europe eventually, and small is the mention made of the ally who did the intervening work ; nor does Mellado even allude to the English at S^{n.} Marcial here. Freire is *the* god of war,

2 s 3

and here *Nosotros* alone fluttered the eagles of Austerlitz; but how stands the truth? The Spaniards, says the Duke, were " *supported and protected* " by the British on all sides; the first division, under Lord Aylmer, was between them and Irun, two brigades of the 4th division, under Cole, were to their r., while the 7th division, under Inglis, was close at hand. The Spaniards " were a *little* desirous of being relieved towards the end of the day, but *I saw* that the enemy were done, and I would not relieve them." (Disp., Sept. 3, 1813.) Venit, *vidit,* vicit; and their presiding tutelar, writing to Castaños, who once commanded this very corps, observed, " *Je* l'ai fait battre Soult toute seule." He readily left the whole glory to the Spaniards, to whom he could well spare some crumbs from his ample banquet. He who had led the Sepoys to victory knew well how the native lights his courage at the example of an English leader's skill and bravery; and gladly did the Spanish PEOPLE trust in the foreigner, whatever might be the prejudice of their own unworthy leaders (see p. 458). Nor ever had the ill-used Spanish soldier a better friend than in the Duke, who in vain, but over and over again stated their cruel wants to their ministers, and now rejoiced in putting them in a good position, and thus demonstrating that their previous disasters had been the result not of the members, but their brainless heads. Here it was the Duke, and none other but the Duke, who commanded and conquered: for this Freire never won a battle before or after, while he had taken a leading part in almost every flight and disgrace (see Index). The French repulse was most complete. Soult, attended by Foy, beheld the rout from the opposite hill of Louis XIV.; while the conflict was going on, the Bidasoa most patriotically swelled its waters, and thus rendered a refording impossible. The beaten, heart and foot sore foe had to retreat round by the bridge of Vera,

and there must have been cut off to a man, had Skerret, instead of remaining half a mile off and inactive, listened to the repeated entreaties of a handful of our rifles to be reinforced (Napier, xx. 3).

And as the boundaries of France and Spain lie at our feet like an opened map, how recollections crowd on the memory; how many spirit-stirring events have disturbed the repose of the now quiet scene; how much brave blood has dyed that clear stream which now winds peacefully to the ocean,

" So calm the water scarcely seems to stray,
And yet it glides like happiness away."

Princely forms and belted knights come and depart like shadows: there slouches the mean false tyrant Louis XI., cheating with sombre smile his gorgeous silly dupe the impotent Henrique IV.; next passes François I., model of French chivalry—he who at Pavia lost all save honour; slowly he treads that bridge, and now, on touching again the sacred soil of France, gathers strength, like Antæus, and shaking off the prison dust of hard Iberia, gallops furiously away, exclaiming, " I am yet a king !" but his second thought is how soonest he can break his plighted word; nor is a Clement VII. wanting to sanctify dishonour by absolving the obligation of a royal oath.

Next advances the stately Louis XIV., in the opening pride of a magnificent monarchy, of which he was the impersonation; with love and pledges on his lips, ambition and perfidy in his heart, he accepts the daughter of Philip IV. for his bride, soon to rob her country of liberty and crown; but the avenger is at hand; now a usurper greater than he sits on the ruins of the Bourbon throne, and grudges to the descendant of *Le Grand Monarque* the sceptre of Spain: that prize of fraud is again seized by treachery, and Ferdinand, lured by Savary, crosses this Rubicon April 20, 1808, welcomed by Buonaparte with a Judas kiss, and dismissed, having tasted his salt, a prisoner and unkinged. And now across that narrow and creaking bridge legions press on legions with dense and heavy tread. How brilliant, this the most splendid soldiery on earth, save that by whom it was driven back: how few destined ever to return to their beloved France! The war begun with perfidy and carried out with terror, was, in the words of the French themselves, a source of fortune to the generals, of misery to the officers, and a grave to the poor soldier. Arguelles ('Hist.' ii. 367) has demonstrated from official statements, that 549,750 Frenchmen entered from Irun alone, of whom only 236,555 came out; while the loss on the Catalonian side exceeded 160,000. The first legions were led across the Bidasoa Oct. 18, 1808, by Generals Laborde and Foy, who were the first to meet the English and defeat at Roleia, while by a poetical justice Foy was the first to regain France Oct. 17, 1813, when Vitoria had consummated a career of uninterrupted victory : then, as Napier says, thousands of the finest and bravest troops in the world fled like sheep before the wolf; say rather from that leopard which their Massénas boasted they would drown in the sea, provided it would dare to await their approach; and how trifling were the means by which this glorious result was obtained! "By having kept about 30,000 men in the Peninsula, the British government gave for five years employment to at least 200,000 French troops of the best Napoleon had; for it is *ridiculous* to suppose that either the Spaniards or the Portuguese could have resisted one moment if the British force had been withdrawn" (ipse dixit Disp., Dec. 21, 1813). The "same who fought at Vimiero and Talavera fought also at Sorauren" (Disp. Aug. 23, 1812). Neither was he adequately supported by *all* the " *Or et Marine* " of England, or the " *Patriotismo invencible* " of Spain, since the " service was always stinted and starved " on land, while the French, credite posteri! were

masters by sea of the Basque coast, and the "conduct of the Spaniards terrible" (Disp., Feb. 7, 1814). He in himself supplied the deficiencies of others, were they wilful or forced ; he husbanded his "*handful* of brave men," which " *struggled* through its *difficulties* for nearly six years " (Disp., April 7, 1814). He was chary of them as of his children; thus while Frederick the Great calculated the loss in every army during each campaign at one-third of its numbers, the average loss of the Duke did not exceed a sixth (see even Foy (i. 315), who is no flatterer either of our general and soldiers), and this against an enemy " every one of whose generals was *prodigal* of men " (Disp., Aug. 23, 1813); and truly and sadly has Foy remarked (i. 58) that the field of battle was the natural death-bed of the French conscript. Buonaparte's murderous strategies consisted either in " En avant, mes colonnes," or in rapidity backed by numerical superiority; he fought at the rate of 10,000 men per day. " Vaincre et trouver des instrumens de victoire était," says Foy (i. 157), "le travail de sa *vie*," and the travail and *death* to millions. Yet so long as wounds were hidden under laurels, and the groans of dying drowned in shouts of victory, France grudged not her valorous children to the altar of her Moloch, military *glory ;* and how much greater is the glory of him who, thwarted at home and abroad, opened with his handful of men a campaign on the most western rock of Europe; and then proceeded, in a steady advance of uninterrupted triumph, to crush marshal after marshal, the bravest of the brave, to rout army after army the previous conquerors of the world, until he perfected the good work by annihilating their mighty master himself, and planting the red banner of St. George on the captured walls of Imperial Paris; then indeed, having cropped all their large honours to make a garland for his brows, he exchanged for a civil wand an untarnished sword.

Those going to Madrid, who have leisure and wish to see San Sebastian, will secure their places beforehand in the diligence for Burgos, to be taken up at Tolosa, allowing three days for the excursion.

ROUTE CXXV.—IRUN TO SAN SEBAS-TIAN AND TOLOSA.

Fuenterrabiá		
Lezo		
Renteria		
Pasages		
S. Sebastian	4¼	
Orio . . . , . .	2	.. 6¼
Zumaya	2	.. 8¼
Azpeitia	3	.. 11¼
Tolosa . . . , .	4	.. 15¼

Ladies may ride this tour *en cacolet*, on quiet and prudent donkeys; there is a direct road by *Renteria*, and it has long been in contemplation to make a carriage road to San Sebastian by *Pasages :* a détour may be made to *Fuenterrabiá*, a name corrupted from the Latin. Fons rapidus, which rises on the *swift* Bidasoa, is 3 short miles from Irun : here Milton placed, somewhat ungeographically, the "dolorous rout" of Charlemagne ; yet such is the gilding power of genius, that his chance expression confers on obscure sites an undying interest, and this *Fuenterrabiá* rivals Vallombrosa. In itself it is a miserable dilapidated spot, although one of the grandiloquent misnomers of Spain, and "a city," which Madrid is not : *Noble de cuatro costades*, its armorial shield, hangs out like a sign-post of an *hay de todo venta*, full of assumption and pretension, but stating the thing that is not. The four quarterings bear an angel holding a key, a whale and two syrens, a castle between two stars. Moya, p. 128, explains these imposing charges, which were bestowed by Philip IV. in 1638, when the Prince de Condé was here repulsed by the admiral of Castile : consult *Sitio y Socorro,* Palafox y Mendoza, 4to. Mad. 1793.

This then important key was under the especial protection of the Virgin of Guadalupe ; vast sums were voted at Madrid *on paper* for the repair of the fortifications, but it need not be said that not one *real* was really paid. The French in 1794 completely dismantled the place, and now Spain's hungry mountains are as ever her natural and best outworks. The Fuenterrabians begrudged during winter time even lodging to our sick ; nay, the authorities wished to take away even the hard boards on which our disabled were stretched ; and these, said the Duke, "are the people to whom we have given medicines, &c., whose wounded and sick we have taken into our hospitals, and to whom we have rendered every service in our power, after having recovered their country from the enemy !" (Disp., Nov. 27, 1813.)

Riding along the coast about 5 miles, is *Lezo*, situated under the Jaizquivel, on what nature had scooped out as a port, but which Spanish neglect has allowed to be choked up. It once was a celebrated dock-yard, and still possesses a *Santo Cristo*, an image to which a grand pilgrimage is made every Sept. 16, which all travellers in this part of the world at that time should join, in order to see Basque costume and manners. *Renteria*, distant about ¼ L. with a popⁿ. of 1600, is placed on its stream, which, running down from the valley of *Oyarzun*, disembogues into the bay of *Pasages :* the once excellent port has from carelessness been much injured by deposits ; the deep land-locked bay is one of the best harbours on this rock-bound coast ; the narrow entrance is defended by the Arando *grande* and *chico ;* when once inside, ships ride safely : the bay narrows at *La punta de las cruzes*, opposite to which is the castle *de Sᵃ· Isabel ;* the anchorage between them is good ; higher up the water gets shallow. Those pressed for time may leave Lezo and Renteria to the l., and cross over from *Pasages*, and so either by the coast or by *Herrera* to San Sebastian. During the Carlist struggle the opposing lines closely approached each other ; the Christino, or *Ametzas* barrier, ran from *Pasages* to *Alza*, joining the Ayete lines below Loyola, and ending S. of San Sebastian: those of the Carlists began at Renteria, included the fort of Sⁿ· Marco, came down to the Urumea, and then crested heights to Oriamendi, with Hernani behind. San Sebastian was gallantly saved, Dec. 13, 1836, from the Carlists by Col. Arbuthnot and the Legion, without whom it must have fallen, for " not a piece of artillery there was fit for service," although a year's time had been given to the Spanish authorities to prepare their defences.

San Sebastian is built on an isthmus under the conical hill *Orgull,* which rises some 400 ft. above the sea, and is crowned by the *mota,* or castle; the place is isolated by the tidal river *Urumea,* up which salmon run: the *marisma,* or marshes, are partly flooded at high water, except the *chofres,* or sand-knolls; the winter wild-fowl shooting is excellent. San Sebastian is much frequented for sea-bathing; then small huts are run up made of reeds, *cañas,* which do the service of machines, and as they have a tent-like look, are called *el campamento:* when the tide is in, San Sebastian seems to rise out of the sea: the Urumea is crossed either by its long wooden bridge, or in boats, which are rowed by women, supposing the feminine gender can be given to such amphibious fish-fags, or *sirens, á la Fuenterrabia;* their red and yellow *sayas* conceal the legs or tails of these mermaids; if however they are not of the true "desinet in piscem mulier" genus, tongues they have at all events, which discourse eloquent Basque Billingsgate.

As the town is the Brighton of Madrid, and near the French frontier, the *posadas* are good; the best are those of Monsʳ· Lafitte, and *el parador real,* and *posada de Sª· Isabel. San Sebastian* used to be the capital of its province; now Tolosa has been substituted, and mutual hatred is the consequence; the town is modern, the older one having been almost destroyed during the war, but has since risen like a phœnix from its

ashes, and was built on a regular plan, which is more convenient than picturesque; the lofty and uniform houses with balconies look rather un-Spanish: the *plaza,* however, with its shops and arcades, is handsome; the town is the residence of local authorities; popⁿ about 13,000, and mercantile: there is little to be seen: the citadel is an irregular fortress, with five fronts. The tombs of several Englishmen who fell here are at the back of the rock. The *partido* of San Sebastian is a jumble of hill and vale; the *Arrobi,* or *Iqueldo,* rises some 3100 ft. high, and commands a panorama over the ocean and sandy *landes* of France: the hills are somewhat denuded on the sea-side, but inland are clothed with oak, chesnut, walnut, and aromatic underwood; a bad *chacoli* is made in sheltered localities, and a better *cider:* the apple *papanduja* is excellent, the sea-fish delicious, abundant, and cheap; fishing indeed is the occupation of the poorer classes.

San Sebastian is memorable for its sieges and libels. It was obtained in March, 1808, by Thevenot, when the French got in under false pretences as at Pamplona and elsewhere; they held it during the war, and being in the rear of the Duke when advancing in 1813 on the Pyrenees, it retarded his progress, and its possession became absolutely necessary; this was a work of great difficulty, for the naturally strong position was garrisoned by 3000 brave French veterans under Gen. Rey, and the Duke, from the usual neglect of our government, was again left to sue the place in formâ pauperis, as at Badajoz and Burgos. In spite of repeated applications to Lord Bathurst, he waited from July 25th to August 26th for *want of means* even to commence operations, during which time the active enemy strengthened their defences, being supplied from France by sea (Disp., Aug. 11, 1813). In vain the Duke had warned Lord Melville, " under whose fatal rule," says Napier, " the navy of England was first exposed to defeat, and who now did his best to ensure a similar misfortune to the army:" read the heart-burning correspondence from Lesaca, especially of the 19th, 20th, and 21st of August; and to make matters worse, Graham, to whom the siege was entrusted, neglected the advice of Sir C. Felix Smith, the defender of Tarifa, and of Sir Rd. Fletcher, the Vauban of the Torres Vedras, who soon was killed here. Graham having failed in a night attack August 24, the Duke was forced to come in person to set matters right, although thereby he was obliged to leave Pamplona exposed to be relieved by Soult, which was all but effected : the Duke's arrival was, as usual, the omen of victory : now the town was assaulted as it ought to have been at first, from the *chofres*, and was taken Aug. 31; the French after a most gallant defence retired to the upper citadel, on which by the almost superhuman efforts of the engineers, backed by the blue jackets, guns were brought to bear, and it surrendered Sept. 9th, two-thirds of the valorous garrison having perished, while nearly 5000 English troops were killed and wounded. The gallant defence of Rey was stained by his behaviour to women and prisoners (Southey, 44), and he forced the English, " contrary to all the rules of war " (the Duke), to labour at the works *sans blindages*, and at points the most exposed to their own countrymen's fire; " of such conduct," said the Duke, " I have never heard" (Disp., Sept. 3rd, 5th, 1813). San Sebastian was sacked by the captors according to all the usages of war, and such ever is the sad fate of all places taken by storm. This event, which gave infinite sorrow and disgust to the Duke, is now made a standing libel against the English, as the *Xefe politico* of San Sebastian, one Conde de Villa Fuentes, accused our officers of purposely burning the town because it traded with France, as if this paltry beggarly Basque port could excite the jealousy of the masters of the world's commerce (compare also p. 743). This gentleman next called on

the Spaniards to *revenge themselves!* but however rude the Basque may be in forging his native iron, few excel him in "forging lies," either in favour of himself or in disparagement of others. These infamous falsehoods were printed by O'Donoju, the war minister at Cadiz, in his *Anti-English* paper *El Duende;* thereupon the Duke called the Regency to account, who formally contradicted the libel in their official gazette of Oct. 20th, 1813. This man, sprung from a refugee Irish Catholic family, was aide de-camp to Godoy and then to Cuesta, and although he rose higher from British protection (Schep. iii. 100), repaid his patrons by bitter anti-English ingratitude, insomuch that the quiet Duke talked of him as the " greatest of all blackguards " (Disp., Nov. 19th, 1813). Such were poor Spain's war ministers; this base scion of the great black chief the O'Donogue Dhuw, died poisoned by his own subalterns in Mexico, *Cosas de España.* The truth, the whole truth, and nothing but the truth, is recorded in the Duke's letters (Disp., Oct. 9th, 23rd, and Nov. 2nd, 1813). These, our unfair inveterate calumniators never quote, while they continue to repeat every refuted falsehood *ad nauseam.* Even the Duke's iron-nerved temper gave way, although he had taken no more notice of angry words hitherto, than the man in the moon does of the swelling tides. Being accustomed in regard to himself to repose on the pedestal of his own glory and good conscience, he intertwined these paper inventions of the enemy amid his victorious laurels, and trusted to time, which reveals everything; yet now stung by the vermin who attacked his officers, his indignation was such "that if he were to direct, he would not have kept the army in Spain for an hour." So when Bernardin Mendoza, the Spanish ambassador at France, converted defeats into victories, and published libels against the officers of Elizabeth, our Drake, who never noticed personal abuse against himself, at once overwhelmed his calumniator, and showed that he could deal with such an enemy as readily with his pen as with his sword.

How stand real facts? San Sebastian was set on fire by the *French* July 22nd, as is admitted by *Rey* in his own dispatch, and it was done for the express purpose of annoying the English by preventing their progress, which it did, and many of our soldiers were actually shot by the Basque townsfolk while extinguishing those very flames which they are now accused of having lighted. The text furnished by Buonaparte, a man who *abhorred* terrorism and falsehood, ran thus, " Les Anglais commettent des horreurs dont les annales de la guerre offrent peu d'exemples, et dont cette nation *barbare* était seule capable dans un siècle de civilisation" (Œuv. de Buon., i. 116). These be hard words, Master Pistol, and scarcely civil without being true; nevertheless the so-called historians on both sides of the Pyrenees who write, as regards England, so much in hate and so little in honour, took up this imperial *thema* with variations, or to use one of the truthful Duke's straightforward facts, with "an improvement of the lies even of the Moniteur" (Disp., Sept. 16th, 1813), and to this day they are warmed up by those very candid persons who befoul their English nests to conciliate the disciples of Voltaire and revolutionary terrorism: these, forsooth, are *unusual* atrocities when British troops are concerned, but only *des horreurs inévitables* when perpetrated by Buonapartists. But the English generals every where repressed these outrages, and so tender was the Duke of Spanish cities, that he never used mortars except when it could not be helped (Disp., July 30, 1813), whereas the invaders, to quote another of their conqueror's quiet truthful expressions, every where and invariably "committed horrors *until then* unheard of" (Disp., Nov. 22nd, 1812), and particularly with the bomb, as Spain in ruins still testifies. Southey (ch. 44) has with

an eloquent indignation refuted these libels, and demonstrated the terrific atrocities habitually perpetrated by our calumniators, these *Victors* à la Medellin. Our general, brave as merciful, wept like Scipio at burning cities, and from his not rejoicing like a Nero in the " beauty of the fire," M. Foy accuses him and his troops of a dull insensibility to the " sublimity of destruction" (see Lérida and Manresa, Ucles, Cuenca, Coria, &c.)

Quitting these sad scenes, lies, and libels, and taking the road to *Zumaya*, we ascend the clear picturesque *Urola*, the " water of smithies," which flows through the delicious green valley of *Loyola*, about 1 short L. from *Azpeitia*. At the head of the valley are the ferruginous baths of *Centona*, which are much frequented from June to September; the accommodations are tolerable, and the building will take in 140 persons; the warm water is conveyed into stone basins, which are sunk in bathing chambers or alcoves.

Azpeitia is pleasantly situated amid its gardens, under the hill *Izarraiz*, pop. 4500. It is a walled place and has four gates; the Doric façade of the church San Sebastian was planned in 1767 by Ventura Rodriguez, and the heavy statue of the tutelar was carved by one Pedro Michel, who was no Angelo. Make an excursion to the *Fonderia de Iraeta* and visit the iron-works, also to the baths at *Centona;* but the marvel of the locality is the large Jesuit college, which was built out of the residence formerly belonging to the family of Ignacio Loyola, and being pleasantly placed under the heights, with a fertile plain in front, exactly suited an order which never was known to found a convent in a barren ground. The *santuario* was founded in 1671 by Mariana of Austria, when Carlo Fontana, a Roman architect, gave the design, in which he wished to represent an eagle; the church was to be the body, the portal the beak, the tail the kitchen and refectory, for the Escorial had anticipated the gridiron. The edifice is now untenanted, excepting a chaplain who shows it to visitors. The church is handsome, and enriched with jaspers from the hill *Izarraiz* "the rock ;" the *cimborio* or cupola supported by pillars is very elegant: observe the marbles and mosaics. The entrance hall to the monastery is noble, and the double corridor beyond handsome; in a large low room up stairs is the spot where San Ignacio was born in 1491, and it is now encased and venerated like the house of the Virgin, which angels moved from Palestine to Loretto. The chapel in which Loyola recovered from his wounds received at the siege of Pamplona, is divided by a *reja*, and is ornamented with bold carvings, some gilt and painted, which illustrate subjects in his life (see Manresa, p. 499).

From Azpeitia to Tolosa (see p. 948) is a charming pastoral, Swiss-like ride, especially the last 4 or 5 miles among the hills, wild woods, and long-leaved chesnuts.

SECTION XIII.

THE KINGDOM OF ARRAGON.

CONTENTS.

The Geography, Constitutional Liberties, and Character of the Natives; Works to Consult.

The warm months are the best periods for visiting Arragon, and especially the Pyrenean districts. Zaragoza, Huesca, and R. cxxxi. are the objects of chief interest.

EL *Reino de Aragon.*—The kingdom of Arragon, once a separate and independent state, was, Castile alone excepted, the most warlike and powerful one in the Peninsula. It extends in length about 140 miles E. to W., and about 200 miles N. and S., and is encompassed by mountains on all sides —viz. the Pyrenees, the Sierras of Morella, Albarracin, Molina, and Soria. The Ebro (see p. 459) flows through the central basin, N. W. to S E., and divides the kingdom almost equally. The climate varies according to locality and elevation: generally speaking the province, from being so exposed to mountains, is much wind-blown; thus the plains over which the cutting blasts descend from the Moncayo (see p. 889) are most miserable. The chief winds are *El Cierzo*, the N. W., *El Bochorno*, the S. E., both of which are keen and cold, while *El Faqueno*, the W. (Favonius), brings showers, warmth, and fertility. The vegetable productions are equally varied, as the soil ranges from the snow-capt mountains to the sunny plain under the latitude 41. The botany and Flora of the Spanish Pyrenees, as well as the natural history, geology, and mineralogy, have yet to be properly investigated. The *Montes* abound with game, and the hill-streams with trout. The population is under a million which is scanty for an area of 15,000 English miles. Accordingly,

as in other portions of the Peninsula, large tracts of fertile land are left in a
state of nature, depopulated and uncultivated; a considerable portion, however,
of these *dehesas y despoblados* is of that hungry description which, according to
the old traveller in Purchas, gives "little corn, but craggez and stonez, that
maketh pilgrymez weary bonez." The Arragonese themselves consider *liberty*
to have been the great compensation by which their ancestors were 'indemnified
for such a hard soil and climate; hence it had few charms for the Moors of the
plain, and was chiefly peopled by the Berber mountaineers, but they were soon
expelled by the children of the Goth, who united together so early as 819, in
the fastnesses of *Sobrarbe*, where their primitive laws were drawn up, which
became the model of the *Fueros* of many other cities. The government was
conducted by patres et *Seniores*, heads of families, and elders, and from the
latter word the Spanish term *Señor* or lord is derived. These *Fueros* were
digested into a code by Vital, bishop of Huesca, and confirmed in that town
in 1246, by Jaime I.; afterwards, about 1294, the celebrated *Justicia*, Simon
Perez Salanova, drew up some additional *Observancias*, which were equivalent
to the *usaticos, usatges*, or *usages* of limitrophe Catalonia. The prerogatives of
the kings, who were scarcely more than presidents, were much curtailed by
these Arragonese Ephori, whose allegiance was but limited and conditional; thus
the crown was but the coronet of the noble, with a somewhat richer jewellery,
for each vassal singly held himself to be as good as his king, and all united, to
be better. About the year 1137 Petronilla, daughter of Ramon el Monge, and
heiress of the crown, married Ramon Berenguer, sovereign count of Barcelona;
thus military Arragon was incorporated with commercial Catalonia, and the
united people extended their conquests and trade alike by sea and land,
becoming masters of the Mediterranean, Naples, and Sicily, while in Spain
Jaime I., about 1238, overran the rich province of Valencia, and dispossessed
the Moors; hence he is called *El Conquistador*, "the Conqueror." All these
acquisitions were carried to the crown of Castile by the marriage, in 1479, of
Ferdinand, heir apparent of Arragon, with Isabella, and from them descended
to their grandson Charles V. As Ferdinand had jealously maintained his
separate rights of a sovereign perfectly independent of Castile, the Arragonese,
after his death, insisted on the continuance of their own peculiar laws and
Fueros, which almost guaranteed republican institutions under an ostensible
monarchy; but such was the peculiarity of most of the early Peninsular popular
liberties, which were enjoyed to a greater extent than any other European nation,
England not excepted.

The Arragonese *Fueros* are now curiosities for legal antiquarians. They
provided, among other points, that the Viceroy could only be of the blood
royal. The Parliament or *Cortes* met in four *Brazos*, branches or orders, to
wit, the clergy, the nobility, the gentry, and the people, and each voted separately, the consent of all four being necessary to pass a law. The greatest
jealousy against the monarch was exhibited in all matters of finance and personal liberty, while a high officer, called *Justicia*, the impersonation of Justice,
Mr. Justice, was the guardian of the laws, and stood a *Juez medio* or go-between
the king and people. In all appeals when the *Fueros* were infringed, the
appellant was said to be *manifestado*, &c.; his person was thus brought under
the custody of the court, as by our Habeas Corpus, and his cause removed from
ordinary tribunals, as by our writ of quo warranto and certiorari. The society
at large was secured by the " *Union*," or a confederacy whose members, in case
the king violated the law, were absolved from allegiance. This element of
disunion was abolished in 1348, when Pedro IV. cut the parchment to pieces
with his dagger, and having wounded himself in his haste, exclaimed, "Such a

charter must cost a king's blood :" hence he was called *El del Puñal.* The French destroyed, in 1808, his curious portrait in this attitude. In 1591 the notorious Antonio Perez fled to Zaragoza, and appealed to Juan Lanuza, the *Justicia,* whereupon Philip II. marched an army into Arragon, and hanged the judge, with whom perished this privilege, the rest of Spain looking tamely on. But never has the Spaniard combined libertatem publice tueri (Florus ii. 17. 2), and whatever liberties were then respected were abolished in 1707 by Philip V. Zaragoza has now an *Audiencia,* with a jurisdiction over 750,000 souls : the number of persons tried in 1844 amounted to 2170, being about one in every 340. The highest court of appeal in Spain is modelled on the French *Cour de Cassation,* and is hence called *de Casacion,* which signifies in Spanish " marriage," not an undoing and annulling.

For the ancient constitutional curiosities of Arragon consult its Coke, Geronimo Zurita; the early edition of his '*Anales*' is rare, 6 vols. fol. Zaragoza, 1562-80-85. It was republished in 7 vols. fol. in 1610-21, and continued by Vincencio Blasco de Lanuza, 2 vols. 1622, and by Bart⁶· Leonardo de Argensola, 1 vol. fol. 1630 ; by Miguel Ramon Zapater, 1 vol. fol. 1663 ; by Diego de Sayas Rabenera y Ortubia, 1 vol. fol. 1666 ; by Diego Joseph Dormer, 1 vol. fol. 1697; and by José de Panyano, 1 vol. fol. 1705. All this series was printed at Zaragoza. Consult also ' *Los Reyes de Arragon,*' Pedro Abarca, fol. 2 vol. Mad. 1682-4, and '*Historia de la Economia Politica,*' D. J. de Asso, 4to. Zar. 1705. The best catalogue of works of Spanish constitutions and jurisprudence, and especially as regards Arragon and Catalonia, is ' *Sacra Themidis Hispanæ Arcana,*' 8vo. Mad. 1780. This work was compiled by the learned Juan Lucas Cortes, but purloined, and first published as his own by Gerard de Frankenau : see our remarks p. 131.

Arragon, a disagreeable province, is inhabited by a disagreeable people, who are as hard headed, hearted, and bowelled as the rocks of the Pyrenees, while for stubborn granite prejudices there is no place like Zaragoza. *Obstinacy,* indeed, is the characteristic of the *testarudo* Arragonese, who are said to drive nails into walls with their heads, into which when anything is driven nothing can get it out. They have, however, a certain serious Spartan simplicity, and are fine vigorous, active men, warlike, courageous, and enduring to the last. They fire up at the least contradiction, which, as Mariana says (xxv. 8), lights up their *increible coraje y furor encendido.* The Arragonese, like the Catalonians (see p. 465), have the antipathies of position and the hankerings after former independence; they detest the Castilians and abhor the French, using them both for their own objects and then abusing them. This love of self and hatred of the foreigner dates earlier than their *Fueros de Sobrarbe,* in which it was provided that the foreigners' aid should be accepted, but never be rewarded by any share in the conquests, *Peregrinus autem homo nihil capito ;* not that this *Españolismo* is a singular trait of character in any portion of the Peninsula.

The Arragonese costume differs from the Catalonian, as knee breeches take the place of pantaloons, and broad-brimmed slouching hats of the red Phrygian cap. The lower classes are fond of red and blue colours, and wear very broad silken sashes. The favourite national air and dance is *La jota Arragonesa,* which is brisk and jerky, but highly spirit-stirring to the native, on whom, when afar from Arragon, it acts like the pibroch on the exiled Highlander, or the Ranz des Vaches on the Swiss, creating an irresistible Nostalgia or home-sickness. The arms of Arragon are " Or four bars gules," said to have been assumed by *Wifred el Velloso,* who, when wounded in battle, drew his bleeding fingers across his golden shield, a truly soldierlike blazon, cruor horrida tinxerat arma.

ZARAGOZA is the capital of Arragon: Inns, *Las Cuatro Naciones*, Casa de Ariño, *El Leon de Oro*, C⁰· de Coso: *El Turco* C⁰· Areocineja. There are good baths at *La Casa de Baños*. Zaragoza was the Celtiberian Salduba, but when Augustus, A.C. 25, became its benefactor, it was called *Cæsarea Augusta*, Καισαραυγουστα (Strabo iii. 225), of which the present name is a corruption. It was always a free city or *Colonia immunis*, having its own charters, and was a *Conventus Juridicus* or seat of judicial assizes. It had a mint, of which Florez, 'M.' i. 186, enumerates 66 coins, ranging from Augustus to Caligula. There are no remains of the Roman city, which Moors and Spaniards have used as a quarry, and whatever antiquities turn up in digging new foundations are, as is too often the case in Spain, reinterred, as "useless old stones:" Cean Ber. Sum⁰· 131.

Zaragoza set an early example of renouncing Paganism, and here Aulus Prudentius, the first Christian poet, was born A.D. 348 (some however say at Calahorra). Then the city could boast of her primitive martyrs, and *real* Christianity, Christus in totis habitat platæis, Christus ubique est (Peris, iv. 71). Now, however, the Virgin reigns paramount. Zaragoza is, and always has been, a city of relics; thus in 542, when besieged by the French, under Childebert, the burgesses carried the stole or *Estola* of San Vicente round the walls, which at once scared away the invaders, just as the cloak of St. Martin did the Normans at Tours. Childebert, however, first begged a portion of the vestment, to receive which he founded the abbey of S⁺ Germain des Prés, near Paris (see E. S. viii. 187, xxx. 127, and Prudentius, Peris v. 10). But the French grew wiser in 1200 years; thus when the Duke of Orleans, in 1707, overran Arragon, beating the Conde de Puebla, the Spanish general assured the Zaragozans that there were no French at all, but that the appearance was a "magical

illusion:" so the old coat was brought out against them in the old style, but the invaders took the town forthwith (Mahon, 'War of Suc.' vi.).

Zaragoza was captured by the Moors in the 8th century, who availed themselves of the local tendency to believe in the supernatural, for Hansh a *Tabi*, or follower of the companions of Mahomet, built a mosque, and the citizens required no other honour than the simple possession of his bones: Moh. D. ii. 4. The Moslem priests had also here a sacred grotto, in which were crowned idols of gold, who were consulted on emergencies (Reinaud, 246). The Zaragozans, being chiefly of Berber extraction, waged war against the Kalif of Cordova. Thus their Sheikh, Suleyman Al-Arabi (the Ifu Alarabi of old Spanish Chronicles), went in 777 to Paderborn, to implore the aid of Charlemagne, who was an ally of Haroon-e-Rasheed, the Kalif of Damascus, and of all enemies to the Cordovese dynasty of Ummeyah, and the especial Christian bulwark of Europe against the Saracens. He entered Arragon in 778, when the perverse people refused to admit their allies into their garrison, and rose upon them when returning to France; but such was precisely the conduct exhibited to the Duke and English. Zaragoza was recovered from the Moors in 1118, by Alonzo *el batallador*, after a siege of five years, when the stubborn population had almost all perished from hunger, and even then it was internal dissension which facilitated the conquest, one Amad-dola having joined the Christians, as Al-Ahmar afterwards aided St. Ferdinand at Seville. These brave Moors were worthy ancestors of the modern Zaragozans; but everything here, as elsewhere in Spain, is *accidental* and uncertain. Thus, in 1591, when Philip II. advanced on Zaragoza, the Arragonese showed as little courage in defending, as they had demonstrated temerity and inconsideration in rebelling; they no sooner came in sight of the king's forces, but they *committed themselves to such safety as their heels might procure them,* abandoning their host, Anto. Perez, and presently after the city of Zaragoza (Cornewayle in Somers tracts, iii. 311). So also in 1823 the patriots swaggered and forthwith surrendered to Molitor; Ballesteros, as usual (see p. 712), being the first to seek safety in his heels (for the sieges see post, p. 968).

Zaragoza is a dull, gloomy, and old-fashioned town,—Pop. about 65,000. Being the capital of the province, it is the residence of a Capⁿ· General, and chief military and civil authorities, and the seat of an *audiencia.* It has a theatre, museo, and university; it is the see of an Archbishop since 1318, whose suffragans are Huesca, Barbastro, Jaca, Tarazona, Albarracin, and Teruel. Zaragoza is placed in a fertile plain which is irrigated by the Ebro. This noble stream separates the city from its suburb, and is crossed by a good stone bridge; seen from outside the place, with its slim towers and spires, has an imposing character, but inside the streets are mostly tortuous lanes, ill-paved and worse lighted, with the exception of the *Coso* or *Pozo* moat, which is the aorta of the town, and the great passage of circulation, or *el curso,* like the Corso at Rome. The houses are indeed castles, being built in solid masonry; but time-honoured Zaragoza has been sacrificed to upstart Madrid, and the mansions of an absentee nobility are either left in a chancery-like dilapidation, or let to agriculturalists, who talk about bullocks in stately saloons, and convert noble *Patios* into farmyards and dung-heaps, for such is the sad change of to-day, when *Bajan los Adarves y alzanse los Muladares.* These rude rustics also block up the city lanes with their cumbersome primitive carts, which they moreover fill with dismal noises, of their own and their creaking wheels making, to which are added certain iron clanking cymbals which give notice of their approach, as

in very few streets can two vehicles pass; hence the din, dirt, stench, and insolent obstructions are intolerable; but these are the bold peasantry who so gallantly defended this town of castles against the French. At Zaragoza the architect will fully comprehend the substantial style of Arragonese building; and observe the superbly carved soffits, rafters, and external cornices, the rich internal cinque cento decorations, and the slim church belfry towers, which are usually constructed in brick, angular in form, and ornamented outside with an embroidered tracery. The artist may here study a school of painting which is little known in Spain, and quite unknown out of it. As the observations of Cean Bermudez are still in MS., the invaders, not having a printed guide, did not know where to go for art-plunder, not but what their fatal bombs destroyed much of what they otherwise would have collected. Look out therefore for the works of *Ramon Torrente,* obt. 1323, and of his pupil *Guillen Fort;* of *Bonant de Ortiga,* who flourished in 1437; *Pedro de Aponte,* painter in 1479 to Ferd., and a pupil in Italy of Signorelli and Ghirlandajo, may be considered as the founder of the Arragonese school; *Tomas Pelegret,* a co-pupil of Polidoro Caravaggio, introduced the cinque cento style, which *Damien Forment,* the Berruguete of Arragon, carried to such perfection in sculpture. *Antonio Galceran,* who painted so much at Barbastro, in 1588; *Geronimo de Mora,* who studied, in 1587, under F. Zuccaro, in the Escorial; *Frº· Ximenes,* obt. 1666, who painted in the *Seu* the life of Sⁿ· Pedro Arbues. Arragonese art ceased with Goya and Bayeu, being then killed by the commonplace R. Academical. Zaragoza bears for arms " Gules, a lion rampant, or," granted, say the natives, by Augustus Cæsar. The lay of the old and smaller town is clearly marked out by the streets, which have since been built on the former boulevards or circumvallation; it began at the river, passed up the *Mercado Nuevo* in the *Coso*, thence to the *Puerta del Sol*, where a few Roman ruins have been traced; here the rivulet Huerba flows into the Ebro; the south side is laid out in public walks, and long lines of poplar trees. The favourite *Alamedas* are *Sᵃ⁻ Engracia*, the *Torero*, and *Casa blanca*; the latter is especially frequented on June 24, *El dia de Sⁿ⁻ Juan*, and June 29, of *San Pedro*.

Zaragoza will not detain the traveller long, for here the invaders, as at Burgos, Salamanca, and Toledo, have ruined palaces, libraries, hospitals, churches, etc. For what the city was before that visitation, consult *Tropheos y Antigüedades*, Juan de Dios Lopez de Lino, 4to., Barcelona, 1639; Ponz, *Viaje*, xv.; for Zaragozan worthies, *Inscripciones en la real sala de la Diputacion*, Geronimo de Blancas, 4to., Zar., 1680; for the ecclesiastical and hagiographical, Florez, E. S. xxx. xxxi., and *Historia de la Iglesia*, Diego Murillo, 4to., Barcᵃ⁻, 1616.

Commence sight-seeing at the noble stone bridge which was thrown across the Ebro in 1437. The two cathedrals now rise in front, for this ultra-religious town is thus doubly supplied, while Madrid is entirely deficient. The chapter reside alternately for six months in each of these cathedrals, which in exterior, interior, and creed, are rather unlike each other. The one is an ancient severe church raised to the Saviour; the other! a modern theatrical temple dedicated to the Great Diana, for now we are in the Ephesus of Spanish Mariolatry. The former edifice rises to the S. or to the l., looking from the bridge, and is called the *Seu* (*Sedes* See, *Cathedra* Cathedral). The style is Gothic. The entrance unfortunately was modernised by Julian Yarza, in the pseudo style of 1683. The white-washed frippery, pillars, and lumbering statues of apostles, by one Giral, contrast with portions of the original arabesque brick-work. One octangular

belfry tower, drawn out into four divisions like a telescope, was finished by Jⁿ⁻ Bᵃ⁻ Contini, with heavy ornaments; the other *está por acabar*. The gate of *La Pavosteria* is of the better period of Charles V. The *Pavorde* is peculiar to Arragon, Catalonia, and Valencia (see p. 498). The word has been derived by some from pascor *pavi*, because certain rations were furnished by this dignitary.

On entering observe the red marble pavement, with rays in black, diverging from the bases of the piers, and the roof studded with gilt rosettes and wheels. The *Retablo* of the high altar was erected in 1456 by B. P. Dalmau de Mur; the three divisions are canopied by Gothic shrines. The mosaic work, Angels bearing Shields, the Adoration, Transfiguration, and Ascension, were wrought in 1350 by Martinez de Donatelo. The under divisions are smaller and somewhat heavy. Observe the *Sedilia* to the r. used by *El Sacerdote*, who consecrates the host, *El Diacono* who reads the gospel, and *El Subdiacono* who reads the epistle. Near is the fine tomb and recumbent figure of Archb. Juan, obt. 1531, and of Archb. Alfonzo, obt. 1520; to the l. is deposited the heart of Don Baltazar, son to Philip IV., the Infante so often painted by Velazquez, who died here of small-pox, Oct. 9, 1616, aged 17. The octangular *Cimborio* was commenced by Benedict III., and finished, as a Gothic inscription records, in 1520. Here Ferdinand, *el Catolico*, born at Sos in 1456, was baptised. The *Coro* is Gothic; observe the archbishop's throne. The fine cinque cento *Trascoro* was executed in 1538 by Tudelilla of Tarazona, who had studied in Italy; and in it Romanism struggles with Paganism, fauns with saints, satyrs with inquisidors, and cupids with martyrs; the materials are clay, stucco, and marble. The workmanship is coarse, but the general effect is strikingly rich. Under a tabernacle of black and white Salominic pillars is the carved crucifix which spoke to the Canon Funes who kneels beside it; but the images of antiquity were even more loquacious. Ovid, Fast. vi. 615: Val. Max. i. 8. Many of the portals inside this Cathedral have quite a Moorish character. The chapels are generally enclosed in their own *Purclose;* among these *Rejas* observe that of S[n.] Gabriel, which, although dark, is of excellent plateresque. Here lies the founder, Gabriel de Zaporta, in his merchant garb, obt. 1579. The marble is of Italian sculpture, and savouring rather of the pantheon than a Christian Cathedral; the *Reja* is excellent. In *S[n.] Bernardo* observe the *Retablo* and carving, especially the Circumcision, and the tutelar to whom the Virgin dictates her book, as Egeria did to Numa. He was an ultra-advocate of Mariolatry, in reward of which the Virgin suckled him, as Juno did Hercules, a subject which Murillo was fond of painting. Yet Bernardo was a very severe saint, for, when her image spoke to him in the Cathedral of Spires, he replied, Mulier taceat in Ecclesiâ. The superb sepulchre and recumbent figure of the founder, Archb. Fernando, grandson of Ferd. the Catholic, is by Diego Morlanes, son of Juan, an excellent Biscayan sculptor, who introduced the tedesque style into Zaragoza in the 15th century. Diego, who inherited his talent, adopted the cinque cento, which was next the prevailing taste. The alabaster "Resurrection" is by Becerra, who gave it to Diego, with whom he lived on his return from Italy; by Diego also is the enriched tomb opposite Aña Gurrea, mother of the prelate. The *Capilla Santiago* is churrigueresque, and in strange contrast with the preceding, especially the tomb of the founder Archb. Herrera; the stucco ornaments are ridiculous, the bad paintings by one Raviela. In that of *Maria la Blanca* are collected the grave stones of early prelates, which were removed when the cathedral was repaved; observe also the arch and pilasters. The tutelar is S[n.] Pedro Arbues de Epila, who was murdered, like Thomas a' Becket, before the altar, by Vidal Duranso, Sept. 15, 1495; his body is buried under the *Baldaquino* of black Salominic pillars, and decorated with a white flag and silver lamps. This ferocious inquisidor had goaded the citizens to madness, yet Charles V. had persuaded Paul III. to make him a saint, and now the Zaragozans endanger their souls by worshipping a man who burnt their fathers' bodies, like the simple Pagans did, "Cæci et imprudentes in contrarium cadunt, adorant itaque hostes suos; interfectores suos, animas suas cum thure ipso cremandas aris detestabilibus imponunt." Lactantius de Just., v. 20. The Kneeling Saint is by Jose Ramirez, and the paintings by F[ro.] Ximenez of Tarazona. This martyrdom was chosen by Murillo for one of his finest pictures, just as Titian selected for his masterpiece another Dominican Peter, who was also a persecutor, and also a victim to popular revenge. Ferdinand caused the murderers of Arbues to be burnt alive, adding sundry Jews to improve the bonfire. Pulgar, Chro. chr. 95. The opposition of the Zaragozans to the holy tribunal arose from there being very few *rich* Jews or Moors living among them, therefore they suspected that this engine was armed against their own persons and properties.

Visit next the *Sacristia*, and observe the plateresque door. Here are some fine *Ternos* (see p. 440); one, a *Pontifical*, cost 14,000 dollars; also a *delante de una Capa*, embroidered with Adam and Eve, which was bought at our Reformation from the old Cathedral of St. Paul's, London. The church plate before the invasion was splendid, but very little escaped from Marshal Lannes. Observe an enamelled chalice of 1655, a plateresque and rather overcharged silver *Custodia* of 1537; some silver busts, with enamel and Gothic inscriptions, given by

Benedict XIII. The once splendid jewel-studded Gothic cross, presented by Archbishop Lope de Luna, and carried before the king at his coronation, was melted by the Liberals in 1820, who took away that bauble. In the *Capilla del Nacimiento* is a classical *Retablo*, and some pictures by Juan Galvan, who painted the cupola in fresco. The Seu is also full of rich marbles, but unfortunately many alterations were made at a period when money was more plentiful than good taste. These old portals and *Retablos* were removed for *desatinos, mamarrachadas y churiguerismo;* specimens of which may be seen in the chapels of *Sⁿ. Vicente, Sⁿ. Valero,* and *Sᵃ. Elena,* which are fitted with choice gilt ginger-bread for grown-up children.

Leaving the Seu to the r. is the vast archiepiscopal palace, which the invaders gutted and plundered. Near it are the remains of the beautiful *Casa de Disputacion,* or Parliament house, which was built in 1437-40 by Alonzo V. The saloons were magnificent, and contained the rich national archives which came down from the earliest period, and the excellent library, while the walls were ornamented with portraits of Arragonese worthies; but everything was utterly destroyed by the French. Opposite is the *Lonja,* the Exchange, built in 1551; remark the projecting and enriched soffit of this square brick edifice, and the heads of kings and warriors let into circular frames in a fine Holbein taste; the towers are tiled with white and green *Azulejo.* The interior is noble; observe the Doric columns, the staircase, and ceilings.

Next visit the second cathedral, *El Pilar,* so called from the identical pillar on which the Virgin descended from heaven; the clustering domes outside, roofed with green, yellow, and white glazed tiling which glitter in the sun, have an Oriental harlequinade look; the edifice has been much modernised, and is still unfinished both inside and outside. These "im-provements," begun in 1677, at a period of vilest taste, were planned by the presumptuous Herrera *el mozo,* and were not amended by the academical Ventura Rodriguez, who, in 1753, rebuilt portions, and left drawings for the façade. The building is quadrangular, in length about 500 feet, with three naves; the pillar and its image are placed in the centre, being thus enclosed like the house of the Virgin which the angels moved from Palestine to Loretto. The unfinished interior is unpleasing, as one half is left plain with whitewashed walls and heavy pilasters picked out in an unsightly blue and buff, and worthy of the poor frescoes in some of the cupolas by Bayeu and Moya, and the tomb of Montemor, a general of Philip, and which is the perfection of abominable rococo. The *Retablo* in San Lorenzo is a poor performance of Vⁿ· Rodriguez. The ancient *Coro* is fine, and of better times; the *Silleria* of 115 seats was admirably carved in oak by Juan Moreto of Florence, in 1542, with subjects principally connected with Mariolatrous legends. The superb *Reja* is the masterpiece of Juan Celma, 1574. The Gothic *Altar Mayor* is composed of alabaster from the quarries of *Escatron.* The all-engrossing subject is the "Assumption of the Virgin," on which *Assumption* Mariolatry is based; the infinite forms and figures baffle pen or pencil. This, the capo d'opera of Damien Forment, is certainly the finest thing of the kind in Arragon; but the detestable new colouring of parts of the cathedral makes this noble old work look somewhat dark and dingy. In the crypt beneath the canons used to be buried, an arrangement common in the cathedrals of Arragon and Catalonia.

Zaragoza is the great pilgrim city of Arragon, as all flock in there from far and wide to see the *Pillar* and the image which came down from heaven, like the *Palladium* of Troy (Paus. i. 26. 6). This modern parallel has been declared so authentic a miracle by so many Popes, that Diego de Astorga, primate of Spain, excommunicated, Aug. 17, 1720, all who even *questioned* it; while Risco, writing in 1775, holds " its truth to be established on such firm grounds that nothing now can shake it." The legend may soon be explained. When the Moors of Cordova cast off their allegiance from the kalif of the East, the reciprocal enmity which ensued rendered a pilgrimage to Mecca impossible; a substitute was therefore established at Cordova, in the *Ceca* of its mosque. Whereupon the imitating Castilians, unable to go to Jerusalem, set up their opposition sepulchre and holy place of pilgrimage at Santiago; but the Arragonese, who were then independent of Castile, did not choose to offer at a *foreign* shrine, and accordingly they invented one of their own, and selected their capital for obvious financial views. As the Castilians had taken St. James for their Hercules, they chose the Virgin for their Astarte. Nothing of all this had been attempted during the Roman and Gothic periods, simply because, as there were then no Moors in Spain, no antagonistic Mecca was wanted; accordingly Prudentius, who wrote so largely on Zaragozan Christianity, omits the *Pilar* altogether, as does S⁰· Isidro (Orig. xv. 1) when describing the geographical and religious advantages of Zaragoza, "Loci amenitate et deliciis præstantius civitatibus Hispaniæ cunctis atque illustrius, *florens sanctorum martyrum sepulturis.*"

The church authorised history is printed at length in the ' E. S.' xxx. 426, and states that Santiago, soon after the crucifixion, applied to the Virgin for *her permission* to preach the Gospel in Spain; having " kissed her hand," he came to Zaragoza, converted eight Pagans, and fell asleep; then the angels of heaven brought her alive from Palestine, and carried her back again, after she had desired him to raise a chapel on the spot, which he did, and to which she often came afterwards to

mass, as Minerva used to do (Od. iii. 435). These Pillars or *Baitulia* (*Bethel*, the house of God) are decidedly Oriental : compare that of the "mother of the gods " at Acrocorinth (Paus. ii. 46); that given by Minerva at Kysicos (Antho. Anath. vi. 342); or the golden one of Juno at Croto (Livy, xxiv. 3).

The *Sanctum Sanctorum*, or chapel of the *Pillar*, is placed in the centre of the cathedral. The oval adytum was designed by Rodriguez, and with its gilt *reja*, lamps, &c. shines like the plateau on a banquet table; it is open on three sides, while the roof being perforated admits the cupola above, on which the Virgin's descent is painted in poor fresco by one Ant⁰· Velazquez, 1793, who was not even distantly connected with his immortal namesake. The pavement is of the richest marbles ; the *Retablo* is much overcharged with statuary and detail; observe among the medallions the Descent of the Virgin, and Vision of Santiago, by José Ramirez; and some others by Manuel Alvarez. The material, from being covered with dust, looks like wood; but it is the purest alabaster, as the hand of Santiago proves, which is cleaned by pious kisses, like the beard of Esculapius (Cic. in Ver. iv. 43). The marble steps are also osculated, as in the days of Apuleius, " exosculatis *Deæ* vestigiis " (Met. xi. 251), and worn " *pedibus volgi*," as in the times of Lucretius (R. N. i. 309). To prevent over-osculation (see Index) and curiosity, a railing keeps off the profane vulgar, inside which none may enter save kings, cardinals, and the appointed priests. Women are expressly prohibited, as in the temple of Hercules at Gades (Sil. Ital. iii. 22). The holy image itself is small, and graven out of a resinous, almost black wood; but the most sacred representations of the Virgin, and especially those carved by St. Luke, are very dark-coloured, " black but comely " (Sol. Song, i. 3), and are said to have been designed when she was tanned during the flight into Egypt. It holds

2 T

the infant in one hand, and collects its drapery with the other. As a work of art it is rude and second-rate, but it inspires the natives with a conventional awe, rather than from wooing the ignorant by the singular diligence of the artificer to more superstition (Wisd. Sol. xiv. 8). On its mode of treatment, dressing, wardrobe, &c. see our remarks at pp. 111, 594. Here, indeed, the worship of the Virgin is openly avowed and practised, in a manner of which our Roman Catholics can form no conception, as with them the juxtaposition of the Bible and free discussion has pared away many an extravagance, which under a religious monopoly have attained a full-blown dimension; here while the names and attributes of the Virgin are multitudinous, the result, as was described by Apuleius, is *one* Mariolatry, "Numen *unicum*, multiformi specie, ritu vario, nomine multijugo, totus veneratur orbis—*Deûm Matrem*" (Met. xi. 241). Her chief festivals are, Feb. 2, *La Purificacion* ; March 25, *La Anunciacion;* Aug. 15, *La Asuncion;* Sept. 8, *La Natividad ;* Dec. 8, *La Purísima Concepcion :* but Oct. 12, the Anniversary of her Descent, is *the* day of Zaragoza, since Innocent III. announced that "God alone can count the miracles which are here then performed ;" 50,000 pilgrims have been known to flock into Zaragoza. Then her shrine is crowded with all ages and sexes of peasants, *Pagani,* who sit, kneel, and pray, falling by pilgrim instinct into most picturesque groups, like the *contadini* at Rome. What a hum and buzz in the church, what a swell of voices, what a smell of garlic! yet all trust to have their petty hopes and wishes granted by her intervention. Thus the Vatican, by providing a miraculous aid for the most vulgar necessities, has secured the million, as to them is offered a system based in sympathy with the humblest wants and infirmities. Such a creed, by being thus lowered to humanity, is rendered palatable and consolatory to

the masses, whose faith therein is the sacrifice of fools.

This *Pillar* is the support of the populace during peace and war, as well as of its caterpillar ministers, who daily preach that it is "La gloriosa Colonna in cui s'appogia nostra speranza." The battle hymn against the invaders ran thus—

> " *La Virgen del Pilar dice,*
> *Que no quiere ser Francesa,*
> *Que quiere ser capitana*
> *De la gente Aragonesa !*"

This doggrel, so little compatible with the reverence due to the Queen of Heaven, is the precise degradation which Plutarch (de Pyth. vii. 604, Reiske) lamented as resulting from scurrilous poetry of the βωμολοχον γενος towards the Pagan mother of the gods.

As at Valencia (p. 441), so here the Virgin was applied to for protection and victory (compare Val. Max. i. 2). " But they that have no knowledge set up the wood of their graven image, and pray unto a god that cannot save " (Isa. xlv. 20). In Spain, however, this religious excitement and supposed supernatural assistance is equal to brandy and double rations with colder Protestants. No wonder, therefore, that the great Jaime I., the conqueror, raised, as Saavedra says, 1000 churches, and all dedicated to the Virgin, and her worship here is almost paramount, and disputes with that of tobacco and money : countless are the mendicants, the halt, blind, and lame, who cluster around her shrine as that of Minerva (Mart. iv. 53), and beg charity for her sake (for the correct mode of refusal see p. 171). The cures worked by this Minerva Medica are almost incredible, and the oil of her lamps is more efficacious than Macassar, since Cardinal Retz relates in his Mémoires (iii. 409) that he saw here in 1649 a man who had lost his leg, which grew again on being rubbed with it; and this portent was long celebrated, as well it deserved, by an especial holiday. The lamps are hung outside in order to preserve the "*simulacro*" (Ponz, xv.

8) from smoke, the " nigra fado *simulacru* fumo " to which Horace alludes (iii. Od. vi. 4): see also Baruch vi. 21. Silver angels also holding candelabra decorate the dainty show. The 22nd of February is also a grand lamp-lighting day here. This candlemass is but an ungraceful copy of the η των λαμπαδων ημερα in honour of Ceres, and of the Egyptian festival at Sain (Herod. ii. 62). Again, Pausanias (i. 26. 6) tells us that the " image of Minerva which came down from heaven " also had lamps fit for the Arabian nights, whose oil burnt miraculously for a whole year without being replenished. No wonder that these *Lychnuchi Pensiles* (Pliny, ' N. H.' xxxiv. 3) and illuminations should have been among the first Pagan superstitions which the primitive Christians put down, believing that idols when so lighted up were inhabited by devils. The pious French accordingly removed most of the silver chandeliers; some, however, have been replaced by Zaragozan *devotos à la Santisima*, and the scene is now precisely that against which Jeremiah (xliv. 15) so much inveighed when " incense was offered to the Queen of Heaven," " to Diana the mooned Astaroth."

All around the shrine are suspended votive tablets, Αναθηματα (see Valencia, p. 441; and Ovid, ' Fast.' iii. 268), which consist, as in the East (1 Sam. vi.), of offerings of models of the members afflicted and healed by the Virgins, *e. g.* eyes, noses, and *legs*, naturally enough here, but so it always was, " pendent tibi crura " (Ovid, ' Am.' iii. 2. 63). Sometimes the parts are presented in silver, whereat the priests rejoice; but wax is the usual material, as being cheaper. Visit, of course, the neighbouring *Plateria* to examine the curious *Pillars*, Virgins, Penates, &c., which are made for the *Pagani*, or male and female villagers, as at Ephesus and Santiago : see our remarks on their saving virtues, p. 671. Rudely engraved prints also are sold of the Virgin's Descent, which, when

hung up in bed-rooms, among other Dii cubiculares, allure Morpheus, and expel Satan and the nightmare. All this indeed is the consecration and apotheosis of error, for such devotion is a sin, and such observance a wickedness.

To give some extent of Spanish female worship, consult Antonio (Bib. Nova, ii. 553), who enumerates 84 works on particular Virgins, and 430 works on her generally. This intolerable quantity of sack, with the halfpenny worth of publications of real religion or of useful knowledge, bears the same ratio as the ordinary condition of Spanish cities, where one public library was allotted in proportion to 30 churches or convents. For the *Virgen del Pilar* and its miracles, consult ' *Fundacion*,' Luis Diaz de Aux, Zara. 1605; the ' *Historia* ' of Murillo (see above, p. 958); and for *official* details, ' *Compendio*,' &c. Villafane, Mad. 1740, pp. 406 to 437. The Spanish authorised biography of the Virgin is ' *La Mystica Ciudad*,' fol. Mad. 1670, which Maria Coronel (*Santa Maria de Agreda*) was " inspired to write by a divine revelation." This work was so ultra absurd that the shrewd Sorbonne and Vatican condemned it, in spite of the efforts and protests of the Spanish ambassador.

The worship of Isis, Astarte, Salambo, and Diana, the invention of the sexual Oriental, was engrafted on the Iberian stock by its Phœnician colonisers, and is better suited to southern latitudes than to northern ones; and here Marianism is the religion of the great bulk of the Spaniards; and notwithstanding that some of the higher classes disbelieve what Popes for gospel do receive, here, indeed, the honour and worship due to the Creator alone is transferred to the creature ; here she rules triumphantly as Empress of heaven and earth, of angels and mortals ; the stern doctrine of retribution for sin is melted down into a soft, easy dependence on this Esther with whom the celestial kingdom is partitioned;

2 T 2

nay, the Deity has all but abdicated in her favour, having given to her all that he could, everything, in short, save his own essence. She is *La Señora de la Merced*, the Lady of *Mercy; La Señora* here being used in the sense of *El Señor*, the Lord God. She administers grace, equity, and remission of sins. Thus the Almighty is robbed of his prerogative, and his sceptre rendered barren, to the exclusion and derogation of the "only one name and none other." The Virgin, as *Regina et Conjux*, "calms the rage of her heavenly husband," and tempers "an angry judge," whose only office is to punish; while as a mother she "commands and compels her son," to whom "she is superior by reason of his humanity, and because as mother she has done more for him than he could have done for her." He saves only by her intercession, for it is *she*, who in the Roman vulgate bruises the serpent's head; she has her rituals, litanies, creeds, offices, festivals, &c.; to her are dedicated almost all the cathedrals of Spain; her graven image is elevated above the high altars in the place of honour, and holds the Son either as a helpless babe or a dying victim, thus made subordinate in both respects, and dependent on her.

The Scriptures are utterly silent of everything which by possibility could raise the "handmaid" into the mistress. Thus even the scantiness of the holy word is instructive; the mystery of the incarnation is indeed plainly revealed, but not one word of the Immaculate Conception, Death, Assumption, Coronation, &c. of the "woman," an expression used purposedly, so thought Bishop Epiphanius, as if in anticipation of this anti-christian Mariolatry. To this foresight also has been referred the apparent neglect and marked distinction between the "Father" and the "woman," the mother of him who was God, which is observable in all the Son's language. She is Θεοτοκος, Deipara, and not Δημητηρ, or Dei *Mater:* compare Luke ii. 49; John ii. 4; Matthew xii.

48; Mark iii. 33; Luke xi. 28. Neither does St. John, after the crucifixion, ever mention the Virgin, nor was she ever present at any of the Saviour's appearances after the resurrection, although so many other females were; nor is any situation assigned her in the Apocalypse.

Mariolatry, utterly unknown in the primitive Christian church, began in Arabia, in the 4th century, where some women like their mothers of old (Jeremiah xliv. 17) "made offerings" to her of cakes. This collyridian heresy was soon put down, but was revived in the 7th century. But how clearly the Romish worship of the Virgin is contrary to Scripture and the practice of the early church, has been proved to demonstration in the reverential, learned, and unanswerable work by Dr. Tyler, Lond. 1844.

The *Sagrario* of the Pillar contains the splendid wardrobe of the image, which is more fitted for a Venus than for her who was so meek, modest, and lowly; the treasures in jewels and gold were once enormous, and rivalled those of Loretto, Monserrat, and Guadalupe; but they were plundered by the invaders, for no "Virgin interfered," as occurred when the old Gaul Brennus attempted to pillage the *Donarium* of Delphi (Cic. ' Div.' i. 37). Mellado (p. 366, Ed. 1843) estimates at 129,411 dollars the "*obsequio,*" or "complimentary *gift,*" made by the chapter to Marshal Lannes: see also Toreno, vii. App. 6. As to these *gifts,* see pp. 671, 697.

Leaving the *Pilar,* proceed to the *Plateria,* and buy honestly a silver Virgin. Observe among the trinkets made for the peasantry the earrings, which are perfectly antique, especially those with three dropping petals made after the identical pattern on the Siracusan medals; occasionally a good old rapier may be purchased, as Andreas Ferrara lived at Zaragoza; the best local blades are those marked with the bear and little dog, *El oso y el perrillo.* For swords, see Toledo, p. 852.

The chief street in Zaragoza is *El Coso;* the houses are still pitted and riddled with shot-marks, the honourable scars of the memorable sieges. Here are many good specimens of Zaragozan architecture : observe No. 168, and *La Casa de los Gigantes.* Among other houses are *La del Comercio,* *C¹· S°· Maria* mayor, with fine *azulejos,* ceilings, and spiral pillars in the *patio;* also those of *Castel Florit* and the Duque del Hijar, and No. 26, *C¹· Zaporta,* with fine mouldings. *The* house, however, is that of the *Infanta,* No. 77, C¹· de S²· Pedro, which was built by the wealthy merchant Gabriel Zaporta in the richest Arragonese cinque-cento style. Enter the beautiful *patio,* and observe the fluted pillars and torsos, the projecting medallions with most Italian-like heads. The magnificent staircase has a rich roof with groups of musicians, but all is hastening to decay.

Among the churches, visit *S²· Pablo,* with its fine façade and columns; the high altar, a grand specimen of the plateresque, is the work of the illustrious Damien Forment. In the *Capilla de S²· Miguel* is the tomb of Diego de Monreal, Bp. of Huesca, obt. 1607. The cupola is painted by Geronimo Secano. A *Museo Nacional* has been recently established in S²· Pedro Nolasco, where it is to be hoped that some brands from the burning may be rescued ere too late. Enquire for the superb Doric and classical *Retablo* made at Genoa for the Dominican convent, with *La Señora del Rosario;* it was originally destined for the sepulchre of Luis de Aliaga. In the same convent was a fine kneeling statue of Cardinal Xavierre.

Visit the *Torre nueva P°· S²· Felipe;* this octangular clock-tower for the city was built in 1504, and leans considerably out of the perpendicular like those of Pisa and Bologna, which is unpleasing, as conveying a feeling of insecurity that is opposed to the essence of architectural principle. It seems to totter to its fall—Ruituraque semper stat mirum ! it is richly ornamented with

brick-work, which at a distance looks Moorish, but it is much coarser both in design and execution. The noble university, with its precious library, was destroyed by the invaders, but a new one has been partly constructed with a fine quadrangle. The grand Hospital, *el general,* is dedicated to the Virgin, and is one of the largest in Spain. The former one was burnt with its patients by the French ; in vain a white flag was hoisted imploring mercy for the wretched inmates, as that very flag was made the especial mark for their bombs ; but the besiegers here spared nothing, and when the town was entered the sick and even lunatics were massacred in their beds (Toreno, v.). The *Casa de Misericordia* is a sort of large hospital and poor-house, in which some 600 to 700 young and old are taken in ; the funds, however, are very inadequate. Near it is the *Plaza de Toros,* where no mercy is shown to bulls or horses. The grand fights are in honour of the Virgin, when the profits go to aid the hospitals. The N. W. gate, *El Portillo,* is the spot where *Agustina,* the maid of Zaragoza, snatched the match from a dying artilleryman's hand, and fired at the French ; hence she was called *La Artillera.* This Amazon, although a mere itinerant seller of cool drinks, vied in heroism with the noble Condeza de Burita, who amid the crash of war tended the sick and wounded, resembling in looks and deeds a ministering angel. But the WOMEN of Spain, worthy mothers of a noble PEOPLE, have always been true "Jaels and wives of Heber." They behaved like men, when the Areizagas and Co. were either running away or trusting to images of the Virgin and S²· Teresa.

Outside the *Portilla* is the *Aljaferia,* the old irregular citadel, built by the Moor Aben Aljafe, as the *Alcazar,* and was therefore assigned to the Inquisition by Ferdinand the Catholic, partly to invest the hated tribunal with the prestige of royalty, and partly for security after the murder of Arbues (see p. 959). Suchet having first damaged the palace with his bombs, made it a barrack; afterwards it became a military hospital, and was degraded into a prison during the civil wars; hence its present deplorable condition. Observe the splendid staircase, which is adorned with the badges of Ferd. and Isab. One room is called *El Salon de S⁰· Isabel;* here where the sainted queen of Hungary was born in 1271, now miserable *bisoños* obtain their happy release and die; above hangs, as if in contrast with present decay, the glorious blue and gold *artesonado* roof with stalactical ornaments, and a rich cornice with festoons of grape leaves; a Gothic inscription bears the memorable date 1492, which was that of the conquest of Granada, and the discovery of the new world; and the first gold brought from it was employed by Ferdinand in gilding this ceiling.

The other gates of Zaragoza best worth notice, are that of *Toledo,* used as a prison, a Newgate; and *La Ceneja,* so called from the ashes of martyrs? found there in 1492, when it was rebuilt by Ferdinand. The public walks, with long lines of poplars, extend on this side of the city, close under the walls, and up to *La Casablanca,* on the canal, where there is a decent *Fonda,* and much frequented by the Zaragozans, who junket here on the festivals of *San Juan,* June 24, and *San Pedro,* June 29; the *El Canal de Aragon* was one of the first to be *begun* in Europe, as it probably will be the last to be finished. This grand conception was projected in 1528 by Charles V., in order to connect the Mediterranean with the Atlantic: vast in promise, slow in execution, and impotent in conclusion, only 8 leagues were cut by 1546, and then the affair was dropped, and languished until 1770, when one Ramon Pignatelli advanced it a few more leagues (compare the canal of Castile, p. 640). It now connects Zaragoza with Tudela, and a boat plies backwards and forwards

with passengers, but this mode of transit is not to be recommended (see p. 991). The engineer may walk out and see the manner in which the canal is carried over the *Jalon,* and consult for details *La Descripcion,* &c., Fⁿ· Zarᵃ· 1796, and Ponz, xv. 102. This canal suggested to Louis XIV. the *Canal du Midi,* which was begun in 1681, and finished with Roman magnificence: thus is Spain ever outstript by those to whom she sets an example. For *Irrigation* and *Hydraulics,* see Index.

Now return to the hill called *El Torero:* below this, Aug. 20, 1710, Stanhope came up with Philip V., flying from his defeat at Lérida; but the German allies hesitated to advance, when the English general charged alone, crying "This is a day to retrieve Almansa," and it did so most effectually; although our troops were footsore and starving, they drove the foe everywhere before them, who abandoned cannon, colours, and everything. Stanhope's first care then was for the disabled French, for "among the wounded," said he, "there are no enemies." (Mahon, viii.) The heavy Austrian Charles now entered Zaragoza in triumph, and the crown might have been his, for Stanhope urged an immediate advance on cowed Madrid, but, like our Duke, he was thwarted by the pottering generals of his ally, and thrifty ministers at home.

The *Torero,* being an elevated and commanding point, was strongly held by the Spaniards in 1808, when the French advanced; instead however of checking the enemy, Col. Falco, the officer in command, fled at their first approach, and thus not only abandoned the key of this front, but left behind him all the tools of the canal company, as if on purpose to furnish the besiegers with instruments in which they were deficient, as at La Coruña and El Ferrol (see p. 655). Accordingly it was from this side that the enemy attacked Zaragoza, and entered at what was the beautiful convent of S⁰· Engracia, which they destroyed: this was of the richest Gothic of Ferd. and Isab., completed in 1517 by Charles V., who could finish convents, but not canals: the portal, in the form of a *Retablo*, was filled with marble sculpture by Juan Morlanes, 1505. The elegant cloisters, with round-headed arches, were the exquisite design and work of Tudelilla, and there reposed the ashes of the learned Zurita, and Blancas, which, with their splendid libraries, were all burnt by the invaders. Sᵃ· Engracia, the tutelar, was a Portuguese virgin, who, accompanied by 18 gentlemen (tu *decem* sanctos revelies et *octo*, Prud. Peri., iv. 53), was on her way to France to be married, but went out of it, to insult Dacian, who put her and her suite to death, April 16, 304; part of her liver was seen and immortalized by Prudentius (Peri. iv. 137), Vidimus partem jecoris revulsam, &c., this relic was long resorted to in Spain, in cases where in England blue pill would have been preferred: the remains of the martyrs were mixed up with the bones of criminals, with which they would not amalgamate, but separated into white *masses*, whence the curious subterranean chapel is called *de las masas santas*, not *misas*, or masses sung there: remark also the well out of which in 1389 the bones were fished up, pink, say all the church authorities, as roses; truth being still left at its bottom: there is a Roman sarcophagus, which is called the tomb of a martyr. This grotto is but an imitation of the Moor (see p. 956), and the type was the caves of Elora in Hindostan, a kylas or paradise: Sᵃ· Engracia is a modern Egeria, and her grand miracle is, that the lamps before her tomb never smoked the low roof. See for details E. S. xxx. 260; Ponz, xv. 49. So the ashes of the altar of Juno Licinia were never moved by the wind (Livy, xxiv. 3). The oil of these lamps rivals that of *El pilar*, and cures *lamparones*, or tumours in the neck.

The medical practice of Pagans and Orientals was more peculiar than scientific: as disease was thought to be a divine punishment for sin, it was wicked to resist by calling in human aid: thus Asa was blamed (2 Chr. xvi. 12); thus Moslems and Spaniards resign themselves to their fate, distrusting, and very properly, their medical men: "Am I a god, to kill or make alive?' (2 Kings v. 7); on Spanish doctors see pp. 173, 774. In the large towns certainly some patients may "suffer a recovery" according to European practice, but in the country and remote villages, although the Government appoints a resident practitioner, the good old reliance on simples, relics, and charms is far from exploded; however Philip III. and Dr. Sangrado might deplore the introduction of perplexing chemistry, mineral therapeuticals still remain a considerable dead letter, as the church has transferred the efficacy of faith from spiritual to temporal concerns, and gun shot wounds. Even Ponz (xiv. 122) was surprised at the number of images ascribed to St. Luke, who, says he, was not a sculptor, but a physician, whence possibly their sanative influence. The old Iberians were great herbalist doctors; thus those who had the herb *vettonica* in their houses, were protected, as a blessed palm branch now wards off lightning (Pliny, N. H., xxv. 8): they had also a drink made of *centum herbæ*, a *bebida de cien herbas*, which, like Morison's vegetable pills, cured every possible disease, and was so palatable that it was drunk at banquets, which modern physic is not: in Spain they cured the gout with flour (Pliny, N. H. xxii. 25), while grandees relieved elongated uvulas by hanging purslain round the patients throat (Pliny, N. H., xx. 20): hydrophobia they relieved by decoctions of dog-roses (Pliny, N. H., viii. 41), and now the *curas y curanderos*, country curates and quacks, furnish charms and incantations, just as Ulysses stopt his bleeding by cantation (Od. T. 457): so a medal of Santiago cures the ague, a handkerchief of the Virgin the ophthalmia, a bone of Sⁿ· Magin, *El mal Frances*, a scrap of Sⁿ· Frutos loss of common sense; the Virgin of Oña destroys worms in royal Infantes, and her sash at Tortosa delivers royal *infantas;* the Zaragozan oils remove goîtres and restore legs,—can the balsam of Fierabras do more? The ancients raised temples to Minerva medica or Esculapius, as Spaniards do altars to *N^a· Señora de los Remedios,* and to S^n. Roque; and both thought that these tutelars did *at least* as much as the doctor (Cic. N. D. iii. 25, 38). *Dios es que sana, el medico lleva la plata;* alas! for the patient credulity of Spanish mankind, which still gulps down such medicinal quackery as all this, and which will continue to do so, however Pliny (N. H., xxviii. 2) might eject the trash "*viritim sapientissimi cujusque respuit fides.*"

The modern martyrs of Zaragoza are those brave peasants who fought and died like men on this site of *S^a· Engracia's* miracles; si monumentum requiras, circumspice: look around at the ravages of the invader, which testify his relentless warfare, and the stubborn defence during the two sieges which have rendered Zaragoza a ruin indeed, but immortal in glory. This city, like other Spanish ones, rose after the executions of Murat on the *dos de Maio,* 1808; on the 25th Guillelmi the governor was deposed, and the lower classes were organised by *Tio Jorge Ibort,* Gaffer George, one of themselves; a nominal leader of rank being wanted, one José Palafox, an Arragonese noble, who had just escaped from Bayonne in a peasant's dress, was selected, partly from accident, and because he was an *hijo de Zaragoza* and *handsome,* for in Spain, as in the East, personal appearance is always influential. "There is none *like* him, long live the king" (1 Sam. x. 24). Palafox had served in the Spanish royal body-guards, and therefore, says Mr. Vaughan, necessarily "knew nothing whatever of the military profession;" according to Toreno (vi.) and Schep. (i. 205), he was totally unfitted for the crisis, nay, even his courage was

doubted, but he was a mere puppet in the hands of better men; thus his tutor Basilio Boggiero wrote his proclamations, the priest Santiago Sas managed the miraculous, while Tio Jorge commanded, with two peasants, Mariano Cerezo and Tio Marin, for his right and left hands: all the means of defence under Guillelmi (says Southey, ch. ix.) were 220 men, 100 dollars, 16 cannon, and a few old muskets; the common condition in which the arsenals and treasures of ill-fated Spain are left by a needy, corrupt, and incapable government; compare p. 742. Lefebvre arrived June 15, 1808, and had he pushed on at once must have taken the place, but he paused, and thus enabled Tio Jorge to prevent a coup de main: Verdier arrived on the 29th with artillery, and began breaching and bombarding: to the French summons of surrender, the bold Tio replied, "War to the knife," and the struggle in the *coso* against their assailants was carried on with that personal prowess and valour for which the Spaniards are unrivalled. Lefebvre in his strategics evinced neither common humanity nor military skill; but the defeat of Dupont at Bailen relieved Zaragoza, which was on the point of surrendering, and then Lefebvre retired Aug. 15, boasting, and with truth, that he had left the city "un amas de decombres," see Belmas (ii. 115): compare the siege of Illiturgis, when Scipio and his disciplined veterans were desperately resisted by brave Iberian peasants (Livy, xxviii. 19). Palafox, *una cabeza llena de viento,* now went madder with vanity than any Gascon or Andaluz; puffed out with smoke, he claimed all the glory to himself in stilty bombast, and reposing under his laurels, neglected every preparation for future defence; meanwhile Buonaparte silently made ready his great revenge, and in three short months, while *Juntas* were talking about invading France, appeared at Vitoria, and crushed all the ill-equipped armies of Spain at one blow, the heroes of

Bailen and Zaragoza being the first to fly, for Castaños at Tudela, Nov. 23rd, scarce gave the French time to charge; and had they then pushed on at once Zaragoza again would have fallen: it was soon invested, and attacked by Buonaparte's sagacious suggestion on both sides, and especially from the Jesuit convent on the other bank of the Ebro, which the careless Spaniards had neglected to secure. Now four marshals conducted the siege, Lannes, Mortier, Moncey, and Junot; and after 62 days of dreadful attack and resistance, plague and famine subdued Zaragoza, which capitulated Feb. 20, 1809, the rest of Spain having looked on with apathy, while Infantado, with an idle army, did not even move one step to afford relief; thus when Joshua attacked Jericho, every other district stood aloof in Oriental and selfish localism; so none co-operated with Samson (Judges xv. 12), but in the words of Florus (ii. 17. 3), never has this unamalgamating land done otherwise,—"nunquam Hispaniæ animus fuit adversus nos universæ consurgere, nunquam conferre vires." Lannes had pledged his honour that Palafox should depart free, and that no one should be molested; and the capitulation was printed in the Madrid Gazette: but, in the words of Southey, "this man was one after Buonaparte's own heart, and with so little human feeling, that he would have carried out the system of terror to any extremity:" accordingly he pillaged the temples, shed innocent blood in torrents, put Boggiero and others to death under prolonged torture, insulted Palafox, robbed him "even of his shirt," although sick, and then sent him to the dungeons of Vincennes; "thus every law of war and humanity was violated," says Toreno, vii. But the Virgin avenged her insulted shrine and massacred people, and ere one short year was fled, she winged a bullet at Essling which sent this man to his dread account, after a life, says Mons. Savary, of kidnapping veracity, "too short for

his friends, although a career of glory and honour without parallel." Lannes, valiant, but not over-refined or scrupulous, had risen from being a journeyman dyer of cloth to be a wholesale dyer in blood. See Michaud, B. U. xxix. 474.

These two sieges cost the lives of nearly 60,000 brave men, and for nothing, as the defence of the town was altogether a military mistake, and entirely the result of popular impulse and accident, the moving powers of things in Spain. The Spaniards now liken Zaragoza to Numantia, but the old Iberians died and did not surrender; then and there 4000 of them resisted 40,000 Romans for fourteen years (Florus, ii. 18), and this in a really weak town, whereas Zaragoza was a city of castles, and how strong it was may be estimated by what has escaped the bomb and mine. The junta of Seville passed a decree to rebuild the place at the public expense. It need not be said that not one real has been forthcoming, except on paper, for a Spanish minister only promises to pay. Ferd. VII. visited Zaragoza after leaving France, and created a *Maestranza*, which, with fine epithets, were all the rewards bestowed. Palafox was not made a *Duque* until 1833, and then not from national gratitude, but because Christina wished to make herself a party; and now Tio Jorge is scarcely mentioned by name, for it would offend the pride of Spain's misleaders to admit the merit of a peasant, whose valour and intelligence shamed the cowardice and incapacity of the Alachas and Imazes. The *Tio* was a true son of the *people* of Spain, and his treatment from his so-called betters is purely Oriental and national. Thus "there came a great king against a small city and besieged it; now there was found in it a *poor wise* man, and he by his wisdom delivered the city, yet no man remembered that same *poor* wise man," Eccles. ix. 15. For details of the sieges consult ' *Memorias*,' &c., Fernando Garcia y Marin, duo., Mad., 1817; ' *Historia de los dos sitios*,' Agustin Alcaide Ibieca, 2 vols. 8vo., Mad., 1830; read also the Narrative of Mr. Vaughan; the French account of Rogniart; the romantic description of Southey; and the scornful truth of Napier, in their respective histories.

Zaragoza is a central point of many roads: beginning S. is the diligence road to Madrid, R. cviii. This branches off at Calatayud for Daroca, R. cvi., and so on to Molina de Aragon, Teruel, and Cuenca, cv., and thence to Murcia and Valencia. R. cvii. leads to Murviedro, and thence to Valencia or Barcelona. For communications with Navarre, see Sect. xiv. There is much talk of a railway which is to connect Madrid and Barcelona via Zaragoza, and also a project of forming a canal from the latter to Lérida.

ROUTE CXXVI.—ZARAGOZA TO BAR-
CELONA.

La Púebla	. . .	3	
Osera	. . . .	3 ..	6
V. de Sª. Lucia	. .	3 ..	9
Bujaroloz	. . .	3 ..	12
Candasnos	. .	3 ..	15
V. de Fraga	. .	2 ..	17
Fraga	. . . .	2 ..	19
Alcarraz	. .	3 ..	22
Lérida	. . . .	2 ..	24
Belloch	. . .	2½ ..	26½
Golmes	. . .	2½ ..	29
Villagrasa	. . .	2½ ..	31½
Cervera	. . .	2½ ..	34
La Pavadella	. .	2½ ..	36½
Al Gancho	. .	2½ ..	39
Igualada	. . .	2 ..	41
Castelloli	. . .	2½ ..	43½
Codul	. . . .	2½ ..	46
Marturell	. . .	3 ..	49
Molins del Rey	. .	2 ..	51
Barcelona	. . .	3 ..	54

This route is extremely uninteresting. Crossing the Ebro is an *arrabal* or suburb, which was almost demolished by the French: here on every Thursday is held a sort of horse-market, which is frequented by picturesque blackguards. Soon the clear Gallego is passed over, while the old brick bridge remains high and dry on the land, a Pons Hispanorum as at Coria and elsewhere; the road now enters the *desert* of Arragon, and dreary is the waste, without trees, life, or cultivation; the soil is poor and chalky, the climate ungenial, and man misgoverned and ignorant. The Ebro flows to the r., and on it is *Velilla*, a village so named from the alarum bell of its church, which tolled of its own accord, like those of Celanova (p. 686), to the comfort of Spanish ringers, who thus while Hercules tugged away smoked their *papelitos* or slept. This toll only took place when coming calamities cast their shadows over Arragon. The bell was cast by the Goths, who threw into the fused metal one of the thirty pieces of silver received by Judas Iscariot. It rang most furiously in 1516, when announcing the death of Ferdinand the Catholic, and again in 1679 for the twentieth and last time, when giving notice in fact of its own dissolution and funeral. The soldier-like Romans, in whose days bells were not invented, were warned of approaching danger by the clashing of arms in heroic sepulchres (Cic⁰· Div., i. 34); but armed men, and not cowled priests, were then the managers of miracles. For authentic details of this bell, see ' *Discursos Varios*,' by Diego Dormêr. The learned Padre Feijoo, in speculating on this miracle, attributed much of the phenomena to hemp. Velilla bears this bell gules on its shield. The tale and toll are now pretty well worn out, or the clapper would indeed have worked hard during the Peninsular war, so multitudinous were Spanish reverses in this valley of the Ebro from Tudela (see R. cxxviii.) downwards. When Bailen had delivered Madrid, and forced the defeated French to fall back on the Ebro, " for the sake only of better water," according to Buonaparte's bulletin; the third Spanish army was advanced on this important line, and destined to cooperate on the r. with Belveder at Burgos in the centre, and with Blake at Epinosa. Castaños was the chief in command, but nothing could exceed the inefficiency of the troops, who were left by the central government in want of everything at the critical moment. The hard but common lot of the poor soldiers was increased by the incapacity of their generals, who vied with each other in playing at war like children. The natural consequence was that the tremendously powerful French everywhere scattered them like sheep at the first attack. At *Maria*, Suchet, with 6000 men, had, June 15, 1809, put Blake and 17,000 men to flight as easily as Samson did the Philistines; one splendid charge of cavalry under D'Aigremont and Burthé being enough. Blake, however, on whom experience was thrown away, halted, for he was a brave man, at Belchite, where the French came up, June 18, and again, by one charge of Burthé, routed the ill-equipped remnant, killing nearly 4000 men, and only losing 40 themselves. Lower down is *Alcaniz*, where, January 26, 1809, Vattier, with 500 men, had with equal ease defeated 4000 Spaniards under Areizaga (of Ocaña infamy); the wretched town was almost demolished in 1813 by Severoli, as his parting legacy when evacuating it after the French rout at Vitoria. 6 L. from Alcaniz, on the road to Morella, is *Monroyo*, a red hill, near which is the hermitage of our Lady of the *fountain*, whose medicinal waters taken with faith cure more diseases than even the lamp-oil of the Pilar, as the votive tablets prove. The chapel once belonged to the Templars, and curious paintings still exist under the Coro alto.

Continuing our route is *Bujaroloz*, pop. 1900, and placed in a fertile valley; hence to ruined *Fraga* (Fragosa, Stony), with a dismantled castle, and built on a slope above the Cinca, over which there is a bridge. This poor rough ill-paved place is worthy of its name, pop. 4900. The environs, however, abound in pomegranate and figs: the small green ones are delicious, and when dried are the staple; but they are diminutive and very inferior to those of Smyrna, although our mediæval

pilgrim in Purchas (ii. 1233) describes them in terms of rapture :—

And figez full gret so God me save,
Thei be like to a great warden,
Blew and faat as any bacon.

There is a bridle-communication with *Mequinenza*, 3 L., and thence by *Flix* to *Tortosa* (see R. xli.). The Cinca divides Arragon from Catalonia. The wearisome country now resembles that near Guadix, and is cut up with ravines and studded with small conical hills. *Lérida* is a well-supplied cheap place. The best inns are *La Posada del Hospital* and *La de Sⁿ· Luis*. There is a local diligence to Barcelona, in case the traveller may wish to halt in this city of classical and military recollections.

Lérida, Ilerda, a name which Bochart derives from the Syriac *Illi*, lofty, is built on the *Segre*, Sicoris, under its acropolis, which rises an imposing mass of lines of fortifications, with an old cathedral and lofty tower. The principal street is one long line of white houses with red and green balconies. The W. side is defended by *Fort Garden* outwork, and the *El Pilar* and *Sⁿ· Fernando*. Lérida, although the second city of Catalonia, is devoid of interest. The new cathedral was built in a Corinthian style in the bad period of Ferd. VI., and contains some second-rate sculpture by Juan Adan. The original cathedral was erected on the upper town by Jaime the Conqueror, who selected an easily defended position; but in the piping times of peace the steep walk proved too much for the stall-fed canons, whose affections were not set on things above: so they abandoned their lofty church, which recently was made a magazine. The citadel was much injured by the invaders; but some vast *algibes* or tanks remain, with a fine view all around.

Ilerda, a Celtiberian city, is well described by Lucan (B. C., iv. 13), "Colle tumet modico," etc., and the foundations of the present fine stone bridge are built on those of the Romans. It was held for Pompey by Afranius and Petreus, who were encamped on Fort Garden until outgeneralled and beaten by Cæsar : here, therefore, read his terse dispatches (B. C., i. 37, etc.), and compare them with those of our Duke before Badajoz, for the iron energy of their swords passed into their pens. Everything was against them both, the elements as well as man, but both, left wanting in means, supplied all deficiency in themselves and triumphed. *Ilerda* soon recoverered its prosperity, and had a mint: for the coinage see Florez (M., ii. 450). It became a *Municipium* and a university, one, however, of such disagreeable "residence" that the recusant youth of Rome were threatened to be rusticated there (Hor. I. 'E.,' xx. 13). In after times Lérida was made the Salamanca of Arragon, and its annalists boast with pride of its pupils, S^n. Vicente Ferrer and Calixtus III. (Borgia), *i. e.*, a bloody inquisidor and a jobbing profligate pope.

The Goths after the downfall of the empire patronised Lérida, and held here a celebrated council, having raised it to a bishopric in 546. Moorish Lérida was sacked by the French in 799, but recovered and rebuilt in 1149 by Ramon Berenguer, who restored the see. It was the site of the death of Herodias and her capering daughter, who were drowned when performing pirouettes on the frozen Segres, when the ice broke and the young lady fell in; but her head got cut off and continued dancing of itself, like the decapitated old apple-woman's on the ice-bound Thames, which still cried " pip, pip, pippin " (see for authentic details ' *Lithologia*,' José V del Olmo, p. 183).

Lérida, in the Catalonian revolt of 1640, chose Louis XIII. for its king, and Leganez, the general of Philip IV., failed in his attempt to retake it, and this entailed the downfall of his kinsman, the great Conde Duque Olivares.

Thereupon Philip IV. came in person to the siege, and having defeated the French under *La Mothe*, entered in triumph (see his Bronze, p. 744). The French in 1644 failed to regain it, whereupon the Grand Conde opened another siege to the tune of violins, but Gregorio Brito, the Portuguese governor, sallied out and drove fiddlers and troopers headlong before him. Next day he sent to the Grand Conde some iced fruits, begging him to excuse his non-return of the serenade-compliment from a want of catgut, but promising, if his previous accompaniment was agreeable, to repeat it as often as his Highness did him the honor to perform before Lérida, which was not long, for the Great Conde soon departed re infectâ, and did *not* print his intended parallel between himself and Cæsar : venit, vidit, et evasit.

Lérida in the War of Succession was long besieged in 1707 by Berwick and Orleans, and capitulated in November; but, nevertheless, was most cruelly and faithlessly sacked. However, it was avenged July 27, 1710, by Stanhope, who near it completely routed Philip V.; and had not the slowness of the Germans delayed the attack, "had there been two hours more daylight, you may be assured that not one foot-soldier of their army would have escaped." So wrote the Duke after Salamanca. Philip V., afterwards writhing under recollections of this disgrace, transferred the university to Cervera, and the two places have detested each other ever since.

Lérida in the Peninsular war was taken by Suchet May 14, 1810. Gen. Harispe having seized upon *Fort Garden* and the town, the unarmed inhabitants, women and children, were driven out on to the glacis, and there exposed to the fire both of the citadel and the invader ; thus they were massacred all night and next day by the French shells, until the Spanish governor, Garcia Conde, overpowered by the frightful scene, hoisted the white flag. Suchet, in his ' Mémoires,' ch. 4, dwells with honest pride on this well-imagined destruction, which he repeated at Tarragona and elsewhere — a proceeding which Col. Napier thought "*politic,* indeed, but scarcely admissible within the pale of civilization." Confound their politics! but Foy (i. 258) sneers at our dull soldiers as being insensible to "Les révélations sublimes du génie de la destruction, qui éveille une puissance de pensée supérieure à celle qui préside aux créations de la poésie et de la philosophie." Suchet, after this splendid feat, which thus outclipsed the sublime of Milton and Burke, removed from Zaragoza to Lérida, where "*Madame*" held her "Court," and ruled him as her hairdresser ruled her, for she was consistent at least, in love for a profession of which her husband had once been a bright ornament. Suchet consoled himself "d'être soumis ainsi à la quenouille par l'oppression de fer du pays." The fortunate coiffeur also rose in the army and became a commissaire de guerre (Schep. iii. 352). Suchet published his 'Mémoires,' and proved himself with his own trumpet to be a paragon of honour and glory, while his lively French editor assures admiring mankind that "his eyes were indicative of the utmost kindness of disposition, and his physiognomy expressed the sentiments of benevolence with which his heart overflowed" (for proofs see also Tarragona, p. 471).

Proceeding onwards between *Golmes* and *Villafranca,* and near *Bellpuig* in the Franciscan convent, is (or was) the most magnificent tomb of Ramon de Cardona, viceroy of Sicily, which was raised by Isabel his widow. The armed noble lies on a splendid ciuquecento *Urna,* which is enriched with mythological and marine deities, while the basement is divided into three portions; in the centre is a sea-battle; the others are inscribed with Latin verses on tablets supported by children; in the l. corner is the name of the Neapolitan sculptor, "Joannes Nolanus,

faciebat 1522." Observe above the Cariatides, and the Virgin and Child in a vesica piscis of clouds upheld by angels.

The dreary country which now ensues, and the interminable leagues, have long been the horror of riding-travellers. *Tarega a Cervera, lequa entera, y si fuere mojada cuentela por jornada.*

Cervera is built on an eminence which descends sharply to Barcelona, pop. 4500. To this place Philip V. transferred the university of Lérida, which recently has again been removed to Barcelona; there he raised the huge unsightly edifice with pointed roofs and French towers, which Suchet and others afterwards gutted, having first burnt the library in order to fit it for a barrack. Cervera is seen from afar on all sides, and its heights command extensive views. The Gothic church has a good chapel of *La Vera Cruz,* and there is a fine cloister in the Dominican convent. At Cervera, Oct. 11, 1811, Eroles defeated the invaders and took their *Corregidor,* one Isidoro Perez Canino, a renegade Spaniard, who placed all his countrymen who did not pay French contributions into a cage, leaving outside their heads besmeared with honey to attract a plague of flies. This *Afrancesado* was torn to pieces by the populace (Toreno, xvi.); but in the words of the Duke (Disp., Nov. 22, 1812), such a wretch had been "guilty of the greatest crime of which any individual in modern times can be guilty, viz., he has aided the French in invading his native country, in which they committed horrors until then unheard of."

From Cervera a poor chalky uneven country leads to *Igualada,* which is also built on an eminence. The older portions are narrow and tortuous, but the *Rambla* is a good street, and the new suburb handsome. Here also is a fine arch constructed to introduce water; here in the summer of 1840 Christina met Espartero, and by persisting in the French scheme of abolishing local *fueros*, prepared the way to her loss of the regency and expatriation. Soon commence rich corn-plains and vineyards, which continue along a busy road (see p. 479) to Barcelona.

SPANISH PYRENEES.—The finest portions are in Arragon. This mountain range was called by the Romans *Montes* and *Saltus Pyrenei*, and by the Greeks Πυρηνη, probably from a local Iberian word, but which they, as usual, catching at sound, not sense, connected with their Πυρ, and then bolstered up their erroneous derivation by a legend framed to fit the name, asserting that it either alluded to a fire through which certain precious metals were discovered, or because the lofty summits were often struck with lightning and dislocated by volcanos. According to the Iberians, Hercules, when on his way to "lift" Geryon s cattle, was hospitably received by Bebryx, a petty ruler in these mountains; whereupon the demigod got drunk, and ravished his host's daughter *Pyrene*, who died of grief, when Hercules, sad and sober, made the whole range re-echo with her name (Sil. Ital., iii. 420); but Pliny (N. H., iii. 1) held this Spanish legend to be an idle fiction. Bochart (Can. i. 35) supposes that the Phœnicians called these ranges *Purani*, from the forest, *Pura* being wood in Hebrew. The Basques have, of course, their etymology, some saying that the real root is *Biri*, an elevation, while others prefer *Bierri enac*, the "two countries," which, separated by the range, were ruled by Tubal (' *Origen*,' Perochegui, p. 19); but when Spaniards once begin with Tubal, the best plan is to shut the book.

This gigantic barrier, which divides Spain and France, is connected with the dorsal chain which comes down from Tartary and Asia. It stretches far beyond the transversal spine, for the mountains of the Basque Provinces, Asturias and Gallicia, are its continuation. The Pyrenees, properly speaking, are placed between 42° 10' and 43° 20' N. latitude, and extend E. to W., in length about 270 miles, and being both broadest and highest in the central portions, where the width is about 60 miles, and the elevations exceed 11,000 feet. The spurs and offsets of this great transversal spine penetrate on both sides like ribs from a back-bone into the lateral valleys. The central nucleus slopes gradually E. to the Mediterranean, and W. to the Atlantic, in a long uneven swell : thus from *Monte Perdido*, which is 11,264 ft. high, it descends, rising again at the *Maledéta* to 11,424 ft.; then it descends into the valley of *Andorra*, rising again in the *Moncal* to 10,663 ft.; dips once more, rising again in the *Canigú* to 9141 ft., and then shelves into the Mediterranean.

The *Maledéta* is the loftiest peak, although the *Pico del Mediodia* and the *Canigú*, because rising at once out of plains and therefore having the greatest apparent altitudes, were long considered to be the highest; but now these French usurpers are dethroned. This central nucleus is a net-work of gigantic masses and heights, which rise almost from the same bases: thus *Neouvielle* (ancient snows) soars 9702 ft., *Marboré* 10,950 ft., *Monte Perdido* 11,264 ft., and *Viguemale* 10,330 ft. : all these are placed between Huesca and Tarbes.

The width of the range is narrowest to the E., being only about 20 miles across near *Figueras*, while the heights are the lowest at the W. extremity, seldom exceeding 9000 ft. The width opposite *Pamplona* ranges at about 40 miles. Seen from a distance the range appears to be one mountain-ridge, with broken pinnacles; but, in fact, it consists of two distinct lines, which are parallel, but not continuous. The one which commences at the ocean is the most forward, being at least 30 miles more in advance towards the south than the corresponding line, which commences from the Mediterranean. The centre is the point of dislocation, and here the ramifications and reticulations are the most intricate, as it is the key-stone of the system, which is buttressed up by *Las Tres Sorellas*, the tria juncta in uno of the sisters *Monte Perdido, Cylindro,* and *Marboré.* Here is the source of the Garonne, *La Garona;* here the scenery is the grandest, and the lateral valleys the longest and widest. The Spanish or S. front is most in advance, and is the steepest, and descends abruptly; while on the French or N. side the acclivities shelve down in tiers with a succession of terraces, dips, and basins. The average height of perpetual snow ranges between 8000 ft. and 9000 ft., a datum which is useful in calculating elevations. In the Alps this line is at 6600 ft., in the Andes 14,000 ft.

In the highest elevations on the French side are glaciers, *Sernelhes,* and frozen lochs; and in general there are more lakes on that side than on the Spanish, which being steeper 'affords fewer positions in which waters can lodge. The lake on *Monte Perdido* is 8393 ft. above the sea. The smaller buttresses or spurs of the great range enclose valleys, down each of which pours a stream: thus the Ebro, Garona, and Bidasoa are fed from the mountain alembic. These tributaries are generally called in France *Gaves,** and in some parts on the Spanish side *Gabas;* but *Gav* signifies a "river," and may be traced in our *Avon;* and Humboldt derives it from the Basque *Gav,* a "hollow or ravine;" cavus, κοιλος. The parting of these waters or their flowing down either N. or S. should naturally mark the line of division between France and Spain: such, however, is not the case, as part of *Cerdaña* belongs to the former, while *Aran* belongs to the latter; thus each country possesses a key in its neighbour's territory. It is singular that this obvious inconvenience should not have been remedied by some exchange when the long-disputed boundary-question was settled between Charles IV. and the French republic (see also E. S., xlii. 236).

The lateral valleys vary in length from 10 to 40 miles; sometimes they narrow into gorges, *gargantas,* or expand into basins, *ollas,* which are encircled by mountains as by an amphitheatre; hence these *oules* are called by the French *Cirques.* These circular recesses were once lakes, from which the waters have burst: the smaller lochs, *Ibones,* abound in trout. The valleys in Arragon are among the most beautiful in the whole range, especially those of *Anso, Canfranc, Biescas, Broto, Gistain,* and *Benasque.*

The highest points or pinnacles are called *Puigs* in Catalonia, *Pueyos* in Arragon, and *Poyos* in Navarre, words which are said to be a corruption of *Podium,* an elevation. *Poyo,* however, in Castilian signifies a stone doorpost. The depressions at the heads of valleys or *necks* of the ridges are called *Colls,* and in Castilian *Collados,* and over them the *passes* of intercommunication are carried; hence they are called *Puertos, gates, doorways, Portæ;* and the smaller ones *Portillos.* The equivalent terms on the French side are *Col,· Hourque, Hourquette, Fourque, Core, Brèche,* and *Porte.* Of these in the whole range there are some 70 or 80, but scarcely a dozen of them are practicable for rude wheel-carriages. They remain much in the same state as in the time of the Moors, who from them called the Pyrenean range *Albort,* the ridge of "gates" or Portæ (see p. 93). Many of the wild passes are only known to the natives and

---

* The word *Gavacho,* which is the most offensive vituperative of the Spaniard against the Frenchman, has by some been thought to mean " those who dwell on Gaves." Marina, however (Mem. Acad. His. iv. 59), derives it, and correctly, from the Arabic *Cabach,* detestable, filthy, or "qui prava indole est, moribusque."

smugglers, and are often impracticable from the snow, while even in summer they are dangerous, being exposed to mists and hurricanes of mighty rushing winds. Generally speaking, the ascents are the easiest from the French side, and to those who cross the barrier the following local names may be useful :— *Cacou, Couilla,* a shepherd's cabin ; *Chaos,* a heap of rocks—" chaos come again;" *Couret,* the course of a river when it leaves a lake; *Estibe,* fine meadows; *Pene,* the extreme point of a mountain ; *Pouey, Puch, Pech, Puy, Sarre, Serre, Sarrat (Sierra Cerro,* Arabicè a back); *Tuc, Tuque,* a mountain; *Turon,* a hillock; *Ramade,* a large flock of sheep.

The two best carriageable lines of intercommunication are placed at each extremity ; that to the W. passes through *Irun,* that to the E. through *Figueras.* On these lines are the best towns and accommodations. The chief secondary passes are the *Puerto de Maya* and *De Roncesvalles* in Navarre ; those of *Canfranc, Panticosa, Gavarnie, Vielsa, Brecha de Roldan* and *Marcadau* in Arragon ; and of *Plan de Ause, Puigcerdá,* and the *Col de Pertus* in Catalonia.

THE SPANISH PYRENEES offer few attractions to the lovers of the fleshly comforts of cities, for the objects of interest relate solely to Nature, who here wantons in her loneliest, wildest forms. The scenery, sporting, geology, and botany are truly Alpine, and will well repay those who can "rough it considerably. The contrast which the southern or Spanish side offers to the northern or French side is great : the mountains themselves are less abrupt, less covered with snow, while the numerous and much frequented baths on the latter have created roads, diligences, hotels, table-d'hôtes, cooks, Cicerones, donkeys, and so forth for the Badaux de Paris ; they indeed babble about green fields and *des belles horreurs,* but seldom go beyond the immediate vicinity and hackneyed " lions ;" for a want of good taste and real perception of the sublime and beautiful is nowhere more striking, says Mr. Erskine Murray, than on the French side, where mankind remains profoundly ignorant of the real beauties of the Pyrenees, which have been chiefly explored by nature-worshipping English. Nevertheless, on the French side many comforts and appliances for the tourist are to be had; nay, invalids and ladies in search of the picturesque can ascend to the *Brèche de Roldan.* Once, however, cross the frontier, and a sudden change comes over all facilities of locomotion. Stern is the welcome of the dura tellus Iberiæ! scarce is the food for body or mind, and deficient the accommodation for man or beast, and simply because there is small demand for either. No Spaniard ever comes here for pleasure; hence the localities are given up to the smuggler and izard. The Oriental inæsthetic incuriousness for *things,* old stones, wild scenery, &c., is increased by political reasons and fears. France, from the time of the Celt down to to-day, has ever been the ravager and terror of Spain. While she therefore has improved her means of approach and invasion, Spain, to whom the past is prophetic of the future, has raised obstacles, and has left her protecting barrier as broken and hungry as when planned by her tutelar divinity. Nor are her highlanders more practicable than their broken fastnesses, as here dwell the smuggler, the rifle sportsman, the *faccioso,* and all who defy the law; here is bred the hardy peasant, who, accustomed to scale mountains and fight wolves, becomes a ready raw material; for the *guerrilleros,* and none were ever more formidable to Rome or France than those marshalled in these glens by Sertorius and Mina, when the tocsin bell rings out, a hornet swarm of armed men, the weed of the hills, starts up from every rock and brake. The hatred of the Frenchman, which the Duke said formed " part of a Spaniard's nature," seems to increase in intensity in proportion to vicinity ; here it is the antipathy of an antithesis, the incompatibility of the saturnine and slow, with the mercurial and rapid ; of the proud, enduring and ascetic, against the vain, the fickle, and sensual; of the enemy of innovation and change to the lover of variety and novelty : and however despots may assert in the gilded galleries of Versailles that *Il n'y a plus de Pyrénées*, this party-wall of Alps, this barrier of snow and hurricane, does and will exist for ever; placed there by Providence, quasi de industriâ, said even the Goths (Sⁿ· Isid. Or. xv. 8), they ever have forbidden and ever will forbid the banns of an unnatural alliance, as in the days of Silius Italicus (iii. 417) :

> Pyrene celsâ nimbosi verticis arce
> Divisos Celtis laté prospectat Hiberos
> Atque æterna tenet magnis divortia terris.

If the eagle of Buonaparte could never build in the Arragonese Sierra, the lily of the Bourbon assuredly will not take root in the Castilian plain; so says Ariosto (xxxiii. 10) :

> —————— Che non lice
> Che 'l giglio in quel terreno habbia radice !

This inveterate condition either of pronounced hostility, or at best of armed neutrality, has long rendered these localities disagreeable to the man of the note-book. Again, these localities consist of a series of secluded districts, which constitute the entire world to the natives, who seldom go beyond the natural walls by which they are bounded except to smuggle. This vocation is the curse of the country, fosters a wild reliance on self-defence, a habit of border foray and insurrection, which almost seems necessary as a moral excitement and combustible element, as carbon and hydrogen are in their physical bodies. No preventive service, no cordon of custom-house officers can put down contraband in these broken ranges, nor guard the infinite tracks which thread the wild rocks, forests, and glaciers. Again, the recent civil wars have been very injurious, by interrupting commerce and arresting honest employment, while the severe regulations regarding the sale of ammunition have interfered with the sportsman by curtailing the chief joy and relaxation of the mountaineer. The habitual suspicion against prying foreigners, which is an Oriental and Iberian instinct, converts a curious traveller into a spy or partisan. Spanish authorities, who seldom do these things except on compulsion, cannot understand the gratuitous braving of hardship and danger for its own sake— the botanizing and geologizing, &c., of the nature and adventure-loving English. The *impertinente curioso* may possibly escape observation in a Spanish city and crowd, but in these lonely hills it is out of the question : he is the observed of all observers, and they, from long smuggling and sporting habits, are always on the look-out, and are keen-sighted as hawks, gipseys, and beasts of prey. Meanwhile the gaping, gazing stranger is as unconscious of the portentous emotions and fears which he is exciting as were the birds of old of the meaning attached to their movements by the Roman augurs, and few augurs ever rivalled a Spanish *Alcalde* in quick suspicion and perception of evil, especially where none is intended. *Be careful therefore to have the passport en règle, and always to call on the Alcalde and frankly state the object of the visit :* refer also to our remarks, p. 9. When, however, the suspicions of these semi-barbarian officials are once allayed, they become civil and hospitable according to their humble means. Latterly some of those who, by being placed immediately under the French boundary, have seen the glitter of the tourist's coin, have become more humanized, and anxious to obtain a share in the profits of the season. Generally speaking, a local guide is necessary : those tourists who can speak

Spanish will of course get on the best, and will easily find some bold smuggler or local sportsman to attend them; those who only speak French must put up with one of those amphibious guides who are always to be found on the French side, and who occasionally, besides being bilingual, are also both rogues and ignorant. For guide-books in the French Pyrenees, consult 'Observations de M. Ramond,' Paris, 1789: he is the Saussure of these Alps: also a 'Summer in the Pyrenees,' by Mr. Erskine Murray, and ' Handbook for France,' by Mr. John Murray.

The geology and botany have yet to be properly investigated. In the metal-pregnant Pyrenees rude forges of iron abound, but everything is conducted on a small, unscientific scale, and probably after the unchanged, primitive Iberian system. Fuel is scarce, and transport of ores on muleback expensive. The iron is at once inferior to the English and much dearer : the tools and imple-ments used on both sides of the Pyrenees are at least a century behind ours; while absurd tariffs, which prevent the importation of a cheaper and better article, prevent improvements in agriculture and manufactures, and perpetuate poverty and ignorance among backward, half-civilised populations. The na-tural woods of these Saltus Pyrenæi have long been celebrated, and Strabo (iii. 245) observed how much more the southern were covered than the northern ones. The timber, however, has suffered much from the usual neglect, waste, and improvidence of the natives, who destroy more than they consume, and never replant. The sporting in these lonely, wild districts is excellent, for where man seldom penetrates the feræ naturæ multiply : the bear is, however, getting scarce, as a premium is placed on every head destroyed. The grand object of the Cazador is the Cabra Montanez, or Rupicabra, the Bouquetin of the French, the Izard (Ibex, becco, bouc, bock, buck). The fascination of this pursuit, like that of the Chamois in Switzerland, leads to constant and even fatal accidents, as this shy animal lurks in almost inaccessible localities, and must be stalked with the nicest skill. The sporting on the French side is far inferior, as the cooks of the table-d'hôtes have waged a guerra al cuchillo, a war to the knife, and fork too, against even les petits oiseaux; but your French artiste persecutes even minnows, as all sport and fair play is scouted, and everything gives way for the pot. The Spaniards, less mechanical and gastro-nomic, leave the feathered and finny tribes in comparative peace. Accordingly the streams abound with trout, and those which flow into the Atlantic with salmon. The lofty Pyrenees are not only alembics of cool crystal streams, but contain, like the heart of Sappho, sources of warm springs under a bosom of snow. The most celebrated issue on the French side, or at least those the most known and frequented, for the Spaniard is a small bather and no great drinker of medicinal waters. Accommodations at the baths on his side scarcely exist, while even those in France are paltry when compared to the spas of Ger-many, and dirty and indecent when contrasted with those of England. The scenery is alpine, a jumble of mountain, precipice, glacier, and forest, enlivened by the cataract or hurricane. The natives, when not smugglers or guerrilleros, are rude, simple, and pastoral; in summer they lead their flocks up to moun-tain huts and dwell with their cattle, struggling against poverty and wild beasts, and endeavouring really to keep the wolf from the door : their watch-dogs are magnificent : the sheep are under admirable control, being, as it were, in the presence of the enemy, they know the voice of their shepherds, or rather the peculiar whistle and cry : their wool is largely smuggled into France, and then re-smuggled back again, manufactured in the shape of coarse cloth.

ROUTE CXXVII.—ZARAGOZA TO URDAX.

Villanueva	2	
Zuera	2	4
Gurrea del Gallego	3	7
Vᵃ de Tulinana	2	9
Ayerbe	3	12
Anzánigo	3	15
Bernues	2	17
Jaca	2¼	19¼
Canfranc	2	22¼
Urdax	3	25¼

There is a sort of diligence communication part of the way in summer, and so on to Oleron in France : generally, however, travellers ride. The mountain-roads are bad, but the scenery is picturesque. The route commences over bald dreary plains, with aromatic wastes extending to the r., while the *Gallego* eats its way to the l. Those who leave Zaragoza late may sleep at a solitary venta about 2 *L.* short of *Gurrea.* Approaching *Ayerbe* the Pyrenees grow in size, as the road grows worse. Crossing a ridge which separates the water-courses of the Aragon and Gallego, and winding through pretty well-watered glens, *Jaca,* Jacca, is reached. This place has immemorially been of some importance, as lying on the frontier. The castle was strengthened by Philip II. The town is tolerably built : popⁿ· about 3000. Near it the river Gas joins the Aragon, and fertilizes the valleys. Jaca is the see of a bishop, suffragan to Zaragoza. The simple solid cathedral was founded by Ramiro in 814. The tutelar is a Sᵃ· Orosia, whose body is venerated in her chapel. Near Jaca is a singular semi-Norman church, called *La Santa Cruz,* with a remarkable door-way.

Jaca was taken from the Spaniards by M. P. Cato, A.C. 195, and spared because a frontier town ; it then became the capital of its district, was fortified, and portions of the Roman wall are yet preserved. It was wrested from the Moors so early as 795, when Don Asnar, its Pelayus, sallied forth from the mountains and dispossessed the infidels, who made a desperate attempt to recover it, but were repulsed, the women fighting like the maids of

Zaragoza. The Moors fled, leaving behind them the heads of four of their kings, *i. e.* shiekhs, which Jaca quarters on her shield to this day. The site of the battle, called *Las Tiendas,* is still visited on the first Friday in May, when these Amazons go gloriously " a-shopping." A church was raised, dedicated to *La Virgen de la Victoria,* just as was done by the Pagans to *Venus Genetrix* or *Fortuna Equestris,* Santiago (App. ' B. C.' ii. 803 ; Val. Max. i. 2). The old castle of Jaca, during the Peninsular war, was repaired and strongly garrisoned by the French under Lomet, a wholesale executioner of prisoners (Schep. ii. 252). After Soult's defeats in the Pyrenees the garrison capitulated, under promise not to serve against the allies ; but no sooner had the troops reached France than this pledge was violated, and the Duke in consequence refused to ratify the capitulations of their countrymen at Santoña (Disp. April 1, 1814). However, this dishonourable practice was quite a thing of course with Buonaparte : so at Aboukir, when Nelson landed the prisoners on a pledge that they were not to serve, before the fleet was out of sight they were all drafted into regiments.

Jaca is interesting to the constitutional antiquarian, as its *fuero,* or municipal charter, is reckoned among the earliest in Spain ; it dates from the Moorish expulsion, and was confirmed in 1063 by Sanchez Ramirez. In Jaca also was held the first parliament on record. All those who have leisure should visit the mines and pine-forests of *Oroel,* and the picturesque ruined Benedictine convent of *San Juan de la Peña,* near which the Arragonese in 760 built their first city, and called it *Panno,* but it was soon destroyed by the Moors, when the natives fled to the cavern, where the convent was afterwards built. Thus it became the rocky cradle of the monarchy, as Covadanga did in the Asturias, and as that of Adullam was to David. Here the early patriots were joined by the mountaineers from *Sobrarbe*, and drew up the so-called *Fueros*. The foundation of the convent was after this wise: a hunter named Voto, while riding after a stag, came suddenly on the chasm under which the building now nestles; while the fore-legs of the galloping steed hung over the gulph, and the hind ones rested on terra firma, Voto, worthy of his name, invoked St. John, and the horse became fixed, hanging in mid-air; in evidence of which miracle the prints of the hoofs on the rock were long shown. Voto then dismounted, and descending into the cave found the stag dead from the fall, and by its side a deceased hermit, on whose stone pillow was inscribed his name, " Juan," and a statement that he had here founded a chapel to the Baptist. This relic was unfortunately lost in 1094, to the grief of the historian Abarca (i. 22), whose account we abridge. While all this was going on, Voto's horse remained suspended over the abyss, a fact afterwards borrowed without acknowledgment by Baron Munchausen: however, when his master climbed up to him the animal became undetached, and prudently turned land-ways. Voto rode to Jaca, persuaded his brother to turn hermit, and both lived and died in the cave, since which " miracles have been continually worked and salvation secured by their intercession." A similar horse-feat and miracle occurred also in Portugal in 1182, where Don Juan discovered the Virgin of Nazareth, whose shrine was pillaged by the invaders under Thomières (Southey, ' Don Rod.' note 28). As *Juan*, the original anchorite, was one of the earliest preachers of a crusade against the Moors, hence few sites were more revered by the Arragonese than this. It became, says Suchet, the " object of popular superstition," and produced a new asserter of liberty, one Sarasa, a local guerrillero ; whereupon the hallowed spot was surprised by the invaders under Musnier, Aug. 25, 1809, who burnt the monastery to the ground, and with it

the precious MSS. and archives of early Arragonese liberties—and melancholy are the picturesque ruins. Observe the singular billet patterns on the arches, and the cloister. The position somewhat recalls the rock-built temples of Petræa. In this primitive sanctuary a long line of the early kings of Arragon down to Alonzo II. were interred, but their ashes were scattered to the winds by the invading soldiers, like those at Leon, Poblet, and elsewhere. In the chapel, on Wednesday, March 30, 1071, was celebrated the first Roman mass performed in the Peninsula. This was effected by Card. Hugo Candido, legate of Alexander II., who influenced the king, Sancho Ramirez. This event, which was cited as the proudest boast by Abarca (i. 119), in reality opened the door to the yoke of Rome. Then the primitive vernacular ritual was exchanged for one in Latin, which the people did not understand, until misgoverned, deluded Spain, having been alternately the inquisitor, executioner, champion, and banker of the Vatican, sunk into bigotry and intolerance, and became a bye-word to the world, enslaved, weak, ignorant, and impoverished. For details, consult ' *Historia de San Juan de la Peña*,' by its abbot, Juan Briz Martinez, Zaragoza, 1620.

Leaving Jaca, the Pyrenean defiles are soon entered, and the road becomes wild and alpine. *Canfranc* is a miserable place, with its castle. The *Puerto* is said to be 6713 ft. above the level of the sea. The overhanging castle commands splendid views. Behind lies Arragon, and above towers the snowy cloud-capped *Can Gran*, one of the most remarkable heights of the range. The inhabitants of *Canfranc* are canes franci, and worthy of their name, being much addicted to smuggling, and this in face of the *Dogana* and custom-house officers of the two countries, des véritables chiens, who worry the honest traveller : how to give a sop to these Cerberi has before been touched on (see p. 205). Canfranc is the last town in Arragon. Adieu, hungry Spain, with thy mountain passes, ilex woods, and fragrant wildernesses, and welcome the talented flesh-pots and superb cuisine of la belle France, of which *Urdax*, however, offers but poor samples. Hence in summer a diligence runs to *Oleron* (see Handbook for France, R. lxxxii.). From the *Puerto de Canfranc* the pedestrian may strike off to the r., under the *Pico del Mediodia*, to *Gabas*, where the French douane is placed, and so on to *Eaux Chaudes.* The Pic du Midi may be ascended from Gabas in from 2 to 3 hours: it is said to be 9500 ft. high. The ascent from *Grip* requires about 6 hours. The views over the rugged Pyrenees contrast with the plains of France.

ROUTE CXXVIII.—JACA TO THE PUERTO DE SALLENT.

Larres .	. . . .	2	
Biescas	. . . .	2 ..	4
Pueyo .	. . . .	2 ..	6
Po. de Sallent.	. . .	2 ..	8

Attend to the provend, and take a local guide, who generally can procure lodgings and some sort of accommodation in private houses in the villages, which are cleaner and quieter than the *Posadas, i. e.* receptacles for smugglers and their beasts. The beautiful valley of *Tena*, with the mineral baths of *Panticosa*, lies between the valley of *Canfranc* W., and that of *Broto* E., and each are divided from the other by ridges or spurs, which shoot down laterally from the Pyrenees; they intercommunicate by wild paths, known however to the natives. The valley of *Tena* is about 4 L. long N. and S., and 3 L. wide, being some 11 L. in circumference; it is watered by the *Gallego; Sallent* is the chief hamlet. Turning W. from *Jaca*, soon after *Larres*, the *Gallego* is neared, which flows on the l. with its tributaries, until crossed and recrossed near the truly Swiss-like village, popⁿ· 800. *Biescas*, with a decent posada near the bridge, is a good sporting quarter; as

in addition to its rivers it communicates both with the valley of *Tena* and *Broto*, which the Izard hunters consider most favourite ground, as lying under the gnarled roots of the *Monte Perdido* group.

Proceeding to *Panticosa* the defiles narrow in, and the scenery increases in Alpine character; about a mile up is the *Barranco de Estaquer*, a wild *rambla* like the bed of a torrent, and thence by another longer mile the sweet glens of *Taguen* and *Laciesa.* Visit the *Fuente Gloriosa*, which, like the fountain of Vaucluse, gushes gloriously from the cave of the *Santuario de Sⁿ· Elena*, in which the daughter of Constantine the Great *is said* to have taken refuge; on the hill above is an intermittent fountain.

Panticosa is a poor village, which owes its celebrity to the mineral baths, which lie distant a mountain league, or a two hours' walk; after ascending a steep ridge, through the rocky gorge *El Escalar*, the site is truly romantic, and severed from the world; all around the dell rise granite ranges, soaring into eternal snow; the place is deserted in winter, but in summer a decent French inn is opened by one Michel: this is one of the highest inhabited spots in the Pyrenees, being some 8500 ft. above the sea. The bathing accommodations are indifferent, the season is from June to September; for an analysis of the waters consult ' *Memoria*,' Fᵐ· Xavier Cabanes, Mad., 1832.

There are several routes to France: one leads to *Eaux Bonnes*, and is tolerable; it may be performed on foot in about 12 hours, but it will try a stout pedestrian: that to *Cauterez* by the *Col de Marcadau*, which is usually preferred, is a wild and difficult ride of about 8 hours; you pass a series of lakes, near the first of which is a large rocking stone; in 2½ hours cross the crest of the Col, and descend in one hour to *Cauterez*, Lion d'or, Hôtel de France; the scenery on the French side is magnificent, especially the *Lac de Gaube* and the *Pont d'Espagne;* the lake is one of the most elevated in the Pyrenees, and abounds in trout: here the *Vignemale* is seen in all its Alpine grandeur and solitude; the *Petit Pic* is said to be 11,000 ft. above the sea, and has been ascended. It will be better to take guides, &c., from Cauterez, as these excursions are all there just as much the fashion as they are *not* among the incurious Spaniards (see ' Hand-book for France,' R. lxxxv.).

Leaving *Panticosa*, a two hours' and steep ride leads to *Sallent*, the capital of the valley of *Tena*, and the seat of the Spanish *Aduana*. The *Posada* is indifferent; consult ' *Sallent Cabeza de el Valle*,' Benito Marton, 4º, Pamplona, 1750. There are several wild passes into France. The W., *Puerto de Formigal*, is the easiest of passage, as those by the *Cuello de Sova* and *La Forqueta* are fitter for smugglers and izard-hunters. The route to Eaux Chaudes in France, by the valley of Ossau, is much frequented, and is highly picturesque; ascend the course of the *Gallego* to the *Port d'Anéou*; the first house in France is called *La Case de Brouselte*, and is a sort of governmental *Hospice*, built for the refuge of storm-lost travellers; afterwards turn amid rocks and firs off to the l. to the *Plateau de Bioux Artiques*, to enjoy the splendid view. The *Pico del Medicdia* soars magnificently; those who wish to ascend it will do well to take a French guide from *Gabàs*, which is the first hamlet in France, and the seat of *la douane*. It has a small *Cabaret* (see ' Handbook for France,' R. lxxxiii.).

ROUTE CXXIX.—JACA TO LA BRECHA DE ROLDAN.

Biescas	4	
Linas	3	7
Broto	3	10
Torla	2	12
Vª. de Bujaruelo	1¼	13¼

Attend to the provend, and take a local guide; to *Biescas* see preceding route. *Broto*, a small hamlet of 300 souls, stands under the *Monte Perdido*,

on the *Ara*, which flows down the wild valley; it has two difficult *Puertos* into France, those of *Cerbillonar* and *Petrañeda*; continuing up the stream-let Cerbillonar to its junction with the Ara, about a L. N., is *Torla*, with 400 souls, and chief of the four *Vicos* or departments into which this district is divided; the forests are magnificent; the timber is floated down from these " Pyrenœi frondosa cacumina Montis," to Tortosa; as this is a central point in these elevations, it is much frequented in summer by shepherds, who drive their flocks to pastures averaging from 7000 to 9000 ft. above the sea. The *Vignemale* and *Monte Perdido*, each the highest mountain in their respective kingdoms, rise from this nucleus base. The precipices are the haunts of the izard, and the lochs and streams abound in trout. The passage into France, by the *Port de Gavarnie*, is truly magnificent. In the *Escala* or ladder-pass into France, a band of 60 mountaineers surprised, in 1510, the Comte de Foix, who was invading Arragon, in order to support Juan Albret of Navarre against Ferdinand the Catholic: they destroyed more than 2000 men, capturing men and baggage; it was a Roncesvalles on a smaller scale.

The *Venta de Bujaruelo*, miserable, while all around is picturesque, is distant from *Torla* about 1¼ L., being at the foot of the three sisters, *Las Tres Sorellas*, or *Sorores*, and *La Brecha de Roldan;* this mighty fissure in the mountain wall is a much-frequented smuggler's pass; it can be seen from Huesca, and some say even from Zaragoza, and then appears only a small notch in the stony ridge, but when approached it becomes a gigantic portal or gate in the natural barrier, which rises more than 9500 ft. above the sea; the formation is somewhat convex on the French side, and really, when beheld from afar, the barrier appears to be an artificial wall, to which that of China is the work of pigmies. It varies in height from 300 to 600 ft., and in thickness from 50 to 80; the breach is shaped like the square opening in the battlement of a frontier defence. This gap, in moments of storms, so frequent in these tempest-haunted heights, becomes truly terrific. Then, indeed, it is the portal of Æolus, or the narrow funnel, through which tear the hurricanes that are checked by the mountains, they sweeping everything away, and rendering impossible any attempt to pass through against them. Some have compared the gap to that in a jaw from whence a tooth has been extracted; this *Brecha*, according to authentic legends, was struck out by Orlando, the redoubtable paladin Roland, at one blow of his trusty blade Durandal, in order to open a passage for his pursuit of the infidel, and his sword is still shown at Madrid (p. 787), but the weapons made in those days far surpassed the fabrics of Toledo or Sheffield, and of such class was the sword of Paredes, with which, like the mace of the Persian Roostem, whole armies were kept at bay.

The descent into France by the *Cirque de Gavarnie* is difficult. Those who wish to ascend the *Monte Perdido*, 11,168 ft. above the sea, are advised to do so from the French side, taking French guides. An active tourist may start from *Gedre*, gain the top, and return the same day. The best route is as follows : leaving Gedre, and its oasis in a rocky desert, make for *Chaos*, an appropriate name for a scene where chaos is come again. The *Cirque de Gavarnie*, at the head of the valley of *Lavedan*, is most romantic, and there is a small inn in the village. Visit the cataract of the *Gave de Pau*, and then proceed to the *Serrades* or sheep pastures under the glorious barrier of the *Marboré*, and thence to the *Brecha de Roldan*; the *Monte Perdido*, which is a secondary formation on primitive rock, is now to be ascended by a series of terrace-like ridges. The summit was first reached in 1802 by Ramond, who was attended by one Rondo, a guide from *Gedre*, some of

whose descendants yet live there, and are well acquainted with every step. Occasionally tourists sleep the first night at *Millaris*, a plain enclosed by the Mont Perdu, Le Cylindre, and Marboré, which form the Spanish *Tres Sorellas ;* and after the summit has been gained, descend into the *Brecha de Roldan*, and thence by *Aragnoet* and the beautiful valley of *Tramesaigues*, and so on to Viel.

Mr. Paris walked from *Bujaruelo* to the baths of *Panticosa*, by the following route; to *Torla* 2½ hours, *Fragin* 1, *Linas* ¾, *Jesera* 2½, *Viescas* 2, *Pueyo* 3, *Panticosa* ½, *Baths* 2½; and as these localities may be considered some of the most interesting in the Spanish Pyrenees, even at the risk of some trifling repetition, we insert some careful details furnished by Mr. Twopeny. Those who start from *Panticosa*, taking a local guide, may, by climbing the *Puerto de Bendenera*, reach in one long day either *Gavarnie*, or *Broto* and *Torla ;* whereas the preceding route by *Viescas* requires two long days, and is far less interesting : leaving *Panticosa* in ascending, you pass on the r. a precipitous mountain like the Balahalish end of Glencoe : the top of the *Puerto* is reached in 3½ hours; a descent of about the same time brings you to the " poor venta of *Bujaruelo*." The scenery is grand, and improves on the road to *Torla*.

From *Bujaruelo* to *Gavarnie*, by the easy *Puerto*, requires 3½ hours, so that a traveller in France might ride from Gavarnie to Bujaruelo ; go on for one hour towards Torla, see all the finest country, and return to Gavarnie the same day ; or proceed from Bujaruelo to Torla, a very picturesque walk, in 2 hours, passing after 2 miles a superb gorge ; then ½ an hour on to *Broto*, and 4 more to *Fanlo*, a village at the back of the *Brecha de Roldan*, from the summit of which it is a descent of 5 hours ; to the r. one looks down into a vast tortuous ravine, hollowed out by the melted snow torrents, which pour down from *Las Tres Sorellas;* near the bottom is a dense mass of forest, the stronghold of the Bouquetin; the precipitous sides are covered with fir. Antonio Sanchez has a decent *Fonda* at Fanlo, and is most anxious to please his guests; his charges for two good meals and bed are one dollar per day; the mutton is capital. Close to Fanlo is a narrow cleft in a rock, as if formed by an earthquake, through which a stream eats its way; ascend above and look down into this *Tajo*, and on the tops of the trees; the river flows beneath, heard but not seen. It may be descended to by means of a rope-ladder. To the E. of Fanlo the wild angular mountain, *Sn. Victorian*, stands forth, and about 5 miles beyond rise tiers above tiers of dark-wooded precipices; between these is one of the grandest ravines of the Pyrenees, which is best to be explored from *Nerin*, a village distant from Fanlo 1½ hours. The Cura Don Joaquin Sanchon will entertain an Englishman for a dollar per day very well; he is a disciple of Isaac Walton, and a good guide, for which service he expects from 3 to 4 francs more a day; from *Nerin* to the hamlet of *Cercuet* 1 hour; the little church is picturesque; ½ an hour more to the mountain shoulder, whence you gaze down on the splendid *Tajo* or chasm hollowed out like a mighty vessel, while the curved strata resemble ribs; deep below boils the emerald-coloured *Billos*, a stream of melted snow, hemmed in by forests, and precipices piled on precipices up to the very sky. Descend to the river by a rude stair-case path; and here behold the primeval forest, safe from the woodman's axe. The firs, yews, oaks, beeches, birches, ashes, &c., are drawn up tall and thin in their search for air and light; their elegant stems contrast with the rugged Salvator-Rosa-like rocks. The caves of the highest precipices are the haunts of eagles, who are always slowly wheeling about. An hour's scramble leads to the picturesque *Puente de Cumac*, beyond which it is needless to proceed. Every artist will make another day's

excursion from *Nerin* to another Alpine bridge, which spans the precipices: crossing this to a chapel in a cave, descend to the bed of the river in the direction of the bridge : return to the bridge and ascend the opposite side to a natural arch of rock, amid a dislocated jumble of rocks called *La Tierra Mala*.

From Fanlo to *Vio* is 3 hours: 1 hour short of Vio the mountains to the E. are very grand. Breakfast at the house of Manuel Cerezuela, who has eggs, wine, and bread; bring your mutton therefore from Fanlo. From *Vio* to *Escalona*, 3 hours; 1 hour short, you descend to the village *Puyarruebo*, whose cultivated slopes contrast with the barren *San Victorian :* at Escalona there is a quaint *Venta* and chapel under the same roof; however dirty and dear, it is much frequented by muleteers : the *Ventero* is careless, and without a conscience—the nearer the church the farther from God. The sunset view of the mountains from the neighbouring fountain is glorious; hence into France by *Vielsa* (see p. 989), 6 hours. To the summit of the *Puerto de Vielsa*, 4 hours; to the l. as you ascend is a very fine cascade; 2 hours' descent lead to the French village *Le Plan ;* thence through *Val d Aure* to *Arreau*, 6 hours.

Another route from *Escalona* runs to the convent of San Victorian, 3 hours of gentle ascent through the village *Espumas*. This monastery is a nobly placed building, although rudely constructed, with a modern church: here some of the early kings of Arragon are interred. When the property was appropriated by the government, they allowed the abbot Don José Gonzalez y Marin to remain here to take care of the building : of course he has never received a farthing of promised aid, or of his miserable stipend. This fine old monk entertains travellers, who pay their expenses. The cave of the tutelar, up in the precipices behind the convent, deserves a visit. From hence a dreary 5 hours leads to *Campo*, through a miserable, bare, slaty, crumbling, and arid district, which in winter is torn by torrents, and in summer burnt up. The clear stream flowing through *Campo*, and the vines trained to the houses, give an artistical character to this poverty-stricken village, in which, however, a bed and dinner is to be got From Campo to *Venasque* is 6 hours. The first portion is inferior to the pass between Bujaruelo and Forla, and afterwards the country becomes tame.

ROUTE CXXX.—ZARAGOZA TO HUESCA.

Villanueva del Gallego .	2		
Zuera	2	..	4
Vᵃ. de Violada . . .	2	..	6
Almudevar	2	..	8
Huesca	3	..	11

There is a diligence, which is the *best*, because the most expeditious, means of getting over the uninteresting and almost abandoned plains; yet the soil is fertile and the climate favourable, and wherever irrigation is adopted the fruits of the earth abound. *La Hoya* or *La Huerta*, near *Zuera*, was doubtless under the Moors a garden, as the name implies. The Gallego is crossed soon after *Zuera*, and the road continues over the bald *Llano de Violada* to *Huesca*, Osca, which is pleasantly situated on the *Isuela*, and looks at a distance somewhat like a ship, with the cathedral tower for a mast. Inns: *El Parador de las diligencias; Posada de Narciso Bruaila, de San Miguel.* This ancient Arragonese city is seldom visited by foreigners, but may be taken by those going to the baths of *Panticosa*, as they will find a regular intercommunication in summer. *Broto* is distant 14 L. through *Solanilla* and *Vegua*. Those going to Barcelona may rejoin the high road (R. cxxvi.) by taking the diligence to *Barbastro*, 8 L. from Huesca, and thence 9½ more to *Lérida*.

Huesca, popⁿ· about 9000, is the chief town of its province and the see of a bishop, suffragan to Zaragoza; it has a university, a *plaza de toros*, and the usual establishments, being the re-

sidence of the local authorities. This decayed and decaying city is one of great antiquity, originally called Ileosca (Strabo, iii. 224), and the capital of the Vascitani. It was chosen by the *guerrillero* Sertorius as the seat of the university which he founded U.C. 677, ostensibly for the education of noble youths, but in reality to hold them as hostages of their fathers' allegiance. The unscrupulous Romans, unable to subdue him by fair fight, set a price on his head, as the French did on that of Mina and others of whom he was a type. At last (U.C. 680) Metellus bribed Perpenna, one of the officers of Sertorius, to invite his chief to a banquet, where, when full of wine, he was murdered. On opening the will of his victim, the assassin was found to be largely remembered therein. Perpenna himself was soon after put to death by Pompeius (App. *B. C.* i. 700), according to genuine Iberian maxims, where the abstract treachery is approved of, but the base agent when used is not. *La traicion aplace, pero no el que la hace.*

Huesca under Sertorius grew to be an important place, insomuch that Plutarch (in Vit. Sert.) calls it "a great city." It became a municipium under the Romans, by name "Osca Urbs Victrix," and had a mint, with a numerous coinage. See Florez, 'M.' ii. 513. The *Nummi Oscences*, of which such quantities are mentioned by Livy as sent to Rome by the plundering and contribution-levying marshals of Rome, have often been referred, but erroneously, to this town. See on this subject p. 785. Huesca not only produced coins, but coin-collectors, as here lived the famous *Vincencio Juan de Lastanosa*, who published a curious catalogue of his cabinet, '*Museo de las Medallas desconocidas*,' 4to., Huesca, 1645, which is enriched with etchings: for an account of the author see p. 295 of the charming '*Voyage d'Espagne*,' Elzevir, à Cologne, 1667, or p. 201 of the English translation printed for Herringman, London, 1670.

2 U

Huesca glories in having given birth to San Lorenzo, of gridiron and Escorial celebrity (see p. 809), but this honour is fiercely disputed by *Huescar*. The rival pretensions are set forth in ' *Vida de Santos de Huesca*,' 8vo., Huesca, 1644, and ' *Discorso Historico*,' Aguas, 4to., Zar., 1676. The better opinion, in which we coincide, assigns the honour to this Huesca.

Roman *Osca* was destroyed by the Moors, and, whenever excavations are made, buried fragments of antiquity turn up, which are either used up as old stones, building materials, or reinterred as rubbish. The Moors rebuilt the place after their fashion, and it became the capital of a sort of independent half-Berber tribe, who, placed between two fires, sided alternately with the French and Cordovese, hating both equally, and only using them for their own local and selfish purposes, and then abusing and ill-treating them. Thus Amoroz, its celebrated Emir, called in the aid of Charlemagne against the Kalif of Cordova, and then refused to admit his allies into the place. Compare *La Coruña*, p. 655, for the other treacheries, assassination, &c. of this Hispano-Oriental chief. See Reinaud, ' Invas. des Sarrasins, 119.

Huesca was recovered by the Christians November 25, 1096, after a siege of two years and a defence of Numantian and Arragonese obstinacy, and, like Jaca, it bears for its arms the heads of four Moorish kings—sheikhs, who were then killed, with the addition of a cross which appeared miraculously in the air, an event by no means of rare occurrence in those days. Consult, however, Chr. 13, ' *Fundacion y excellencias de Huesca*,' Fro. Diego de Aynsa y Iriarte, fol., Huesca, 1619, which is a curious local volume.

Huesca is a fine specimen of an old Arragonese city, being solidly built, and picturesque. The chief street, as at Zaragoza, is called *El Coso*. The town is cheap, and well supplied with the products of hill and plains, or the

Campos, which are irrigated by the rivers *Flumen* and *Isuela*. The hydraulist should visit the grand reservoir or *Pantano*, near *Arquis*, 4 L. N. of Huesca, where the *Isuela* is dammed up in a gorge by a stupendous wall, built by Fro. Artigas.

The see of Huesca, which dates from the 6th century, was restored in 1096 by Pedro I. The beautiful Gothic cathedral was built in excellent masonry, by Juan de Olotzaga, a Biscayan, in 1400. The grand entrance is studded with statues of apostles, &c.; below are 14 larger than life, and above, 48 smaller ones, in niches. Above the portal the Virgin occupies the position of chief honour, and on the sides the Adoration of Kings, and the Saviour appearing to the Magdalen. Higher up, under a sort of canopy, is a model of the cathedral as it was originally designed by Olotzaga: the interior is simple, with three naves. The alabaster grand *Retablo*, one of the finest things in Arragon, is the masterpiece of Damien Forment. Begun in 1520, it was not finished until 1533, tantæ molis erat! This Cellini-like, most cinque-cento work, is divided into three partitions. Observe the Passion of the Saviour, carved in full relief, and the medallion portraits of the artist and his wife. In the cloister is the monument of one of his pupils, Pedro Muñoz, put up by his master in 1522. The rich vessels of silver and gold were carried off by the invaders. Ascend the belfry tower, for the panoramic view is glorious.

Huesca was the Salamanca of Arragon. The modern university, which, in reference to the ancient one, bears the name of *Sertorio*, was founded in 1354, by Pedro IV. The *Colegio de Santiago* was founded by Charles V., that of *Sn. Vicente* by Jayme Callen, in 1587, and the *Seminario* or *Sa. Cruz*, in 1580. The schools, libraries, &c., were ravaged by the invaders during the war, and never have recovered.

Next visit the ancient *Palacio de los Reyes de Aragon*, and descend into the vault called *La Campana*, the "bell," from the following classical and Spanish event. In the year 1136 King Ramiro II., being thwarted by his turbulent aristocracy, consulted Frotardo, abbot of Sn. Pedro de Tomeras: the learned priest, who either had read Ovid's 'Fasti' (ii. 704), or possessed naturally a Tarquinian instinct, was walking in his garden when the royal messenger arrived, and simply by way of answer cut off with his stick the tallest cabbages, lilia summa metit. Ramiro thereupon summoned his grandees to consult on the casting a bell, which should be heard all over Arragon, and as each man arrived singly, he cut off his head, casting the bodies into the vault, from whence they were afterwards taken out, and buried in *San Juan de Jerusalem*, a very curious old church, which once belonged to the Templars, some of whose sepulchres exist. Abarca (i. 190) questions this bell massacre: see, however, Mariana (x. 16), and Mem. Acad. Hist. iii. 508.

The architect may also look into the parish church of *Sn. Pedro*, and at the house of the Conde de Huaza, and the *Casa del Ayuntamiento*, with its two *miradores*, and open connecting gallery.

Near Huesca are two remarkable monasteries: one is the *Ermita de Sn. Miguel de Foces*, which contains some most ancient tombs, with singular arched work, and early paintings, of a Byzantine style, which, long doomed to neglect, will soon be among the things that were; the other, the *Monasterio real*, is placed at *Monte Aragon*, 1 L. from Huesca. Here, in a crypt, is the simple but very singular tomb of Alonzo el Batallador: the engrailed arches deserve notice.

ROUTE CXXXI.—ZARAGOZA TO GISTAIN.

Villamayor	1½	
Perdiguera	2	3½
Lecinaña.	1	4½
Alcubierre	2	6½
Poliniño	2½	9
Va. de Vallerias . .	2½	11½
Berbegal	2½	13
Barbastro	2½	15½
Naval	4	19½
Ainsa.	6	25½
Puertolas	3	28½
Gistain	3	31½

The first portion of this route runs over the dreary plains of the desert of Arragon. Passing *Perdiquera*, to the E. rises the *Monte Oscuro*. At *Lecinaña* the *Guerrillero* Mina overtook Genl. Paris, who had evacuated Zaragoza July 8th, 1813, on the first news of the battle of Vitoria; but his progress was impeded by the accumulated plunder, and here again, like the Aurum Tolosanum of old, the crime entailed its punishment, and brought a just judgment on this Paris: compare pp. 304, 916 (Toreno, xxii.).

Poliniño is placed near the *Flumen*, which comes down from the hills; next the *Alcanadre* is crossed, which, just above *Huerta*, has been joined by the *Guatizalesma*, and both are excellent fishing rivers. *Barbastro*, popn. about 7000, is placed on the *Vero*, which intersects it. This ancient city is the see of a cathedral, which contains some paintings by Anto. Galceran, 1588. Here the traveller about to proceed into the mountains should furnish his commissariat. The road now turns N., with the *Cinca* flowing to the E., which is joined by the *Ara*, at *Ainsa*, an ancient town, and once the court of the kings of *Sobrarbe*, some remains of whose *Alcazar* yet exist. The church is collegiate. About 1½ mile distant is the cross of Sobrarbe, placed on a stone shaft, which imitates the trunk of a tree, and is canopied by a Doric cupola. This marks the site where Garcia Ximenez or Inequez fastened a cross on an oak as his battle standard, when he defeated the Moors about the year 750, and founded the kingdom of Sobrarbe, taking for its arms, "or, a cross gules, on an oak vert;" and in these Ainsa still rejoices, as the clergy there saw a miraculous cross, an event of ordinary occurrence then, although less so in our days.

Now we quit the plains, and enter into the Pyrenean spurs. *Puertolas* stands in a narrow valley, watered by the *Bellos*, while on each side ridges divide it from the valleys of *Vio* and *Vielsa ;* a communication with the latter is carried by the wild pass *El Portillo de Tella*, and thence to the French frontier, by the *Puerto de Folqueta*, and on to Arreau.

Gistain, on the *Cinqueta*, is the chief village of the valley *Gistan*, which is intersected by the spurs of the *Barbachina*. Here are some celebrated cobalt mines : a fragment of one was originally discovered by a peasant, and taken to Zaragoza, whence, as none could tell what it was, it was sent to Germany to be analysed. The assayer, however, kept his secret, came in person and persuaded the peasant to sue for a licence to work the mine, as if being a lead one, and then purchased it all, sending some 600 quintals a-year to Strasbourg until the fraud was discovered.

Gistain has several communications with France, by the *Puerto de la Madera*, the *Aura de Plan*, and by *La Pez*, which is 9930 ft. high, and practicable only for foot passengers. *La Clarabida* is still wilder, and is often blocked up with snow. Up in heights on the French side is a singular tunnel, which was cut in order to convey the Spanish pine-timber of *Gistan* into the *Val de Louron*. The mountains in this locality are superb, as the *Monte Perdido* rises to the l. of *Vielsa*, while the *Malédeta* soars to the r., over *Benasque*.

The beautiful valley of *Benasque* is 7 L. in length, and 18 L. in circumference, and is bounded to the W. by that of *Gistan*, and to the E. by that of *Aran*, with which it communicates by the *Puerto de la Picada*, and is separated by the river *Rivagorzana*. It contains several mineral springs, of which little use is made; one near the *Pueblo del Barranco*, and called *de los Padellasos*, is cold and ferruginous. There is also a silver mine in the hill,

or the *cod de Toro*, and others of copper and coal, but all are much neglected. *Benasque*,Vercelia, the capital, contains 1000 inhabitants, and is situated on the Esera about 3829 ft. above the sea level. It has two parish churches, one of a Romanesque style, a small picturesque castle, and some Prout-like old houses : the place was cruelly sacked by the French in 1809. There are many wild Alpine communications with France, of which the *Puerto de Benasque* is the easiest, and ladies may be carried across in *literos*, or portable chairs. The route ascends the Esera, and passing through a woody slope reaches a valley with a waterfall to the l. The *camino real*, as this royal muletrack is called, winds on, through a rocky scene, to the *Baños de Sⁿ. Roque*, which are only used by peasants : ascending continually until it reaches the *Hospitalet*, 5542 ft. above the sea, which affords an imperfect shelter from the winds and cold. Now the *Malédeta* rises in all its " glorious horrors," and denuded masses, to the height of 11,426 ft.; but its apparent elevation is diminished, like that of the Sierras of Central Spain, from its being a mountain rising out of a mountain base : the highest peak ever ascended, the *Puig de Nethou*, was reached in 1842 by a Russian. Malédeta is called the *accursed*, because, devoid itself of pasturage, it severs the valleys of *Benasque* and *Aran*, thus cutting off their natural inter-communication. This skeleton of a mountain, which is a fine *subject* for the naturalist who wishes to investigate Alpine conformation and developement, is an offset from the great dorsal chain. The *Puerto* is cut through the *Peña Blanca* 7917 ft. high, and in storms the mighty winds rush fearfully through the funnel fissures, while in the depths below the Esera springs and tumbles into the lake *del Toro*, from whence, after a short underground course, it re-emerges near the *Hospitalet*.

The *Malédeta* rises in Spain, as the boundary between France here makes an angle inwards N., and including the *Valle de Aran,* which, if the flow of waters had been taken as a demarkation, ought to have belonged to France. Here, again, is the point of dislocation in the two great ranges of the Pyrenees. From the *Puerto* we descend to Bagneres de Luchon. A zigzag staircase track leads to a stone hut, the *Hospice de France,* but the hospitality is miserable. For the Frozen Lochs and Glaciers, see ' Hand-book for France, R. lxxxvii.

To the l. of Venasque rises the *Puerto d'Oo,* which leads to the village of Oo in France. The pass is 9850 ft. above the sea, and is extremely wild and difficult, being chiefly used by smugglers. It however is full of interest, especially on the French side, where are the lakes or tarns of *Seculejo* set deeply in their mountain-frames : observe the frozen loch *La Sehl de la Vaque.* The valley of Lys is a miniature Arcadia, while the gorge of *Esquierry* is celebrated for its flowers and botany ; nor can anything be more pastoral than the valley of *Lasto.* All these localities, however, will be best visited from Bagneres de Luchon.

The communications with Aran are carried under the *Pena Blanca,* and behind the *Malédeta ;* they break off to the E. by the *Puerto de la Picada,* which is 7872 ft. high, and is so called from a rock-like obelisk. This route communicates also with the Hospice de France ; and thus in a few hours the traveller may pass from France into Arragon, and return through part of Catalonia. Another longer, but easier track, leads to Aran, which winds under the apple-headed *Pomeron,* and is very wild, and varied with lakes, torrents, and cascades: It descends through the woods of *Balican* to *Vielsa,* which is the chief place of the *Valle de Aran.*

This beautiful valley lies as it were a shell encompassed by the spurs of the Malédeta. It is 7 L. long, by 6 L. wide, and belongs to the bishoprick of Urgel. It is damp and cold in winter,

and hot in summer, being exposed to the S. Here again, if the fall of waters were to be taken as an indication of boundary, this corner should belong to France, as indeed it once did before it passed by marriage in 1192 to Arragon. It abounds in fine woods, that are floated down the Garona, which rises in this valley. The rivers which run into Spain are the *Noquera, Ribagorzana,* which separates Aran from Benasque, and the *Pallaresa,* a tributary of the *Segre,* which rises near the *Puerto de Pallas,* and runs into the *Valle de Esterri.* A ridge of hills divides the two valleys, and is passed by the *Puerto de Caldas,* or *Bonaguia.* These *Cordilleras* are continuations of the Spurs of the Malédeta, and wall out the Aran from Spain. The communications in winter are much blocked up by snow, and many lives are lost, from the necessity of crossing them for supplies.

Vielsa, where there is a tolerable *Posada,* is the chief place ; pop. about 800. The *Garona* rises from many sources, especially under the *Montgarri ;* many other springs, which are fed by the glaciers of the *Malédeta,* ooze out of their rocky pores: some again disappear for a time among the broken rocks, and then burst up anew ; hence they are called *los Ojos de la Garona* (comp. those of *La Guadiana,* p. 309). The chief communications with France are to the E. by the *Puerto de las Aulas,* which leads to *Castillon* and S. Girons. Another which passes to *Sⁿ. Beat,* follows the *Garona* by *Castel Leon,* which the French ruined, and *Les,* an ancient barony, with a dismantled castle of Roman foundation, where are some mineral baths: advancing, the rocks narrow in, and a wooden bridge over a tributary of the *Garona,* and called *El puente del Rey,* separates the two kingdoms.

The communication with the *Valle de Luchon* passes over the *Portillon,* and commands glorious views. The usual excursion made from *Bagneres de Luchon* into Spain, may be just described. Leaving Luchon a 2 hours' ride up the Pique river leads to the Hospital, a stone shealing for the Preventive Guard, who go through the farce of stopping smuggling. The views of the two gorges or chief passes, the Port de Picade and Port de Venasque, are superb; the latter almost appears an artificial slit in a wall of mountain rock. The Malédeta rises in a huge sugar-loaf form, with its dark crest emerging from a mantle of snow and glaciers: its real height is however greater than the apparent, for it is seen from elevated ground. The Pic de Nethou is 10,050 ft. high; the summit it is said has never yet been reached, yet it might be accomplished in August. Now descend to the basin, and cross the Port de Pomeron; near it the Port de Picade leads back again to Luchon. Continue, however, to the valley of Artique Telline, which is in Spain: observe the Trou de toro, or gulf of dissolved glacier-water. Next thread the pastoral valley after passing the waters which reappear from the Trou after their subterraneous course; a noble forest leads to the Trou de Geneou, from whence, as at Vaucluse, the waters gush out as over a river. The scenery on to Bosorte is truly Ruysdael-like: down this stream vast supplies of wood are floated into France, to be sawed into planks at the mills of Foz and St. Beat; the latter place is remarkable for its marbles. The waste of these noble forests is truly scandalous: hence to miserable Bosorte, and crossing the Pont du Roi, back again into France. Thus, by this valley of Aran, Spain has a ready approach into her neighbour's territory.

The following rather longer Spanish excursion may be made from Bagneres de Luchon to Venasque and back again. Passing through the beech woods, reach the French hospice at the foot of the Puerto in 2½ hours; and gain in 2½ hours the heights, enjoying splendid views of the Malédeta, with its rampant lines of precipices. Thence in 1 hour into Spain, to the vile posada at the hospitalet. Observe three singular

cone-like pinnacles. There are some sulphur baths in an isolated house. Hence in 3 hours to Venasque. Now strike to Vitalles, passing the village of Sarli and mountain of Castaneze, where the botany is remarkable. In 3 hours you reach the dreary Puerto; and thence descend over green hills and into the romantic defile of Castaneze, 4 hours; and then in 2½ to Vitalles, having now entered Catalonia. Hence to Viella, striking N. up a rambla or valley, hedged by bold barren mountains, to the village of Anatou. The scenery is a superb jumble of rock and forest, and the haunt of bears and bouquetins. In 4 hours you reach the hospice in its park-like Vega, and thence ascend the Port de Viella, an austere tremendous pass of 8300 ft. high, where the glaciers of Malédeta contrast with the plains of Catalonia; thence descending into the village-studded valley of Aran to Viella. The beech woods of Baracoude and valley of Joncou are charming. Visit the ojos de la Garona; and quitting the road to Luchon, ascend the valley to the Hospice de Artique Telline, where you can sleep: the valley is delicious. Having examined the gushing streams and beech woods, ascend to Artique de Pomairo in its green mountain basin. On leaving the valley, pass through Las Bordes, Castel Leon, and over the wooded heights of the Port de Portillon to Bagneres de Luchon.

The Pyrenean districts are the cream of Arragon. The traveller is earnestly advised to avoid all the tract of country between Zaragoza, Burgo de Osma, Logrofio, and Tudela, as the towns are poor, and devoid alike of social or artificial interest, while the wearisome plains are inhabited by a backward, uninteresting peasantry.

ROUTE CXXXII.—ZARAGOZA TO TUDELA.

Las Casetas				.	.	.	.	2		
Alagon .	.	.	.	.	.	.	2	..	4
Cabañas	.	.	.	.	.	1	..	5
Pedrola	.	.	.	.	.	1	..	6
Malleu .	.	.	.	.	.	3	..	9
Cortes .	.	.	.	.	.	1	..	10
Tudela .	.	.	.	.	.	4	..	14

There is also a passage-boat by the canal (see p. 996): the vessels are long and narrow, and are drawn by mules at about four miles an hour. You embark at *Casablanca.* A halt is generally made at *Gallur*, half way, where there is a good *posada.* Thence to *El Bocal*, which is four miles from Tudela, to which carriages are always ready to convey passengers. The *Palacio imperial*, however grand the name, is not worth visiting. *La obra*, or the work for letting out the waters, may interest the hydraulist. The water hatches generally are named after saints, like the wine vaults at Xerez, or salt pans in the *Isla.* The irrigation about *Gallur* is well conducted.

The Navarrese company runs diligences to Tudela, and thence to Bayonne. The road follows between the lines of the canal and the Ebro, but the country is uninteresting. At *Alagon*, June 14, 1808, Lefebvre Desnouettes routed Palafox, as completely and as easily as he had the day before defeated his brother at *Mallen*, the worthy pair in both instances being the first to set an example of flight to their unfortunate troops.

Soon the frontier of Navarre is crossed, in which kingdom *Cortes* is situated. Near Tudela, Castaños, La Peña, and Cartoajal had united their armies, and were *talking* of invading France; but when Lefebvre and Maurice Mathieu advanced, Nov. 23, 1808, they ran before the enemy could get near them; nor did the hero of Bailen halt until he reached Calatayud; and had Ney used the commonest expedition in his pursuit, instead of delaying to plunder, not a man would have escaped. *Tudela*, Tutela, is situated on an angle formed by the *Queyles.* The diligence inn is the best. Here the Ebro is crossed by a good stone bridge, once defended by three towers, which the city bears on its shield, enclosed with the chains of Navarre. Tudela, popⁿ· 8000, is a tidy town, but dull; the streets are narrow, and the houses solidly built and lofty:

there is, however, a good plaza, and some pleasant walks near the river. Tudela was taken from the Moors in 1114 by Alonzo I. The ancient Gothic collegiate church was raised to be a see in 1783. The river is celebrated for its sturgeon and eels, and its island *Mejana* for fruit. Tudela is the birthplace of the learned Jew Benjamin, who flourished in the twelfth century: his works have been translated into Latin by Arias Montano. This town is the central point of many branch roads.

ROUTE CXXXIII.—TUDELA TO SORIA
AND ARANDA DEL DUERO.

Cascante	2	
Tarazona	2	.. 4
Agreda	4	.. 8
Aldea del Pozo . . .	4	.. 12
Fuen Sanco . . .	2	.. 14
Soria	2	.. 16
Villa Cuervos . . .	3	.. 19
Val de Albillo. . .	4	.. 23
Burgo de Osma . . .	3	.. 26
Osma	½	.. 26½
Sⁿ· Esteban de Gormaz .	1½	.. 28
Lauga	3	.. 31
Badecondes . . .	2½	.. 33½
Aranda · . . .	2	.. 35½

Cascante, Cascantum, hangs over the Queyles, which has two bridges; popⁿ· 3000. The church, dedicated to the Assumption of the Virgin, was built in 1476 by Luiz de Gramondi and Anton Albizturiz; the *Retablo*, which is one of the few fine things in these parts, was carved in 1596 by Pedro Gonzalez de Sⁿ· Pedro and Ambrosio de Vengochea; the three divisions contain subjects from the Virgin's life. Observe the Holy Rood, and the statues of St. Peter, St. Paul, and the Magdalen. The *Sagrario* is enriched with the mysteries of the Passion. A pleasant walk under a covered way leads up to an old church, also sacred to *La Santisima Maria*, in which is an image called *La Virgen del Romero*, to which "High Place" pilgrimages are made. In Cascante is a mineral spring which is beneficial in visceral complaints, notwithstanding its ill-omened name, La Fuente del *Matudor.*

Tarazona, Turiaso, is a fine old town, placed on a wind-blown plain, and exposed to the blasts of the bleak *Moncayo* (see p. 889). Here a handful of disciplined Romans routed with the same ease and success a Celtiberian army, led by incompetent chiefs, as the French did in our own times (Livy, xv. 51). Turiaso became a municipium under the conquerors : protected by the Goths, it was celebrated for its steel. It is now the see of a bishop suffragan to Zaragoza, has a Gothic cathedral, a Moorish *alcazar*, three bridges over the Queyles, and a picturesque wear or *Azuda*. Pop^n· about 10,000, and chiefly pastoral and agricultural.

Agreda, Grœcubis, also is placed on the Queyles, and is much exposed to the Moncayo : pop^n· about 3500. The river here is carried under ground as at Granada, with the *Plaza*, a fountain, and the *Casas consistoriales* over it. Observe the mansions of the Ayamonte and Velamazan families. Agreda vies with Avila in its holy sybil (see p. 805), as this *Maria de Jesus* was another of the "spouses" in the concubinage of Spanish hagiography : she was abbess here of the convent of "The Immaculate Conception." Her biography, by Jos. Xim. Samaniego, 4to. Mad. 1720, is indeed rich and rare.

Now the traveller has re-entered the bald regions of Old Castile, and the best thing is to get out of them again as quickly as possible. *Soria*, which calls itself Numantia, filching the honours of others, is the chief place of its denuded province, and was ceded to Castile by Arragon in 1136. The city is very ancient, and is still surrounded with its walls, which were raised in 1290, and are well preserved. To the E. rises the *Alcazar*, once a strong castle, but now a ruin. *Soria* is placed on the Duero, and has a fine bridge : pop^n· about 5500. It is a dull place, and inhabited by agriculturists. The environs are rugged and broken. Among the rocks is placed a celebrated sanctuary dedicated to *San Saturio*, the

local tutelar. The environs are cheerless and treeless. The wide *valdios y dehesas*, especially the common of *Valdonsadero*, are grazed by hungry flocks, which produce much and excellent wool. The corn plains are very fertile, and the pastures maintain a dairy, the butter of which, celebrated in Spain, is to our tastes rank and ill-tasted. Coal-beds exist near *Oblega* and *Prejano*; but a Bœotian incubus of apathy and inactivity hangs over this rarely visited province. Soria is 34 L. from Madrid. For details consult vols. xx. and xxi. of the '*Memorias Politicas*,' by Eugenio Larruga, and ' *Compendio Historial*,' Pedro Tutor y Melo, 4to., Alcalá de Henares, 1690. Soria was dreadfully sacked in 1808 by Ney, who, allured by plunder, forgot his military duties, and thus allowed Castaños and a remnant of the Spanish forces to escape (Pen. Camp., i. 387).

Numantia, of classical fame, is said to lie 1 L. N. of Soria; but all this is mere conjecture, as the terrorist Romans passed a ploughshare over the site of a city which defied their arms. The character of the present natives remains unchanged ; they, like the Arragonese and Zaragozans, are distinguished for obstinacy, endurance of privations, and a dogged resistance to the yoke of a foreign invader.

From Soria there is a bridle road to *Logroño*. The localities to the N.W. abound in immemorial pine forests, *Los pinares de Soria*, which rival those of Cuenca, and produced the fine material which the chisels of Juni and Hernandez converted into such splendid forms of art and religion.

Passing a dreary country, we reach *Osma*, Oxoma, another of these decayed agricultural towns: pop^n· about 1000. It was once of great importance, being a frontier city, and was taken from the Moors in 746 by Alonzo II. of Leon and destroyed : it was rebuilt in 938 by Gonzalo Tellez, and fortified in 1019 by Sancho Garcia, Count of Castile. It stands on the Ucero and Abion, tributaries of the Duero ; but the Roman city was placed on the hill, and some traces of their buildings yet remain. The cathedral was erected in 1232 by Juan, chancellor of St. Ferdinand. The *Capilla mayor* is very grand, and the *Retablo* and *Trascoro* were excellently carved in 1556 by Juan de Juni. This grand work represents the passion of Christ. The superb *reja* was wrought in 1505 by Juan Frances, and at the cost of the princely primate of Toledo, Alonzo de Fonseca. The façade, tower, and *Sacristia* of this interesting cathedral were unfortunately "beautified" in the last century by Juan de Sagarvinaga; then too was raised the *Capilla de Palafox*, designed by the commonplace Sabatini. Consult for *Osma*, Florez, 'E. S.' vii. 265, the account in the 2d vol. of Canon Loperraez, and '*El Teatro Ecclesiastico de Osma*,' by Gil Gonzalez. The ancient city of *Clunia* lay near *Coruña del Conde*, about 5 L. west of Osma; and here, as at *Peñalva*, are some few ill-treated remains of antiquity. The old theatre, however, being cut in the rock, has resisted the farmer and builder. Osma lies 13 L. from Siguenza, and 9½ from Aranda del Duero, and nothing can be more uninteresting than the intervening country.

The ferocious Inquisador Domenick, called in this land of misnomers El *Santo* Domingo, was born near Osma, at Calavega, Aug. 4, 1060; his mother having previously dreamt that she was pregnant of a dog with a torch in his mouth, a symbol that the order of Dominicans which he was destined to found should, as *Domini canes*, hunt heretics to hell; while the blazing implement of the Furies alluded not to the furnaces of the *holy* tribunal, but to the eloquence of these Preachers, whose sermons were to enlighten the world. The godmother of the babe next saw a star on his forehead at his baptism, and his nurse was scared by bees which clustered round his mouth, like Pindar's, when his cradle. He rose to be a canon of Osma, and at thirty became an itinerant preacher. One of his first miracles

was performed with his rosary (see p. 672) on Sancha, queen of France, who, previously barren, now became the mother of St. Louis. The operator was afterwards commissioned by the Pope and French king to deliver them from the Albigenses, or Protestants; and thus, by the aid of the bloody Simon de Montfort, "100,000 lost souls were converted," 20,000 persons being killed at Moruel alone. But he raised almost as many others from the dead, and amongst them a young Italian named *Napoleon*, who had fallen from his horse: however, his miracles were so numerous that a volume would not contain them. See, however, Ribadeneyra (ii. 424), from whence we have extracted these few facts. Spain became the head-quarters of this order, the corollary of whose convincing sermons was the *quemadero* or furnace: not contented with the angelic virtues of their patron, his disciples have, like true Spaniards, eulogised his illustrious descent, which they have traced to the Guzmanes, the *good* men (see Tarifa, p. 225); so it was said of Byron, that he was prouder of his seat in the House of Lords than of his niche in the temple of Apollo. The heraldic collector should by all means study the '*Dissertacion — del Santissimo Patriarcha*,' Lorenzo Roberto de la Linde, 4to. Sevilla, 1740.

ROUTE CXXXIV.— TUDELA TO LOGROÑO.

Alfaro	. . . . .	3
Aldea Nueva	. . . .	2 .. 5
Calahorra	. . . . .	2 .. 7
Vᵃ. de Ansejo	. . . .	4 .. 11
Vᵃ. de Tamarices	. . .	2 .. 13
Logroño	. . . . .	2 .. 15

The road ascends the basin of the Ebro; the country on each side of the banks is sufficiently fertile. *Alfaro*, a largish town, is placed on the borders of Navarre, under a hill, which is washed by the *Alhama*, a tributary of the Ebro. The church is collegiate. *Calahorra*, the Calagurris Nasica of the Vasconi and Celtiberi, is a most ancient town; popⁿ· about 6500. It rises on a gentle hill at the extremity of Navarre and Arragon, and is watered by the *Cidacos*, which empties itself close by into the Ebro. These sources of irrigation fill the fields with corn and fruits: the cherries and cauliflowers are renowned. Ancient Calagurris rivalled Numantia, and both were types of desperate Arragonese defence. Pompey besieged it u.c. 678, but was compelled to retire by Sertorius, after a loss of 3000 men; four years afterwards it was taken and burnt by Afranius, after a dreadful famine, and such straits as passed into a proverb: then husbands fed on their wives, while mothers killed and salted their children, but they died rather than surrender. The ancient Handbooks are full of this " longæ dira obsidionis Egestas," of this " Calagurris in fame nihil non experta " (see Juv. xv. 93; Val. Max. vii. 6 ; Florus, iii. 22); but so when Ben Hadad went up against Samaria, women boiled and ate their sons (2 Kings vi. 29); and as the bloody atrocities of Sylla drove the Celtiberians into arms, so in our times the butcheries of the Murats, Augereaus, &c., infuriated their descendants, nor were Minas wanting to lead the *Guerrilla* bands after the fashion of Sertorius.

Modern Calahorra blazons on her shield, " two naked arms fighting with swords, from which sparks issue," in reference to a vision which Hannibal beheld when he captured the city. The crest is a woman wielding a sabre in one hand and a naked arm in the other, with the motto " *Prevaleci contra Cartago y Roma.*" A modest untruth, seeing that the town was beaten both by Carthaginian and Roman. On the *Plaza* were rudely painted this woman eating a human arm. The constancy, however, of the Calagurritans was proverbial; Bebricus, one of the *Devoti* or liegemen of Sertorius, would not survive his master's murder, but offered himself to his manes, true in death as in life. Augustus Cæsar (Suet. 49) chose his body-guard from

the city of Fidelity : the natives, however, then, as now, fought better behind walls than on the plain, for here, u.c. 568, a mere handful of disciplined Romans routed as easily and completely a countless rabble of Iberians, as our Black Prince did at Navarrete, or Suchet at Tudela.

Of ancient Calagurris some portions of towers, a circus maximus, an aqueduct, and of a *Naumachia*, have been traced ; but the remains have long been worked up as a quarry by Moor and Spaniard.   Florez (M. i. 255) describes 30 coins of the mint. This is the birth-place of Quintilian, and, according to some, of Aulus Prudentius, the first Christian poet, who has left a hymn in honour of the city tutelars, Emeterio and Celedonio. These martyrs were decapitated, but their heads, on being thrown into the Ebro, floated away together, cheek by jowl, into the Mediterranean, and having coasted Spain, passed the Straits, and worked up to Santander, where they became the pride and defence of the city (see for details E. S. xxxiii. 272); but no live sailors in the world can vie with the self-navigating Saints of Spain when dead (see pp. 449, 662, 663, 901).   A cathedral was erected at Calagurris, over their headless bodies, which were the object of holy pilgrimage every Aug. 31.   When the Moors captured the city the corpses rose from the graves and marched away into the hills, from whence they were marched back again in grand pomp in 1395 : " Ce n'est que le premier pas que coute " (see p. 253); the bodies were found perfectly well preserved after 1000 years, nor could they have lasted longer, even if salted à la Celtibérienne.

Calahorra was retaken in 1045 by Garcia VI., who raised it to be a see, conjointly with S^{o.} Domingo de Calzada ; the ancient cathedral was almost destroyed in one of those inundations to which the city is subject, from 'the confluence of the Cidacos, Ega, and Ebro. It was restored in 1485 by El Maestre Juan ; it is now a thing of patch-work: the additions beyond the transept are of the 17th and 18th century : the principal portal and facade, as well as the chapel of *La Epifania,* were altered in the bad period of Philip V., when the *Coro* also was disfigured. Calahorra is a dull, decayed and decaying, but genuine old Castilian town. The celebrated warm baths of *Arnedillo* lie distant about 4 L. S.S.E., following up the course of the river Cid ; they are much frequented from June 14 to Sept. 20, and are considered the Bareges of La Rioja. The average heat is 42° Réaum. : the principal ingredient is muriate of soda ; consult, however, the chemical ' *Ensayo* ' of them by Proust.

A flat, uninteresting, but fertile cereal country, subject however to inundations, continues up the Ebro ; for *La Rioja Alta y Baja* see R. cxiv. *Logroño, Julia Briga,* has a decent posada of the diligence : the town is placed on the Ebro, in a hill-enclosed rich plain, on the confines of Navarre, Alava, and Old Castile. It is the chief town of its province, and from its position, was once of great importance ; it is surrounded by walls and a moat, which can be flooded. The Old Castle is a ruin : the town is freshened by the rivulet *Irequa ;* it has a good *Plaza " del Coso,"* and pretty walks, especially *La Alameda de los Muros ;* popⁿ· about 10,000. It has a theatre and *Liceo.* The fertile plains abounding in corn and fruit render this place cheap and well provided, while its central position makes it a mart of considerable traffic. *Logroño,* accordingly, is a fair specimen of a prosperous Castilian country town, and many of its inhabitants are in easy circumstances. There is not much to interest a stranger ; the *Colegiata* is dedicated to *Sᵃ· Maria la Redonda,* and has some frescoes in the New *Trascoro,* by Josef Vexes, ob. 1782, by whom also are the Passion of Christ, painted for the cloister of the parish church *Del Palacio Imperial.* The convent of *Carmelitas Descalzas* is memorable in

monastic annals. It was discovered that the friars of an opposite convent had burrowed a subterraneous communication, by which they visited the sisterhood somewhat unspiritually. This commerce continued from the years 1712 to 1737 before it was found out ; it resulted, from an ecclesiastical inquiry, that out of 21 nuns, 17 at one period had repented of their vows of vestal chastity.

The bridge over the Ebro deserves notice, having been built in 1138 by the hermit San Juan de Ortega, who is now worshipped by the peasantry as a river-god, just as San Juan Nepomucene is in Bohemia ; and the city bears for arms this wonderful bridge in a border of fleurs de lys, granted by Charles V. in 1523, in honour of the citizens, who, led by the Duque de Najera, signally repulsed the French under Andre de Foix. The invaders had penetrated thus far, taking advantage of Spain's infirmity during the civil wars of the *Comuneros ;* but the past, in this strange land of contradictions and accident, was no prophet of the future, for in our times Verdier, after his sack of Vitoria, arrived here June 5, 1808, when, in the words of Foy (iii. 267), " Les Espagnols furent mis en déroute, avant que les troupes Françaises eussent le temps de les attaquer. Verdier fit quelques exemples" —that is, sacked the unresisting place without mercy. The routed army completed their disgrace by murdering their general, Pignatelli, a very common Carthaginian and Spanish finale (see p. 891). Logroño was again taken by Ney, Oct. 27, 1808, without resistance, and again utterly sacked. Again in 1823, the French, under Obert, instantaneously routed the patriots and took the city without the loss of even one man.

Here Espartero married Jacinta de Sᵃ Cruz, a wealthy heiress ; and here again, in 1838, he fixed his head-quarters, when proposing to take *Estella,* the strong Carlist hold of Maroto ; as, however, both these notabilities only waged war with paper pellets, cigars, and frothy bombast bulletins, it has been suspected that some mutual understanding existed, which ripened into the convention of Vergara. At the same time both armies were equally hors de combat, and " wanting in everything at the critical moment," while their condition was rendered more pitiable by the " marchings and counter-marchings," and other much-ados-about-nothing of their generals. Many men perished on both sides from hunger, more fatal than bullet or bayonet.

It was at Logroño that Villalonga executed, Jan. 20, 1845, the redoubtable Christino general, Zurbano, and this without any form of trial beyond identification : such was the order of Zurbano's former colleague Narvaez, as usual in Spain (see p. 934). He was shot in the back, when almost out of his mind from privations and grief at the death of his brother-in-law, Caye-

tano Muro, and his two sons, Benito and Feliciano, accomplices in his ill-advised revolt. Villalonga, in order to add to the bitterness of a father's death, selected for the site of the execution the spot where his children had been killed. Zurbano was the son of a small farmer of Barea, near Logroño, and from being a smuggler rose in the civil wars to high command. He was a brave active guerrillero, but false and sanguinary. Navarrete el Mudo (see p. 813) was born at Logroño.

From central Logroño many branch roads diverge; they are none of the best, nor possess the least interest, excepting R. cxv. A diligence runs to Burgos, R. cxv. A bridle and cart track leads to Soria, 17 L. ; to Miranda del Ebro, by Haro, 10 L.; to Vitoria, by Peñacerrada, 10 L.: this is carriageable; the shorter bridle-road by Bernedo is only 9 L. The road to Pamplona by Estella is carriageable, 14½ L.

SECTION XIV.

THE KINGDOM OF NAVARRE.

CONTENTS.

The Province; Agotes, Guerrilleros, and Works to consult.

The best periods for visiting Navarre are the summer months, as the springs are rainy, and the winters cold in the hilly regions: the cities are devoid of attraction, but the wild country possesses charms for the sportsman, artist, and naturalist ; while to the British soldier the frontier-line offers the sites of some of the hardest-fought battles and most glorious triumphs by which the Duke concluded the Peninsular Campaign.

El Reino de Navarra is another of the small early independent kingdoms of which the bundle of the present Spanish monarchy is composed. It is the ancient *Vasconia. Nav,* a common Iberian prefix, signifies a "plain under hills," and this is the best description of the province. Shaped in an irregular square, 80 miles in length by 60 in width ; it is bounded to the N. by the Pyrenees: the whole population scarcely exceeds 300,000, and is chiefly pastoral and agricultural. The Ebro, which flows to the S.E., and the Bidasoa, which runs to the W., are the main trunks that receive the smaller mountain tributaries. The kingdom is divided into five *Merindades,* or departments, each of which has its petty capital ; they lie thus—*Pamplona,* N., *Tafalla,* S., *Olite,* in the centre, *Estella,* E., and *Sangueza,* W. The northern barrier is very mountainous, being composed of the western slopes of the Pyrenees, which dip down to the ocean from *Monte Perdido,* and these wild and broken glens became the natural fastnesses of the unconquered natives, when retiring before the Romans and Moors. They found their Pelayus against the latter in Garci Ximenez, and made common cause with the highlanders of Arragon, until about 842, when Inigo Arista was chosen king of Navarre at Pamplona, while the national liberties were guaranteed by the celebrated *Fueros de Sobrarbe* (p. 944). The kingdom bears for arms " gules and chains or," in memorial of the achievement of Sancho III. *el fuerte,* who broke down the chains of the Moorish general's tent at *Navas de Tolosa.* Navarre was annexed to Castile in 1512, by Ferdinand *el catolico,* partly by force and partly by fraud (see Prescott, Ferd. and Isab. ch. 24): Jean d'Albret, the rightful heir, being abandoned by his French allies, who profited by his ruin, as the territory was partitioned, Ferdinand seizing all S. of the Pyrenees, while the N. portion ultimately passed with Henri IV. into the crown of France. The French side is interesting to Englishmen, as having been long possessed by the Black Prince, and being the scene of many of Froissart's delightful narrations.

The intercommunications between Navarre and Arragon, N. of the Ebro, are carried over a desolate country, while those S. of the Pyrenees are extremely mountainous and difficult, being seldom traversed except by smugglers. The Navarrese live very much to themselves, each in their valley, which is to them the whole world; here in the green meadow or wooded hill-side they tend their flocks, while in the warmer plains they till the earth, and labour in the vineyard, and the wines of *Peralta, Azagra* and *Cascante,* are deservedly popular. These simple peasants, far from cities, have few wants and few vices; with them the "chief thing is water, bread, clothing, and a house to cover shame," and their bane is the all-corrupting habit of smuggling, which their intricate frontier favours. The scenery is alpine and picturesque. The trout-fishing and wild shooting excellent; the mountains are not so high as those in Arragon; the *Altobiscar* reaches however 5380 ft., and the *Adi* 5218; the valleys are beautiful, especially those of *Bastan* (Arabice, the *Garden*), *Santisteban,* and *Cincovillas.* In the former lived the *Agotes,* who, resembling the *Cagots* of Luchon, have long been a stumbling-block to antiquarians; persecuted on both sides of the Pyrenees as "an accursed thing," in Spain the proscribed caste was held to be wanting in *Limpieza de Sangre,* none therefore would intermarry or associate with beings of " unclean blood;" thus the outcasts were in some instances denied even the sacraments, and were not allowed to enter churches except at a side door. Mons. Ramon absurdly derives the word *cagot,* quasi *Caas Goth,*" sons of the Goth," which, so far from being a disgrace, is the most honoured source of descent in Spain. De Maria reads in *Caas Goth, Caçadores,* "hunters of the Goth." Ducange in voce *Gagoti* gives as other names *Cacosi, Caqueux,* which are probably only unseemly French epithets, and not more connected with the true etymology than with the Greek word κακος. They are termed in the old *For de Navarra* of 1074, *Caffos;* Gafo means a leper, from the Hebrew *Cafah,* distorted, a cripple, from whence the Arabic term of opprobrium *Kafir,* a rebeller against God. *Gafo* took precedence in the five actionable words of slander in old Spanish law, because combining the horrors of a physically infectious leprosy with the moral taint of heresy, which affected body and soul. Thus the curse of *Gehazi* was the common penalty in mediæval Spanish deeds to all who broke the covenants. Time, which has cured this leprosy (substituting the *goitre*), has softened the hearts of persecutors, and as the odium theologicum decreased, pity reappeared, until the *Agotes* became merged among the peasantry, and now are more talked about than really existing, and furnish materials for essays, not persecution; indeed there is so little difference in their appearance and treatment, that they are all but absorbed: some of them are millers in the *Baztan,* while others occupy the quarter *Bozate* in the valley of *Aizcun.* Some think them the remnant of the Arians who fled here in the sixth and seventh centuries; others, and with greater probability, think them the descendants of the Protestant *Albigenses,* who hid themselves in these mountains six centuries later when flying from the sword of Simon de Montfort and the faggot of St. Domenick. Being treated as heretics, they obtained the additional name *Gafo,* because it is the worst in the Spanish language (comp. Gavacho, p. 975), just as they were sometimes called by the Moors *Christaos*, or Christian dogs; others held them to be remnants of persecuted Jews and Moors; a taint, however, of some *heresy* is evident. The highlanders of Navarre are remarkable for their light active physical forms, their temperate habits, endurance of hardships and privation, individual bravery, and love of perilous adventure; the pursuits of the chase, smuggling, and a dash of robbery, form their moral education: thus their sinewy limbs are braced, and their hawk-eyed self-reliance sharpened. Naturally, therefore, they have always been first-rate *guerrilleros*. Placed by position on the borders of France, Arragon, and Castile, and alternately the dupe and victim of each, necessity has forced them to be always on their guard against neighbours whom they fear and abhor. Thus a spirit of nationality burns in every heart, which broods with retentive memory over wrongs that are never forgotten or forgiven. A watch and ward system of an armed armistice dates from their earliest laws; as by the *Fueros de Sobrarbe* a provision was made that by a given signal of danger the whole male population should hurry to the first place of meeting (Abarca, i. 115). This preparation still exists along the Pyrenean frontier; and the Catalan borderer is called *Somaten*, from the summoning tocsin-bell. As Sertorius made Huesca his stronghold, so Mina sallied forth from "his country," from the glens of Navarre, with his bold followers, a race that never will be extinct in these hills, whose weed is man in all his native unsophisticated energy. Imitating the example of the Romans, the French endeavoured to exterminate these irregular opponents by every means, whether fair or foul. They burnt their houses, set prices on their leaders' heads, and executed them when taken like Hofer in the Tyrol. It suited them also to consider these patriot insurgents as "bandits," not soldiers, because wearing no uniform; but a cross and gold lace are not necessary to make an honest defender of native hearths and altars, nor is uniform a thing of Spain or the East, where "*regulation*" niceties are scouted. The French severities, as in the days of the Romans (Livy, xv. 39), led to just and terrific retaliations, and swelled the bands with infuriated recruits, as those whose homes are in ashes must take to arms for existence and revenge: hence the personal ferocity of Navarrese reprisals against their invaders and ill-users. These hornet swarms caused, as the Duke said (Disp. June 18, 1812), "the utmost annoyance to the French," exactly as they had done to the Romans (Livy, xxviii. 22), by being a thorn in their paths, interrupting communications, cutting off convoys and stragglers; but they were utterly unable, from want of organization and every sinew of war, to carry out any sustained operation, or do anything against the enemy when in position; nor have great contests ever been successfully concluded by undisciplined numbers. The Maldonados, &c., being well aware of the unvaried failures of the Cuestas and Blakes, are reduced to ascribe the salvation of Spain to the desultory bush-fightings of some thousand half-armed peasants, which is as ridiculous as it is humiliating to those arms at which Europe once trembled. The Duke, sagacious as just, knew that the *guerrillero* was "*the only useful arm;* he is better acquainted with his trade than *what is called* the officer of the regular Spanish army; he knows the country better, and is better known to the inhabitants, and, *above all*, has no pretensions to military character."—Disp., May 3, 1812. And this sound conclusion is borne out by every page of Spanish history, past and present. The dislocation of the Peninsula seems to suggest that desultory warfare which is so congenial to the temperament of Bedouin and Highlander. These armed freebooters multiply like wild animals in their safe retreats, the cradles of the *guerrillero*, the wolf, and vulture; active, quicksighted, bold, cruel, and predacious (see Livy, xxii. 18), they sweep down into the plains, for never here has the raid or foray been deemed a *disgrace*, which consists rather, as among the Greek pirates, in the returning *empty handed* (Strabo, iii. 223, 231). But, as our old author observes, this " robbing propensity " incapacitated the Iberians from producing a great general, and rendered them only fit for "a petty war," τα μικρα τολμωντες. Such was the school and career of Viriatus (Florus, ii. 17. 15), the type of the Cids, Minas, and other Rob Roys and *Robbing Hoods* of the Peninsula. The plunder obtained by the Navarrese at Arlaban proved a powerful magnet to new followers, and *Viva Fernando y vamos robando* expressed the warcry of loyalty combined with pillage : thus the scion of patriotism was often grafted on the stock of plunder, just as the olive branch is on the wild oleaster, and the sacred cause of country gave a dignity to a buccaneering thirst for gold and a reckless bloodshedding.

In vain the Duke urged on the Spanish governments the adoption of a defensive partizan warfare; but the pride of the regular generals would take nothing less than fighting and losing pitched battles. Yet the Navarrese, warlike but not military, preferred their native rude although *poetic* form of war; their roving habits and love of personal independence rejected the *prosaic* yet effective system of drill and discipline, by which the individual is merged in order to create an *exercitus*, an exercised and really formidable machine. Again, their point of honour was that of the Iberian, not of the modern soldier : they counted it no disgrace to turn and run when a disorderly attempt failed (Cæs., ' B. C.' i. 44), nor deemed any unfair advantage dishonourable (Geogr. iii. 408). See Index, *Guerrillero*, and pp. 305, 892, 905.

The best works to consult on Navarre are the ' *España Sagrada*,' xxxiii. ; ' *Historia del Reyno de Navarra*,' Garᵃ· de Gongora, fol., Pamplona, 1628 ; ' *Anales del Reyno*,' Josef de Moret, fol., Pamplona, 1665, or the later edition of 5 vols. fol., Pamp. 1766 ; ' *Congressiones Apologeticas*,' Pedro de Moret, 4to., Pamp. 1678. There is a paper on the royal genealogy, by Joaquin Traggia, in the 3rd vol. of the ' *Memorias de la Academia de Historia*.'

The district to the N.W. of Zaragoza is called *De las Cincovillas*, and these "*five* " towns are *Tauste, Ejea, Sadava, Castillo*, and *Sos*. They were raised to the rank of *Villa*, which is higher than *Pueblo* and lower than *Ciudad*, by Philip V., to reward them for assistance rendered during the War of Succession; they are very uninteresting.

Ejea de los Caballeros lies about 13 L. N.W. of Zaragoza. This ancient city, with some 2000 inhab., retains the tower on its walls in which Queen Urraca was confined by Alonzo I. of Arragon (see p. 610). Here a tauromachian *Suerte*, or trick, was played off against the French. In July, 1808, a detachment arrived on a plundering expedition, when the inhabitants shut all the gates except one, through which about 150 of the enemy entered, meeting with no resistance ; but when they reached the *plaza*, a herd of bulls were let loose on them. The invaders not being *matadores*, or *picadores*, retreated before these unusual opponents, when the inhabitants fired at them from the windows, and all not killed were taken prisoners (see Ibieca, ' *Sitios de Zaragoza*,' sup., 153 ; and Schep., i. 194). Let Ejea be no longer called a city of knights, but of bulls, and raised to the honour of *muy heroica y invicta*. This bull-fighting strategy is purely Iberian; thus the Spaniards defeated Amilcar by driving bullocks against his troops (App., ' B. H.,' 428). The Carthaginians also took a leaf out of this Peninsular tauromachia, as Hannibal baffled Fabius by making his Spanish rear-guard drive against the Romans 2000 oxen, to whose horns lighted torches had been tied, as was done by Samson to the foxes' tails (Polyb., iii. 93 ; Livy, xxii. 16 ; and compare Carrion, p. 615).

ROUTE CXXXV.—ZARAGOZA TO
PAMPLONA.

Tudela	14	
Valtierra	3	17
Caparroso	4	21
Tafalla	4	25
Va. del Piojo	3	28
Pamplona	3	31

For *Tudela* see R. cxxviii.; leaving
it and crossing the Ebro the dreary
common *La Bardena* expands to the
r. *Valtierra*, with 3000 inhabitants,
has a ruined Moorish castle. Hence
a bald country stretches to *Caparroso*,
with its church and Alcazar on an
eminence. Crossing the Arragon by a
fine bridge, and quitting a few vineyards and olive-grounds, the waste re-
commences; improving, however, as
Olite and the Cidacos are approached.
Peralta, famous for its wines made
from Berbez grape, lies to the l.
Olite is built on the Cidacos. The
Alcazar, once the residence of the
kings of Navarre, was destroyed by the
French republicans in 1792.   *Olite*
and *Tafalla* were the flowers of the
Navarrese crown, *Olite y Tafalla—
Flor de Navarra;* now they are both
in the sear and fall.

Tafalla, Tubalia, because founded
by Tubal, was once the court of the
kings. Here Semen Lezano in 1419
built for Charles III. a fine palace,
now a sad ruin. The old city walls
have escaped better. The *Plaza de
armas* is on an eminence. The climate
is delicious and the place salubrious,
and there is good shooting in the
Montes, near *Artajona,* at *El Plano*
and *El bosque del Condestable,* near
which flows the Arga, coming down
from the Baztan, and an excellent
trout stream. *Tafalla* is now much
impoverished : pop. under 5000. Visit
the hermitage Sa. Catalina, where the
Bishop of Pamplona, Nicolas Eche-
varri, the head of the Agramont party,
was murdered Nov. 23, 1469, during
the sitting of the Cortes, by the constable Pierres de Peralta, the chief of
the Beaumont faction. Parties ran so
high that this deed was done even in

the presence of the Infanta. The *Parroquia de Sa. Maria* has a fine cinque-
cento *Retablo,* by Miguel de Ancheta,
representing the lives of the Saviour
and the Virgin. Observe the Doric
and Ionic tabernacle, and the bassi-
rilievi, especially the Saviour exhibiting his wounded side.

Crossing the Cidacos, whose banks
are pretty, we reach *Belascoin,* where
Diego Leon defeated the Carlists in
the spring of 1839, the English legion-
ary battalion really doing the brunt of
the work. Diego, when the day was
won, could not be induced to cross the
bridge, which he ought to have done,
and thus the enemy was only partially
destroyed. He was made a *Conde* for
this affair, but met with a melancholy
end, being shot for treason (see p. 784).
Diego, or, as the Spaniards called him,
El Leon de los Leones, was a pseudo-
Murat, vain, generous, and chival-
rously brave; he delighted in national
boato, or ostentatious show, and was, in
fact, a genuine Arab Mameluke, *muy
bizarro y fanfarron,* and few Spaniards
ever were more distinguished in dashing cavalry-charges. Emerging from
the defiles of *Olarzy,* near *Noain,* to
the l. of Arlequy, is the fine aqueduct
of Pamplona, which we now enter,
crossing the Monreal. Best inns, *El
Parador general, Posada* de la Viuda
de Florentino Echevarria, and Posada
de Antonio Cortes.

Pamplona is the capital and fron-
tier-key of Navarre, being the first
city of the plains. The *Relate* chain
of the Pyrenees is distant 4 L. It is
situated on the l. of the Arga, which
here forms a horse-shoe bend N., and
is one of the chief tributaries which
" make a man " of the Ebro :—

Arga Ega y Aragon,
Hacen al Ebro, Baron.

The Arga flows through the beautiful
Cuenca, 7 L. in circumference, the *Concha,* the shell of which Pamplona is the
pearl. The climate is somewhat damp
and cold, but the gardens are fruitful
and the meadows verdant. The position

is well adapted for a fortress, as it commands the level plain, while its own sloping eminence is not commanded itself. The hills and spurs of the Pyrenees rise charmingly in the distance, especially when seen from the citadel and *El Mirador* on the walk. The sons of Pompey were induced by local considerations to rebuild this place in the year 68 B.C., whence it was called Pompeiopolis (Strabo, iii. 245). This the Moors corrupted into *Bambilonah*, whence the present name. The city remained faithful to the cause of its founders, and was therefore slighted by Augustus. In the middle ages it was called *Irunia*, " the good town." It was conquered from the Romans by Euric in 466, and again by the French in 542, under Childibert, who sacked it and laid waste the whole country. The French again destroyed it in 778 under Charlemagne. That great emperor had been invited by the Berber chiefs of Navarre to assist them against the Moors of Cordova, but when the Franc troops arrived they were refused admittance into the garrisons, just as occurred in regard to ourselves during the Peninsular war (see *Cadiz*, p. 209 ; and *La Coruña*, p. 655). Pamplona beat off the Moors in 907, and the Castilians in 1138 ; but has always yielded to the more military French. Buonaparte, whose policy was *ruse doublée de force*, followed the example of the Romans, who obtained the Spanish frontier almost before the natives suspected their vile perfidy, or were aware of their own strength, "Ante obsessa quam se ipsa cognoverat" (Florus, ii. 17. 3); accordingly in Feb., 1808, he sent Gen. D'Armagnac under the guise of an alliance with Charles IV., when the Spanish authorities were weak enough to serve out rations to their friends in the citadel itself : thereupon some French grenadiers, under the pretence of playing at snowball, secured the drawbridge and captured the place, like Barcelona (p. 481, etc.). Thus Lucullus deceived the Iberians ;

first he professed amity with the garrison of Cauca, and begged the officers to trust to his honour; and when his dupes were off their guard sent in select soldiers in disguise, who massacred 20,000 men (App., ' B. H.,' 479). The French held Pamplona during the war; it was blockaded by the Duke after their defeat at Vitoria. Soult made a desperate attempt to relieve it, but was signally repulsed : then Gen. Cassan threatened to blow up the defences; but the decided Duke was near, and wrote at midnight to the Conde de España (Disp., Oct. 20, 1813) in case of such an act, " contrary to the laws of war," to " order him, without further orders," to shoot the governor and all the officers, and decimate the garrison. Cassan, who perceived that there was no mistake, surrendered the next day, and thus the citadel of Pamplona escaped destruction, the usual parting legacy of the invader, whose policy was to dismantle the defences of a neighbour. Pamplona accordingly, thanks to the Duke, is the chief *Plaza de armas* of this frontier, and the Cortes voted a statue to be erected there in honour of the preserver, which it need not be said this, like all the others decreed on paper, was never even begun; but governmental *gratitude* in Spain loves the paulo post futurum tense (see p. 162).

Pamplona has grand titles; it is denominated *Muy noble, muy leal, y muy heroica*, and bears for arms a lion rampant with a sword in dexter paw, and the chains of Navarre as an orle: the town is clean and well built; pop^{n.} about 15,000. It is the residence of a Captain-General, who was formerly called the Viceroy. It is the see of a bishop, founded in 1130, and suffragan to Burgos : it possesses an *Audiencia*, with jurisdiction over 230,900 souls: the numbers committed for trial in 1844 were 1201, which gives about one in every 190 : here also reside the usual provincial authorities. It has a theatre, a *Liceo*, a *Casa de Espositos*, two good fives-courts, and a *plaza de*

Toros. There are charming *alamedas* or public walks on the roads leading to Madrid, France, and La Rioja; that called *La Taconera* in the town is the most frequented : the streets are well paved, but dull, and the uniformity is increased by the similarity of the projecting eaves, balconies, and *rejas*, which are all generally painted at the same time. There are many family houses, *casas solares*, which the heraldic shields denote. The fountains are well supplied from the noble aqueduct, which was built in a Roman style and solidity by Ventura Rodriguez; the water is brought from the hills of *Subiza*, 3 L. distant : visit one portion of about 2300 ft. in length, which contains 97 arches of 35 feet in span and 65 in height : the town is cheap and well provisioned; the principal square, *La plaza del Castillo*, is converted into a *plaza de Toros* on great festivals. Visit *La plaza de abajo*, or the market-place, which is well supplied; observe the buxom peasant girls, *Las Pajesas*, with their long *trensas*, and the *Boyna*, or *Bereta* cap of the males : the river is crossed by several bridges ; the suburb *de Rochapea* was almost destroyed by the French, and suffered much during the O'Donnell Christino outbreak in 1841, when it was fired at for three days from the citadel, by which Sⁿ· Lorenzo and the *Casa del Ayuntamiento* were almost ruined.

Pamplona is soon seen : the Gothic cathedral was built in 1397 by Charles III. of Navarre, who then took down the older edifice of 1100 ; he left however a portion of the beautiful cloisters, whose double galleries, quaint capitals to pillars, and iron palisado, a relic from the battle of *Navas de Tolosa*, deserve notice : the grand entrance is in a heavy incongruous Corinthian, and was put up in 1783 by Vᵃ· Rodriguez during the pseudo-classical and R. Academical mania; the portal is the Assumption of the Virgin, and the tutelar of the city, Sⁿ· Fermin : this saint, although very much unknown out of Navarre, is the great patron of Pamplona, "Urbis Patronus;" the 7th of July is sacred to him : then *Los Gigantes*, or Gog and Magog images, representing Moors, Normans, &c. (see p. 240), visit the town-hall, "the mayor and corporation;" dance before the cathedral, and then pay their respects to Sⁿ· Fermin's image at *San Lorenzo* : the period to visit Pamplona is during this *Feria* or fair, which is held every year in his honour, from June 29 to July 18; the place is then thronged with villagers, *pagani*, and mountaineers, who come to combine a little business with devotion and pleasure. Sⁿ· Fermin was born in Pamplona, went to preach in France, and was put to death at Amiens Sept. 25, 303. According to Ribadeneyra (iii. 92), the body while underground worked so many miracles, that Salvio, Bishop of Amiens, prayed that the site might be revealed to him; and after one of his sermons supernatural lights illumined the spot; on digging, the aromas of Araby the blessed issued forth (sure sign of a dead Spanish saint, see p. 576), and such, says one annalist, as no perfumer, not even a French one, ever devised : the congregation thought that they were in Elysium, and sung extemporaneous hymns : when the body was raised, although it was deep winter, the weather became so warm that the townsfolk imagined the rest of the world to be on fire; trees burst forth into leaf, plants into flower, and all the sick who gathered them were immediately healed, as in the old days of the Iberian vegetable panaceas (see p. 967). This and much more of the same value was printed at Madrid in 1790, and authorized by the church for pious belief; such a saint verily deserves a whole hetacomb of bulls: *Taurum Neptuno, Taurum tibi pulcher Apollo.*

The cathedral is small, but the interior is of a good light Gothic. The *coro* has some excellent carvings of saints, patriarchs, &c., by Miguel Ancheta, wrought, it is said, out of English oak. Observe the tombs of Carlos el

Mayor and his queen Leonor of Castile. The *rejas* both of the quire and high chapel are excellent. Visit the *basilica* or chapel of Ignacio Loyola, who was wounded before Pamplona. The burial crypt of the canons is in the cruciform *sacristia*. In the *sala preciosa* is a remarkable tomb of the Conde de Ganges, which was removed in 1813 from the Capuchinos. A part of the ancient refectory and kitchen of the canons is preserved in the cloisters : formerly the chapter lived in a conventual community. The cathedral library is tolerable; the books are arranged with their edges, not backs, turned to the spectator. Look out of the window at the fine view. The traveller will often see in this cathedral the offerings made of loaves, corn, &c., to the manes of the deceased, whose souls are thus supposed to be extracted from purgatory (see p. 170). For these oblations, see p. 927.

In the *Diputacion*, where the Cortes of Navarre sat, are some second-rate royal portraits. The bridges over the river are picturesque; but beware of sketching the citadel without observing previously our recommendations (see p. 9). This strong defence is separated from the town by a glacis or esplanade. The works were much strengthened in 1521, for Charles V., by Pedro Machuca, and enlarged by Philip II. The citadel is pentagonal; two bastions, *La Rochapea* and *La Magdalena*, front the river. Foreigners are not readily admitted, but may cònsole themselves with the assurance that "everything is wanting," which Alaix officially reported to Espartero, in words which Ribera, the painter of horrors and starvation, alone could have portrayed in a picture (' *Campo de Don Carlos,*' 3rd ed. p. 18) : but so it always was. " They showed us here," says an old traveller, " the magazines, not very well furnished either with ammunition or victual, and a very fair tower built to keep powder, *of which it is altogether unprovided*" (' Journey into Spain,' Herringman,

London, 1670, p. 223). To hear, however, what the Navarrese officials say, one would imagine that all the contents of Woolwich was here stowed away; but, as the Duke writes, they are " all visionaries and enthusiasts, who will not look at things as they really are; and although they cannot be ignorant of the truth of all we say of the miserably inefficient state of their army, they talk and act as if it were an army, till some dreadful disaster happens; and they are highly offended if in any discussion the truth, which ought never to be concealed in such a discussion, is even hinted " (Disp. July 20, 1811).

When was this otherwise? So our William III. told Bishop Burnet (' Mem.' fol. ed. i. 405), " that in their campaigns the Spaniards were both so ignorant and so backward, so proud and yet so weak, that they never would own their feebleness or their wants to him ; they pretended they had stores when they had none, and thousands when they scarce had hundreds. He had in their councils desired that they would give him only a *true* state of their garrisons and magazines, but they always gave it false; so that for some campaigns all was lost merely because they had deceived him in the strength they pretended to have. At last he believed nothing they said, but sent his own officers to examine everything."

The government, either from apathy or want of means, have thus constantly exposed their soldiers and allies to the risk of disasters. How was it to be expected that regular sieges could be sustained against the organised French when, in the words of the Duke to a Spanish general, " vous savez que vous n'avez ni argent, ni *magasins*, ni rien de ce qu'il vous faut pour tenir une armée en campagne " (Disp. Dec. 24, 1813). This offers some palliating explanation to those Spanish garrisons which too often surrendered strongly fortified towns even to a charge of French cavalry, like Toro, Zamora, and others; as the garrisons, well aware of the inefficiency of their incompetent leaders, like Imaz, Alacha, &c., and empty arsenals, despaired; yet when well commanded, in spite of every want, their defences, such as Gerona, Astorga, Ciudad Rodrigo, &c., rivalled those of ancient Saguntum and Numantia; but from the earliest period the Iberians have fought well behind walls, and have defied hunger and the elements (Sil. Ital. iii. 326): well therefore did Musa describe them as *Leones in sus Castillos* ('Conde,' i. 59).

It was in defending this citadel in 1521, that Ignacio Loyola was wounded, and conceived, during the tedious progress of his cure, the idea of founding his semi-soldier order for the especial defence of the Papacy, and to rule politics through polemics, having crushed the rights of mind (see Manresa, p. 499). Pamplona was at that time besieged by the French, under Andre de Foix, who had been sent by François I., under the pretence of assisting Henri D'Albret of Navarre, in the recovery of his hereditary dominions; but the real motive was to profit in a moment of Spain's infirmity, when during the absence of Charles V. and his armies, and when the country was torn by the civil discontent, which ended in the *Comunero* outbreak. The citadel being, as usual, unprepared and unfinished, soon surrendered; then the French threw off the mask, and invaded Castile, but they were defeated at Logroño, and forced to evacuate the Peninsula, when François I. most perfidiously deserted his friend Henry, whose country was partitioned between Spain and France. In the fosse of this citadel Santos Ladron de Guevara (see p. 931) was shot, Oct. 15, 1839; he had proclaimed Don Carlos at *Estella,* and was one of the first victims of the "plus quam civile bellum."

The vicinity of Pamplona is of the highest interest to the British soldier. The Duke, after defeating Jourdan at Vitoria, was obliged to blockade Pamplona, instead of besieging it, his plans having been marred by Sir John Murray's gross failure before Tarragona (see p. 472). Suchet was thereby left at liberty to co-operate with Soult, and fall on the English flank, which he did not do, from the usual jealousies between rival marshals. On the 23rd July, 1813, Soult crossed the frontier, having had every possible advantage in choice of time, easy communications, and an overwhelming numerical superiority; he judiciously poured his greatest force on our weakest points, and attacked Byng and Cole at Roncesvalles, who fell back at *Zubiri,* while Drouet, with 2000 men, was arrested a whole day at the *Maya* pass, by Stewart, with only 1500: the Duke, who was absent at San Sebastian, setting the blunders of others to right, only heard of the French advance on the night of the 25th. Picton and Cole had retired on Pamplona, and were posted between *Sorauren* and *Zabaldica;* had the French pushed on at once, Pamplona must have been relieved, and the Duke's advance into France arrested; the enemy's hesitation induced "Fighting old Picton" to stand firm, and thus precious time was gained, and the Duke arrived on the 27th; he had ridden from the *Baztan,* almost alone, when he reached *Sorauren,* and saw at once the real state of things; he pencilled a few wizard orders on the parapet of the bridge, and then galloped up the hill, the French entering the village, "luckily," as he said, "about two minutes" after he had left it. On what trifles do the destinies of nations turn! Had this one man been taken, all would have been lost. And now, as this one man rode up alone, the whole army saw and knew him; every soldier felt what Foy (i. 81) describes as the *magic* of the mere presence of Buonaparte. "A l'approche du danger, ce qu'on sentait pour lui, était plus que l'admiration; on lui rendait un *culte,* comme au Dieu tutélaire de l'armée," and the great Emperor knew his power. "A la Guerre," said he, "les hommes ne cont rien, c'est *un* homme qui est tout." Εισ εμοι μυριοι, wrote Cicero to Atticus (Ep. xvi. 11). Thus the spirit of a single master-mind makes that of multitudes take one direction. The Spaniards felt fully the inspiring influence, and shouted, *Allà va trenta mil hombres ;* such was their estimate of the value of a real " Head," the thing wanting in their camps and councils. The British army responded in that true English cheer, the certain omen of victory, whereupon the Duke, who could see Soult, remarked, " He will hear that cheer, and, from caution, will hesitate attacking, this will give time for the 6th division to arrive, and I shall beat him." Having made his dispositions, he amused himself with reading the newspapers. He knew his man, and his prudent strategies (see p. 568), and Soult knew his man too, and heard the knell like cheer : accordingly, although commanding 25,000 splendid French, he hesitated to attack 16,000 English, and thus lost a day, which, as usual, lost him (compare Lugo, p. 650, and Albuera, p. 320).

The next morning, while the Duke was writing to Graham, Soult attacked in force, then the pen was thrown down for the bayonet, and the foe was repulsed at every point. The 40th, 7th, 20th, and 23rd, charging the superb French masses no less than four times each ; Soult gave way, and retreated, abandoning with Gen. Foy their almost impregnable positions (for details see R. cx., xxix.). The Duke, when he had " settled" Soult, quietly resumed his letter, withot even adding the postscript of Cæsar, *Veni, Vidi, Vici ;* but Zubiri was but a repetition of Salamanca (see p. 565).

Soult's plan of relief was daring, and well conceived, but feebly carried out ; repeated defeats had cowed his troops, and the presence of the Duke, which raised the English from despondency to confidence, had the contrary effect on their assailants. Soult indeed, even in the words of his stanch friend Napier (xxi. 5), failed

from " slowness and indecision, which seemed injudicious." Monsʳ· Savary, however, attributes the failure to "a deluge of rain in the mountains, which compelled Soult to recall his columns;" but it did not compel the Duke to order his to advance and follow. The news of this important repulse reached the Allied Sovereigns, while conferring on making terms with Buonaparte, and much influenced their final rejection : thus, the non-relief of Pamplona led to the first capture of Paris.

ROUTE CXXXVI.—PAMPLONA TO LOGROÑO.

Astrain	2	
Po. de la Reina	2	4
Estella	3¼	7¼
Los Arcos	3	10¼
Viana	3	13½
Logroño	1	14½

This is the best route to Burgos, and was one of the grand lines taken by pilgrims on their road to Santiago, and owes, in common with many others, its bridges, hospitals, and accommodations to pious benefactors who wished to facilitate the progress of the devout. Near *Astrain* is a "high place" on which is a temple of *La Virgen de la Reniega,* or *el Perdon,* much visited by the peasantry. A good wine is made near *Puente de la Reina,* where several streams meet in the plain. The place has about 3300 inhab. Visit the convent *San Juan de Crucifijo ;* it originally belonged to the Templars : in the chapel is the marble tomb of Juan de Beaumont.

The ancient city of *Estella,* the capital of its *Merindad,* is built on the Ega, which is joined here by the Amescoa, and both are good trout-streams ; pop. under 6000, and chiefly agricultural. A tolerable wine is made on the rocky slopes. The walnut *Alameda* is pretty ; there are two old churches and a ruined *Alcazar* on an eminence. Estella was long the head-quarters of Don Carlos, who was proclaimed King here in Nov. 1833, by Santos Ladron de Guevara ; it was beleaguered in June, 1838, by Espartero, who lingered at Logroño with some 30,000 ill-equipped men, in such inactive vacillation that some secret understanding has been suspected with Maroto, the Judas of Vergara (see p. 929). Both, in short, remained firing much powder at each, when out of shot; "marching and counter-marching," *more Hispano*, as the Duke says (see p. 221). It was at Estella, on Feb. 17, 1839, that Maroto arrested six of his brother commanders and executed them without even the form of a trial; so Moreno despatched Torrijos and his party at Malaga; so Roncali dealt with Benot and Co. at Alicante. One of them, Gen. Garcia, was put to death in the dress of a clergy-man, in which he was taken when attempting to escape. Another, Gen. Carmona, was lured into the trap by a friendly invitation from Maroto, with whom *he breakfasted*, after which his host begged him to "speak with his adjutant on business," who took him to *El Puig* and had him shot instantly, thus violating the sacred laws of hos-pitality. See *Campo de Don Carlos*, p. 192. But here, as in the East, the man in power has ever been jealous of a rival as a Turk, and suspicious as of standing on mined ground. Competitors are made short work of. Thus Joab greeted Amasa with a kiss and "my brother," and then smote him in the fifth rib, such a *one* blow that he died (2 Sam. xx. 9). So before had he dealt with Abner (1 Sam. iii. 27). So the Carthaginian Agathocles invited Aphellas to supper, "blando alloquio et humili adulati-one," and killed him when off his guard (Justin, xxii. 7). So Perpenna feasted Sertorius and then murdered him (see Huesca, p. 985). So True-ba II. had his nobility to a banquet and then had them imprisoned and slaughtered (Mariana, viii. 2). So Rami-ro II., like Tarquinius, cut off his pro-minent nobles (see p. 987). So Me-hemet Ali enticed his Mamelukes to a splendid entertainment and then caused them to be butchered. So Buonaparte welcomed Ferdinand VII.

to dinner at Bayonne, and offered him for dessert the choice between abdi-cation or death. So the same Ferdinand often received a minister with caresses and cigars, while the order was drawn up for his dismissal and banishment.

While Maroto was decoying and executing his brother officers, Don Carlos, timid and uncertain as usual, neglected, although previously warned, to hurry to Estella, where several faith-ful battalions would have turned upon the traitor. He at first resented the massacre, whereupon Maroto marched to his residence, and when an officer was sent out to ask his intentions, re-plied, "You know them, and may act as you choose." So when Jehu con-spired against his master, the king sent a messenger, "Is it peace?" and so, when too late, Joram exclaimed, "There is treachery, O Ahaziah!" (2 Kings, ix. 18).

The uneven plains, or upper *Ames-coas* between Estella and Salvatierra, and the country in the *Valle de Ara-quil* near the pass of *Borunda*, were the scenes of the victories gained by that fine *Guerrillero* Zumalacarreguy in 1835, over the bungler Valdes and other Christino *regular* generals. *Los Arcos* is another of these hill-fort cities with its ancient castle and *torre de homenaje*. *Viana* is an ancient city in a rich corn country, with the Ebro flowing S.; it was founded in 1219 by Don Sancho el Fuerte, as a frontier place against the Castilians: pop. about 3000. It is a cheerful town, has a good plaza and fine church, *La Sa. Maria*. For Logroño see R. cxxxiv. and for Pamplona to Vitoria see R. cxv.

The company of diligences of Na-varra run coaches between Bayonne, Tolosa, Tudela, Pamplona, and Zara-goza. There are four routes from Pamplona to Bayonne and France; that by *Tolosa* long was the only one carriageable, but recently a new and shorter route has been opened by *Vera*; the other passes are merely bridle and mountain roads.

ROUTE CXXXVII.—PAMPLONA TO
TOLOSA.

Irungum 3
Lecumberri . . . . 2¼ .. 5¼
Arribas . . . . . 2¼ .. 8
Tolosa . . . . . 3 .. 11

You quit Pamplona by a bad road,
over arid and bald plains, but after
passing *Berrio* the ascent commences
and the scenery improves. The valley
of *Araquil* is Swiss-like, and you enter
the mountains at the pass of the two
sister rocks *Las dos Hermanas*. *Tour-
zan* is one of the 14 villages of Ara-
quil. *Lecumberri*, where mine host of
the *Posada*, Don Sebastian, is a fine
hearty fellow, stands in its valley, the
Larraun, as *Arribas* does in that of
Ariaz, under the noble hill Elvira and
by the rapid torrent *Aspiroz*. The royal
road soon enters Guipuzcoa, and Tolosa is reached by a mountain defile,
through which a crystal stream flows
pleasantly : from thence to Irun see R.
cxxi.

ROUTE CXXXVIII.—PAMPLONA TO IRUN.

Ostiz 2¼
Latasa . . . . . 1¼ .. 4
Sⁿ. Esteban . . . 4 .. 8
Sumbilla . . . . . 1 .. 9
Vera . . . . . . 4 .. 13
Irun . . . . . . 4 .. 17

We now turn into the Pyrenees of
Navarre, into its passes and defiles,
those natural fortresses out of which
the Duke drove Soult in 1813. These
localities have been officially surveyed
by English engineers ; the maps were
published on a grand scale by Wyld,
in 1840. The volume is, however, far
too cumbrous for the traveller, and
almost for the library. The apple-
bearing valley of which Sⁿ· *Esteban de
Lerin* is the chief hamlet, is truly
Swiss-like. Here two streams, one
coming down from *Elisondo*, unite into
the *Bidasoa*, which some hence interpret *Vida*, two, *Osoa*, united in one
(see p. 942). The delicious valley of
Baztan is (as the word implies in Arabic) a " garden." The plains abound

in fruit and pasture, the rivers in trout ;
the hills are wooded and the mountain
cottages, which are here called *Bordas*,
resemble the *Chalets* of Switzerland
and the *Brenas* of the Asturias. The
peasantry are simple, purely primitive,
and pastoral. Now we enter the *Merindad de Cinco villas* : these five hamlets are *Echalar, Lesaca, Vera, Yanci,*
and *Aranaz*. Iron is found in
the hills, which is smelted and
wrought in *Fraguas y Ferrerias*, forges
and smithies, as rude and picturesque
as those of the old Cantabrians. The
Bidasoa flows through the village of
Sumbilla, pursuing its sweet course to
Janci, at the bridge of which, had the
Spaniards Longa and Barcenas done the
shadow of their duty, Aug. 31, 1813,
not a Frenchman could have escaped,
when Soult, after the splendid repulse
of what the Duke termed a "mauvaise
opération," was forced to retreat with
six divisions along the narrow defile ;
but here, as at Salamanca, (p. 656)
our worthy allies offered a pont d'or to
the common enemy. The retreating French were so beaten, morally
and physically, and their cries for
quarter were so piteous, that our rifles,
merciful as brave, and victorious,
scorned to destroy a foe half-dead from
panic alone. Napier (xxi. 5).

Lesaca was for many months the
head-quarters of the Duke; from
hence are dated those memorable de-
spatches which reveal in true colours
the miserable ministerial mediocrities of
England and Spain, who were dragged
out of their mire by his triumphal
car. In vain did he din into Lord
Bathurst that " the brave little army
was stinted in everything;" in vain
did he reiterate to Lord Melville that
the French were masters of the sea.
The dull ear of official red-tapism was
deaf to his prayers, as it had before been
to those of Nelson. Our Cabinet was
lavishing millions on jobbing Spanish
juntas and paltry German princes, who
neither had the means nor even the intention of repayment or doing their
duty. Stores and gold were cast into

the lap of foreigners, while the brain, blood, and bone of England was pining for dry bread, whilst our starving countrymen were being hung on trees for robbing beehives, when they had no rations and no money to procure food!

Soon we approach the charming valley of *Vera*. Hic ver purpureum. Here again were the sites of new triumphs of the invincible light division. Here Soult, July 31, 1813, made a second and desperate attempt to force the English lines, but was splendidly repulsed in every direction; and now, had Skerrett supported the rifles, not a Frenchman could have escaped. Here again, Oct. 7, the enemy was utterly and magnificently routed, the English army passing triumphantly into France, Soult and Foy flying before them. The whole ride on to Irun, by the beautiful Bidasoa, is all that the artist or angler can desire. For La Rhune (La Runa), Sn. Marcial, and military events, see pp. 941-2-5.

ROUTE CXXXIX.—PAMPLONA BY MAYA TO BAYONNE.

Ostiz	2½	
Lanz	2	4½
Berrueta	3	7½
Elizondo	1	8½
Maya	2	10½
Urdax	2	12½
Añoa	1	13½
Bayonne	4½	18

This is the central of the 3 mountain routes, and all are alike wild, Alpine, and full of military interest. Now we tread the ground where the Duke foiled Soult in his attempt to relieve Pamplona. Sorauren is the hamlet which witnessed his narrow escape (see p. 1005). Look at that bridge, reader, on which he pencilled the death-warrant of his enemy. In this now quiet village many most desperate encounters took place; the first occurred on the 4th anniversary of the victory of Talavera; then our 27th and 48th regiments fell three times on the whole brigade of Reille, "rolling back his crowded masses in disorder, and throwing them violently down the mountain's side; it was no child's play" (Nap., xxi. 5). Meanwhile, on the hill above, the Spanish regiment of Pravia, distrusting their officers, disbanded and gave way, leaving the 40th alone to bear the brunt. That regiment "in stern silence" received four separate attacks of a whole French brigade, repulsing them every time, until three companies alone drove the depressed enemy headlong down with the bayonet. This indeed, in the Duke's words, was "bludgeon-work." Both parties, as at Waterloo, were "gluttons," but in the death-struggle the better man prevailed, as at Mayorga and elsewhere..

The second combat began two days afterwards at daylight, when "fighting old Picton" advanced against Foy, while Inglis, with 500 men of the 7th division, broke at "one shock" the two French regiments which covered Clausel's right, and drove them pell mell down the valley of Lanz. Then the 28th, under Byng, charged up the village, taking 1400 prisoners. The enemy now retreated in sad disorder, flying for refuge with Foy, who had remained safe on the top of a hill, from whence he too fled next, into the woods (Napier, xxi. 5), while nothing could induce him to face the British bayonet, which he survived to attack with his pen. How if the Duke could then have foreseen the calumnies of this *historian*, would he not have smiled contemptuously? It is pleasant, said Lord Bacon, "to stand in the window of a castle, and to *see* a battle, but no pleasure is comparable to the standing on the vantage ground of *truth*, a hill not to be commanded."

At *Ostiz* the road branches off to the l., to *Ayoca;* keep on, however, by the r., to *Olaque*, from whence another track strikes off by the r., to *Roncesvalles*. Bearing to the l. we reach *Lanz*, where the 7th division beat the French at the same moment as the 6th division did the same at *Sorauren*, Morillo *co-operating* by keeping out of the way to the N.E., on the hill of *Sa. Barbara*, the patroness of Spanish artillery, and who this day preserved him safely. "What does he in the north, when he should serve his sovereign in the west?" The ascent now to *Berrueta* is long and steep: from *Elisondo*, a central point in its valley, many rude mountain paths diverge. Keeping to the r., we cross and recross the Bidasoa, and emerging from the sweet valley, wind up the rocky path to the *Puerto de Maya;* from this lofty eminence the country towards the Bayonne is displayed as an opened map. Here the English army, catching sight of France, cheered, as the victorious troops of Hannibal, when they beheld from the Alps that Italy which they were about to invade. But their courage was cooled by the necessity of guarding these bleak and exposed heights, during the long delay occasioned by the siege of Pamplona. The cold was piercing, the night duties severe, and clothes and supplies were *not* forwarded by Lord Bathurst. Meanwhile the warm, sunny plains of France lay in sight, tempting even Englishmen to desert. This important pass was held July 25, 1813, by Gen[l.] Stewart, when Soult attempted to relieve Pamplona. According to Napier (xxi. 5), our general mistook the real point of the French attack, and marched up his regiments singly, against the enormous masses of the enemy, but the magnificent defence of Barnes's brigade and the 82nd checked Drouet, who was so stunned by their soldier welcome that he remained 24 hours doing nothing, with 20,000 men, instead of seizing the nick of time, and joining Soult before Pamplona; thus the whole well-devised plan of the enemy was frustrated.

ROUTE CXL.—PAMPLONA TO FRANCE BY RONCESVALLES.

Zavaldica	2¼	
Zubiri	2¼	4½
Burguete	3	7½
Roncesvalles	1	8½
Valcarlos	4	12¼
S[t.] Jean Pied du Port	2¼	14¾

Crossing the Arga, and then the Esteribar 3 times, we reach *Huarte,*

in its narrow valley, by which the 3rd division advanced July 30, 1813, driving the French to *Roncesvalles,* the scene of a former "dolorous rout." Keeping to the r. after *Zubiri,* cross a stream before *Zizoain* and another beyond *Viscarret,* and descend into the pastoral valleys of *Burguete* and *Roncesvalles.* At *Burguete* a track branches off to the l., to the Alduides, and another from Roncesvalles to the r., to *Orbaiceta,* 3 L., where the royal foundries were almost destroyed by the French.

Roncesvalles, Roscida vallis, a small hamlet with a great name, stands in the park-like valley de Valcarlos; the road passes under the now untenanted Augustine convent, which was dedicated to our Lady of the Valley, by whom the army of Charlemagne was cut off. The church is still used as a parochial one. The winter cold in these exposed localities is severe, and the hardships which were endured by the army of the Black Prince, when entering Spain, was intense. Hence to *Urdax :* a small trout-stream, about two miles on, divides Spain from France. The fine oak woods form the wealth of the peasantry ; of these, in 1793, the French republicans wantonly cut down 23,000 trees. Here, Sep. 14, 1839, Don Carlos, after the *transaccion* of Vergara, passed a second time into the prisons of France ; first confined at Valençay by the usurper Buonaparte, and secondly at Bourges by his Bourbon cousin Louis Philippe.

At *Urdax,* Vicente Moreno, of Torijos infamy (see p. 354), was murdered Sep. 6, 1839. His death, according to the letter of his aide-de-camp, An[to.] Acena (see p. 215 ' *Campo de Don Carlos*'), was a premeditated crime. Moreno, after the crowning treachery of Maroto, retreated to the French frontier, with his wife and family. During a delay, occasioned by a failure of a promised escort, and in the presence of one Mendoza, their officer, and the miserable women, he was shot and bayoneted, by some soldiers of the

11th battalion of Navarre. It is said that he prayed for a confessor and a short grace, " Kill me to-morrow; let me live to-day; but half-an-hour!" " Die," exclaimed his executioners'; " such mercy as you showed to Torrijos shall be shown to you" (see p. 354).

It was at *Roncesvalles*, in 778, that the army of Charlemagne, with all "his peerage, fell." The invasion of the Peninsula by this great emperor of the west is involved in some obscurity. It would seem that this arbiter of nations was invited to Zaragoza, to settle the dissensions of the rival houses of Abbas and Omar, just as Buonaparte interfered between Charles IV. and Ferd. VII. Charlemagne gladly raised the banner of the cross against the crescent, for the Infidel was then the dread of Europe; hence the religious character given by Dante to the crusade—

Dopo la dolorosa rotta, quando
Carlo magno perde la *santa* gente.

But the Spaniards and Moors, Christians as well as Mahomedans, were little influenced by the *sanctity* of the French invaders; nay, their hatred of foreign dictation reconciled all previous differences, which were merged in one common greater loathing of the *Gavacho*, a name said to have then been first applied to the French. In vain did Alonzo *el Casto* of Leon make over Spain to Charlemagne, as Charles IV. did to Buonaparte. The noble people, then, as now, worthy of better rulers, rose, as in our times, to a man, and found a leader in Bernardo del Carpio, the reputed nephew of Alonzo; probably he, as well as Orlando, who was slain by him, are, like Achilles, the pure creatures of romance, but they truly depict the spirit of the age, and so far are historical. The ballads are among the finest in any language. The march of Bernardo (Duran, iv. 157) tells the gathering, the uprising of the nation; the cry was, "Arm for your independence!' has the Frenchman peradventure already conquered the

land? does he expect a bloodless victory? never! It may be said of the Leonese that 'they die, but never that they surrender :' " and this was a truth, not the idle boast of a runaway, the first to be taken prisoner and alive. The French, retiring from Spain, were caught in the mountain gorges, where superior discipline and manœuvre are of no avail; but this, the prototype of Bailen, was lost on the silly juntas and generals of Spain, who, in spite of the Duke's earnest advice to adopt a Fabian, mountain, and defensive warfare, left their broken hills to descend into the plains, with ill provided, undisciplined troops, and thus courted certain unavoidable defeat.

The Spaniards now claim *all* the glory of Roncesvalles for themselves: but here, as elsewhere, *foreigners* at least bore their share of the real brunt : and the Moors go so far as to assert that it was *their* victory (Conde i. 201). Nor are the Moors the only disputers of Spanish glories, since even the defeated French ingeniously claim the deed as theirs. Les Arabes, *et même* les Espagnols, *prétendent* à l'honneur de cette victoire; il n'appartient ni aux uns, ni aux autres : les Français de la Seine ne furent vaincus que par les Français de l'Adour et de la Garonne! Marles (Conde i. 234). So Mons. Foy (i. 205) discovered that the victories " de Creci, de Poitiers, et d'Azincourt" were *not* won by Englishmen, but by French troops, composed of "Normans, Poitevins, and Gascons." Be these things and *Gascons* as they may, the English, under Gen¹. Byng, were cheered on these identical spots by the Spaniards, who sang the old ballads of Bernardo, nor will the *religio loci*, even be it a "romance," ever be explained away. This time-honoured locality was marked with a pillar, which commemorated the defeat of Charlemagne, but the monument was pulled down in 1794, to the tune of a "musique touchante," by two commissioners of the French republic, who entered the

2 x 2

valley with a column of men, called by themselves *La Infernale,* who carried fire and sword everywhere : see even the French account, ' V. et C.' iii. 180. The parish church was then pillaged, where long had hung the identical chains which guarded the Moorish chief's tent at Navas de Tolosa, and through which Sancho el Fuerte broke. Now they only exist in the armorial shield of Navarre. It was through this memorable valley that the Black Prince led his legions in Feb. 1367, to the victory of Navarrete ; and it was over the same site that Joseph Buonaparte fled, after the

"dolorous rout," and the Duke's victory at Vitoria. Alas! poor Pepé! Here also was Don Carlos proclaimed king, by Eraso, Oct. 12, 1833.

Three mountain routes branch hence; the best is the central, which goes up the *Valcarlos.* A small rivulet, a tributary of the *Nive,* divides Spain and France. The boundary line is indicated by land-marks, placed in 1792 by mutual referees. One league leads to *St. Jean Pied du Port.* The frontier on both sides is marked by custom-house officers : for how to deal with this gentry, see pp. 205, 513.

HIC FINIS CHARTÆQUE VIÆQUE.

"Da veniam scriptis, quorum non gloria nobis
Causa, sed *utilitas* officiumque fuit."
OVID. iii. *Ex Pont.* ix. 55.

TRAVELLING MAP
OF
SPAIN
TO ACCOMPANY THE HANDBOOK
FOR TRAVELLERS

The material originally positioned here is too large for
reproduction in this reissue. A PDF can be downloaded
from the web address given on page iv of this book, by
clicking on 'Resources Available'.

INDEX.

An *asterisk* is placed at those references which are of most general interest for the convenience of readers at home.

Sp., *Spain, Spaniards*. En., *England, English*. Fr., *France, French*.

2 x 3

1034 INDEX.

Iberi, truces, 459
Ibex, 978
Ibi, 425
Ibones, 975
Ibnu-l-abmar, 329, 361
Ices, 69
*Indifference, Sp., to constitutions, 862
*—— to death, 993
Idiot enlightened, 610
Indigites, 508
If and but, 631, 696
Iglesia estenta, 698
*—— jurandera, 609, 806, 899
Igualada, 973
*Ildefonso, S., his legend, 844
*Ildefonso, San, palace, elevation and position; Philip V.'s character, la colegiata, tombs, events, intrigues, revocation of Salic law, Garcia, gardens, fountains, manufactories, 821
Illescas, 831
Illi, 971
Illiberis, 361
Illiturgis, 523, 968
Images, graven, 109, 112, 113, 114, 269*, 442, 494, 538, 608*, 901*, 961*, 902*, 963
Imaz, Jose, 522
*Immaculate concepcion, 265, 267
Impertinente curioso,977
*Impedidos, los, 877
Incense to Queen of Heaven, 963
Incensario, 848
*Indecency, Sp., to dead, 349, 560, 567
Inglis, Gen., 1009
——, Mr., 43; blunder, 256
Inhospitality, Sp., 725
Infidels and bigots, 168, 881
*Ingratitude, Sp., 162, 209, 214, 233, 239,

279, 285, 316, 327, 348, 393, 526, 532, 541, 568, 574, 689, 752, 796, 839, 878, 882, 884, 908, 911, 913, 922, 955, 1002
Inigo, Arista, 997
*Inns, 21 ; cost at, 945
Inquisition, Sp., 270, 278, 283, 371
Intimos, 213
Inscriptions, Moorish, 372
Instituto Asturiano, 705
Intolerance, Sp.,167,168
*Introduction of Romanism in Sp., 846, 980
*Invention, 317
*Invincible Armada, 312, 552, 653, 817
John, of Austria, Don, 552
—— of Gaunt in Sp., 659, 913
Ionios, genii, 826
Iriarte, 760
*Irrigation,Moorish,430
Iron mines, 350, 938
Irurac bat, 922
Irun, 944
—— to Bayonne, 940
—— to Pamplona, 1008
—— to San Sebastian, 948
—— to Vitoria, 928
Irving, W., 132, 239, 326, 364
*Isabella, 177, 258, 329, 388, 397, 408, 619, 622, 623, 787, 827
*Isidoro, San, 31, 244, 305, 414, 608, 609
Isis, 257
*Isla, Padre, on Gil Blas, 707
*—— de los Faisanes, 943
——, de Leon, 218
Isquierdo, 514
*Isolation, social, 161
*Italica, 283 ; amphitheatre, 284

Izard, 978
Izarraiz, 940, 952
Izan, S. Pedro de, 893

J.

Jaca, 779
—— to Brecha de Roldan, 982
—— to Sallent, 981
Jack Cade, 581, 827
Jaen, 329
—— to Adra, 400
Jaime El conquistador, 954
Jaimè de Crevillente, 421
Jalea, 140 ; Jaleos, 285
Jalon, Salo, 889
Jamones, see Hams, 519
James, Lord of Douglas, 333
James, Col., 339
Jaurequi, Gaspar, 924
Jara, 148
Jaraiseco, 539
Jardin Ingles, 857
Jaspers, 266, 870
*Jaula de Mugeres, 186
Javali, 105
*Jealousy, 153
Jean de Albret, 998
Jephthah, 905
Jereed, 385
Jerica, 878
Jervis, Adm., 204
*Jerome, St., flogged by angels, 577
*Jeronomite monks, 812
Jesebel, 837
*Jesuits, philosophy of Sp., 499 ; costume, suppression, how painted, 500
*Jews, Sp., blood, 223, 267, 295, 269, 342, 353, 361, 596, 636, 806, 835, 836; accusations, 849 ; Jewesses, 343, 348 ; synagogues, 835, 911
Jicara, 71
Joab, 1007

3 A

Puebla deMontalban,543
*Puente de Alcantara,
Toledo, 839
*———— Alcantara, 547
———— Arenas, 918
———— Arzobispo, 541
———— Domingo Flo-
rez, 601
———— del Cardenal, 539,
550
*Puentes del diablo,
Devil's bridges, 473,
493, 825
Puente de Zuazo, 217
Puercas, las, 215
*Puerco, 519
Puerta de Alcalá, 738
———— Lodada, 833
Puerto d'Oo, 989
———— de la Picada, 989
———— de Sª· Maria, 215
———— Marin, 686
———— Real, 216
Puertos, 93
Puigcerda, 503
*Pulgas, 158
Pulgar, Hernando de,
359, 388, 559
*Pulli, 910
*Puls punica, 67
*Pulmonia, 95, 722
Pulpitos, 125
*Puñal, Puñaleco, 858,
859
Punctilious, 2
*Pundonor, 152, 604
Punic faith, Sp., see
Breach of word
Purchena, 402
Purification, 665
*Pyrrhica saltatio, 189
Pyrrhus, 325
Purani, 974
Purchas, 281, 675, 971
*Purgatory, doctrine of
ceremonies, blessed
souls, 168; painting,
corporations, Sp. ten-
derness for souls,
how delivered from
fire, 169
Purification, 108, 364,
665

Purkiss, David, 728
Putos, 295
Pyrene, 974
*Pyrenean Key, 943
*Pyrenean local terms,
975, 976
*Spanish Pyrenees ;
name, legends, con-
figuration, heights,
breadth, local names,
bad accommodations,
hatred of neighbours,
natural history and
sporting, baths,
scenery, natives, 974

Q.

Quails, 106
*Quarantine, 205, 342
Quarrels, Sp. generals,
618
Quercus pedunculata,
703
*Quemadero, 278
*Queen of Heaven, 963
*Queens Regent, 450,
798,840,879; Sp., 610
*Quesada, 223, 309, 316
Queso, 28
Quicksilver mines, 291
*Quidnuncs at Madrid,
733
Quien es, 158
Quinones, Suero de, 604
Quinta, 923
———— de quita pesares,
824
Quintana, 327
———— de los Muertes, 671
Quintilian, 994
*St. Quintin, battle, 809
*Quinto, 837
Quixada, Luis de, 552
*Don Quixote, critique
on, 314 ; best editions,
317

R.

*R. A's. Sp., 734
Rabida, 238
*Rábitos, 296, 529

Rabbits, 63
*Race, influence, 144,
353, 934; Madrid, 779
*Rachel and Vidas,
Jews, 898
Raffles, 734
Rafol, Ms. de, 442
Ragged staff, 345
*Railways in Spain,
number, projects, pro-
spects of success, 800;
probable benefits, 612,
696
Rain, scarcity, 92
*Rain, Christ, 773
Raisins (Malaga), 355
Raleigh, Sir W., 572
Ramales, 932
Rambles, 12 ; *La Ram-
bla, 479
Ramiro, 11, 987, 1007
*Ramon Nonat, St. and
accoucheur, miracles,
501
*Raphael, 10 pictures
at Madrid, 757
Raphael ware, 818
Raso, 431
Rasura Nuno, 894
Rasgo de Moya, 130
Ratero, 40
*Ratones, casa de, 350,
365, 385
Raumur, 820
Re Casto, 698
Real, 3
*Rebeccas, 348, 369,
408, 689
Recogidas, las, 792
Recommendations, 10
*Reding, Gen., 303,
477, 479
Redondela, 681
*Refranes, 318
Regalada, la, 302
*Regla de Santiago, 262
Reille, Gen., 1009
Reina Propnetaria, 716
Reinaud, Monsʳ·ʼ 278,
340, 528, 986;
O'Reilly, Gen., 211,
218
Reinosa, 909
3 A 3

3 B

3 B 2

ERRATA.

P., *page*. l., *line*. c., *column*.

P. 8, l. 48, *for* Algesiras, *read* Algeciras.
P. 22, l. 18, *for* Junio, *read* Junco.
P. 24, l. 48, *for* Vender le, *read* Venderle.
P. 25, l. 11, *for* Christiano, *read* Cristiano.
P. 25, l. 7, *for* Punhonor, *read* Pundonor.
P. 30, l. 46, *for* Purones, *read* Porrones.
P. 31, l. 25, *for* 14th, *read* 13th.
P. 67, l. 49, *for* an, *read* is an.
P. 80, l. 43, *for* Babel, *read* Bable.
P. 82, l. 51, *for* tres, *read* cuatro.
P. 82, l. 52, *for* three, *read* four.
P. 87, c. 1, l. 11, *for* Purissima, *read* Purisima.
P. 111, l. 47, *for* imagines, *read* imagenes.
P. 111, l. 45, *for* Camerin, *read* camarin.
P. 113, l. 42, *for* te, *read* tu.
P. 113, l. 42, *dele* iii. 43.
P. 113, l. 44, *for* he, *read* the.
P. 113, l. 44, *for* Santissima, *read* Santisima.
P. 114, l. 8, *for* Cazulla, *read* Casulla.
P. 114, l. 26, *for* authentic, *read* most approved.
P. 116, l. 36. *for* galleria. *read* galeria.
P. 121, l. 16, *for* Virgines, *read* Virgenes.
P. 122, l. 28, *for* Taragona, *read* Tarragona.
P. 126, l. 4, *for* Santissima, *read* Santisima.
P. 127, l. 45, *for* Περιστρε φομενος, *read* Περιστρεθομενος.
P. 134, l. 33, *for* love, *read* loves.
P. 137, l. 11, *for* guerillos, *read* guerrilleros.
P. 137, l. 45, *for* his, *read* their.
P. 146, l. 48. *for* arana, *read* jarana.

P. 148, l. 27, *for* Alghad, *read* Algihad.
P. 148, l. 45, *for* Coscoja, *read* Coscojo.
P. 158, l. 18, *for* Purissima, *read* Purisima.
P. 158, l. 21, *for* peccado, *read* pecado.
P. 160, l. 15, *for* continental, *read* most continental.
P. 161, l. 2, *for* handkerchief, *read* handkerchiefs.
P. 161, l. 26, *for* sistor, *read* visitor.
P. 163, l. 31, *for* cheminea, *read* chiminea.
P. 164, l. 2, *for* women, *read* housewives.
P. 166, l. 2, *for* aff^{mo.} *read* af^{mo.}
P. 167, l. 36, *for* Christiano, *read* cristiano.
P. 170, l. 10, *for* Promptuarios, *read* Prontuarios.
P. 171, l. 30, *for* Santissima, *read* Santisima.
P. 212, c. 2, l. 5, *for* cressatura, *read* crissatura.
P. 212, c. 2, l. 20, *for* those, *read* he.
P. 212, c. 2, l. 20, *for* investigate, *read* investigates.
P. 281, c. 1, l. 6, *for* four, *read* five.
P. 237, c. 1, l. 47, *for* Masmora, *read* Mazmorra.
P. 250, c. 1, l. 29, *for* Santissima, *read* Santisima.
P. 258, c. 1, l. 33, *for* Berruguette, *read* Berruguete.
P. 227, c. 2, l. 8, *for* Algeciras, *read* Algeciras near Tarifa.
P. 233, c. 2, l. 75, *to* devuelto *add* sent back from England.
P. 257, c. 1, l. 35, *for* art am, *dele* art.
————————— *for* and iii. *read* art and iii.
P. 277, c. 2, l. 15, *for* Tobaco, *read* Tabaco.

P. 279, c. 1, l. 11, *for* Philip, *read* Philippe.

P. 293, c. 2, l. 41, *for* Monteil, *read* Montiel.

P. 313, c. 1, l. 38, *for* for, *read* before.

P. 313, c. 1, l. 48, *dele* Narvaez.

———— *add* Seoane, Tacon.

P. 381, c. 1, l. 6, *for* tingling, *read* tinkling.

P. 389, c. 2, l. 30, *for* Chancelleria, *read* Chancilleria.

P. 452, c. 2, l. 1, *for* Covarrobias, *read* Covarrubias.

P. 452, c. 2, l. 10, *for* Covarrobias, *read* Covarrubias.

P. 494, c. 2, l. 27, *for* Wilfred, *read* Wifred.

P. 511, c. 1, l. 70, *for* Swartz, *read* Schwartz.

P. 523, c. 2, l. 29, *for* Victor as at Ucles, *tr.*

P. 531, c. 2, l. 44, *for* Confessionario, *read* Confesionario.

P. 547, c. 2, l. 36, *for* aliam, *read* alium.

P. 553, c. 1, l. 32, *for* hand, *read* hands

P. 592, c. 2, l. 41, *for* Santissima, *read* Santisima.

P. 622, c. 1, l. 13, *for* Carnecerias, *read* Carnicerias.

P. 625, c. 2, l. 32, *for* Chancelleria, *read* Chancilleria.

P. 638, c. 2, l. 41, *for* Francisca, *read* Francisco.

P. 639, c. 1, l. 40, *for* Chancelleria, *read* Chancilleria.

P. 675, note, *for* 14th, *read* 13th.

P. 681, c. 2, l. 29, *for* Colonel, *read* Captain.

P. 697, l. 18, *after* Bable, *add* comes down.

P. 723, l. 4. *for* Embosandose, *read* Embozandose.

P. 735, c. 1, l. 28, *for* were, *read* seem.

P. 769, c. 2, l. 24, *for* Darphes, *read* D'Arphes.

P. 771, c. 2, l. 28, *after* Toledo, *read* we hear that it is still in that city, in the Palacio Arzobispal.

P. 794, c. 2, l. 26, *for* al, *read* at.

P. 796, c. 1, l. 26, *for* plaza, *read* plazuela del Rey, No. 2, Calle de las Infantas.

P. 795, c. 1, l. 33, *for* there, *read* then.

P. 816, c. 1, l. 32, *for* Cuello, *read* Coello.

P. 839, c. 1, l. 4, *for* Brabante, *read* Bradamante.

P. 843, c. 2, l. 13, *for* Carrera, *read* Carrara.

P. 847, c. 1, l. 26, *for* the latter, *read* into the latter.

P. 850, c. 1, l. 16, *after* home, *add* enquire for the grand picture of El Conde de Orgar (see p. 771), by El Greco.

P. 864, c. 1, l. 9, *for* harassed, *read* harnessed.

P. 872, c. 2, l. 40, *for* Medellen, *read* Medellin.

P. 879, c. 2, l. 19, *for* raised, *read* was to have been raised.

P. 886, c. 2, l. 4, *for* Sⁿ· *read* Sᵃ·

P. 904, *for* Cerdena, *read* Cardena.

P. 907, c. 2, 828, *for* Cerdena, *read* Cardena.

P. 907, c. 1, l. 23, *for* Cerdeña, *read* Cardeña.

P. 908, c. 1, l. 54, *for* Leibana, *read* Liebana.

P. 908, c. 2, l. 44, *for* Leibana, *read* Liebana.

P. 914, c. 2, l. 12, *for* perdita, *read* perdida.

P. 915, c. 1, l. 82, *for* Murillo, *read* Morillo.

P. 925, l. 28, *for* Machinas, *read* Maquinas.

P. 934, c. 2, l. 17, *for* Assegurales, *read* Asegurales.

P. 935, c. 1, l. 30, *for* Ponte, *read* Puente.

P. 935, c. 1, l. 33, *for* Bello Vas, *read* Bello Vao.

P. 935, c. 2, l. 24, *for* Carneceria, *read* Carniceria.

P. 948, c. 1, l. 36, *for* Costades, *read* Costados.

P. 963, c. 1. l. 1, *for* fado *read* fædo.

P. 973, c. 2, l. 8, *for* lequa, *read* legua.

P. 976, l. 32, *for* Breche, *read* Brecha.

P. 987, c. 1, l. 30, *for* Hueza, *read* Guara.

P. 988, *for* Gistan, *read* Gistau.

P. 1007, c. 1, l. 15, *for* Benot, *read* Bonet.

9 781108 037549